Economics, Law, and Institutions in Asia Pacific

The Asia Pacific region is expected to steadily enhance its economic and political presence in the world during the twenty-first century. At the same time, many serious economic and political issues remain unresolved in the region. To further academic enquiry and enhance readers' understanding about this vibrant region, the present series, Economics, Law, and Institutions in Asia Pacific, aims to present cutting-edge research on the Asia Pacific region and its relationship with the rest of the world. For countries in this region to achieve robust economic growth, it is of foremost importance that they improve the quality of their markets, as history shows that healthy economic growth cannot be achieved without high-quality markets. High-quality markets can be established and maintained only under a well-designed set of rules and laws, without which competition will not flourish. Based on these principles, this series places a special focus on economic, business, legal, and institutional issues geared towards the healthy development of Asia Pacific markets. The series considers book proposals for scientific research, either theoretical or empirical, that is related to the theme of improving market quality and has policy implications for the Asia Pacific region. The types of books that will be considered for publication include research monographs as well as relevant proceedings. The series show-cases work by Asia-Pacific based researchers but also encourages the work of social scientists not limited to the Asia Pacific region. Each proposal and final manuscript is subject to evaluation by the editorial board and experts in the field.

All books and chapters in the Economics, Law and Institutions in Asia Pacific book series are indexed in Scopus.

Junji Nakagawa · Taro Hamada ·
Yoshimichi Ishikawa
Editors

Geopolitical Risks and Geoeconomics in International Economic Law

Asian Perspectives and Beyond

Springer

Editors
Junji Nakagawa
Chuo Gakuin University
Tokyo, Japan

Taro Hamada
Faculty of Law
Senshu University
Tokyo, Japan

Yoshimichi Ishikawa
School of International Relations
University of Shizuoka
Shizuoka, Japan

ISSN 2199-8620 ISSN 2199-8639 (electronic)
Economics, Law, and Institutions in Asia Pacific
ISBN 978-981-95-6995-3 ISBN 978-981-95-6996-0 (eBook)
https://doi.org/10.1007/978-981-95-6996-0

This Springer imprint is published by the registered company Springer Nature Singapore Pte Ltd.
The registered company address is: 152 Beach Road, #21-01/04 Gateway East, Singapore 189721, Singapore

Preface

This book grew naturally out of the conversations we shared at the 9th AIELN Conference in Tokyo in June 2025. Anyone who was there will remember the sense of urgency that filled the room—the feeling that the world of international economic law was shifting faster than our usual analytical frameworks could catch up with. For many of us, there was also a quieter sense of continuity. AIELN held its very first conference in Tokyo back in 2009, and gathering again in the same city more than fifteen years later felt like returning to the place where a long conversation first began. Rather than letting the energy of this latest meeting fade, we wanted to capture it, refine it, and give it a form that others could engage with.

The details of the conference, AIELN's history, and the intellectual background of this volume are already explained in the Introductory Part, so we will not repeat them here. From the editors' side, our role was simply to create a space where contributors could develop their ideas further, respond to one another, and shape their work into chapters that speak across the four sections of this book. The online workshop in October 2025 played an especially important role in this process, helping us see how diverse perspectives could fit together into something coherent.

Our hope is modest but sincere: that this collection provides readers with a clearer sense of how scholars in and around Asia are thinking about geopolitical risk, security, technology, and economic governance—and that it encourages further dialogue across the topics addressed in the chapters that follow.

Tokyo, Japan
Tokyo, Japan
Shizuoka, Japan
December 2025

Junji Nakagawa
Taro Hamada
Yoshimichi Ishikawa

Acknowledgments

Many people helped make this book possible, and we would like to express our appreciation in a simple and genuine way.

Our first thanks go to everyone who joined the 9th AIELN Conference at Senshu University. The energy and openness of the discussions were what convinced us that a volume like this would be worthwhile. We are also grateful to the contributors who took on the extra work of revising their papers—sometimes more than once—after the October workshop.

We are especially grateful to Senshu University, which generously hosted the conference, provided the venue and on-site support, and offered additional financial assistance. Their support created the environment that made the discussions possible and ultimately helped shape this volume.

We also gratefully acknowledge the support of the Japan Society for the Promotion of Science (JSPS), Grants-in-Aid for Scientific Research (KAKENHI), Project No. 23K22056, which helped make it possible to organize the 9th AIELN Conference.

We also wish to thank Anderson Mori & Tomotsune, the main sponsor of the 9th AIELN Conference. Their contribution enabled us to bring participants from across the region to Tokyo and made the meeting feasible.

Finally, we thank the students of Senshu University, whose onsite logistical support during the two days of the conference ensured that everything ran smoothly.

Any remaining errors are, of course, our own responsibility.

Contents

1 Introduction 1
Junji Nakagawa, Taro Hamada, and Yoshimichi Ishikawa

Part I Geopolitical Risk, Supply Chains, and Sustainable Digitalization

2 Geopolitical Conflict, Geoeconomic Manoeuvring, and the Law of the Jungle: Are We Witnessing the End of the Liberal Trading Order? 11
Jianfu Chen and Zhiqiong June Wang

3 Sustainable Digitalization and Cyber Resilience on the Supply Chain 33
Rolf H. Weber

4 How to Capture "Supply Chain Resilience" Under Justifications of the WTO Law 53
Mari Shimizu

5 Geopolitical Risk and International Economic Law: An Empirical Framework for Designing Resilient Trade and Investment Rules 73
Yoshimichi Ishikawa

6 How Geopolitics Shape New Forms of International Economic Ordering 95
Alexandros Bakos

Part II National Security, Regulatory Space, and Investment Risk Governance

7 Investment Screening Mechanisms Under the Investment Treaty Law: The Case of the UK's National Security and Investment Act 119
Apoorva Vishnoi

8 Does the Frequent Invocation of the National Security Exception Render WTO Disciplines Meaningless? Exploring Viable Options Under the Current WTO Dispute Settlement Mechanism 139
Tomohiko Kobayashi

9 Beyond Investment Protection: A Theory of Political Risk Governance in International Investment Law 149
Teerawat Wongkaew

10 National Security Concerns and Data Governance: Export Restrictions on Data and Its Implications for International Economic Law 177
Shota Watanabe

11 Conflict Between Environmental Protection and Investment Protection 197
Satomi Shintani

Part III Data Governance, Digital Sovereignty, and Regional Norm-Building in Asia

12 Digital Silk Road or Cyber Silk Curtain? Geo-Economics and Legal Dynamics of China's Belt and Road Initiative Within ASEAN Under the RCEP Framework 215
Intan Innayatun Soeparna and Sheva Atha Nugroho

13 Bamboo in the Storm: A Vietnamese Perspective on Data Sovereignty and Trust in the Digital Economy 235
Hien Xuan My Nguyen and Vy Thao Nguyen Ngo

14 "Soft" Law on Cybersecurity and Data Governance: Strengthening Asia's Digital Economy 255
Trang Anh Mac

15 Normative Reconstruction of Data Governance in Asia Amid Geopolitical Shifts 291
Hiroshi Kataoka

Part IV Emerging Regulatory Challenges: AI, Health, and Finance

16 The Case for the Development of an Asian Regional AI Framework—Expanding the Discussion on "Sovereign AI" to a Regional Level 315
Sungjin Kang

17 Technology Transfer in the Health Sector: Between Voluntary Licenses and Competition 339
Francisco Hernández Fernández

18 Principles of Sustainable Finance Regulation and Their International Investment Law Implications: The Case of Hong Kong and Its Taxonomy for Sustainable Finance 361
Lee Soo-Hyun

19 Forging Trade Rules in the Age of AI: The Case for Special Labor Safeguards 379
Tsai-fang Chen

Editors and Contributors

About the Editors

Junji Nakagawa is a Professor at the Faculty of Liberal Arts at Chuo Gakuin University. He is also a Professor Emeritus of the University of Tokyo. He is Of Counsel at Anderson, Mori & Tomotsune. He received his B.A., M.A., and Ph.D. from the University of Tokyo. Before assuming the current positions, he was a Professor of International Economic Law at the Institute of Social Science at the University of Tokyo. He is a Chairperson of the Asia International Economic Law Network (AIELN) and the Asian WTO Research Network. His research covers a wide range of public international law regulating transnational economic transactions. His major recent publications include: *RCEP Commentary,* Japan Tariff Association, 2022, in Japanese; *A Post-WTO International Legal Order*, Springer, 2020; *TPP Commentary*, Japan Tariff Association, 2019, in Japanese; *International Economic Law, 3rd edition*, Yuhikaku, 2019, in Japanese; *Asian Perspectives on International Investment Law*, Routledge, 2019; *Nationalization, Natural Resource and International Investment Law*, Routledge, 2017; and *International Harmonization of Economic Regulation*, Oxford University Press, 2011.

Taro Hamada is Professor at the Faculty of Law at Senshu University, Japan. He examines the evolving legal and institutional frameworks that govern global trade, with particular attention to how states balance economic integration, domestic regulatory autonomy, and the protection of workers. His recent publications include *International Law and the Global Economy,* co-ed., Shinzan-sha, 2021, in Japanese; *The Frontier of International Law,* co-ed., Nippon Hyoron Sha, 2019, in Japanese; "*International Trade and Labor*" in *International Economic Law*, 31, 2022, in Japanese; and "*Are Korea's Import Bans on Japanese Foods Based on Scientific Principles?*", co-author, in *European Journal of Risk Regulation*, 11(1), 2020. He previously served at the Ministry of Foreign Affairs of Japan and at the Permanent

Mission of Japan in Geneva, where he was responsible for WTO and EPA negotiations. He also worked at the National Institute for Research Advancement, conducting feasibility studies on the China–Japan–Korea FTA.

Yoshimichi Ishikawa is Associate Professor at the School of International Relations at the University of Shizuoka, Japan. Before entering academia, he served in the Ministry of Foreign Affairs of Japan, working on WTO dispute settlement. He received his Ph.D. in Law from the University of Bern, Switzerland, where he completed his dissertation, *International Trade in Food after a Nuclear Accident*, with the distinction of *magna cum laude*. His research focuses on evidence-based analysis of international trade regulation, with particular interest in the quantification of risk and the design of effective risk governance frameworks. He currently serves as a Board Member of the Japanese Society of International Economic Law and as a Member of the Government Procurement Review Board of the Cabinet Office. He is also Associate Editor of the *Chinese (Taiwan) Yearbook of International Law and Affairs*.

Contributors

Alexandros Bakos College of Law, Hamad Bin Khalifa University, Doha, Qatar

Jianfu Chen University of Melbourne School of Law, Melbourne, Australia;
La Trobe University, Melbourne, Australia

Tsai-fang Chen National Yang Ming Chiao Tung University, Hsinchu, Taiwan

Taro Hamada Faculty of Law, Senshu University, Tokyo, Japan

Francisco Hernández Fernández Unified Patent Court, Luxembourg City, Luxembourg

Yoshimichi Ishikawa School of International Relations, University of Shizuoka, Shizuoka, Japan

Sungjin Kang Kim & Chang, Seoul, South Korea

Hiroshi Kataoka Azabudai Kataoka Legal and Economic Affairs Office, Tokyo, Japan

Tomohiko Kobayashi Otaru University of Commerce, Otaru, Japan

Soo-Hyun Lee College of Management Engineering, University of Suwon, Hwaseong-Si, South Korea;
Asia Centre, Future Earth Programme, Seoul National University, Seoul, South Korea

Trang Anh Mac Ho Chi Minh City University of Law, Ho Chi Minh City, Vietnam

Junji Nakagawa Faculty of Liberal Arts, Chuogakuin University, Abiko, Japan

Vy Thao Nguyen Ngo Vietnamese Journal of Legal Sciences, Ho Chi Minh City University of Law, Ho Chi Minh City, Vietnam

Hien Xuan My Nguyen International Law Faculty, Ho Chi Minh City University of Law, Ho Chi Minh City, Vietnam

Sheva Atha Nugroho Faculty of Law, Universitas Airlangga, Surabaya, Indonesia

Mari Shimizu Graduate School of Law and Politics, University of Osaka, Osaka, Japan

Satomi Shintani University of Tokyo, Tokyo, Japan

Intan Innayatun Soeparna Faculty of Law, Universitas Airlangga, Surabaya, Indonesia

Apoorva Vishnoi LSE Trade Policy Hub, London School of Economics, London, UK

Zhiqiong June Wang Western Sydney University Law School, Sydney, Australia

Shota Watanabe Nomura Research Institute, Tokyo, Japan

Rolf H. Weber Faculty of Law, University of Zurich, Zurich, Switzerland

Teerawat Wongkaew Ministry of Foreign Affairs of Thailand, Bangkok, Thailand

Chapter 1
Introduction

Junji Nakagawa, Taro Hamada, and Yoshimichi Ishikawa

Abstract This introduction traces the Asian International Economic Law Network (AIELN) from its 2009 founding to the 9th AIELN Conference held in Tokyo (14–15 June 2025). Drawing on Asian experiences, the volume addresses how geopolitical risk and geoeconomic strategy now run through the core of trade, investment, and digital governance. The contributions examine whether the liberal trading system is fragmenting into regional blocs, how legal frameworks allocate the costs of regulatory risk, and whether Asian states can act as norm entrepreneurs rather than objects of great-power strategies. Ultimately, the volume asks how international economic law can accommodate demands for resilience, security, and sustainability without abandoning rule-based multilateralism.

Keywords Geopolitical risk · Geoeconomic strategy · Fragmentation · Asian International Economic Law Network (AIELN) · Rule-based multilateralism · Resilience

1.1 The Origins and Evolution of AIELN

For international economic lawyers, starting the day with news of new tariffs, sanctions, investment screening measures, export controls, or restrictions on data flows has become routine. What once looked like background noise in the global economy has moved firmly to center stage. Geopolitical risk and geoeconomic

J. Nakagawa (✉)
Faculty of Liberal Arts, Chuogakuin University, Abiko, Japan
e-mail: nakagawa@fla.cgu.ac.jp

T. Hamada
Faculty of Law, Senshu University, Tokyo, Japan
e-mail: thamada@isc.senshu-u.ac.jp

Y. Ishikawa
School of International Relations, University of Shizuoka, Shizuoka, Japan
e-mail: y.ishikawa@u-shizuoka-ken.ac.jp

J. Nakagawa et al. (eds.), *Geopolitical Risks and Geoeconomics in International Economic Law*, Economics, Law, and Institutions in Asia Pacific,
https://doi.org/10.1007/978-981-95-6996-0_1

Table 1.1 AIELN conferences (2009–2025)

	Date	Venue	Conference theme
1.	3 August 2009	Tokyo	Multilateralism and regionalism in global economic governance: trade, investment, and finance
2.	15–16 July 2011	Hong Kong	The global financial and economic crisis and the post-crisis international economic law environment
3.	18–19 July 2013	Seoul	The WTO at 20 and the future of the international law on trade, investment and finance
4.	20–21 July 2015	Bali	Regionalism in Asia–Pacific and beyond: challenges and opportunities
5.	16–17 June 2017	Xiamen	Asian Perspectives on international investment law
6.	26–27 October 2019	Taipei	International Trade regime for the data-driven economy: how will Artificial Intelligence Transform International Economic Law ?
7.	9–10 December 2021	Online	Building a sustainable future: new Asian regionalism in International Economic Law
8.	1–2 December 2023	Taipei	The new generation of economic agreements in the Asia–Pacific
9.	14–15 June 2025	Tokyo	Geopolitical risks and Geoeconomics in international economic law: Asian perspectives and beyond

strategy are no longer external shocks to an otherwise stable legal order; instead, they now run through the core of trade, investment, and digital governance. This volume grew out of a shared sense that Asian perspectives have a great deal to say about this transformation—and that they should be heard more clearly in the global conversation.

The Asian International Economic Law Network (AIELN) traces its roots back to 2009, long before these modern challenges took shape. Established by Asia-based members of the Society of International Economic Law (SIEL), it operates as an open, non-partisan network connecting scholars, practitioners, government officials, and international organizations working on international economic law in and on Asia. Since its inception, AIELN's aim has been to promote research, education, and practice of international economic law in the region. Over the years, this mission has produced not only a series of lively conferences but also a substantial body of collective publications that have tracked the evolution of the global economy. As summarized in Table 1.1, AIELN has so far held nine major conferences across Asia—each with its own theme, venue, and resulting book or special issue.[1]

Tokyo has been central to AIELN's story from the very beginning. The inaugural AIELN/SIEL Conference on Asian Perspectives in International Economic Law was

[1] Nakagawa (2011), Lim and Mercurio (2015), Choi (2015), Nakagawa (2019), Peng et al. (2021), and AJWH (2022).

held at the University of Tokyo on 3 August 2009, spearheaded by AIELN Chair Professor Junji Nakagawa and a steering committee of leading scholars from across the region. Since then, the conferences listed in Table 1.1 have moved from Hong Kong and Seoul to Bali, Xiamen, and Taipei, and even into a fully online format during the pandemic. Each meeting has added new perspectives and broadened the network's reach across Asia.

Against this background, it was more than a matter of convenience that the 2025 conference returned to Tokyo. By holding the 9th AIELN conference at Senshu University's School of Law, the network returned to the city where it began, providing a fitting setting for the discussions that ultimately shaped the present volume.

1.2 The 9th AIELN Conference: A Return to Tokyo

Convened in this historic setting on 14–15 June 2025, the 9th AIELN Conference was organized under the theme "Geopolitical Risks and Geoeconomics in International Economic Law: Asian Perspectives and Beyond." The Call for Papers invited contributors to explore how recent global turbulence—trade wars, armed conflicts, sanctions, political instability, and resulting disruptions to trade, investment, and supply chains—is reshaping the environment in which international economic law operates. At its core, the conference asked what these developments mean for the future direction of international economic law and what legal or policy responses may be possible in Asia and beyond.

The organizers were overwhelmed by a substantial and international response, receiving proposals arriving from across Asia as well as Europe, North America, and other regions. Faced with far more high-quality abstracts than available presentation slots, the Organizing Committee[2] navigated a demanding selection process, resulting in a programme that brought together scholars and practitioners at different career stages. Over two intensive days in Tokyo, discussions ranged from national security measures and trade restrictions to data governance, digital economy regulation, financial stability, and supply chain strategy.

From the outset, the organizers envisioned the conference as the beginning of a broader collaborative effort. Following the meeting, the editors secured publication support from Springer and reconvened the authors on 11 October 2025 for an online contributors' workshop. This second round of discussion allowed authors to refine their arguments, respond to peer feedback, and identify cross-cutting themes that informed the structure of this volume.

[2] The 9th AIELN Conference was organized by a committee consisting of Junji Nakagawa, Heng Wang, Taro Hamada, Yoshimichi Ishikawa, and Henry Gao. Professors Heng Wang and Henry Gao, both from the Yong Pung How School of Law at Singapore Management University, joined forces with the Tokyo-based organizers to shape the programme, review proposals, and chair sessions.

Ultimately, this book is the outcome of that process—a Tokyo conference followed by an online workshop that allowed the contributors to refine their ideas and develop them into the chapters that follow.

1.3 Structure of the Book

1.3.1 Part I: Geopolitical Risk, Supply Chains, and Sustainable Digitalization

Part I brings together four chapters examining how rising geopolitical risk, fragile supply chains, and accelerating digitalization are reshaping the basic architecture of international economic law. **Jianfu Chen** and **Zhiqiong June Wang** (Chap. 2) frame the contributions within the context of an eroding "liberal" trading order. They trace how geopolitical conflict and geoeconomic maneuvering are undermining the normative and institutional foundations of GATT/WTO, risking a return to the "law of the jungle" where power overrides rules. The chapter questions whether this turbulence marks the end of the post-war consensus or a transition toward fragmented regional blocs. **Rolf H. Weber** (Chap. 3) explores the double-edged sword of digitalizing supply chains. While technologies like blockchain enhance transparency, he warns that they also spike energy demand and create new cyber vulnerabilities, necessitating harmonized standards like the EU's Cyber Resilience Act. Turning to trade measures, **Mari SHIMIZU** (Chap. 4) focuses on policies adopted in the name of "supply chain resilience" and asks to what extent such measures—which often restrict imports from specific sources—can be justified under existing WTO rules, including general exceptions (GATT Article XX/GATS Article XIV) and security exceptions, without collapsing into disguised protectionism.

Building on a quantitative perspective, **Yoshimichi Ishikawa** (Chap. 5) introduces the Geopolitical Risk (GPR) Index and surveys empirical work on how spikes in geopolitical risk affect trade flows, foreign investment, and the configuration of global value chains (promoting "inward-looking" policies and fragmentation). His chapter argues for integrating "risk" more systematically into the design of trade and investment rules to enhance predictability. **Alexandros Bakos** (Chap. 6) then turns to the EU–India Trade and Technology Council and the Indo-Pacific Economic Framework to show how geopolitical competition is driving the creation of new, deliberately flexible forms of economic ordering. He argues that these "minilateral" initiatives prioritize strategic alignment and supply chain security over binding market access commitments.

Collectively, the chapters in this part show that the world of "rules-based trade" is increasingly negotiated under conditions of persistent geopolitical shock and structural uncertainty.

1.3.2 *Part II: National Security, Regulatory Space, and Investment Risk Governance*

Part II addresses the uneasy marriage between national security, regulatory autonomy, and the protection of foreign investment. Using the United Kingdom's National Security and Investment Act as a case study, **Apoorva Vishnoi** (Chap. 7) examines how ostensibly nationality-neutral screening mechanisms can in practice operate as selective filters targeting specific countries (notably China) and sectors, raising complex liability questions under bilateral investment treaties regarding expropriation and fair and equitable treatment. **Tomohiko Kobayashi** (Chap. 8) revisits the WTO security exception, asking whether its frequent invocation by major powers risks rendering WTO disciplines meaningless, and explores what pragmatic options remain under the current dispute settlement mechanism (such as Alternative Dispute Resolution) in the absence of a functioning Appellate Body.

The part then moves to the governance of data and political risk. **Teerawat Wongkaew** (Chap. 9) develops a comprehensive theory of international investment law as a mechanism for allocating political risk—including sanctions, climate transition policies, and broader geopolitical shifts—rather than as a simple "investor protection" device. His "political risk governance" framework offers a structured methodology for tribunals to balance regulatory change against investor expectations. Next, **Shota Watanabe** (Chap. 10) analyzes export restrictions on data motivated by national security concerns, focusing on China's comprehensive data security regime and "government access" risks, and examines reciprocal responses by the US and Japan. He considers how far such measures can be justified under trade and investment rules like the GATS and CPTPP. Finally, **Satomi SHINTANI** (Chap. 11) scrutinizes conflicts between environmental regulation and investment protection, especially in extractive industries in Latin America, and highlights the potential for regulatory chill when environmental measures trigger large compensation claims, proposing procedural reforms like state counterclaims.

Collectively, these contributions show that security and sustainability discourses are increasingly being channeled through legal concepts that determine who ultimately bears the cost of regulatory risk.

1.3.3 *Part III: Data Governance, Digital Sovereignty, and Regional Norm-Building in Asia*

Part III turns to data governance and digital sovereignty, with a particular focus on Asia as a laboratory for regional norm-building. **Intan Innayatun Soeparna** and **Sheva Atha Nugroho** (Chap. 12) analyze China's Digital Silk Road and its deepening role in ASEAN's digital infrastructure, arguing that it can function both as an engine of connectivity and as a "cyber silk curtain" that entrenches technological dependence despite RCEP's framework. Offering a Vietnamese perspective, **Nguyen**

Xuan My Hien and **Ngo Nguyen Thao Vy** (Chap. 13) discuss data sovereignty and trust, showing how GDPR-inspired models are being transplanted into domestic law and where they clash with local institutional capacities, arguing for a gradual convergence with Japan's "Data Free Flow with Trust" (DFFT) approach.

Taking a broader view across 58 jurisdictions, **Trang Anh Mac** (Chap. 14) surveys the highly uneven landscape of cybersecurity and data protection laws across 58 jurisdictions in the Asia–Pacific and examines the role of soft law instruments—standards, guidelines, and voluntary frameworks—in closing capacity gaps that hard law alone cannot address. **Hiroshi Kataoka** (Chap. 15) then situates CPTPP, RCEP, and initiatives such as Data Free Flow with Trust within a broader discussion of how to distinguish legitimate data protection from digital protectionism. He proposes a "Contextual Risk-Based Minimization Model" and discusses how middle powers in the region might use minilateral agreements to reconstruct data governance norms (the "Tokyo Effect").

Together, the chapters in this part ask whether Asian states will remain objects of great-power digital strategies, or whether they can act as autonomous norm entrepreneurs in the evolving data order.

1.3.4 Part IV: Emerging Regulatory Challenges: AI, Health, and Finance

Part IV examines how emerging technologies and sustainability objectives intersect with sectoral regulation in AI governance, health, and finance. **Sungjin Kang** (Chap. 16) expands the debate on "sovereign AI" by arguing that national-level self-sufficiency is structurally unrealistic given Asia's interdependent AI tech stacks. He therefore makes the case for an Asian regional AI framework that would move beyond the thin ethical language of existing digital trade agreements and toward more concrete cooperation on infrastructure, data resources (including local-language repositories), workforce development, and cybersecurity. The chapter's quiet message is that "sovereignty" in AI will remain a slogan unless it is redesigned as a regional project. In the health sector, **Francisco Hernández Fernández** (Chap. 17) interrogates the meaning—and frequent emptiness—of "technology transfer" under the TRIPS Agreement. He contrasts voluntary licensing initiatives such as the Medicines Patent Pool and the WHO mRNA hub with the underused but legally meaningful role of competition law, especially TRIPS Article 40, in addressing licensing practices that impede genuine know-how diffusion. The chapter thus reframes access to medicines not as a matter of benevolence, but of regulatory design and enforcement. **Soo-hyun LEE** (Chap. 18) concludes the volume by examining Hong Kong's taxonomy for sustainable finance and its implications for international investment law. He shows how the taxonomy's cautious treatment of "do no significant harm" reflects a prioritization of market usability and interoperability, while leaving a doctrinal gap that may weaken Hong Kong's ability to justify public-interest regulation in investment disputes. **Tsai-fang Chen** (Chap. 19) examines the challenges that AI-induced labor displacement poses to existing WTO rules. It argues that the current safeguard regime is ill-equipped to address systemic employment shocks linked to trade in AI-intensive goods and services, and proposes a special AI labor safeguard mechanism to manage such disruptions within a rules-based framework.

Collectively, this part shows that AI, public health, and sustainable finance are not peripheral add-ons but central testing grounds for whether international economic law can handle modern regulatory demands without pretending that slogans are governance.

References

AJWH (2022) Special Issue on Building a Sustainable Future: New Asian Regionalism in International Economic Law. Vol 17(1)

Choi W-M (ed) (2015) International Economic Law: The Asia-Pacific Perspective. Cambridge Scholars Publishing, Newcastle upon Tyne

Lim CL, Mercurio B (eds) (2015) International Economic Law after the Global Crisis: A Tale of Fragmented Disciplines. Cambridge University Press, Cambridge

Nakagawa J (ed) (2011) Multilateralism and Regionalism in Global Economic Governance: Trade, Investment and Finance. Routledge, London

Nakagawa J (ed) (2019) Asian Perspectives on International Investment Law. Routledge, London

Peng S, Lin C, Streinz T (eds) (2021) Artificial Intelligence and International Economic Law: Disruption, Regulation, and Reconfiguration. Cambridge University Press, Cambridge

Part I
Geopolitical Risk, Supply Chains, and Sustainable Digitalization

Chapter 2
Geopolitical Conflict, Geoeconomic Manoeuvring, and the Law of the Jungle: Are We Witnessing the End of the Liberal Trading Order?

Jianfu Chen and Zhiqiong June Wang

Abstract This chapter argues that the postwar liberal trading order is being destroyed by geopolitical conflict and geoeconomic manoeuvring. Developing country preferences politicised and fragmented the WTO. Major powers now struggle over rule-making through super-RTAs (TPP/CPTPP, RCEP, IPEF) serving geopolitical aims, while geoeconomic coercion—exemplified by superpowers' bullying behaviour towards smaller countries—exploits WTO gaps by avoiding formal measures. Trump 2.0 represents a qualitative shift: open disregard for multilateral rules through unjustified tariffs and attacks on the system itself. The chapter concludes that we are witnessing the end of the liberal trading order, with fragmentation into regional blocs (EU, CPTPP, RCEP) likely unless states relearn the dangers of abandoning multilateral disciplines.

Keywords Liberalism · Fairer Trade · Geopolitics · Geoeconomics · Economic Coercion · Trump 2.0

It is acknowledged that this chapter draws, in summary form, some materials from our earlier work on geopolitics and geoeconomics in global trade: Wang and Chen (2023) International trade regulation: evolving dynamics and shifting foundations. Routledge, London. Open access at https://www.taylorfrancis.com/books/oa-mono/https://doi.org/10.4324/9781003275510/international-trade-regulation-zhiqiong-june-wang-jianfu-chen.

J. Chen (✉)
University of Melbourne School of Law, Melbourne, Australia
e-mail: J.Chen@latrobe.edu.au

La Trobe University, Melbourne, Australia

Z. J. Wang
Western Sydney University Law School, Sydney, Australia
e-mail: Zhiqiong.Wang@westernsydney.edu.au

J. Nakagawa et al. (eds.), *Geopolitical Risks and Geoeconomics in International Economic Law*, Economics, Law, and Institutions in Asia Pacific,
https://doi.org/10.1007/978-981-95-6996-0_2

2.1 Introduction: An Unprecedented Time

Ever since the 'establishment' of the GATT in 1947, the international trade regulatory system, principally consisting of rules and mechanisms under the GATT/WTO, regional trade agreements and other bilateral/intergovernmental cooperative agreements, has faced various challenges and undergone continuing changes, mostly in the name and direction of trade liberalisation while struggling for fairer trade, however the latter might be defined.

More recently, however, a new dimension to the struggle has emerged, with its nature having become clearer with the rise of Asian giants such as China and India. Thus arises a new struggle that is geopolitical in nature, principally fought in the form of regional agreements, but it has also been reflected in demands for WTO reforms. Although it is geopolitical in nature, it is nevertheless, on its surface, fought in the name of a fairer trade order. Fundamentally, geopolitical struggle was fought under the existing rules-based order and was largely fought for the power to make rules and to lead governance reforms.

To aid and support geopolitical contention, there came geoeconomic manoeuvring. Until recently, geoeconomic manoeuvring or even economic coercion had only tried to sidestep rules, and justifications were most often made by arguing that measures taken were still within the agreed international framework. Avoidance of rules or rules-based order is the key to understanding geoeconomic manoeuvring.

Then there came Trump 2.0, with its so-called Liberation Day, America First, and Make America Great Again (MAGA) ideology and policies which have often caused chaos in international markets and, more importantly, some serious (if not fatal) damage to the existing international economic order.

Although the international trade regulatory system has always been contentious and dynamic, with different forces propelling its development at different times throughout its history,[1] the more recent development, that is, geopolitical conflict, geoeconomic manoeuvring, and economic coercion and bullying, has posed some historically unprecedented challenges that are no longer about freer and fairer trade. Although it is cruel to talk about the end of the liberal trade order, the reality is that the universal system (i.e. the WTO) and some of the regional and bilateral cooperative agreements are being made ineffective, irrelevant, and even redundant.

As far as international economic order is concerned, the most serious question that we must now ask is: should the Liberation Day and subsequent actions taken by the Trump Administration, and more broadly the MAGA movement, be understood as 'liberating' the United States from a rules-based order? And, if so, are we witnessing the end of the liberal trading order that has facilitated international trade and global economic prosperity for the past 80 years or so?

History is, in most cases, our best guide, but its lessons are seldom learnt, often forgotten or lost in the chaos. In this chapter, we would like to place what is happening today in a historical perspective. For this purpose, we shall start with the status quo, the liberal foundation for an international trade regulatory system as established in

[1] Wang and Chen (2023).

1947 and further strengthened, moderated and weakened throughout its history. We will then explain the struggle for fairer trading, that is, the gradual 'improvement' of the rules and the accommodation of the needs of developing countries. Both of these are well-known stories and, hence, will be only briefly addressed. This is followed by an introduction to the practice of regional agreements, which were clearly not intended by the GATT/WTO design, and the emergence of historically unprecedented geopolitical and geoeconomic struggles that politicise international trade regulation and fragment the global trade regulatory system, at our peril. Finally, we shall place our present chaos caused by Trump 2.0 in a historical context. This will assist us in determining the nature of the present struggle and why we are, or we are not, witnessing the destruction of the existing international economic order, and whether a new international economic order is being reshaped or rebuilt.

2.2 A Liberal Trading Order Established and Maintained (Until Recently)

As mentioned above, the establishment of a liberal trade order is now a well-known 'story' that needs not be retold. However, in light of recent developments, some key points (historical lessons) are highlighted below.

2.2.1 Separating the Economic from Political, but Political and Economic Intertwined

At the outset, it is important to point out that one of the most significant postwar developments was the establishment, in 1945, of the United Nations (UN) to replace the ineffective League of Nations. While the most important task of the UN is to prevent future wars by maintaining peace and security throughout the world, it is important to keep in mind that the UN also serves to promote international economic and social cooperation, as evidenced in the title of Chap. 9 of the UN Charter (International Economic and Social Cooperation). Details of its functions in this regard are set out in Art. 55 of the Charter, which includes the promotion of 'solutions of international economic, social, health, and related problems; and international cultural and educational cooperation'.[2]

Today, it is particularly important to note that the inclusion of international economic and social cooperation in the UN's fundamental tasks reflected one of the main strands of thinking about the possible causes of World War II at the end of that war. A prominent WTO scholar has pointed out that

[2] Charter of the United Nations Art. 55(b).

> the mistakes concerning economic policy during the interwar period (1920–1940) were a major cause of the disasters that led to the WWII. … During this interwar period, nations, particularly after the damaging 1930 US Tariff Act, took many protectionist measures, including quota-type restrictions, which choked off international trade. Political leaders of the US and elsewhere made statements about the importance of establishing postwar economic institutions that would prevent these mistakes from happening again.[3]

Now the 'old story' that needs to be kept in mind is that the World Bank and the IMF of the Bretton Woods institutions are part of the UN structure but, by accident rather than by design, the GATT/WTO was established and operates outside the UN (and, as such, is sometimes referred to as the economic UN).

2.2.2 The Liberal Trading Order Established and Maintained by the Power of a Hegemon and Its Allies

As world politics in the postwar period was dominated by the US and its allies, the international order was, unsurprisingly, a product of Western powers. However, liberalism as the then dominant Western ideology was only partially embedded in the UN—its fundamental philosophy is state cooperation and intervention while individualism was reflected in its objectives to protect human rights. On the other hand, with the US being the then economic hegemon, the global economic order that the Bretton Woods system pursued was a liberal economic order. In this liberal order, we are reminded, the 'pride of place is given to market rationality', even though '[t]his is not to say that authority is absent from such an order. It is to say that authority relations are constructed in such a way as to give maximum scope to market forces rather than to constrain them'.[4] In other words, the postwar international economic order was founded on a liberal market ideology that places its faith in market rationality while limiting government roles to, essentially and ideally, fostering such a market order.

This ideology is most clearly reflected in the GATT approach to trade liberalisation and regulation (the essence of the order)—free and open market (reducing trade barriers) under transparent regulation and operating on a non-discriminatory basis—as reflected in its Preamble. In other words, the liberal economic order is not an abstract notion that could easily be discarded; it is embedded in the underlying principles of international economic institutions. Further, liberalism as reflected in the principal and supporting agreements was not and still is not absolute free trade; it is about *freer* trade—regulated free trade. However, like most trade theories or justifications for free trade, the liberal market ideology that underpins the pursuit of the postwar international economic order has been criticised and challenged from time to time, and different narratives have been advanced through the history.[5]

---

[3] Jackson (1989, p. 31).

[4] Ruggie (1982, p. 381).

[5] Cohen (2019, p. 326).

2.2.3 And, the Order is Meant to Evolve—Freer and Fairer

Indeed, ever since its establishment, the GATT (and later WTO) has been an evolving mechanism that pushes for further liberalisation while also struggling to make its principles and mechanisms *fairer* for all, with the increasing emphasis placed on the notion of fair trade by the shift of trade regulation from reduction of tariffs to non-tariff measures as trade barriers. Ultimately, the Uruguay Round consolidated the efforts on non-tariff measures and, in doing so, hugely expanded the scope of regulation, and transformed the whole tariff-based system into a comprehensive yet contentious system in which tariff is but a component part.

The efforts on non-tariff measures were fought, as usual, in the name of free and fair trade, with liberalisation as its foundational philosophy. As such, the liberal economic order is further entrenched into global regulation of trade: freer trade on equal footing for all members.

However, it is important to note that this continuing entrenchment of the liberal economic order is not without interruption. The expanded membership of the GATT/WTO and the emergence of new economic powers have each created some unique problems that led to some less-than-comfortable struggles that continue today: preferential treatment for developing countries; regional agreements; and the rise of economies under authoritarian regimes. Each of these significantly challenges (but of a different nature) the liberal foundation of the GATT/WTO, especially its core principle of non-discrimination and the faithful compliance with the GATT/WTO rules.

2.3 Moderating for a Fairer Trade System

One of the first serious demands for reform and changes of the then GATT came from the developing countries, as part of their aspiration to establish a 'New International Economic Order (NIEO)', after the export-led development strategy failed to deliver what was promised as part of the liberal trade order. Not surprisingly, developing countries demanded certain concessions to be given to them so that the liberal order would be fairer in that the disadvantages of developing countries would be part of the consideration in the global trade order. Thus began the principal battle for fairer trade that was to provide some special treatment to developing countries (by implication, countries with weak capacity for trade) in global trading systems. Essentially, that battle was (and still is) to translate a political status (developed at the UN through UNCTAD) into a trading right (the so-called S&D treatment under the GATT/WTO), ending with the politicisation of the GATT/WTO.[6]

When the notion of 'developing countries', a political notion developed at the UN, was introduced to the GATT/WTO in trading right negotiations, a confusion between a political status/right and an economic/trading right in the UN's efforts to establish

[6] We had earlier analysed this issue elsewhere. See Wang and Chen (2023), Chap. 2.

an NIEO based on entirely different philosophical foundations was introduced into trade negotiations. Its end results became thus: a political victory for developing countries, with very little tangible economic benefits; the creation of ambiguous and ineffective exceptions to liberal trading order; the fragmentation of the GATT/WTO; and, most importantly, the severe undermining of principles of non-discrimination.[7]

The lesson here is that a politico-economic status must not be confused with a trading right/rule,[8] and an aspirational idea may not easily be translated into a binding and operational mechanism. In fact, such incorporation of a political right into a trade regulatory regime might cause more damage to trade than benefits and unnecessary complications for effective solutions to an identified problem—the problem of how to achieve fairer trade. It is important to always keep in mind that WTO is a trading regulatory organisation that performs best when it focuses on its core functions, and WTO must neither be the other UNCTAD nor follow the fate of it.

2.4 The Geopolitical Struggle and the Unintended Use of Regional Agreements

2.4.1 The Battle for Domination: Geopolitical Battles over Rules and Order

If the fight for fairer trade for developing countries ended up with the fragmentation of the GATT/WTO, another battle was also being fought simultaneously, with even more severe consequences for global trade. And though the battle might be of a different kind, it was still about rules and order; that is, geopolitics in global trade, which has been described as 'politics based on considerations of location and physical geography'.[9] Cruelly, it is about power, rivalry, domination, containment and, if all else fails, balance or sharing of powers in international relations. Until very recently, it is mostly 'bloc' politics in which one hegemon (a dominant force) leads and coordinates a group of countries (a 'bloc') for a common or shared objective(s) in international relations. In international economic relations, geopolitical conflict is fought mostly, but not exclusively, by way of regional trade agreements (RTAs). Although the battle takes the form of a contest between multilateralism and regionalism, the real battle is for domination, especially in international rule-making.

On paper, concluding an RTA does not violate GATT/WTO rules. Indeed, the original GATT—Article XXIV—allows for the formation and operation among contracting parties of customs unions, free trade areas, and interim agreements leading to either of these arrangements to be made outside and alongside the GATT.

[7] For detailed analysis, see Wang and Chen (2023), Chap. 2.

[8] We concede that the separation of politics from economics is difficult, but the confusion of a political status with a trading right is a different issue.

[9] Scholvin (2016, p. 13).

Similarly, the GATS (Article V) under the WTO also made the allowance for the formation of additional arrangements outside the GATS. Additionally, agreements such as those that grant special benefits by developed nations to developing countries have further extended the application of the exception to WTO rules,[10] including the use of waiver under the GATT/WTO.[11] These provisions, in their legal nature, make special exceptions to the non-discrimination principles under the GATT/WTO by limiting preferential treatment among participating members of the relevant agreement. As such, they are generally seen as being complementary to efforts for global trade liberalisation even though it is also contested as to whether these provisions produce benefits or disadvantages or damages to the multilateral trade regime (i.e. the GATT/WTO).[12]

While multilateral, regional, and bilateral agreements and arrangements have coexisted in international trade law ever since, perhaps, the emergence of trade law, the interrelationship among them and their relative weight in trade liberalisation have been in a constant state of flux, and each of them has often been controversial as to its nature as well as its relationship vis-à-vis the others. Further, even though the initial RTA development did not challenge the liberal foundation of the GATT/WTO, the existence of a large number of RTAs—some 375 as of August 2025[13] does lead to the erosion of the integrity and coherence of the WTO. Most importantly, the emergence of the ever-expanding regime of RTAs but especially the negotiation and the conclusion of some of them, the super-RTAs—the TPP/CPTPP,[14] TTIP,[15] RCEP,[16] and more recently the IPEF[17]—suggest something more sinister was going on, namely, the geopolitical contention between existing and rising powers, to call it out, even though the US withdrew from the TPP in 2017 and some of the super-RTAs never came to fruition.

Fundamentally, super-RTAs have always had a geopolitical element that is also intra-regional in nature, and they are clearly meant for domination and primacy in international economic order, as many contain exclusive membership requirements. With a large number of countries and regions in their membership (while also being members of the WTO), it would be very naïve to describe them as being complementary to the traditional global trade (WTO) regulatory regime. Indeed, the geopolitical nature makes a mockery of the RTA's original purpose, that is, as an interim agreement or special exception for developing countries or as complementary means for

---

[10] See the 1979 Decision on Differential and More Favourable Treatment, Reciprocity and Fuller Participation of Developing Countries (the Enabling Clause).

[11] GATT, Art. XXV; Understanding in Respect of Waivers of Obligations under the General Agreement on Tariffs and Trade 1994.

[12] For a summary of the controversy and debate, see Lester et al. (2018, pp. 331–338), Matsushita et al. (2015, pp. 509–512).

[13] See WTO (2025).

[14] Trans-Pacific Partnership/The Comprehensive and Progressive Agreement for Trans-Pacific Partnership (concluded).

[15] Transatlantic Trade and Investment Partnership (negotiations discontinued in April 2019).

[16] Regional Comprehensive Economic Partnership (concluded).

[17] Indo-Pacific Economic Framework for Prosperity (status uncertain).

free trade. One must remember that RTAs are special exceptions to the most important principle of the GATT/WTO: non-discrimination. The reality, however, is that it is a showdown between existing and rising powers as a result of the shifting balance of economic powers, and of the search for a new equilibrium in the international economic order.[18]

2.4.2 It Is Polite Contention Under the Law Until It Is Not

To be precise, the geopolitical contention in the form of super-RTAs is one between US-led Western powers and China, the latter's rise poses some very different challenges due to its very different political and economic system as well as its strong economy, which is also capable of challenging the US hegemony.

The China story is a long and complicated one. Suffice it to say, China's efforts in regionalism have always been strategic and geopolitical, having regional domination (over rivals Japan and India) but, more recently, global domination (or at least counter-balancing the US hegemony) in mind.[19] As such, the race to regionalism inevitably shaped up as a showdown between the existing and emerging powers. The competition for regionalism then effectively changed the nature of the race to regionalism as the rivalry became of a global nature. While economic powers and interests still worked in the background, backing up claims for regional leadership, the global geopolitical rivalry was the force that pushed the existing powers and rising powers to a showdown in their efforts to establish a new international economic order. Thus, geopolitical contention was about controlling the development of international economic order, or more precisely the right to rule/decision-making. This is most clearly revealed when then-US President Barack Obama declared in 2016:

> As a Pacific power, the United States has pushed to develop a high-standard Trans-Pacific Partnership, a trade deal that puts American workers first and makes sure we write the rules of the road for trade in the twenty-first century. … America should write the rules. America should call the shots. Other countries should play by the rules that America and our partners set, and not the other way around. … The United States, not countries like China, should write [the rules].[20]

Not surprisingly, the existence of the deeply rooted rivalries among major powers (Japan, China, and India) in Asia, and the geopolitical competition among world powers (China, US (and EU), Japan, and India) eventually led to an entirely different set of considerations for Asia–Pacific nations. Thus arose a new initiative, the creation

[18] Obviously, some super-RTAs are of a clear geopolitical nature (such as TPP/CPTPP as further analysed below), others appear to be less so (such as RECEP). However, when the timing and leadership (the forces behind such a push) in forming these RTAs are taken into consideration, all are clearly geopolitical in nature. For detailed analysis of the emergence and the nature of the super-RTAs, see Wang and Chen (2023), Chap. 3; and Chen (2014).

[19] For detailed analysis of China's rise and its approaches to RTAs, see Wang and Chen (2023), Chap. 3.

[20] Obama (2016).

or, more precisely, the then work-in-progress project of creating the concept of Indo-Pacific.[21]

There were different conceptions as to what Indo-Pacific is, and the notion remains controversial and contested. Essentially, however,

> [t]he idea of an Indo-Pacific region involves recognising that the growing economic, geopolitical, and security connections between the Western Pacific and the Indian Ocean regions are creating a single 'strategic system'. At its simplest, this can be understood as a set of geopolitical power relationships among nations where major changes in one part of the system affect what happens in the others. In this sense, the Indo-Pacific can be understood as a maritime 'super-region' with its geographical centre in Southeast Asia.[22]

And,

> the overwhelming rationale of the Indo-Pacific thus far has been strategic and geopolitical and designed to extend and reinforce American-led military primacy and to balance against the rise of China'.[23]

Indeed, when the Indo-Pacific Strategy (February 2022) and the Indo-Pacific Economic Framework for Prosperity (IPEF; May 2022) were finally launched, security considerations prevailed over economic cooperation. While the US and its like-minded allies would 'decide on rules of the road', little was about trade liberalisation.

In that context, it was not unreasonable for China to question whether the US was politicising, weaponising, and ideologising economic issues and coercing regional countries to take sides by economic means.[24] In short, the RTA showdown between political powers was becoming open geopolitical warfare.

In short, the search for a new balance of power in the international economic order has led to a twisted development—the rapid development of RTAs, but especially the so-called super-RTAs, and the concept of Indo-Pacific with a geopolitical balance of power in mind. There is little doubt that such a development has a potential to fundamentally undermine multilateralism in favour of opposing trade blocs more for geopolitical consideration than for trade liberalisation and thus a potential to start a trade-led 'cold war'. We should keep this in mind when we consider Trump 2.0.

---

[21] There is yet no indication whether the current Trump Administration (Trump 2.0) has abandoned the strategy, but the Trump tariff war seems to treat 'enemies' and allies alike.

[22] Medcalf (2015) (citations omitted).

[23] Beeson and Lee-Brown (2017).

[24] Wang (2022).

2.5 Geoeconomic Manoeuvring and Sidestepping Rules

2.5.1 Geoeconomics: A 'War by Other Means'

Geoeconomics, as a notion, emerged in the early 1990s. While it has been widely used as a term to describe power politics by economic means, or 'war by other means',[25] its meaning is not precisely defined. It is sometimes seen as a sub-variant of geopolitics. However, at least in its early usage, it envisages a geopolitical strategy in which capital replaces firepower, civilian innovation replaces military advancement, and markets replace garrisons and military bases.[26] Based on this understanding, geoeconomics is defined as 'the use of economic instruments to promote and defend national interests and to produce geopolitical results'.[27] In other words, it implies the advancement of the geostrategic goals of one party, and is *not seen* as a mutually beneficial relationship.[28]

In the Asian context, geoeconomics is often used to analyse China's Belt and Road Initiatives as well as to describe China's reaction to political disagreements from smaller countries such as, most notably, Norway, South Korea, Australia, and Lithuania.[29]

2.5.2 Geoeconomics: The Power of the Powerful, and the New Species—Economic Coercion

More broadly, there are always formidable difficulties in attempting to subject powerful countries to international rules, even though international law is precisely meant to address the problem. In this context, one is reminded of the fact that the US Trade Representative (USTR) frequently determined, unilaterally, violations of US rights by foreign governments and imposed retaliation measures without the involvement of GATT/WTO. And, of course, there are the 'American Exceptionalism' and 'America First' ideologies.[30] We mention these here to caution that geoeconomic behaviours in the Asian context are not unique in the world; it is just part of the ugly power politics in our world.

Back to Asia, China's geoeconomic practices (and, of course, US practices) suggest that geoeconomic manoeuvring has two entirely different faces. The Belt and Road Initiatives can be seen, in some senses, as 'carrots', though not subject to

---

[25] Blackwill and Harris (2016).

[26] Scholvin and Wigell (2018).

[27] Blackwill and Harris (2016).

[28] Wigell and Vihma (2016).

[29] Zhang (2018), Wiśniewski (2021), Blumenthal (2018), Chen (2019), and Uren (2020).

[30] Trebilcock et al. (2012), Deudney and Meiser (2012), Sanger and Haberman (2016), Sheldon et al. (2018), and Petersmann (2018).

multilateral or even regional agreements but regulated through bilateral agreements. While such arrangements contain the potential for coercion and, indeed, have led to some less-than-desirable practices,[31] it is difficult to deny that many less developed countries (or their governments, more precisely) do welcome the Belt and Road Initiatives and many of the specific projects therein.

China's geoeconomic practices towards political disagreements with some smaller countries or less powerful (but developed) countries (e.g. Norway, South Korea, Australia, and Lithuania) are, to say the least, less than civil. Recent China–Australia relations provide a case in point—an ugly aspect of using newly acquired economic powers in an extra-legal manner that also shows the impotence of the international law.[32]

Australia was one of the first Western countries to establish diplomatic relations with China, with its recognition of the People's Republic of China (PRC) in 1972. A bilateral relationship between the two countries developed reasonably smoothly and, in 2014, the bilateral relationship was defined as a 'comprehensive strategic partnership', with the China–Australia Free Trade Agreement (ChAFTA) entering into force in December 2015. By then, China had been Australia's largest trading partner in goods and services for several years, accounting for nearly one-third of Australia's global trade in 2019.

Suffice to say that the relationship between the two countries began to deteriorate rapidly from around 2018, due to a series of events: Australia's decision to ban the participation of Huawei in Australia's 5G construction in 2018; the introduction of a comprehensive package of legislative reforms by Australia in relation to foreign interference, also in 2018; and in 2020, Australia's call for an international inquiry into the origin of the Covid-19 virus.

China did not hide its anger with Australia and, through the government-controlled media, began to disseminate a message that China will exercise its economic muscle to punish Australia. 'Sanctions' then began to emerge, not through any government announcement or measures, but rather through various reports of go-slow practices at Chinese customs to hold up the clearance of Australian goods; new administrative hurdles imposed on the importation of Australian beef, lobster, fruit, cotton, and timber; and the massive delays or plain refusal of Australian coal shipments at Chinese ports. Most of these 'bans' or 'sanctions' were imposed by China without any formal notice being issued (some legal measures were later imposed by China, such as anti-dumping and anti-subsidy duties on Australian barley in May 2020 and on Australian wines a few months later); thus, officially and in many instances, there were no 'bans' or 'sanctions'.

The only avenue to address such informal sanctions was consultation, a traditional and long-held practice in Chinese dispute resolution. However, China simply closed its doors to such consultation, despite the existence of a bilateral trade and investment treaty which provides methods for dispute resolution, including consultation. In fact, China blocked all official communication channels.

---

[31] Wang and Chen (2020).

[32] The next few paragraphs are a further updated summary of Wang and Chen (2023), Chap. 5.

It is important to stress, in the absence of any government-to-government consultation and formal government measures imposing sanctions, the impotence of bilateral agreements and WTO dispute resolution (DR) mechanisms.[33] This is because the injured party simply does not have a cause of action nor indeed any formal evidence to support complaint or its legal action (if any taken).

This so-called China–Australia trade dispute was described as 'the most salient present instance of trade coverage being weaponised for political ends',[34] representing a new form of geoeconomic manoeuvring by the blatant use of trade as a means of economic coercion,[35] yet avoiding the ascertainment of legality under international law.

In short, DR mechanisms in international law (e.g. WTO) assume that parties will act in a bona fide manner and comply with the law in good faith, but that is often not the case in geoeconomic manoeuvring. Clearly, what China did was to avoid the laws, not to openly break them—at least China appeared to aim at such an outcome by refusing any communication with Australia. China's actions on restricting/hindering Australia's trade were, put simply, extra-legal measures for which there are few legal channels to challenge their legality nor, indeed, methods to gather evidence as required by the WTO or other international (including bilateral) agreements.

2.6 The Law of the Jungle: The Abandoning of and Total Disregard for Rules

2.6.1 We Were in Trouble Well Before Trump 2.0

As analysed above,[36] the world before Trump 2.0 was already in a precarious place: the fault lines in the global trade order, including the flawed design in the WTO DR scheme,[37] had already been showing, and the geopolitical conflict and geoeconomic manoeuvring had fragmented the integrity of the global trade system, paralysing the WTO as a negotiation forum and as a dispute resolution mechanism.

Domestically, in the US and in many other (developed or developing) nations, the increasing gap between rich and poor, the decline of manufacturing, and hardly

---

[33] It should be made clear that the bilateral and multilateral (e.g. WTO) DR arrangements are impotent not because of the arrangements *per se*, but because some authoritarian (centrally controlled) countries are willing to and capable of manoeuvring outside the established rules. In the case of China, there are many cases concerning China that had been referred to the WTO for 'adjudication', but there are also many cases that had not been so as China had taken extra-legal measures that were outside the established rules of the WTO or other bilateral/regional arrangements.

[34] Financial Times (2022).

[35] Hanson et al. (2020), Zhang (2018), Wiśniewski (2021), Blumenthal (2018), Chen (2019), and Uren (2020).

[36] For more detailed analysis, see Wang and Chen (2023).

[37] See Wang and Chen (2023), Chap. 5.

sustainable trade and budget deficits, etc., were there for all to see. Clearly, the world was in desperate need for leadership to undertake repairs and reforms, and to address challenges brought about by globalisation. Instead, we got Trump 2.0 which so far has brought about chaos, uncertainty, and unpredictability.

2.6.2 *The Final Nail in the Coffin?*[38]

Much has been said about Trump 2.0, especially its first 100 days.[39] In relation to international economic order, the shock came on 2 April 2025, a day President Trump called 'Liberation Day',[40] when the Trump Administration announced a minimum 10% tariff on all imports to the US, and higher 'reciprocal'[41] tariffs (ranging from 15% on imports from Norway to 49% on imports from Cambodia) on some 57 countries: friends (20% on EU, 24% on Japan, etc.), foes, and non-inhabited islands,[42] but with some shocking exclusions, including Russia, Belarus, North Korea, and Cuba. This was followed by a 90-day postponement for the implementation of the 'reciprocal' tariffs,[43] selected exceptions,[44] the escalation of 'trade war' between the US and China, and then the apparent backdown from the US.[45] Chaos ensued, and

[38] For some, there should be no question mark to this title. See Froman (2025).

[39] For overviews, see The New York Times (2025a, b). For assessment by legal scholars, see The New York Times (2025c).

[40] But a day others call the day the global trading regime ended. See Curran (2025).

[41] At least since the conclusion of the Uruguay Round negotiations of the WTO, 'reciprocity' has been seen as a 'dirty word'. See Kelly (2025a). A 'dirty word' or not, there is no legal basis for reciprocal tariffs in WTO or regional trade agreements; all tariffs are based on the result of negotiations (hence trade-offs) which involve much more than the consideration of tariffs.

[42] White House (2025c) and the Annexes therein. The non-inhabited islands include Australia's external territory of Heard Island and McDonald Islands. See Lyon and Evershed (2025).

[43] Jones et al. (2025).

[44] Halpert M (2025).

[45] Tariffs on China reached 125% by 10 April 2025, with some up to 245%. On 22 April 2025, President Trump seemed to suggest that the US and China were in negotiations and he promised to substantially cut tariffs on China. See Koziol (2025b). China, however, soon stated that there had been no contact or negotiations with the US. See Xinhua (2025a). And then there were negotiations. See White House (2025b). The result of the negotiations was to postpone, for 90 days (which was further extended for another 90 days from 12 August 2025) all tariffs imposed on 'Liberation Day' and the subsequent retaliation and counter-retaliation tariffs and measures, effectively bringing the US and China back to the pre-Liberation Day relationship (but with the US retaining the extra 10% tariff announced on Liberation Day for all imports into the US. After this backdown, tariffs between the US and China would still amount to 30–50%, depending on the products. Not surprisingly, the consecutive postponements have given China more time and, importantly, optimism that it is winning the conflict and contention. See Sun (2025). The US-China *tic-for-tat* trade war is, at the time of publication, on-going with no clear end in sight.

uncertainty and unpredictability soon became the norm, causing massive losses and damages to global stock markets.[46]

As to the 'Liberation Day', one wonders from what the US wants to liberate itself, and who would be liberated. The reality is that the US has been the very hegemon since the end of WWII, and it has been the principal architect and a main promoter of the postwar international economic order. In this context, it is most ironical for the US President to claim that, '[f]or decades, our country has been looted, pillaged, raped and plundered by nations near and far, both friend and foe alike'.[47]

And, of course, much has been said about the illogical basis for the application of tariffs,[48] the irrationality for the imposition of tariffs, the bizzare calculation method for the so-called 'reciprocal' tariffs, and the economic coercion in doing so.[49] One may also talk about economic losses, the self-defeating nature of the 'policies', and the unlikelihood of achieving any of the supposed objectives—revenue raising, trade balance, manufacturing, renegotiating terms of trade, and, of course, constraining China.[50]

The real question for the global economic order is: are we witnessing the end of the liberal trade order?

2.6.3 The Essential Nature of Trump 2.0

The most lethal aspect of Trump's tariff war, in terms of international economic order, is the total disregard for multilateral, regional, and bilateral agreements which have taken some 80 years to develop and the subsequent, potentially permanent, damage to the international economic order. Though it may sound overly pessimistic, the question we must ask ourselves is whether Trump's 'liberation' means liberating from a rules-based international order. The reality is, the phrase 'rules-based international order' seems to have completely disappeared in the 142 or so executive orders issued by the Trump 2.0 Administration by the end of its first 100 days in office.[51] And so far, we do not ascertain any rules that the 'American Liberation' is willing to comply with (and one must not forget that even in a military war there are some rules to

---

[46] For the US market alone, more than USD6 trillion was wiped out within two days of the announcement. See Huang et al. (2025). It should be pointed out that as of mid-June 2025 the stock markets had all recovered. This does not, however, mean that uncertainty has disappeared. For further expert views, see Council on Foreign Relations (2025).

[47] Crew and Clarke (2025), Kelly (2025a, b, c).

[48] After many negotiations with various countries, on 8 August 2025 the US imposed new tariffs over some 90 countries, representing the highest tariffs on imports since 1934. See Budget Lab at Yale (2025).

[49] See e.g. Bartholomeusz (2025a), Koziol (2025a), The Australian (2025), Bown and Irwin (2025), and Prasad (2025).

[50] Additionally, there are major issues as to the constitutionality of the executive order that imposes the tariffs. See Room (2025).

[51] The Age (2025).

go by) other than coercing countries to comply with America's will. Further, as we have just discussed above, the global liberal trading order had already been fractured; compliance with it has at times been distorted or ignored by countries (including, of course, China and the US) when it is convenient to do so. In other words, the global trading system (i.e. WTO) had already been in serious trouble by the time of Trump 2.0, as a negotiation forum or a mechanism for compliance and enforcement of rules.[52]

If Trump's tariff war is aiming at creating a new international economic order, as some observers have suggested,[53] it is then even more puzzling as to how it is conducted. The fundamental nature of Trump 2.0 is the open disregard of international law which had never happened other than by rogue states.[54] In relation to geopolitics and geoeconomics, Trump 2.0 openly disdains its allies and alliances—the latter the constant feature in geopolitical and geoeconomic contention. The damage to the Western alliance is so severe that European Commission President Ursula von der Leyen recently declared that '[t]he West as we knew it no longer exists'.[55]

More broadly, it is important to remember that there was a bipartisan reappraisal of the liberal trading order well before Trump 2.0.[56] One should not forget that the paralysis of the WTO DR system started under the Obama presidency, intensified during Trump 1.0, and continued into the Biden Administration.[57] In this context, Trump 2.0 does not start the destruction of the global liberal trading order; its actions constitute another, potentially final, nail in the coffin, and that is worrying.

Not surprisingly, the end of an era has now been pronounced by many. A national newspaper in Australia declared that Trump's 'executive order seeks to dismantle the world trade system originating from 1947, threatening disruption, recessions, and a new protectionist Fortress America. Trump's new tariff regime is the final termination of the age of trade liberalisation and globalisation that has lifted incomes around the world'.[58] Others have announced that the global trading system as we know it has now ended and there is no going back.[59]

One may argue, of course, that all is not lost and we should be a little bit more optimistic; after all, Trump 2.0 may only last four years. The trouble is, assuming the global liberal trading order survives Trump 2.0, will the order be the same, will the US have any credibility left (considering that the US has been less than supportive since Obama), and will nations still trust it? Indeed, a major commentator in the

[52] See Hopewell (2024).

[53] Rosalsky (2025), Hurlburt (2025), and White House (2025a) 2025c

[54] Not so long ago it would have been unimaginable for anyone to describe the US as a rogue state, but this is exactly the label some commentators now give to the US. See, e.g. Kelly (2025a, b, c) and Beckley (2025).

[55] Swanson (2025).

[56] See also Pettis (2025). It should be pointed out that part of the damage was caused by Trump 1.0. See Beckley (2020). On the bipartisan reappraisal of the liberal international trade order, especially during Biden Administration, see Bade (2023).

[57] See Wang and Chen (2023), Chap. 5.

[58] Kelly (2025a, b, c).

[59] Froman (2025).

Australian media summed up thus: 'Trump has successfully blown up the global trading system. America, regardless of the nature of successor administrations, will never be as trusted as an ally or trade partner again'.[60]

In short, it is safe to assume that the global economic order will never be the same in the foreseeable future and, in this context, we are indeed witnessing the end of the global liberal trading order.

2.7 Conclusion: Lessons Learnt and Lost

When the international trading system, as symbolised in GATT/WTO and regional/bilateral trade agreements, is focused on reducing trade barriers in a non-discriminatory manner, even though it has largely neglected issues in relation to export (including those of control and restriction),[61] it works reasonably well. However, it has never been effective in dealing with issues other than trade barriers. Indeed, GATT/WTO records on 'trade-related' issues are mixed. It has proven mostly ineffective when it addresses politically charged issues, such as special treatment for developing countries, regional trade agreements, or geopolitical contentions.[62] In other words, attempts to address issues other than trade barriers have caused more damage to the global trading system than facilitating trade and its liberalisation. It is therefore important to remember that removing trade barriers in a non-discriminatory manner is the cornerstone of global trade order, an order that has reduced poverty, created prosperity, and maintained global peace. Despite its inherent problems, we have much to be thankful for the establishment and continuation of this liberal trading order. It is equally important to recognise that, since its establishment in 1947, the global trading system has been weakened, fragmented, and sometimes ignored in its attempts to deal with fairer trade, geopolitical and geoeconomic conflict, compliance, and enforcement of rules. Nevertheless, a rules-based international order was never openly abandoned, despite the constant struggles among major powers for domination and control of rule-making, reform, and repair.

This international liberal trading order is now facing a number of unprecedented and threatening challenges. Unless other evidence emerges, it is doubtful that the Trump 2.0 has any longer-term game or any clear vision for the future: 'It is just

[60] Bartholomeusz (2025b).

[61] This weakness was gravely exposed during the Covid-19 crisis when many countries competed for limited availability of basic medical and health materials and equipment, including vaccines. To date, there have not been any effective measures that address issues related to export controls at the WTO.

[62] More recently, efforts to address 'social issues'—issues that are not trade in nature but having potential impact on certain human rights (e.g. labour standards, environment protection, trade and gender, etc.) brought about by trade liberalisation, as highlighted since the Uruguay Round (1986–93) of the GATT/WTO negotiations—have all proven to be ineffective, but these are separate stories that need to be addressed elsewhere.

making it up as it goes',[63] and probably '[the President] has no clue what he is doing'.[64] As such, Trump 2.0 is unlikely to go about building any new order.[65] Trump 2.0 has changed everything, and 'America First' (or whichever country comes first) goes against the underlying philosophy of the international liberal trading order that has so far operated and served us reasonably well (despite the various difficulties and problems) for some 80 years. History has always reminded us that those who brutally and ruthlessly destroy the past won't be the ones who build a new one, let alone a better one. Under these circumstances, we must seriously ask: if the global liberal trading order won't survive Trump 2.0, what will the future trading system look like?

Ideally, of course, we still need the economic superpowers to work together in managing the next process, be it re-globalisation or de-globalisation. If we are to strengthen globalisation, as Stiglitz pointed out, US, China and all '[t]hose seeking closer economic integration have a special responsibility to be strong advocates of global governance reforms'.[66] Even if the next phase of international economic collaboration is not about closer integration but de-globalisation, the global community still needs to manage the process better than it managed globalisation,[67] as there are no alternatives to collaboration when the world's nations are already interdependent.

It is likely that we will be in a de-globalisation process in the foreseeable future, with the WTO idle. In this process, regional arrangements will be the main currency, with the EU (Europe), the CPTPP[68] (Pacific), and the RCEP[69] (Asia) as the new tripod in the fragmented global trading system, but none will be in the form of coalitions of the like-minded.[70] In this new world, the trouble is that the poorest countries in Africa and in Asia will be the largest losers, and the Americas will be in limbo.

Even if we assume Trump has some geopolitical aims in mind, his abrasive actions on tariffs and the Administration's subsequent negotiations are likely to push some Asian countries to gather around China.[71] Indeed, China is exercising its economic powers by warning other countries that it will take countermeasures if they make deals with the US 'at China's expense'[72]—this is not particularly civil either, and it is not a particularly promising future to anticipate.

---

[63] Bartholomeusz (2025c).

[64] Friedman (2025).

[65] Kelly (2025b).

[66] Stiglitz (2016).

[67] Stiglitz (2022).

[68] The Comprehensive and Progressive Agreement for Trans-Pacific Partnership (CPTPP) is the latest version of the TPP.

[69] Regional Comprehensive Economic Partnership Agreement (RCEP).

[70] See e.g. Froman (2025), Atkinson and Ezell (2025).

[71] Kuok (2025).

[72] See Xinhua (2025b), Hodge (2025), and Lee (2025).

References

Atkinson RD, Ezell S (2025) Toward globalization 2.0: a new trade policy framework for advanced-industry leadership and national power. Information Technology and Innovation Foundation, Mar 24. https://itif.org/publications/2025/03/24/globalization2-a-new-trade-policy-framework/. Accessed 16 Aug 2025

Bade G (2023) Joe Biden wants a 'new economic world order': It's never looked more disordered. Politico, 25 May. https://www.politico.com/news/2023/05/25/joe-bidens-economy-trade-china-00096781. Accessed 25 Apr 2025

Bartholomeusz S (2025a) Donald Trump's dumb war just got much, much dumber. The Age, 3 Apr. https://www.theage.com.au/business/the-economy/donald-trump-s-dumb-trade-war-just-got-much-much-dumber-20250403-p5lor6.html. Accessed 22 Apr 2025

Bartholomeusz S (2025b) Trump has successfully blown up the global trading system. The Age, 15 Apr. https://www.theage.com.au/business/markets/trump-has-successfully-blown-up-the-global-trading-system-20250415-p5lrsa.html. Accessed 23 Apr 2025

Bartholomeusz S (2025c) The Trump administration is just making it up as it goes. The Age, 24 Apr. https://www.theage.com.au/business/markets/the-trump-administration-is-just-making-it-up-as-it-goes-20250424-p5ltwu.html. Accessed 24 Apr 2025

Beckley M (2020) Rogue superpower. Foreign Aff, 6 Oct. https://www.foreignaffairs.com/articles/united-states/2020-10-06/illiberal-american-century-rogue-superpower. Accessed 24 Apr 2025

Beckley M (2025) The age of American unilateralism: how a rogue superpower will remake the global order. Foreign Aff, 16 Apr. https://www.foreignaffairs.com/united-states/age-american-unilateralism. Accessed 26 Apr 2025

Beeson M, Lee-Brown T (2017) The future of Asian regionalism: not what it used to be? Asia Pac Policy Stud 4(2):195–210

Blackwill R, Harris J (2016) War by other means: geoeconomics and statecraft. Belknap Press, Cambridge

Blumenthal D (2018) Economic coercion as a tool in China's grand strategy. Statement before the US Senate Committee on Foreign Relations, 24 Jul. https://www.foreign.senate.gov/imo/media/doc/072418_Blumenthal_Testimony.pdf. Accessed 5 Apr 2022

Bown CP, Irwin DA (2025) The incoherent case for tariffs: Trump's fixation on economic coercion will subvert his economic goals. Foreign Aff, 11 Mar. https://www.foreignaffairs.com/united-states/incoherent-case-tariffs-trump. Accessed 22 Apr 2025

Budget Lab at Yale (2025) State of U.S. tariffs: July 28, 2025. https://budgetlab.yale.edu/research/state-us-tariffs-july-28-2025. Accessed 14 Aug 2025

Chen D (2019) Countering China's economic coercion: no fear but resolve, no illusion but diversification. Discussion Paper, Macdonald-Laurier Institute. https://macdonaldlaurier.ca/files/pdf/20190827_China_Economic_Coercion_Chen_PAPER_FWeb.pdf. Accessed 5 Apr 2022

Chen J (2014) Regional Trade Agreement in Context, in Hu J & Vanhullebusch (Eds) Regional Cooperation and Free Trade Agreements in Asia (Leiden/Boston:Brill/Nijhoff), 377–402

Cohen HG (2019) What is international trade law for? Am J Int Law 113(2):326–346

Council on Foreign Relations (2025) What Trump trade policy has achieved since 'Liberation Day', 7 Jul. https://www.cfr.org/article/what-trump-trade-policy-has-achieved-liberation-day. Accessed 16 Aug 2025

Crew J, Clarke J (2025) What Trump has done — and why it matters. BBC, 4 Apr. https://www.bbc.com/news/articles/c0qnd2x1nn3o. Accessed 24 Apr 2025

Curran J (2025) The day the international economic system died in the Rose Garden, 3 Apr. https://www.afr.com/policy/foreign-affairs/the-day-the-international-economic-system-died-in-the-rose-garden-20250403-p5losx. Accessed 25 Apr 2025

Deudney D, Meiser J (2012) American exceptionalism. In: Cox M, Stokes D (eds) US foreign policy, 2nd edn. OUP, Oxford

Executive Order (2 April 2025). 'Regulating Imports with a Reciprocal Tariff to Rectify Trade Practices that Contribute to Large and Persistent Annual United States Goods Trade Deficits', and the Annexes therein. Available at https://www.whitehouse.gov/presidential-actions/2025/04/regulating-imports-with-a-reciprocal-tariff-to-rectify-trade-practices-that-contribute-to-large-and-persistent-annual-united-states-goods-trade-deficits/ (last accessed 21 April 2025)

Financial Times (2022) Australia offers timely lessons in resisting Chinese trade coercion, 9 Feb. https://www.ft.com/content/fcb3590b-e468-4b88-9fba-217f54bd49d8. Accessed 10 Feb 2022

Friedman TL (2025) Why Trump's bullying is going to backfire on him. The Age, 19 Feb. https://www.theage.com.au/business/markets/why-trump-s-bullying-is-going-to-backfire-on-him-20250219-p5ldcv.html. Accessed 19 Feb 2025

Froman MBG (2025) After the trade war: remaking rules from the ruins of the rules-based system. Foreign Aff, 11 Aug. https://www.foreignaffairs.com/united-states/after-trade-war-michael-froman. Accessed 12 Aug 2025

Halpert M (2025) Trump exempts smartphones and computers from new tariffs. BBC, 13 Apr. https://www.bbc.com/news/articles/c20xn626y81o. Accessed 22 Apr 2025

Hanson F, Currey E, Beattie T (2020) The Chinese Communist Party's coercive diplomacy. Australian Strategic Policy Institute. https://www.aspi.org.au/report/chinese-communist-partys-coercive-diplomacy. Accessed 4 Apr 2022

Hodge A (2025) China's threat to Asia on US tariff deals. The Australian, 22 Apr. https://www.theaustralian.com.au/world/chinas-threat-to-asia-on-us-tariff-deals/news-story/4efc9dc723f01ce83ba8aa0d3f85ffd6. Accessed 23 Apr 2025

Hopewell K (2024) The world is abandoning the WTO and America and China are leading the way. Foreign Aff, 7 Oct. https://www.foreignaffairs.com/united-states/world-abandoning-wto-china-leading-way-kristen-hopewell. Accessed 28 Apr 2025

Huang V, Hur K, Banerji G (2025) Trump's tariffs wipe out over $10 trillion on Wall Street in epic two-day rout. The Australian, 5 Apr. https://www.theaustralian.com.au/business/the-wall-street-journal/trumps-tariffs-wipe-out-over-10-trillion-on-wall-street-in-epic-twoday-rout/news-story/7459d2d9ad59b2e4cdea1c0145cdd4f2. Accessed 21 Apr 2025

Hurlburt H (2025) Trump's 'Liberation Day' tariffs are likely just the beginning of a longer-term vision. Chatham House, 3 Apr. https://www.chathamhouse.org/2025/04/trumps-liberation-day-tariffs-are-likely-just-beginning-longer-term-vision. Accessed 25 Apr 2025

Jackson JH (1989) The world trading system: law and policy of international economic relations. MIT Press, Cambridge

Jones C, Rankin J, Davidson H, Mason R (2025) Trump pauses plans to hike US tariffs on most countries except China. The Guardian, 10 Apr. https://www.theguardian.com/us-news/2025/apr/09/trump-tariffs-pause-china. Accessed 21 Apr 2025

Kelly J (2025a) Trump embraces reciprocal tariffs in a bid to rebalance the global trading system. The Australian, 14 Feb. https://www.theaustralian.com.au/world/trump-embraces-reciprocal-tariffs-in-a-bid-to-rebalance-the-global-trading-system/news-story/94d67b21195f1e104a14ee9e3f77c04a. Accessed 19 Sep 2025

Kelly J (2025b) Donald Trump has no road map for remaking the global order. The Australian, 1 May. https://www.theaustralian.com.au/world/donald-trump-has-no-road-map-for-remaking-the-global-order/news-story/a150ca7891427e0c4f9d9d618397056c. Accessed 1 May 2025

Kelly P (2025c) Unleashed Trump goes rogue before the world. The Australian, 4 Apr. https://www.theaustralian.com.au/inquirer/unleashed-trump-goes-rogue-before-the-world/news-story/48de448b22f69dfdf749be5591685ab9. Accessed 24 Apr 2025

Koziol M (2025a) Trump hits Australia with 10 per cent tariff on all exports to the US. The Age, 3 Apr. https://www.theage.com.au/world/north-america/trump-hits-australia-with-10-per-cent-tariff-on-all-exports-to-the-us-20250403-p5lopx.html. Accessed 3 Apr 2025

Koziol M (2025b) Trump says he will 'substantially' cut China tariffs as trade war bites. The Age, 23 Apr. https://www.theage.com.au/world/north-america/trump-says-he-will-substantially-cut-china-tariffs-as-trade-war-bites-20250423-p5ltl8.html. Accessed 23 Apr 2025

Kuok L (2025) How Trump's coercion could backfire in Asia: forcing the region to choose sides risks pushing it toward China. Foreign Aff, 14 Apr. https://www.foreignaffairs.com/united-states/how-trumps-coercion-could-backfire-asia. Accessed 26 Apr 2025

Lee L (2025) China warns countries against striking trade deals with US at its expense. The Age, 21 Apr. https://www.theage.com.au/world/asia/china-warns-countries-against-striking-trade-deals-with-us-at-its-expense-20250421-p5lt62.html. Accessed 21 Apr 2025

Lester S, Mercurio B, Davies A (2018) World trade law: text, materials and commentary, 3rd edn. Hart Publishing, Oxford

Lyon K, Evershed N (2025) 'Nowhere on Earth is safe': Trump imposes tariffs on uninhabited islands near Antarctica. The Guardian, 3 Apr. https://www.theguardian.com/us-news/2025/apr/03/donald-trump-tariffs-antarctica-uninhabited-heard-mcdonald-islands. Accessed 21 Apr 2025

Matsushita M, Schoenbaum T, Mavroidis P, Hahn M (2015) The World Trade Organization: law, practice, and policy, 3rd edn. OUP, Oxford

Medcalf R (2015) Reimagining Asia: from Asia-Pacific to Indo-Pacific. The Asan Forum, 26 Jun. http://www.theasanforum.org/reimagining-asia-from-asia-pacific-to-indo-pacific/. Accessed 27 Jun 2019

Ministry of Foreign Affairs (2022) Wang Yi: We need to impose a big question mark over US 'Indo-Pacific Economic Framework', 22 May. http://www.mfa.gov.cn/wjbzhd/202205/t20220522_10690866.shtml. Accessed 28 June 2022

Obama B (2016) The TPP would let America, not China, lead the way on global trade. Washington Post, 2 May. https://www.washingtonpost.com/opinions/president-obama-the-tpp-would-let-america-not-china-lead-the-way-on-global-trade/2016/05/02/680540e4-0fd0-11e6-93ae-50921721165d_story.html. Accessed 5 May 2016

Petersmann EU (2018) The 2018 American and Chinese trade wars risk undermining the world trading system and constitutional democracies. EUI Working Paper Law 2018/17. https://cadmus.eui.eu/bitstream/handle/1814/59444/LAW_2018_17.pdf. Accessed 27 Mar 2022

Pettis M (2025) The global trading system was already broken. Foreign Aff, 21 Apr. https://www.foreignaffairs.com/world/global-trading-system-was-already-broken. Accessed 21 Apr 2025

Prasad E (2025) The age of tariffs: Trump is launching a turbulent new era for the global economy. Foreign Aff, 3 Apr. https://www.foreignaffairs.com/united-states/age-tariffs-trump. Accessed 4 Apr 2025

Room T (2025) Trump's tariffs prompt wave of lawsuits as states and businesses fight back. The New York Times, 27 Apr. https://www.nytimes.com/2025/04/27/us/politics/trump-tariffs-lawsuits.html. Accessed 28 Apr 2025

Rosalsky G (2025) Are Trump's tariffs a bargaining chip for a new global economic order. NPR, 11 Apr. https://www.npr.org/sections/planet-money/2025/04/11/g-s1-59772/are-trumps-tariffs-a-bargaining-chip-for-a-new-global-economic-order. Accessed 25 Apr 2025

Ruggie JG (1982) International regimes, transactions, and change: embedded liberalism in the postwar economic order. Int Organ 36(2):379–415

Sanger DE, Haberman M (2016) In Donald Trump's worldview, America comes first, and everyone else pays. The New York Times, 26 Mar. https://www.nytimes.com/2016/03/27/us/politics/donald-trump-foreign-policy.html

Scholvin S (2016) Geopolitics: an overview of concepts and empirical examples from international relations. FIIA Working Paper No 91. https://www.files.ethz.ch/isn/196701/wp91-Geopolitics.pdf. Accessed 8 Aug 2018

Scholvin S, Wigell M (2018) Geo-economics as concept and practice in international relations: surveying the state of the art. FIIA Working Paper No 102. http://www.fiia.fi/en/publication/geo-economics-as-concept-and-practice-in-international-relations. Accessed 7 Aug 2018

Sheldon IM, Chow DC, McGuire W (2018) Trade liberalization and constraints on moves to protectionism: multilateralism vs regionalism. Am J Agric Econ 100(5):1375–1390

Sun Y (2025) China is enjoying Trump 2.0: how the trade war is helping Beijing prepare for long-term competition. Foreign Aff, 15 Aug. https://www.foreignaffairs.com/china/china-enjoying-trump-20. Accessed 15 Aug 2025

Stiglitz JE (2016) The new geo-economics. Project Syndicate, 8 Jan. https://www.project-syndicate.org/commentary/hope-for-better-global-governance-by-joseph-e--stiglitz-2016-01

Stiglitz JE (2022) Getting deglobalization right. Project Syndicate, 31 May. https://www.project-syndicate.org/commentary/deglobalization-and-its-discontents-by-joseph-e-stiglitz-2022-05. Accessed 7 Jun 2022

Swanson A (2025) Trump takes on improbable task in seeking trade deals across the globe. The New York Times, 23 Apr. https://www.nytimes.com/2025/04/23/business/economy/trump-tariffs-trade-deals.html. Accessed 24 Apr 25

The Age (2025) How Trump changed America in 100 days – with just a pen. 30 Apr. https://www.theage.com.au/world/north-america/order-142-and-counting-how-trump-has-used-his-pen-to-change-america-in-100-days-20250428-p5lumi.html. Accessed 30 Apr 2025

The Australian (2025) Trump's voodoo tariffs from the witchdoctor-in-chief will hurt all Australians. 3 Apr. https://www.theaustralian.com.au/nation/trumps-voodoo-tariffs-from-the-witchdoctorinchief-will-hurt-all-australians/news-story/6bb85b3bc41198b30966ea96d082abc1. Accessed 3 Apr 2025

The New York Times (2025a) Trump's 100-day report card, 29 Apr. https://www.nytimes.com/2025/04/29/business/dealbook/trump-100-days-economy.html. Accessed 30 Apr 2025

The New York Times (2025b) 100 days in, 29 Apr. https://www.nytimes.com/interactive/2025/04/28/us/trump-100-days-actions.html. Accessed 30 Apr 2025

The New York Times (2025c) The 'recklessness itself sends a message': 35 legal experts assess Trump's return, 28 Apr. https://www.nytimes.com/2025/04/28/opinion/trump-constitution-rule-of-law.html. Accessed 30 Apr 2025

Trebilcock MJ, Howse R, Eliason A (2012) The regulation of international trade, 4th edn. Routledge, London/New York

Uren D (2020) Economic coercion: boycotts and sanctions—preferred weapons of war. Australian Strategic Policy Institute. https://www.aspi.org.au/report/economic-coercion-boycotts-and-sanctions-preferred-weapons-war. Accessed 5 Apr 2022

Wang Yi (2022), 'Wang Yi: We need to impose a big question mark over US 'Indo-Pacific Economic Framework', 22 May, available at https://www.mfa.gov.cn/wjbzhd/202205/t20220522_10690866.shtml (last accessed 28/6/22)

Wang ZJ, Chen J (2020) BRI 2.0: cosmetic repairs or a change of course? J World Trade 54(5):791–812

Wang ZJ, Chen J (2023) International trade regulation: evolving dynamics and shifting foundations. Routledge, London. https://doi.org/10.4324/9781003275510

White House (2025a) CEA Chairman Steve Miran Hudson Institute event remarks. Statement, 7 Apr. https://www.whitehouse.gov/briefings-statements/2025/04/cea-chairman-steve-miran-hudson-institute-event-remarks. Accessed 26 Apr 2025

White House (2025b) Joint statement on US–China economic and trade meeting in Geneva. Statement, 12 May. https://www.whitehouse.gov/briefings-statements/2025/05/joint-statement-on-u-s-china-economic-and-trade-meeting-in-geneva/. Accessed 12 May 2025

White House (2025c) Regulating imports with a reciprocal tariff to rectify trade practices that contribute to large and persistent annual United States goods trade deficits. Executive order, 2 Apr. https://www.whitehouse.gov/presidential-actions/2025/04/regulating-imports-with-a-reciprocal-tariff-to-rectify-trade-practices-that-contribute-to-large-and-persistent-annual-united-states-goods-trade-deficits/. Accessed 21 Apr 2025

Wigell M, Vihma A (2016) Geopolitics versus geoeconomics: the case of Russia's geostrategy and its effects on the EU. Int Aff 92(3):605–624

Wiśniewski R (2021) Economic sanctions as a tool of China's hybrid strategies. Polish Pol Sci YB 50:91–103

World Trade Organization (2025) Regional Trade Agreements Database. https://rtais.wto.org/UI/PublicMaintainRTAHome.aspx. Accessed 4 Aug 2025

Xinhua (2025a) China, US have not held consultations or negotiations on tariff-related issue: Chinese FM spokesperson. Xinhua, 24 Apr. https://english.news.cn/20250424/20cc3566809b4d96b639b4b61ea43856/c.html. Accessed 24 Apr 2025

Xinhua (2025b) Ministry of Commerce responding to US coercing other countries to make deals that restrict them from cooperating with China. 25 Apr. http://www.news.cn/world/20250421/4bfa78e63f3f45e7818055bb66518ebb/c.html. Accessed 21 Apr 2025
Zhang K (2018) Calculating bully: explaining Chinese coercion. Dissertation, MIT. https://dspace.mit.edu/handle/1721.1/122472. Accessed 5 Apr 2022

Chapter 3
Sustainable Digitalization and Cyber Resilience on the Supply Chain

Rolf H. Weber

Abstract Digitalization and sustainability are important far-reaching policy objectives that need to be reconciled. Since the WTO legal framework is partly outdated, this task is now "transferred" to regional instruments often having extraterritorial effects, mainly covering due diligence obligations and cyber resilience requirements. But further harmonization of standards remains important.

Keywords Brussels Effect · Cyber Resilience · Digitalization · International Digital Trade Law · Responsible Business Conduct · Sustainability

3.1 Introduction

Digitalization was a main driver of international trade during the last decade[1]: (i) the trans-border delivery of goods has at least partly been replaced by the cross-border offering of services; besides, traditional physical goods are now often available in the form of digital assets; (ii) in addition, the new distributed ledger technologies (DLT) provide for additional infrastructures that are suitable to pave the way for an increased digital trade. The appearance of geoeconomics is substantially influenced by digitalization, but mostly outside the normative WTO framework.

In parallel, digitalization can also contribute to the achievement of the *United Nations Sustainable Development Goals* (SDG); the objective of sustainable development and the shift toward a secure, climate-neutral, and resource-efficient economy are both focal points of numerous expanding international endeavors.[2] The concept of an environment-friendly digital transformation has emerged to harness technology

[1] Bacchus (2022, pp. 136–137).

[2] UN General Assembly, Transforming our world: the 2030 Agenda for Sustainable Development, A/RES/70/1 (2015).

R. H. Weber (✉)
Faculty of Law, University of Zurich, Zurich, Switzerland
e-mail: rolf.weber@ius.uzh.ch

J. Nakagawa et al. (eds.), *Geopolitical Risks and Geoeconomics in International Economic Law*, Economics, Law, and Institutions in Asia Pacific,
https://doi.org/10.1007/978-981-95-6996-0_3

toward sustainable outcomes.[3] Looking at traditional goods, the digitalization of border trade procedures by way of paperless trade formalities could lead to substantial CO^2 savings.

Sustainable digitalization must encourage the development and use of technologies having sustainability considerations in mind, i.e., sustainable digitalization should ensure that technological advancements prioritize ethical considerations and environmental sustainability aspects throughout the life cycle of such technologies. Furthermore, digitalization for sustainability emphasizes the proactive development and use of digital tools to achieve environmental targets and to foster positive outcomes for both the environment and its inhabitants.[4] Thereby, it should not be overlooked that digitalization depends on the existence of cyber resilience measures on the supply chain.

This article is structured as follows: In part 2, the chances and challenges of sustainable digitalization are discussed by addressing potential promotion measures supporting sustainability and the energy implications of digitalization. The subsequent part 3 analyzes the digitalization in the international trade law environment as well as the attempts to adapt the existing regulatory framework to the new digital needs. Part 4 sheds a closer look at the practically important issue of cyber resilience on supply chains; cybersecurity has been a regulatory issue for decades, but only recently, cyber resilience has come into the focus of legislators. The article discusses the regulatory cyber resilience regime in the European Union (EU) and tackles the question, to what extent global developments could be based on the existing EU regulatory framework.[5] The article closes with an outlook showing how digitalization and sustainability can be reasonably reconciled.

3.2 Digitalization and Sustainability: Chances vs. Challenges

The near-marginal costs of digital information and of transactions open new possibilities for conducting business across borders on an increasing scale. Looking from a technological perspective, digitalization is suitable to contribute to sustainability; however, mainly due to the big energy consumption it also causes detrimental effects to the environment. Therefore, the two tendencies must be balanced in an appropriate way.

---

[3] United Nations Environment to Programme (UNEP), *Digitalization for Sustainability* (2024), https://www.unep.org/topics/digital-transformations/digitalization-sustainability. Accessed 28 August 2025.

[4] According to UNEP (No. 3), all SDG can be affected by digital technology; of the 17 SDG and 169 targets, not even one is detached from digital technology; 103 out of the 169 targets can be directly influenced by a combination of seven digital technologies ("Facts").

[5] For a good overview of the relevant EU law see Aueamnuay et al. (2024), passim.

3.2.1 Promotion of Sustainability by Digitalization

DLT infrastructures and digital assets can play an important role in advancing sustainable development by enabling efficient, transparent, and inclusive global supply chains. To achieve these objectives, efforts must be undertaken (i) to transition digital assets into more energy-efficient consensus mechanisms and (ii) to implement clean energy production powers.[6]

Sustainable digitalization is improved if alternative consensus mechanisms being less energy-intensive are used. In contrast to the Proof of Work (PoW) consensus mechanism, the alternative of the Proof of Stake (PoS) technique does not require participants to conduct computationally intensive work.[7] Initial assessments of Ethereum's transition from PoW to PoS show that a reduction of the energy consumption in the range of 99% could be achieved.[8] In addition, as PoS has lower energy demands and lacks any dynamic increases in electricity consumption, PoS hardware requires 10 to 500 times less power than the power used for mining a Bitcoin.[9]

So far, the energy intensity of digitalization has mainly been discussed in relation to cryptocurrencies (i.e., mining of Bitcoins). On the supply chain, however, digital assets in the form of tokenized goods are transferred from the seller to the buyer. Therefore, energy consumption in the respective tokenization process is relevant; specific research into this aspect is not yet widely available.

Digitalization makes global trade more inclusive from a communications perspective. The near-zero marginal costs of digital information exchanges and of transactions open new possibilities for conducting businesses across borders on an increasing scale.[10] While trade previously was for the most part driven by advanced economies and their large multinational companies, digital platforms allow more countries and smaller enterprises to participate.[11] In fact, B2C e-commerce has substantially increased over the last years; the biggest markets and growth potential in e-commerce accrue in developing countries, particularly East Asian nations like China, Indonesia, Vietnam, and the Philippines.[12]

---

[6] See also Schacherer and Weber (2026), Ch. 2.3; a similar analysis not in respect of the supply chain, but in respect of Central Bank Digital Currencies (CBDC), has been done by Wang (2024, pp. 647–661).

[7] United States Energy Information Administration (EIA), *Tracking electricity consumption from U.S. cryptocurrency mining operations* (1 February 2024), https://www.eia.gov/todayinenergy/detail.php?id=61364. Accessed 28 August 2025.

[8] For further details see Saraji (2023), passim.

[9] United States Office of Science and Technology Policy (OSTP), *Climate energy implications of crypto-assets in the United States* (2022), 13–14, https://bidenwhitehouse.archives.gov/wp-content/uploads/2022/09/09-2022-Crypto-Assets-and-Climate-Report.pdf. Accessed 28 August 2025; the OSTP Report also refers to the difficulties to directly monitor the total power usage of digital asset networks since many computing or mining centers do not disclose their location.

[10] Weber (2023, pp. 73–74).

[11] Burri and Kugler (2023, p. 4).

[12] Burri and Kugler (2023, p. 5).

3.2.2 Energy Implications of Digitalization

Energy consumption is central to the use of DLT infrastructures and the creation of digital assets, with electricity being needed for their production, generation, ownership, and exchange, as well as to power the essential functions of a DLT network, including data storage, computing, and data communications. This development is further accentuated by the widespread application of artificial intelligence (AI); so far, energy-intensive high-performance chips are running the AI programs; however, alternative computers, as for example developed by the German enterprise SpiNNcloud,[13] and processors executing operations based on light can contribute to a higher degree of efficiency. In addition, arguments are presented that "expensively" produced AI would be able to achieve efficiency gains and savings in the traditional electricity and other energy production methods.[14]

The rise in the use of digital infrastructures and assets has been accompanied by a significant growth in energy consumption, with the global total annual electricity usage estimated to have doubled or even quadrupled from 2018 to 2022, thereby exceeding that of individual countries such as Australia.[15] According to academic research, Bitcoin network's yearly electricity usage is estimated at an amount comparable to the total annual electricity consumption of Austria and Finland together.[16] Therefore, some countries forbid cryptocurrency mining or at least limit electricity use in this context to combat the increased energy consumption and its environmental impacts.[17]

Nevertheless, some miners reportedly rely on renewable energy sources to power their operations, such as solar/wind farms and hydropower.[18] But broader sustainability concerns are justified since digital assets do not only contribute to greenhouse gas emissions, but also generate additional pollution, noise, and other localized negative effects.[19]

Beyond the environmental impacts, the digital economy poses further economic and social threats to sustainable development. The comparative advantage of developing countries in the costs of production processes is increasingly being eroded by the automation of low-skilled work that disrupts traditional pathways to economic

---

[13] The new-generation AI computer is called SpiNNaker2, see https://spinncloud.com. Accessed 28 August 2025.

[14] See The Economist, April 12th 2025, 12, pp. 67–71.

[15] OSTP Report (No. 9), p. 5.

[16] Cambridge Center for Alternative Finance, *Cambridge Bitcoin Electricity Consumption Index*, https://ccaf.io/cbnsi/cbeci. Accessed 28 August 2025.

[17] See New York State Senate, Senate Bill S6486D, https://www.nysenate.gov/legislation/bills/2021/S6486. Accessed 28 August 2025; China has also forbidden the mining of cryptocurrencies for general policy reasons.

[18] OSTP Report (No. 9), p. 13.

[19] Schacherer and Weber (2026), Ch. 2.2; see also the most recent figures in the newest report of the International Energy Agency, *Energy and AI*, pp. 19 et seq., https://www.iea.org/reports/energy-and-ai. Accessed 28 August 2025.

improvement and threatens to increase the inequality gulf among countries that has been decreasing lately.[20]

3.2.3 Reconciling Chances and Challenges

Experience has shown that digital sustainability cannot only be realized through the voluntary adoption of technological innovations by industry participants but should also be incentivized by tailored regulatory frameworks encompassing a mixture of incentives and behavioral guidelines for enterprises.[21] Prohibition regulations are usually less efficient and forward-looking, i.e., governmental interference into the markets should rather guide than restrict.

Moreover, alternative regulatory approaches must be developed. First and foremost, the existing regulations on carbon border adjustment measures (CABM) need to be amended and revised to become more efficient.[22] In addition, the imposition of taxes on transactions concluded on the blockchain could be considered; the amount of tax levied would have to depend on the energy consumption involved.[23] Alternatively, the invention of energy-sensitive technologies is possibly worth to be financially supported. In a nutshell, a mixture of incentives and behavioral guidelines for enterprises can bring added value.

The reconciliation of chances and challenges in the tensioned relation between digitalization and sustainability could also rely on a new understanding of moral commitments in complying with the UN SDG and of voluntarily adopting technological innovations. Public policy is a term that plays an important role in most international legal instruments; the objective of sustainable development and the shift toward a resource-efficient economy are both focal points of expanding international endeavors.[24]

3.3 Digitalization in the International Trade Law Environment

The digitalization of the last decade has substantially influenced the framework of international trade law. Non-physical services have gained importance; these services are not addressed in the *General Agreement on Trade in Services* (GATS) of the *World*

---

[20] Burri and Kugler (2023, pp. 5–6) with further references.

[21] Schacherer and Weber (2026), Ch. 2.4.

[22] The existing main legal instrument is the Regulation (EU) 2023/956 establishing a carbon border adjustment mechanism of 10 May 2023, OJ 2023 L 130/55–104.

[23] OSTP Report (No. 9), pp. 6, 25–26.

[24] For further details see UNEP (No. 3), "What we do".

Trade Organization (WTO). The normative WTO framework is based on classifications that have been relevant in the early nineties of the last century; therefore, they would need to be amended, which has not been sufficiently done so far.[25] The newer *Preferential Trade Agreements* (PTA) are more open to the recent technological developments and often contain some digitally oriented provisions.

3.3.1 Digital Economy in the WTO and PTA Framework

Digital trade is not defined in the WTO framework, and a definition of digital trade that is recognized and accepted worldwide does not exist. According to the OECD, a growing consensus exists that digital trade encompasses digitally enabled transactions of trade in goods and services; since the WTO trade rules should be interpreted in a technologically neutral way, the mere fact that trade is conducted otherwise than by means of a physical transaction should not change WTO obligations.[26]

In 1998, the WTO Council adopted the "Work Programme on e-Commerce"[27]; this document describes the term e-commerce as "the production, distribution, marketing, sale or delivery of goods and services by electronic means". Many attempts have been undertaken to further develop the Work Programme, often being called an "unfinished" agenda.[28] However, reality has shown that improvements and amendments could not be achieved. Only on the physical product side, the *Information Technology Agreement* was updated to a limited extent.

In the context of digital goods and services, some academic voices plead for the application of an interpretative concept called the "predominant purpose" test; this approach looks at the characteristics of digital services as intangible/heterogeneous/inseparable/perishable (non-storable)[29]; such kind of services taxonomy with additional characteristics helps to identify the closest relationship to the given services classification, but the general dilemma of allocating each digital service to a specific category remains largely unresolved.

The problem with the outdated goods and services classification has become subject to negotiations between the States, mainly among the developed countries. In the context of the 11th Ministerial Conference (December 2017, Buenos Aires), a short "Joint Statement on Electronic Commerce" (JSEC) has been adopted inviting the participating WTO members to further work on digital trade.[30] However, in the

---

[25] Bacchus (2022, pp. 137–138).

[26] Weber (2023, pp. 73–74).

[27] WTO, General Council, Work Programme on Electronic Commerce, September 24, 1998, WT/L/274, para. 1.3.

[28] Weber (2023, p. 75).

[29] Peng (2020, pp. 669–726).

[30] WTO/WT/MIN(17)/60 of December 13, 2017; following this Statement, 80 countries have agreed to join the negotiations: WTO, Joint Statement on Electronic Commerce, WT/L/1056, January 25, 2019.

meantime, the negotiations did not advance substantially even if several attempts have been undertaken to agree on new provisions.[31]

As a reaction to both the stalemate in the multilateral forum of the WTO and the extended scope of regulatory issues concerning the digital economy, States are increasingly using PTA to regulate digital trade. The so far agreed PTA show the dynamics of the cross-border services needs and of the data-driven economy.[32] About half of the PTA signed since 2020 contain provisions relevant to digital trade.[33] But the disadvantage of this approach consists in the lack of a coherent legal environment due to the differing priorities and the piecemeal character of the introduced rules.

Such negative impacts can at least partly be avoided by regional legal instruments. The most important East Asian accord containing digital services and data flow provisions is the *Comprehensive and Progressive Agreement for Trans-Pacific Partnership* (CPTPP). Eleven countries in the Pacific Rim signed the CPTPP, being in force since 30 September 2018 and representing almost 15% of the global cross-domestic products.[34] Data transfers and digital trade are addressed; however, the level of harmonization is not very high. As a second East Asian accord, the *Regional Comprehensive Economic Partnership* (RCEP) was signed in November 2020 and came into force on 1 January 2022[35]; it is composed of China, Japan, South Korea, Australia, New Zealand, and 10 ASEAN members. The topic of "cross-border transmission of information by electronic means" is addressed, but the scope of harmonization in respect of digital trade rules does not go far.[36] More recently, first ideas have been exchanged to "merge" (in whatever way) the CPTPP and the RCEP; whether such a move would be successful appears to be unclear.

3.3.2 Challenges Caused by New Trade Barriers

The regulatory challenges due to the increasing digital trade, particularly for (data) privacy and national (cyber) security, have become a justification for the introduction (or "invention") of a new generation of trade barriers' provisions.[37] As the main instrument, localization measures are implemented providing for requirements that compel companies to conduct certain digital trade-related activities within a country's borders (as, for example, introduced by China, Russia, Iran, Turkey).[38] The localization measures do have an impact on the data sharing activities being partly

[31] See Weber (2023, p. 77), Bacchus (2021, pp. 5–6, 9).

[32] Burri (2023, pp. 9–27).

[33] See also Burri (2023, pp. 19–21).

[34] Additional countries, for example China, are applying for becoming a CPTPP member; after a potential accession of China the market share would substantially increase.

[35] For further details see Bacchus (2021, pp. 145–146), Burri (2021, pp. 34–36).

[36] Weber (2023, p. 78).

[37] Burri and Kugler (2023, pp. 7–8).

[38] Peng (2024, pp. 66–67, 199–201).

jeopardized by privacy and national security provisions. Very obviously, measures protecting data privacy do directly impact data flows; however, experience has shown in the meantime that most regulatory provisions can be implemented in compliance with international trade law.[39] Further problems are potentially caused by IP-related measures, particularly in the context of artificial intelligence and machine learning.[40]

The growth in digital trade has also raised issues related to cybersecurity; the protection of ICT systems and their contents from cyberattacks is of major importance. In principle, the measures combating cyberattacks, being attempts by unauthorized persons to access ICT systems, are broadly acknowledged; however, cybersecurity should not become an instrument that is used to foster specific economic interests of a State; governmental measures must rather adhere to the given international legal concepts (such as the concepts of cooperation duties, of global public goods, of shared spaces, of common heritage of mankind, and of State responsibility).[41]

Moreover, interventions of States must be in line with the security exemptions of the WTO framework, namely Art. XXI of the *General Agreement on Tariffs and Trade* (GATT) and particularly Art. XIVbis of the GATS.[42] Equally, such reconciliation must be achieved in view of the exception "to protect human, animal plant life or health" (Art. XX lit. b GATT) and in view of the exception "to protect public morals or to maintain public order" and "to secure compliance law or regulations" (Art. XIV lit. a and lit. c GATS).[43]

Practice of the Dispute Settlement Body as well as of legal doctrine is available for the interpretation of the security exemption. In principle, States cannot claim absolute discretion in reading too much into the security exemption; the intrinsic idea of any exemption provision calls for a narrow interpretation, i.e. an overbroad or abusive application of national policy interests under the heading of "security" should be avoided.[44] Similar considerations are expressed in assessing the mentioned specific exception clauses.[45]

So far, the mentioned new regulatory trade barriers mainly concern data flow and cybersecurity measures. The sustainability challenges are much less discussed notwithstanding the fact that climate change problems appear to be obvious. It remains to be seen to what extent and when the perspective is going to change, possibly also due to the efforts undertaken by the OECD.

---

39 Weber (2023, p. 83).

40 Burri and Kugler (2023, p. 10).

41 Weber (2024a, nos. 28–55).

42 For further details to the origins and contents of the security exemptions see Weber and Baisch (2018, pp. 379–382).

43 For a case law overview see Weber and Baisch (2018, pp. 383–385); the WTO justifications are also addressed by Shimizu (2026) in this book.

44 See Diebold (2008, pp. 43 et seq., in particular p. 56).

45 See also Weber (2024b, pp. 242–244).

3.3.3 Responsible Business Conduct Guidelines of OECD

In view of the fact that the WTO normative framework gives little guidance to the treatment of cyber resilience aspects, other international legal instruments must also be considered.

On 8 June 2023, 51 countries adopted the revised text of the "OECD Guidelines for Multinational Enterprises on Responsible Business Conduct"[46]; the prolongation of the title of the Guidelines with the specific reference to "Responsible Business Conduct" clearly shows the general emphasis on responsible conduct issues. Chapter VI of the OECD Guidelines on "Environment" experienced substantial changes during the revision; the avoidance of negative impacts on a sustainable environment has become a key challenge for many enterprises around the globe. The new Guidelines are also relevant for the East Asian region since two countries (Japan, South Korea) adhered to the OECD and two other countries are in the accession process (Thailand, Indonesia).

The OECD Guidelines are intended to encourage reasonable trade activities as well as to realize benefits that are needed for society to achieve sustainable development. In view of potential sustainability challenges, enterprises can be involved in a wide range of adverse impacts, e.g., climate change, biodiversity loss, degradation of land, marine and freshwater ecosystems, deforestation, air, water and soil pollution, and mismanagement of waste. According to the OECD Guidelines, enterprises are obliged to identify and assess adverse impacts associated with their operations, products or services based on a risk-oriented due diligence process.[47] Thereby, compliance with globally developed "understandings" and guidelines in this field is important. The OECD Guidelines refer to the internationally agreed standards and concepts with the objective of harmonizing the applicable regulations to the benefit of the enterprises.[48]

The OECD Guidelines apply approaches to foster a sustainability-friendly behavior of enterprises; therefore, business entities have the task to implement an "Environmental Management". This term should be interpreted in a broad sense, (i) embodying all activities related to adverse impacts and risks, (ii) avoiding and addressing sustainability "conflicts", and (iii) supporting the potential improvement of the sustainability performance.[49] The OECD Guidelines define the term "cause" as a corporate activity that could in itself result in an adverse impact and the term "contribute to" as a part of its activities, in combination with activities of other entities.[50]

---

[46] OECD Guidelines for Multinational Enterprises on Responsible Business Conduct, OECD Publishing (2023), https://www.oecd.org/en/publications/oecd-guidelines-for-multinational-enterprises-on-responsible-business-conduct_81f92357-en.html. Accessed 28 August 2025.

[47] OECD Guidelines (No. 46), Chapter VI, introduction, p. 33.

[48] Weber (2026, ch. B.I.).

[49] OECD Guidelines (No. 46), Chapter VI, comm. no. 67.

[50] OECD Guidelines (No. 46), Chapter VI, comm. no. 67.

To materialize the environmental management, a risk management regime must be implemented by the enterprises.[51] Increased sustainability is an element of an improved resilience within the structures of large business entities, not at least since adverse impacts are often closely interlinked with other matters (health, safety, cybersecurity). Therefore, the due diligence concept should also include and involve a risk-based prioritization of achievable objectives that are based on an interdisciplinary perspective.[52] In the digital context, the use of the best available technologies on mutually acceptable terms in a technology-neutral environment is of utmost importance. In addition, interoperability between different infrastructures must be realized; supply chains only are efficient if the product can be channeled through noninterrupted technical infrastructures.[53]

In a nutshell, the OECD Guidelines consider sustainability issues to a much further extent than the present WTO legal framework and the existing PTA (on a regional or bi-/trilateral basis); the Chapter on "Environment" could be a model for future PTA discussions or should at least be thoroughly considered in future negotiations.

Because it has become increasingly clear during the last few years that supply chains need to be protected against cyberattacks and cyber resilience incidents, and since the OECD should not remain the only international organization addressing the respective issues, their importance in the broadened digital environment needs to be discussed and substantially analyzed in more detail hereinafter, not least since remarkable progress has been achieved in Europe.

3.4 Cyber Resilience on the Supply Chain

Cybersecurity was a (partly hotly debated) regulatory topic for almost three decades.[54] More recently, cyber resilience (among others on the supply chain) has become an issue that has gained importance; cyber resilience goes further than cybersecurity, i.e., the avoidance and/or mitigation of cyberattacks. Cyber resilience has the objective to generally provide for a stable, safe, and undisturbed supply chain environment.

---

[51] Weber (2026, ch. B.II.).

[52] OECD Guidelines (No. 46), Chapter VI, item 3, p. 34.

[53] OECD Guidelines (No. 46), Chapter VI, comm. nos. 70–79.

[54] Weber (2024b, nos. 8 et seq.).

3.4.1 Cybersecurity: Legal Framework and Governance

On the global level, legal instruments intending to combat cybercrime have been discussed for quite some time.[55] Already several *United Nations Group of Governmental Experts* (UNGGE) have exchanged ideas and published reports on cybersecurity, however, without agreeing on binding principles.[56] The more recent UN *Open-Ended Working Group* (OEWG) elaborating on the security of and in the use of information and communications technologies issued a report proposing confidence-building and capacity-building measures, without agreeing on specific cybersecurity standards.[57] In 2022, the UN General Assembly adopted a *Programme of Action* (PoA) to advance responsible State behavior in the use of information and communications technologies in the context of international security.[58] Furthermore, a new Ad Hoc Committee to "Elaborate a Comprehensive International Convention on Countering the Use of Information and Communications Technologies" for criminal purposes has taken up its work[59]; however, not least due to the war in Ukraine, the outcome of the discussions remains uncertain.[60] As an important step, however, the General Assembly of the United Nations adopted the (general) UN Convention against Cybercrime on 24 December 2024 which can serve as cybersecurity guideline even if it does not contain binding obligations.[61]

The OECD also included resilience considerations in the Guidelines for Multinational Enterprises on Responsible Business Conduct (revised version of June 2023),[62] being of importance for all kinds of supply chains.

Particularly in Europe, multilateral legal instruments do exist and are also applied in practice. The Council of Europe adopted the (Budapest) Convention on Cybercrime in 2001,[63] now encompassing more than 60 ratifying States (also outside of Europe, including Argentina, Australia, Canada, Chile, Israel, Japan, and the United States of America). As set forth in the Preamble, the main objective of the Budapest Convention is to pursue a common criminal policy against cybercrime by adopting appropriate legislation and by fostering international cooperation.[64] The ongoing efforts to revise the Convention and to include additional provisions on new digital cybercrimes are not yet concluded.

---

[55] For an overview see Weber (2025, pp. 34–37).

[56] For further details see UNGEE Report of July 2021, UN Doc. A/76/135; Weber (2024b, nos. 8–12); Kulesza and Weber (2021, pp. 5–6).

[57] OEWG Report of March 2021, UN Doc. A/AC.2090/2021/CRP.2.

[58] UN Doc. A/C.1/77/L.73.

[59] UN Doc. A/RES/75/282; information about the activities of the Ad Hoc Committee can be found under https://www.unodc.org/unodc/en/cybercrime/ad_hoc_committee/home. Accessed 28 August 2025.

[60] See also Weber (2025, p. 35).

[61] UN Res. 79/243, A/79/460.

[62] See above Sect. 3.3.3.

[63] Council of Europe, Convention on Cybercrime, ETS no. 185, Budapest, November 2001.

[64] Weber (2025, p. 37).

The European Union (EU) implemented not only the *General Data Protection Regulation* (GDPR) in 2016,[65] containing several provisions on data security, but also the *Network and Information Society* (NIS) Directive in 2019 which has been revised and amended in November 2022 (NIS 2)[66]; their objectives are to improve national cybersecurity capabilities, cooperation, and security/incident notification requirements. The importance of the *European Union Agency for Cybersecurity* (ENISA) has increased in recent years, and the established *National Computer Security Incident Response Teams* (CSIRT) have attempted to improve cross-border cooperation.[67]

Notwithstanding the fact that cybersecurity remains a crucial regulatory objective in an increasingly digitized world, practical experience during the last few years has shown that not only "security" as such is important but also "stability" and "resilience" of digital infrastructures in a broader sense merit attention. The early discussions about stability and resilience concerned the Internet; particularly the *Global Commission on the Stability of Cyberspace* (GCSC) published a Report in 2019[68] identifying the most important regulatory needs in this context. The first and main principle envisages avoiding harmful acts that undermine the resilience and stability of cyberspace. Furthermore, developers and producers of digital goods and services having an impact on the resilience of cyberspace should (i) prioritize security and stability, (ii) take reasonable steps to ensure that their goods and services are free from significant vulnerabilities, and (iii) take measures to timely mitigate vulnerabilities.[69] Such an approach corresponds to the concept of "norm-development" that includes the observation of and compliance with international legal principles.[70]

In addition, the EU adopted the Cyber Resilience Act in November 2024,[71] being applicable from December 2027, which will be discussed in more detail hereinafter.

3.4.2 Cyber Resilience Act of EU

The Cyber Resilience Act (CRA) is the first horizontal regulation on cybersecurity in the EU; this approach intends to avoid fragmentation and to ensure a coherent cybersecurity framework. The CRA contains provisions applicable for products with digital elements. Its main purpose consists in the setting of cybersecurity standards

[65] OJ 2016 L 119/1 of May 4, 2026.

[66] OJ 2022 L 333/80 of December 27, 2022.

[67] See Weber (2024b, no. 16).

[68] Global Commission on the Stability of Cyberspace (GCSC), Advancing Cyberstability, Final Report, IGF Berlin, November 2019.

[69] GCSC (No. 68), pp. 20 et seq.

[70] See also Segura-Serrano (2021, pp. 722 et seq.).

[71] Regulation (EU) 2024/2847 of 23 October 2024 on horizontal cybersecurity requirements for products with digital elements, OJ 2024 L 1 of 20 November 2024.

for hardware and software products that connect to networks and devices.[72] Up to the CRA, the EU has only known vertical, i.e., sector-specific cybersecurity measures, for example addressing medical devices, motor vehicles, civil aviation, and marine equipment.[73] The CRA is in force since December 2024; however, it is set up to apply from 11 December 2027 onward. To facilitate the adoption of the CRA provisions, additional details will be regulated in harmonized standards addressing both horizontal and sector-specific perspectives.[74]

3.4.2.1 Covered Products

The CRA refers to the so-called "products with digital elements". This term is neither very precise nor further defined in the CRA. In general, its scope is quite wide; it encompasses hardware and software products which are intended or foreseeable to operate with connectivity to other devices or networks, i.e. hardware and hardware components also fall into the scope of the CRA.[75] Possible examples are smartphones, laptops, tablets, drones, routers, browsers, fitness trackers, baby phones, surveillance cameras with remote access, smart home appliances, and remote-controlled or connected machinery and factory equipment. As one can see from this enumeration, the variety of products is very wide.[76]

The CRA defines its application scope in a broad sense: not only is the connected product with digital elements covered but also its remote data processing solutions. Consequently, cloud-enabled functionalities of connected products enabling users to control the product at distance are also within the scope of the CRA. For other cloud computing services, the cybersecurity requirements of the NIS 2 are applicable; these provisions govern, for example, cloud computing services such as software as a service (SaaS), platform as a service (PaaS), and infrastructure as a service (IaaS).[77]

---

[72] For a general overview see Burri and Zihlmann (2023, pp. B 13 et seq.).

[73] For an analysis of the regulatory approaches (horizontal, risk-based, and product safety) underlying the CRA see Chiara (2025, pp. 1 et seq.); https://doi.org/10.1017/err.2025.9. Accessed 28 August 2025.

[74] A new study attempts to identify the most relevant existing cybersecurity standards and guidelines for each CRA requirement: European Commission/European Union Agency for Network and Information Security (ENISA), *Cyber Resilience Act Requirements Standards Mapping*, Publication Office of the European Union 2024; https://www.enisa.europa.eu/sites/default/files/2024-11/Cyber%20Resilience%20Act%20Requirements%20Standards%20Mapping%20-%20final_with_identifiers_0.pdf. Accessed 28 August 2025.

[75] Art. 3 CRA contains many definitions concretizing the products being in the scope of the CRA.

[76] See also Burri and Zihlmann (2023, p. B 16).

[77] An IaaS cloud computing model provides virtualized computing resources over the internet. PaaS means that there is a platform for developing, deploying, and managing applications managed by the cloud provider. With a SaaS the subscribed software application is delivered over the Internet.

3.4.2.2 Main Obligations of Providers

The CRA imposes various obligations on the manufacturers of products with digital elements. In particular, the following obligations are noteworthy:

- *Product requirements*: The produced goods must comply with the essential cybersecurity requirements as outlined in Annex I to the CRA; manufacturers may only place a good with digital elements on the market if such compliance is ensured.[78] The design and production of digital goods must avoid known vulnerabilities; regular updates should address newly upcoming security flaws.[79] If components of third parties are integrated into the digital good, the producer is obliged to exercise due diligence in respect of the cybersecurity of such components.[80]
- *Continuous risk assessment*: Manufacturers have an obligation to perform a cybersecurity risk assessment related to the relevant goods containing digital elements.[81] This cybersecurity risk assessment is to be documented and updated during the support period. As in other consumer protection regulations, the support period must take into consideration the length of time during which the product is expected to be used, but at least five years.[82] Obviously, depending on the digital good, the support period needs to reflect its characteristics, particularly if the digital goods are relatively durable (fridge equipment compared to smartphones). In addition, the marketing language should be adapted to the maintenance obligations of the manufacturer.
- *Documentation and information*: The producer of the digital good is obliged to prepare a technical documentation with all relevant details of the means used by the producer regarding compliance of the product with the CRA.[83] This technical documentation must be kept by the producer at the disposal of the market surveillance authorities for a duration of at least 10 years after the product placement in the market or the elapse of the support period, respectively, whichever is longer. The producer of digital goods is also obliged to ensure that the product is accompanied with the minimum information and instructions as set forth in Annex II of the CRA.[84]
- *Reporting*: The producers of digital goods are obliged to report any actively exploited vulnerability contained in the product and any severe incident having an

[78] Annex I of the CRA describes the "essential cybersecurity requirements" and particularly also mentions the vulnerabilities.

[79] 'Security by design' means to consider the systems' security needs upfront and integrate these needs into the systems' subsequent design and construction; for further details see Bygrave (2021a, pp. 126–177); https://www.scup.com/doi/10.18261/olr.8.3.2. Accessed 28 August 2025.

[80] This provision refers to the supply chain risks as addressed by the OECD Guidelines (see above Sect. 3.3.3).

[81] The CRA requires a risked-based classification of products, Burri and Zihlmann (2023, pp. B 25 et seq.).

[82] Art. 13(8) CRA; see also Rec. 60 CRA.

[83] Burri and Zihlmann (2023, p. B 6).

[84] Annex II of the CRA bears the title "Information and Instructions to the User".

impact on the security of the product to a designated CSIRT and to ENISA.[85] The producer must also submit an early warning notification of an incident without undue delay and, in an event, within 24 h after its occurrence, as well as, at a later stage, submit a detailed incident report.[86]
- *Conformity assessment* (Art. 32 CRA): The producers equally need to perform a conformity assessment of the goods with digital elements to determine whether the essential security requirements as set forth in Annex I to the CRA are met.[87] For many of such digital goods, a self-assessment by the producer will be sufficient to assess the safety; however, in the case of important and critical products, an assessment by a third party is required.

As the above list of obligations clearly shows, the production of goods with digital elements will be confronted with much higher cybersecurity requirements as soon as the CRA is applicable. But the description also evidences that a complex interplay with other regulations in the digital environment must be solved in the future. The effectiveness of the obligations imposed on manufacturers depends on the actual enforcement of the comprehensive market surveillance.[88]

3.4.2.3 Impact on International Trade Law

Notwithstanding the fact that the CRA is a regional legal instrument, its impact on cross-border international trade in general should not be underestimated since the CRA has, similarly to the GDPR of 2016, manifold extraterritorial effects:

- EU companies doing global cross-border business will have to comply with the cyber resilience requirements throughout the whole supply chain also in non-EU countries. Consequently, as a matter of compliance, EU companies importing goods from East Asia will impose these requirements on the manufacturers at the place of their origin.[89]
- Foreign manufacturers, for example companies in East Asia, will have to comply with the CRA if they place goods with digital elements on the EU market or make them available to EU purchasers.[90] The territorial scope of the CRA extends to the offering of products for distribution or for use in the EU market in the course

[85] See above Sect. 3.4.1 with No. 67.

[86] Art. 14 (2a) and (4a) CRA; see also Rec. 120 CRA.

[87] 'Conformity assessment' is defined in Art. 3 (27) CRA as "the process of verifying whether the essential cybersecurity requirements set out in Annex I have been fulfilled"; see also rec. 91 CRA: "Under the internal control conformity assessment procedure, the manufacturer ensures and declares on its sole responsibility that the product with digital elements and the processes of the manufacturer meet the applicable essential cybersecurity requirements set out in this Regulation."

[88] See Chapter V of the CRA: "*Market Surveillance and Enforcement*", Art. 52–60 CRA.

[89] A similar effect occurred under the EU Green Deal instruments on the supply chains; non-EU producers are often contractually obliged to comply with the due diligence requirements introduced in EU law.

[90] Burri and Zihlmann (2023, p. B 24).

of a commercial activity (regardless of whether this is done for payment or free of charge).[91]
- Experience has shown that modern civil society, or more specifically consumer protection legislation, which has been implemented in the EU, is often, at least partly, taken over in other countries; the main example for this scenario is the GDPR of the EU, which has served as "model law" in many countries, i.e., the EU has shaped the global privacy regime impacting web technologies and privacy requirements.[92]

As far as the "model law" impact is concerned, *Anu Bradford* having analyzed this effect in the relationship between the EU and the USA refers to the so-called "Brussels Effect".[93] As in the case of data protection, the EU would also be interested in becoming a "cyber resilience champion", however, the two environments, namely in data protection and in cyber resilience, are not identical.

The EU consumer market is large and too wealthy to ignore; nevertheless, supply chains and the importance of imports from East Asia into Europe should also not be underestimated. In parallel, in respect of both areas it is cheaper to apply one high standard globally rather than create deviating standards for similar products and the separation of different areas is equally difficult. Therefore, EU importers might try to "impose" their cyber resilience standards on East Asian exporters. Since the CRA will only come into force in December 2027, East Asian countries could try to develop their own cyber resilience standards on a national or regional level at an earlier stage; however, such an approach would have to be implemented very quickly by overcoming usual time-consuming delays in harmonization exercises to take advantage of the "first mover" effect.

In assessing these factors, it appears to be likely that the "Brussels Effect" will also play a role in the cyber resilience environment even if it might be slightly less "dominant" than in the data protection context. A respective influence can particularly be expected in the following areas:

- Compliance with generally acknowledged cyber resilience standards throughout the whole supply chain by all concerned companies irrespective of the goods or services at stake.
- Implementation of civil society or consumer protection measures (transparency, accountability, observability, responsibility requirements) directed to safeguarding cyber resilience.

---

[91] Art. 3(13) CRA defines the "manufacturer" as "a natural or legal person who develops or manufactures products with digital elements or has products with digital elements designed, developed or manufactured, and markets them under its name or trademark, whether for payment, monetisation or free of charge". In Art. 3(22) CRA the definition of 'making available on the market' also includes the supply of a product with digital elements for distribution or use on the EU market during a commercial activity, whether in return for payment or free of charge.

[92] See Peukert, Bechold, Batikas and Kretschmer (2022, p. 319); for the influence of the Council of Europe's Data Protection Convention see Bygrave (2021b, pp. 1 et seq.).

[93] See Bradford (2020); for a case study related to Brazil and the EU Digital Services Act see Bueno and Gadoni (2024, pp. 2 et seq.).

- Application of reporting and early warning notifications (to the actual and potential purchasers of the goods as well as to the supervisory authorities) in case of a serious incident.

The development of international cyber resilience standards would be a helpful tool for the concerned enterprises involved in cross-border trade. Such a development could constitute a further factor reflecting an international regulatory spillover.[94]

3.4.3 Global Cyber Resilience Developments

As outlined, cyber resilience has become an important issue in many countries. Politically, the ongoing discussions about cybersecurity are more difficult than the development of cyber resilience standards that are more of a technical and economic nature and that do have a lower impact on politics. In the future, manufacturers of goods with digital elements will have to prioritize resilience issues and take reasonable steps to ensure that these goods are free from significant vulnerabilities.[95]

Experience has shown that self-regulation by the concerned participants of supply chains can play a role, "substituting" governmental legal rules.[96] Self-regulation has several benefits: among others, rules created by the people being involved in the given market environment are usually efficient since they respond to real needs, mirror the technological challenges, and provide the opportunity to flexibly adapt the legal framework if needed.[97] A further benefit of self-regulation consists in the fact that such a model develops and establishes rules independently of the principle of territoriality, thereby realizing a global reach.[98]

Self-regulation also carries some risks since private rules are not always transparent and not every relevant group is necessarily involved. Furthermore, a "free rider" problem can occur and, particularly, non-compliance with private rules might be confronted with enforcement problems (no coercive measures, no sanctions). Nevertheless, it must equally be considered that a loss of reputation in case of a "dark sheep" situation often turns out very negatively for a non-complying company[99]; reputation usually is a good driver for the attempt to prevent cascading failures on the supply chain.[100]

In addition, self-regulation should not be envisioned to replace the mandatory CRA framework; moreover, private rules can serve as a complement to governmental

---

[94] To this concept see Davis and Marotta-Wurgler (2024, pp. 79 et seq.).

[95] GCSC (No. 68), pp. 24–25.

[96] For a general overview see Weber (2021, pp. 25 et seq.).

[97] Weber (2021, p. 28).

[98] Weber (2025, p. 49).

[99] Weber (2021, p. 28).

[100] The Japanese firm Asahi recently made the negative experience that successful cyber incidents can have substantial negative impact in the business environment; see https://www.bbc.com/news/articles/cly64g5y744o. Accessed 13 October 2025.

regulation. In respect of such a complementing approach, academics have coined the notion of "co-regulation" meaning that self-regulation is approved to become effective and to constitute a generally accepted standard of good compliance.[101]

To strengthen self-regulation and co-regulation, industry organizations should become more active in the elaboration and further development of harmonized technical standards (beginning with ISO 27001) and best practices guidelines (including model contracts providing for resilience obligations). Slightly more extensive measures would be voluntary audits of cyber resilience conditions, voluntary certification schemes related to protocols, protection regimes, etc., and alternative compliance mechanisms. Efforts in this direction would strengthen the cyber resilience of responsible supply chains.

3.5 Outlook

Supply chains are exposed to fast-developing new technologies (e.g., digitalization, tokenization of assets) and to far-reaching policy requirements related to sustainability objectives. These two "tracks" do not always run in parallel but cause challenges. As shown hereinabove, reconciliation between the diverging objectives can be achieved.

International trade law (i.e. the WTO normative framework) is not (anymore) up to date. The more than thirty-year-old classifications of goods and services need a thorough adaptation to the present business models. Since the respective efforts are politically not successful, PTA and regional agreements have replaced the WTO rules (at least to a certain extent). In addition, the new OECD Guidelines on Responsible Business Conduct might play an increasingly important role, also due to their extended geographical scope.

Furthermore, regional regulations with extraterritorial effects do have an impact on cross-border transactions of goods and services. This aspect particularly concerns due diligence obligations and cyber resilience requirements being applicable to the supply chain. Therefore, stronger emphasis must be put on compliance and corporate governance requirements. In this respect, a certain harmonization of generally acknowledged standards is underway; however, additional efforts are needed for constituting a desirable legal environment.

[101] See Weber (2021, p. 30).

References

Aueamnuay C, et al. (2024) Digital Regulation in the EU, 03 EuZ, passim; https://eizpublishing.ch/artikel/euz/03-2024/digital-regulation-in-the-european-union/. Accessed 28 August 2025
Bacchus J (2021) The Digital decide. How to agree on WTO Rules for Digital Trade
Bacchus J (2022) Trade Links. New Rules for a New World
Bradford A (2020) The Brussels Effect: How the European Union Rules the World
Bueno TM and Gadoni R (2024) The Brussels Effects in Brazil: Analysing the impact of the EU digital services act on the discussion surrounding the fake news, 48 Telecommunications Policy 102757, passim
Burri M (2021) Data Flows and Global Trade Law. In: Burri (ed), Big Data and Global Trade Law, pp 11–36
Burri M (2023) Digital trade rulemaking in free trade agreements. In: Collins D and Geist M (eds) Research Handbook on Digital Trade, pp 9–27
Burri M and Kugler K (2023) Digitization, Regulatory Barriers and Sustainable Development, University of Lucerne, Trade Law 4.0 Working Paper no. 03/2023
Burri M and Zihlmann L (2023) The Cyber Resilience Act – The EU's proposal for a horizontal regulation on cybersecurity for products with digital elements, 02 EuZ, pp B 1–B 45
Bygrave LA (2021b) The 'Strasbourg Effect' on data protection in light of the 'Brussels Effect': Logic, mechanics and prospects, 40 CLSR, 105460, passim
Bygrave LA (2021a) Security by Design: Aspirations and Realities in a Regulatory Context, 8/3 Oslo L. Rev., pp 126–177; https://www.scup.com/doi/https://doi.org/10.18261/olr.8.3.2. Accessed 28 August 2025
Chiara PG (2025) Understanding the Regulatory Approach of the Cyber Resilience Act: Protection of Fundamental Rights in Disguise?, E.J.R.R., pp 1–16; https://doi.org/10.1017/err.2025.9. Accessed 28 August 2025
Davies KE and Marotta-Wurgler F (2024) Filling the Void: How E.U. Privacy Law Spills Over to the U.S., 1 J. L. & Econ. Anal., pp. 77–97
Diebold NF (2008) The Morals and Order Exemptions in WTO Law: Balancing the Toothless Tiger and the Undermining Mole, 11 J. Int'l Econ. L., pp 43–74
Kulesza J and Weber RH (2021) Protecting the Internet with international law, 40 CLSR 195531, passim
Peng S-y (2020) A New Trade Regime for the Servitization of Manufacturing: Rethinking the Goods-Services Dichotomy, 54 J.W.T., pp 669–726
Peng S-y (2024) International Economic Law in the Era of Datafication
Peukert Ch, Bechtold St, Batikas M and Kretschmer T (2022) Regulatory Spillovers and Data Governance: Evidence from the GDPR, 41 Marketing Science, pp 318–340
Saraji S (2023) Blockchain and Sustainable Energy. In: Saraji S and Chen S (eds) Sustainable Oil and Gas Using Blockchain, pp 121–143
Schacherer S and Weber RH (2026) Digital Assets and Sustainable Development. In: Allen JG et al. (eds) The Oxford Handbook of Digital Assets and the Law (forthcoming)
Segura-Serrano A (2021) Cybersecurity and Cybercrime: Dynamic Application versus Norm Development, 81 Heidelberg J. Intl. L., pp 701–732
Shimizu M (2026), How to Capture Economic Resilience under Justiffications of the WTO Law, in: …
Wang H (2024) Addressing governance challenges of digitalisation and sustainability: The case of central bank digital currency, 33 Rev. Europ. Comp. & Int. Environm. L., pp 647–661; https://doi.org/10.1111/reel.12571. Accessed 28 August 2025
Weber RH (2021) Sectoral Self-Regulation as Viable Tool. In: Mathis K and Tor A (eds) Law and Economics of Regulation, pp. 25–36
Weber RH (2023) WTO law and cross-border data flows for digital trade. In: Collins D and Geist M (eds) Research Handbook on Digital Trade, pp 73–89

Weber RH (2024a) Cybersecurity Governance – international law as policy driver? Weblaw Jusletter IT, 27 May 2024
Weber RH (2024b) Financial Inclusion as a Public Policy Issue in the Global Digital Economy, 19 AJWH, pp 231–252
Weber RH (2025) Cybersecurity and internet governance. In: Balleste R et al. (eds) Research Agenda for Cybersecurity Law and Policy, pp 33–54
Weber RH (2026) Climate Justice and the Supply Chain Tasks. In: De Franceschi A and Boyd W (eds) Sustainability and Climate Change, part II (forthcoming)
Weber RH and Baisch R (2018) Revisiting the Public Moral/Order and the Security Exceptions under the GATS, 13 AJWH, pp 375–394

Chapter 4
How to Capture "Supply Chain Resilience" Under Justifications of the WTO Law

Mari Shimizu

Abstract This paper examines whether supply chain resilience measures that may violate WTO non-discrimination principles can be justified under WTO exception clauses. Analyzing security exceptions, FTA/EPA exceptions, and general exceptions through recent case law, the paper concludes that general exceptions (GATT Article XX/GATS Article XIV) provide the most appropriate framework. For trade in services, GATS Article XIV(a) offers the best routes for justification. Even for trade in goods, GATT Article XX(d) with proper domestic legislation and other subparagraphs such as (b)—to the extent a stable supply of certain products leads to fulfilling the policy objectives provided for in such subparagraphs—may provide justifications. However, in any route of justification, appropriate limitations are indispensable to avoid the risk of over-generalization that could create loopholes for protective measures under the guise of supply chain resilience. The paper proposes an analytical framework based on two core elements: (1) likelihood of supply disruption risk, and (2) degree of adverse impact from shortages. These objective criteria distinguish legitimate resilience measures from protectionism. Actual supply disruptions, especially through economic coercion, strengthen justification, while hypothetical or over-generalized risks should be rejected. Product-specific analysis is essential.

Keywords Supply Chain Resilience · Economic Security · General Exceptions · Security Exception · FTA Exception · Equitable Share

4.1 Introduction

As trade tensions and geopolitical risks have increased in recent years, countries are increasingly discussing and introducing measures to strengthen the resilience of their supply chains, often under the concept of economic security. While the definition or

---

M. Shimizu (✉)
Graduate School of Law and Politics, University of Osaka, Osaka, Japan
e-mail: mari-shimizu.law@osaka-u.ac.jp

J. Nakagawa et al. (eds.), *Geopolitical Risks and Geoeconomics in International Economic Law*, Economics, Law, and Institutions in Asia Pacific,
https://doi.org/10.1007/978-981-95-6996-0_4

scope of "economic security" and "(economic) resilience" can vary depending on the context and discussant,[1] for the purposes of this paper, resilience of the supply chain or "supply chain resilience" will be used to mean the ability of the supply chain to cope with the risk of importing countries being cut off from supplies from particular countries on which those importing countries have become dependent.[2]

Some measures taken for supply chain resilience are comparatively decent in the sense that while they state the need to diversify sources of supply and often provide a framework for specific measures to be taken in the future, they do not provide (or at least, do not explicitly refer to) concrete measures to exclude or restrict imports from specific sources.[3] On the other hand, there are other versions of measures (seemingly) taken for supply chain resilience that appear on their face to be discriminatory or restrictive to imports from certain sources. For example, the two recent Section 301 measures by the United States, i.e., the four-year review on Chinese technology transfer and the investigation on China's targeting the maritime, logistics, and shipbuilding sectors for dominance have both highlighted the risk that China's actions pose to the supply chain resilience for the United States.[4] One can argue that the United States' Section 232 measures on steel and aluminum, which were based on the finding that increased imports of steel and aluminum were weakening domestic production capacity and threatened to impair the national security, are also aimed to ensure supply chain resilience, although the concept of "supply chain resilience" was not explicitly mentioned in the reports.[5] Another example in service area is a measure to assess whether diversification of energy supply sources will be ensured upon certifying foreign energy transmission service suppliers, as seen in *EU–Energy Package*[6] case, which will be discussed in Sect. 4.4 below.

The discriminatory aspects of such measures against foreign goods or services that an imposing country currently depends on make some sense for supply chain resilience purposes. Indeed, to diversify sources of supply, it may ultimately be effective to exclude and/or restrict products from certain competitive but risky sources, by prioritizing products or inputs sourced domestically or from other less risky sources. However, such restriction of sources necessarily raises the question of whether its discriminatory aspect is consistent with the principles of non-discrimination (i.e.

[1] For example, the OECD states that "[s]upply chain resilience can … be defined as the ability of a supply chain to return to normal operations following a disruption." (OECD 2025, p. 2).

[2] The parallel pattern of "demand" disruptions, which is caused to exporting countries by importing countries suspending imports, needs separate discussion and is not addressed in this paper.

[3] *See* e.g. Japan's Economic Security Promotion Act.

[4] The United States Trade Representative [USTR], Four-Year Review of Actions Taken in the Section 301 Investigation: China's Acts, Policies, and Practices Related to Technology Transfer, Intellectual Property, and Innovation, pp. 78–82 (14 May 2024); USTR, Report on China's Targeting of the Maritime, Logistics, and Shipbuilding Sectors for Dominance, pp. 61–63, 132–138 (16 January 2025).

[5] U.S. Department of Commerce [USDOC], Bureau of Industry and Security [BIS], The Effect of Imports of Steel on the National Security, (11 January 2018); USDOC, BIS, The Effect of Imports of Aluminum on the National Security, (17 January 2018).

[6] Panel Report, *EU—Energy Package*, WT/DS476/R, circulated on 10 August 2018 (under appeal).

national treatment and most-favored nation treatment)—which are among the most fundamental rules of the WTO Agreement. Measures without explicit distinction by country of origin would still risk being *de facto* discrimination to the extent that they are structured and/or applied in such a way to alter the competitive conditions to the detriment of products from particular countries. This paper will refer to the measures taken to ensure the supply chain resilience that may be inconsistent with non-discrimination principles (or sometimes with tariff concessions, when tariffs are used) as the "supply chain resilience measures".

The inevitable question to be pursued is whether and how supply chain resilience measures could be justified under the exception clauses of the WTO law. The essence of the underlying concern is whether and how a line could be drawn, irrespective of specific applicable provisions, between the "legitimate" policy of ensuring supply chain resilience and the policy of protecting the domestic industry or forming a block of certain countries to the detriment of others. The latter has been considered as an obvious example of unjustifiable policy objective under the WTO law, but it is hard to deny that the protection of domestic industry or a block with less risky countries would decrease the reliance on risky imports, and thus somehow contribute to the resilient supply chain. At the same time, no matter how obvious the need for supply chain resilience in today's world with various risks of supply disruption,[7] if supply chain resilience measures are pursued excessively, there will be a risk of recurrence of block economies, i.e. fragmented and economically inefficient markets, which is detrimental to all stakeholders and fundamentally against the *raison d'être* of the WTO law.

With that concern in mind, I am going to discuss the following possible justifications incorporated in the WTO Agreement: (1) security exceptions (Sect. 4.2); (2) FTA/EPA exceptions (Sect. 4.3); and (3) general exceptions, with particular focus on the analysis of dispute settlement cases that dealt with the relevant general exceptions (Sect. 4.4).

4.2 Security Exceptions

Supply chain resilience would contribute to the economic security—e.g., in terms of the stability of the country's economic environment as a fundamental basis for social and economic activities—of the Member imposing the measure. The obvious question then is whether supply chain resilience measures can be justified under the security exceptions.

---

[7] OECD (2025, p. 2) ("Supply chain disruptions are becoming the new normal. Conflicts, wars, extreme weather events leading to natural disasters, ongoing geopolitical tensions, regulatory uncertainty and economic fluctuations and threats of cyber-attacks have highlighted the importance of boosting resilience. Increased pressure on the logistics and transport industry coupled with frequent congestion, labour and container shortages and rising prices have put additional strain on supply chains").

According to the interpretation taken by the past panels, the scope for the objective of ensuring supply chain resilience to be covered by subparagraph (b)(iii) of GATT Article XXI and GATS Article XIV bis:1 ("other emergency in international relations") is still open. Indeed, the latest findings on this issue by the panels in *US—Steel and Aluminium Products*[8] and *US—Origin Marking (Hong Kong, China)*,[9] while both concluded that the measures at issue did not fall within the scope of subparagraph (b)(iii) because the particular situations at issue did not reach the level of gravity required as an "emergency",[10] left open the possibility that economic situations could be covered.

The panel in *US–Steel and Aluminium Products (China)* found that, among the three factors identified by the USDOC as the basis for its finding that the "weakening of [the United States'] internal economy may impair the national security" for the steel and aluminium 232 measures, only "global excess capacity" of steel and aluminium fell under "international relations" in subparagraph (b)(iii).[11] In *US–Origin Marking (Hong Kong, China)*, although the matter was not particularly relevant to supply chain resilience, the panel notably indicated that a broad range of events and/or interests can be protected under subparagraph (b)(iii) by finding that "(international) relations" thereunder may "involve diverse matters, such as political, *economic*, social, or cultural exchanges".[12]

From these findings, it could be argued that a situation where there is a risk of disruption of supply (to be addressed by supply chain resilience) can be covered by subparagraph (b)(iii), provided that the situation has an "international" aspect and is "grave" enough. While a mere consideration of the protection of domestic industry is excluded by the requirement of "internationality", whether a particular event is classified as domestic or international may sometimes be ambiguous, considering that the disruption of "international" supply is a risk to a "domestic" market.

However, while certain risks with an obvious "international" event of a certain "gravity" may be covered, I believe that these two thresholds should be applied strictly, and that the coverage of supply chain resilience measures under the security exception should be very limited and exceptional, for the following reasons.

Firstly, the interpretation of the scope of incidents covered under the term "emergency in international relations" by different panels has not been necessarily consistent (in part because the Appellate Body is not currently functioning to integrate these

---

[8] Panel Reports, *US–Steel and Aluminium Products*, WT/DS544/R *(China)*, WT/DS552/R *(Norway)*, WT/DS556/R *(Switzerland)* and WT/DS564/R *(Turkey)*, circulated on 9 December 2022 (under appeal). Hereinafter, with respect to this case, I refer to the paragraphs in Panel Report, *US—Steel and Aluminium Products (China)*, WT/DS544/R,.

[9] Panel Report, *US–Origin Marking (Hong Kong, China)*, WT/DS597/R, circulated on 21 December 2022 (under appeal).

[10] Panel Report, *US– Steel and Aluminium Products (China)*, ¶7.147–148; and *US—Origin Marking (Hong Kong, China)*, ¶7.290.

[11] Panel Report, *US– Steel and Aluminium Products (China)*, ¶7.142. The panel dismissed the other two elements ("displacement of domestic industry" and "adverse impact on the economic welfare of domestic industry") as they focused primarily on "developments relating to the domestic situation".

[12] Panel Report, *US–Origin Marking (Hong Kong, China)*, ¶7.280 (emphasis added).

interpretations). The panel in *US–Origin Marking (Hong Kong, China)* specifically rejected the other panel's finding in *Russia–Traffic in Transit* that an emergency in international relations generally refers to "a situation of armed conflict, or of latent armed conflict, or of heightened tension or crisis, or of general instability engulfing or surrounding a state", and that "such situations give rise to particular types of interests for the Member in question, i.e. defence or military interests, or maintenance of law and public order interests".[13] Subsequent panels are not obliged to follow the aforementioned criteria of "internationality" or "graveness", and even if they would *de facto* follow, it is not predictable how it would be applied in specific cases. Secondly, the term "consider" would at least qualify the chapeau of paragraph (b). And supply chain resilience, however important and sensitive, is so close to industrial policy. Therefore, the risk of abuse by disguising the permanent industrial policy in peacetime as a security issue to circumvent the standard under general exceptions is real. Thirdly, the interpretation of paragraph (b) of the security exception is not stable considering the self-judging approach pursued by the United States. Although this approach has been rejected by panels in all previous WTO cases, the United States is explicitly seeking an authoritative interpretation of it, along with suggested rebalancing measures based on the non-violation clause.[14] The United States has also indicated that this issue must be addressed in order to reform the dispute settlement system.[15] However, applying the security exception with a self-judging interpretation to supply chain resilience measures in general, even with the suggested rebalancing measures, would create a significant loophole in the rules and render restrictions under the security exceptions more or less unenforceable. Finally, as I will argue in Sect. 4.4 below, supply chain resilience can also be appropriately considered under general exceptions.

4.3 FTA/EPA Exception

Since it is often economically unviable to procure supplies entirely on one's own, any country may wish to structure and join a framework of allied countries to secure supplies, in particular of certain strategic goods. I would like to touch briefly on whether such a supply framework among allied countries can be justified under FTA/EPA exceptions (GATT Article XXIV and GATS Article V).

---

[13] Panel Report, *US-Origin Marking (Hong Kong, China)*, footnote 438 (rejecting Panel Report, *Russia–Traffic in Transit*, WT/DS512/R, adopted on 26 April 2019, ¶7.76).

[14] Communication from the United States, Reflection from the United States on the Handling of Disputes Involving Essential Security Measures, JOB/DSB/10 (11 December 2024).

[15] E.g. Statements by the United States at the Meeting of the WTO Dispute Settlement Body (25 April 2025), https://geneva.usmission.gov/wp-content/uploads/sites/25/2025/04/Apr25.DSB_.Stmt_.as_.deliv_.fin_.pdf (Accessed 14 September 2025), p. 11 (in the agenda item of "Appellate Body Appointments", pointing to the panel's finding on the security exception in *US–Origin Marking (Hong Kong, China)* as a specific example of the WTO dispute settlement process exceeding its limitation and making new rules to which the United States had not agreed).

GATT Article XXIV:5 provides that in forming a “free-trade area”, the constituent territories shall not raise external trade barriers.[16] Whether a framework of allied countries can meet this condition may depend on specific measures/actions to be taken under it. In this regard, traditional measures seen in various FTA/EPAs such as (i) cooperative facilitation (e.g. the provision of a matching program for businesses), (ii) commitments not to impose export taxes on participants, and (iii) preferential tariffs for participants may not be considered as raising external trade barriers. On the other hand, more trade-restrictive measures such as (i) favorable treatment of imports from participants under domestic regulations, subsidies, etc. and (ii) common tariff increases against non-participants are likely to be considered as raising external trade barriers.

More fundamentally, however, “customs union” and “free-trade area” under GATT Article XXIV (and “economic integration” under GATS Article V) seem to presuppose a more *integrated* relationship (as reflected in the “closer integration” referred to in GATT Article XXIV:4 and the title of GATS Article V) than a supply chain resilience framework focused on specific strategic goods or industries. Whether the latter framework can be justified under FTA/EPA exceptions may be debatable considering such a substantial difference in nature. A relevant and specific condition is provided in GATT Article XXIV:8(b), which requires the elimination of duties and other restrictive regulations of commerce on “substantially all the trade” within the free-trade area.[17] Supply chain resilience frameworks focused on specific strategic industries or goods may not meet this condition.

4.4 General Exceptions

4.4.1 Overview

While the protection of economic resilience itself is not explicitly provided for in the subparagraphs of the general exceptions (GATT Article XX and GATS Article XIV), some recent WTO dispute settlement cases have dealt with defenses under the general exceptions for measures allegedly taken to ensure stable supplies of relevant products and services.

These cases can be classified into four categories as follows:

1. cases of GATT Article XX(j) (“essential to the acquisition/distribution of products in general or local short supply”)–specifically, *India–Solar Cells*[18] and *EU—Energy Package*;
2. a case of GATS Article XIV(a) (“necessary to … to maintain public order”)—specifically, *EU—Energy Package*;

[16] A parallel provision in GATS is GATS Article V:4.

[17] A parallel provision (“substantial sector coverage”) in GATS is GATS Article V:1(a).

[18] Appellate Body Report, *India – Solar Cells*, WT/DS456/AB/R, adopted on 14 October 2016.

3. cases where supply chain resilience was specifically argued as an element to support the justification under specific subparagraphs that provide (relevant but) different legitimate objectives, such as GATT Article XX (b) ("necessary to protect human ... health") in *Turkey—Pharmaceutical Products (EU)*,[19] since, if a particular product on the market contributes to a specific legitimate policy objective covered by the general exceptions (human health, environmental protection, public moral etc.), a *stable and affordable supply* of such products would reinforce this contribution; and
4. a case of GATT Article XX(d) (and possibly GATS Article XIV(c)) ("necessary to secure compliance with laws and regulations")–specifically, *India–Solar Cells*.

4.4.2 Category 1: GATT Article XX(J) (Essential to the Acquisition or Distribution of Products in General or Local Short Supply)

In *India—Solar Cells*, India invoked GATT Article XX(j) to justify domestic content requirements (the DCR measures) that required solar power developers to use domestically produced solar cells and modules, arguing that "general or local short supply" would occur when there is no indigenous production, as "sole dependence on imported solar cells and modules brings risk associated with supply side vulnerability and fluctuations".[20]

In *EU—Energy Package*, the EU invoked GATT Article XX(j) for the "TEN-E measure", which identified certain infrastructure projects to be prioritized for administrative facilitation and financial incentives with the aim of diversifying the supply of natural gas to include sources other than Russia, arguing that natural gas is a product "in general or local short supply" because of genuine and serious risks of disruption of gas supply.[21]

The panels and the Appellate Body in both cases rendered the strict reading and application of the requirement of "short supply". The Appellate Body in *India–Solar Cells* found that "a panel should examine the extent to which a particular product is "available" for purchase in a particular geographical area or market, and whether this is sufficient to meet demand in the relevant area or market", and that "due regard should be given to the total quantity of imports that may be 'available'".[22] The Appellate Body further clarified the temporal dimension of the "availability" analysis that it requires "a holistic consideration of trends in supply and demand as they evolve over time, as well as whether the conditions giving rise to short supply have ceased

[19] Panel Report, *Turkey—Pharmaceutical Products (EU)*, WT/DS583/12, attached to Türkiye's notice of recourse to arbitration and circulated on 28 April 2022; and Award of the Arbitrators, *Turkey—Pharmaceutical Products (EU) (Article 21.5)*, WT/DS583/ARB25, circulated on 25 July 2022.

[20] Appellate Body Report, *India—Solar Cells*, ¶5.46.

[21] Panel Report, *EU—Energy Package*, ¶7.1336.

[22] Appellate Body Report, *India—Solar Cells*, ¶5.71.

to exist."[23] Consequently, India's defense was rejected for disregarding supply from international sources.[24] Explicitly following the Appellate Body's finding in *India–Solar Cells*, the panel in *EU–Energy Package* rejected the EU's Article XX(j) defense, as the EU had not demonstrated that natural gas was *currently* in short supply in the EU, despite that, "due to certain risks of natural gas disruptions, natural gas *may become* a product 'in short supply'."[25] The panel also found that the EU had not provided evidence of the relevant trends that could indicate the inherent risks of supply disruptions.[26]

However, though the panel in *India—Solar Cells* found that the terms "products in … short supply" do not cover products that are *at risk* of becoming in short supply,[27] the Appellate Body found that potential risks of disruption arising from the continued dependence on imports could, in principle, be relevant to the issue of "availability", while ultimately did not admit the existence of such risks in this case by referring to the panel's findings that there was no demonstration of actual supply disruptions of the relevant products.[28]

4.4.3 Category 2: GATS Article XIV(a) (Necessary to Maintain Public Order)

EU—Energy Package also addressed the third-country certification measure implemented by certain EU Member States taken under the EU Gas Directive. The measure imposed an additional condition for the certification of a transmission system operator (TSO) in light of the security of energy supply (SoS) of the Member State and the Community where the TSO or the owner of the transmission system is controlled by non-EU third countries. In response to Russia's claim under GATS Article XVII (national treatment), the EU invoked Article XIV(a), arguing that the measure was necessary to ensure the EU's SoS and thus to maintain public order. The panel found the measure to be provisionally justified under subparagraph (a), but ultimately unjustified under the chapeau.

First, with respect to the policy objective of the measure, the panel found that SoS is a "fundamental interest[] of society" within the meaning of footnote 5 to Article XIV(a), given the potential severe social, economic, and political effects of

---

[23] *Id.* ¶5.70.

[24] *Id.* ¶5.89–90.

[25] Panel Report, *EU—Energy Package*, ¶7.1350 (emphasis added). Russia did not contest the existence of risk of supply disruption and the EU's characterization of such risks as "genuine and serious" (*Id.* ¶7.1345).

[26] *Id.* ¶7.1351–1352.

[27] Panel Report, *India—Solar Cells*, ¶7.250.

[28] Appellate Body Report, *India—Solar Cells*, ¶5.76.

disruptions of energy supply.[29] Then the panel elaborated the meaning of "genuine and sufficiently serious threat" under footnote 5 that a "genuine" threat relates to the degree of *likelihood* of the threat materializing, and a "sufficiently serious" threat refers to the potential *consequences* or *gravity* of the effects of a threat materializing.[30] Based on this understanding, the panel found that the EU had demonstrated a real and true—not merely hypothetical—possibility that foreign governments would require or induce foreign controlled TSOs to undermine the EU's SoS and, accordingly, that foreign control of TSOs posed a "genuine and sufficiently serious threat" to the EU's SoS.[31] The panel stated that evidence of the materialization of threat is not a prerequisite for demonstrating that a threat is "genuine", and that the EU's allegation was not mere conjecture, since it identified a number of actual situations in which the three "indispensable" circumstances would occur. These circumstances are: (a) foreign governments having incentives to undermine the EU's SoS; (b) foreign controlled TSOs effectively undermining the EU's SoS, by failing to comply with legal obligations under the EU law or by acting contrary to their own commercial interests; and (c) foreign governments having the means to require or induce foreign controlled TSOs to undermine the EU's SoS. One example of this would be where a foreign government may be interested in ensuring its own security of energy supply at the expense of the EU's, in particular in case of parallel shortage.[32]

Second, the panel found that the measure was "necessary" to achieve this objective, considering that: (i) the objective was of fundamental importance; (ii) the measure was manifestly apt to address *ex ante* the threat to security of energy supply posed by foreign control of TSOs; (iii) trade-restrictiveness of the measure was limited, as it would only restrict trade if such a threat was found to exist; and (iv) there were no reasonably available alternatives.[33]

However, the panel concluded that the measure was not justified because it violated the chapeau, as the measure lacked any assessment of threats posed by foreign governments in requiring or inducing *domestically controlled* TSOs to undermine the security or energy supply in the EU, which constitutes arbitrary and unjustifiable discrimination in violation of the chapeau.[34]

[29] Panel Report, *EU—Energy Package*, ¶7.1154. Russia did not dispute this issue other than that the EU's definition of SoS was not clear enough.

[30] *Id.* ¶7.1162–1163.

[31] *Id.* ¶7.1194, 1202.

[32] *Id.* ¶7.1171–1191.

[33] *Id.* ¶7.1212–1238.

[34] *Id.* ¶7.1251–1253.

4.4.4 Category 3: Supporting Element for Other Explicitly Provided Interests

In *Brazil—Taxation,*[35] for Brazil's tax exemptions on digital television transmitting equipment with a requirement to go through certain production process in Brazil, Brazil invoked GATT Article XX(a), arguing that the measure was taken to bridge the digital divide and to promote social inclusion.[36] In *Turkey—Pharmaceutical Products (EU),*[37] Türkiye invoked GATT Article XX(b) as one of the justifications for the localization requirement incorporated in the government reimbursement of pharmaceutical products. A notable common feature of these defenses is that the respondents argued that it was necessary to enhance domestic capacity of the relevant products in order to ensure their supply and prepare for possible import disruption.

In both cases, the alleged objectives with this common intermediate feature were recognized to be covered by the policy objectives set out in subparagraphs GATT Articles XX(a) (public morals) and (b) (human health).[38] In *Turkey—Pharmaceutical Products (EU),* the panel noted that there was no disagreement between the parties that, among others, (i) the objective of ensuring adequate access to pharmaceutical products was related to the protection of human life or health under Article XX(b) and was vital and important, and (ii) Members may, in the context of Article XX(b), take measures to address the risk of future shortages of supplies before such shortages actually arise.[39]

However, neither panel ultimately found the measure to be justified, as the risk of import disruption leading to lack of availability in the market was found to be hypothetical, noting that the respondent had not provided any actual instances of import disruptions.

Specifically, in *Brazil—Taxation,* the panel rejected the "necessity" of the measure, as the decline in import supply resulting from the discrimination would be either equivalent to or less than the increase in domestic supply, and therefore the measure was unlikely to make much contribution, if any, to the objective.[40] The panel noted

---

[35] Panel Reports, *Brazil–Taxation,* WT/DS472/R and WT/DS/497/R, adopted on 11 January 2019, as modified by Appellate Body Reports WT/DS472/AB/R and WT/DS497/AB/R. The panel's findings under GATT Article XX(a) were not appealed.

[36] *Id.* ¶7.544, 552, 572.

[37] The appeal arbitration award maintained the panel's findings on GATT Article XX(b).

[38] Panel Reports, *Brazil–Taxation,* ¶7.568 (The panel disagreed with the EU's argument that accepting that general objectives to improve the social and economic conditions of its community may fall within "public morals" would in practice tantamount to say that Article XX is virtually available to justify any governmental action which is taken in the public interest.); and *Turkey–Pharmaceutical Products (EU),* ¶7.142–143.

[39] Panel Report, *Turkey—Pharmaceutical Products (EU),* ¶7.161–162. The panel noted that all third parties that expressed a view agreed on the element (ii) *(Id.* ¶7.162 and footnote 589).

[40] *Id.* ¶7. 601–602, 622. The panel accepted in advance that the measure was not incapable of contributing to the objective, and was therefore designed for that objective, as the discriminatory measure could potentially lead to a situation where the protected domestic producers could become

that Brazil had not provided any evidence of the alleged risk that transmitting equipment would not be made adequately available in the domestic market and Brazil had not substantiated its argument that imported products could not supply the market.[41] In *Turkey—Pharmaceutical Products (EU)*,[42] the panel rejected Türkiye's argument that the measure was designed to protect human life or health as it addressed a risk of long-term shortage arising from over-reliance on imports. The panel held that a risk of over-reliance on imports must be more than a mere hypothetical possibility.[43] Then the panel found that the risk identified by Türkiye was only hypothetical, given that Türkiye had not identified any instance of supply shortage caused by the alleged circumstances relating to the cost of imports, namely that (a) foreign producers shifting to other markets with higher prices, and (b) imports becoming unaffordable due to exchange rate fluctuations.[44]

It is also worth noting that the panel in *Turkey—Pharmaceutical Products (EU)* specifically addressed the excessive generality of the respondent's arguments. The panel stated that "the situation described by Turkey is characterized by a level of temporal and sectoral generality that is at odds with the concept of risk under Article XX(b)" and "[t]he generality of Turkey's argument is in fact such that the risk identified by Turkey could be present in any sector and concern any market" and would lead to the conclusion that "international trade liberalization in products and sectors that are necessary for the protection of human life or health creates a permanent risk to human life or health under Article XX(b)".[45]

4.4.5 *Category 4: GATT Article XX(D) & GATS Article XIV(C) (Necessary to Secure Compliance with Non WTO-Inconsistent Laws)*

Lastly, in *India—Solar Cells*, India invoked GATT Article XX(d) to justify the DCR measures on the basis of a substantial common ground with Article XX(j) (see Sect. 4.4.2), arguing that the measures were to comply with India's obligation under domestic law to "ensure ecologically sustainable growth while addressing India's energy security challenge, and ensuring compliance with obligations relating to climate change" by ensuring an adequate reserve of domestic manufacturing capacity for solar cells and modules in case of import disruptions.[46]

---

competitive in the market, and thus could achieve a net welfare benefit in terms of social inclusion and information access through lower prices for consumers (*Id.* ¶7.583).

[41] *Id.* ¶7. 573–580, 597, 600.

[42] *Id.* ¶7.165, 172.

[43] *Id.* ¶7.166–170 (referring to findings in *India—Solar Cells*, *Brazil—Taxation* and *EU—Energy Package*).

[44] *Id.* ¶7.171–177.

[45] *Id.* ¶7.178.

[46] Panel Report, *India—Solar Cells*, ¶7.189, 268.

The Appellate Body rejected India's defense, finding that the domestic instruments identified by India lacked the "degree of normativity" required for "laws or regulations" with which "compliance" can be "secure[d]" under Article XX(d).[47] This was because various general laws and provisions identified by India were not specifically linked to the DCR measures, and appeared to be *ex post* at the dispute settlement stage.

While the focus of its overall analysis was not on the substantive elements regarding supply chain resilience, the panel conducted a limited analysis (without weighing and balancing) of whether the DCR measures were "essential" or "necessary" in terms of Articles XX(j) or (d), in case of modification or reversal on appeal. The panel assessed the alleged objective of ensuring a continuous and affordable supply of solar cells and modules as "important", given that these products are needed to generate solar power.[48] However, the panel assessed the contribution by the measures negative, as the measures were unlikely to make any short-term contribution and could arguably undermine the said objective, and the long-term contribution was still hypothetical and doubtful.[49]

4.4.6 Analysis

4.4.6.1 Comparison of the Four Categories

With Categories 2 to 4, panels and the Appellate Body have generally been positive at the initial stage of the analysis of general exceptions, namely, accepting that the alleged objectives, which essentially relate to supply chain resilience, fall within the scope of the legitimate objectives set out in various subparagraphs of general exceptions. Complainants have often not contested that the objectives are covered by the subparagraphs at issue, which may indicate that not a few Members recognize the need to justify certain, if not all, measures taken for supply chain resilience.

On the other hand, with respect to Category 1 (GATT Article XX(j)), "short supply" is hardly affirmed when there has not been actual disruption of import supply (see Sect. 4.4.2). This strict reading may be reasonable given that GATT Article XX(j) can be understood to strike a balance by setting no textual limitation with respect to product types and the degree of impact of the shortage, on the one hand, but limiting the applicable situations through the strict reading of "short[age]" along with the proviso regarding the measure's termination and the requirement of "essential[ness]"

[47] Appellate Body Report, *India—Solar Cells*, ¶5.136–137 (upholding the panel's finding).

[48] Panel Report, *India—Solar Cells*, ¶7.335, 353–354, 367. The United States did not contest the issue.

[49] *Id.* ¶7.335, 353–354, 367. For the long-term contribution, the panel noted that: (i) the measure's effect on increasing domestic manufacturing capacity was not demonstrated; (ii) related measures taken to ensure the input supply for domestic production were not identified; and (iii) it was not clear whether domestic solar cells or modules would be sold to Indian producers, as opposed to foreign competitors, in the event of supply disruptions.

of the measure, on the other. Nevertheless, the findings indicating (i) the need to assess "trends" in supply and demand, and (ii) the relevance of risks inherent in the continued dependence on imports for the "availability" analysis, may still leave scope for covering certain imminent risks of supply disruption.

The other categories also have their own textual limitations regarding coverage. Of these, Category 2 (GATS Article XIV(a)) seems best suited to addressing supply chain resilience measures.[50] Notably, unlike GATT Article XX(j), footnote 5 of GATS Article XIV(a) can unarguably cover the risk (of disruption) since its terms include "threat". However, "public order" cannot be invoked for measures affecting trade in goods, as the parallel provision in GATT (Article XX(a)) does not contain this term. This textual difference between GATT Article XX(a) and GATS Article XIV(a) may be explained by the consideration that the prevention of disruption to the host country's order upon entry and operation of foreign services deserves specific classification in GATS Article XIV(a), given that trade in services naturally involves a substantial degree of integration of foreign service into the domestic market. Nevertheless, this does not necessarily negate the need for the protection of certain aspects of public order under GATT Article XX, provided it contributes to achieving the policy objectives set out in the subparagraphs.

With respect to Category 4 (GATT Article XX(d) and GATS Article XIV(c)), there may still be unaddressed issues regarding coverage. These include (i) whether these subparagraphs apply to measures taken by a government to secure its *own* compliance with its laws or regulations[51]; and (ii) whether the terms "laws or regulations" include domestic legislation primarily designed to regulate trade itself (e.g. supply chain resilience), despite the non-exhaustive examples provided (e.g. custom enforcement, monopoly enforcement, and intellectual property protection) may imply that these subparagraphs address the consequential trade-restrictive effect of domestic regulatory measures or stand-alone trade measures like tariffs.

Despite the ambiguity in Category 4, Categories 3 and 4 with fewer textual limitations are more likely to be invoked for supply chain resilience measures. In this regard, the lack of contemporaneous evidence (including "specific" domestic legislation with normativity), as highlighted in Category 4, may be addressed *ex ante* by elaborating on the legal basis in the domestic legislative process. However, the concern of over-generalization as specifically noted in Category 3 (see Sect. 4.4.4)—that any product and any sector have some hypothetical long-term risk of shortage due to potential import disruption—is particularly applicable to Categories 3 and 4 with fewer textual limitations. Therefore, certain substantive criteria or elements for assessing supply chain resilience measures are necessary in any category to avoid such over-generalization.

[50] The defense under GATS Article XIV(a) in *EU–Energy Package* is the only one as of September 2025 for which a provisional justification under general exceptions was accepted for supply chain resilience measures.

[51] The issue was raised by the United States in *India—Solar Cells*, but the panel exercised judicial economy (Panel Report, *India—Solar Cells*, ¶7.324, 329).

4.4.6.2 Core Elements to Assess Supply Chain Resilience Measures Under General Exceptions: Likelihood and Degree of Adverse Impact of the Risk of Shortage

The core elements for assessing the justification for supply chain resilience measures can be boiled down to (i) the likelihood of the risk of supply shortage caused by import disruptions and (ii) the degree of adverse impact caused by such supply shortage. These elements correspond to the terms "genuine" and "sufficiently serious", respectively, in footnote 5 of GATS Article XIV(a) as rendered in Category 2. But they have also been reflected in the availability analysis in Category 1 and the analysis of linkage between the measure and the objective (design or contribution) in Categories 3 and 4.

The First Element: Likelihood of the Risk of Supply Shortage

Likelihood of the risk has been examined in Category 3 (and in Category 4, on assumption), through findings that, if the risk is hypothetical, there is no risk to be addressed by the measure, and thus the measure *cannot* be considered as being designed for the objective or as making a material contribution to the objective.

In Category 1 (GATT Article (j)), the relevant factors were addressed to examine the "availability" of the products in question. In this regard, the Appellate Body in *India—Solar Cells* listed specific factors to assess the "availability", which are also relevant to the likelihood of shortage risk. They are: the nature of the products; the level of domestic production; the relevant market; potential price fluctuations in the market; the purchasing power of foreign/domestic consumers; the role of foreign and domestic producers (including the extent to which domestic producers sell their production abroad); and, notably, stability and accessibility of international supply (including the reliability of local or transnational supply chain).[52] In this regard, certain additional or overlapping factors/aspects would be particularly relevant to examine supply chain resilience measures, such as (i) structure and nature of supply chains (e.g. whether international supply is monopolized or oligopolized), (ii) availability of alternative sources, and (iii) existence of geopolitical risk and/or susceptibility of the relevant products to such risk.

The Second Element: Degree of Adverse Impact by Supply Shortage

The second element of adverse impact depends heavily on the nature and scope of the product in question. One of the key reasons why the defense under GATS XIV(a) succeeded in *EU—Energy Package* (Category 2) may be that the case concerned natural gas, a shortage of which would directly impact social and economic infrastructure.

[52] Appellate Body Report, *India—Solar Cells*, ¶5.89.

On the other hand, the "availability" analysis in Category 1 may not fit to consider this element. Also, in Categories 3 and 4, the adverse impact of shortage has been addressed only in an indirect manner, either to support the relevance of the products at issue to the objectives provided in subparagraphs (see Sect. 4.4.4) or to assess the importance of the objective in the necessity analysis (see Sect. 4.4.5).

However, to address the concern of over-generalization, it may be appropriate to consider this second element more explicitly, and to ask whether the shortage of the products in question seriously affects the fundamental line of economy or lives. This may be assessed in Categories 1, 3, and 4 by evaluating the link between the measure and the objectives under the relevant subparagraphs (i.e. whether the measure is "designed" for or "necessary"/"essential" to achieving these objectives). If the impact of shortage is not serious enough, the linkage or contribution of the supply chain resilience measure to the ultimate objectives under the subparagraphs will be limited.

Inter-Relations of the Two Elements and the Weight of Actual Instances

These two core elements are interrelated and require a holistic assessment. In particular, products for which a shortage would have a serious adverse impact—such as strategic upstream goods with limited alternative sources (e.g. energy resources and critical minerals)—may necessitate preventive measures. In other words, the likelihood of a shortage due to supply disruption for such products can be assessed positively *ex ante*.

One relevant question is how actual instances of import disruption should be weighed. As the panel in *Brazil—Taxation* indicated (see Sect. 4.4.4), in the absence of a probable risk of import disruption, supply chain resilience measures that limit import supply undermine the objective of ensuring market supply. However, it is impractical and unreasonable to wait for an actual instance of disruption to occur when the risk is likely and serious, for example when a country depends on strategic imports from limited sources and has no domestic production capacity.[53]

In *EU—Energy Package*, for instance, the *ex ante* effect of the measure was assessed positively, and it was found that the energy supply risk was covered by GATS Article XIV(a). This was based on the identification of reasonable simulative situations involving geopolitical elements (i.e., interference by foreign governments) that could lead to supply disruption. It was explicitly clarified that materialization of the risk was not necessary. Conversely, in the same case, the risk of short supply, supported by past import disruption events, was denied being covered under GATT Article XX(j) (see Sects. 4.4.2 and 4.4.3).[54] Also, in *Turkey—Pharmaceutical Products (EU)*, the risk explained using possible scenarios but without providing

[53] *See* note 40 for Members' recognition of the necessity of certain preventive measures.

[54] For its defense under GATT Article XX(j), the EU argued that the supply disruption risks materialized in the past, referring to disruptions of gas supplies from Russia via Ukraine that occurred in 2006 and 2009 (Panel Report, *EU—Energy Package*, ¶7.1338 and footnote 2167).

actual instances was found hypothetical and denied coverage under GATT Article XX(b). The different treatment of actual instances in the two defenses in *EU—Energy Package* may be explained by the strict textual limitation of GATT Article XX(j), as discussed. The uniqueness of the finding under GATS Article XIV(a) in *EU—Energy Package*, which does not question the lack of actual instances, may be because the subject product is limited to strategic goods, the disruption of which would have a serious adverse impact. Though not specifically mentioned, the increased geopolitical risk between the EU and Russia may also have influenced the panel's assessment.

In this respect, if the supply is actually disrupted, especially without valid reason or transparency, this should highly support the affirmative determination of the likelihood of supply disruption risk. In particular, a history of economic coercion on the part of a supplying Member would indicate a certain level of geopolitical risk and unreliability in that part of the supply chain. And if those disruptive actions by exporting countries are taken for products that would seriously affect the fundamental line of economy or life of importing countries if they were in short supply, the importing countries' supply chain resilience measures should be furthermore likely to be justified. This understanding could act as a deterrent to Members using economic coercion through their supply power.

4.4.6.3 Other Elements

Trade-Restrictiveness

As assessed by the panel in *EU—Energy Package* in relation to GATS Article XIV(a) (see Sect. 4.4.3), the trade-restrictiveness of the measure will undoubtedly be relevant and will be assessed through the linkage between the measure and the objectives set out in the subparagraphs (e.g. the "necessary" analysis). The relevant elements to be considered would be similar to those discussed in Sect. 4.3 regarding the requirement of whether the measure raises external trade barriers in FTA/ETA exceptions.

Chapeau of General Exceptions

The chapeau of GATT Article XX and GATS Article XIV will not materially affect the assessment in this paper, since the essence of the relevant assessment is common to the subparagraphs (which is on the measure itself) and the chapeau (which is on the application of such a measure), in that it requires a linkage between the provided policy objectives and the measure.[55] If such linkage can be found for the measure itself but not for its application, then the application is not justified under the chapeau,

[55] *See* e.g. Appellate Body Report, *European Communities–Measures Prohibiting the Importation and Marketing of Seal Products*, WT/DS400/AB/R and WT/DS401/AB/R, adopted on 18 June 2014, ¶5.306 ("one of the most important factors [under the chapeau] is ... whether the discrimination can be reconciled with, or is rationally related to, the policy objective [provided in the subparagraphs].").

as was seen for the defense under GATS Article XIV(a) in *EU–Energy Package* (see Sect. 4.4.3). However, generally, the WTO-inconsistency finding regarding the application of measure is comparatively addressable for a Member that imposed and applied the measure, as the core structure of the measure is intact by such finding.

Equitable Share and Termination upon the Cessation of Relevant Conditions

While the two core elements discussed in Sect. 4.4.6.2 will be examined to introduce supply chain resilience measures, it may be necessary to consider further whether such measures should be maintained or terminated. This is particularly pertinent considering that measures based on the risk of supply disruption would be difficult to remove voluntarily once in place.[56] To this end, two specific conditions under the proviso of GATT Article XX(j) may be indicative. These conditions do not apply to other subparagraphs of general exceptions, but they may still be relevant when assessing the requirement of "necessary"/"essential" in Categories 2–4.

The first condition of the proviso under GATT Article (j) is that a measure shall be consistent with the principle that all Members are entitled to "an equitable share of the international supply". This condition typically envisions a situation where a Member wishes to secure a certain share of the supply in its market by imposing *export* restrictions upon a current shortage. However, the idea of an equitable share of the supply *that addresses the risk of import disruption* may make sense for measures that have restrictive effects on *imports*.

In turn, the second condition of the proviso is that the measure should terminate when the conditions that gave rise to it cease to exist. The panel in *India—Solar Cells* referred to this second condition as an immediate context to support its interpretation that the terms "in … short supply" under GATT Article XX(j) only cover the *current* shortage.[57] However, the idea that a measure should terminate when the circumstances that led to it ceased to exist is generally applicable. Indeed, if an import-restrictive measure were to be *permanently* imposed to address the supply disruption risk, then other options, such as tariff renegotiation under GATT Article XXVIII[58] and preferential tariffs under FTAs (including a combination of them), might be more appropriate.

In other words, the two ideas that (a) the measure should not be structured to secure more than an equitable share of the international supply, and that (b) the measure should terminate once the risk of supply disruption is addressed sufficiently (including when the equitable supply share has been secured), may help to establish a threshold and termination point for measures, so that the measures would not be excessive.

---

[56] *See* Hestermeyer and Nielson (2014, p. 591), pointing out that "local content measures may help to upstart an industry, but they rarely are endowed with sunset clauses and soon become a measure of government perk, sustaining an increasingly inefficient industry."

[57] Panel Report, *India—Solar Cells*, ¶7.245.

[58] *See* Pauwelyn (2025, pp. 4–5), Kometani (2025).

However, the obvious problem is that, without further elaborations, the objective criteria of these two conditions are not clear *per se* and would be very difficult for Members to implement and for adjudicators to assess.[59]

Some relevant discussion was seen in *Turkey—Pharmaceutical Products (EU)*, where the panel found that there was no rational relationship between the domestic production target (i.e. 60% by value of domestic demand to be met by domestic production) and the objective of ensuring the supply of pharmaceutical products.[60] It remains to be discussed whether there is scope for setting a specific target for domestic production or imports from alternative sources that can be explained by the objective of ensuring supply chain resilience, which may depend on the elaboration by imposing Members.

At least as a practice, it would be worth considering requiring the government to set a specific target upon the implementation of supply chain resilience measures, with objective reasons why such a target is necessary to ensure supply chain resilience, and to terminate the measure once that target has been met. Ideally, however, these concepts—which require at least a product-based analysis—could be further developed through discussion among Members, and eventually could be monitored by Members as well.

4.5 Conclusion

The examination undertaken in this paper suggests that there is reasonable scope to capture supply chain resilience measures under the general exceptions of the WTO Agreement. While GATT Article XX(j) (acquisition or distribution of products in short supply) may not provide sufficient coverage for preventive measures, at least for trade in services, GATS Article XIV(a) (public order), with its footnote 5, fits for the purpose. Even for trade in goods, GATT Article XX(d) (compliance with non WTO-inconsistent laws) may cover certain supply chain resilience measures, provided that the relevant domestic laws are properly structured *ex ante*. Also, if a stable supply

[59] This proviso itself has not been interpreted in the WTO dispute settlement proceedings so far. However, with respect to the terms "equitable share of world export trade" under GATT Article XVI:3, the GATT panel in *EEC—Subsidies on Export of Wheat Flour* was unable to conclude on whether the export subsidy in issue had resulted in "more than an equitable share", given "the difficulties inherent in the concept of 'more than equitable share'." (Report of the Panel, *EEC–Subsidies on Export of Wheat Flour*, SCM/42, circulated on 21 March 1983 (not adopted), ¶5.3). Also, Paulsen points out that, although not subject to third-party adjudication, the principle of "equitable" distribution or allocation was at the center in (i) the GATT disputes regarding the United States' export license measures withdrawal of MFN tariff treatment against Czechoslovakia, and (ii) the operation of International Materials Conference, which was convened from 1951 to 1953 to allocate strategic materials among western allied countries (Paulsen 2025, pp. 248, 258, 261).

[60] Panel Report, *Turkey—Pharmaceutical Products (EU)*, ¶7.201–208. The panel in *India–Solar Cells* dismissed India's argument that a lack of (sufficient) domestic manufacturing capacity establishes that a product is in "short supply" under GATT Article XX(j), as India's argument lacked any objective point of reference (Panel Report, *India—Solar Cells*, ¶7.225–226).

of certain products leads to fulfilling other policy objectives specifically provided for in the subparagraphs of GATT Article XX (e.g. GATT Article XX(b) (human health etc.)), a measure taken to ensure supply chain resilience for the product may be justified under that specific subparagraph. However, in any route of justification, appropriate limitations are indispensable to avoid the risk of over-generalization that could create loopholes for protective measures under the guise of supply chain resilience. The crucial points that need to be worked out are these "appropriate limitations", which represent the particular value that can be achieved by making use of the general exceptions rather than the security exception. These limitations can be imposed by the criteria of likelihood and degree of short supply risk, as well as other elements that indicate temporal and/or substantive threshold (e.g. "equitable" share) (see Sects. 4.4.6.2 and 4.4.6.3).

In this respect, the discussion in this paper is still very broad for the purpose of analyzing various actual measures. The required considerations would differ substantially depending on, *inter alia*, the products, the structure of supply chains, the design of specific measures, and the possible circumstances in which the supply disruption could occur. Such considerations require an accurate understanding of specific supply chains in question and may evolve over time.

Ultimately, such elaboration would help to answer the fundamental question of what kind of measures would work to achieve long-term supply stability. As Professor Hudec once stated on the exceptions to the non-discrimination principles in GATT 1947, the crucial role of the exception is to "control and contain discrimination rather than to eliminate it", and the exceptions need to be fixed and defined "so that other countries could plan commercial policy around them", namely, to enhance a stable trade environment from which all countries and businesses should benefit.[61]

References

Hestermeyer H and Nielsen L (2014) The Legality of Local Content Measures under WTO Law. Journal of World Trade 48, no. 3: 553–592

Hudec R (1990) The GATT Legal System and World Trade Diplomacy, 2nd edition. Butterworth Legal Publishers

Kometani K (2025) Considering Middle Powers' Position on the Trump Administration's Tariff Policies [Japanese only]. RIETI Special Report https://www.rieti.go.jp/jp/special/special_report/221.html accessed 14 September 2025

OECD (2025) Keys to Resilient Supply Chains policy (Toolkit: Increasing Supply Chain Resilience). https://www.oecd.org/content/dam/oecd/en/events/2024/3/forum-on-critical-supply-chains--policy-tools-for-preparedness-and-responsiveness/Resilient-Supply-Chains_Brochure-2025.pdf accessed 14 September 2025

Paulsen M (2025) The Past, Present and Potential of Economic Security. Yale Journal of International Law 50, no. 2: 222–297

Pauwelyn J (2025) How the US Reciprocal Tariff Plan May Save the Global Trading System. World Trade Review, 1–6

[61] Hudec (1990, p. 221).

Chapter 5
Geopolitical Risk and International Economic Law: An Empirical Framework for Designing Resilient Trade and Investment Rules

Yoshimichi Ishikawa

Abstract This article examines how rising geopolitical risk is reshaping international economic law (IEL) and proposes an empirical framework for institutional design. Drawing on recent empirical studies, it demonstrates that spikes in geopolitical risk depress international trade, particularly in services, energy, and agriculture, and reduce foreign direct investment, especially in states with weak governance and regulatory quality. Building on these findings, it argues that IEL requires more predictable rules, more tailored sectoral disciplines, and more transparent investment governance to manage the systemic pressures created by heightened geopolitical risk. In doing so, the article contributes to the "empirical turn" in IEL by linking quantitative measurement of geopolitical risk with normative debates on the future architecture of trade and investment rules.

Keywords Geopolitical Risk Index (GPR Index) · Trade contraction · FDI fragmentation · Institutional predictability · Governance quality · Empirical turn

5.1 Introduction

The international economic order faces a structural rise in geopolitical tensions, evidenced by Russia's invasion of Ukraine in February 2022, intensifying U.S.-China strategic competition, and the proliferation of economic security concepts. The

---

This article is part of the research project supported by JSPS KAKENHI Grant-in-Aid for Scientific Research (C) (FY 2024–2026, Principal Investigator: Yoshimichi Ishikawa). The author is grateful to Professor Junji Nakagawa (Chuo Gakuin University) and Professor Taro Hamada (Senshu University) for their valuable comments on earlier drafts. All remaining errors are the author's own.

Y. Ishikawa (✉)
School of International Relations, University of Shizuoka, Shizuoka, Japan
e-mail: y.ishikawa@u-shizuoka-ken.ac.jp

J. Nakagawa et al. (eds.), *Geopolitical Risks and Geoeconomics in International Economic Law*, Economics, Law, and Institutions in Asia Pacific,
https://doi.org/10.1007/978-981-95-6996-0_5

World Trade Organization (WTO) warned in its 2023 Annual Report that deepening geopolitical confrontation risks "fragmenting" the international trading system, with potentially severe negative consequences for the global economy.[1] The International Monetary Fund (IMF) similarly highlights how rising geopolitical risk encourages "friend-shoring" of foreign direct investment (FDI), potentially marginalizing developing countries from the international economic system.[2] These warnings reflect a shared recognition that geopolitical factors are driving institutional and structural transformation of the international economic order.

In international economic law scholarship, the tension between national security and economic order has long been a central issue. Considerable analytical work addresses specific problems such as abuse of security exception clauses,[3] the legal legitimacy of economic sanctions,[4] and invocation of national security exceptions in investment treaty arbitration.[5] However, most studies remain normative and interpretive, failing to adequately address the challenge of clearly defining, measuring, and quantitatively verifying the institutional effects of "geopolitical risk." Consequently, debates over institutional design have proceeded without empirical grounding regarding the extent to which proposed frameworks might actually mitigate the negative impacts of geopolitical risk.

In contrast, economics has made it possible to quantify geopolitical risk on a monthly basis through the development of the "Geopolitical Risk Index" (GPR Index) by Caldara and Iacoviello.[6] The GPR Index measures the standardized frequency of geopolitical tension-related terms in major English-language newspapers. Numerous empirical studies have already demonstrated that geopolitical risk, as measured by this index, significantly affects international economic activity, including trade contraction and FDI reduction. The international economic law field can now empirically examine how institutional design responds to and potentially mitigates the effects of geopolitical risk by employing such quantitative indicators.

This article aims to introduce the GPR Index into international economic law research to quantitatively assess geopolitical risk's impact on international trade and FDI, and to examine what legal institutions might mitigate these negative effects. By integrating empirical findings from economics with institutional analysis from international economic law, this study seeks to complement traditional normative and interpretive approaches by connecting institutional design debates to data-driven empirical verification. Recent calls for an "empirical turn" in international economic law scholarship[7] have highlighted this need; this article represents an attempt to apply that methodological shift to the contemporary challenge of geopolitical risk.

---

[1] World Trade Organization (2023, pp. 12–18).

[2] International Monetary Fund (2023, pp. 93–95).

[3] On the invocation of GATT Article XXI, see e.g., Shaffer (2023).

[4] On the legality of economic sanctions, particularly secondary sanctions, see, e.g., Ruys and Ryngaert (2020).

[5] On security exceptions in investment arbitration, see, e.g., Henckels (2024).

[6] Caldara and Iacoviello (2022).

[7] See, e.g., Shaffer and Ginsburg (2012), Shaffer (2014), and Alschner et al. (2017).

This article proceeds as follows. Sect. 2 reviews the evolution of geopolitical risk since 1985 using the GPR Index. Sect. 3 surveys existing empirical research demonstrating geopolitical risk's impact on international trade and FDI, while verifying that institutional factors such as governance quality and the presence of trade agreements can mitigate risk's negative effects. Sect. 4 draws on these empirical findings to propose institutional design principles for international trade and investment rules that respond to geopolitical risk. The conclusion discusses the significance and limitations of this research.

5.2 The Evolution of Geopolitical Risk

In international economic law, "geopolitical risk" has long served as a descriptive convenience term encompassing geopolitical tensions and international crises. However, this usage has been conceptually vague and inadequate for rigorously assessing risk levels and fluctuations. Caldara and Iacoviello addressed this limitation by systematically measuring media coverage of geopolitical tensions, developing the GPR Index as a quantitative indicator. The index is widely used in economics and incorporated into analyses by international organizations including the IMF.[8] Yet it remains underutilized in international economic law research, delaying the connection between empirical examination and institutional design debates. This section, as a foundation for subsequent discussion, reviews the GPR Index's characteristics and evolution since 1985.

5.2.1 *What is Geopolitical Risk?*

Caldara and Iacoviello define geopolitical risk as "the threat, realization, and escalation of adverse events associated with wars, terrorism, and any tensions among states and political actors that affect the peaceful course of international relations."[9] This definition has two distinctive features.

First, it expands the scope of coverage. While classical geopolitics focused on territorial military confrontations, the risks captured by the GPR Index include tensions and power struggles that fall short of armed conflict, as well as terrorism that destabilizes international order. In other words, it provides a framework for capturing "broadly defined geopolitical factors" that affect contemporary international economic activity.

Second, it expands the temporal dimension. While risk generally refers to uncertain future events, the GPR Index definition encompasses three temporal stages: (i) future threats, (ii) current occurrences, and (iii) escalating tensions. This reflects that

[8] See, e.g., International Monetary Fund (2025).

[9] Caldara and Iacoviello (2022, p. 1195).

geopolitical tensions evolve continuously from potential risk to manifest crisis, all of which can affect international economic activity.[10]

The GPR Index, which is built on this definition, measures the monthly frequency of geopolitical risk-related terms in ten major English-language newspapers[11] as a proportion of total articles.[12] Two series exist: Historical GPR covering from 1900 onward and Recent GPR Index from 1985 onward. This article uses the more detailed Recent GPR data, referring to it as the GPR Index.

5.2.2 Evolution of the GPR Index Since 1985

Figure 5.1 shows GPR Index trends from 1985 to 2024. The index is standardized to a baseline of 100 representing the monthly average from 1985 to 2019, enabling historical comparisons.[13] Major spikes correspond to the Gulf War (1991), the 9/11 attacks (2001), the Iraq War (2003), and Russia's invasion of Ukraine (2022), while the post-2022 period exhibits a persistently elevated baseline. For analytical clarity, this forty-year period is divided into six phases and characterized as follows.

a. **Late Cold War Through Gulf War (1985–1991)**: During the late Cold War (1985–1989), the average index stood at approximately 110, reflecting persistent East–West tensions. Following Iraq's invasion of Kuwait in August 1990, the index surged, reaching approximately 390 during the January 1991 Gulf War outbreak. This represented the first major spike since 1985, revealing new instabilities in the post-Cold War order.
b. **Period of Relative Stability (1992–2000)**: After the Gulf War, the GPR Index declined rapidly, averaging around 90 from the mid-1990s onward. This period can be characterized as a "stable era" of post-Cold War international order.
c. **9/11 and Iraq War (2001–2005)**: The September 2001 terrorist attacks drove the GPR Index to approximately 498, the highest level since 1985. The index also rose to approximately 420 during the March 2003 Iraq War outbreak. Together with the Gulf War, these events—the Gulf War, 9/11, and the Iraq War—constitute the three major spikes since 1985.[14]
d. **Second Stability Period (2006–2016)**: Following the Iraq War, the GPR Index again declined, maintaining a relatively moderate average of approximately 85.

---

[10] Id.

[11] The covered newspapers are Chicago Tribune, Daily Telegraph, Financial Times, Globe and Mail, Guardian, Los Angeles Times, New York Times, USA Today, Wall Street Journal, and Washington Post (six U.S., three U.K., and one Canadian newspaper).

[12] The authors also manually read approximately 44,000 front-page articles from the New York Times to assess whether each article reflected high geopolitical risk. This validation exercise confirmed that the algorithmic measurement closely tracked human judgment (correlation coefficient of 0.86). The index indeed spikes during major international crises such as the Gulf War, the 9/11 terrorist attacks, and the Iraq invasion. Id. pp. 1206–1207.

[13] Id. pp. 1197–1198, 1202.

[14] Caldara and Iacoviello (2022, p. 1197).

While individual events such as the 2011 Libya military intervention (approximately 150) and Russia's 2014 Crimea annexation (approximately 180) produced short-term increases, the period remained structurally stable.

e. **Sustained Elevated Period (2017–2021)**: From 2017 onward, the GPR Index's baseline rose markedly even absent distinct triggering events, with the average jumping to approximately 130. Continuous tensions such as U.S.-North Korea confrontations (2017–2018, approximately 200) and the Syria crisis (2018, approximately 180) occurred in succession. Sustained media coverage extended these "tensions without resolution," accounting for the elevated baseline.[15]
f. **Ukraine Invasion and After (2022–Present)**: Russia's February 2022 invasion of Ukraine drove the GPR Index to 318.[16] After a temporary decline, elevated levels averaging 125–130 have persisted from late 2022 through 2024. The post-invasion average (140.04) substantially exceeds the full 1985 onward period average (102.68) and approximates the 90th percentile (142.26).[17] In other words, what was historically "exceptional" high-risk has become "normalized," clearly marking the end of the post-Cold War stability era.

5.3 The Impact of Geopolitical Risk

This section reviews the impact of geopolitical risk on international trade, foreign direct investment (FDI), and invocation of security exceptions in trade, drawing on major empirical studies. Specifically, it clarifies the magnitude by which geopolitical risk affects trade volumes and investment flows, and identifies institutional and structural factors that can mitigate these effects. It further examines the extent to which rising geopolitical risk increases states' invocation of security exceptions. The findings in this section provide the empirical foundation necessary for the institutional design discussion in Sect. 5.4.

5.3.1 *Impact on International Trade*

Mulabdic and Yotov[18] conducted a comprehensive analysis of geopolitical risk's impact on international trade by combining the GPR Index with the U.S. International

[15] Id. pp. 1201–1202.

[16] Caldara and Iacoviello's article was published in 2022 and uses data only through December 2020. More recent data have since been updated monthly by the authors and are publicly available.

[17] The 90th percentile is the value below which 90% of all monthly observations fall. In other words, it represents a high-risk level that historically occurred only about 10% of the time.

[18] Mulabdic and Yotov (2025).

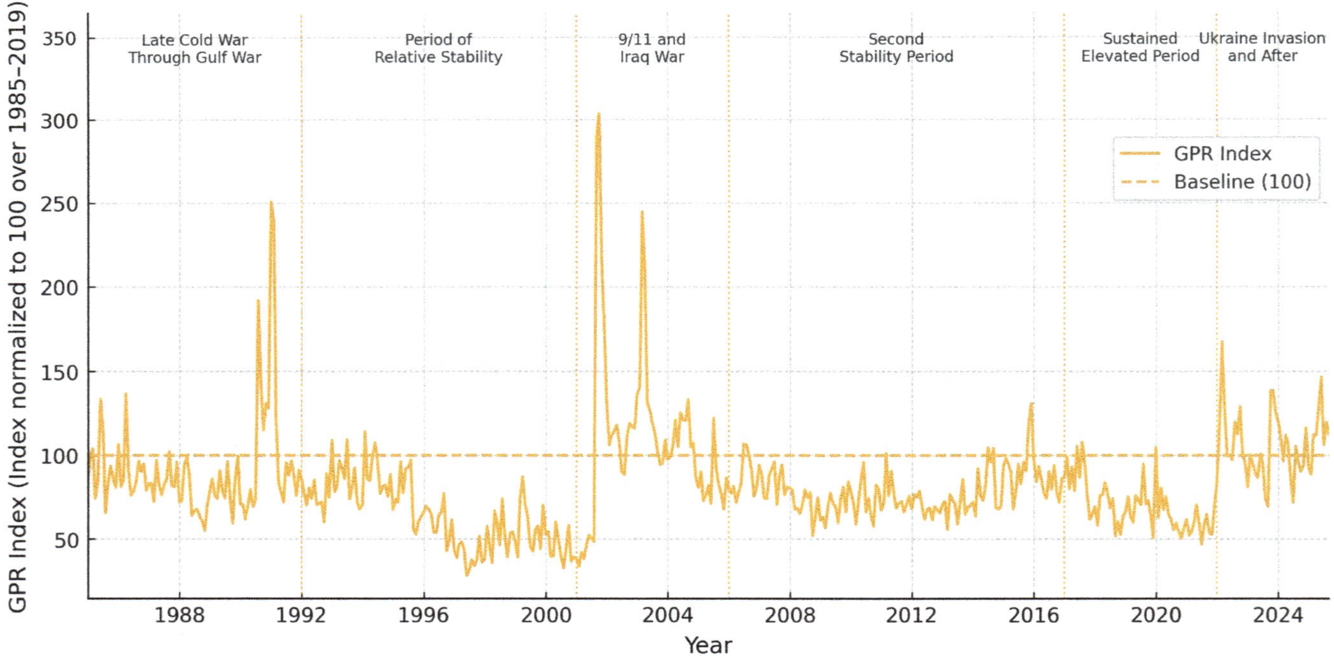

Fig. 5.1 Geopolitical Risk (GPR) Index, 1985–2024[19]

[19] Figure 5.1 is based on the Recent GPR Index compiled by Dario Caldara and Matteo Iacoviello, using data downloaded from the authors' website (https://www.matteoiacoviello.com/gpr.htm).

Trade Commission's International Trade and Production Database for Estimation (ITPD-E).[20]

5.3.1.1 The "Inward Orientation" Effect

Mulabdic and Yotov demonstrate that during periods of "extremely high" geopolitical risk (years containing months when the GPR Index reaches the top 5% of its historical distribution), international trade contracts substantially relative to domestic trade. Specifically, international trade falls approximately 27% below domestic trade across all industries on average, and approximately 40% in the most affected industries.[21] This finding indicates that geopolitical tensions selectively impose strong negative shocks on cross-border transactions, causing trade to be redirected toward domestic markets—an "inward orientation."[22]

Converting this effect into tariff equivalents yields approximately 8–14% in additional tariffs, demonstrating that geopolitical risk functions as a "hidden trade cost" operating outside institutional frameworks. This magnitude could substantially offset the effects of WTO tariff reductions.

Importantly, this inward orientation effect does not emerge linearly with risk levels. While statistically significant negative effects appear in the top 10% of GPR levels, they become insignificant at the top 25%.[23] In other words, trade structures do not change substantially under moderate tension; the relative suppression of international trade versus domestic trade occurs only during periods of extremely high geopolitical tension.

While the IMF and WTO have qualitatively noted this strengthening "inward orientation," Mulabdic and Yotov's distinctive contribution lies in incorporating both domestic and international trade into a single model, thereby quantifying inward orientation as their relative change.[24]

---

[20] ITPD-E (International Trade and Production Database for Estimation) is an international trade database constructed by the U.S. International Trade Commission (USITC) covering over 200 countries, 170 industries, and the period 1986–2019. Because it includes both international and domestic trade data, it enables researchers to distinguish whether geopolitical risk affects cross-border transactions specifically or economic activity generally.

[21] Mulabdic and Yotov (2025, pp. 4, 8, 12–13), tables 1 and 2. The top 5% of the GPR Index roughly corresponds to index values of 200 or above, covering six years: 1990–1991 (Gulf War), 2001 (9/11 terrorist attacks), 2002, 2003 (Iraq War), and 2005 (London bombings).

[22] Id. pp. 2–3, 7, 21.

[23] Id. pp. 16, table 3.

[24] Geopolitical risk affects not only exporting countries but also importing countries. Khalil et al. analyze how geopolitical risk in partner countries acts as a "supply shock" affecting U.S. and Eurozone imports, finding that a one-standard-deviation increase in a partner country's GPR Index reduces real import volumes from that country by approximately 0.3% and raises import prices by approximately 0.15%. They also identify differential adjustment patterns between the U.S. and Eurozone in response to rising Chinese risk: while the U.S. substitutes decreased direct imports from China with increased imports from third countries, the Eurozone experiences reduced imports even from third countries deeply integrated into Chinese supply chains. Khalil et al. (2025, pp. 12–14).

5.3.1.2 Sectoral Impacts

Mulabdic and Yotov further demonstrate that geopolitical risk produces differential impacts across sectors according to industrial structure. Analysis covering 170 industries reveals that services trade is most vulnerable: during periods of heightened geopolitical tension, international trade in services falls approximately 43% relative to domestic trade.[25] Services trade depends heavily on professional mobility and regulatory environments, making travel restrictions and visa regulations direct obstacles during geopolitical tensions.

The next most affected sectors are beverages and tobacco (declining approximately 26% relative to domestic trade), mining and energy (approximately 21% lower), and agriculture (approximately 20% lower).[26] Beverages and tobacco are sensitive to regulatory changes and logistical disruptions. Mining and energy include resources such as crude oil and natural gas that frequently become geopolitical focal points, making supply uncertainty rise sharply during heightened tensions. In agriculture, negative effects are significant for most products, with geopolitical risk operating strongly through food security concerns and transport constraints.

Manufacturing, by contrast, experiences relatively moderate effects, with international trade declining only 15–20% relative to domestic trade in most sectors. This reflects manufacturing's resilience to short-term shocks through mechanisms such as inventory adjustment, alternative sourcing, and long-term contracts.[27] However, variation within manufacturing remains substantial, with textiles and wood products experiencing particularly small impacts.[28]

5.3.1.3 Mitigating and Amplifying Factors

The relative suppression of international trade caused by geopolitical risk (inward orientation) is amplified or mitigated by interstate relationships and institutional frameworks. Mulabdic and Yotov examine how four factors—physical distance, common language, economic sanctions, and regional trade agreements (RTAs)—affect this outcome.[29]

First, closer geographic proximity weakens geopolitical risk's negative impact, while greater distance strengthens it. Trade between distant locations has limited alternative transport options, making it more susceptible to logistical disruptions during heightened tensions. Second, countries sharing a common language experience significantly mitigated geopolitical risk effects across nearly all sectors. Common language reduces costs of contract negotiation, information transmission, and dispute resolution, enhancing resilience to increased uncertainty. Third, when

[25] Mulabdic and Yotov (2025, pp. 15–16), table 2.

[26] Id. pp. 12, 14–15, table 1.

[27] Id. pp. 15–16.

[28] Id. p. 16.

[29] Id. pp. 17–18.

exporting countries face economic sanctions, geopolitical risk's negative effects are amplified. Exports from sanctioned countries already face high uncertainty; additional tension further contracts transactions.[30]

Fourth, regional trade agreements (RTAs) systematically mitigate geopolitical risk's negative effects. RTAs provide political and legal commitments including dispute avoidance and consultation procedures, functioning as "institutional buffers" against uncertainty shocks through reduced transaction costs and enhanced predictability. Limão and Maggi's research[31] is instructive on this point, theoretically demonstrating that trade agreements enhance economic welfare not only by reducing average tariffs but also by mitigating trade policy uncertainty.[32] In the contemporary era when geopolitical risk remains structurally elevated, the value of predictability and certainty provided by trade agreements is even greater.

5.3.2 Impact on Foreign Direct Investment (FDI)

Recent research demonstrates that rising geopolitical risk affects not only international trade but also foreign direct investment (FDI). This section first examines the impact on corporate capital expenditure and then analyzes effects on FDI.

5.3.2.1 Corporate Capital Expenditure

According to Wang et al. (covering approximately 9,000 publicly traded U.S. firms, quarterly data, 1987–2016),[33] when the GPR Index doubles, firms' capital expenditure rate declines by approximately 14% in the following quarter.[34] Geopolitical risk suppresses investment because capital expenditure involves highly fixed investments with difficult recovery; when uncertainty rises, postponing investment becomes rational.[35] Even when controlling for other factors that could affect investment—such as business cycles and policy uncertainty—rising geopolitical risk retains a significant negative effect on corporate capital expenditure.

This investment contraction effect manifests most strongly in firms with low asset redeployability. Firms with low redeployability (bottom 25th percentile) experience

[30] Khalil et al. (2025, pp. 12–14). Khalil et al. similarly demonstrate that geopolitical risk's impact on trade is strongly linked to sanctions.

[31] Limão and Maggi (2013, pp. 3–6, 26–28), table 1.

[32] Id. pp. 6, 22–24.

[33] Wang et al. (2024).

[34] Id. p. 2025. Firms typically allocate approximately 1.4% of total assets to capital expenditure. Id. p. 2026.

[35] Id. p. 2025.

markedly larger capital expenditure declines when geopolitical risk rises compared to firms with high redeployability (top 25th percentile).[36]

5.3.2.2 FDI Decline

Bussy and Zheng's analysis (monthly FDI flows in 19 emerging market countries, 2003–2019)[37] demonstrates that a one-standard-deviation increase in the GPR Index (a commonly occurring magnitude) reduces FDI inflows by approximately 9.4%.[38] However, this decline varies substantially depending on host country governance levels.[39]

Specifically, among the World Bank WGI's six indicators,[40] countries with high "government effectiveness" and "regulatory quality" experience statistically significant mitigation of geopolitical risk's adverse effects.[41] Government effectiveness refers to administrative capacity to formulate and implement consistent public policies with some independence from political pressure, and to maintain policy commitments. Regulatory quality, meanwhile, represents the capacity to design and operate rules that do not impede private sector development, thereby limiting arbitrary and ad hoc regulatory changes. In countries with high government effectiveness (top 25th percentile), FDI decline is limited to approximately 5.9%, whereas in low-effectiveness countries it reaches approximately 10.4%. Moreover, in countries with high regulatory quality, concerns about arbitrary regulatory changes are mitigated, weakening the negative impact on FDI (reducing investors' risk perception).[42]

This indicates that countries with weaker governance experience amplification of geopolitical shocks as political risk, leading to greater FDI decline. Maintaining FDI requires improving administrative capacity and regulatory predictability.

---

[36] Id. pp. 2024, 2038. Generally, specialized equipment designed for specific products (e.g., semiconductor manufacturing equipment or specialized chemical plants) is difficult to repurpose, while general-purpose machinery, office equipment, and transport vehicles are relatively easy to redeploy.

[37] Bussy and Zheng (2023).

[38] Id. p. 8, table 2.

[39] Bussy and Zheng identify two additional moderating factors beyond governance. First, firms with greater information about host countries (neighboring countries, common language, accumulated investment experience) tend to exercise greater caution in investment decisions during periods of heightened geopolitical risk. Second, FDI in R&D-intensive industries is largely unaffected by geopolitical risk due to the transferability of intangible assets and strategic importance. Id. pp. 4–10.

[40] The World Bank's World Governance Indicators (WGI) is an annual dataset evaluating government governance capacity across six dimensions: government effectiveness, regulatory quality, rule of law, voice and accountability, political stability and absence of violence, and control of corruption. Data and methodology are available at the World Bank's official website (https://info.worldbank.org/governance/wgi/).

[41] Bussy and Zheng (2023, p. 6).

[42] Id. pp. 6–7, table 3.

5.3.2.3 FDI Fragmentation

The IMF's *World Economic Outlook* (2023) notes that heightened geopolitical tensions accelerate FDI reallocation, with investment concentrating in geopolitically proximate countries and regions—a phenomenon termed "FDI fragmentation."[43] Since 2018, with U.S.-China confrontation as a catalyst, U.S. FDI has increasingly concentrated toward countries and regions with alliance relationships. U.S. outward FDI contracted by approximately 24% between Q2 2020 and Q4 2022, primarily driven by a sharp decline in FDI to China.[44] Meanwhile, investment in geopolitically proximate countries such as Canada and South Korea has remained relatively robust. This trend is more pronounced in strategic sectors such as semiconductors. As of Q4 2022, China's semiconductor-related FDI inflows had declined by approximately half compared to 2015 levels, while European and U.S. FDI in the same sector roughly doubled over the same period.[45] This demonstrates that FDI is being restructured toward "alliance blocs," particularly in strategic industries.[46]

This bias largely stems from governments' investment restrictions justified by national security. Examples include U.S. strengthening of inbound investment screening (FIRRMA)[47] and the EU investment screening framework.[48] Additionally, U.S. restrictions on investment in advanced sectors in China[49] and semiconductor subsidy policies (U.S. and EU)[50] create pressure guiding corporate investment in strategic sectors toward allied countries.

The IMF measures countries' vulnerability to such friend-shoring through an "Aggregate Vulnerability Index."[51] According to this measure, approximately 86% of emerging and developing countries exhibit vulnerability exceeding the advanced-country median.[52] Consequently, FDI fragmentation is estimated to reduce global real GDP by approximately 2% in the long term, with emerging and developing countries bearing the greatest losses.[53]

---

[43] International Monetary Fund (2023).

[44] Id. p. 96.

[45] Id. p. 95.

[46] According to Aiyar et al., FDI is clearly concentrated within "alliance blocs," with the FDI ratio between countries with the highest geopolitical alignment reaching over twice the expected baseline (~20%), at 40–50%. This bloc bias has intensified further since 2018, particularly in strategic industries. Aiyar et al. (2024). Similarly, the European Central Bank demonstrates that FDI within geopolitical blocs is increasing while FDI to non-aligned and third countries is relatively declining. European Central Bank (2024).

[47] Foreign Investment Risk Review Modernization Act of 2018 (FIRRMA), Pub. L. 115–232 (2018).

[48] Regulation (EU) 2019/452 of the European Parliament and of the Council of 19 March 2019.

[49] Executive Order 14105 (Addressing United States Investments in Certain National Security Technologies and Products in Countries of Concern, 2023).

[50] CHIPS and Science Act of 2022, Pub. L. 117–167 (2022); Regulation (EU) 2023/1781 (European Chips Act).

[51] International Monetary Fund (2023, p. 99).

[52] Id. p. 99.

[53] Id. p. 94.

5.3.3 *Impact on Invocation of Security Exceptions*

In recent years, against the backdrop of U.S.-China confrontation and the Russia-Ukraine war, invocation of GATT Article XXI security exceptions has surged. This trend has been consistently identified in prior scholarship and international organization reports.[54] This section examines the extent to which this increase in invocations is attributable to rising geopolitical risk.

5.3.3.1 GPR Index and Number of Invocations

The WTO Secretariat's *World Trade Report 2023* notes that global economic policy uncertainty has been rising since 2008, a development not unrelated to the contemporaneous increase in geopolitical crises.[55] According to the report, the number of quantitative restriction measures notified by Members under GATT Article XXI increased from approximately 40 in 2012 to nearly 180 in 2022—roughly quadrupling over this decade.[56] In 2022, the GPR Index surged to 157.6 following the Russia-Ukraine war, with the number of measures in force simultaneously reaching peak levels, suggesting a correlation between the two phenomena.

However, historical examination reveals a contrary pattern. According to the Historical GPR Index, the two world wars (1914–1918, 1939–1945) averaged 271.6, and the Cold War period (1946–1989) averaged 97.8—both substantially higher than the present (2012–2024 average: 81.6). Despite these far higher levels of geopolitical risk, Article XXI invocations during the GATT era were exceedingly rare. This demonstrates that high geopolitical risk alone does not directly drive security exception invocations.

Indeed, the fact that security exception invocations have surged in the contemporary era—when GPR levels are not historically exceptional—cannot be explained by a simple "higher geopolitical risk leads to more invocations" logic. This phenomenon instead reflects structural changes in the international economic order, specifically two factors: the entrenchment of an economic security paradigm and the declining effectiveness of the WTO dispute settlement system.

---

[54] See, e.g., Voon (2019).

[55] World Trade Organization (2023, pp. 46–47).

[56] Id. p. 48.

5.3.3.2 Two Contributing Factors

First, a new "economic security" paradigm has become entrenched.[57] During the Cold War, economic interdependence was generally understood to mitigate military tensions.[58] However, from the 2010s onward, critical technologies and materials—semiconductors, AI, 5G, rare earths—have come to occupy the core of security concerns, with supply chain vulnerabilities and dependence on specific countries increasingly recognized as security threats.[59] This paradigm shift has made it easier for Members to justify invoking GATT Article XXI under the banner of "economic security."

Second, the WTO dispute settlement mechanism has weakened. The Appellate Body ceased functioning in 2019,[60] but even before then, the mechanism had been experiencing institutional fatigue due to U.S. blocking of member reappointments and prolonged proceedings.[61] Moreover, while the panel in *Russia—Traffic in Transit* rejected complete self-judging discretion under GATT Article XXI(b), it adopted a standard affording Members relatively broad discretion in necessity assessments.[62] However, with the Appellate Body's absence, opportunities to refine this standard and ensure uniform application were lost. Consequently, judicial restraint mechanisms have weakened, lowering psychological and institutional barriers to Article XXI invocation.

In sum, the recent surge in Article XXI invocations stems not from rising geopolitical risk per se, but rather from structural changes—namely, the entrenchment of the economic security paradigm and the weakening of WTO dispute settlement. Accordingly, this issue must be distinguished from "institutional design to mitigate geopolitical risk's adverse effects," which the next section will address.

---

[57] Heath argues that the concept of national security is expanding beyond the military domain to encompass a broad range of areas including climate change, pandemics, infrastructure vulnerabilities, data, and financial system risks, fundamentally transforming the premises of the international economic order. Heath (2020).

[58] Keohane and Nye (1977).

[59] See, e.g., Roberts et al. (2019).

[60] The Appellate Body has been unable to function since December 11, 2019, due to lack of quorum.

[61] Shaffer (2018).

[62] Panel Report, *Russia – Measures Concerning Traffic in Transit*, WT/DS512/R, paras. 7.138–7.140. The panel adopted a lenient "not implausible" standard for assessing GATT Article XXI(b) claims, declining to apply the strict necessity test of the GATT Article XX type, thereby affording Members broad discretion in substantive determinations.

5.4 Institutional Responses to Geopolitical Risk's Negative Impacts

The previous section confirmed that while rising geopolitical risk produces negative effects such as inward orientation of international trade and FDI reduction and fragmentation, the magnitude of these effects is substantially influenced by institutional factors including governance quality and the existence of trade agreements. This section examines institutional measures to improve international trade and investment rules to mitigate these negative impacts.

5.4.1 International Trade Rules

As demonstrated in Sect. 5.3, rising geopolitical risk promotes contraction of international trade and inward orientation among countries. Mulabdic and Yotov showed that when the GPR Index reaches the top 5%, international trade falls 30–40% below domestic trade levels, and that regional trade agreements (RTAs) significantly mitigate this negative effect. Limão and Maggi revealed that trade agreements suppress policy uncertainty independently of tariff reduction effects, with benefits equivalent to 16–32% of average tariff reductions. These findings demonstrate that institutionally securing trade policy predictability is essential precisely in environments of heightened geopolitical tension.

5.4.1.1 Strengthening Predictability

RTAs can mitigate geopolitical risk's negative effects because agreements suppress policy uncertainty and provide institutional frameworks that restrain unilateral trade restriction measures even during heightened tensions. This function is not limited to specific agreements but represents a fundamental role common to international trade rules generally. With tensions becoming normalized, strengthening predictability has become the paramount priority for international institutions.

First, introducing and expanding disciplines preventing rollback of liberalization levels. Standstill clauses freeze liberalization levels at the time of agreement entry into force, prohibiting introduction of new trade barriers thereafter.[63] Ratchet clauses, meanwhile, prohibit in principle rollback of liberalization measures once implemented.[64] During periods of heightened geopolitical risk, countries' incentives

[63] A typical example of a standstill clause is Article 2.13 of the EU-Japan Economic Partnership Agreement, which freezes customs duty rates on goods originating in the other party at the scheduled levels under the agreement, prohibiting any increases beyond that level, thereby legally securing the "freeze" of market access levels. EU–Japan Economic Partnership Agreement, art. 2.13.

[64] For example, the CPTPP includes annexes titled "Non-Conforming Measures Ratchet Mechanism" in its investment and services-related chapters, introducing a mechanism that prevents parties

to roll back liberalization in the name of security or industrial policy intensify; thus, applying these disciplines more broadly and strengthening mechanisms to institutionally maintain liberalization levels becomes necessary. However, appropriate exceptions and reservations must be established to avoid impeding legitimate regulatory changes based on environmental, public health, or security policy objectives, with transparency and accountability ensured when invoked.[65]

Second, expanding transparency obligations. While the WTO Trade Facilitation Agreement (TFA)[66] primarily targets customs procedure transparency, under geopolitical risk conditions, transparency coverage must extend to trade restriction measures themselves. When geopolitical tensions rise, countries tend to become excessively wary of partner intentions, rushing to preventive trade restrictions. To institutionally restrain this, mandating advance notification, publication of regulatory impact assessments (RIA),[67] and stakeholder consultations when introducing trade restrictions proves effective; particularly for measures justified by geopolitical risk, requiring specification of objectives, scope, and duration plus periodic review is beneficial. Such transparency safeguards provide the foundation for restraining arbitrary application and enhancing international trade predictability.[68]

5.4.1.2 Sector-Specific Institutions

As Sect. 5.3 showed, geopolitical risk's impact varies by sector. Services trade in particular depends on movement of people and data flows, making it sensitive to heightened geopolitical confrontation. The energy and agriculture sectors are likewise vulnerable to "weaponization" of exports by supplier countries. Accordingly, uniform institutions prove insufficient; institutional design must respond to structural characteristics of each sector.

---

from rolling back regulatory liberalization below pre-liberalization levels once relaxed. CPTPP, Annex 9-I; Annex 10-C; Annex 11-C.

[65] For concerns that rollback prohibition clauses such as ratchet and standstill provisions may permanently constrain regulatory space in public policy areas including health care, necessitating policy space preservation through exceptions and exclusions, *see* Koivusalo et al. (2021).

[66] Agreement on Trade Facilitation, WT/L/931 (July 15, 2014).

[67] Regulatory Impact Assessment (RIA) is a standard government analytical tool for ex ante evaluation of costs, benefits, and policy alternatives of new regulations. According to OECD surveys, 32 of the then 34 member countries had introduced some form of RIA. Organisation for Economic Co-operation and Development (2015).

[68] On transparency obligations functioning as a tool to reduce uncertainty regarding trade policy and enhance its predictability, see Collins-Williams and Wolfe (2010).

Services Trade

First, under geopolitical confrontation, measures such as visa issuance suspension are readily employed as retaliatory tools.[69] While GATS Article XIV*bis*(a) contemplates security exceptions, its broad scope means invocation barriers are not necessarily high, creating abuse risks. To address this, imposing procedural obligations on invocation—advance notification, specification of target period and region, explanation of rationale—can somewhat restrain politically motivated application.[70]

Second, internet shutdowns and cross-border data transfer restrictions (e.g., data localization) have recently become typical retaliatory measures.[71] If such measures are arbitrarily invoked, international service provision immediately ceases. Therefore, institutional frameworks requiring measures restricting cross-border data transfer to demonstrate reasonable relevance to stated policy objectives and mandating prompt disclosure of measure content, scope, and justification prove necessary.[72]

Third, for services with strong humanitarian character such as health care and education, avoiding situations where confrontation unjustly infringes citizens' basic needs becomes necessary. Accordingly, establishing "humanitarian clauses" in GATS to maintain certain service provision levels even during wartime and sanctions, ensuring cross-border transfer and provision of medical technology and educational resources in emergencies, merits consideration. The crosscutting humanitarian exceptions introduced in recent UN Security Council sanctions provide useful design references.[73]

[69] An example of visa issuance suspension due to geopolitical confrontation is the 2020 mutual restriction of journalist visas between the U.S. and China. U.S. Department of State, "Designation of Additional Chinese Media Entities as Foreign Missions" (June 22, 2020).

[70] For institutional control over security exceptions, Lester and Manak propose establishing a National Security Committee that would mandate early notification, continuing oversight, and technical consultations for security measures. Lester and Manak (2020).

[71] For instance, in March 2022, the Russian government blocked domestic access to Facebook and Twitter as a countermeasure against Meta's restrictions on Russian state media content regarding Russia's war against Ukraine. Milmo (2022).

[72] Arguments for applying GATS Article XIV-type necessity tests to cross-border data transfer restrictions have been repeatedly advanced. Burri in particular argues that data localization and cross-border transfer restrictions should be subject to review of relevance, necessity, and proportionality to policy objectives within the international economic law framework. Burri (2017).

[73] Ensuring access to basic services including health care and education during wartime and under sanctions has been repeatedly emphasized in international humanitarian law. UN Security Council Resolution 2664 (2022) introduced a humanitarian exception framework that comprehensively exempts from asset freeze measures the provision of funds, materials, and services necessary for humanitarian assistance activities (health care, food supply, and other activities supporting basic needs). This article's proposal to add humanitarian clauses to services trade aligns with this international trend. United Nations Security Council, S/RES/2664 (2022), adopted 9 December 2022.

Energy and Food Products

Energy and agriculture sectors are vulnerable sectors where trade substantially contracts during geopolitical risk increases. They also possess characteristics making supplier countries prone to "weaponizing" exports as political tools. Russia's natural gas supply cutoffs and Ukrainian grain export restrictions exemplify this.[74]

While GATT Article XI prohibits export restrictions in principle, exceptions exist for food security and other reasons; thus, when tensions rise, countries risk "preventively" invoking export restrictions on these grounds, creating cascading effects that worsen supply crises. During COVID-19, many countries restricted pharmaceutical and food exports, with export controls relying on exception provisions ultimately amplifying supply disruption risks.[75]

Based on this experience, clarifying international principles restraining unilateral export suspensions for geopolitical reasons becomes essential.[76] However, mandating perpetual export obligations proves unrealistic; exceptions for securing minimum domestic demand should be permitted restrictively from necessity and proportionality perspectives. Furthermore, imposing procedural requirements on exception invocation—advance notification, specified duration, periodic review—can institutionally promote distinguishing genuine security purposes from political retaliation.

Additionally, establishing international stockpiling and emergency allocation mechanisms to address bilateral supply relationship disruptions proves effective. If multilayered stockpiling and allocation systems like the International Energy Agency (IEA) coordinated stockpile system[77] or ASEAN + 3 Emergency Rice Reserve (APTERR)[78] exist, alternative supply through third countries during confrontation-related supply disruptions can be secured, mitigating civilian impacts.

5.4.2 *International Investment Rules*

As demonstrated in Sect. 5.3, rising geopolitical risk substantially suppresses FDI by amplifying uncertainty regarding regulatory environments. The impact manifests

---

[74] Food and Agriculture Organization of the United Nations (2023).

[75] See, e.g., World Trade Organization (2020).

[76] For proposals to impose procedural requirements such as transparency, specified duration, and periodic review on export restrictions based on the COVID-19 experience of cascading export prohibitions, see Pauwelyn (2020).

[77] The IEA emergency response system centers on requiring member countries to hold "oil stocks equivalent to at least 90 days of net imports from the previous year" and implementing coordinated stock releases and demand restraint during major supply disruptions.

[78] APTERR (ASEAN + 3 Emergency Rice Reserve) is a regional emergency rice reserve system established by ASEAN + 3 countries under an agreement (signed in Jakarta in 2011) that facilitates intra-regional distribution of pre-committed rice stocks when food security is threatened by natural disasters or price surges.

more strongly in countries with weak governance, where investment decline proves more pronounced. Moreover, expansion of selective investment regulation in the name of security promotes FDI "fragmentation," biasing investment toward allied countries. This section examines investment rules that encourage host country governance improvements and frameworks restraining arbitrary application of security exceptions to address these two problems.

5.4.2.1 Governance Improvement

FDI reacts more sensitively than trade during periods of heightened geopolitical risk because investment involves formation of fixed assets premised on long-term recovery, making regulatory changes and administrative measure opacity directly linked to value impairment.[79] As Bussy and Zheng showed, what determines this risk amplification is "government effectiveness" and "regulatory quality"; countries weaker in these two elements experience larger FDI declines from the same geopolitical shocks.

Given this, institutional design required of investment agreements proves insufficient if merely reiterating transparency obligations discussed in trade contexts. Because regulatory changes in investment directly link to value impairment risks, procedural frameworks stabilizing regulatory formation and operation processes themselves must be positioned more explicitly. Elements such as advance notice, rationale provision, and securing reasonable transition periods constitute core institutions supporting investor predictability, not merely administrative accountability.[80] Moreover, requiring implementation and publication of regulatory impact assessments (RIA) for investment-related regulations contributes to reducing policy uncertainty by constraining arbitrary regulatory formation and making consistency with policy objectives externally verifiable. These procedural elements represent a vision incorporating good regulatory practices required of general regulations by CPTPP Chapter 25 and USMCA Chapter 28 into the investment sphere.[81]

---

[79] For instance, India's Press Note 3 (2020 Series) of April 2020 changed the system to require government approval for all FDI from countries sharing land borders with India (effectively targeting China). While nominally justified as preventing "hostile takeovers" during COVID-19, it is widely understood as discriminatory regulation targeting Chinese investment on national security and economic security grounds. Government of India, Ministry of Commerce & Industry, Department for Promotion of Industry and Internal Trade, FDI Policy Section, Press Note No. 3 (2020 Series), 17 April 2020.

[80] Investment arbitration practice and scholarship note that regulatory change predictability and procedural transparency can be factors in determining fair and equitable treatment (FET) violations. This suggests that improving regulatory change processes can enhance administrative stability while also reducing unnecessary dispute risks. See, e.g., Potestà (2013).

[81] Both chapters target generally applicable regulatory measures concerning the entire agreement (including investment), aiming to improve regulatory quality through regulatory impact assessment and enhanced transparency. However, in current agreements, many such provisions remain soft or cross-cutting administrative cooperation clauses rather than hard obligations within investment chapters.

Furthermore, empirical research demonstrating that countries with weaker governance experience larger FDI declines indicates that institutional arrangements alone prove insufficient; elevating administrative capacity itself becomes essential. Capacity building—enhancing expertise of authorities handling investment screening and regulatory operations, supporting RIA system introduction and operation, developing regulatory information infrastructure—substantively improves both government effectiveness and regulatory quality, strengthening institutional resilience to geopolitical shocks.[82]

5.4.2.2 Addressing FDI Fragmentation

In step with heightened geopolitical tensions, strengthened inward investment screening and outward investment regulation for advanced technology sectors are rapidly expanding across countries. While these measures can formally conflict with investment treaty obligations, many treaties broadly recognize security exceptions; thus countries increasingly perceive they can justify such measures through exception invocation.[83] Consequently, investment regulation becomes selectively operated from geopolitical perspectives, promoting so-called FDI fragmentation whereby FDI becomes biased toward politically "trusted" allied countries.

However, given current international circumstances, narrowing security exceptions themselves at the treaty level holds almost no feasibility.[84] Accordingly, the realistically available direction involves making the excercise of exception clause externally verifiable and constructing institutional frameworks restraining exceptions from operating as de facto permanent regulations or political retaliation.

From this perspective, introducing transparency obligations and peer review systems concerning investment regulation and related subsidies becomes important. Regarding inward investment screening and subsidies for strategic sectors, the approach involves mandating advance and ex post notification of information—objectives, target sectors and countries, measure content, application duration, review procedures—according to common templates, and establishing mechanisms for periodic evaluation of such content in forums such as the G20, OECD, and WTO Trade

[82] For example, Chap. 15 (Economic and Technical Cooperation) of the Regional Comprehensive Economic Partnership Agreement (RCEP) aims to support "inclusive, effective and efficient implementation and utilization" of the agreement, positioning capacity building and technical assistance for developing and least-developed country parties as priorities for economic and technical cooperation activities covering trade and investment sectors (Articles 15.3, 15.5, and 15.6).

[83] However, Voon argues that recent FDI screening expansion stems from countries overestimating the scope of security exceptions. According to Voon, FDI screening can conflict with numerous investment treaty obligations including non-discrimination principles (national treatment and most-favored-nation treatment), FET, indirect expropriation, and prohibitions on performance requirements; thus countries cannot exercise such screening as freely under the "security" banner as they assume. Voon and Merriman (2024).

[84] For arguments advocating judicial reviewability of exceptions and objective review standards to prevent abuse of security exceptions in investment treaties, see Shelbaya (2024).

Policy Reviews.[85] While not directly constraining state discretion, this avoids exception "black-boxing" and exerts restraining effects against introducing excessively comprehensive or permanent measures.

5.5 Conclusion

Conventional international economic law scholarship has addressed the relationship between geopolitical risk and international economic rules without clearly defining or measuring the concept of "geopolitical risk." This article, by contrast, introduces the GPR Index to quantitatively grasp geopolitical risk's negative impacts on the international economy and proposes international economic institutional reforms based on empirical evidence to mitigate these impacts. Such analysis embodies a concrete realization of the "empirical turn" in international economic law scholarship.

Drawing on prior research, empirical analysis demonstrated that rising geopolitical risk strengthens countries' inward orientation, substantially contracting international trade in vulnerable sectors such as services, energy, and agriculture. It also showed that FDI declines more severely in countries with weaker governance, and that selective strengthening of investment regulation may advance FDI fragmentation. Conversely, the surge in security exception invocations was shown to stem not from geopolitical risk itself but from structural factors—the entrenchment of an economic security paradigm and weakening of the WTO dispute settlement system.

Building on these findings, this article presented institutional designs to ensure trade predictability and stability by establishing procedural disciplines for vulnerable sectors, centered on preventing rollback of liberalization levels and enhancing transparency, thereby preventing trade retreat even under geopolitical risk. For FDI, it proposed frameworks combining host country governance improvement with investment regulation transparency and verification systems to restrain regulatory uncertainty and arbitrary application, thereby suppressing FDI decline and fragmentation.

However, immediate realization of these institutional reforms cannot be taken for granted. Major powers involved in geopolitical confrontation are unlikely to consent to strengthening international rules constraining their own discretion, and under multilateralism's weakening, universal rule formation becomes increasingly difficult. Moreover, in circumstances where economic security paradigms dominate policy-making, countries tend to prioritize short-term security interests.

Nevertheless, geopolitical risk's negative impacts are measurable, and scope exists for institutional responses to mitigate portions thereof. Realistically, an approach

---

[85] Regarding investment regulation for security reasons, the OECD emphasizes the importance of principles of transparency, predictability, and accountability, along with policy monitoring through peer review. Organisation for Economic Co-operation and Development (2009). Lorfing argues that integrating security-based investment screening into an internationally verifiable framework is essential. Lorfing (2021).

beginning with partial institutional construction by willing countries, with participation gradually expanding as effectiveness is confirmed, merits consideration. Now that geopolitical tensions have become the "new normal," international economic law faces a novel role: maintaining interdependence under geopolitical uncertainty while institutionally managing risks. This article aspires to provide a foundation for such institutional design.

References

Aiyar S, Malacrino D, Presbitero AF (2024) Investing in Friends: The Role of Geopolitical Alignment in FDI Flows. IMF Working Paper

Alschner W, Pauwelyn J, Puig S (2017) The Data-Driven Future of International Economic Law. J Int Econ Law 20:217–231

Burri M (2017) The Regulation of Data Flows through Trade Agreements. Georgetown J Int Law 48:407–448

Bussy A, Zheng H (2023) Responses of FDI to Geopolitical Risks: The Role of Governance, Information, and Technology. Int Bus Rev 32(4):102136

Caldara D, Iacoviello M (2022) Measuring Geopolitical Risk. Am Econ Rev 112(4):1194–1225

Collins-Williams T, Wolfe R (2010) Transparency as a Trade Policy Tool: The WTO's Cloudy Windows. World Trade Rev 9(4):551–581

European Central Bank (2024) Geopolitical fragmentation in global and euro area greenfield FDI. ECB Economic Bulletin, Issue 4

Food and Agriculture Organization of the United Nations (2023) The Importance of Ukraine and the Russian Federation for Global Agricultural Markets and the Risks Associated with the War in Ukraine. FAO, Rome

Heath JB (2020) The New National Security Challenge to the Economic Order. Yale Law J 129(4):1020–1098

Henckels C (2024) Whither Security? The Concept of 'Essential Security Interests' in Investment Treaties' Security Exceptions. J Int Econ Law 27:114–129

International Monetary Fund (2023) Geoeconomic Fragmentation and Foreign Direct Investment. In: World Economic Outlook, Chapter 4. IMF, Washington DC

International Monetary Fund (2025) Global Financial Stability Report: Enhancing Resilience amid Uncertainty. IMF, Washington DC

Keohane RO, Nye JS (1977) Power and Interdependence. Little, Brown and Company, Boston

Khalil M, Osten D, Strobel F (2025) Trade Dynamics under Geopolitical Risk. Deutsche Bundesbank Discussion Paper, No. 03/2025

Koivusalo M, Heinonen N, Tynkkynen LK (2021) When Actions Do Not Match Aspirations – Comparison of the European Union Policy Claims against What Has Been Negotiated for Health Services, Trade and Investment. Globalization and Health 17(98):1–11

Lester S, Manak I (2020) A Proposal for a Committee on National Security at the WTO. Duke J Comp Int Law 30:267–281

Limão N, Maggi G (2013) Uncertainty and Trade Agreements. NBER Working Paper No. 18703

Lorfing PA (2021) Screening of Foreign Direct Investment and the States' Security Interests in Light of the OECD, UNCTAD and Other International Guidelines. In: Titi C (ed) Public Actors in International Investment Law. Springer, Cham, pp 179–199

Milmo D (2022) Russia blocks access to Facebook and Twitter. The Guardian, 4 March 2022

Mulabdic A, Yotov YV (2025) Geopolitical Risks and Trade. CGPA Working Paper, No. 2025–32, Center for Global Policy Analysis, Drexel University

Organisation for Economic Co-operation and Development (2009) Building Trust and Confidence in International Investment. OECD Investment Committee Report DAF/INV(2008)11/REV1. OECD Publishing, Paris

Organisation for Economic Co-operation and Development (2015) OECD Regulatory Policy Outlook 2015. OECD Publishing, Paris

Pauwelyn J (2020) Export Restrictions in Times of Pandemic: Options and Limits Under International Trade Agreements. J World Trade 54(5):727–748

Potestà M (2013) Legitimate Expectations in Investment Treaty Law: Understanding the Roots and the Limits of a Controversial Concept. ICSID Rev 28:88–122

Roberts A, Moraes HC, Ferguson V (2019) Toward a Geoeconomic Order in International Trade and Investment. J Int Econ Law 22(4):655–689

Ruys T, Ryngaert C (2020) Secondary Sanctions: A Weapon Out of Control? The International Legality of, and European Responses to, US Secondary Sanctions. Br Yearb Int Law 24:1–116

Shaffer G (2014) The New Empirical Turn in International Law Scholarship. Proc Annu Meet (Am Soc Int Law) 108:369–372

Shaffer G (2018) A Tragedy in the Making? The Decline of Law and the Return of Power in International Trade Relations. Yale J Int Law Online 44:37–53

Shaffer G (2023) Retooling Trade Agreements for Economic Security. Am J Int Law 117:561–615

Shaffer G, Ginsburg T (2012) The Empirical Turn in International Legal Scholarship. Am J Int Law 106:1–46

Shelbaya M (2024) Security Exceptions. ICSID Rev 39(2):263–283

Voon T (2019) The Security Exception in WTO Law: Entering a New Era. Am J Int Law Unbound 113:45–50

Voon T, Merriman D (2024) Incoming: How International Investment Law Constrains Foreign Investment Screening. J World Investment Trade 24:75–114

Wang X, Wu Y, Xu W (2024) Geopolitical Risk and Investment. J Money Credit Bank 56(8):2023–2059

World Trade Organization (2020) Export Prohibitions and Restrictions: Information Note, 23 April 2020

World Trade Organization (2023) World Trade Report 2023: Re-globalization for a Secure, Inclusive and Sustainable Future. WTO, Geneva

Chapter 6
How Geopolitics Shape New Forms of International Economic Ordering

Alexandros Bakos

Abstract This chapter analyses how geopolitics is shifting international economic relations from binding multilateral treaties towards flexible frameworks. Two case studies—the EU-India Trade and Technology Council and the Indo-Pacific Economic Framework for Prosperity (US-Vietnam focus)—show how both form (soft, minilateral, flexible) and content (digital sovereignty, economic security, supply chains) are driven by security considerations. For the EU-India TTC, the logic is hedging against China and reducing India's dependence on Russia, constrained by divisions within the EU regarding India's structural ties to Russia. For IPEF, variable geometry facilitates US-Vietnam cooperation, but US domestic politics, President Trump's tariffs, and Vietnam's hedging limit deeper rule-making. The chapter concludes that these frameworks institutionalise flexibility—helping states react to geopolitical shocks but weakening multilateralism, non-discrimination, and predictable enforcement. The emerging order is a geoeconomic middle ground where informal, plurilateral arrangements substitute for WTO-style rules.

Keywords Geoeconomic turn · Minilateralism · Soft governance · Plurilateralism · Geopolitics · New geoeconomic order

6.1 Introduction

Increased geopolitical tensions have had a structural impact on international economic law and, more broadly, on international economic governance.[1] While geopolitical realities have always influenced the features and paradigms of trade

[1] See, generally, Roberts and Müllerson (2016), Roberts et al. (2019), Shaffer (2021), Ramos Codeço (2022), Babić et al. (2024), Hurrell (2024), Malkin and He (2024), Mclaughlin (2024), Collins (2025), Verdier (2025), and Qiu et al. (2025).

A. Bakos (✉)
College of Law, Hamad Bin Khalifa University, Doha, Qatar
e-mail: abakos@hbku.edu.qa

J. Nakagawa et al. (eds.), *Geopolitical Risks and Geoeconomics in International Economic Law*, Economics, Law, and Institutions in Asia Pacific,
https://doi.org/10.1007/978-981-95-6996-0_6

and investment global ordering frameworks,[2] the widespread increase in (perceived) security threats arising from the deepening of geopolitical cleavages has had an unprecedented impact on the global economic order.[3] Taking this reality as a starting point, the chapter expands upon how states drift away from traditional binding instruments, such as treaties, towards more flexible and less binding instruments of international economic ordering. Focusing on two major initiatives, the European Union (EU)-India Trade and Technology Council (TTC),[4] and the Indo-Pacific Economic Framework for Prosperity (IPEF),[5] the chapter demonstrates that both the content *and* the form of such global (economic) ordering initiatives are increasingly influenced by geopolitical considerations and alignment. Moreover, geopolitics also plays a major inhibiting role in the development and consolidation of such frameworks, as seen especially with the uncertainty surrounding IPEF's future.

The pursuit of digital development and sovereignty plays an essential role in shaping both the form and content of such new instruments of economic ordering.[6] Considering the inherent link between geopolitics and the goals of various states to achieve technological supremacy,[7] the analysis emphasises the role of such objectives as essential considerations for the adoption of novel frameworks of global economic governance. Additionally, as the digital economy presents cross-border characteristics (despite the attempt of some states to territorialise it and emphasise their sovereignty over the digital economy[8]),[9] it forces states to be responsive to geopolitical developments and constraints. The cross-border nature of the internet,[10] coupled with the opacity of many digital technologies, such as artificial intelligence,[11] changes existing paradigms. Most importantly, they render international coordination more relevant than ever to addressing security threats. A siloed, purely sovereigntist, view of a state's security interests (assuming that security threats impact only that specific state and that they are possible to address by acting from within the concerned state's borders) cannot facilitate effective responses to contemporary security risks. This is the case, for instance, with cyberattacks from servers located outside a state's own borders,[12] foreign election interference,[13] or the risks that arise with cross-border data transfers.[14] While some of these examples transcend aspects of direct relevance

[2] Orford (2021, pp. 160, 170–1).

[3] Cohen (2020), Heath (2020), Vidigal and Schill (2021), Heath (2024), and Henckels (2024, pp. 118–9).

[4] European Commission (2023a).

[5] Office of the United States Trade Representative (2022), Natalegawa and Poling (2022).

[6] Ji (2024, pp. 394–5), Sharma (2025, pp. 342–4).

[7] Dear (2021), Wong (2021), Glencross (2024), and Farrand et al. (2024).

[8] Generally, see Aaronson (2019). Focusing on the European Union, see Broeders et al. (2023).

[9] Dimitropoulos (2022, p. 53).

[10] Ibid.

[11] Chesterman (2021, pp. 81–2).

[12] Qian (2024, pp. 298–9).

[13] Kello (2022), p. 95.

[14] Hong (2020, pp. 94–6), Tan (2024, pp. 370, 373).

to the global economy, it is impossible to not acknowledge how an important number of transactions and economic engagement can only occur when the security of the underlying digital infrastructure and of the essential input (data) is guaranteed.[15]

In addition, digital security is heavily connected to economic security,[16] with the expansion of the scope of security interests into the economic realm still ongoing and the borders of economic security not clearly drawn. The latter encapsulates aspects such as the security and resilience of supply chains,[17] freedom from trade coercion,[18] or security of access to critical resources,[19] increasingly relevant for digital development. Thus, despite the deepening of geopolitical tensions, the nature of the global (digital) economy forces states to engage internationally. It is because of this constraint that a transition can be seen in international economic governance. However, this transition does not entail isolation. It is one that brings about a change in the nature, structure, and even content of the ordering frameworks that govern economic relations.[20]

This chapter addresses such aspects by zooming in on two novel instruments that are illustrative of the transition to an increasingly geopoliticised and geoeconomic world order: the EU-India TTC (discussed in Sect. 6.2.1) and IPEF, with a focus on US-Vietnam relations (discussed in Sect. 6.2.2). It explores how geopolitics determine the initiation and adoption of such forms of cooperation, their nature, form, and their content. It particularly explores the inherent flexibility of such frameworks and the weakening of binding commitments made in instruments adopted under the umbrella of such initiatives. It also explains how geopolitical tensions can have a constraining effect—preventing the future development of those frameworks, thus creating a risk of irrelevance for initiatives such as IPEF or the EU-India TTC. This chapter, however, does not focus on the increasingly unilateral turn in the global economy and the ensuing geoeconomic paradigm that results from states exceedingly engaging in statecraft (for instance, through the imposition of export controls to dominate strategic supply chains).[21] The goal of this chapter is much narrower, mainly to show what forms new types of global economic ordering frameworks take in an increasingly geopolitical world, what is their content, and what are the prospects for the deepening of such forms of cooperation.

---

[15] Mishra (2024, p. 66), Kim (2024, pp. 110, 112).

[16] Reiterer and Houng (2023, p. 172) ("[T]he EU's *Strategy on Economic Security* (…) includes the essential lifeblood of today's economies: data, high-end technology (e.g., semiconductors), new raw materials like rare earths and minerals critical to emerging technologies, and (still crucial) energy.").

[17] Shiquan and Deyi (2023, p. 401).

[18] Farrell and Newman (2019, pp. 43–7), American Journal of International Law (2023, pp. 723–4).

[19] For instance, the Minerals Security Partnership has been adopted to reinforce supply chain resilience in this area, with the initiative including economies such as the US, EU, Japan, or Australia. See U.S. Department of State (2022), Logan (2024), and Crochet and Zhou (2024, p. 148).

[20] See, similarly, Chaisse and Dimitropoulos (2021, p. 249) (referring to legal deglobalisation).

[21] Chaisse and Dimitropoulos (2021, pp. 232–40), Hurrell (2024, p. 225).

6.2 New Forms of International Economic Ordering

This section discusses two examples of innovative frameworks that can each offer an adequate platform for states and regional organisations to cooperate to safeguard their security interests: firstly, the EU-India TTC; secondly, the IPEF. The analysis explains how such initiatives maintain flexibility by design, which facilitates future strategic decision-making that might entail undoing the progress achieved in the first place. As such, the focus is not only on the geopolitical causes that have led to the adoption of those instruments, but also on how geopolitical considerations shape their forms and content. Most importantly, the analysis explores the geopolitical constraints that can act as a counterweight to the goal of deeper coordination and cooperation through such frameworks.

6.2.1 The EU-India TTC

Through the TTC, the EU and India have established a semi-institutionalised strategic cooperation mechanism, which addresses issues of common interest for both entities in their pursuit of digital development and sovereignty.[22] This includes aspects such as policy coordination on semiconductors,[23] or achieving the technological interoperability of the two partners' digital public infrastructures.[24] A feature of the TTC's flexible nature is its structuring along Working Group (WG) lines, as they permit targeted focus on areas in which the partners can pursue enhanced coordination. The Working Groups are: (i) strategic technologies, digital governance and digital connectivity; (ii) green and clean energy technologies; and (iii) resilient value chains, trade and investment.[25] Despite the focused nature of the TTC's WGs, an overarching recurring goal is to address (economic) security threats arising from the increasingly volatile geopolitical dynamics.[26]

One of the guiding causes that has instilled a sense of urgency in pursuing deeper cooperation through the EU-India TTC has been the US-China tech rivalry and the perceived risk for both the EU and India of failing to address Washington's and Beijing's increasingly structural dominance.[27] This explains why one of the leading goals of the initiative has been to bridge the digital divide between the two partners, as an attempt to avert dependence on states that hold a privileged position in the race to achieve technological supremacy.[28] The EU also sees India as an important partner in deepening its coordination efforts on securing access to critical minerals, which

[22] For an assessment of a similar framework, the EU-US TTC, see Fahey (2024).

[23] Panda (2023, p. 54).

[24] European Commission (2025b).

[25] Delivorias (2024a, b).

[26] European Commission (2025b), Kathuria and Sánchez-Cacicedo (2025, p. 1).

[27] Idem, p. 5.

[28] Delivorias (2024a, b).

seek to address China's dominance over different supply chains and avert Beijing's imposition of its own standards for supply chain governance.[29] At the same time, the TTC's potential success is even more impressive when considering India's status as a traditionally swing state that does not approach strategic engagement as a result of a binary division between Western and Eastern blocs.[30] India normally responds to geopolitical developments through selective engagement with other powers and blocs, ready to both cooperate with Western actors, such as the EU, and engage in initiatives such as the Quad, but also being a founding member of BRICS.[31]

The EU-India TTC also holds significant promise to address core security interests, such as those having a military and defence nexus, and to achieve structural benefits in this area. This is despite the lack of any major reference to such goals in the foundational documents and official communications surrounding the TTC. For instance, a clear security pivot around which objectives such as reducing Brussels' reliance on China and New Delhi's reliance on both China and Russia can be seen.[32] Geopolitical imperatives, such as India's reliance on Russia for defence purposes,[33] dictate how the TTC has been shaped to potentially enable the co-development and co-production of defence equipment. This is reflected predominantly in the activities of WG1 on Strategic Technologies, which also address military technologies.[34]

Furthermore, China's privileged position in global supply chains and the risk of exploitation of such vulnerabilities have been a major concern for both India and the EU.[35] Cooperation in areas such as research and development on semiconductors and policy coordination are a result of trying to address such geopolitical chokepoints.[36] To this end, WG1 has adopted a Memorandum of Understanding (MoU) on Semiconductors.[37] Considering the limited role that both Brussels and New Delhi play in shaping the features of the semiconductor supply chain,[38] the MoU seeks to address both partners' goals of redrawing supply chain lines to reduce dependence on actors that are perceived to constitute geopolitical threats.[39]

Nonetheless, the official communications from the European Commission on the adoption of the TTC and on its workings did not adopt language that reflected military or defence goals, this being more reflective of think-tank accounts of the EU-India

---

[29] Crochet and Zhou (2024, pp. 161–2).

[30] Leoni and Tzinieris (2024, p. 43).

[31] Ibid. See, also, Chatham House (2025), Patrick et al. (2025).

[32] European Commission (2022) ('This strategic coordination mechanism will allow both partners to tackle challenges at the nexus of trade, trusted technology and security, and thus deepen cooperation in these fields between the EU and India.'); Cogo Morales and Jorge Ricart (2023).

[33] Benaglia and Fanni (2023, p. 61).

[34] Okano-Heijmans and Kranenburg (2023, p. 2).

[35] European Commission (2022), Cogo Morales and Jorge Ricart (2023).

[36] European Commission (2023b).

[37] Memorandum of Understanding on Working Arrangements on Semiconductors Ecosystem, its Supply Chain and Innovation under the Framework of EU-India Trade and Technology Council.

[38] Narian (2024, pp. 4–5).

[39] Glencross (2024, pp. 729, 733).

TTC. Such choice of language would be understandable if TTCs only represented instances of specific applications of the EU's trade policy and nothing else. According to Art. 3 of the Treaty on the Functioning of the European Union, the Common Commercial Policy (which includes trade policy) is an area of exclusive competence for the Union, situating the European Commission as a central executive decision-maker in this sphere.[40] In reality, TTCs represent complex governance frameworks that span different areas of competence, some of which do not even entail Union competence (defence policy, for instance).[41]

Other avenues, such as the envisioned EU-India Security and Defence Partnership,[42] would be more suitable to address defence and military cooperation. However, as technological development is increasingly intertwined with security, defence, and military objectives,[43] it is not always clear where to draw the line. Moreover, in the Union's recent Strategic EU-India Agenda, the Commission emphasises the importance of deeper cooperation and coordination along security and defence lines, emphasising aspects such as maritime security or boosting defence industrial cooperation.[44] It also emphasises aspects such as 'rising geopolitical tensions and technological change,' the emerging risks in the cyber domain, and especially the military use of disruptive technologies, such as AI, as fundamental building blocks in the development of strategic relations with India.[45] In addition, owing to the flexibility and the often porous nature of different strategic coordination mechanisms and partnerships that increasingly characterise the global (economic) order,[46] it is arguably less than ideal to create a siloed approach to how they are leveraged. Otherwise, partners end up avoiding or reducing the scope for potential synergies between their strategic coordination mechanisms.

Aspects such as the EU's institutional set-up and its competences are beyond the scope of this chapter. Nonetheless, it is worth noting that the Union's geopolitical awakening has had an empowering effect on supranational actors such as the Commission. This has enabled it to pursue policymaking that influences areas of fundamental interest to the Member States, such as security and defence, which remain within their own sphere of competence. In this context, the Commission has leveraged the 'Open Strategic Autonomy' doctrine.[47] The doctrine, owing to its vague nature, empowers the Union to achieve geoeconomic resilience and to develop an ability to respond to geopolitical threats. These include, for instance, addressing the exploitation of interdependencies in a globally connected economy, even if done

[40] Freudlsperger and Meunier (2024, p. 1064).

[41] Fahey (2024, p. 480).

[42] European Commission (2025a, p. 10).

[43] Kennedy (2023, pp. 117–20), Gompert (2024, pp. 79–82), and Calabria (2025).

[44] European Commission (2025a, pp. 10–12).

[45] Idem, p. 10.

[46] Moran (2025, pp. 1–2).

[47] European Commission (2020a, pp. 13–4), European Commission (2021), Miró (2023, p. 330), and Varna (2024, p. 65).

through the leveraging of trade instruments by the Commission.[48] TTCs represent one such example, as they pursue trade, digital sovereignty, and economic security goals, all under the broader umbrella of the Union's geopolitical awakening.[49]

TTCs represent an important way through which the Union's digital diplomacy is realised, by pursuing engagement with like-minded partners to enable the proper functioning of the digital economy and to create the context for a truly 'global and open cyberspace.'[50] More specifically, the digital world's borderless nature brings with it the risk of exploiting vulnerabilities in one country that can eventually affect even digitally developed states. In response, the EU's Cybersecurity Strategy emphasises the importance of capacity building efforts. '[P]artner countries experiencing a rapid digital development' are singled out.[51] This underscores the dialectics of the Union's digital development goals. On the one hand, its values dictate openness, multilateralism, and the pursuit of an open and free internet.[52] On the other hand, geopolitical risks and the possibility of exploiting interdependencies become determinative of the EU's *selective* external engagement and the forms through which it engages. Interdependencies become critical, for instance, in the pursuit of interoperability between the EU's and India's Digital Public Infrastructures (DPI).[53] While DPI interoperability enhances structural integration between two, or more, economies, they also expose each party to the security risks affecting the other, often a result of geopolitical threats. Such threats are exacerbated by the failure of multilateralism, the increasingly securitised global order, and the role of private actors in cybersecurity developments.[54] As a result, threats in this area create risks of irreversible damage, such as the now-infamous data breach that affected the Indian digital ID database, *Aadhaar*, and which resulted in the personal data recorded therein being sold on the dark web.[55]

Despite its promise, progress made through the TTC can also stall as a result of geopolitical developments. For instance, while China's rise and its exploitation of vulnerabilities have resulted in increased cooperation between Brussels and New Delhi, EU Member States do not always converge on how to approach critical issues related to China.[56] A relevant example is Hungary, which has established close ties to Beijing through the former's involvement in the Belt and Road Initiative and as a receiver of Chinese foreign direct investment (FDI) for infrastructure development.[57]

---

[48] Juncos and Vanhoonacker (2024), p. 968.

[49] Jacobs et al. (2023, p. 16).

[50] Council of the European Union (2022), paras. 5 and 11 (explicitly singling out the EU-India TTC); European Commission (2020b, pp. 21–3).

[51] Idem, pp. 22–3.

[52] Smith (2018, p. 542).

[53] Ministry of External Affairs. Government of India (2023).

[54] Sukumar et al. (2024, p. 25).

[55] Safi (2018). See, also, Cluley (2023).

[56] Cogo Morales and Jorge Ricart (2023). See, also, Ramalho Alves (2024), García-Herrero and Vasselier (2024, pp. 8–9).

[57] Downes and Lai (2025, p. 12).

In fact, in 2024 Hungary accounted for almost half of Chinese FDI into the Union.[58] This is part of Budapest's broader 'Eastern Opening' strategy, initially established to build closer ties with Russia and Turkey, but which has also led to the development of structural ties with China.[59] Divisions also arise between Western European and Central and Eastern European (CEE) Member States. One area where this plays out is in the level of support shown for Taiwan. For the most part, Western European states refuse to engage with Taiwanese high-ranking officials.[60] CEE states, despite their traditional openness to China, have been more critical of its policies towards Taiwan, especially after Russia's invasion of Ukraine and Beijing's support for Moscow.[61] Since the Union's Common Foreign and Security Policy cannot replace that of the Member States and any initiative pursued in this area at EU level requires unanimity as a rule, then coordination between the 27 Member States may not always be readily achievable.[62] This raises serious questions about the cogency of the Union's strategy towards China.

At the same time, the EU's China strategy, to the extent that one coherent approach can be identified, is currently one of hedging.[63] This emphasises de-risking, addressing dependencies such as those affecting strategic sectors like chemicals, electronics, or critical raw materials,[64] or addressing the risk of Chinese support for Russia.[65] It does not, however, prioritise balancing or containment, unlike Washington's strategy towards the East Asian country.[66] And, most importantly, it entails selective approaches, based on different structural realities. In its 2019 strategy towards China, the EU saw Beijing as a partner in addressing certain international challenges, but also as an economic and technological competitor, and even a systemic rival that promotes alternative models of governance.[67] At the same time, two major events have further nuanced the Union's approach towards Beijing—the latter's lack of transparency during the COVID-19 pandemic, and its support for Russia pursuant to Moscow's invasion of Ukraine.[68] In fact, it is precisely this latter development that has had a major impact on how CEE Member States perceive China, bringing the 27 Member States further into alignment on how to engage with Beijing.[69] As such, to the extent that the Union emphasises a hedging and de-risking strategy towards China, with the continuous pursuit of selective cooperation, it risks

---

58 Krumbein (2025, p. 302).

59 Song and Li (2024, pp. 592, 594–6).

60 Krumbein (2025, p. 302).

61 Ibid. See, also, Huang (2024, pp. 264–5, 269).

62 Krumbein (2025, pp. 302–3).

63 Tunsjø (2025, p. 1).

64 Chimits (2024), Foucar and Grzeszkowiak (2024), and Vandermeeren (2024, p. 10).

65 Tunsjø (2025, p. 1).

66 Idem, p. 2.

67 European Commission, High Representative of the Union for Foreign Affairs and Security Policy (2019, pp. 1, 3), Tunsjø (2025, p. 2).

68 García-Herrero and Vasselier (2024, p. 2), Krumbein (2025, pp. 294–5).

69 Idem, p. 4.

antagonising certain Member States less, considering that such an approach entails enhanced flexibility and refinement. This more readily accommodates the interests of those Member States for which cooperation with China is high on their strategic agenda.

When it comes to the other main geopolitical goal of the TTC, to address structural dependence on Russia, especially India's, the TTC arguably offers less opportunities. Such ambitious goals must be understood in the broader context in which the structural features of India-Russia defence ties have arisen. They go back to the Cold War, where India has manoeuvred between Sino-Soviet tensions and its own conflict with China, especially the 1962 military escalation that resulted from the border dispute between Beijing and New Delhi. This has led to India establishing closer ties to the Soviet Union.[70] Security ties between Moscow and New Delhi followed a *realpolitik* logic, seeking to influence the regional balance of power—China's threat and the US engagement with Pakistan under Richard Nixon made Indian engagement with the Soviet Union an almost foregone and unavoidable conclusion.[71] Defence cooperation between Moscow and New Delhi continues to this day. Existing structural features such as Russia remaining India's largest arms supplier to this day and the existing stockpile of Russian military equipment which requires spare parts from Russia for maintenance mean that India is effectively locked into defence cooperation with Russia.[72] While sanctions regimes have led to Russia conducting trade with India in rupees, thus giving New Delhi an additional leverage in their relationship,[73] the existing structural ties will keep New Delhi in Moscow's orbit for the foreseeable future. This shows the geopolitical limits of the EU-India TTC, whose developments, at least in the medium term, entail being receptive, and often reactive, to geopolitical contingencies rather than actively and structurally shaping them.

One criticism of the EU-India TTC has been that it risked amounting to little more than just a diplomatic forum, thus failing to produce concrete results. Commentators would point to the lack of clear strategic goals or roadmaps to achieving them.[74] However, there are other considerations that should also inform any assessment of the TTC's prospects for success. Most importantly, as new forms of international economic ordering are designed along flexible lines, emphasising cooperation and coordination, and not the adoption and implementation of hard, binding rules, their role should be assessed in the broader context. Regarding EU-India relations, the TTC is part of an ecosystem that also includes a potential Security and Defence Partnership,[75] and possibly an eventual free trade agreement (FTA),[76] negotiations for which started in 2021.[77] In fact, the European Commission has emphasised in its

---

[70] Mohan (2025, p. 36).

[71] Idem, pp. 36–7.

[72] International Institute for Strategic Studies (2024a, p. 1).

[73] Ibid.

[74] Nachiappan (2024).

[75] European Commission (2025a, p. 10).

[76] Seshadri (2023, p. 354).

[77] Delivorias (2024b).

most recent EU-India Strategic Agenda that both partners aimed to *conclude* negotiations for the FTA by the end of 2025.[78] This would be a considerable achievement, especially in an era in which states negotiate and conclude FTAs to an increasingly lower extent than until 2015, when their adoption peaked.[79]

The negotiation of treaties with hard, binding rules has been sidestepped by the ushering in of novel and flexible economic ordering frameworks, such as minilateral deals.[80] Those are heavily focused on targeted areas of coordination, such as standardisation agreements.[81] They also give states additional flexibility to navigate geoeconomic and geopolitical uncertainty.[82] For instance, minilateralism, owing to its *ad hoc* nature that focuses on small achievements and flexibility, more readily accommodates engagement even when geopolitical interests might diverge—in any case, more than any multilateral framework could.[83] Trilaterals such as the Japan-South Korea-US one potentially enable regional strategic coordination to enhance deterrence capabilities and enhance collective defence integration—but are ultimately a result of consistent diplomatic engagement and, thus, reflective of evolving geopolitical contingencies.[84] As a result of economic interdependence and the need to engage internationally in a world order increasingly characterised by strategic and geoeconomic competition, minilaterals offer an innovative form of addressing the inherent tension between the two.[85]

The likelihood of adoption of new FTAs depends on existing deep structural ties between the negotiating parties, often a result of geopolitical alignment. For instance, the EU's recently concluded FTA with Chile displays such patterns. One of the guiding considerations behind the Union's engagement was its goal of securing access to critical raw materials, such as lithium and copper.[86] This is in pursuit of the EU's Economic Security Strategy,[87] which represents an essential guide to the Union's geopolitical and geoeconomic strategy. Similarly, the imperative of achieving autonomy for both India and the EU lays the building blocks for strategic

---

78 European Commission (2025a, p. 3).

79 Kolsky Lewis (2025, p. 95), Moran (2025, pp. 1–2, 3).

80 Claussen (2022).

81 Idem, 329–30.

82 Dimitropoulos (2025, pp. 355–60).

83 Panda and Park (2024, p. 937).

84 Kanodia (2025).

85 Heiduk and Wilkins (2024, p. 808).

86 Moran (2025, p. 3).

87 European Commission (2023c, pp. 2–3) (The EU's Economic Security Strategy priority include: '[p]artnering with countries who share [the Union's] concerns on economic security as well as those who have common interests and are willing to cooperate with [the Union] to achieve the transition to a more resilient and secure economy. In practice this means working together with the broadest possible range of partners to reinforce economic security, foster resilient and sustainable value chains, and strengthen the international rules-based economic order and multilateral institutions. It also means partnering with countries on similar de-risking paths, furthering and finalising free trade agreements, and investing in sustainable development and secure links throughout the world through Global Gateway.')

convergence between the two.[88] With the recent adoption by the Union of the EU-India Strategic Agenda,[89] deeper cooperation between the two partners is high on both their agendas, with newfound political impetus for consolidation. This is arguably driven by both India and the EU's attempts to structurally de-risk from China and to address New Delhi's reliance on Russia for its defence strategy, but also by more recent geopolitical dynamics, such as US President Donald Trump's geopolitical manoeuvres towards Russia.[90] In fact, President Trump's engagement with Russia and especially the weaponisation of tariffs to achieve trade and investment concessions from partners such as the EU have sped up the Union's pursuit of autonomy in different spheres. This includes security and defence but also economic security and resilience from trade coercion. Engagement with New Delhi can play a major role in addressing both.[91] Coupled with the workings of the TTC, the newfound will for deepening cooperation between India and the EU will have a structural impact on strategic coordination between the two partners. It is likely that an update and refinement of the ties that have been already consolidated through the Strategic Partnership between Brussels and New Delhi dating back to 2004 will be seen, potentially preceding the conclusion of negotiations for the FTA.[92] In other words, the success of an eventual EU-India FTA will likely depend on progress made in other *fora*, including the TTC, which can consolidate (geopolitical) alignment between Brussels and New Delhi.

6.2.2 IPEF's Role in the Development of US-Vietnamese Relations

Similarly to how geopolitical considerations are driving the deepening of EU-India strategic cooperation mechanisms, IPEF initially represented Washington's response to China's rise and its increasing assertiveness in the Indo-Pacific.[93] In fact, supply chain resilience has played a major role in the design and implementation of IPEF,[94] with the first instrument adopted under its broader framework being the Supply Chain Resilience Agreement.[95] Unlike EU-India relations, however, IPEF shows

---

[88] Kumar (2025).

[89] European Commission (2025a).

[90] Kumar (2025).

[91] Sachdeva (2025).

[92] Commission of the European Communities (2004).

[93] For more details on IPEF, see Bachand (2023), Ji (2024).

[94] Generally, on how Southeast Asia has become a major area for geopolitical contestation and how supply chains represent an area of particular concern for both the US and China, see Yeo (2025). See, also, Freund et al. (2023, pp. 2–3, 5, 15).

[95] Indo-Pacific Economic Framework for Prosperity Agreement Relating to Supply Chain Resilience (signed 14 November 2023, entered into force 24 February 2024). See, also, Delev (2025).

less potential for further development, with US President Donald Trump explicitly singling it out as one of the frameworks that he considered withdrawing from.[96]

IPEF's novelty lies in the flexibility of its framework, allowing states to selectively participate and choose the instruments that they are ready to become parties to. This reflects IPEF's plurilateral nature, displaying a variable geometry by design.[97] The resulting plurilateral agreements are also issue specific,[98] emphasising an understanding of the participants' unique developmental and geopolitical needs. This renders a context where bilateral relations still matter, with IPEF having the potential to deepen them even if the broader framework does not show much promise for future development. A case in point is the US-Vietnam bilateral (security) relationship, which has been considerably shaped by China's position in the Indo-Pacific.[99] It is IPEF's second pillar, Resilient Economy, where such geopolitical dynamics play out most clearly. Washington's goal through the development of this pillar has been the pursuit of supply chain diversification. Vietnam has been a major catalyst to this pursuit, and the signing of the Supply Chain Resilience Agreement in June 2024 represents an opportunity for Hanoi to further benefit from such dynamics.

It is also IPEF's first pillar, Connected Economy, that can theoretically be leveraged to achieve regional security by pursuing the digital development of US allies such as Vietnam. The focus of this pillar is on digital trade, cross-border data flows, and cybersecurity.[100] In 2023, US Ambassador to Vietnam, Marc E. Knapper, reiterated Washington's support for Hanoi in the latter's pursuit of digital development, linking such outcomes to economic security in the Indo-Pacific.[101] Realistically, the chances of further developments under the umbrella of the Connected Economy pillar are moderate to small. For electoral reasons, the US was unwilling to conclude the trade pillar, a development which unfolded during former President Biden's term.[102] The extent to which US-Vietnamese relations would have deepened in the pursuit of IPEF's first pillar is questionable also because one of the expected approaches to its development was through the imposition of restrictions on data localisation, prohibitions on the imposition of customs duties on digital products, and banning any restrictions to cross-border data flows.[103] Vietnam's balancing act between China and the US might have proven an obstacle in this regard as well, as Hanoi's data governance model follows a similar pattern to that of Beijing. It emphasises state control over data and cross-border data flows.[104]

---

[96] Olson (2025). See, also, Kuo (2025).

[97] Katada (2025, p. 69).

[98] Dimitropoulos et al. (2025, pp. 21–2).

[99] Hiep (2021, pp. 1–2). See, also, Dung (2022), Vu et al. (2023).

[100] Gunasekara-Rockwell (2023, p. 36).

[101] U.S. Embassy & Consulate in Vietnam (2023).

[102] Chen (2024).

[103] Manak (2023). But see Natalegawa and Poling (2022), International Institute for Strategic Studies (2024b), and Bakos et al. (2025).

[104] Natalegawa and Poling (2022, p. 5). See, also, Zhang (2024, pp. 11–2), Rana and Azeez (2025).

At the same time, US-Vietnam dynamics represent an example of geopolitics being a major obstacle to the development of IPEF, as they are reflective of the strategic choices that US partners in the Indo-Pacific must make in such a volatile region. Hanoi's strategic choices entail pivoting between the US and China. At the same time, such balancing acts benefit Vietnam, which is strategically placed to leverage its position at the confluence of great power politics between major poles such as the US and China. Another development affecting the continuous deepening of US-Vietnam relations has been the imposition of reciprocal tariffs on Vietnamese goods. Initially, a 46% tariff was planned to take effect on 9 April 2025 but had been temporarily suspended for three months.[105] On 7 August 2025, Washington announced a 20% reciprocal tariff rate on all Vietnamese goods, pursuant to a tariff agreement concluded with Hanoi.[106] A different tariff rate of 40% applies for rerouted goods from China—called 'transshipment' tariffs.[107] Nonetheless, the declared cause for the imposition of the tariff rate on Vietnamese imports has a geopolitical origin—President Trump cited both trade imbalances and concerns with the rerouting of Chinese goods through Vietnam to avoid tariffs.[108] According to some, US-Vietnamese relations might even be structurally affected by increasing engagement between Hanoi and Beijing.[109] While it is still too early to declare such a radical change in foreign policy (at least) for Vietnam, whose approach has always been informed by its own geopolitical realities and constraints, seeking to maintain balanced relations between competing powers,[110] one aspect becomes clear. The geopolitical awakening that has led to a re-shuffling of the global economic order and brought about novel instruments such as IPEF represents the same force that can prevent their future development. In any case, Washington's commitment to regional stability in SE Asia has diminished, leading countries such as Vietnam to engage beyond US-centric frameworks, including closer cooperation with the BRICS by joining as a Partner Country in June 2025.[111]

Often, geostrategic choices made by countries such as Vietnam require precisely the type of flexibility inherent in novel forms of global economic ordering. An example can be seen with Hanoi's approach to digital development (driven, in part, by its security interests), which has ultimately resulted in significant benefits for the Southeast Asian country. In its balancing act between Beijing and Washington, Vietnam has initially rejected using Huawei equipment for its 5G network.[112] This partially results from the negative light in which Chinese investments are perceived

[105] Takahashi (2025).

[106] Hayton (2025), Hoang (2025).

[107] Lopez (2025).

[108] Lakshmi (2025).

[109] Stratfor (2025).

[110] Vu (2023).

[111] Ministério das Relações Exteriores (2025), Yeo (2025, pp. 118–9).

[112] Hiep (2021, p. 26). Eventually, Vietnam resumed relations with the Chinese telecommunications giant, Huawei returning to construct telecommunications equipment in the South-East Asian nation. See EIAS (2024).

in Vietnam.[113] Subsequently, Hanoi's choice prompted engagement with US chipmaker Qualcomm.[114] This has enabled Vietnam to develop its own 5G base station equipment.[115] The Southeast Asian country turned into one of the few states which have 5G network equipment manufacturing capabilities (the others include Sweden, China, or South Korea).[116] It was Hanoi's geostrategic flexibility that allowed it to manoeuvre around geopolitical constraints and even leverage them to pursue digital development.

The US-Vietnamese example represents a perfect instance of how geopolitics shape not only the form and content of new international economic ordering frameworks. More importantly, *after* such frameworks are set up, geopolitical constraints shape their future development. IPEF is characterised just as much by what has been put in place (the Supply Chain Agreement) as it is by what has stalled, which is the development of the three other pillars. In conjunction with the tensions that have arisen as a result of the US tariff policy and the geopolitical uncertainty that they entail, such changes perfectly illustrate how states engage with new forms of international economic ordering in a way that fundamentally retains flexibility—including the possibility of withdrawal. This even renders plausible the risk of retaliation in a geopolitically volatile world. But it also assuages the geopolitical concerns of the involved parties. In this regard, it signals a veritable shift towards enhanced unilateralism and qualified engagement in international (legal) frameworks.[117]

At the same time, such considerations raise questions about certainty, the future of multilateralism, and the continuous shaping of a rules-based international order. Even in the best-case scenario in which the new types of instruments assessed in this chapter have a positive impact on pushing forward the regulatory and governance agenda in areas such as digital trade and AI governance, this does not render realistic the prospect of a return to multilateralism and its foundational principle of non-discrimination.[118] Such structural developments will likely remain a feature of the new global economic order, where geopolitics and geoeconomics have created the impetus for seeking flexibility in global rules-making processes. This is why plurilateral initiatives such as IPEF should be seen as a middle ground between complete isolation and the ideal of a multilateral global order that is consistently shaped and applied in accordance with principles such as the most-favoured-nation one.[119]

The newfound geopolitical awareness of different states, correlated with the weakening of institutions that contribute to compliance with multilateral rules, such as World Trade Organization's currently non-functional Appellate Body, raises another

---

[113] Tung (2022, p. 906).

[114] Sangam (2024).

[115] Nitta (2024).

[116] Dharmaraj (2025).

[117] Chaisse and Dimitropoulos (2021).

[118] But see, on the geopolitical causes of the multilateral global economic order and the most-favoured-nation principle, O'Rourke (2025, pp. 22–3).

[119] Dimitropoulos (2025, p. 152).

challenge: the risk of a decrease in the cogency of enforcement mechanisms.[120] This is a natural, albeit unwanted, consequence of the changing global economic order. It primarily signifies a shift in the function of international rules adopted as a result of geopolitical realignment. States are not seeking to outright develop certain areas of (economic) governance (for instance, by liberalising market access as a reflection of a dominant neoliberal paradigm) anymore. They are looking to rebalance the governance *status quo*, just as a geopolitical rebalance transforms global power relations.[121] Additionally, the enforcement of new types of global ordering frameworks and their instruments rely on conditioning access to mechanisms that result from such frameworks, as is the case with IPEF's Supply Chain Council. Non-compliance will lead to an exclusion from the benefits associated with engagement in such mechanisms, including the sharing of data, evaluation of supply chain weaknesses, and the coordination of measures taken to address those weaknesses.[122]

6.3 Conclusion

By focusing on EU-India relations as reflected in the TTC between the two partners and on US-Vietnamese IPEF engagement, this chapter has explored the characteristics of novel frameworks of international economic ordering that are a result of geopolitical realignment. While the conclusions are drawn to a large degree from focusing on specific forms of cooperation that pursue digital development, they paint a broader picture. This picture unveils a pattern of change in the features of international economic ordering: in the current global economy, states cannot isolate themselves if they seek to respond to geopolitical threats and to address their security interests. They still need to engage internationally. Nonetheless, as geopolitical realities consistently change, what may have driven cooperation in the past may hinder it in the future or even reverse the progress that has been made. While EU-India relations have received an additional boost because of the increased geopolitical alignment between the two partners, reflected in a broader ecosystem where the TTC is starting to resemble a stepping stone, this is not the case with IPEF. The latter is equally a story of geopolitical alignment as it is one of geopolitics hindering the deepening of existing cooperation and coordination frameworks. Perhaps the most palpable effect on global economic ordering of the geopolitical turn seen with multiple actors is enhanced flexibility in both the design and content of the existing instruments. This is highly welcome to the extent that it enables states to more readily react to geopolitical threats and geoeconomic chokepoints. Yet, this newfound flexibility also increasingly represents a threat to multilateralism, any forms of rules-based international ordering, and predictability.

---

[120] Zhou and Crochet (2025, pp. 293–4).

[121] Idem, p. 293.

[122] Hoekman and Mavroidis (2025, p. 45).

Acknowledgements Postdoctoral researcher in International Economic Law at Hamad Bin Khalifa University, College of Law. This research was supported by the *Industrial Policy for Digital Development (IPDD) Project* (ARG01-0524-230314), funded by the Qatar National Research Fund (QNRF). I would like to thank Junji Nakagawa, Taro Hamada, and Yoshimichi Ishikawa for their helpful suggestions. All the mistakes remain mine.

References

Aaronson SA (2019) What Are We Talking about When We Talk about Digital Protectionism? World Trade Review 18:4–541

American Journal of International Law (2023) The United States Seeks to Counter China's "Economic Coercion" Through Enhanced Cooperation and Coordination. American Journal of International Law 117:4–723

Babić M, de Graaff N, Linsi L, and Weinhardt C (2024) The Geoeconomic Turn in International Trade, Investment and Technology. Politics and Governance 12–1 https://www.cogitatiopress.com/politicsandgovernance/article/view/9031 accessed 19 September 2025

Bachand R (2023) International Economic Institutions After Neoliberalism: The Indo-Pacific Economic Framework for Prosperity as a Blueprint? London Review of International Law 11:3–405

Bakos, Zaman, Dimitropoulos (2025) From the Ashes of the "Empires": Towards Global Convergence in Approaches to Data Governance? Opinio Juris https://opiniojuris.org/2025/01/20/from-the-ashes-of-the-empires-towards-global-convergence-in-approaches-to-data-governance/ accessed 30 September 2025

Benaglia S and Fanni R (2023) A View from Europe on the Role of Technology in EU– India Relations: The Trade and Technology Council. Kranenburg V, Okano-Heijmans M (eds) How Strategic Tech Cooperation Can Reinvigorate Relations between the EU and India. Clingendael Report https://docs.clingendael.org/sites/docs/files/2023-03/Report_Strategic_tech_cooperation_between_EU_India.pdf accessed 19 September 2025, 60–5

Broeders D, Cristiano F and Kaminska M (2023) In Search of Digital Sovereignty and Strategic Autonomy: Normative Power Europe to the Test of Its Geopolitical Ambitions. Journal of Common Market Studies 61:5–1261

Calabria M (2025) Offensive Cyber Attacks and Conventional Warfare. Survival 67:4–67

Chaisse J and Dimitropoulos G (2021) Special Economic Zones in International Economic Law: Towards Unilateral Economic Law. Journal of International Economic Law 24–229

Chatham House (2025). Back-to-Back BRICS and Quad Meetings Highlight India's Increasingly Difficult Balancing Act. Chatham House https://www.chathamhouse.org/2025/07/back-back-brics-and-quad-meetings-highlight-indias-increasingly-difficult-balancing-act accessed 30 September 2025

Chen S (2024) Reflecting on IPEF's Impact and Charting the Future: A Perspective of US Domestic Politics. China International Strategy Review 6–319

Chesterman S (2021) We, The Robots? Regulating Artificial Intelligence and the Limits of the Law. Cambridge University Press, Cambridge

Claussen K (2022) Trade's Mini-Deals. Virginia Journal of International Law 62:2–315

Cluley G (2023) India's Biggest Data Breach? Hacking Gang Claims to Have Stolen 815 Million People's Personal Information. Bitdefender Blog https://www.bitdefender.com/en-au/blog/hotforsecurity/indias-biggest-data-breach-hacking-gang-claims-to-have-stolen-815-million-peoples-personal-information accessed 19 September 2025

Cogo Morales P, Jorge Ricart R (2023) (Elcano Royal Institute) (2023) https://www.realinstitutoelcano.org/en/commentaries/the-eu-india-trade-and-technology-council-opportunities-and-challenges-ahead/ accessed 19 September 2025

Cohen HG (2020) Nations and Markets. Journal of International Economic Law 23:4-793
Collins D (2025) Plurilateralism and the New Geoeconomics of International Law. Journal of World Investment & Trade 26:1–2–54
Commission of the European Communities (2004) EU-India Strategic Partnership COM(2004) 430 final
Council of the European Union (2022) EU Digital Diplomacy: Council Conclusions, Foreign Affairs Council, 11406/22
Crochet V and Zhou W (2024) Critical Insecurities? The European Union's Strategy for a Stable Supply of Minerals. Journal of International Economic Law 27:1-147
Dear K (2021) Beyond the 'Geo' in Geopolitics. The Digital Transformation of Power. The RUSI Journal 166:6–7–20
Delev C (2025) Economic Resilience under the Indo-Pacific Economic Framework Supply Chain Agreement: Treading between Geoeconomic Ambitions and World Trade Organization Compatibility? World Trade Review accessed 27 September 2025
Delivorias A (2024a) (European Parliament Research Service) EU-India Trade and Technology Council https://www.europarl.europa.eu/RegData/etudes/ATAG/2024/757587/EPRS_ATA(2024)757587_EN.pdf accessed 19 September 2025
Delivorias A (2024b) (European Parliament Research Service) EU-India Free Trade Agreement https://www.europarl.europa.eu/RegData/etudes/BRIE/2024/757588/EPRS_BRI(2024)757588_EN.pdf accessed 20 September 2025
Dharmaraj S (2025) Vietnam: 5G Launch a Game-Changer for Digital Transformation. Open Gov https://opengovasia.com/2025/01/04/vietnam-5g-launch-a-game-changer-for-digital-transformation/ accessed 24 September 2025
Dimitropoulos G (2022) Law and Digital Globalization. University of Pennsylvania Journal of International Law 44:1–41
Dimitropoulos G (2025) Industrial Policy and the New Internationalism: After the Liberal International Order. Cornell International Law Journal 57:2–295
Dimitropoulos G, Chen RC, Chaisse C (2025) Plurilateralism. A New Form of International Economic Ordering? Journal of World Investment & Trade 26:1–2–1
Downes JF and Lai K (2025) EU-China Relations in a Post-COVID-19 World Order: The Context of the BRI Project. Frontiers in Political Science https://www.frontiersin.org/journals/political-science/articles/10.3389/fpos.2025.1644327/full accessed 21 September 2025
Dung PX (2022) "No One Can Force Vietnam to Choose Sides": Vietnam as a Self-Reliant Middle Power. Asia Policy 17:4–151
EIAS (2024) Bamboo Diplomacy Meets 5G: Europe's High-Stakes Bid on Vietnam's Telecommunications Transformation. EIAS https://eias.org/publications/op-ed/europes-high-stakes-bid-on-vietnams-telecommunications/ accessed 30 September 2025
European Commission (2020a) A New Industrial Strategy for Europe. COM(2020)102
European Commission (2020b) The EU's Cybersecurity for the Digital Decade. JOIN(2020) 18 final
European Commission (2021) Updating the 2020 New Industrial Strategy: Building a Stronger Single Market for Europe's Recovery. COM(2021) 350 final
European Commission (2022) EU-India: Joint Press Release on Launching the Trade and Technology Council https://ec.europa.eu/commission/presscorner/detail/en/ip_22_2643 accessed 19 September 2025
European Commission (2023a) EU-India: New Trade and Technology Council to Lead on Digital Transformation, Green Technologies and Trade, https://ec.europa.eu/commission/presscorner/detail/en/ip_23_596 accessed 19 September 2025
European Commission (2023b) First EU-India Trade and Technology Council Focused on Deepening Strategic Engagement on Trade and Technology. Press Release https://ec.europa.eu/commission/presscorner/detail/en/ip_23_2728 accessed 19 September 2025

European Commission (2023c) European Economic Security Strategy JOIN(2023) 20 final https://eur-lex.europa.eu/legal-content/EN/TXT/PDF/?uri=CELEX:52023JC0020 accessed 20 September 2025

European Commission (2025a) Joint Communication to the European Parliament and the Council on a New Strategic EU-India Agenda. JOIN(2025) 50 final

European Commission (2025b) Key Outcomes of the Second EU-India Trade and Technology Council https://digital-strategy.ec.europa.eu/en/news/key-outcomes-second-eu-india-trade-and-technology-council accessed 19 September 2025

European Commission, High Representative of the Union for Foreign Affairs and Security Policy (2019) EU-China – A Strategic Outlook. JOIN(2019) 5 final

Fahey E (2024) Legal Convergence Through Soft Law? The EU-US Trade and Technology Council (TTC) European Foreign Affairs Review 29:4–471

Farrand B, Carrapico H and Turobov A (2024) The New Geopolitics of EU Cybersecurity: Security, Economy and Sovereignty. International Affairs 100:6–2379

Farrell H and Newman AL (2019), Weaponized Interdependence. How Global Economic Networks Shape State Coercion. International Security 44:1-42

Foucar J and Grzeszkowiak J-L (2024) Realignment of the EU-China Political Strategy: An Analysis of the EU's Asymmetrical Interdependences. In: Andreosso-O'Callaghan B and Rajmil D (eds) Geopolitical Uncertainty and International Business. Shaping Our Future World. Edward Elgar, Cheltenham

François Chimits (2024) Growing Asymmetry: Mapping the Import Dependencies in EU and US Trade with China. Mercator Institute for China Studies https://merics.org/en/report/growing-asymmetry-mapping-import-dependencies-eu-and-us-trade-china accessed 20 September 2025

Freudlsperger C and Meunier S (2024) When Foreign Policy Becomes Trade Policy: The EU's Anti-Coercion Instrument. Journal of Common Market Studies 62:4–1063

Freund C et al. (2023) Is US Trade Policy Reshaping Global Supply Chains. World Bank Policy Research Working Papers, Working Paper 10593

García-Herrero A, Vasselier A (2024), Updating the EU Strategy on China: Co-existence while Derisking through Partnerships. Bruegel https://www.bruegel.org/policy-brief/updating-eu-strategy-china-co-existence-while-derisking-through-partnerships accessed 20 September 2025

Glencross A (2024) The Geopolitics of Supply Chains: EU Efforts to Ensure Security of Supply: EU Efforts to Ensure Security of Supply. Global Policy 15:4–555

Gompert DC (2024) Winning the US-China Technology Race. Survival 66:4–77

Gunasekara-Rockwell A, Dr. (2023) Friendship in the Shadow of the Dragon. The Challenge of Upgrading US-Vietnam Ties Amid Tensions with China. Journal of Indo-Pacific Affairs 24

Hayton B, Dr. (2025) Vietnam's Tariffs Deal with Trump Reflects Balancing Act between US and China. Chatham House https://www.chathamhouse.org/2025/07/vietnams-tariff-deal-trump-reflects-balancing-act-between-us-and-china accessed 30 September 2025

Heath JB (2020) The New National Security Challenge to the Economic Order. The Yale Law Journal 129:4–1020

Heath JB (2024) Neutrality and Governance in a Weaponized World. The American Journal of International Law 118:3–566

Heiduk F & Wilkins T (2024) Minilateralism and Pathways to Institutional Progression: Alliance Formation or Cooperative Security Governance? Australian Journal of International Affairs 78:6–808

Henckels C (2024) Whither Security? The Concept of 'Essential Security Interests' in Investment Treaties' Security Exceptions. Journal of International Economic Law 27:1–114

Heokman B, Mavroidis PC (2025). Plurilateral Agreements, Multilateralism and Economic Development. Journal of World Investment & Trade 26:1–2–31

Hiep LH (2021) The Vietnam-US Security Partnership and the and the Rules-Based International Order in the Age of Trump (ISEAS–Yusof Ishak Institute)

Hoang L (2025) Vietnam Offers Factory Perks as US Tariffs Hit Chinese Suppliers. Nikkei Asia https://asia.nikkei.com/economy/trade-war/trump-tariffs/vietnam-offers-factory-perks-as-us-tariffs-hit-chinese-suppliers accessed 30 September 2025

Hong Y (2020). The Institutional Logic of Security Assessment of Cross-Border Data Transfers in China: Context and Progress. International Cybersecurity Law Review 1–93

Hong Y (2024) The Institutional Logic of Security Assessment of Cross-Border Data Transfers in China: Context and Progress. International Cybersecurity Law Review 1–93

Huang J (2024) China's Role in the EU's Search for Strategic Autonomy: Nonhegemonic Power Relations During World Order Transition. China International Strategy Review 6–254

Hurrell A (2024) Geopolitics and Global Economic Governance. Oxford Review of Economic Policy 40:2-220

International Institute for Strategic Studies (2024a) India's Relationship with Russia. Strategic Comments 30:5–1

International Institute for Strategic Studies (2024b) Washington's Hesitancy on Digital-Trade Diplomacy https://www.iiss.org/publications/strategic-comments/2024/09/washingtons-hesitancy-on-digital-trade-diplomacy/ accessed 30 September 2025

Jacobs T et al (2023) The Hegemonic Politics of 'Strategic Autonomy' and 'Resilience': COVID-19 and the Dislocation of EU Trade Policy. Journal of Common Market Studies 61:1–3

Ji X (2024) Securitising Regionalism: Mega-Regional Trade Blocs, Indo-Pacific Economic Framework and Supply Chain Alliances in Asia. Asia Europe Journal 22–383

Juncos AE, Vanhoonacker S (2024) The ideational power of strategic autonomy in EU security and external economic policies. Journal of Common Market Studies 62:4–955

Kanodia K (2025) The Unpromising Future of Japan-South Korea-US Trilateral Cooperation https://www.chathamhouse.org/2025/02/unpromising-future-japan-south-korea-us-trilateral-cooperation accessed 1 November 2025

Katada SN (2025) The Rise of Plurilateral Trade Agreements and the Future of Trade in the Indo-Pacific. Asia Policy 20:2-61

Kathuria R and Sánchez-Cacicedo A (2025) Tapping into the Momentum: The EU-India Trade and Technology Council https://in.boell.org/sites/default/files/2025-07/tapping-into-the-momentum-the-eu-india-trade-and-technology-council.pdf accessed 19 September 2025

Kello L (2022), Striking Back: The End of Peace in Cyberspace – And How to Restore. Yale University Press, New Haven, CT

Kennedy AB (2023) The Resilience Requirement: Responding to China's Rise as Technology Power. Survival 65:1–115

Kim H-C (2024) Industrial Digital Transformation and a Proposal to Rebuild Digital Trade Agenda. Journal of World Trade 58:1–87

Kolsky Lewis M (2025) Plurilateralism and Free Trade Agreements. Journal of World Investment & Trade 26:1–2–82

Krumbein F (2025) Less Panda, More Dragon – Moving Towards Realism in EU–China Relations. International Journal of Asian Studies 22.2–293

Kuo MA (2025) Trump 2.0 and US Leadership in the Indo-Pacific, The Diplomat https://thediplomat.com/2025/02/trump-2-0-and-us-leadership-in-the-indo-pacific/ accessed 30 September 2025

Lakshmi AA (2025) Vietnam Faces the Heat Over Chinese Tariff 'Backdoor' to US. Financial Times https://www.ft.com/content/41788509-f7ce-4d1a-ba90-29ce9b682dec accessed 24 September 2025

Leoni Z and Tzinieris S (2024) The Return of Geopolitical Blocs. Survival 66:2-37

Logan S (2024) Material World: How Europe Can Compete with China in the Race for Africa's Critical Minerals. European Council on Foreign Relations https://ecfr.eu/publication/material-world-how-europe-can-compete-with-china-in-the-race-for-africas-critical-minerals/ accessed 19 September 2025

Lopez J (2025) In Vietnam's Case, What, Exactly, is the Target of Trump's "Transshipment" Tariffs? https://www.lowyinstitute.org/the-interpreter/vietnam-s-case-what-exactly-target-trump-s-transshipment-tariffs accessed 30 September 2025
Malkin A & He T (2024) The Geoeconomics of Global Semiconductor Value Chains: Extraterritoriality and the US-China Technology Rivalry. Review of International Political Economy 31:2–674
Manak I (2023) Unpacking the IPEF: Biden's Indo-Pacific Trade Play. Council on Foreign Relations https://www.cfr.org/article/unpacking-ipef-bidens-indo-pacific-trade-play accessed 24 September 2025
Mclaughlin M (2024) The Geoeconomics of Belt and Road Disputes: A Case Study on the China-Pakistan Economic Corridor. Asian Journal of International Law 14:1–94
Ministério das Relações Exteriores (2025) Vietnam Joins BRICS as a Partner Country https://www.gov.br/mre/en/contact-us/press-area/press-releases/vietnam-joins-brics-as-a-partner-country accessed 30 September 2025
Ministry of External Affairs. Government of India (2023) India – EU Joint Statement 1st Meeting of the Trade and Technology Council https://www.mea.gov.in/bilateral-documents.htm?dtl/36553/India__EU_Joint_Statement_1st_Meeting_of_the_Trade_and_Technology_Council accessed 19 September 2025
Miró J (2023), Responding to the Global Disorder: the EU's Quest for Open Strategic Autonomy. Global Society 37:3-315
Mishra N (2024) International Trade Law and Global Data Governance: Aligning Perspectives and Practices. Bloomsbury Publishing, New York, NY
Mohan CR (2025) India and the rebalancing of Asia. Great transitions. Adelphi Series 65:517–523
Moran N (2025) New Frontiers in EU Trade Policy: Moving Beyond Conventional Trade Agreements. Global Policy https://onlinelibrary.wiley.com/doi/full/10.1111/1758-5899.70074?campaign=woearlyview accessed 20 September 2025
Nachiappan K (2024) EU-India Trade and Technology Council: The Path Ahead. National University of Singapore, Institute of South Asian Studies https://www.isas.nus.edu.sg/papers/eu-india-trade-and-technology-council-the-path-ahead/ accessed 20 September 2025
Narian S (2024) Balancing Interests and Promoting Democracy – The India-EU Trade and Technology Council. Austrian Institute for European and Security Policy Focus Paper Papers, Focus Paper 2024/5
Natalegawa A and Poling GB (2022) The Indo-Pacific Economic Framework & Digital Trade in Southeast Asia. Center for Strategic and International Studies https://www.csis.org/analysis/indo-pacific-economic-framework-and-digital-trade-southeast-asia accessed 19 September 2025
Nitta Y (2024) Viettel and Qualcomm Launch Open RAN 5G Network in Vietnam. Nikkei Asia https://asia.nikkei.com/Business/Telecommunication/Viettel-and-Qualcomm-launch-Open-RAN-5G-network-in-Vietnam accessed 30 September 2025
Office of the United States Trade Representative (2022) Indo-Pacific Framework for Prosperity, https://ustr.gov/trade-agreements/agreements-under-negotiation/indo-pacific-economic-framework-prosperity-ipef accessed 19 September 2025
Okano-Heijmans M and Kranenburg V (2023) Executive Summary. In: Kranenburg V, Okano-Heijmans M (eds) How Strategic Tech Cooperation Can Reinvigorate Relations between the EU and India. Clingendael Report https://docs.clingendael.org/sites/docs/files/2023-03/Report_Strategic_tech_cooperation_between_EU_India.pdf accessed 19 September 2025, pp. 1–4
Olson S (2025) The Economic Implications of Donald Trump's Presidency for Southeast Asia. Fulcrum https://fulcrum.sg/the-economic-implications-of-donald-trumps-presidency-for-southeast-asia/ accessed 30 September 2025
Orford A (2021) Regional Orders, Geopolitics, and the Future of International Law. Current Legal Problems 74:1–149
O'Rourke KH (2025) The Global Economic Order A Brief History. In: Ing LY and Rodrik D (eds) The New Global Economic Order. Routledge, Abingdon

Panda J (2023) The Prospects of Critical and Emerging Technology Cooperation between India and the EU. In: Kranenburg V, Okano-Heijmans M (eds) How Strategic Tech Cooperation Can Reinvigorate Relations between the EU and India. Clingendael Report https://docs.clingendael.org/sites/docs/files/2023-03/Report_Strategic_tech_cooperation_between_EU_India.pdf accessed 19 September 2025, pp. 51–9

Panda J & Park JJ (2024) Minilateralism and Global Governance: Effectiveness of Hybrid Models. Australian Journal of International Affairs 78:6–929

Patrick S et al. (2025) BRICS Expansion and the Future of World Order: Perspectives from Member States, Partners, and Aspirants. Carnegie Endowment for International Peace https://carnegieendowment.org/research/2025/03/brics-expansion-and-the-future-of-world-order-perspectives-from-member-states-partners-and-aspirants?lang=en accessed 30 September 2025

Qian X (2024) Redefining International Law Paradigms: Charting Cybersecurity, Trade, and Investment Trajectories within Global Legal Boundaries. Journal of World Investment & Trade 25:3–295

Qiu H, Xia D and Yetman J (2025) The Role of Geopolitics in International Trade. Bank for International Settlements Working Papers, Working Paper No 1249

Ramalho Alves D (2024) The EU's Discourse Coherence and its Relationship with China: A New Normative Actor? SN Social Sciences 4 https://link.springer.com/article/10.1007/s43545-024-00862-4 accessed 20 September 2025

Ramos Codeço R (2022) WTO Crisis Through the Lens of Hegemony Theories: When International Trade Law and Geopolitics Collide. New Global Studies 16(3)-251

Rana V and Azeez GK (2025) Southeast Asia's Quest for Digital Sovereignty. The Diplomat https://thediplomat.com/2025/03/southeast-asias-quest-for-digital-sovereignty/#:~:text=Smaller%20economies%20are%20following%20suit,hub%20of%20the%20Mekong%20region accessed 30 September 2025

Reiterer M, Houng LI (2023) The Economic Security Tightrope: EU Economic Security Strategy, Friend-Shoring, and European Relations with Indo-Pacific States. The Journal of East Asian Affairs 36:2–169

Roberts A, Choer Moraes H and Ferguson V (2019) Toward a Geoeconomic Order in International Trade and Investment Law. Journal of International Economic Law 22:4–655

Roberts A, Müllerson R (2016) Ideology, Geopolitics and International Law. Chinese Journal of International Law 15:1–47

Sachdeva G (2025) Can India-EU Ties Withstand Global Geopolitical Fragmentation? EU-Renew https://eu-renew.eu/can-india-eu-trade-ties-withstand-global-geopolitical-fragmentation/ accessed 20 September 2025

Safi M (2018) Personal Data of a Billion Indians Sold Online for £6, Report Claims. The Guardian https://www.theguardian.com/world/2018/jan/04/india-national-id-database-data-leak-bought-online-aadhaar accessed 20 September 2025

Sangam P (2024) Op-Ed: This is Why Qualcomm's Viettel Win is a Big Deal. Tantra Analyst https://www.tantraanalyst.com/ta/op-ed-this-is-why-qualcomms-viettel-win-is-a-big-deal/ accessed 30 September 2025

Seshadri VS (2023) Free Trade Agreements. India and the World. Oxford University Press, Oxford

Shaffer G (2021) Governing the Interface of U.S.-China Trade Relations. The American Journal of International Law 115:4–622

Sharma DC (2025) Cooperation Between the EU and India with a Focus on Standardisation. In: Freimuth J, Kaiser S, Schädler M (eds) Standardization Strategies in China and India Industrial Policy and Geopolitics and Implications for Europe. Springer, Wiesbaden, pp. 341–56

Shiquan D, Deyi X (2023) The Security of Critical Mineral Supply Chains. Mineral Economics 36–401

Smith M (2018) The EU, the US and the Crisis of Contemporary Multilateralism. Journal of European Integration 40:5–539

Song W & Li X (2024). "Eastern Opening" Policy as Political Marketing: Populism and Hungary's Relations with China under the Orbán Government. Problems of Post-Communism 71:6–592

Stratfor (2025) Trump's Tariffs Pose a Structural Threat to Vietnam's Economy. Stratfor, https://worldview.stratfor.com/article/trumps-tariffs-pose-structural-threat-vietnams-economy accessed 24 September 2025

Sukumar A, Broeders D & Kello M (2024) The Pervasive Informality of the International Cybersecurity Regime: Geopolitics, Non-State Actors and Diplomacy. Contemporary Security Policy 45:1–7

Takahashi T (2025) How Tariff-Hit Vietnam Could Signal Dawn of a Post-U.S. Asia. Nikkei Asia https://asia.nikkei.com/Spotlight/Comment/How-tariff-hit-Vietnam-could-signal-dawn-of-a-post-U.S.-Asia accessed 30 September 2025

Tan W (2024) National Security as the Trump Card: Assessing China's Legal Regime on Cross-Border Data Transfer. Information & Communications Technology Law 33:3–368

Tung NC (2022) Uneasy Embrace: Vietnam's Response to the U.S. Free and Open Indo-Pacific Strategy Amid U.S.-China Rivalry. The Pacific Review 35:5-884

Tunsjø Ø (2025) The EU's China Strategies: A Hedging Framework for Analysis. Journal of Common Market Studies https://onlinelibrary.wiley.com/doi/10.1111/jcms.13749 accessed 20 September 2025

U.S. Department of State (2022) Minerals Security Partnership https://www.state.gov/minerals-security-partnership accessed 19 September 2025

U.S. Embassy & Consulate in Vietnam (2023), Elevating the U.S.-Vietnam Economic Relationship https://vn.usembassy.gov/elevating-the-u-s-vietnam-economic-relationship/ accessed 24 September 2025

Vandermeeren F (2024) Understanding EU-China Exposure. Single Market Economics Briefs https://single-market-economy.ec.europa.eu/system/files/2024-01/EconomicBrief_4_ETBD_23_004ENN_V2.pdf accessed 20 September 2025

Varma T (2024) European Strategic Autonomy: The Path to a Geopolitical Europe. The Washington Quarterly 47:1–65

Verdier P-H (2025) International Finance and the Return of Geopolitics. The American Journal of International Law 119:2–229

Vidigal G & Schill SW (2021) International Economic Law and the Securitization of Policy Objectives: Risks of a Schmittean Exception. Legal Issues of Economic Integration 48:2–109

Vu K (2023) The China Factor in Vietnam's Multidirectional Foreign Policy. The Diplomat https://thediplomat.com/2023/04/the-china-factor-in-vietnams-multidirectional-foreign-policy/ accessed 24 September 2025

Vu V-H, Soong J-J & Nguyen K-N (2023) The Political Economy of Vietnam and Its Development Strategy under China-USA Power Rivalry and Hegemonic Competition: Hedging for Survival, 56(4) The Chinese Economy 56:4–256

Wong PN (2021) Techno-Geopolitics. US-China Tech War and the Practice of Digital Statecraft. Routledge, London

Yeo A (2025) Supply Chains and Southeast Asia: The Sino-American Shadow. Survival 67:4–113

Zhang C (2024), China's Privacy Protection Strategy and its Geopolitical Implications. Asian Review of Political Economy 3 https://link.springer.com/article/10.1007/s44216-024-00028-2 accessed 30 September 2025

Zhou W and Crochet V (2025) Confronting Fragmentation: A Quest for a Plurilateral Appellate Mechanism under the WTO. Journal of World Investment & Trade 26:1–2–275.

Part II
National Security, Regulatory Space, and Investment Risk Governance

Chapter 7
Investment Screening Mechanisms Under the Investment Treaty Law: The Case of the UK's National Security and Investment Act

Apoorva Vishnoi

Abstract Investment screening has become a popular tool in "derisking" efforts from the People's Republic of China (China) and protecting strategic interests from Chinese influence or acquisition through investment. A notable example of such an investment screening mechanism is the National Security and Investment (NSI) Act 2021 in the United Kingdom (UK). The NSI Act allows the government to screen both foreign and domestic investments in a "qualifying" entity or asset for national security risks. If risk is discovered, the UK government can issue orders to mitigate national security risks. These orders can vary from imposing performance conditions on the acquisition to completely blocking the acquisition. Seven deals have been blocked or reversed so far under the NSI Act, either with a Chinese or Russian connection. This chapter will focus on 5 cases with a Chinese connection that enable examination of the NSI Act's interaction with the UK's investment treaty regime. These cases involve direct acquisitions by mainland Chinese investors as well as indirect acquisitions through non-Chinese companies based in Hong Kong and the Netherlands. Given the huge network of international investment agreements (IIAs) signed by the UK, a conflict may arise between the UK's drive towards national security and its obligations towards investors as a host State under its IIAs. This chapter will assess whether risk for such a conflict exists and, if yes, how the UK should respond. The first part of the chapter will briefly examine the details of the NSI Act and the orders issued under it. The second part will examine whether these cases fall under the scope of a UK IIA. If yes, it will explore if there is a risk that the investment screening orders violate UK's obligations as a host state and whether the UK can justify its actions under international investment treaty law. The chapter will then conclude with broad lessons that can be derived from the UK's example. It will also highlight some of the best practices the UK has already adopted (e.g., its country-neutral design of the NSI Act and its approach in the UK-Australia FTA). Further, the UK's investment screening mechanism and national security approach

A. Vishnoi (✉)
London School of Economics and Political Science, London, UK
e-mail: apoorvasvishnoi@gmail.com

J. Nakagawa et al. (eds.), *Geopolitical Risks and Geoeconomics in International Economic Law*, Economics, Law, and Institutions in Asia Pacific,
https://doi.org/10.1007/978-981-95-6996-0_7

will be contextualised within the broader discussion on investment screening and investment treaty law.

Keywords Investment Screening · Economic Security · UK Investment Law · International Investment Agreements (IIAs) · National Security · Chinese Outbound Investment

7.1 Introduction

Investment screening has become a popular tool for countries around the world worried about the control of critical infrastructure or the acquisition of advanced technologies by unfriendly states.[1] This popularity of investment screening is attributable to many reasons, not least among them being the geopolitical tension (or the new "cold war")[2] between the People's Republic of China (or "China") and Western countries, and China's growing status as a major capital-exporting country.[3] Voon and Merriman (2022a) broadly define investment screening as "*scrutiny and approval processes that need to be completed before certain investment-related actions by foreign individuals or entities will be allowed*".[4] Given the complexity of corporate ownership structures covering multiple countries, investment screening can also include investment by domestic entities with foreign links.

The UK's National Security and Investment (NSI) Act 2021[5] belongs to this family of investment screening measures enacted in the EU, Australia, Canada, and the USA in response to the "swift growth of Chinese investments in strategic high-tech industries".[6] These countries had previously "championed economic liberalization"[7] and signed hundreds of investment treaties with China and other countries. The complexity and sheer number of these investment treaties or international investment agreements (IIAs) make it hard to scrutinise if and to what extent a conflict exists between the investment screening mechanisms and national security policies on the one hand, and the regime of IIAs on the other hand. So, the article will focus on the NSI Act, with particular consideration of 5 cases with connection to the PRC. This will allow for the examination of the NSI Act's interaction with the UK's investment treaty regime in terms of both its design and implementation.

These NSI Act cases involve direct acquisition by PRC investors as well as indirect acquisitions through non-PRC companies based in Hong Kong and the Netherlands. They show that not only mainland Chinese companies, but companies with indirect

[1] Schild (2025, p. 3).

[2] Ford (2023, p. 423).

[3] McCalman et al. (2023, p. 82).

[4] Voon and Merriman (2022a, p. 76).

[5] National Security and Investment Act 2021 (NSI Act), c. 25 (UK).

[6] Erdal (2022, p. 13).

[7] Gáspár-Szilágyi (2024, p. 195).

connections to the PRC are also under scrutiny. But given the huge network of IIAs signed by the UK, a conflict may arise between the UK's drive towards national security and its obligations towards investors as a host State under its IIAs, whether its older generation Bilateral Investment Treaties (BITs) or modern treaties with investment provisions (TIPs). This article will assess whether risk for such a conflict exists and, if yes, how the UK should respond. The first part of the article will examine the details of the NSI Act, and the orders issued under it. The second part will examine whether these cases will fall under the scope of the China-United Kingdom BIT (1986)[8] and Hong Kong, China SAR-United Kingdom BIT (1998).[9] If yes, the article will further explore whether there is any risk of conflict and whether the UK can justify its actions under international investment treaty law. The article will then conclude with broad lessons that can be derived from the UK's example. It will also highlight some of the best practices the UK has already adopted (e.g., its country-neutral design of the NSI Act, and its approach in the UK-Australia Free Trade Agreement[10]). Moreover, the UK's investment screening mechanism and national security approach will be contextualised within the broader discussion on investment screening and investment treaty law.

7.2 The Design and Implementation of the UK's National Security and Investment Act

7.2.1 The Design of the NSI Act

The NSI Act was enacted in 2021 and came into force in January 2022.[11] It introduced an investment screening regime focused purely on one purpose—national security. Before this, the Enterprise Act 2002[12] enabled the government to intervene

[8] Agreement Between the Government of the United Kingdom of Great Britain and Northern Ireland and the Government of the People's Republic of China for the Promotion and Protection of Investments, U.K.–China, May 15, 1986, 1496 U.N.T.S. 33 (UK-China BIT).

[9] Agreement Between the Government of the Hong Kong Special Administrative Region of the People's Republic of China and the Government of the United Kingdom of Great Britain and Northern Ireland for the Promotion and Protection of Investments, U.K.–H.K. SAR, July 30, 1998, available at https://investmentpolicy.unctad.org/international-investment-agreements/treaty-files/1522/download (UK-Hong Kong BIT).

[10] Free Trade Agreement Between the United Kingdom of Great Britain and Northern Ireland and Australia (UK-Australia FTA), Dec. 17, 2021, [2023] ATS 1.

[11] Cabinet Office, *The National Security and Investment Act alongside Regulatory Requirements* (July 20, 2021), https://www.gov.uk/government/publications/the-national-security-and-investment-act-alongside-regulatory-requirements/the-national-security-and-investment-act-alongside-regulatory-requirements.

[12] Enterprise Act 2002, c. 40 (UK).

in mergers and acquisitions (M&A) cases on grounds of national security.[13] The UK government began a review of its national security infrastructure in 2017 and introduced a White Paper on "National Security and Investment" in 2018[14] as it wanted to widen the scope of economic activities that can be scrutinised on national security ground.[15] Other considerations were separating competition-focused assessments of M&A transactions from national security assessments and ensuring regulatory independence of the CMA.[16] The White Paper also cited inspiration from allies like the USA, Australia, France, Germany, and Japan for "modernising" national security safeguards on international investments.[17]

The NSI Act is concerned with two situations: first, when a legal person gains control of a qualifying entity, and second, when a person gains control of a qualifying asset.[18] These two situations are classed as "trigger events". The Secretary of State can intervene when a trigger event giving rise to a national security risk has happened or when arrangements are in progress or contemplation which will result in such a trigger event taking place.[19] A "qualifying entity" must be an entity either formed or recognised under the UK law or it must carry on activities or supply goods or services in the UK.[20] A "qualifying asset" could be land, tangible moveable property, or ideas, information or techniques which have industrial, commercial, or other economic value.[21] The last category of "ideas, information or techniques" includes trade secrets, databases, source code, algorithms, formulae, designs, plans, drawings, specifications, and software.[22] The concept of "gains control" is defined in the NSI Act as a situation where a person acquires a right or interest in (or in relation to) a qualifying entity, increasing their share percentage (say from less than 75% to more than 75%) or voting rights.[23]

Under the NSI Act, the government begins its scrutiny process by giving a "call-in" notice. The government can call in transactions notified by mandatory notifications, retrospective validation applications, and voluntary applications, or even transactions

---

[13] The Secretary of State here means the Secretary of State for Business and Trade in charge of the Department for Business and Trade in May 2025. A Secretary of State is any senior minister in the UK government. It is the Prime Minister who can decide which Secretary of State has what portfolio and what duties. UK Government, *Secretary of State for Business and Trade*, https://www.gov.uk/government/ministers/secretary-of-state--2.

[14] Cabinet Office, supra note 11.

[15] *Department for Business, Energy & Industrial Strategy* (BEIS), *National Security and Investment: Proposed Legislative Reforms*, Cm 9635 (2018), https://assets.publishing.service.gov.uk/media/5b564807e5274a3fce485918/20180723_-_National_security_and_investment_-_final_version_for_printing__1_.pdf.

[16] *Id.*

[17] *Id.*

[18] NSI Act, *supra* note 5, § 5.

[19] NSI Act, *supra* note 5, § 1.

[20] NSI Act, *supra* note 5, § 7(3).

[21] NSI Act, *supra* note 5, § 7(4).

[22] NSI Act, *supra* note 5, § 7(5).

[23] NSI Act, *supra* note 5, § 17(2)(a).

that were not notified. The Secretary of the State may give a call-in notice for a closer scrutiny when a "notifiable acquisition" acquiring a qualifying entity falling under mandatory notification requirement.[24] A notifiable acquisition cannot take place without the approval of the Secretary of State, or it is void.[25] A person may also give a voluntary notification regarding an acquisition that would result in a trigger event.[26] Retrospective validation in the form of a validation notice is needed for a trigger event that happened between 12 November 2020 and the commencement day (the day the Act came into force).[27] A validation notice by the Secretary of State means that the notifiable acquisition is considered as being completed with the approval of the Secretary of State, i.e., it is not considered void.[28] The Secretary of the State has retrospective power up to 5 years after the commencement day (or 6 months from the day when Secretary of State becomes aware of the trigger event).[29]

After the call-in of an acquisition, the Secretary of the State has to undertake an assessment within a given period. By the end of the assessment period, the Secretary of State must either give a final notification that no further action will be taken, or a "final order".[30] The final order is given in case a trigger event has taken place,[31] and if the Secretary of State is satisfied that a "risk to national security" has arisen[32] and "reasonably considers" that a final order is "necessary and proportionate" for preventing, remedying or mitigating risk. The final order can include a wide range of instructions.[33] It may include conditions requiring a person to observe certain actions or prohibit them from certain activities. It may require the appointment of a person to supervise activities. Or the order may demand non-disclosure of the content of the order (except to the extent the order itself allows disclosure).

As of September 2025, the government has designated 17 sensitive areas as areas requiring "mandatory notifications" under the National Security and Investment Act 2021 (Notifiable Acquisition) (Specification of Qualifying Entities) Regulations 2021.[34] These include areas like AI and advanced materials, previously covered by short-term measures under the Enterprise Act.[35]

---

[24] NSI Act, *supra* note 5, § 14(8)(b)(ii).

[25] NSI Act, *supra* note 5, § 13(1).

[26] NSI Act, *supra* note 5, § 18.

[27] NSI Act, *supra* note 5, § 71.

[28] NSI Act, *supra* note 5, § 15.

[29] NSI Act, *supra* note 5, § 2(2) and 15(2).

[30] NSI Act, *supra* note 5, § 26(1).

[31] Or an arrangement will result in a trigger event.

[32] Or will arise.

[33] NSI Act, *supra* note 5, §26.

[34] UK Statutory Instrument 2021 No. 1264, *The National Security and Investment Act 2021 (Notifiable Acquisition) (Specification of Qualifying Entities) Regulations 2021*, made 10 Nov 2021, commenced 4 Jan 2022, https://www.legislation.gov.uk/uksi/2021/1264/contents/made.

[35] Department for Business, Energy & Industrial Strategy, *Enterprise Act 2002: Guidance on Changes to the Turnover and Share of Supply Tests for Mergers (Orders 2020)*, GOV.UK (21 July 2020), https://www.gov.uk/government/publications/enterprise-act-2002-guidance-on-changes-to-the-turnover-and-share-of-supply-tests-for-mergers-orders-2020.

An interesting feature of the NSI Act is that it does not differentiate between domestic and foreign acquirers by design, i.e., it is country-neutral. Even though the government does mention concern about foreign investment, covering acquisitions by domestic entities makes sense in case of ultimate foreign ownership or control of the domestic entity.

Another notable feature is that the NSI Act does not impose any requirements regarding the publication of government scrutiny before a final order. If a final order is made, then the government has to publish a notice about it being made or about it being varied or revoked. This notice must state the date of the order, the description of the acquirer, target (entity or asset), trigger event, and a summary of the order.[36] Anything that prejudices the commercial interest of any person or is contrary to national security can be exempted from publication. This means that there is limited transparency about the proceedings under the NSI Act.

7.2.2 Cases Under the NSI Act

The government received 1740 notifications between January 2022 and March 2024 and called in 123 business activities.[37] Out of these 123, 72 were either mandatory notifications or retrospective validation applications, 37 were voluntary notifications, and 14 were non-notified acquisitions identified by the government through market monitoring.[38] Between 2022 and 2024, the government published final orders (along with variations or revocations) in 13 cases in 2022, dropping to 4 cases in 2023 before climbing to 15 cases in 2024.[39] Between January and May 2025, final orders were published in 4 cases.[40] Out of these 36 cases with final order notifications, there were 6 cases where a transaction was not approved or where an order imposed the requirements to reverse a transaction. Other cases had their transactions approved subject to conditions like appointing a Chief Information Security Officer approved by the Secretary of State (*Truphone Limited* case)[41] or keeping the target company's

---

[36] NSI Act, *supra* note 5, §26.

[37] Cabinet Office (2024) Report on the National Security and Investment Act 2021 (Notifiable Acquisition) (Specification of Qualifying Entities) Regulations 2021. https://www.gov.uk/government/publications/report-on-the-nsi-act-notifiable-acquisition-regulations/report-on-the-national-security-and-investment-act-2021-notifiable-acquisition-specification-of-qualifying-entities-regulations-2021-html.

[38] *Id.*

[39] *Id.*

[40] *Id.*

[41] Cabinet Office & Department for Business, Energy & Industrial Strategy (2022a) Acquisition of the Assets and Subsidiaries of Truphone Limited by TP Global Operations Limited: Notice of Final Order. https://www.gov.uk/government/publications/acquisition-of-the-assets-and-subsidiaries-of-truphone-limited-by-tp-global-operations-limited-notice-of-final-order/acquisition-of-the-assets-and-subsidiaries-of-truphone-limited-by-tp-global-operations-limited-notice-of-final-order.

research, development, and manufacturing capabilities in relation to atomic clocks in the UK (*CPI TMD Technologies Limited* case).[42]

However, in this article, we will focus our attention on 5 cases involving the prohibition of acquisition by China-linked companies for scrutiny. These cases are the HiLight case, the Nexperia case, Pulsic case, the Beijing Infinite case and the FTDI case. The first four cases are from 2022 while the fifth case is from 2024.

In the **HiLight** case, SiLight (Shanghai) Semiconductor Limited was going to acquire 100% shares in HiLight Research Limited.[43] SiLight, as the name suggests, is a company from mainland China. The government assessed that there was a risk of HiLight's technology being used to build technological capabilities that may pose a national security risk to the UK. So, it prohibited the acquisition.

In the **Nexperia** case, Nexperia BV had increased its share from 14% of the share capital in Newport Wafer Fab to 100% ownership and renamed it Nexperia Newport Limited (NNL). Nexperia BV is a Dutch company owned by Wingtech Technology, a Chinese computer and telecom equipment manufacturer.[44] Wingtech Technology was itself partially owned by the state-owned Assets Supervision and Administration Commission of the State Council (SASAC).[45] This case was also related to semiconductors. The acquisition happened on 5 July 2021. It initially received approval from the UK Business Secretary, but after concerns were raised by various sources, the government began an investigation.[46] The UK government judged that there was a risk that compound semiconductor activities might be reintroduced at the site, considering the site had been associated with this niche but upcoming technology. Another risk was that the acquisition of the site would facilitate access to the South Wales Cluster, a hotbed of semiconductor activity in the UK. The government decided to order Nexperia BV to sell "at least" 86% of shares in Nexperia Newport Limited.[47]

---

[42] Cabinet Office & Department for Business, Energy & Industrial Strategy (2022b) Acquisition of CPI Intermediate Holdings, Inc by Iceman Acquisition Corporation: Notice of Final Order. https://assets.publishing.service.gov.uk/media/6335c6718fa8f506587dd173/acquisition-of-cpi-intermediate-holdings-notice-of-final-order.pdf.

[43] Cabinet Office & Department for Business, Energy & Industrial Strategy (2022c) Acquisition of HiLight Research Limited by SiLight (Shanghai) Semiconductors Limited: Notice of Final Order. https://www.gov.uk/government/publications/acquisition-of-hilight-research-limited-by-silight-shanghai-semiconductors-limited-notice-of-final-order/acquisition-of-hilight-research-limited-by-silight-shanghai-semiconductors-limited-notice-of-final-order.

[44] Nexperia (2022) New Ownership Opens up Opportunities for Nexperia, 8 Feb. https://www.nexperia.com/about/news-events/press-releases/new-ownership-opens-up-opportunities-for-nexperia.

[45] Shead S (2021a) Nexperia Owner Wingtech Is Backed by Chinese Government, Analysis Says. CNBC, 7 July. https://www.cnbc.com/2021/07/07/nexperia-owner-wingtech-is-backed-by-chinese-government-analysis-says.html.

[46] Shead S (2021b) Tech Consortium Prepares Bid to Buy the UK's Biggest Chip Plant Back Off Chinese-Owned Nexperia. CNBC, 29 July. https://www.cnbc.com/2021/07/29/nexperias-newport-wafer-fab-could-be-bought-by-consortium.html.

[47] Cabinet Office & Department for Business, Energy & Industrial Strategy (2022a) Acquisition of Newport Wafer Fab by Nexperia BV: Notice of Final Order, 16 Nov. https://assets.publishing.service.gov.uk/media/6375ef068fa8f5771111bd60/NWF_Final_Order_Public_Notice_16112022.pdf.

In the **Pulsic** case, the acquirer Super Orange HK Holding Limited proposed to acquire the entire share capital of target Pulsic Limited. Super Orange is a Hong Kong company but it is controlled by mainland China-based Shanghai UniVista Industrial Software Group which in turn is backed by the Chinese government's National Integrated Circuit Industry Investment Fund.[48] The UK government considered that Pulsic's IP on EDA and integrated circuits (again related to semiconductors) was dual-use and there was a risk that EDA tools could be used to build defence capability. The acquisition was prevented from proceeding.[49]

The **Beijing Infinite** case is slightly different from others as the potential Chinese investor was going to acquire an asset, and not an entity. Beijing Infinite Vision Technology Company Ltd is a mainland Chinese company that entered into a licencing agreement with the University of Manchester to use intellectual property relating to SCAMP-5 and SCAMP-7 vision sensing technology to manufacture and sell products. However, the technology had dual-use applications, and so, the government prevented the Beijing Infinite company from acquiring the IP rights.[50]

In the **FTDI** case, FTDI Holding Limited (FTDIHL) gained control of Future Technology Devices International Limited (FTDI) by increasing its acquisition from less than 75% to more than 75% (causing a trigger event). FTDIHL is owned by 5 limited partnerships based in China, with Beijing Jianguang Asset Management Co. Ltd being the general partner and which in turn is owned by state-owned China Jiayin Investment Ltd.[51] The Chancellor of the Duchy of Lancaster ordered FTDIHL to sell 80.2% of FTDI due to the risk of semiconductors IP being deployed in "ways that are contrary to UK national security" and FTDI posing a risk to critical national infrastructure.[52]

---

[48] Taipei Times (2022) UK Orders China's Nexperia to Sell Chip Factory, 20 Aug. https://www.taipeitimes.com/News/front/archives/2022/08/20/2003783830.

[49] Cabinet Office & Department for Business, Energy & Industrial Strategy (2022b) Acquisition of Pulsic Ltd by Super Orange HK Holding Ltd: Notice of Final Order, 17 Aug. https://www.gov.uk/government/publications/acquisition-of-pulsic-ltd-by-super-orange-hk-holding-ltd-notice-of-final-order/acquisition-of-pulsic-ltd-by-super-orange-hk-holding-ltd-notice-of-final-order.

[50] Department for Business, Energy & Industrial Strategy (2022) Acquisition of Know-How Related to SCAMP-5 and SCAMP-7 Vision Sensing Technology: Notice of Final Order, 20 July. https://assets.publishing.service.gov.uk/media/62d83b1ae90e071e768aa514/aquisition-scamp5-scamp7-know-how-final-order-notice-20220720.pdf. Rose Fulbright+7.

[51] R. (on the application of Nexperia B.V.) v. Sec'y of State for Bus. & Trade [2025] EWHC (Admin) 241 (Eng.). https://www.bailii.org/ew/cases/EWHC/Admin/2025/241.html.

[52] Cabinet Office (2024) Acquisition of 80.2% of Shares in Future Technology Devices International Limited by FTDI Holding Limited: Notice of Final Order, 6 Nov. https://www.gov.uk/government/publications/acquisition-of-802-of-shares-in-future-technology-devices-international-limited-by-ftdi-holding-limited-notice-of-final-order/acquisition-of-802-of-shares-in-future-technology-devices-international-limited-by-ftdi-holding-limited.

Other than these 5 cases, there is one case linked to Russia.[53] However, this article only focuses on these 5 cases because China has extensive and mostly normal commercial relations with the UK, unlike Russia, which is sanctioned due to the Ukraine war. In fact, the UK received an FDI of GBP 4.2 billion in 2023 from China.[54] Another reason behind choosing these 5 cases is due to the fact that Chinese acquisitions are most frequently called in. In the 2022–23 period, 42% of call-ins of acquisitions were "associated" with China, 32% were domestic ones associated with the UK and 20% were associated with the USA.[55] In 2023–24, the trend continued, with 41% of called-in acquisitions being from China, followed by the UK (22%) and the USA (21%).[56]

This paper will now examine how the NSI Act itself and its implementation, as exemplified through these 5 cases, may interact with the UK's obligations as a host State under the UK-China BIT and the UK-Hong Kong BIT.

7.3 NSI Act v. UK's IIA Regime

7.3.1 Applicability of UK BITs to the Five Cases Under the NSI Act

The first thing to determine is whether these cases fall under the scope of the two BITs the UK has with China and Hong Kong. Both these treaties follow a more traditional BIT model, compared to modern TIPs, as well as allow for investor–state dispute settlement (ISDS). Traditional BITs generally did not grant any pre-establishment rights, a trend that has become more common in modern BITs or TIPs.[57] Instead, an investor was granted protection after he had made an investment.

So, the question arises: whether an investment was made in the 5 cases? This is where the NSI Act presents an interesting and diverse set of examples. In the HiLight

---

[53] As of June 2025. Cabinet Office & Department for Business, Energy & Industrial Strategy (2022) Acquisition of Upp Corporation Ltd by L1T FM Holdings UK Ltd: Notice of Final Order, 19 Dec. https://www.gov.uk/government/publications/acquisition-of-upp-corporation-ltd-by-l1t-fm-holdings-uk-ltd-notice-of-final-order/acquisition-of-upp-corporation-ltd-by-l1t-fm-holdings-uk-ltd-notice-of-final-order.

[54] Department for Business, Energy & Industrial Strategy (2025) Trade and Investment Factsheets: China, 2 May. https://assets.publishing.service.gov.uk/media/6812449bc47c2060a91216dc/china-trade-and-investment-factsheet-2025-05-02.pdf.

[55] UK Cabinet Office (2023) National Security and Investment Act 2021: Annual Report 2022–23, CP 821. https://assets.publishing.service.gov.uk/media/65c21672688c39000d334c12/National_Security_and_Investment_Act_2021_annual_report_2022-23__PDF_.pdf.

[56] UK Cabinet Office (2024) National Security and Investment Act 2021: Annual Report 2023–24, CP 1030. https://assets.publishing.service.gov.uk/media/66fff9a6e84ae1fd8592ee62/National_Security_and_Investment_Act_-_Annual_Report_2023-24.docx.pdf.

[57] Voon and Merriman (2022b, p. 10).

case, the final order notice stated, "*The acquirer did not previously hold any shareholding in HiLight Research Limited*".[58] In Pulsic case, the acquirer, Super Orange HK, "*proposed to acquire the entire share capital of Pulsic Limited*" and the final order prevented "*the acquisition of Pulsic Limited from proceeding*".[59] In Beijing Infinite case also, the order prevented "*the acquisition of the intellectual property from proceeding*".[60] In these 3 cases, no investment was made, but only an attempt at "establishing" investment was made. As Voon and Merriman say for traditional Australian BITs, the "*strongest protections for foreign investment screening in these BITs are exclusion of the pre-establishment stage of an investment*".[61] This appears to be a strong argument if we take a look at how the 3 cases fare under the BITs with China and Hong Kong.

Contrast this to language employed in a modern TIP like the Investment chapter in the UK-Australia FTA, where certain pre-establishment rights are granted under the provisions on Market Access,[62] National Treatment,[63] Most-Favoured-Nation (MFN) Treatment,[64] and Performance Requirements.[65] These provisions lay down obligations on the host State with respect to the "*establishment, acquisition, expansion, management, conduct, operation, and sale or other disposition of investments*".[66]

But, as Wagner (2023a) has stated, the term pre-investment is "*somewhat diffuse and in a legal sense only exists as an antipode to the notion of investment*".[67] What this means is that in certain situations, the pre-investment phase can involve preparatory activities that may constitute an investment even in more traditional BITs. Wagner describes 3 cases: one where contractual obligations or binding commitments exist in the preparatory stage. Second, the prohibited investments may be one part of an ongoing investment. Third, some traditional IIAs may use "*broadly formulated provisions on admission and promotion*".

Now, the first two scenarios depend on the facts of each case. For the three cases here, namely, the HiLight case, the Pulsic case, and the Beijing Infinite case, there is not enough information to determine whether there were any contractual obligations or binding commitments before the acquisition that could qualify as an investment. Nor is there enough information to determine if their attempt at acquisitions was part of an ongoing investment. However, from the UK government's perspective, it may be interesting to also consider activities or transactions related to the prohibited acquisitions. These related activities or transactions may not give rise to national

---

[58] Cabinet Office & Department for Business, Energy & Industrial Strategy (2022a).

[59] Cabinet Office & Department for Business, Energy & Industrial Strategy (2022b).

[60] Department for Business, Energy & Industrial Strategy (2022).

[61] Voon and Merriman (2022b, p. 10).

[62] UK-Australia FTA (2021), art. 13.4.

[63] UK-Australia FTA (2021), art. 13.5.

[64] UK-Australia FTA (2021), art. 13.6.

[65] UK-Australia FTA (2021), art. 13.11.

[66] UK-Australia FTA (2021), arts. 13.4, 13.5, 13.6, 13.11.

[67] Wagner (2023a, p. 127).

security concerns, but they may give rise to the risk of breach of the UK's IIA obligations as a host State. As for the third scenario pointed out by Wagner, both the UK-China BIT and UK-Hong Kong BIT have obligations related to "admission".

UK-China BIT has a provision stating:

> "**Article 2. Promotion and Protection of Investment**
>
> (1) Each Contracting Party shall encourage and create favourable conditions for nationals or companies of the other Contracting Party for investment in its territory and, subject to its right to exercise powers conferred by its laws, shall admit such investment".

This is part of a general European trend towards a controlled entry model where host States are obligated to "encourage" and "create" favourable conditions and also grant the right to admission but subject to the laws of the host State.[68] So, it remains an open question whether the UK encouraged and created favourable conditions for Chinese and Hong Kong investors. Further, the provision does grant a right of admission to Chinese and Hong Kong investments. But this right is subject to the laws of the parties, such as the NSI Act. It is unlikely dispute may arise on this point as there have been challenges to the NSI Act orders where the courts ruled in favour of the UK government and affirmed that these orders were exercised consistent with the UK laws.[69]

The two cases of FTDI and Nexperia offer a more interesting perspective. In both cases, there was a forced disinvestment by the order of the UK government through retrospective investment screening. Moreover, in both cases, even before the acquisition, the investing companies had some shares in FTDI and Nexperia. So, this was a case of investment expansion being reversed.[70] This means that even before the expansion, the Chinese companies qualified as investors and could benefit from the protection granted to investors under the UK-China BIT and UK-Hong Kong BIT. I will analyse how the NSI Act and the UK government's conduct in FTDI and Nexperia cases fare under the obligations related to non-discrimination, expropriation, and fair and equitable treatment.

7.3.2 Non-Discrimination Obligation

Many investment screening mechanisms are designed to screen investments from foreign investors, especially investors from particular countries. Both the UK-China BIT and the UK-Hong Kong BIT have provisions for non-discrimination, namely MFN and National Treatment.[71]

---

[68] Chaisse (2012), p. 56.

[69] R. (L1T FM Holdings UK Ltd & Anor) v. Chancellor of the Duchy of Lancaster [2024] EWHC 2963 (Admin); R. (FTDI Holding Ltd) v. Chancellor of the Duchy of Lancaster [2025] EWHC 241 (Admin).

[70] Wagner (2023a, p. 133).

[71] UK-China BIT (1986), art. 3(1) and 3(2); UK-Hong Kong BIT (1986), art. 4(1).

However, the NSI Act is designed in a way that it is not targeted against one particular country, making a claim of MFN or National Treatment violation unlikely. Additionally, even in its conduct under the NSI Act, the UK has acted with constraint. In Final Orders, the companies targeted come from diverse backgrounds, like the US, Luxembourg, Jersey, and the UAE, and not just China.[72] Similarly, for the National Treatment obligation, in the Annual Reports for NSI Act, after Chinese companies, the UK companies were the most common investors for called-in acquisitions. This design is advantageous for two purposes. First, it makes it hard for a foreign investor to simply set up a company in the UK or an "allied" nation and then undertake investments that would not have been approved in the case of some other nations not allied with the UK. Second, it also makes it hard for an investor to argue for a case of violation of discrimination principles under the IIAs.

As stated in the *Pope & Talbot Inc v Canada* case, "rational government policies" justifying differential treatment must "not distinguish, on their face or de facto, between foreign-owned and domestic companies".[73] The record shows that China, the UK, and the USA are identified as top countries for call-ins and final orders,[74] so it will be hard to argue that the implementation of the NSI is leading to de facto discrimination. Contrast this to the EU or Australia. The EU Foreign Screening Regulation[75] provides a framework focused on "foreign investors" and investments made by Member State investors.[76] Australia's Foreign Investment Policy is also at risk of a claim of National Treatment and MFN violation, as Voon and Merriman highlighted.[77] On its face, this appears as less favourable treatment than the treatment given to similarly situated Member State investors. This makes a claim of violation of the National Treatment principle more likely for the EU and Australia than the UK. The EU and Australia can, of course, argue that foreign investors, such as those from China and Russia, are not "similarly situated". But there is a risk that this reasoning may not be accepted by an ISDS panel. So, the neutral UK design remains a good safeguard against a non-discrimination claim.

[72] UK Cabinet Office (2023), Section Four: Final Orders. https://www.gov.uk/government/publications/national-security-and-investment-act-2021-annual-report-2023/national-security-and-investment-act-2021-annual-report-2022-23-html#section-four-final-orders.

[73] Pope & Talbot Inc. v. Canada, NAFTA Chapter 11 Arb. Trib., Award on the Merits of Phase 2, ¶ 78 (10 Apr. 2001).

[74] UK Cabinet Office (2023), Section Four: Final Orders.

[75] Regulation (EU) 2019/452 of the European Parliament and of the Council of 19 Mar. 2019, 2019 O.J. (L 79I) 1.

[76] Pohl (2020, pp. 725–768).

[77] Foreign Investment Review Board (2021), Australia's Foreign Investment Policy, pp. 8–11; Voon and Merriman (b, p. 15).

7.3.3 Expropriation

Both Nexperia and FTDI cases do not present cases of "direct expropriation" as the government ordered them to sell their shares but did not forcibly take over their shares themselves. Nexperia was bought by Vishay Intertechnology, an American company,[78] while FTDIHL is contesting the Final Order to sell its share in the UK High Court.[79] So, we will focus on whether a case can be made out of indirect expropriation. There is a recognition in the UK-China BIT that expropriation can be allowed for "*a public purpose related to the internal needs of that Contracting Party and against reasonable compensation*".[80]

Provision on expropriation in UK-China BIT covers "*measures having effect equivalent to expropriation or nationalisation*", i.e., indirect expropriation too.[81] However, the question of what counts as indirect expropriation is far from settled. Different arbitration tribunals have applied different criteria to determine whether a measure leads to indirect expropriation. These include the detrimental effect, proportionality, and legitimate public interest. So, if a tribunal applies the criterion of "detrimental effect', also known as the criterion of "injurious effect" or "sole effect doctrine', it asks whether or not a "taking" has occurred.[82] *Tippets v. Iran*, for instance, applied this criterion and stated that the "effects of the measure on the owner of the assets" or "reality of impact" are more important than the government's intention or the form of measures or control.[83] The Final Orders leading to retrospective deprivation of investments in Nexperia and FTDI deprived the Chinese investors of their assets and caused injurious effects to them. So, under this criterion, there is some possibility of a case being made.

Under the proportionality criterion, the question the tribunal would ask is if these measures of forced disinvestment were proportionate. On this front, the LetterOne case investors already filed a case in the UK High Court challenging the proportionality of the Final Order under the NSI Act.[84] The investors claimed that the disinvestment order was disproportionate and breached section 6(1) of the Human

---

[78] Vishay Intertechnology Inc. (2023). Vishay Intertechnology to acquire Nexperia's Newport Wafer Fab for $177 million, 8 Nov. https://www.nexperia.com/about/news-events/press-releases/vishay-intertechnology-to-acquire-nexperias-newport-wafer-fab-for-177-million.

[79] Solicitors Journal (n.d.) FTD Holdings Ltd's challenge against the Chancellor of the Duchy of Lancaster. https://www.solicitorsjournal.com/sjarticle/ftdi-holding-ltds-challenge-against-the-chancellor-of-the-duchy-of-lancaster?category=Court%20Report.

[80] UK-China BIT (1986), art. 5; Kohona (1987), p. 165.

[81] UK-China BIT (1986), art. 5.

[82] Johnson L & Volkov O (2003) Best Practices: Indirect Expropriation. Int'l Inst. for Sustainable Dev., Mar. https://www.iisd.org/system/files/publications/best_practice_indirect_expropriation.pdf.

[83] Johnson and Volkov (2003); Tippetts, Abbett, McCarthy, Stratton v. TAMS-AFFA Consulting Engineers of Iran, Award No. 141-7-2, 6 Iran-U.S. Cl. Trib. Rep. 219, 225–26 (1984).

[84] R. (L1T FM Holdings UK Ltd & Anor) v. Chancellor of the Duchy of Lancaster [2024] EWHC 2963 (Admin).

Rights Act 1998.[85] The court concluded that the public interest of national security prevailed over the private financial interest of the claimant, and that it was not disproportionate for the financial burden of disinvestment to fall on claimant rather than public purse through compensation by the government.[86] While a tribunal may disagree with the approach taken by the court, it is unlikely, given the sensitivities surround national security interest and deference to a state's policy space in cases like *Tecmed v. Mexico* on proportionality.

The third criterion focuses on "police power measures" or "legitimate public regulations". As Voon and Merriman stated, the police powers doctrine will likely "*enable justification of legitimate regulatory measures*".[87] Both the NSI Act and its application in cases involving advanced technologies like semiconductors or quantum technology, or public infrastructure like the telecom sector, present a strong case of legitimate regulatory measures. Further, given that NSI's retrospective powers began from the day after the NSI Bill was introduced in the UK Parliament, observation by Voon and Merriman on Australian investment screening also applies here: "[*A]n investor is unlikely to have reasonable investment-backed expectations that call-in or last resort powers will not be used*".[88]

7.3.4 Fair and Equitable Treatment (FET)

The FET standard offers the broadest and also the most controversial standard of protection in international investment law.[89] It is composed of reasonableness, consistency, non-discrimination, transparency, due process, and legitimate expectations, among other elements.[90] But these elements can pose a challenge for a host State due the inherent nature of investment screening proceedings requiring confidentiality, secrecy, and discrimination. As Wagner (2023b) noted in his commentary on the *Global Telecom v. Canada* case, the FET standard includes the state's obligation to "respect due process rights in administrative and judicial proceedings, to act in a consistent and transparent manner and to protect an investor's legitimate expectations" and that investment screening mechanisms may fall short of the level of transparency required under the FET standard.[91] So, in both Nexperia and FTDI

[85] Human Rights Act 1998, c. 42 (UK).

[86] Herbert Smith Freehills (2024) First Judicial Review Under UK National Security and Investment Act Rejected: Lessons for Future Challenges, 4 Dec. https://www.herbertsmithfreehills.com/notes/crt/2024-posts/first-judicial-review-under-UK-National-Security-and-Investment-Act-rejected--lessons-for-future-challenges.

[87] Voon and Merriman (2022a, p. 96).

[88] Voon and Merriman (2022b, p. 34).

[89] Ryan (2011, p. 925), Burgstaller and Negret (2025, p. 85).

[90] Erdal (2022, p. 38).

[91] Wagner (2023b).

cases, the question is if the government has acted in unfair, inconsistent, discriminatory, non-transparent, or arbitrary manner, or acted against investors legitimate expectations?

On arbitrariness or unfairness, in these cases, or in future cases, there is some risk that an investor can show a case of inconsistent or arbitrary application. After all, in other Final Orders, including some involving Chinese companies, the acquisitions were approved after imposing some conditions on management, maintenance of infrastructure or similar conditions. The Final Order notices have not disclosed the reasoning behind their assessment of national security risk or how they decide what conditions will be imposed. This is echoed in FTDI's statement: "[...] *the UK Government has never explained the basis for its concerns related to national security*".[92] Moreover, the FTDI proposed "*remedies which would have been sufficient to address any [national security] concerns in a proportionate manner*" but the UK government "*did not engage in any dialogue with FTDI on its proposals*".[93]

Similarly, there is a concern regarding transparency in the NSI review process. Due to sensitivities involving national security, the UK government has understandably not followed an open and transparent decision-making process. As Voon and Merriman have rightly pointed out, FET requires transparency in the decision-making process which might often be lacking in "*investment screening processes where the decision-maker is unwilling to disclose the nature or details of the national security concerns precisely because they are (by definition) confidential or classified. Many arbitral tribunals have identified transparency as a component of FET, for example, suggesting that the host State should act 'totally transparently in its relations with the foreign investor*'".[94] This points to a conflict between the obligation of transparency on the host State and the host State's legitimate need for confidentiality regarding its investment screening process, national security concerns, and the kind of data it considers.

On the point of legitimate expectations, it may be hard for investors in newer and more recent cases like the FTDI to argue that they did not expect government intervention in investments by Chinese companies with links to the Chinese government in sensitive sectors like semiconductors. However, with the older acquisitions like the Nexperia case, things may be different. The government may argue that the acquisition happened in July 2021 and at that point, Nexperia must have been aware that the NSI Act had been enacted. Also, the government had been pursuing a stricter policy on the national security front since 2018.[95] But Nexperia can argue

---

[92] FTDI Chip (2024) Recent Press Speculation Regarding Requirement by UK Government to Divest 80.2% Shareholding in FTDI, 11 Nov. https://ftdichip.com/recent-press-speculation/.

[93] *Id.*

[94] Voon and Merriman (2022b, p. 102).

[95] UNCTAD (2018) United Kingdom Strengthens Control Over Mergers in Critical Sectors Due to National Security Considerations, 11 June. https://investmentpolicy.unctad.org/investment-policy-monitor/measures/3247/united-kingdom-the-united-kingdom-strengthens-its-control-over-mergers-in-critical-sectors-due-to-national-security-considerations.

that the UK government had initially approved the transaction and had done a retrospective review after a few voices raised concerns.[96] The tribunal in *Global Telecom v. Canada* took a more lenient view on legitimate expectations and sided with the government, declaring that the investor "*had all the means to know, at the time of making its investment, that the ownership of a Canadian wireless business was subject to foreign investment restrictions*".[97] But, the reversal of a government decision does raise concern about arbitrariness and legitimate expectations an investor may hold.

7.3.5 Minimising the Risk of Investor Claims Due to the NSI Act

The UK government could minimise the risk of an ISDS claim due to the NSI Act through carve-outs, non-precluded measures, or national security exceptions. Voon and Merriman recommended that "explicit exclusions regarding foreign investment policy (with respect to dispute settlement and non-discrimination obligations) provide the clearest protections for foreign investment screening".[98] While the neutral design of the NSI Act minimises the risk with respect to non-discrimination obligations, there is still some risk with respect to FET obligation as well as indirect expropriation claim.

The UK government is already aware of the risk as evident in the Investment chapter in the UK-Australia FTA, where it included the following carve-out[99]:

> "**Annex 13C Foreign Investment Framework**
>
> 2. A decision or requirement by the United Kingdom under the National Security and Investment Act 2021 or on public interest grounds under Part 3 of the Enterprise Act 2002, shall not be subject to dispute settlement under Chapter 30 (Dispute Settlement). [...]"

This can "*remove the potential for challenges to decisions taken pursuant to its domestic legal framework for the screening of foreign investments*".[100] In addition, it contains a carefully drafted National Security Exception applicable to the Investment Chapter.[101] This exception not only allows the UK and Australia to pursue measures that "it considers necessary" for "international peace or security" or "essential security interests", but also to not to be forced to disclose information and maintain transparency with investors in cases of "essential security interests". So, even if the carve-out in Annex 13C had not existed, the UK could resort to the National Security

---

[96] Shead (2021).

[97] Global Telecom Holding S.A.E. v. Canada, ICSID Case No. ARB/16/16, Award, ¶603 (2020). https://www.italaw.com/sites/default/files/case-documents/italaw11434.pdf.

[98] Voon and Merriman (2022a, b, p. 10).

[99] UK-Australia FTA (2022), Annex 13C.

[100] Paine (2022, p. 11).

[101] UK-Australia FTA (2022), art. 31.2.

Exception. While there are not many IIA cases on national security exceptions, the arbitral tribunal is likely to follow a good faith review of this exception.[102]

However, the UK's traditional BITs or its investment chapters in FTAs do not cover such carve-outs. Moreover, unlike some of the modern TIPs, the UK's traditional BITs lack security exceptions. However, there is a possibility that even if a BIT does not have a security exception provision, an arbitral tribunal may consider legitimate public rationales when interpreting and applying investment protection standards.[103] So, even if a case arose from traditional BIT like UK-China BIT, an arbitral tribunal may consider the national security rationale behind the orders under the NSI Act, as happened in *Global Telecom v. Canada* case.[104]

7.4 Key Lessons from the UK's Approach to Investment Screening and IIA

Some of the key takeaways from the analysis are things that the UK has done right in terms of minimising the risk of conflict between its investment screening mechanism and international investment law obligations.

First, in terms of the design of the NSI Act, by making it country-neutral and including both domestic and foreign investors under its ambit, the UK has decreased the risk of violating its National Treatment and MFN obligations under its investment treaty regime. From a security point of view, having a wider scope than the EU's and Australia's investment screening mechanisms also allows it to stop any indirect investment, e.g., through a UK subsidiary of a foreign company, that may raise national security concerns.

Second, its actions under the NSI Act so far also allow little scope for accusations of de facto discrimination. It has issued call-ins as well as final orders for many non-Chinese and even domestic investors too. Also, the area it has targeted so far, e.g., semiconductors or infrastructure, present a strong link to national security concerns.

Third, the model adopted by the UK in the Investment chapter of the UK-Australia FTA adds multiple layers of protection for its investment screening activities, such as through a carve-out and a broad national security exception. The carve-out allows it to protect an action taken under one particular law, while the exception allows it to protect its national security policy space for any future laws or actions it may decide to take.

But, most of the UK's IIA obligations arise from traditional BITs where some risk exists under the FET obligation, particularly from concerns about arbitrariness and lack of transparency, as well as some risk from claims of indirect expropriation in cases of retrospective screening. The UK is exposed to an investor claim under traditional BITs for two reasons. One, the lack of carve-outs and security exceptions

102 Wagner (2023b), Wagner (2024).

103 Wagner (2023b).

104 Global Telecom Holding S.A.E. v. Canada, ICSID Case No. ARB/16/16, Award, ¶616 (2020).

makes the UK government will be more exposed to these claims. Two, the UK is taking action against investment expansion as well as a retrospective review, i.e., at the post-establishment stage. This means that despite the lack of any significant coverage of the pre-establishment stage, the range of investment covered by its investment screening law makes it more exposed to a claim. It should also be noted that the performance or management requirements imposed under the NSI Act Final Orders (and not explored in this article) may potentially add another area of risk for the UK government.

The UK government can still rely on arguments about legitimate public rationale or interest and customary international law defence, but it creates more uncertainty for the UK. However, the UK should ensure that it gives serious consideration to the risk of IIA claims in its investment screening approach as a whole.

But observing past trends, the actual risk for the UK from Chinese investor claims is decreased because of the general aversion of Chinese investors to bringing ISDS claims. Between 2007 and 2024, Chinese nationals only initiated 7 ICSID cases and 4 PCA cases.[105] Also, 5 cases we covered involved areas identified by the UK government as "sensitive areas of the economy" and at least some of the Chinese companies had links to the Chinese government. So, the UK government has used a very broad investment screening law in a constrained manner and with genuine concern, rather than using the law for purely commercial reasons. Given the constrained and genuine approach of the UK government and the limited chance for success, one can question whether the Chinese investors will shed off their usual aversion and bring a case against the UK government.

In conclusion, the UK must form a long-term approach towards reconciling its IIA regime with its national security concerns, particularly in light of China's increasing status as a capital-exporting country. While the risk of a claim due to investment screening may not be high, there is some risk. The lessons from *Global Telecom v. Canada* and any ruling that happens in *Huawei Technologies Co. v. Sweden*[106] will need to be taken into account.

The UK's approach in the UK-Australia FTA provides a model not just for the UK's future approach to international investment law, but also for other countries that have or want to adopt investment screening mechanisms, while also committing to and promoting investment protection. But the UK and its allies must assess whether their traditional IIA approach complements their priorities on national security issues, especially in a world where more and more economic issues are coming under the purview of national security[107] and as economic security gets intertwined with national security.[108]

China and its investors, on the other hand, need to reconsider what their newfound role as a capital-exporting country means in terms of international investment law. Do they wish to make full use of investment law protection they are entitled to,

---

[105] Boza and Plaza (2024).

[106] Huawei Technologies Co., Ltd. v. Kingdom of Sweden, ICSID Case No. ARB/22/2; Pohl (2023).

[107] Something that has already happened at a large scale in international trade law. Bacchus (2022).

[108] Slawotsky (2024), Slawotsky (2021).

or would they rather avoid disputes, as they have done so far? If they wish to enjoy investment protection, especially when investing in areas where they face uncertainty about government intervention, they need to plan their investments with the network of investment treaties in mind.

Overall, the world of international investment law is likely to see interesting developments in next few years from the rise of China as a capital exporter, due to expansion of national security concept to include greater economic issues and because of the derisking efforts of the Western nations.

References

Bacchus J (2022) The black hole of national security: striking the right balance for the national security exception in international trade. Cato Institute, Policy Analysis No. 936. https://www.cato.org/policy-analysis/black-hole-national-security. Accessed 29 Sept 2025

Boza RT, Plaza DC (2024) Chinese participation in the investor-state dispute settlement system. ITA in Rev 6:23. https://itainreview.org/articles/2024/vol6/issue1/chinese-participation-in-the-investor-state-dispute.html. Accessed 29 Sept 2025

Burgstaller M, Negret A (2025) Investment protection standards: Can EU law fill the shoes of investment treaties? Arbitration International 41:85–85

Chaisse J (2012) Promises and pitfalls of the European Union policy on foreign investment—how will the new EU competence on FDI affect the emerging global regime? J Int Econ Law 15:51–68

Erdal ÖB (2022) Investment screening mechanism and its interplay with investment treaty obligations. Master's Thesis, Uppsala University. https://www.diva-portal.org/smash/get/diva2:1664756/FULLTEXT01.pdf. Accessed 29 Sept 2025

Ford S (2023) The new Cold War with China and Russia: same as the old Cold War? Case W Res J Int Law 55:423–460. https://scholarlycommons.law.case.edu/jil/vol55/iss1/16. Accessed 29 Sept 2025

Gáspár-Szilágyi S (2024) When the dragon comes home to roost: Chinese investments in the EU, national security, and investor–state arbitration. J Int Disp Settlement 15:195–220. https://doi.org/10.1093/jnlids/idad028

Johnson L, Volkov O (2003) Best practices: indirect expropriation. International Institute for Sustainable Development. https://www.iisd.org/system/files/publications/best_practice_indirect_expropriation.pdf. Accessed 29 Sept 2025

Kohona PTB (1987) Some major provisions in modern investment protection agreements. Third World Legal Studies 6:151–165

McCalman P, et al. (2023) Inward foreign investment screening targets China: interdisciplinary perspectives. Cambridge Int Law J 12:82–105. https://doi.org/10.4337/cilj.2023.01.06

Paine J (2022) An analysis of the UK–Australia FTA's investment chapter. Bristol Law Research Paper Series No. 003/2022. https://www.bristol.ac.uk/media-library/sites/law/research/An%20Analysis%20of%20the%20UK%E2%80%93Australia%20FTA%E2%80%99s%20Investment%20Chapter.pdf. Accessed 29 Sept 2025

Pohl JH (2020) The impact of investment treaty commitments on the design and operation of EU investment screening mechanisms. In: YSEC Yearbook of Socio-Economic Constitutions 2020. Springer, pp 725–768

Pohl JH (2023) The impact of investment treaty commitments on the design and operation of EU investment screening mechanisms. SSRN. https://papers.ssrn.com/sol3/papers.cfm?abstract_id=4341368. Accessed 29 Sept 2025

Ryan MC (2011) Glamis Gold, Ltd. v. United States and the fair and equitable treatment standard. McGill Law J 56:919–945

Schild J (2025) Towards a geopoliticization of investment policy? Investment screening in the European Union. Jean Monnet Working Papers No. 2/2025. https://www.researchgate.net/publication/389810925. Accessed 29 Sept 2025

Shead S (2021a) Nexperia owner Wingtech is backed by Chinese government, analysis says. CNBC, 7 July 2021. https://www.cnbc.com/2021/07/07/nexperia-owner-wingtech-is-backed-by-chinese-government-analysis-says.html. Accessed 26 Feb 2026

Shead S (2021b) Tech consortium prepares bid to buy the UK's biggest chip plant back off Chinese-owned Nexperia. CNBC, 29 July 2021. https://www.cnbc.com/2021/07/29/nexperias-newport-wafer-fab-could-be-bought-by-consortium.html. Accessed 26 Feb 2026

Slawotsky J (2021) The fusion of ideology, technology and economic power: implications of the emerging new United States national security conceptualization. Chi J Int Law 20:3–30

Slawotsky J (2024) Conceptualizing national security in an era of great power rivalry: implications for international economic law. East Asia 41. https://doi.org/10.1007/s12140-024-09434-y

UK–Australia FTA (2021) Agreement in Principle between the Government of the United Kingdom of Great Britain and Northern Ireland and the Government of Australia for a Free Trade Agreement. UK Department for International Trade. https://www.gov.uk/government/publications/uk-australia-free-trade-agreement-agreement-in-principle.. Accessed 26 Feb 2026

UK–Australia FTA (2022) Free Trade Agreement between the United Kingdom of Great Britain and Northern Ireland and Australia. UK Department for International Trade. https://www.gov.uk/government/publications/uk-australia-free-trade-agreement. Accessed 26 Feb 2026

UK–China BIT (1986) Agreement between the Government of the United Kingdom of Great Britain and Northern Ireland and the Government of the People's Republic of China for the Promotion and Reciprocal Protection of Investments. UK Treaty Series. https://www.legislation.gov.uk/uksi/1988/1949/made. Accessed 26 Feb 2026

UK–Hong Kong BIT (1986) Agreement between the Government of the United Kingdom of Great Britain and Northern Ireland and the Government of Hong Kong for the Promotion and Protection of Investments. UK Treaty Series. . Acceshttps://www.legislation.gov.uk/uksi/1991/1790/madesed 26 Feb 2026

Vishay Intertechnology Inc. (2023) Vishay Intertechnology to acquire Nexperia's Newport Wafer Fab for $177 million. https://www.nexperia.com/about/news-events/press-releases/vishay-intertechnology-to-acquire-nexperias-newport-wafer-fab-for-177-million. Accessed 29 Sept 2025

Voon T, Merriman D (2022) Incoming: how international investment law constrains foreign investment screening. J World Invest Trade 24:75–104. https://doi.org/10.1163/22119000-12340253

Voon T, Merriman D (2022) Is Australia's foreign investment screening policy consistent with international investment law? Melb J Int Law 23:1–25

Wagner K (2023a) Determining the role of FDI screening in international investment law. In: Sattorova M (ed) Weaponising investments, vol 2. Springer, pp 127–145

Wagner K (2023b) Global Telecom Holding S.A.E. v. Canada – investment arbitration as a potential remedy against negative FDI screening decisions? CELIS Blog, 23 Oct 2023. https://www.celis.institute/celis-blog/global-telecom-holding-s-a-e-v-canada-investment-arbitration-as-a-potential-remedy-against-negative-fdi-screening-decisions/. Accessed 29 Sept 2025

Wagner K (2024) Angel Samuel Seda and others v. Colombia: new pathways in the application of security exceptions? Kluwer Arbitration Blog, 7 Oct 2024. https://arbitrationblog.kluwerarbitration.com/2024/10/07/angel-samuel-seda-and-others-v-colombia-new-pathways-in-the-application-of-security-exceptions/. Accessed 29 Sept 2025

Chapter 8
Does the Frequent Invocation of the National Security Exception Render WTO Disciplines Meaningless? Exploring Viable Options Under the Current WTO Dispute Settlement Mechanism

Tomohiko Kobayashi

Abstract This article asks whether frequent invocation of the national security exception—especially by the United States—renders WTO disciplines meaningless amid Appellate Body paralysis. Despite U.S.' insistence that GATT Article XXI is wholly self-judging and its use of "appeals into the void," the article argues WTO disciplines retain normative significance: panel proceedings continue to function, unadopted reports carry persuasive weight, and alternative dispute-resolution mechanisms remain available. It concludes that safeguarding the WTO's effectiveness requires drawing upon the full range of existing procedures rather than excluding security matters from all forms of discipline.

Keywords National security exception · Appellate Body paralysis · Self-judging · Alternative dispute resolution (ADR) · Appeal into the void · Economic security

8.1 Introduction: Background of the Problem

Digital economy is reshaping the society as well as the international flows of trade and investment.[1] The rapid development of artificial intelligence (AI) is expected to enable a substantial reduction in production costs for goods and services, thereby stimulating international trade and investment. On the other hand, AI may also exert

[1] Chaisse et al. (2025, p. 1). See also chapters written by Rolf H. Weber, Heng Wang, Hiroshi Kataoka, Nguyen Xuan My Hien and Trang Anh Mac in this book.

T. Kobayashi (✉)
Otaru University of Commerce, Otaru, Japan
e-mail: tkobayashi@res.otaru-uc.ac.jp

J. Nakagawa et al. (eds.), *Geopolitical Risks and Geoeconomics in International Economic Law*, Economics, Law, and Institutions in Asia Pacific,
https://doi.org/10.1007/978-981-95-6996-0_8

a profound impact in various respects—not only in technology and engineering, but also across multiple domains of international law. These include the risks of copyright and human rights violations, the environmental harm associated with rising electricity consumption, and the exacerbation of the digital divide.[2] As emphasized in the preface by World Trade Organization (WTO)'s Director-General Ngozi Okonjo-Iweala, a carefully designed policy mix encompassing trade, investment and related sectors is essential.[3]

In addition, it is well established that there has been a consistent trend toward the proliferation of regional trade agreements (RTAs)—including free trade agreements (FTAs), economic partnership agreements (EPAs), and issue-specific international arrangements. Yet, the question of how to structure their relationship with the WTO in a mutually complementary manner remains unresolved. While regional agreements such as the Trans-Pacific Partnership (TPP) and its successor, the Comprehensive and Progressive Agreement for Trans-Pacific Partnership (CPTPP), have introduced more detailed and higher-standard rules than those found in the WTO, they cannot replace the WTO's function as a common institutional foundation. Accordingly, the relationship between the WTO and RTAs remains fundamentally complementary.

Although numerous challenges have emerged from advances in science and technology and the expansion of new sectors, the evolution of existing legal frameworks—particularly multilateral regimes such as the WTO—appears to be significantly lagging behind. Nevertheless, if trade disputes were to arise from these emerging issues, the WTO Agreements and the dispute settlement mechanism established thereunder would likely provide the most comprehensive framework for addressing them, especially when compared to RTAs, which may contain broader substantive rules but have far more limited membership.

However, along with these new trends, the WTO is facing a crisis on multiple fronts. Since its establishment in 1995, phenomena such as the expansion of digital trade and the increasing complexity of global value chains have emerged, yet the content and scope of its rules have not been meaningfully updated or improved. The failure of the so-called Doha Round negotiations (Doha Development Agenda) symbolized this stagnation. Because decision-making at the WTO is, in principle, based on consensus, the expansion of membership to over 160 countries and the rise of powers such as the coalition of Brazil, Russia, India, China, and South Africa (BRICS) have made it increasingly difficult to respond flexibly to diverse and sometimes conflicting interests. That said, simply shifting to majority voting is not a straightforward solution, and no viable breakthrough has yet been identified.

Another challenge is that the WTO dispute settlement system—once a cornerstone in ensuring compliance—has been constrained since the end of 2019, when the Appellate Body ceased functioning. The United States has been particularly critical, contending that the Appellate Body has overstepped its mandate in interpreting and

[2] WTO Secretariat (2025, p. 14ff). See also chapters written by Jianfu Chen, Sungjin Kang, James Cooper, Francisco Hernández Fernández and Adrien Schifano in this book.

[3] WTO Secretariat (2025, p. 7). See also chapters written by Teerawat Wongkaew, Satomi Shintani, Soo-hyun Lee and Intan Innayatun Soeparna in this book.

applying the agreements. Since 2016, the United States has persistently blocked consensus decisions needed for the appointment of Appellate Body members.[4]

Against this backdrop, recent years have seen growing attention to a new development: the increasing recourse to the national security exception when adopting trade-restrictive measures.[5] This trend is not limited to the United States. With the diversification of national security concepts, the invocation of the exception is becoming an attractive option for other WTO members as well. Yet, because the provision's text appears to permit, at least in part, subjective or self-judging determinations, and because it covers a wide range of potential measures, excessive reliance by a major power such as the United States risks creating a gaping loophole. Such developments could ultimately undermine the constraining force of WTO rules.

This paper focuses on one of the pressing challenges facing the dispute settlement system: the concern that frequent U.S. reliance on the national security exception may erode the system's functioning. It examines the extent to which the mechanisms currently available under WTO agreements can provide a response. Section 8.2 surveys recent WTO disputes in which the national security exception has been invoked, with particular emphasis on the United States' position. Section 8.3 then considers what options remain available under the existing WTO dispute settlement framework—most notably the Understanding on Rules and Procedures Governing the Settlement of Disputes (Dispute Settlement Understanding: DSU)—given both the reliance on the security exception and the Appellate Body's paralysis. Section 8.4 offers some concluding observations.

8.2 The United States' Position on the Invocation of the Security Exception in WTO Dispute Settlement

8.2.1 Previous Interpretations of the Security Exception in WTO Disputes

A comprehensive analysis of the position of the security exception within WTO agreements and recent trends in its invocation is addressed elsewhere in this volume. This paper focuses specifically on the stance taken by the United States. The reason is that U.S. attitudes toward the invocation of the security exception are closely linked to its broader concerns about the WTO dispute settlement system itself—concerns that predate the first Trump administration.

It is, of course, not only the United States that has invoked the security exception. The first WTO dispute in which Article XXI of the GATT was formally invoked

---

[4] *Dispute Settlement Body—Minutes of meeting—Held in the Centre William Rappard on 23 June 2025*, WT/DSB/M503 (15 July 2025), para. 4.3.

[5] See chapters written by Mari Shimizu, Apoorva Vishnoi, Shota Watanabe and Alexandros Bakos in this book.

was the *Russia—Measures Concerning Traffic in Transit* case (DS512), in which the panel report was circulated in April 2019.[6] This panel report was not appealed and thus became final upon adoption by the Dispute Settlement Body (DSB). This marked the first interpretation and application of GATT Article XXI by a WTO panel. The second was the *Saudi Arabia—Measures Concerning the Protection of Intellectual Property Rights* case (DS567), in which the panel report was circulated in June 2020.[7] Although Saudi Arabia noticed its intention to appeal, the two countries subsequently agreed to suspend and terminate the dispute in a manner satisfactory to both sides.[8]

Subsequently, during the first Trump administration, the United States imposed additional tariffs under Section 232 of the Trade Expansion Act on imports of steel, aluminum, and derivative products. The rationale was that a high dependence on foreign products in these sectors created vulnerabilities for U.S. national security. When China and other WTO members challenged these measures before the WTO, the United States invoked GATT Article XXI, arguing that the provision was entirely "self-judging" and thus not subject to review by panels or the Appellate Body.

In December 2022, however, a panel report circulated to WTO members rejected this sweeping claim. While acknowledging that the evaluation of national security necessity was largely self-judging, the panel held that questions such as whether the measures fell within the situations listed under Article XXI(b)(i)–(iii) were subject to review by a panel or the Appellate Body.[9] The United States filed a notice of appeal, but because of the paralysis of the Appellate Body, the case remains in limbo.

A similar issue arose when the United States imposed origin marking requirements on products from Hong Kong, requiring them to be labeled as "Made in China" on the grounds that Hong Kong's autonomy had been eroded under pressure from China. When Hong Kong challenged this measure before the WTO, the United States again invoked Article XXI as wholly self-judging. A separate panel report circulated in December 2022 rejected this claim, albeit with slightly different reasoning.[10] As with the earlier report, the case has been suspended due to a U.S. appeal into the void.

8.2.2 The United States' Stance

The disputes involving Russia and Saudi Arabia arose from measures taken under extremely serious circumstances, such as armed conflict over territory and the

---

[6] Panel Report, *Russia – Measures Concerning Traffic in Transit*, WT/DS512/R, adopted 26 April 2019.

[7] Panel Report, *Saudi Arabia – Measures Concerning the Protection of Intellectual Property Rights*, WT/DS567/R, circulated to WTO Members on 16 June 2020, then terminated by mutual consent.

[8] *Saudi Arabia—Measures concerning the Protection of Intellectual Property Rights—Communication from Qatar*, WT/DS567/11 (25 April 2022), p. 1.

[9] Panel Report, *United States—Certain Measures on Steel and Aluminium Products*, WT/DS544/R, para. 7.128.

[10] Panel Report, *United States—Origin Marking Requirement*, WT/DS597/R, paras. 7. 160 & 7.185.

severance of diplomatic relations. By contrast, the recent U.S. invocations have been made in the name of economic security. Under both the Republican Trump administration and the Democratic Biden administration, measures such as additional tariffs have been justified on grounds that trade deficits, deterioration of the balance of payments, and the weakening of domestic manufacturing capacity due to international competition all raise national security concerns.

What is particularly distinctive about the U.S. position is its insistence that GATT Article XXI is wholly self-judging and therefore not amenable to judicial review. For example, with respect to Hong Kong's complaint in DS597, the United States repeatedly criticized the very act of bringing the case to the WTO, continuing this line of argument at meetings of the DSB into early 2025.[11] Notably, there has been little divergence between the Trump and Biden administrations in this regard. While panel reports have already been issued in disputes concerning measures imposed during the first Trump administration, additional tariffs imposed during the second Trump administration have also been challenged by China, Canada, and Brazil.[12] These disputes remain ongoing, but it is expected that the United States will continue to rely on the security exception.[13]

Thus, the United States has not only paralyzed the Appellate Body by blocking consensus on the appointment of its members but also appears committed to broad reliance on the national security exception. Taken together, these actions risk undermining the WTO dispute settlement mechanism both substantively and procedurally.

That said, the national security exception and the use of the "appeal into the void" tactic are not panaceas. First, the security exception constitutes an affirmative defense invoked to justify violations of other provisions, such as GATT Articles I, II, III, V, and XI. A respondent state cannot invoke the national security exception at the outset of a dispute to evade the entire WTO dispute settlement mechanism. It must follow the procedures established in the DSU, whether under Article 4, Article 5, or through panel proceedings, and present its case before invoking the exception clauses.

Secondly, once a panel report is circulated to WTO Members, it may possess normative weight even if it is not adopted by the DSB. This does not mean it has precedential value, since even adopted panel reports do not create binding precedent. Nevertheless, an appeal cannot nullify the entire panel process, including the persuasiveness of the parties' arguments and the analytical clarity of the panel's reasoning.

Curiously, the United States does not deny the value of the WTO dispute settlement system as such. Nor does it openly endorse unilateral measures absent DSB authorization, which presupposes adoption of panel or Appellate Body reports. Indeed,

[11] See the US statements in WT/DSB/M477, M478, M482, M483, M484, M486, M487, M491, M497, M499, M500.

[12] For details, see WTO disputes DS633, DS634, DS635, DS637, DS638, and DS640.

[13] See *United States—Additional Tariff Measures on Goods from China—Communication from the United States*, WT/DS633/3 (18 March 2025), pp. 1–2; *United States—Tariff Measures on Goods from Brazil—Communication from the United States*, (18 August 2025), p. 1.

the United States has criticized other WTO members when they resorted to unilateral countermeasures outside of the WTO framework.[14] Nevertheless, Washington's tendency to prioritize short-term and immediate victories raises serious concerns.

Given that amending the DSU is not a realistic option at present, the question becomes: what responses remain feasible under the current system? Sect. 8.3 explores the options available within the existing WTO dispute settlement framework.

8.3 Institutional Options for Response

8.3.1 Exploring New Mechanisms

Two types of initiatives have emerged in response to the current crisis facing the WTO dispute settlement system.

First, following the paralysis of the Appellate Body in December 2019, a group of like-minded members established the Multi-Party Interim Appeal Arbitration Arrangement (MPIA) in April 2020. Although formally based on arbitration under Article 25 of the DSU, the MPIA enables parties to a dispute to agree in advance that a party dissatisfied with a panel report may appeal to arbitration. The arbitrators are selected from a pool of ten individuals nominated by participating members, with half of the roster renewed in early 2025.

As an emergency response to the immediate loss of the Appellate Body, the MPIA played a significant role. By August 2025, nearly one-third of WTO members had joined, and the mechanism has provided a functional substitute for appellate review among those members. In the case *Turkey—Certain Measures concerning the Production, Importation and Marketing of Pharmaceutical Products* (DS583), even non-participating members have agreed to follow procedures modeled on the MPIA, effectively extending its reach. Nonetheless, the United States has shown no indication that it would accept appellate proceedings under this framework. Moreover, because the legal basis for the MPIA lies in the parties' prior consent to arbitration, panel reports appealed under the MPIA do not require adoption by the DSB through the negative consensus rule.

Second, informal negotiations have been pursued regarding DSU reform as part of broader efforts to reform WTO dispute settlement. Beginning in January 2019—just prior to the Appellate Body's paralysis—informal meetings chaired by Ambassador Walker of New Zealand were convened. These did not result in agreement on concrete measures. After the Appellate Body's suspension and the disruptions caused by the COVID-19 pandemic, informal negotiations resumed in February 2024 under the facilitation of Minister Molina of Guatemala.

---

[14] Hanna Monicken, "U.S. accuses China of 'specious' use of WTO dispute settlement against Canada," *Inside US Trade* (27 June 2025), 2025 WLNR 15,914,740, p. 26.

As an interim outcome, draft text led by Mr Molina was submitted to the DSB in February 2024.[15] The draft did not directly address restoration of the Appellate Body, leaving that as a future issue. Instead, it proposed clarifying and promoting the use of alternative dispute-resolution (ADR) mechanisms already provided for in the DSU, as well as introducing improvements and clarifications to panel proceedings. These proposals reflected a pragmatic, incremental approach to strengthening the system. However, following Minister Molina's removal from office for domestic political reasons, progress has stalled, and it cannot be said that negotiations are moving smoothly at present.[16]

8.3.2 Feasibility Within the Existing Framework

Given these circumstances, what responses are possible under the current DSU, assuming that the Appellate Body remains non-functional?

First, it is important not to overlook the fact that panel proceedings remain operational and are actively used. Under the DSU, if neither party appeals a panel report, the report is adopted by the DSB through negative consensus and thus becomes final. While during the DSU's drafting, appeals were expected to be rare, in practice roughly two-thirds of panel reports after the WTO's establishment were appealed, leading to an emphasis on the Appellate Body's role. Nonetheless, if a panel report is adopted by the DSB without appeal, the Appellate Body's paralysis is immaterial. Indeed, even after the Appellate Body ceased functioning, there have been numerous cases in which panel reports were adopted without appeal, including: *Costa Rica—Measures Concerning the Importation of Fresh Avocados from Mexico* (DS524), *European Union—Certain Measures Concerning Palm Oil and Oil Palm Crop-Based Biofuels* (DS593), *European Union and Certain Member States—Certain Measures Concerning Palm Oil and Oil Palm Crop-Based Biofuels* (DS600), *China—Anti-Dumping Measures on Stainless Steel Products from Japan* (DS601), and *Australia—Anti-Dumping and Countervailing Duty Measures on Certain Products from China* (DS603).

Of particular interest is *United States—Safeguard Measure on Imports of Large Residential Washers* (DS546), brought by Korea against the United States. In February 2022, the panel report rejected many of the United States' key arguments and found violations in its measures, including in relation to the interpretation of GATT Article XIX and Article 3.1 of the Safeguards Agreement. Given that the dispute concerned a major traded product (one also subject to additional tariffs since August 2025 on "derivatives" of steel and aluminum under Section 232 of the Trade Expansion Act), both governments continued bilateral consultations. Ultimately, the DSB adopted the panel report in April 2023. At the meeting, the United States, while

[15] *Consolidated Text Referred to in Mr. Molina's Report*, JOB/GC/385 (16 February 2024), Annex 1.

[16] Monicken (2025, p. 25).

criticizing several aspects of the report's reasoning, nevertheless accepted adoption "on balance."[17] This demonstrates that panel proceedings continue to play an important role even in disputes involving the United States.

Another illustrative example is Brazil's recent recourse to WTO procedures. In August 2025, Brazil requested consultations with the United States (DS640) after Washington announced additional tariffs in response to the Brazilian Supreme Court's prosecution of a former president.[18] Although Brazil simultaneously pursued bilateral negotiations and domestic countermeasures, it also turned to the WTO system, reflecting continued confidence in the dispute settlement mechanism.

Second, the increasing use of ADR, highlighted in the Molina draft shown in Sect. 8.3.1, is also noteworthy. From the outset, ADR was envisaged as complementing the quasi-judicial functions of panels and the Appellate Body. Article XXIII of the GATT 1947 already allowed disputes to be raised regardless of whether a violation had occurred. The DSU subsequently provided for arbitration under Article 25 and for good offices, conciliation, and mediation under Article 5. This is consistent with the DSU's objective of promoting amicable dispute resolution rather than strict judicialization. Article 3.7 of the DSU states:

> "Before bringing a case, a Member shall exercise its judgment as to whether action under these procedures would be fruitful. The aim of the dispute settlement mechanism is to secure a positive solution to a dispute. A solution mutually acceptable to the parties to a dispute and consistent with the covered agreements is clearly to be preferred."

Although the precise meaning of a "positive solution" remains ambiguous in WTO jurisprudence, the emphasis on practical outcomes is evident. In recent years, there have been cases where, even after an appeal, the DSB chair or other facilitators assisted in adjusting the parties' interests, thereby contributing to dispute resolution in practice, albeit not formally under DSU Article 5.

Admittedly, further discussion is required on how ADR could be applied in highly sensitive disputes involving vital national interests, such as those concerning the security exception. That said, even the United States has, in certain disputes involving national security, encouraged the use of ADR rather than panel proceedings.[19] This suggests that options under the DSU remain available for addressing disputes concerning the interpretation and application of the security exception (including whether such disputes should be adjudicated at all). This may likewise be the case in addressing emerging issues such as AI, cross-border subsidies, and

[17] *Dispute Settlement Body—Minutes of meeting—Held in the Centre William Rappard on 28 April 2023—Chairman: H.E. Mr Petter Ølberg (Norway)*, WT/DSB/M/478 (16 June 2023), para. 3.7.

[18] *United States—Tariff Measures on Goods from Brazil—Request for consultations by Brazil*, WT/DS640/1 (11 August 2025), p. 1.

[19] "The parties may consider engaging in good offices, conciliation, or mediation pursuant to DSU Article 5." See *United States—Certain Measures on Steel and Aluminium Products—Notification of an appeal by the United States under article 16 of the Understanding on Rules and Procedures governing the Settlement of Disputes (DSU)*, WT/DS552/16 (30 January 2023), p. 1; *United States—Certain Measures on Steel and Aluminium Products—Notification of an appeal by the United States under article 16 of the Understanding on Rules and Procedures Governing the Settlement of Disputes (DSU)*, WT/DS556/21 (30 January 2023), p. 1.

e-commerce, which await the establishment of multilateral rules within the WTO framework. Alongside efforts to clarify and refine existing rules, greater use of these mechanisms should be considered.

8.4 Conclusion

The foregoing analysis suggests that, at least for the time being, the normative significance of WTO rules has not yet been lost. To be sure, as discussed earlier, the concept of "national security" has become increasingly diverse and complex, and considerable uncertainty remains regarding how existing provisions should be interpreted. As emphasized from the outset of this paper, the U.S.' tendency to prioritize its own short-term interests continues to generate serious concern. Nevertheless, it cannot be said that other WTO members are following the U.S. approach of treating any measure as permissible simply by labeling it a matter of national security.

At the same time, attempts to clarify the interpretation of national security exceptions—whether judicially or legislatively—raise concerns from the standpoint of compliance. When a state adopts a trade-restrictive measure on grounds of national security, it may prove politically difficult to withdraw that measure even if a panel or the Appellate Body determines that it violates WTO rules and cannot be justified under such exception. Moreover, it is doubtful whether compliance could realistically be secured through countermeasures taken by the complainant.

Does this mean, as the United States has argued, that security exceptions must be treated as entirely beyond the scope of dispute settlement? Historical precedent offers useful context. For example, the League of Nations' 1927 Convention on the Abolition of Import and Export Prohibitions and Restrictions allowed measures to safeguard "vital interests" under "extraordinary and abnormal circumstances" (Article 5) and explicitly excluded such measures from dispute settlement procedures.[20] More recently, certain regional trade agreements and investment treaties also exclude disputes concerning national security exceptions from adjudication.

Yet, it must not be overlooked that WTO dispute settlement is not confined to quasi-judicial proceedings before panels and the Appellate Body. In today's world, where security has become a multifaceted concept implicating many countries, it may at times be more appropriate to resort to alternative dispute-resolution mechanisms. The crucial question, therefore, is whether security issues should be categorically excluded from all disciplines, or whether, even if they are not subject to judicial review, they might still be addressed through other forms of WTO dispute settlement. This multifaceted challenge requires analysis from an equally multidimensional perspective.

---

[20] The text of the treaty is available in the archive referenced below. https://archives.ungeneva.org/convention-pour-labolition-des-prohibitions-et-restrictions-a-limportation-et-a-lexportation-signature-et-ratification-par-lempire-britanique.

Ultimately, ensuring the effectiveness of WTO disciplines requires an inclusive and comprehensive approach that draws upon the full range of available procedures: panels and the Appellate Body, Trade Policy Reviews (TPRs), the raising of Specific Trade Concerns (STCs), negotiations, and ADR. There is no doubt that the WTO is in crisis. If WTO members continue to cling to quasi-judicial dispute settlement procedures while neglecting the ADR mechanisms embedded in the existing WTO rules, interest in the WTO dispute settlement system is likely to decline further, with attention shifting toward its counterparts under RTAs. Moreover, some members might even become interested in relying on AI-based arbitral mechanisms rather than the WTO's own institutional bodies.

Precisely for this reason, in order to maintain the trust of a wide range of stakeholders—including not only member governments but also businesses and civil society—it is essential to continue reform efforts, including of the dispute settlement mechanism, in the spirit of "like a rolling stone."[21]

References

Chaisse J, Dimitropoulos G, Mosquera I (2025) Law and Digital Transformation in the Indo-Pacific, Journal of World Investment and Trade 26: 575-620.

Kobayashi T, Fukunaga Y (2020) Like a Rolling Stone: Exploring Viable Options for the WTO Dispute Settlement Mechanism to Evolve Forward in the Post-WTO Era. In Lewis M K, Nakagawa J, Neuwirth R J, Picker C B, Stoll P-T (eds), A Post-WTO International Legal Order: Utopian, Dystopian and Other Scenarios, Springer International Publishing, pp. 133-147.

Monicken H (2025) U.S. accuses China of 'specious' use of WTO dispute settlement against Canada. Inside US Trade (27 June 2025), 2025 WLNR 15914740, p. 26.

WTO Secretariat, World Trade Report 2025: Making Trade and AI Work Together to the Benefit of All (2025), p. 14ff.

[21] Kobayashi and Fukunaga (2020, p. 147).

Chapter 9
Beyond Investment Protection: A Theory of Political Risk Governance in International Investment Law

Teerawat Wongkaew

Abstract International Investment Law (IIL) confronts unprecedented challenges from climate transition policies, geoeconomic competition, and digital governance. These evolving risks transcend the regime's traditional focus on discrete acts of host state misconduct. This article proposes a reconceptualisation of IIL's fundamental purpose: the regime should be understood not merely as a mechanism for investor protection, but as a comprehensive system for the governance and allocation of political risk between host states and foreign investors. Drawing upon theories of political risk, risk governance, and efficient risk allocation, this article develops a comprehensive analytical framework that reinterprets core treaty obligations—fair and equitable treatment, expropriation, and full protection and security—as dynamic instruments of risk allocation. The framework advances a structured four-step methodology for arbitral decision-making, critically engages with competing approaches in the literature (particularly proportionality-based and legitimate expectations frameworks). The utility of the proposed framework is demonstrated through its application to the Spanish renewable energy cases and the Argentine financial crisis jurisprudence. By articulating and operationalizing the inherent risk allocation function within treaty interpretation, this approach offers a principled pathway towards greater consistency, transparency, and legitimacy in international investment arbitration, with concrete implications for the ongoing UNCITRAL Working Group III reform process.

Keywords Political risk governance · Risk allocation · Legitimate expectations · Knightian uncertainty · Four-step analytical methodology · Systemic and external risks

---

T. Wongkaew (✉)
Ministry of Foreign Affairs of Thailand, Bangkok, Thailand
e-mail: teerawat.w@mfa.go.th

J. Nakagawa et al. (eds.), *Geopolitical Risks and Geoeconomics in International Economic Law*, Economics, Law, and Institutions in Asia Pacific,
https://doi.org/10.1007/978-981-95-6996-0_9

9.1 Introduction: International Investment Law in a Fragmented World—In Search of a Principled Justification

9.1.1 Setting the Scene: A Changing Risk Landscape and a Contested Regime

Since its inception, International Investment Law (IIL) has been pervasively understood as a regime for the protection of foreign investors against the misconduct of the host state. Despite this recognition, the global investment landscape confronts unprecedented complexity. The foundational assumptions of the international investment protection regime are being challenged by contemporary political risks that extend far beyond traditional concerns such as direct expropriation. These modern risks encompass a vast array of state measures, including those related to climate transition,[1] pandemic responses, weaponisation of economic interdependence, digital governance, and geopolitical tensions between major powers.[2]

It is pertinent to recall the acute consequences of these developments. The Russia–Ukraine conflict, for instance, triggered sweeping unilateral sanctions and asset seizures, which demonstrated clearly how geopolitical conflict can rapidly erase investment value. Similarly, the strategic competition between the United States and China has given rise to national security-driven industrial policies, such as the U.S. CHIPS Act, which put strategy before market logic.[3] A wave of ambitious climate regulation, from the European Union's Carbon Border Adjustment Mechanism (CBAM) to national laws mandating the phase-out of fossil fuels, has created profound transition risks for investors.[4]

In the absence of a coherent rationale for how to address these new realities, tribunals have developed jurisprudence in a conflicting and unstructured manner. While modern treaties often contain general exceptions, arbitral tribunals have struggled to apply them consistently to multi-faceted risks that blur the lines between legitimate regulation and compensable state interference. This has led to significant jurisprudential inconsistency, as seen in the divergent outcomes of the Spanish solar saga, where different tribunals arrived at opposing conclusions on similar sets of facts.[5]

Such uncertainty, coupled with a perceived pro-investor bias, has fuelled a powerful backlash from states. The result is a fragmented and contested regime, marked by nations terminating their investment treaties and key states withdrawing

---

[1] Zhang and Li (2024, pp. 1471–1489), Segger and Gleason (2025, pp. 1–18).

[2] Farrell and Newman (2019, pp. 42–79), Dimitropoulos et al. (2025, paras 15–28).

[3] De la Rasilla and Cai (2024, pp. 245–267), Blackwill and Harris (2016, pp. 89–112).

[4] Brewin et al. (2021, pp. 15–32), Cotula (2023, pp. 766–789).

[5] See Eiser Infrastructure Ltd v. Spain, ICSID Case No. ARB/13/36, Award (4 May 2017), paras 362–389; Charanne BV v. Spain, SCC Case No. 062/2012, Award (21 January 2016), paras 483–517.

from multilateral instruments like the Energy Charter Treaty.[6] This institutional turmoil underscores the urgent need for a new conceptual approach for navigating the risks of a multipolar and fragmented world.

9.1.2 *The Argument: Reframing IIL as Political Risk Governance*

This article aims to develop a theory for IIL from the perspective of political risk governance. It argues that the fundamental purpose of the regime is not merely to protect investors, but to systematically allocate and manage political risks between host states and foreign investors. In other words, the core function of treaty obligations such as fair and equitable treatment, expropriation, and full protection and security can be better understood as risk allocation mechanisms.

To substantiate this claim, the article addresses a series of interrelated questions. It begins by asking: *How does recognising IIL's function as political risk governance clarify the regime's core purpose and improve treaty interpretation in an era of complex regulatory and geopolitical risks?* To answer this question, the inquiry proceeds through four subsidiary questions: (1) why are the prevailing theoretical foundations of IIL inadequate for addressing contemporary risks? (2) to what extent do core substantive obligations function as legal instruments for allocating political risks and the ISDS mechanism as a risk governance institution? (3) how does treaty drafting and arbitral jurisprudence provide evidence for this function? and (4) what are the normative and policy implications of explicitly recognising this function for the future of the regime?

The methodology employed to address these questions is multi-faceted. The article first constructs a theoretical framework drawing on three distinct bodies of scholarship. Specifically, it draws upon Frank Knight's foundational distinction between risk and uncertainty, Ortwin Renn's comprehensive theory of risk governance, and Ronald Coase's insights into efficient risk allocation. This political risk governance framework is then applied through a doctrinal and textual analysis of legal sources, reinterpreting core substantive obligations not as static rules but as dynamic instruments of risk allocation. To ground these theoretical claims empirically, the analysis turns to a close reading of key arbitral awards and trends in treaty practice, bridging the gap between the abstract framework and its real-world application.

This article's primary contribution is the development of a systematic and coherent theoretical framework to explain the core function of risk allocation in IIL. While tribunals may implicitly engage in risk allocation, it is often done on an ad hoc basis without a unifying theory.[7] This article addresses that gap by moving the concept from an implicit practice to an explicit, principled framework. Specifically, the article makes three contributions. First, it provides a *diagnostic* contribution by

---

[6] Monti and Fermeglia (2024, pp. 189–215), Tienhaara (2011, pp. 606–627).

[7] Bonnitcha et al. (2017, pp. 50–78), Howse (2019, pp. 363–389).

demonstrating that much of the inconsistency in investment jurisprudence can be explained by tribunals' implicit and unarticulated disagreements about risk allocation. Second, it offers a *prescriptive* contribution by developing a structured four-step methodology that tribunals can employ to make risk allocation decisions transparent and principled. Third, it provides a *design* contribution by demonstrating how risk governance thinking can inform treaty drafting and institutional reform. The article also provides a revised typology of modern political risks—including regulatory, geopolitical, and climate-related risks—that is currently lacking in IIL scholarship.[8] In doing so, it seeks to provide a more balanced and predictable basis for navigating future investment disputes and aligning the IIL regime with broader public policy goals.

Following this introduction, Sect. 9.2 critically examines why prevailing theoretical foundations of IIL prove inadequate for addressing contemporary multidimensional risks, engaging particularly with economic liberal theory, institutionalist approaches, and existing scholarship on legitimate expectations. Building upon this critique, Sect. 9.3 develops the political risk governance framework, establishing its theoretical foundations in Knight's risk-uncertainty distinction, Renn's risk governance theory, and Coasean analysis, while proposing a systematic risk categorisation. Section 9.4 demonstrates how both substantive treaty obligations and the ISDS system function as risk allocation mechanisms, presenting the four-step analytical methodology. The framework is then applied in Sect. 9.5, which provides empirical evidence through systematic analysis of the Spanish renewable energy cases and the Argentine financial crisis jurisprudence, culminating in application to climate-related investment disputes. Section 9.6 addresses potential challenges and critiques of the theory, including concerns about indeterminacy, democratic legitimacy, and institutional capacity. Finally, Sect. 9.7 concludes by examining the normative and policy implications of the framework for treaty design, arbitral practice, and ISDS reform, with particular attention to the ongoing UNCITRAL Working Group III process.

9.2 The Inadequacy of Prevailing Theoretical Foundations: A Critique

This section provides a critical analysis of three prevailing theoretical approaches to IIL, exposing their fundamental weaknesses in the face of contemporary challenges.[9] The first, grounded in economic liberalism, proves obsolete as its assumption of discrete political risks cannot account for today's systemic and interconnected challenges. The second, drawing from institutionalism, offers a focus on procedural legitimacy and institutional efficiency, yet fails to resolve the fundamental substantive conflicts that procedural improvements alone cannot address. The third approach

---

[8] Robock (1980, pp. 6–20), Kobrin (1979, pp. 67–80).

[9] Sornarajah (2015, pp. 112–145), Bonnitcha (2014, pp. 56–89).

engages with traditional political risk theory, demonstrating how international relations scholarship reveals the categorical obsolescence of Cold War-era risk frameworks. The inadequacy of these frameworks reveals a significant theoretical gap, necessitating a new approach capable of addressing today's multidimensional and rapidly evolving risks.

9.2.1 Economic Liberal Theory and Its Limits

The dominant conception of international investment law, articulated by scholars such as Rudolf Dolzer and Christoph Schreuer, Kenneth Vandevelde, and Jeswald Salacuse, understands the regime primarily as facilitating capital flows through credible protection commitments.[10] On this view, investment treaties solve a time-inconsistency problem: states wish to attract foreign investment but face incentives to act opportunistically once investments are sunk. Treaties provide credible commitments by enabling investors to enforce protection standards through international arbitration, thereby reducing political risk and encouraging investment.[11]

This framework captures something important about the regime's historical origins and its function in certain contexts. However, it proves inadequate for contemporary challenges in three respects. First, economic liberal theory assumes that political risks are discrete, identifiable events—expropriation, breach of contract, and discriminatory treatment—that can be managed through legal commitments.[12] Contemporary risks are fundamentally different in character: they are systemic, interconnected, and arise from legitimate policy responses to global challenges rather than from opportunistic state misconduct.[13] When a state phases out fossil fuels in response to climate commitments, this is not the kind of discrete 'political risk' that the theory contemplates.[14]

Second, economic liberal theory operates with a binary framework that distinguishes legitimate regulation (no compensation) from illegitimate interference (full compensation). This binary cannot accommodate the 'grey zone' where most contemporary disputes arise.[15] Climate transition measures, pandemic responses, and digital governance regulations typically pursue legitimate objectives through means that may nonetheless impose significant costs on investors.[16] The question is not whether these measures are 'legitimate' but how their costs should be distributed—a question the binary framework cannot answer.[17]

---

[10] Dolzer and Schreuer (2012, pp. 1–25), Vandevelde (2010, pp. 23–67), Salacuse (2015, pp. 56–89).

[11] Moehlecke and Wellhausen (2021, pp. 515–548), Rubins et al. (2020, pp. 45–78).

[12] Robock (1980, pp. 6–20).

[13] Sarvarian (2023, pp. 422–448), Wortmann (2024, pp. 742–768).

[14] Kobrin (1979, pp. 67–80), Wells and Ahmed (2007, pp. 11–45).

[15] Zhang and Li (2024, pp. 1471–1489).

[16] Johnson and Sachs (2012, pp. 23–45), UNCTAD (2014, pp. 10–25). Ortino (2021, pp. 287-291).

[17] Krajewski (2016, pp. 23–45).

Third, economic liberal theory's focus on investor protection overlooks the interests of host states and affected communities.[18] The theory assumes that maximising investment protection maximises welfare, but this assumption is increasingly contested. The empirical literature on whether investment treaties actually increase FDI flows is inconclusive, while the costs of the regime—in terms of regulatory chill, fiscal exposure, and constraints on policy space—have become increasingly apparent.[19]

9.2.2 Institutionalist Approaches and Their Substantive Gaps

Institutionalist approaches have made significant contributions to understanding IIL's governance dimensions. Global Administrative Law (GAL) theorists have illuminated how investment arbitration functions as a form of global governance, emphasising procedural legitimacy, transparency, and accountability in arbitral decision-making.[20] Legal institutionalists have shown how ISDS operates not merely as an adjudicative mechanism but as a norm-generating institution that shapes state and investor behaviour through its interpretive function.[21] Institutionalist scholarship reveals how tribunals create de facto precedent despite the formal absence of stare decisis. New Institutional Economists have contributed insights into how treaty frameworks reduce transaction costs and enhance credible commitment, explaining why states enter into agreements that constrain their future regulatory freedom.[22]

These contributions are valuable but incomplete. GAL's procedural focus—emphasising due process, reasoned decisions, and participatory rights—cannot resolve fundamental substantive disagreements about who should bear the costs of regulatory change.[23] A procedurally perfect award may still rest on contestable assumptions about risk allocation. Legal institutionalism describes how tribunals generate norms but offers no principled basis for determining what those norms *should* be. The observation that ISDS functions as a governance institution does not answer the question of how that institution should govern. New Institutional Economics explains why states commit to investment protection but not where the boundaries of that protection should lie.

The institutionalist tradition, in short, improves the *process* of investment governance but provides no *substantive principles* for the allocation decisions that tribunals

---

18 Mearsheimer (2014, pp. 34-78), Brands (2022, pp. 112–156).

19 Luttwak (1990, pp. 17–23), Farrell and Newman (2019, pp. 42–79).

20 Kingsbury, Krisch, and Stewart (2005, pp. 15–61). GAL scholars have analysed investment arbitration as a site of global administrative governance subject to principles of transparency, participation, and reasoned decision-making.

21 Roberts (2010, pp. 179–225), Pauwelyn and Elsig (2013, pp. 445–473). See also Commission (2007, pp. 129–158), Kaufmann-Kohler (2007, pp. 357–378).

22 North (1990, pp. 34–89), Williamson (2000, pp. 595–613).

23 Van Harten (2007, pp. 78–112), Schneiderman (2008, pp. 78–112).

must make. When a tribunal must decide whether an investor should bear the costs of climate transition policy or whether the state should compensate for regulatory change, institutionalist frameworks offer procedural guidance but no substantive criteria.[24] This gap leaves tribunals to make consequential allocation decisions without explicit normative foundations.

9.2.3 Traditional Political Risk Theory's Categorical Obsolescence

Traditional scholarship on political risk employs outdated categories that cannot capture the complex risks of the contemporary era.[25] Classic typologies distinguishing between macro and micro risks, direct and indirect risks, or host state and home state risks were developed during the Cold War and assume state-centric political systems with clear sovereign decision-making.[26] These frameworks served their purpose when the primary threats to foreign investment were nationalisation, expropriation, and currency inconvertibility—discrete acts by identifiable host state actors.

International relations scholarship illuminates why these categories have become obsolete. The shift from unipolarity to multipolarity has transformed the investment landscape, with great power competition creating new categories of risk that transcend traditional frameworks.[27] Economic instruments increasingly serve geopolitical objectives—'geoeconomics' or the 'weaponisation of economic interdependence'.[28] States now deploy investment screening mechanisms, export controls, technology transfer restrictions, and targeted sanctions as tools of strategic competition. Investment risks therefore originate not only from host states but from home states and third countries, fundamentally challenging frameworks premised on bilateral host state/investor relationships.

Contemporary political risks challenge traditional categories. Climate risks arise from global scientific realities and international governance frameworks—the Paris Agreement, COP decisions, and transnational regulatory networks—that cannot be attributed to any single state's decision-making.[29] Digital governance presents similar challenges, with data localisation requirements, AI regulations, and cybersecurity

---

[24] Johnson and Sachs (2018, pp. 8–15).

[25] Robock (1980, pp. 6–20).

[26] Kobrin (1979, pp. 67–80); Wells and Ahmed (2007, pp. 11–45). See also Moran (1998, pp. 1–24); Minor (1994, pp. 1–24).

[27] Mearsheimer (2014, pp. 34–78), Brands (2022, pp. 112–156).

[28] Farrell and Newman (2019, pp. 42–79), Luttwak (1990, pp. 17–23). See also Blackwill and Harris (2016, pp. 89–134), Roberts et al. (2019, pp. 655–684).

[29] Zhang and Li (2024, pp. 1471–1489).

measures responding to technologies and business models that did not exist when traditional risk frameworks were created.[30]

Geopolitical competition has evolved beyond traditional classifications. When investment risks stem from multilateral sanctions regimes or strategic economic competition between major powers, a theory focused narrowly on host state actions proves inadequate. The Russia–Ukraine conflict vividly demonstrates this limitation: investors face risks arising from EU and US sanctions, Russian counter-measures, asset freezes, and the broader geopolitical realignment of global supply chains—none of which fit neatly into traditional political risk categories that assume a bilateral relationship between investor and host state.[31]

9.2.4 The Theoretical Gap: The Need for a Risk Governance Approach

These theoretical inadequacies leave a fundamental gap between the available analytical frameworks and the complex realities of contemporary international investment. Economic liberal theory protects investors but ignores regulatory nuance. Institutionalist approaches improve procedures but offer no substantive principles for allocation decisions.[32] Traditional political risk theory, as international relations scholarship reveals, relies on categorical frameworks that cannot accommodate risks originating from multiple state actors, transnational governance regimes, and geoeconomic competition.

The consequences of this gap are serious. Arbitral tribunals decide cases inconsistently because they lack a systematic methodology for balancing legitimate regulatory change against legitimate investment expectations. States cannot predict which measures might trigger disputes, producing regulatory chill that constrains necessary policymaking.[33] Investors, in turn, cannot distinguish between risks they must manage themselves and those the treaty renders compensable. This uncertainty undermines both investment protection and regulatory effectiveness. This theoretical inadequacy necessitates a new framework that addresses multidimensional, interconnected, and rapidly evolving risks. Risk governance theory provides this foundation.

[30] Krajewski (2016, pp. 23–45), Burri (2017, pp. 1–28).

[31] de la Rasilla and Cai (2024, pp. 245–289), Hindelang and Moberg (2022, pp. 1–34).

[32] Roberts (2017, pp. 137–178).

[33] Tienhaara (2011, pp. 606–627).

9.3 The Conceptual Foundations of Political Risk Governance

This section develops the political risk governance framework, which is proposed to provide a more coherent conceptualisation of IIL's core function. Political risk governance is defined herein as the systematic identification, assessment, and allocation of uncertainties arising from the exercise of political authority that may affect an investment.[34] The framework conceives of treaty provisions as dynamic legal instruments that delineate the boundaries between compensable and non-compensable risks.[35] The framework draws on three distinct bodies of scholarship on political risk: Frank Knight's foundational distinction between risk and uncertainty, Ortwin Renn's comprehensive theory of risk governance, and Ronald Coase's insights into efficient risk allocation.

9.3.1 Risk, Uncertainty, and the Limits of Probabilistic Reasoning

Frank Knight's distinction between 'risk' and 'uncertainty' provides the conceptual foundation for understanding what investment treaties can and cannot accomplish.[36] For Knight, 'risk' refers to situations where outcomes are unknown but can be assigned meaningful probabilities based on experience or calculation. 'Uncertainty', by contrast, refers to situations where probabilities cannot be meaningfully assigned—where we face, in Knight's phrase, outcomes that are 'not susceptible to measurement'.[37] This distinction has profound implications for investment treaty design and interpretation.

Traditional political risks—expropriation, discriminatory taxation, and breach of contract—can often be treated as 'risks' in Knight's sense.[38] Insurance markets and historical experience provide bases for assigning probabilities and pricing these risks commercially.[39] Investment treaties can be understood as mechanisms for shifting such risks from investors to states, with the shift justified by states' superior ability to control their own conduct.[40] This risk-shifting function explains the historical development of the investment protection regime.

---

[34] Renn (2008, pp. 8–45), Renn and Klinke (2005, pp. 749–774).

[35] Moehlecke and Wellhausen (2021, pp. 515–548).

[36] Knight (1921, pp. 19–20, 197–232).

[37] Knight (1921, p 233). Knight argued that uncertainty, unlike risk, cannot be reduced to actuarial calculation because it involves genuinely unique situations.

[38] Robock (1980, pp. 6–20). Traditional political risks were amenable to probabilistic assessment based on historical patterns.

[39] Wells and Ahmed (2007, pp. 11–45), Kobrin (1979, pp. 67–80).

[40] Salacuse (2015, pp. 56–89).

Contemporary political risks, however, increasingly fall into the category of Knightian 'uncertainty'. It may be difficult to assign probabilities to the risk of climate-driven regulatory change, the weaponisation of economic interdependence, and pandemic response measures because they involve genuinely novel situations where past experience provides limited guidance.[41] The proliferation of 'unknown unknowns' in the contemporary investment environment means that treaties cannot simply allocate pre-identified risks but must establish frameworks for managing uncertainties whose character is not fully known at the time of drafting.

This insight has important implications for treaty interpretation. When tribunals assess 'legitimate expectations', they are not asking whether investors correctly predicted specific regulatory changes but whether they appropriately accounted for the *uncertainty* inherent in the regulatory environment.[42] An investor in a highly regulated sector cannot claim surprise at regulatory change as such, even if the specific form of change was unpredictable. The baseline for assessing expectations must account for the difference between foreseeable categories of risk and unforeseeable specific events.

9.3.2 Risk Governance as a Framework for Managing Uncertainty

Ortwin Renn's work on risk governance provides the operational framework for applying Knight's insights to investment law. Renn defines risk governance as 'the totality of actors, rules, conventions, processes, and mechanisms concerned with how relevant risk information is collected, analysed and communicated, and how regulatory decisions are taken'.[43] This definition emphasises that risk governance involves normative choices about how risks should be identified, assessed, and allocated across society.[44] By applying this lens to IIL, the framework views investment treaties and arbitral tribunals not merely as instruments of investor protection, but as key elements of a governance regime for managing political risk and uncertainty.

Renn distinguishes between four categories of risk, each requiring different governance approaches: (1) 'simple' risks with reliable probability estimates and established management approaches; (2) 'complex' risks involving causal chains that are difficult to trace; (3) 'uncertain' risks where scientific knowledge is incomplete or contested; and (4) 'ambiguous' risks where the interpretation of risks—their meaning, significance, and appropriate response—is itself contested.[45]

---

41 Zhang and Li (2024, pp. 1471–1489).

42 Bonnitcha (2014, pp. 156–189).

43 Renn (2008, pp. 8–45). Renn's comprehensive framework addresses both technical and normative dimensions of risk governance.

44 Renn and Klinke (2005, pp. 749–774).

45 Renn (2008, pp. 52–78), Renn and Klinke (2005, pp. 749–774).

Contemporary political risks in international investment increasingly fall into the 'uncertain' and 'ambiguous' categories.[46] Climate transition risks are 'uncertain' because we lack reliable models for predicting the pace and character of regulatory change. They are 'ambiguous' because their meaning is contested: are they properly understood as regulatory risks inherent in carbon-intensive investment, or as expropriatory measures requiring compensation?[47] The risk governance framework requires that tribunals explicitly identify which category of risk they are addressing and apply appropriate analytical tools for that category.

9.3.3 Coasean Insights into Efficient Risk Allocation

Ronald Coase's foundational work provides the economic basis for the risk governance framework.[48] His central insight, known as *the Coase Theorem*, is that if transaction costs were zero, the initial assignment of legal rights would not affect the final, efficient allocation of resources, as parties would simply bargain their way to the best outcome. However, the crucial corollary for the real world is that because transaction costs *do* exist, initial allocations of rights matter significantly for efficiency.[49]

Applying Coasean analysis to investment treaties suggests that risks should be allocated to the party best able to bear them—the 'least-cost risk bearer'.[50] This principle forms a normative foundation for allocation decisions. Generally, states are the least-cost bearers of risks arising from their own arbitrary or discriminatory conduct, as they control that conduct. Conversely, investors are typically best suited to bear general regulatory risks because they can diversify their investments and incorporate regulatory uncertainty into their decisions.[51]

This analysis highlights a key difficulty with climate-related risks: neither states nor investors are clearly the 'least-cost risk bearers'.[52] Investors cannot diversify away the risk of a global energy transition, which affects all carbon-intensive assets. Similarly, states cannot unilaterally avoid transition costs driven by international commitments and global necessities. Therefore, the Coasean framework suggests these risks may require innovative allocation mechanisms—such as burden-sharing

---

[46] Renn (2008, pp. 73–98), Renn and Klinke (2005, pp. 749–774).

[47] On the application of risk governance frameworks to climate policy, see Renn and Klinke (2013, pp. 1–24), Walker et al. (2014, pp. 728–738).

[48] Coase (1960, pp. 1–44).

[49] On the application of Coasean analysis to risk allocation in contract law, see Posner and Rosenfield (1977, pp. 83–118), Kronman (1978, pp. 1–32).

[50] The 'least-cost risk bearer' principle has been developed in the law and economics literature by Calabresi (1970, pp. 135–173), and applied to insurance and contract law by Priest (1981, pp. 1045–1090).

[51] On the application of Coasean principles to international investment law, see Bonnitcha (2014, pp. 89–134), Sykes (2005, pp. 539–570).

[52] Robock (1980, p. 7), Kobrin (1979, pp. 67–69).

arrangements, transition periods, or compensation schemes—rather than simple allocation to one party.

9.3.4 *Defining Political Risk in a Contemporary Context*

Building on these theoretical foundations, political risk is defined as the real or perceived threat that the exercise of political authority will adversely affect the value, security, or operational viability of foreign investment.[53] This definition encompasses both objective aspects—measurable events like expropriation—and subjective dimensions, including investor perceptions, expectations, and the interpretive contexts through which risks are understood.[54]

Crucially, political risk is not just about what states do, but also how that conduct is interpreted. This interpretation is influenced by the investor's sophistication, the specific industry (sectoral context), and the timing between the investment decision and the regulatory change.[55]

For example, a regulatory change might be 'unexpected' to an inexperienced investor but entirely foreseeable to a sophisticated actor familiar with the sector's dynamics. This nuanced understanding allows for a better risk allocation analysis than simple, binary approaches that only distinguish between 'legitimate regulation' and 'compensable interference.

9.3.5 *A Systematic Risk Categorisation Framework*

The political risk governance framework requires a more expansive and nuanced typology of risks that reflects the contemporary investment landscape.[56] A coherent categorisation based on the source and nature of the risk provides greater analytical clarity. This framework organises risks into three main categories: state-centric risks, systemic and external risks, and system-generated risks.

State-centric risks encompass risks that emanate directly from the host state's exercise of political authority.[57] *Classic sovereign risks* include the foundational risks that IIL was created to address: direct, indirect, or creeping expropriation; breaches of governmental contractual commitments; and denial of justice through failure to provide fair judicial remedies.[58] *Modern regulatory risks* constitute an expanding

---

[53] Beck (1992, pp. 21-56) (1986, Wellhausen (2015, pp. 34–67).

[54] Salacuse (2015, pp. 56–89), Schill (2009, pp. 25–67). Investment treaties function as instruments for stabilising expectations and governing conduct.

[55] Beck (1992, 21-56) (1986,

[56] Robock (1980, pp. 6–20), Kobrin (1979, pp. 67–80).

[57] Borchard (1933, pp. 51–64), Dolzer and Schreuer (2012, pp. 89–134).

[58] Newcombe and Paradell (2009, pp. 201–245), Salacuse (2021, pp. 178–223).

category encompassing unexpected changes in laws and policies that adversely affect investments.[59] These range from good-faith environmental and public health measures to sudden tax reforms, emergency crisis responses, and novel governance challenges including climate transition measures, digital economy regulations, and ESG-related mandates.[60]

Systemic and external risks arise from the broader political and economic environment, often extending beyond the host state's direct control.[61] Geopolitical and geoeconomic risks have moved to the forefront of investor concerns, including risks from international conflicts, economic sanctions, and strategic decoupling between major powers.[62] Socio-political instability presents a distinct risk category, with threats originating from civil unrest, public protests, or organised opposition to investment projects.[63]

System-generated risks are created by the IIL regime itself.[64] Regulatory chill occurs when fear of costly ISDS claims deters states from enacting necessary public interest regulations.[65] Inconsistent jurisprudence creates uncertainty about how obligations will be interpreted.[66] These risks are particularly troubling because they undermine the regime's legitimacy and effectiveness—states are mitigating risks created by the very framework designed to manage other risks.[67]

9.4 The Architecture of Risk Governance: Treaty Obligations and Analytical Methodology

This section analyses the functional architecture of the political risk governance framework, focusing on its two principal components: substantive treaty obligations and the ISDS system. It argues that core treaty obligations, such as fair and equitable treatment, are not static protection rules but are the primary legal instruments for allocating political and regulatory risks. The analysis will then examine the ISDS system as the central institution of risk governance. Finally, the section will present the four-step analytical methodology that operationalises the framework.

---

59 Alvarez (2011, pp. 223–264), Johnson and Sachs (2012, pp. 23–45).

60 Zhang and Li (2024, pp. 1471–1489), Krajewski (2016, pp. 23–45). Hodgson et al. (2025, 45-78).

61 Caldara and Iacoviello (2022, pp. 1194-1225).

62 See Ukrnafta v. Russia, PCA Case No. 2015-34, Award on Jurisdiction (4 June 2020); Stabil LLC v. Russia, PCA Case No. 2015-35.

63 Johnson and Coleman (2016, pp. 8–15).

64 Tienhaara (2011, pp. 606-627), Vadi (2015, pp. 1285–1332).

65 Tienhaara (2011, pp. 611–627).

66 Roberts (2017, pp. 137–178).

67 Van Harten (2007, pp. 78–134), Sornarajah (2015, pp. 323–367).

9.4.1 *Substantive Treaty Obligations as Risk Allocation Instruments*

Substantive treaty obligations function as instruments for allocating political risks between host states and investors.[68] The adoption of this framework reframes the manner in which tribunals resolve disputes. Rather than asking simply whether the conduct of the state constitutes a breach of a treaty rule, a tribunal must instead determine where the treaty requires the burden of a specific risk to lie: is this a political risk the treaty allocates to the state, making it compensable, or is it a regulatory or commercial risk that the investor was expected to manage?[69] This functional approach shifts the analysis from a formal determination of breach to a principled allocation of risk, thereby aligning treaty interpretation with the core governance function of international investment law.

9.4.1.1 The Fair and Equitable Treatment (FET) Standard as a Risk Allocation Filter

The FET standard, specifically its core component, the doctrine of legitimate expectations, functions as the primary tool for distinguishing between compensable, state-allocated risks and non-compensable, investor-assumed risks.[70] State-allocated risks typically include arbitrary conduct, denial of due process, and radical, non-transparent regulatory changes. Conversely, risks assumed by the investor encompass general, good-faith regulatory evolution.[71]

The doctrine of legitimate expectations applies this distinction by analysing foreseeability.[72] Tribunals assess whether a prudent investor should have anticipated the regulatory change given the sector's regulatory history, the host state's development level, and any specific state assurances.[73] Radical or arbitrary changes that defy reasonable expectations constitute state-allocated risks. Evolutionary, proportionate regulatory changes in the public interest constitute investor-assumed risks. This framework mediates the tension between regulatory stability and policy adaptation.

---

[68] Dolzer and Schreuer (2012, pp. 89–134), Newcombe and Paradell (2009, pp. 321–378).

[69] See Philip Morris Brands Sàrl v. Uruguay, ICSID Case No. ARB/10/7, Award (8 July 2016), paras 287–305; Methanex Corp. v. United States, UNCITRAL, Final Award (3 August 2005), Part IV, Chapter D, paras 7–15.

[70] Bonnitcha (2014, pp. 234–267), Howse (2019, pp. 363–389).

[71] Newcombe and Paradell (2009, pp. 337–367).

[72] See Azurix Corp. v. Argentina, ICSID Case No. ARB/01/12, Award (14 July 2006), paras 408–410.

[73] Salacuse (2021, pp. 312–345).

9.4.1.2 Expropriation as an Economic Risk Allocation Mechanism

Expropriation provisions serve to allocate the risk of severe economic loss from state measures.[74] The 'police powers' doctrine is the central analytical tool for determining who bears the economic cost of public policy.[75] If a state's measure constitutes a compensable taking, the state bears the cost through compensation. If the measure represents a legitimate exercise of police powers, the investor is deemed to have borne the cost as a foreseeable business risk. Such an analysis requires a rigorous assessment of the measure's purpose, its proportionality, and its economic impact on the investment.

9.4.1.3 Full Protection and Security (FPS) and Other Standards

The FPS standard is a risk allocation mechanism focused on institutional and systemic failure.[76] The evolution of this standard to encompass legal security means that states now bear the risk of a breakdown in the rule of law. States bear the risk of their own negligence or systemic collapse, while investors bear the risk of unforeseeable third-party acts beyond the reasonable control of the state.[77] Non-discrimination obligations are designed to allocate the risk of politically motivated economic harm.

Umbrella clauses shift the risk of domestic institutional failure from the investor to the state. They achieve this by elevating breaches of government contracts to the level of treaty violations, thus protecting investors against opportunistic state conduct or the risk of inadequate domestic remedies.[78]

9.4.2 The Investor-State Dispute Settlement (ISDS) System as a Risk Governance Institution

The ISDS system is the central institution for managing—and sometimes creating—political risk.[79] It functions as a decentralised norm-generating system where landmark awards clarify how future risks will be allocated. This gives ISDS a prospective governing role, clarifying the rules of risk allocation rather than just resolving past disputes.[80]

---

[74] Salacuse (2021, pp. 281–311).

[75] Dolzer and Schreuer (2012, pp. 178–201).

[76] Schreuer (2004, pp. 231–256), Reinisch (2004, pp. 1–15).

[77] Reinisch (2004, pp. 5–12), Gazzini T and Tanzi A (2013, pp. 978-994).

[78] Dolzer and Schreuer (2012, pp. 166–177), Schreuer (2004, pp. 245–256).

[79] Roberts (2017, pp. 137–178), Titi (2015, pp. 205–230).

[80] Schill (2009, pp. 25–67), Roberts (2017, pp. 137–178).

The broadly worded standards in investment treaties grant tribunals substantial interpretive discretion.[81] Arbitrators act as normative gatekeepers, using principles like reasonableness and proportionality to distinguish between compensable and non-compensable risks. This is an inherent systemic function necessary because the treaty text leaves certain words indeterminate.

For this role to be legitimate, decisions must be based on transparent reasoning that explicitly acknowledges the risk allocation choices made, grounding them firmly in the treaty's framework. Tribunals are not independent 'risk allocators'; their legitimate function is to interpret and apply the risk allocation structure already agreed to by the state parties within the treaty framework.

9.4.3 The Four-Step Analytical Methodology

Tribunals often lack a consistent methodology for applying these principles, especially in 'grey-zone' cases where legitimate state objectives conflict with improper state conduct.[82] To address the inconsistency that arises when tribunals lack a systematic way to apply these principles, the political risk governance framework uses a structured, four-step analytical process. This process turns risk allocation from an implicit, ad hoc exercise into an explicit, principled inquiry.

9.4.3.1 Step One: Identify and Categorise the Political Risk

The tribunal first identifies and categorises the nature of the political risk at stake, using the framework's typology. This initial step determines the subsequent analysis by asking: is it a state-centric risk (classic sovereign or modern regulatory), systemic/external risk, or system-generated risk? This initial categorisation is crucial as it informs the entire subsequent analysis. For instance, a climate phase-out law (modern regulatory risk) is analysed differently from arbitrary conduct of the classic sovereign risk.

9.4.3.2 Step Two: Determine Specific State Assurances (Assurance Override)

The tribunal determines whether the host state provided a clear, specific, and unconditional assurance of regulatory stability that the investor reasonably relied upon.

If such a specific assurance exists, the state has explicitly shifted a particular risk onto itself. The risk is allocated to the state, and the inquiry largely concludes, as the

[81] Kucik and Puig (2023, pp. 145–170).

[82] Tienhaara (2011, pp. 611–627).

state must be held to its promise. The reasoning used in the *Eiser* tribunal, which found Spain's specific guarantees of a stable tariff regime, is an example of this pathway.[83]

9.4.3.3 Step Three: Establish the Baseline Regulatory Risk

If no specific assurance is found, the tribunal establishes the baseline regulatory risk a prudent investor should have reasonably foreseen at the time of investment. This objective, context-specific assessment considers (a) sectoral volatility—was the investment in a sensitive or highly regulated sector, such as fossil fuels or public health? (b) temporal context—what was the prevailing scientific, political, and legal consensus at the time? (c) host state context—what were the host state's development level, regulatory history, and public policy signals? and (d) treaty architecture—does the treaty itself contain specific clauses that shape the risk environment? This baseline defines the 'investor-assumed risks'—those good-faith, evolutionary, and proportionate regulatory changes for which no compensation is due.

9.4.3.4 Step Four: Evaluate the State Measure Against the Baseline

Finally, the tribunal must characterise the state measure itself by evaluating it against four independent factors: (1) its regulatory purpose, (2) its procedural propriety, (3) its discriminatory effect, and (4) its proportionality. This step provides the hierarchical decision rules needed to resolve 'grey-zone' conflicts.

If the evaluation reveals a fundamental defect—systematic discrimination targeting foreigners or a complete denial of due process, the risk is allocated to the state, regardless of any legitimate purpose. A legitimate purpose does not excuse improper, arbitrary conduct. In the absence of a fundamental defect, the tribunal conducts a final proportionality balancing of the four factors against the baseline risk to achieve a principled and transparent final allocation.

9.5 Practical Application: Evidence from Treaty and Arbitral Practice

This section applies the political risk governance framework to treaty practice and arbitral jurisprudence, demonstrating both its diagnostic power (explaining divergent outcomes) and its prescriptive potential (suggesting how cases should be analysed).[84] The analysis focuses on three areas: treaty design, Spanish renewable energy cases,

83 See Eiser Infrastructure Ltd v. Spain, ICSID Case No. ARB/13/36, Award (4 May 2017), paras 362–389; Charanne BV v. Spain, SCC Case No. 062/2012, Award (21 January 2016), paras 483–517.

84 UNCTAD (2014, pp. 10–25), Gaukrodger (2021, pp. 10–35).

and the Argentine financial crisis cases—before applying the framework to climate-related disputes.

9.5.1 Evidence from Treaty Practice: A Conscious Allocation of Risk

The conceptual framework of IIL as a system of risk governance is not merely a theoretical proposition. It is evident in the design of investment treaties themselves.[85] The drafting of an investment treaty is a deliberate act of risk allocation by the state parties, using textual choices to delineate the boundaries of foreseeable risk for both investors and the state. Early generations of BITs emphasised robust investor protection, featuring broad, open-ended obligations and expansive definitions of investment.[86] This design allocated a significant degree of regulatory and political risk to the host state.

Modern treaty practice, however, shows a significant shift towards a more symmetrical allocation of risk. In response to expansive interpretations by arbitral tribunals, states are reclaiming policy space by clarifying substantive obligations, explicitly defining indirect expropriation to protect 'police powers', and adding comprehensive general exceptions for public policy goals.[87] The ASEAN Comprehensive Investment Agreement (ACIA),[88] CETA's Investment Court System,[89] CPTPP's detailed annexes,[90] and USMCA's elimination of ISDS between parties[91] all reflect this sophisticated risk allocation in treaty design. This trend is also visible in emerging plurilateral initiatives that incorporate ESG-related obligations and investor responsibilities into arbitral frameworks (Hodgson et al. 2025, pp.45–78).

9.5.2 The Spanish Renewable Energy Cases: A Systematic Analysis

The Spanish renewable energy cases present a natural experiment for testing the risk governance framework.[92] Between 2007 and 2013, Spain established a generous support scheme for renewable energy. Beginning in 2010, Spain progressively

[85] Vandevelde (2010, pp. 23–67), Salacuse (2015, pp. 56–89).

[86] UNCTAD (2014, pp. 10–25), Johnson and Sachs (2012, pp. 23–45).

[87] Chaisse and Bellak (2015, pp. 79–115), Dimitropoulos et al. (2025), paras 15–28.

[88] For analysis of ACIA provisions, see Chaisse and Bellak (2015, pp. 89–115).

[89] For analysis of CETA's Investment Court System, see Kucik and Puig (2023, pp. 145–170).

[90] For analysis of CPTPP. investment chapter, see UNCTAD (2014, pp. 20–35), Monardes et al. (2021, pp. 288–313).

[91] For discussion of USMCA's approach to ISDS, see Gaukrodger (2021, pp. 35–50).

[92] Roberts (2017, pp. 137–178), Bonnitcha et al. (2017, pp. 50–78).

reduced and restructured these supports in response to a tariff deficit crisis. The outcomes across over fifty arbitrations have been strikingly inconsistent. Some tribunals, including *Charanne*,[93] *Isolux*,[94] and *Stadtwerke München*,[95] dismissed claims. Others, including *Eiser*, *Novenergia*,[96] *Masdar*,[97] and *Foresight*,[98] found violations and awarded substantial damages.[99]

The risk governance framework explains these divergences as reflecting different implicit assumptions at each step of the analysis.[100] Regarding disagreement on specific assurances (Step Two), tribunals disagreed on whether Spain's regulatory framework constituted specific assurances of stability.[101] *Eiser* found specific assurances in the regulatory design[102]; *Charanne* found only general provisions subject to change.[103]

Regarding disagreement on baseline risk (Step Three), tribunals adopted fundamentally different views on the baseline regulatory risk.[104] *Charanne* established a high baseline—investors in a heavily regulated sector should anticipate significant regulatory evolution. *Eiser* established a low baseline—Spain's representations created expectations that subsequent changes were unforeseen.[105]

This analysis shows that the divergences stem from disagreements over appropriate risk baselines, not errors in settled doctrine. The risk governance framework would require tribunals to make these baseline judgments explicit and to justify them with reference to the factors specified in Step Three, which would focus the dispute on normatively relevant questions and facilitate consistency.

---

[93] See Eiser Infrastructure Ltd v. Spain, ICSID Case No. ARB/13/36, Award (4 May 2017), paras 362–389; Charanne BV v. Spain, SCC Case No. 062/2012, Award (21 January 2016), paras 483-517.

[94] See Isolux Netherlands BV v. Kingdom of Spain, SCC Case No. V2013/153, Award (17 July 2016), paras 765–841.

[95] See Stadtwerke München GmbH v. Kingdom of Spain, ICSID Case No. ARB/15/1, Award (2 December 2019), paras 256–312.

[96] See Novenergia II - Energy & Environment (SCA) v. Kingdom of Spain, SCC Case No. 2015/063, Final Award (15 February 2018), paras 654–723.

[97] See Masdar Solar & Wind Cooperatief U.A. v. Kingdom of Spain, ICSID Case No. ARB/14/1, Award (16 May 2018), paras 485–556.

[98] See Foresight Luxembourg Solar 1 S.à.r.l. v. Kingdom of Spain, SCC Case No. 2015/150, Final Award (14 November 2018), paras 342–423.

[99] For analysis of divergent outcomes in Spanish solar cases, see Monti and Fermeglia (2024, pp. 189–215).

[100] Alvarez (2011, pp. 240–264).

[101] See Isolux Netherlands BV v. Kingdom of Spain, SCC Case No. V2013/153, Award (17 July 2016), paras 765–841.

[102] See Stadtwerke München GmbH v. Kingdom of Spain, ICSID Case No. ARB/15/1, Award (2 December 2019), paras 256–312.

[103] See Novenergia II—Energy & Environment (SCA) v. Kingdom of Spain, SCC Case No. 2015/063, Final Award (15 February 2018), paras 654–723.

[104] See Masdar Solar & Wind Cooperatief U.A. v. Kingdom of Spain, ICSID Case No. ARB/14/1, Award (16 May 2018), paras 485–556.

[105] See Foresight Luxembourg Solar 1 S.à.r.l. v. Kingdom of Spain, SCC Case No. 2015/150, Final Award (14 November 2018), paras 342–423.

9.5.3 The Argentine Financial Crisis Cases

The Argentine financial crisis cases from the early 2000s provide a second testing ground, focusing on how tribunals allocate the risk of systemic economic crisis.[106] Argentina's economic collapse in 2001–2002 generated over forty investment arbitration claims. The outcomes diverged significantly. *CMS v. Argentina* rejected Argentina's necessity defence, finding that Argentina had contributed to the crisis. *LG&E v. Argentina* accepted the necessity defence for a limited period.[107] *Continental Casualty v. Argentina* adopted a nuanced temporal approach.[108] The annulment committee in *CMS* criticised the original tribunal's analysis but declined to annul the award.[109]

The risk governance framework suggests these cases as struggles over baseline determination.[110] The key question was: should investors in Argentine utilities during the 1990s have anticipated catastrophic economic collapse? The framework suggests that for systemic crisis risks, baseline determination should focus on whether the crisis was beyond Argentina's control or resulting from Argentina's own policies.[111] This distinction aligns with Coasean least-cost risk bearer principles: if a state causes a crisis through its own misconduct, it cannot invoke that crisis to escape responsibility.

9.5.4 Climate-Related Disputes: Applying the Framework Prospectively

Climate-related investment disputes represent the most significant emerging application for the risk governance framework.[112] The global effort to combat climate

---

[106] See CMS Gas Transmission Co. v. Argentina, ICSID Case No. ARB/01/8, Award (12 May 2005), paras 304–394; LG&E Energy Corp. v. Argentina, ICSID Case No. ARB/02/1, Decision on Liability (3 October 2006), paras 226–266.

[107] See Suez, Sociedad General de Aguas de Barcelona S.A. v. Argentina, ICSID Case No. ARB/03/19, Decision on Liability (30 July 2010), paras 220–260.

[108] See Continental Casualty Co. v. Argentina, ICSID Case No. ARB/03/9, Award (5 September 2008), paras 160–236.

[109] See CMS Gas Transmission Co. v. Argentina, ICSID Case No. ARB/01/8, Decision on Annulment (25 September 2007), paras 89–136, critiquing the original tribunal's analysis of the necessity defence.

[110] Newcombe and Paradell (2009, pp. 337–367).

[111] For analysis of the exogenous/endogenous distinction in crisis jurisprudence, see Burke-White and von Staden (2008, pp. 284–355), Kurtz (2010, pp. 325–379).

[112] Zhang and Li (2024, pp. 1471–1489), Sarvarian (2023, pp. 422–448).

change represents precisely the kind of complex, multi-faceted risk that strains traditional IIL frameworks.[113] Climate disputes are fundamentally about allocating the immense economic costs of global energy transition.[114]

In *Rockhopper v. Italy*, the tribunal found Italy liable for breaching legitimate expectations after banning offshore oil drilling.[115] Applying the four-step methodology produces a different analysis. Step One identifies the risk as 'modern regulatory risk'. Step Two asks whether preliminary permits constituted specific assurances—under rigorous analysis, non-final permits would likely be insufficient in a rapidly evolving regulatory environment. Step Three establishes the baseline: what should a prudent investor in offshore fossil fuel extraction have anticipated given the 2015 Paris Agreement, the EU's climate commitments, and Italy's own sustainability policies? The framework suggests a high baseline of regulatory risk.[116]

The *RWE v. Netherlands* case, challenging the Dutch coal phase-out law, represents another critical test.[117] The case was eventually discontinued following RWE's request, which came after the German Federal Court of Justice ruled the arbitration inadmissible as an intra-EU proceeding.[118] Had it proceeded to a decision, the risk governance framework would have required careful analysis of whether investors in coal-fired power generation should have anticipated accelerated phase-out timelines given evolving climate science and policy. The framework suggests that investors who entered the market after the Paris Agreement or other clear policy signals should bear a higher baseline of transition risk than those who invested before such signals emerged.[119]

9.6 Addressing Objections: Challenges and Limitations

This section addresses three potential primary objections to the political risk governance approach: the indeterminacy challenge, democratic legitimacy concerns, and questions about institutional capacity.[120]

---

[113] Cotula (2023, pp. 766–789).

[114] Sarvarian (2023, pp. 422–448), Wortmann (2024, pp. 742–768).

[115] See Rockhopper Exploration Plc v. Italian Republic, ICSID Case No. ARB/17/14, Award (23 August 2022), paras 133–234.

[116] Sarvarian (2023, pp. 430–448), Cotula (2023, pp. 775–789).

[117] See RWE AG v. Kingdom of the Netherlands, ICSID Case No. ARB/21/4, Notice of Arbitration (20 January 2021).

[118] See RWE AG v. Kingdom of the Netherlands, ICSID Case No. ARB/21/4, Order of Discontinuance (12 January 2024).

[119] Cotula (2023, pp. 766–789), Monti (2024, pp. 456–478).

[120] Bonnitcha (2014, pp. 56–89), Howse (2019, pp. 363–389).

9.6.1 The Indeterminacy Challenge

Critics might argue that the risk governance framework merely replaces one form of indeterminacy with another.[121] If tribunals currently struggle to apply standards like 'legitimate expectations', will they do any better with 'baseline risk'? This objection has force but ultimately proves unpersuasive.[122] The framework does not eliminate judgement calls but channels them into explicit, structured inquiry.[123] The four-step methodology requires tribunals to articulate precisely which category of risk they are addressing, what baseline they are establishing and why, and how the specific measure deviates from or conforms to that baseline.[124] This transparency enables meaningful review and iterative refinement of doctrine across cases.

9.6.2 Democratic Legitimacy Concerns

A second objection challenges the democratic legitimacy of arbitral tribunals making risk allocation decisions that affect public policy.[125] Investment arbitration already faces criticism for enabling unelected arbitrators to second-guess democratically adopted regulations.[126] Does reconceptualising their role as 'risk allocators' exacerbate this concern?[127] The framework actually addresses rather than aggravates legitimacy concerns in several ways.[128] By making risk allocation explicit, the framework enables democratic accountability.[129] When tribunals articulate the risk allocation choices implicit in their decisions, states and publics can assess whether those choices align with their preferences and, if not, modify treaty commitments accordingly.[130] The opacity of current doctrine obscures these choices, insulating them from democratic scrutiny.

---

[121] On indeterminacy in international law more broadly, see Kennedy (1987, pp. 1–36).

[122] On indeterminacy in investment treaty standards, see Sornarajah (2015, pp. 323–367), Schneiderman (2008, pp. 78–112).

[123] Bonnitcha (2014, pp. 234–267), Renn and Klinke (2005, pp. 749–774).

[124] Bonnitcha (2014, pp. 267–298).

[125] On the democratic legitimacy critique of investment arbitration, see Van Harten (2007, pp. 152–184), Schneiderman (2008, pp. 178–212), Sornarajah (2015, pp. 445–489).

[126] Ortino (2025, pp. 45–89). Ortino's proportionality framework draws on constitutional law literature, particularly Alexy (2002, pp. 44–110), Möller (2012, pp. 179–210).

[127] Kennedy (1987, pp. 1–36).

[128] On the interpretive function of arbitrators in treaty application, see Roberts (2010, pp. 179–225), Pauwelyn and Elsig (2013, pp. 445–473).

[129] Van Harten (2007, pp. 152–184), Schneiderman (2008, pp. 178–212), Sornarajah (2015, pp. 445–489).

[130] Kingsbury and Schill (2010, pp. 75–104).

9.6.3 *Institutional Capacity Limitations*

A third objection questions whether arbitral tribunals possess the technical capacity to engage in sophisticated risk governance analysis.[131] Risk assessment involves technical judgments about probability, causation, and future developments that may exceed arbitrators' expertise.[132] This concern is legitimate but overstated.[133] Tribunals already engage in risk-related reasoning when they assess foreseeability, proportionality, and the legitimacy of expectations.[134] The framework does not require tribunals to become actuaries or risk scientists; it requires them to structure their existing reasoning more explicitly and to draw on available evidence about risk characteristics. Where technical expertise is needed, tribunals can and do appoint expert witnesses and technical advisors.

9.7 Conclusion: Implications for Treaty Design, Arbitral Practice, and ISDS Reform

This article has argued that international investment law is better understood as a system of political risk governance than as a regime of investor protection. The political risk governance framework developed here provides both diagnostic power—explaining why existing approaches generate inconsistent outcomes—and prescriptive potential—offering a structured methodology for more principled decision-making.[135]

The framework has significant implications for three domains. For *treaty design*, the framework suggests that states should draft treaties with explicit attention to risk allocation.[136] Rather than relying on open-ended standards interpreted by tribunals, states can specify which categories of risk are allocated to investors, which to states, and which require burden-sharing. Modern treaty practice already moves in this direction; the framework provides a conceptual foundation for these developments.

For *arbitral practice*, the four-step methodology offers a pathway towards greater consistency and legitimacy.[137] Tribunals that explicitly identify the category of risk, assess baseline expectations, and evaluate measures against that baseline will produce awards that are more transparent, more reviewable, and more likely to generate coherent doctrine over time.[138]

---

[131] See Yukos Universal Ltd v. Russia, PCA Case No. AA 227, Final Award (18 July 2014); Bear Creek Mining Corp. v. Peru, ICSID Case No. ARB/14/21, Award (30 November 2017).

[132] Roberts (2010, pp. 179–225), Pauwelyn and Elsig (2013, pp. 445–473).

[133] Schlink (2012, pp. 293–308), Tsakyrakis (2009, pp. 468–493).

[134] Burke-White and von Staden (2008, pp. 284–355), Kurtz (2010, pp. 325–379).

[135] Bonnitcha et al. (2017, pp. 50–78), Howse (2019, pp. 363–389).

[136] Moehlecke and Wellhausen (2021, pp. 515–548), Renn (2008, pp. 8–45).

[137] Zhang and Li (2024, pp. 1471–1489), Segger and Gleason (2025, pp. 1–18).

[138] Schill (2009, pp. 25–67), Roberts (2017, pp. 137–178).

For *ISDS reform*, the framework contributes to ongoing discussions in UNCITRAL Working Group III about the future of investment dispute settlement.[139] Current reform proposals focus largely on procedural innovations—a multilateral investment court, an appellate mechanism, a code of conduct for arbitrators. These reforms address important legitimacy concerns but do not resolve the substantive inconsistency that stems from divergent approaches to risk allocation. The framework suggests that procedural reforms should be complemented by substantive guidance that helps decision-makers apply a consistent analytical methodology.[140]

International investment law stands at a crossroads. The traditional paradigm of investor protection, while capturing important aspects of the regime's function, proves inadequate for a world of climate transition, geoeconomic competition, and digital transformation. The political risk governance framework offers a pathway beyond this impasse—not by abandoning protection for investors or regulatory space for states, but by providing a principled approach to balancing these legitimate interests. By making explicit the risk allocation function inherent in treaty interpretation, the framework offers the possibility of a more coherent, transparent, and legitimate international investment law for the challenges ahead.

* * *

References

Alexy R (2002) A theory of constitutional rights. Oxford University Press, Oxford

Alvarez JE (2011) The Return of the State. Minn J Int Law 20:223–264

Beck U (1992) Risk society: towards a new modernity. Sage, London

Blackwill RD, Harris JM (2016) War by other means: geoeconomics and statecraft. Harvard University Press, Cambridge

Bonnitcha J (2014) Substantive protection under investment treaties: a legal and economic analysis. Cambridge University Press, Cambridge

Bonnitcha J, Poulsen L, Waibel M (2017) The political economy of the investment treaty regime. Oxford University Press, Oxford

Borchard E (1939) The "Minimum Standard" of the treatment of aliens. Am Soc'y Int'l L Proc 33:51–74

Brands H (2022) The twilight struggle: what the cold war teaches us about great-power Rivalry Today. Yale University Press, New Haven

Brewin S, Morgera E, Cianci E (2021) Climate change and international investment agreements: a scoping paper. International institute for sustainable development, winnipeg

Burke-White W, von Staden A (2008) Investment protection in extraordinary times: the interpretation and application of non-precluded measures provisions in bilateral investment treaties. Virginia J Int Law 48:307–410

Caldara D, Iacoviello M (2022) Measuring Geopolitical Risk. American Economic Review 112(4):1194–1225

[139] Kucik and Puig (2023, pp. 145–170), Gaukrodger (2021, pp. 10–50).

[140] Bonnitcha et al. (2017, pp. 250–289), UNCTAD (2014, pp. 30–45).

Chaisse J, Bellak C (2015) Navigating the expanding universe of international treaties on foreign investment: creation and use of a critical index. J Int Econ Law 18:79–115
Coase RH (1960) The Problem of Social Cost. J L & Econ 3:1–44
Cotula L (2023) International Investment Law and Climate Change: Reframing the ISDS Reform Agenda. J World Inv Trade 24:766–791
de la Rasilla I, Cai C (2024) The Cambridge Handbook of China and International Law. Cambridge University Press, Cambridge
Dimitropoulos G, Chen RC, Chaisse J (2025) Plurilateralism: a new form of international economic ordering? J World Inv Trade 26:1–30
Dolzer R, Schreuer C (2012) Principles of International Investment Law, 2nd edn. Oxford University Press, Oxford
Farrell H, Newman AL (2019) Weaponized interdependence: how global economic networks shape state coercion. Int Security 44 (1):42–79
Gaukrodger D (2021) The future of investment treaties—possible directions. OECD working paper on international investment No. 2021/03. OECD Publishing, Paris
Gazzini T, Tanzi A (2013) Handle with care: umbrella clauses and MFN treatment in investment arbitration. J World Invest Trade 14(6):978–994
Hodgson M, Duggal K, Horne K, Pirnia AS (2025) The dawn of a new era: advancing ESG obligations in arbitration through plurilateralism. J World Invest Trade 26(1–2):301–331
Howse R (2019) International investment law and arbitration: a conceptual framework. In: Ruiz Fabri H (ed) International Law and Litigation: A Look into Procedure. Nomos, Baden-Baden, pp 363–389
Johnson L, Coleman J (2016) Political risk insurance and bilateral investment treaties: an overview. Columbia Ctr on Sustainable Inv, New York
Johnson L, Sachs L (2014) International investment agreements, 2011–2012: a review of trends and new approaches. In: Bjorklund AK (ed) Yearbook on international investment law and policy 2012–2013. Oxford University Press, New York
Johnson L, Sachs L (2018) Investor-state dispute settlement: what are we trying to achieve? CCSI policy paper. Columbia Ctr on Sustainable Inv, New York
Kennedy D (1987) International legal structures. Nomos, Baden-Baden
Kingsbury B, Krisch N, Stewart RB (2005) The emergence of global administrative law. Law Contemp Probs 68:15–62
Kingsbury B, Schill SW (2010) Public law concepts to balance investors' rights with state regulatory actions in the public interest—the concept of proportionality. In: Schill SW (ed) International Investment Law and Comparative Public Law. Oxford University Press, Oxford, pp 75–104
Knight FH (1921) Risk, uncertainty, and profit. Houghton Mifflin, Boston
Kobrin SJ (1979) Political risk: a review and reconsideration. J Int Bus Stud 10:67–80
Koskenniemi M (2005) From apology to utopia: the structure of international legal argument, reissue edn. Cambridge University Press, Cambridge
Krajewski M (2016) Model clauses for the exclusion of public services from trade and investment agreements. Chamber of labour Vienna (AK Wien) and European Federation of Public Service Unions (EPSU), Vienna
Krajewski M (2017) Ensuring the primacy of human rights in trade and investment policies: Model clauses for a UN treaty on transnational corporations, other Businesses and human rights, CIDSE
Krisch N (2010) Beyond constitutionalism: The pluralist structure of postnational law. Oxford University Press, Oxford
Kucik J, Puig S (2023) Towards an effective appellate mechanism for ISDS tribunals. World Trade Rev 22(5):562–583
Kurtz J (2010) The merits and limits of comparativism: national treatment in international investment law and the WTO. J Int Econ Law 13:537–568. https://doi.org/10.1093/jiel/jgq026
Lang A (2011) World trade law after neoliberalism: reimagining the global economic order. Oxford University Press, Oxford

Luttwak EN (1990) From geopolitics to geo-economics: logic of conflict, grammar of commerce. Nat'l Interest 20:17–23
Mearsheimer JJ (2014) The tragedy of great power politics, updated edn. W.W. Norton, New York
Moehlecke C, Wellhausen RL (2022) Political risk and international investment law. Ann Rev Polit Sci 25:485–507
Möller K (2012) The global model of constitutional rights. Oxford University Press, Oxford
Monardes R, Novik A, Portales C (2021) Addressing the Right to Regulate in the CPTPP Investment Chapter: identifying new treaty practice. In: Huerta-Goldman JA, Gantz DA (eds) The comprehensive and progressive trans-pacific partnership: analysis and commentary (pp. 288–313). Cambridge University Press, Cambridge
Monti A (2024) Climate change and investor-State disputes: protecting stranded assets or promoting green investments? In: Sindico F, McKenzie K, Medici-Colombo GA, Wegener L (eds) Research handbook on climate change litigation. Edward Elgar Publishing, Cheltenham, pp 344–363
Monti A, Fermeglia M (2024) The FET standard between treaty reform and ISDS practice: an analysis of the modernized ECT. J Int Arb 41(2):155–178
Morgenthau H (1978) Politics among nations: the struggle for power and peace, 5th edn. Alfred A. Knopf, New York
Newcombe A, Paradell L (2009) Law and practice of investment treaties: standards of treatment. Kluwer Law International, Alphen aan den Rijn
North D (1990) Institutions, Institutional Change and Economic Performance. Cambridge University Press, Cambridge
Ortino F (2021) Investment treaty law and the COVID-19 pandemic. AJIL Unbound 115:287–291
Ortino F (2025) The development of international investment law by arbitral tribunals and the strange case of the "Fair and Equitable Treatment" Standard. King's LJ 36(1):36–47
Pauwelyn J, Elsig M (2013) The politics of treaty interpretation: variations and explanations across international tribunals. In: Dunoff JL, Pollack MA (eds) Interdisciplinary Perspectives on International Law and International Relations: The State of the Art. Cambridge University Press, Cambridge, pp 445–473
Reinisch A (2004) The interpretation of umbrella clauses in bilateral investment treaties. Transnat Dispute Manag 1(3)
Renn O (2008) Risk governance: coping with uncertainty in a complex world. Earthscan, London
Renn O, Klinke A (2005) A framework of risk governance. J Risk Res 8:749–774
Roberts A (2010) Power and persuasion in investment treaty interpretation: the dual role of states. Am J Int Law 104:179–225
Roberts A (2017) Is international law international? Oxford University Press, Oxford
Robock SH (1971) Political risk: identification and assessment. Colum J World Bus 6:6–20
Rubins N, Papanastasiou TN, Kinsella NS (2020) International investment, political risk, and dispute resolution: a practitioner's guide, 2nd edn. Oxford University Press, Oxford
Salacuse JW (2015) The law of investment treaties, 2nd edn. Oxford University Press, Oxford
Salacuse JW (2021) The law of investment treaties, 3rd edn. Oxford University Press, Oxford
Sarvarian A (2023) Invoking the Paris agreement in investor-state arbitration. ICSID Rev—Foreign Inv LJ 38 (2):422–440
Schill SW (2009) The multilateralization of international investment law. Cambridge University Press, Cambridge
Schneiderman D (2008) Constitutionalizing economic globalization: investment rules and democracy's promise. Cambridge University Press, Cambridge
Schreuer C (2004) Travelling the BIT route: of waiting periods, umbrella clauses and forks in the road. J World Inv Trade 5:231–259
Segger MCC, Gleason T (2025) Introduction to the research handbook on investment law and sustainable development. In: Segger MCC, Gleason T (eds) Research handbook on investment law and sustainable development. Edward Elgar, Cheltenham, pp 1–18
Sornarajah M (2015) Resistance and change in the international law on foreign investment. Cambridge University Press, Cambridge

Tienhaara K (2011) Regulatory chill and the threat of arbitration: a view from political science. In: Brown C, Miles K (eds) Evolution in investment treaty law and Arbitration. Cambridge University Press, Cambridge, pp 606–627

Titi C (2015) Are investment tribunals adjudicating political disputes? J Int Arb 32 (3):261–288

UNCTAD (2014) Reform of the IIA regime: four paths of action and a way forward. IIA issues note No. 3. UNCTAD/WEB/DIAE/PCB/2014/6. United Nations, Geneva

UNCTAD (2020) Investment policy responses to the COVID-19 pandemic. Investment policy monitor special issue No. 4. United Nations, Geneva

Vadi V (2015) Beyond known worlds: climate change governance by arbitral tribunals? Vand J Transnat'l L 48:1285–1351

Van Harten G (2007) Investment treaty arbitration and public law. Oxford University Press, Oxford

Vandevelde KJ (2010) Bilateral investment treaties: history, policy, and interpretation. Oxford University Press, Oxford

Waltz KN (1979) Theory of international politics. Addison-Wesley, Reading MA

Wellhausen RL (2014) The shield of nationality: when governments break contracts with foreign firms. Cambridge University Press, Cambridge

Wells LT Jr (2005) The new international property rights: can the foreign investor rely on them? In: Moran TH, West GT (eds) International political risk management: looking to the future, Vol III. World Bank (MIGA), Washington, DC

Wells LT, Ahmed R (2007) Making foreign investment safe: property rights and national sovereignty. Oxford University Press, Oxford

Wortmann C (2024) Conflicts between international climate law and investment arbitration: a proposed exception to the full reparation standard without moving the goalposts. J World Inv Trade 25(5/6):742–766

Yackee J (2010) Do Bilateral investment treaties promote foreign direct investment? Virginia J Int Law 51:397–439

Zhang S, Li N (2024) Addressing climate change through international investment agreements: obstacles and reform options. Sustainability 16:1471

Chapter 10
National Security Concerns and Data Governance: Export Restrictions on Data and Its Implications for International Economic Law

Shota Watanabe

Abstract This chapter examines the proliferation of cross-border data transfer restrictions adopted on national security grounds, analyzes their legal implications under international economic law, and proposes solutions. While prior analyses have focused on privacy-based restrictions under WTO and FTA frameworks, this chapter demonstrates through case studies of China, the United States, and Japan that security-based measures are rapidly expanding. China's expansive national security conception and use of domestically held data for security and industrial purposes have prompted the US and Japan to intensify their own transfer restrictions. The chapter identifies key legal and systemic concerns including transparency deficits, regulatory fragmentation, data re-export risks, and potential WTO/FTA incompatibilities. Drawing analogies to export control regimes for goods, the chapter argues that frameworks like the Wassenaar Arrangement offer valuable guidance for addressing these challenges through common control lists, enhanced information sharing, and convergence in restriction design. It concludes by proposing a forum among like-minded states to facilitate policy coordination between export control and digital regulation communities.

Keywords Cross-border data flows · Digital trade · Data governance · Export control · Economic security · Government access

10.1 Introduction

In today's increasingly digitalized society, ensuring the smooth flow of data is essential for corporate business operations. For example, sharing human resources data across borders or exchanging supply chain-related data such as production volume

S. Watanabe (✉)
Nomura Research Institute, Tokyo, Japan
e-mail: s4-watanabe@nri.co.jp

J. Nakagawa et al. (eds.), *Geopolitical Risks and Geoeconomics in International Economic Law*, Economics, Law, and Institutions in Asia Pacific,
https://doi.org/10.1007/978-981-95-6996-0_10

and CO_2 emissions can enhance the efficiency of business activities. Digital data also plays a vital role in addressing societal challenges, including healthcare applications such as infectious disease prevention and pharmaceutical development, as well as urban planning efforts like mitigating traffic congestion.

However, growing awareness of the need to protect data has prompted states to implement data localization requirements and cross-border data transfer restrictions to retain control over data flows. While such measures are often grounded in legitimate public policy objectives, they can impede the aforementioned corporate activities. Though respecting national sovereignty over data regulation is essential, it must be balanced against the need for cross-border data flows.

Traditionally, data protection has been discussed primarily in the context of privacy and personal data protection. Particularly within the framework of international trade law, there has been extensive analysis on the consistency between instruments such as the EU Data Protection Directive or the General Data Protection Regulation (GDPR) and provisions on data flows under the WTO's General Agreement on Trade in Services (GATS)[1] and Free Trade Agreements (FTAs).[2] However, a new and remarkable trend has emerged in recent years—the intersection of data and national security.

This trend originated from China's unique concept of national security, under which domestic data flows are tightly controlled to prevent cross-border transfer of data deemed critical to national security. For instance, high-resolution mapping data collected during autonomous driving operations falls under this category[3] and is restricted even for foreign entities operating in China.

By ensuring that security sensitive data remains within national borders and granting the government compulsory access—so-called "government access"—the Chinese state can utilize data held by private entities to support policy implementation and industrial development.[4] In response, other countries have begun introducing similar measures aimed at counterbalancing China's approach. For example, although the initial focus was on preventing the transfer of data to China during foreign investment screenings, US restrictions have gradually expanded to cover broader categories of cross-border data transfers. The United States has recently implemented new regulations concerning the handling of sensitive personal data.

This paper aims to examine the current state of cross-border data transfer restrictions for the purpose of national security—an area that remains underexplored compared to personal data protection—and to identify the key challenges associated with such restrictions. Furthermore, it explores the potential of international trade law as a framework for addressing these challenges. The analysis includes a comparative assessment of export control regimes of trade in goods grounded in national security, given the structural similarities, and evaluates how international legal mechanisms might contribute to resolving emerging frictions over data governance.

---

[1] Burri (2021, pp. 15–20), Weber (2012, pp. 25–47), Irion K et al. (2016, pp. 27–33).

[2] Burri (2021, pp. 34–40).

[3] NASG (2017).

[4] Regarding general debate on government access, please see: OECD (2022).

10.2 Data Transfer Restrictions for the Purpose of National Security

To clarify the core issues, this paper first examines the current landscape of cross-border data transfer restrictions imposed by various countries on national security grounds. Specifically, it aims to identify the types of risks that individual governments associate with the cross-border transfer of domestic data. In conclusion, the analysis here reveals that one of the primary concerns is the risk of foreign governmental access to sensitive data—particularly by the Chinese government.

Subsequently, the paper investigates how states are responding to this perceived risk. It focuses on identifying the categories of data that are designated as critical to national security, the extent and severity of transfer restrictions imposed on such data, and whether any exceptions to these restrictions exist.

10.2.1 China

China has long recognized the strategic importance of controlling the flow of information within its borders, particularly with respect to political dissent such as movements critical of the Chinese Communist Party (e.g., the Tiananmen Square protests). This awareness has manifested in policies such as the construction of the "Great Firewall" and the exclusion of foreign service providers from the Chinese digital ecosystem. While China's accession to the World Trade Organization (WTO) raised expectations for liberalization in the realm of services and information exchange, these expectations have not materialized.[5] Instead, China has continued to maintain strong sovereign authority over domestic information flows.

In parallel, China has also paid early attention to the potential national security implications of data held by private entities, including foreign firms operating within China. This perspective is deeply rooted in China's unique security doctrine, notably influenced by the concept of "Unrestricted Warfare," which advocates the strategic use of all available resources—both domestic and foreign—in pursuit of victory.[6] Within this framework, data generated or stored in China, including that held by foreign enterprises, is viewed as a critical asset for enhancing domestic industry, supporting defense, and conducting intelligence operations.

This thinking has culminated in General Secretary Xi Jinping's doctrine of "Comprehensive National Security," which extends beyond traditional security areas (e.g., political, military, and territorial sovereignty) to include non-traditional domains such as the economy, technology, and society.[7] Based on this expansive view of security, China has introduced a sophisticated legal regime governing data flows,

---

[5] Pauwelyn (2010).

[6] Barno and Bensahel (2016).

[7] Kwan (2024).

consisting of the Cybersecurity Law (CSL), the Data Security Law (DSL), and the Personal Information Protection Law (PIPL)—collectively known as China's "three data laws."

Enacted in 2017, the CSL was China's first comprehensive legislation to introduce data localization requirements. It mandates that Critical Information Infrastructure Operators (CIIOs) must store within China any personal information and "important data" collected or generated domestically. Moreover, cross-border data transfers are only permitted following a national security review administered by designated authorities. Notably, at the time of enactment, the CSL did not define key terms such as "important data" or "CIIO," creating legal uncertainty.

Promulgated in 2021, the DSL addressed this gap by establishing clearer definitions and mechanisms. Articles 21, 27, 30, and 31 of the DSL provide for the classification of "important data" and delegate the creation of detailed data catalogs to sectoral authorities. The DSL requires risk assessments for cross-border transfers of important data and mandates export control–like measures. It also prohibits the production of domestically stored data to foreign judicial or law enforcement authorities without prior government approval.

Following the CSL's entry into force, the Chinese government rapidly expanded its regulatory infrastructure beginning in 2021. The CII Protection Regulations, issued in September 2021, define the scope of CIIOs and outline supervisory mechanisms. In 2022, the Measures for the Security Assessment of Cross-Border Data Transfers further specified the data categories subject to review, procedural requirements, and evaluation criteria for such transfers.

The United States, in a submission to the WTO Services Council, expressed concern that these rules, if fully implemented, would significantly impact cross-border service delivery by foreign commercial entities.[8]

China has complemented its data localization regime with statutes enabling governmental access to localized data. The most notable example is the National Intelligence Law, enacted in 2017.[9] The law imposes a mandatory cooperation obligation on all organizations and citizens:

> All organizations and citizens shall support, assist, and cooperate with national intelligence efforts in accordance with law, and shall protect national intelligence work secrets they are aware of.[10]

Violations of this obligation may lead to administrative detention of up to 15 days, and where applicable, criminal liability.[11] Moreover, the law defines the objectives of national intelligence work in sweeping terms:

---

[8] Tiles (2017).

[9] In this paper, the English translation of the text of the National Intelligence Law is based on "China Law Translate", https://www.chinalawtranslate.com/en/national-intelligence-law-of-the-p-r-c-2017/#_Toc486408893.

[10] National Intelligence Law, Art. 7.

[11] *Ibid..*, Art. 28.

> National Intelligence work adheres to the overall national security perspective, provides intelligence as a reference in major national decision-making, provides intelligence support for the prevention and mitigation of threats endangering national security, and preserves the national political power, sovereignty, unity, and territorial integrity, the welfare of the people, sustainable social and economic development and other major national interests.[12]

This broad framing allows for data collected within China—including data held by foreign firms—to be mobilized not only for traditional state security purposes, but also to serve economic and developmental policy objectives, which, under Chinese perception, are also legitimate national security purposes.

10.2.2 United States

In the United States, concerns over cross-border data transfers from a national security perspective have been largely driven by the risk of government access (GA) by foreign authorities—particularly the Chinese government. Until around 2020, the United States addressed such GA-related risks primarily through measures such as strengthening foreign investment screening, establishing infrastructure security standards, and excluding Chinese firms from 5G networks.

For example, the U.S. government blocked attempted acquisitions by Chinese entities targeting companies that handled sensitive information, such as personal data of federal employees[13] or large volumes of financial data on U.S. citizens,[14] by U.S. foreign direct investment screening reviews of the Committee on Foreign Investment in the United States (CFIUS). These interventions were grounded in national security concerns, specifically the risk that—post-acquisition—such U.S.-origin data could be subject to compulsory disclosure to Chinese firms or the Chinese government. In essence, the underlying concern was that data deemed vital to U.S. interests could be accessed under foreign legal compulsion after a foreign acquisition.

Similarly, the United States has introduced multiple initiatives aimed at eliminating the influence of the Chinese Communist Party from its domestic 5G networks.[15] On August 5, 2020, Secretary Pompeo announced the expansion of the Clean Network program: Clean Carrier, Store, Apps, Cloud, Cable, and Path. All of these were designed to exclude CCP's influence on the US.

Amid the intensifying strategic rivalry between the United States and China in recent years, the U.S. government has moved to further tighten its regulatory measures. This trend is most clearly exemplified by Executive Order 14,117, issued in February 2024, titled "Preventing Access to Americans' Bulk Sensitive Personal Data and United States Government-Related Data by Countries of Concern."

---

[12] *Ibid.*, Art. 2.

[13] Executive Office of the President (2020).

[14] Roumeliotis (2018).

[15] USDOS (2021).

The United States has justified the issuance of this Executive Order as a direct response to the government access (GA) risks posed by so-called "countries of concern." According to the order, "governments of countries of concern may seek access to and exploit bulk sensitive personal data in ways that are inconsistent with democratic values, the protection of privacy, and other human rights and freedoms." This practice, the order notes, stands in stark contrast to the principles reflected in democratic norms and the OECD Declaration on Government Access to Personal Data Held by Private Sector Entities.

In line with similar concerns, the United States also enacted the Protecting Americans' Data from Foreign Adversaries Act (PADFA) in April 2024. This statute imposes restrictions on the transfer of a broader range of sensitive personal data—particularly by data brokers—to countries of concern. It complements Executive Order 14,117 by targeting commercial data flows outside of specific government contexts.

Key Elements of the EO 14,117 is below;

Covered Data[16]

Bulk sensitive personal data of U.S. persons: This includes individual identifiers, geolocation and sensor-related data, biometric identifiers, personal health and financial information, and any combinations thereof that meet threshold criteria established by rules issued by the Attorney General.

U.S. government-related data: Regardless of volume, data designated by the Attorney General as highly likely to be exploited by countries of concern in ways that could harm U.S. national security, also defined through implementing rules.

Covered Entities (Data Recipients)

Foreign persons who are employees or contractors of, or entities controlled by, countries of concern—currently defined by regulation to include China, Russia, Iran, and North Korea.

Foreign persons who reside primarily in such countries, or others designated by the Attorney General.

Restricted Transactions[17]

U.S. persons are prohibited from knowingly engaging in certain types of transactions involving sensitive data—including data brokerage, vendor contracts, employment agreements, and investment-related arrangements—if such transactions involve covered data and counterparties linked to countries of concern.

The regulation also prohibits entering into such transactions without requiring contractual safeguards to prevent onward transfer of data to countries of concern or designated individuals.

[16] Section 3 of the EO14117.

[17] Section 2 of the EO14117.

10.2.3 Japan[18]

In Japan, academic discourse began raising concerns about government access by China around 2019,[19] but the issue gained widespread public and policy attention following the 2021 incident involving LINE Corporation. LINE, the provider of Japan's most widely used messaging application, came under scrutiny when it was revealed that, contrary to its explanations to Japanese government agencies, it had stored message content not within Japan but in South Korea, and that such content had been made accessible to a Chinese subcontractor.

Although user consent for cross-border data transfers had been obtained, and thus the transfers to South Korea and China did not constitute a violation of Japan's Act on the Protection of Personal Information (APPI), the revelation sparked significant public criticism. In response, an independent third-party committee was established to investigate the matter. The committee emphasized that a messaging service as critical as LINE—given its central role in Japan's communication infrastructure—must implement robust safeguards aligned with economic security imperatives.[20] The company's handling of the incident was deemed insufficient in this regard.

In 2022, Japan enacted its key legislative framework for economic security: the *Act on the Promotion of Economic Security by Integrated Implementation of Economic Measures* (hereinafter, the Economic Security Promotion Act).[21] This law introduced four major institutional pillars[22]:

1 a system to ensure stable supplies of critical materials (Articles 6 to 40);
2 a system to ensure stable provision of services using critical infrastructure (Articles 40 to 59);
3 a system that supports the development of critical technologies (Articles 60 to 64);
4 a secret patent system (Articles 65 to 85).

Among the four pillars introduced under Japan's Economic Security Promotion Act, the measure most directly related to cross-border data flows is the second: ensuring the stable provision of core infrastructure services. This regime officially entered into force in May 2024.

Under this framework, the competent ministries overseeing respective sectors of critical infrastructure serve as regulatory authorities. They are responsible for designating Specified Critical Equipment—defined by ministerial ordinance as equipment essential to the stable provision of services and potentially exploitable as a means of disruptive conduct. Regulatory authorities assess whether such equipment is resilient to so-called Specified Disruptive Acts (e.g., cyberattacks), and may issue recommendations or orders based on the outcome of this assessment.

---

[18] Watai (2023, pp. 448–453).
[19] Watanabe (2019).
[20] LY Corporation (2021, p. 6).
[21] GOJ (2022).
[22] European Parliament (2023).

Notably, the scope of the review applies to the introduction of new Specified Critical Equipment and to the outsourcing of key maintenance and management functions. Existing equipment already in use is not subject to the screening. However, equipment upgrades that effectively constitute new introductions may also fall under the scope of review, depending on their nature and extent.

Furthermore, some of the items covered in the review process appear to address concerns related to data transfers. For instance, when filing for review, operators must disclose the country or region in which the factory or business facility manufacturing the equipment is located. This enables authorities to assess potential government access risks associated with foreign jurisdictions.

In addition, the review process is grounded in a self-assessment model, wherein designated core infrastructure operators are expected to evaluate risks independently and adopt risk mitigation measures proportionate to the nature and severity of identified threats. To facilitate this, a standardized checklist of risk control items is provided.[23] Among the key checklist items are the following (numbers in parentheses refer to the checklist item numbers):

> Checklist ⑤-1 and ⑤-2: Equipment suppliers must ensure that access to the manufacturing environment (including research and development environment) is restricted to authorized personnel only, through both physical (e.g., surveillance cameras and access control systems) and logical (e.g., data and system access controls) means.
>
> Checklist ⑭-1 and ⑭-2: Suppliers must not have violated domestic regulations or internationally recognized standards, including those implemented under national regimes, within the three years preceding the filing data.
>
> Checklist ⑯: If the equipment is used to monitor or manage infrastructure (such as surveillance cameras or drones), the operator must ensure that the legal environment of the supplier's country of incorporation (including the headquarters of any majority shareholder) does not affect the appropriate handling of video data.

Checklist item ⑯ most explicitly reflects concerns related to GA risk. It stipulates that when surveillance devices such as cameras or drones are used, the legal environment in the supplier's home jurisdiction must not adversely affect the proper management of visual data. Given the context, the term legal environment is likely intended to reference jurisdictions outside Japan, potentially including those with weak personal data protection standards compared to Japan.

However, a lower level of personal data protection alone does not necessarily constitute a national security threat. For example, the mere transfer of employee data to a country of concern would not typically be viewed as a threat to national security. In contrast, if surveillance footage or other sensitive visual data related to the management of critical infrastructure—such as the operational status of electric or gas utilities, or security conditions at nuclear power facilities—were transferred to a foreign manufacturer based in a country of concern, such data could potentially be accessed by that country's government under its domestic laws. The data could then be analyzed by state agencies and used to plan or conduct attacks on infrastructure.

---

[23] Cabinet Office (2025) (translated by the author).

Thus, it is more reasonable to interpret this provision as being directed at GA risks. In this sense, the regulation reflects a recognition of the potential for data, once transferred abroad through suppliers of critical equipment, to be subject to foreign governmental access and subsequently weaponized in ways that pose national security threats.

Among the provisions under item ⑤, particular attention should be given to the access control requirements. These provisions can reasonably be interpreted as being formulated with GA risks in mind. Similarly, item ⑭ requires compliance with "internationally accepted standards," which may implicitly reference the *OECD High-Level Principles on Government Access to Personal Data Held by Private Sector Entities*—a document frequently cited by the United States in its policy rationale.

In addition to equipment introduction, a comparable checklist is applied to the *maintenance and management* phase, which also requires an assessment of GA risks associated with foreign legal environments. Operators of designated core infrastructure services must confirm that the adequacy of critical outsourced maintenance services (including subcontracting and re-subcontracting) is not affected by such legal environments. More specifically, the checklist instructs operators to verify the following items (numbers in parentheses refer to the corresponding checklist entries)[24]:

> Checklist ⑩-1: In cases where a foreign legal environment or the instructions of external entities—whether explicit or implicit—could cause a contractor to violate its agreement with the infrastructure operator, the operator must contractually ensure that such incidents are reported.
>
> Checklist ⑩-2: The same reporting obligation must apply to subcontractors or re-subcontractors under similar circumstances, requiring them to notify either the infrastructure operator or the primary contractor.
>
> Checklist ⑪: When surveillance equipment such as cameras or drones is installed or used at maintenance sites, the operator must ensure that the legal environment of the supplier's home jurisdiction (including that of any entity holding a majority of the supplier's voting rights) does not affect the proper handling of visual information.

Items ⑩ and ⑪ specifically address risks that arise from extended supply chains, particularly those involving foreign contractors and subcontractors. These provisions are directly aimed at mitigating the GA risks inherent in such arrangements. Notably, they appear to have been shaped in part by the lessons learned from the LINE incident, which exposed the vulnerabilities of entrusting critical data processing to foreign-based entities potentially subject to government access obligations.

This explanation is based on the author's sole analysis, as there is no public information on governmental review practices on such infrastructures. Japanese governmental review does care about risks associated with transferred data, however, its actual operations, especially what kinds of data and what types of countries are concerned in this process, are still unclear.

---

[24] *Ibid.*, 17.

10.3 Problems Identified

How do the recent developments in national regulations on cross-border data transfers for security purposes impact global data governance?

10.3.1 Lack of Transparency

One of the foremost issues surrounding national security–driven restrictions on cross-border data transfers is the lack of transparency.[25] A key example is the ambiguity surrounding the scope of data categories subject to protection—such as what constitutes "important data." In China, the definitions of terms such as "important data" and "Critical Information Infrastructure Operators (CIIOs)" remain vague and open to broad interpretation.

In addition, the implementation of these regulatory regimes also presents challenges. In China, there has been a significant time—several years—lag between the enactment of primary laws and the issuance of detailed implementing rules or ministerial guidelines to define such foundational terms. Consequently, businesses are often left without sufficient information at the time of enactment to properly interpret the legal requirements and ensure compliance. This leads to excessive compliance costs, as companies err on the side of caution. Moreover, although filing or reviewing mechanisms by authorities have been introduced, the criteria and procedures for such reviews are not clearly disclosed.

While it is understandable that certain levels of confidentiality are inherent in national security measures, current practices in several countries exhibit an excessive lack of transparency, going beyond what is reasonably necessary.

10.3.2 Regulatory Fragmentation

As illustrated in Sect. 10.2, the scope of national security concerns differs substantially across countries. China adopts an extremely broad interpretation of national security, encompassing a wide range of data categories. By contrast, the United States focuses primarily on the risk of GA by foreign adversaries. As a result, the types of data subject to restrictions, as well as the conditions for transfer, vary significantly by jurisdiction. This tendency can be also seen in countries other than China and the United States. For example, Vietnam has a regulation similar to China. In Viet Nam, Decree No. 53/2022/ND-CP, which outlines implementing regulations of the Cyber

[25] From the perspectives of businesses, transparency is one of the main issues and barriers on the cross-border flow of data. *Please see*, Digital Agency (2023).

Security Law, stipulates that foreign and domestic online service providers in Viet Nam must store both personal and non-personal data within the country.[26]

Multinational corporations that operate global data flows across borders are thus required to comply with a fragmented and inconsistent patchwork of national regulations. They must analyze detailed rules in each country and implement jurisdiction-specific compliance frameworks. This regulatory divergence imposes substantial administrative burdens and increases compliance costs for businesses.

10.3.3 Re-export Risk

The fragmentation of regulations also gives rise to another challenge from a government perspective: re-export risk. In corporate practice, it is common for data to be transferred from one country to another and subsequently to a third jurisdiction. For example, data from a regional office may be transferred to a company's headquarters and then onward to another foreign subsidiary.

Among the regimes outlined in Sect. 10.2, only the United States explicitly regulates the re-export of data. This means that even if a country initially approves a data transfer to a "trusted" jurisdiction, the receiving country may not impose the same level of restrictions, allowing for potential circumvention of the original regulatory intent.

In contrast, export control regimes in areas like dual-use goods or sensitive technologies often involve harmonized international standards, enabling consistent enforcement of re-export restrictions across jurisdictions.[27] Similar international coordination is currently lacking in the context of data flows.

10.3.4 Compatibility with WTO and FTA Rules

Finally, we need to assess whether measures outlined in Sect. 10.2 conform to international trade rules under the WTO and FTAs. As noted earlier, there is already a substantial body of scholarship analyzing the consistency between restrictions on cross-border personal data transfers and obligations under the WTO's GATS and bilateral or plurilateral FTAs.

In substance, the same types of trade rule violations could be invoked in the context of security-related data transfer restrictions. However, a key difference lies in the likely invocation of national security exceptions as a legal justification. In such cases, measures may be assessed under Article XIV bis of the GATS or comparable clauses in FTAs, which provide broader discretion for states to adopt measures for the protection of essential security interests.

---

[26] Watanabe et al. (2025).

[27] Please see *infra.*, 4.1.

10.3.4.1 WTO Consistency[28]

Under WTO law, there is no provision that directly regulates cross-border data transfers. Nevertheless, prior research has acknowledged that restrictions on data flows may constitute barriers to trade in services and therefore be subject to obligations under the GATS. Depending on the nature of the measure and the commitments listed in a Member's schedule, such restrictions may violate the most-favored-nation (MFN) obligation, national treatment, or market access obligations.[29] For instance, a U.S. policy that prohibits data transfers to specific countries—but permits them to others—could potentially violate the MFN principle.

Such violations may, however, be justified under GATS Article XIV, which provides general exceptions. In case of a measure like the U.S. data transfer restrictions, if the stated objective is the protection of personal data, they could fall within the exception for "the protection of the privacy of individuals in relation to the processing and dissemination of personal data."[30]

However, in the context of this paper, the measures in question are primarily motivated not by privacy concerns, but by national security. As such, Article XIV bis (Security Exceptions) is a more relevant provision. Nonetheless, applying this article presents interpretive difficulties. Article XIV bis(2)(b) lists three specific exceptions: (i) the supply of services to military establishments, (ii) the supply of services relating to nuclear materials, and (iii) emergencies in international relations. The data transfer restrictions discussed here do not appear to fall neatly into any of these categories. Therefore, the most plausible legal basis, then, would be Article XIV bis(1)(a), which states:

> Nothing in this Agreement shall be construed to require any Member to furnish any information, the disclosure of which it considers contrary to its essential security interests.

A central interpretive issue arises as to whether the term "information" can include data held by private entities. The text seems to assume that the information is in the possession of the government itself, implying that measures regulating private-sector data flows might fall outside the intended scope of this exception. On this basis, reconciling current national security–motivated data transfer restrictions with WTO obligations appears to be legally challenging.

That said, even if WTO-consistency is questionable in legal terms, it is unlikely to pose a significant practical risk. As discussed earlier, many countries have shown a strong interest in maintaining sovereign authority to restrict outbound data flows for national security reasons. In this political climate, a WTO ruling against one country's security-based data regulation could set a precedent that undermines the legitimacy of similar measures adopted by other Members. Consequently, states may refrain from initiating disputes, even if legal grounds for a challenge exist.

---

[28] *See generally*, Mitchell and Mishra (2021, pp. 83–112).

[29] Abe (2021, pp. 9–17).

[30] *Ibid.*, pp. 17–20.

10.3.4.2 FTA Compatibility

While numerous FTAs address digital trade and data flows, this section focuses on two advanced frameworks with multiple Asia–Pacific signatories: the Comprehensive and Progressive Agreement for Trans-Pacific Partnership (CPTPP) and EU-Japan Economic Partnership Agreement (EJEPA).

CPTPP[31]

The CPTPP advances beyond the GATS in explicitly addressing cross-border data flows. Article 14.11 (Cross-Border Transfer of Information by Electronic Means) provides:

> 1. The Parties recognize that each Party may have its own regulatory requirements concerning the transfer of information by electronic means.

This acknowledges the regulatory sovereignty of each Party. However, it is followed by a binding obligation:

> 2. Each Party shall allow the cross-border transfer of information by electronic means, including personal information, when this activity is for the conduct of the business of a covered person.

In principle, then, CPTPP Member States must permit data transfers necessary for business operations. Nevertheless, this obligation is subject to exceptions.

While national security–motivated restrictions on cross-border data flows may arguably conflict with Article 14.11, they may also be subject to objective assessments—especially if challenged under the CPTPP's dispute settlement mechanism. Whether a given restriction qualifies for an exception would depend on its proportionality and necessity under the agreement.

Importantly, the CPTPP includes horizontal security exceptions that apply across all chapters, including Chap. 14 as follows:

> Nothing in this Agreement shall be construed to:
>
> (a) require a Party to furnish or allow access to any information the disclosure of which it determines to be contrary to its essential security interests; or
>
> (b) preclude a Party from applying measures that it considers necessary for the fulfillment of its obligations with respect to the maintenance or restoration of international peace or security, or the protection of its own essential security interests.[32]

Compared to GATS Article XIV bis, the CPTPP's security exception is broader and affords greater discretion to Member States. The phrase "measures that it considers necessary" grants wide leeway for Parties to adopt restrictive measures, provided they can plausibly link them to essential security interests. Accordingly,

---

[31] Bryztwa et al. (2021, pp. 452–453).

[32] CPTPP, Article 29.2 (Security Exceptions).

many of the restrictions discussed in Sect. 10.2 could likely be justified under this clause. This provision is also contained in subsequent US-led digital trade agreements like Agreement Between the United States of America and Japan Concerning Digital Trade (USJDTA).[33]

EU-Japan Economic Partnership Agreement

The EU–Japan Economic Partnership Agreement (EJEPA) entered into force in February 2019. Although discussions on cross-border data flows initially stalled due to differences in positions between Japan and the EU, a formal agreement was finally reached at the end of 2023. It stipulates as a general principle that "Party shall not adopt or maintain measures which prohibit or restrict the crossborder transfer of information."[34]

This principle has an exception as below;

> Nothing in this Article shall prevent a Party from adopting or maintaining measures inconsistent with paragraphs 1 and 2 to achieve a legitimate public policy objective, provided that the measure:
>
> (a) is not applied in a manner which would constitute a means of arbitrary or unjustifiable discrimination between countries where like conditions prevail, or a disguised restriction on trade; and
>
> (b) does not impose restrictions on transfers of information that are greater than necessary to achieve the objective.

EJEPA also has WTO-like general exceptions, horizontally applicable to all articles, which are similar to those of GATT/GATS.[35]

Based on the foregoing analysis, this section has demonstrated that, under WTO rules, certain national security–based restrictions on cross-border data transfers may conflict with obligations under the General Agreement on Trade in Services (GATS). While it is difficult to justify such restrictions through the narrowly construed security exceptions provided under the GATS, in practice, few disputes arise. This is primarily because many WTO Members are themselves seeking to preserve regulatory discretion in this area and are therefore disincentivized from initiating formal challenges. In contrast, the Comprehensive and Progressive Agreement for Trans-Pacific Partnership (CPTPP) offers a more expansive security exception, granting greater discretion to member states. As a result, cross-border data transfer restrictions imposed for national security purposes are less likely to be inconsistent with CPTPP obligations.

---

[33] USJDTA, Article 4.

[34] EJEPA, Article 8.81.

[35] EJEPA, Article 1.5.

10.4 Possible Solutions

Can international economic law offer effective solutions to the challenges identified in Sect. 10.3?

10.4.1 International Cooperation on Data Export Controls

Many of the issues raised in Sect. 10.3 closely resemble challenges already addressed in the context of export controls for goods. In that realm, study on multilateral export control regimes—such as the Wassenaar Arrangement and the Australia Group, both of which evolved from the former Coordinating Committee for Multilateral Export Controls (COCOM)—plays a central role. For example, the Australia Group states its objective as follows:

> Through the harmonization of export controls based on common control lists and the exchange and publication of information, cooperation among AG participants aims to prevent would-be proliferators and terrorists from exploiting differences or ambiguities in national export control arrangements.[36]

By analogy, similar arrangements may be beneficial in the area of data exports. For instance, a common control list could be established to define what types of data—such as bulk sensitive personal data—constitute national security risks. Furthermore, information-sharing frameworks could clarify whether such data is subject to blanket export bans, licensing regimes, or conditional restrictions, depending on the jurisdiction.

Such cooperation would mitigate regulatory fragmentation and reduce compliance costs for multinational enterprises. At the same time, it would enhance consistency in the application of data transfer rules and functionally resemble re-export controls, thus also helping governments prevent indirect or unauthorized data flows.

That said, there is currently no global consensus on which categories of data are likely to impact national security, or how such risks materialize. While concerns such as foreign interference in elections or surveillance of government personnel through transferred personal data are acknowledged by some countries, many others have yet to adopt similar threat perceptions. Accordingly, a first step may be for like-minded countries to begin sharing their respective risk assessments concerning the intersection of cross-border data transfers and national security.

Given the sensitive nature of such information, a practical starting point may be to build coalitions among trusted partners, such as countries participating in the Clean Network Initiative, and to establish a secure framework for confidential information exchange. Within such frameworks, participating states could also explore mechanisms to ensure transparency—drawing lessons from export control regimes

---

[36] WTO (2023, p. 11 5).

in goods, such as the regular updates of control lists and protection of confidential technical information in line with technological progress.

It must be noted, however, that export control regimes on goods themselves are not without challenges. For instance, the Wassenaar Arrangement has been criticized for failing to keep pace with emerging technologies such as AI, prompting countries like the United States to adopt unilateral measures that go beyond the agreed framework.[37] These limitations underscore the need for renewed international coordination. Platforms such as the U.S.–EU Trade and Technology Council (TTC)—which already discusses the modernization of export controls[38]—may serve as useful institutional models.

10.4.2 International Rulemaking on Government Access[39]

As demonstrated in previous sections, countries such as the United States and Japan increasingly view the possibility of GA to transferred data in recipient countries as a national security threat. Restrictions on data transfers to such jurisdictions are based on this concern. Therefore, if recipient countries were to adopt appropriate rules on GA, the associated risks could be substantially reduced. This represents a more fundamental and long-term solution.

At present, efforts are underway within the OECD to establish international principles governing government access to data. In December 2022, the OECD adopted the "Declaration on Government Access to Personal Data Held by Private Sector Entities," which sets out seven high-level principles related to government access for national security and law enforcement purposes.

However, these principles are limited in scope to personal data and to GA for national security and law enforcement. Rules governing GA to non-personal data or GA for the purposes other than national security or law enforcement have yet to be developed. Recognizing this gap, the G7 Trade Ministers' Statement (2023) affirmed:

> We welcome the OECD Declaration on Government Access to Personal Data Held by Private Sector Entities as an important tool to increase trust in, and facilitate, cross-border data flows... We acknowledge that unjustified government access to non-personal data, including confidential information, undermines the credibility of, and presents substantial obstacles to, cross-border data flows.[40]

Thus, expanding international rulemaking to cover non-personal data and non-security/law enforcement access is essential. In Japan, an expert group published a report in 2022 that addresses rulemaking on GA to both personal and non-personal

[37] Shivakumar et al. (2023).

[38] TTC (2021).

[39] *See generally*, Mishra (2024, pp. 115–122).

[40] G7 (2023).

data. Many of the concepts applicable to personal data could be extended to non-personal data, and the OECD may be a logical forum for this work.[41] In addition, we should take note that OECD is also working on governmental access on non-personal data, which started recently.[42]

Nonetheless, the OECD's membership is limited and excludes countries that are often categorized as "countries of concern" (e.g., China and Russia). Expanding participation beyond the OECD will be crucial in ensuring broader relevance and effectiveness.

Additionally, OECD principles are currently non-binding under international law. Yet, there is precedent for such soft law instruments gaining legal significance when referenced in trade agreements. For instance, both the OECD Privacy Guidelines and the ILO Declaration on Fundamental Principles and Rights at Work have been referenced in FTAs, thereby becoming subject to dispute settlement mechanisms. A pertinent example is the EU–Japan Economic Partnership Agreement (EPA), which includes a provision stating:

> The Parties also recognise that high standards of privacy and data protection as regards government access to privately held data, such as those outlined in the OECD Principles for Government Access to Personal Data held by Private Sector Entities, contribute to trust in the digital economy.[43]

While this provision does not impose binding obligations, it sets an important precedent for the incorporation of GA principles into trade law. Moving forward, FTAs could include more concrete obligations, such as clauses authorizing data transfer restrictions against countries that fail to adhere to such principles—either through general or national security exceptions.

10.4.3 Clarifying WTO Rules

As noted in Sect. 10.3, the current security exceptions under GATS may not provide sufficient flexibility to justify cross-border data transfer restrictions based on national security grounds. Given that formal amendments to WTO agreements are politically infeasible, alternative interpretative or procedural approaches should be explored.

One such approach may involve seeking consensus interpretations within the Council for Trade in Services, clarifying that GATS Article XIV bis can be applied to cover national security concerns relating to cross-border data flows. Even committee-level, not at the Ministerial level, consensus decisions can be qualified as "subsequent agreement" under Article 31(3)(a) of the Vienna Convention on the Law of Treaties, which establishes interpretive guidance among treaty parties as well as dispute settlement bodies.[44]

---

[41] CFIEC (2022).

[42] López González et al. (2025).

[43] EUJEPA, Article 8.82(3).

[44] WTO (2012), paras. 241–275.

That said, international debate on this issue remains limited. Thus, as emphasized in Sect. 10.4.1, the initial priority may be to establish forums for consensus-building among like-minded countries, which could eventually lead to broader acceptance and clarification of WTO rules in this domain.

10.5 Conclusion

This paper has examined how the expanding concept of national security is increasingly influencing global data flows. In particular, it has highlighted how restrictions on cross-border data transfers are being implemented as countermeasures against the risk of unrestricted government access by so-called countries of concern. These measures are being introduced unilaterally by individual states, leading to a lack of transparency and growing regulatory fragmentation. This fragmentation also creates the risk that data transferred to a trusted country may be subsequently re-exported to a third country lacking equivalent regulatory safeguards—potentially circumventing the intent of the original restriction.

As discussed in Sect. 10.4, many of these challenges mirror those previously addressed in the context of export controls on goods. There are valuable lessons to be drawn from multilateral export control regimes, which have developed structured approaches such as common control lists, licensing systems, and information-sharing frameworks. These forums are also important mechanisms to enhance common understandings of national security risks and unnecessary restrictions on data transfers, an important factor to secure policy space while maintaining day-to-day commercial transactions. However, a significant divide remains between the communities involved in digital data governance and those traditionally engaged in export control of tangible goods. This lack of interdisciplinary engagement has impeded the cross-pollination of ideas, even where structural similarities exist.

Going forward, academic exchanges between these two communities should be actively encouraged. On the practical level, collaboration between corporate departments responsible for data governance and those managing export compliance should be strengthened. Similarly, interagency cooperation between governmental units tasked with export control and those handling security-related data transfer restrictions is also crucial.

At the same time, the export control community must increasingly consider developments in the digital domain. This includes the regulation of networked devices, surveillance technologies, connected products, and semiconductors used in AI. Mutual learning and cooperation between the two policy domains may help foster a more integrated regulatory framework for both tangible and intangible assets under the umbrella of national security.

From a legal perspective, this paper has only briefly touched upon a more fundamental question that merits deeper engagement within the field of international economic law: how should cross-border data transfer restrictions grounded in national security be evaluated under WTO law? Compared to the WTO's narrow security exceptions, recent FTAs—such as the CPTPP—adopt much broader security exceptions, suggesting an emerging trend toward greater regulatory autonomy for national security measures.

This raises a new challenge: how should the relationship between the WTO and these more permissive WTO-minus FTAs be conceptualized? In disputes between CPTPP members within the WTO framework, could a party invoke the CPTPP's broader national security exception to justify an alleged WTO violation? While past WTO jurisprudence does not categorically rule out such arguments, it would likely be extremely difficult to succeed.

Security-related restrictions on cross-border data flows thus represent one of the most pressing contemporary challenges at the intersection of trade law, national security, and digital governance. Continued academic, institutional, and legal efforts are essential to address this evolving and complex policy frontier.

References

Abe Y (2021), Data Localization Measures and International Economic Law: How Do WTO and TPP/CPTPP Disciplines Apply to These Measures? Public Policy Review 16 5 1 29

Barno D. and Bensahel N (2016), A New Generation of Unrestricted Warfare. https://warontherocks.com/2016/04/a-new-generation-of-unrestricted-warfare/

Burri M (2021), Data Flows and Global Trade Law Big Data Global Trade Eds Mira Burri Oxford University Press Law 11 41

Brzytwa E, N Cory S Ezell 2021 Understanding the TPP Agreement E-Commerce Chapter DA Gantz Eds Huerta-Goldman JA Analysis and Commentary. Cambridge University Press The Comprehensive and Progressive Trans-Pacific Partnership 443 457

Cabinet Office (2025), Regarding System for Ensuring Stable Provision of Essential Infrastructure Services, 13–15, https://www.cao.go.jp/keizai_anzen_hosho/suishinhou/infra/doc/infra_gaiyou.pdf (translated by the author)

CFIEC (2022), Report of the Study Group on Government Access and Trade Rules] Rulemaking for Government Access: Toward Appropriate International Distribution of Personal and Non-Personal Data, https://www.cfiec.jp/wp-content/uploads/pdf/gov/gov-2022-11-complete.pdf

China Law Translate (2017), National Intelligence Law. https://www.chinalawtranslate.com/en/national-intelligence-law-of-the-p-r-c-2017/#_Toc486408893

Corporation LY (2021), Final Report of the Special Advisory Committee on Global Data Governance, https://www.lycorp.co.jp/ja/privacy-security/special-advisory-committee/Final-Report-by-the-Specioal-Advisory-Committee_full.pdf

Digital Agency (2023), Issues and Barriers of Cross-border Flow of Data, https://www.digital.go.jp/en/policies/dfft/dfft-issues-and-barriers

European Parliament (2023), Japan's economic security legislation, https://www.europarl.europa.eu/RegData/etudes/ATAG/2023/751417/EPRS_ATA(2023)751417_EN.pdf

Executive Office of the President (2020), Regarding the Acquisition of StayNTouch, Inc. by Beijing Shiji Information Technology Co., Ltd., https://trumpwhitehouse.archives.gov/presidential-actions/order-regarding-acquisition-stayntouch-inc-beijing-shiji-information-technology-co-ltd/

G7 (2023), G7 Trade Ministers' Statement Osaka-Sakai, 29 October 2023, https://www.meti.go.jp/press/2023/10/20231029001/20231029001-a.pdf

Government of Japan (GOJ) (2022), Outline of the Economic Security Promotion Act (Act on the Promotion of Ensuring National Security through Integrated Implementation of Economic Measures), https://www.japaneselawtranslation.go.jp/outline/75/905R403.pdf

Irion K, Yakovleva S and Bartl M (2016), Trade and Privacy: Complicated Bedfellows?. https://www.ivir.nl/publicaties/download/trade_and_privacy.pdf
Kwan C H (2024), Strengthening National Security Has Become a Top Priority for the Xi Jinping Administration —Can it be compatible with economic development?, https://www.rieti.go.jp/en/china/24031301.html
López González, J., C. Del Giovane and J. Ferencz (2025), "A Preliminary Mapping of Measures Affecting the Cross-Border Flow of Non-Personal Data", OECD Trade Policy Papers, No. 295, OECD Publishing, Paris, https://doi.org/10.1787/0825c57c-en.
Mishra N (2024), International Trade Law and Global Data Governance: Aligning Perspectives and Practices, Hart Publishing
Mitchell AD, N Mishra (2021), WTO Law and Cross-Border Data Flows An Unfinished Agenda Big Data Global Trade Eds Mira Burri Oxford University Press Law 83 112
National Administration of Surveying, Mapping and Geoinformation of China (NASG) (2017), Surveying and Mapping Law of the People's Republic of China. https://web.archive.org/web/20170525200020/http://en.nasg.gov.cn/article/Lawsandregulations/201312/20131200005471.shtml
OECD (2022), Declaration on Government Access to Personal Data Held by Private Sector Entities, https://legalinstruments.oecd.org/en/instruments/OECD-LEGAL-0487
Pauwelyn J (2010), Squaring Free Trade in Culture With Chinese Censorship: the WTO Appellate Body Report on China - Audiovisuals Melbourne Journal of International Law 11 1 119 140
Roumeliotis G (2018), U.S. blocks MoneyGram sale to China's Ant Financial on national security concerns. https://www.reuters.com/article/business/us-blocks-moneygram-sale-to-chinas-ant-financial-on-national-security-concern-idUSKBN1ET039/
Shivakumar S, Wessner C, Tomoshige H (2023), Toward a New Multilateral Export Control Regime, https://www.csis.org/analysis/toward-new-multilateral-export-control-regime
Tiles T (2017), U.S. Asks China not to Enforce Cyber Security Law, Reuters, September 2017.
TTC (2021), Working Group 7 - Export Controls, https://futurium.ec.europa.eu/en/EU-US-TTC/wg7
US Department of State (USDOS) (2021), The Clean Network, https://2017-2021.state.gov/the-clean-network/
Watai R (2023), Digital Trade and Economic Security: considerations on the Japan-US Digital Trade Agreement. In Research Handbook on Digital Trade (David Collins and Michael Geist ed., 2023), pp. 439–454.
Watanabe S (2019), Restrictions on outbound data transfer based on Government Access in foreign countries -The current situation, Regulation by International Trade Law and Implications for DFFT-, https://www.rieti.go.jp/en/publications/summary/19120008.html
Watanabe S, Ogura E and Oikawa K (2025), Current Status of ASEAN Data Governance and Its Implications for the Digital Economy Framework Agreement. https://www.eria.org/uploads/Current-Status-of-ASEAN-Data-Governance-and-Its-Implications-for-the-DEFA.pdf/
Weber RH (2012), Regulatory Autonomy and Privacy Standards under the GATS Asian Journal of WTO and International Health Law and Policy 7 25 47
WTO (2012), Report of the Appellate Body, US-Clove Cigarettes
WTO (2023), International Export Regulations and Controls, https://www.wto.org/english/res_e/booksp_e/international_exp_regs_e.pdf

Chapter 11
Conflict Between Environmental Protection and Investment Protection

Satomi Shintani

Abstract This chapter explores the tension between environmental and investment protection in international investment arbitration, particularly in resource-rich Latin America. While no normative conflict exists between environmental and investment treaties, *de facto* conflicts arise: states risk large compensation when environmental measures breach investment agreements, deterring regulation. Treaty exceptions fail to shield states because tribunals impose additional criteria—good faith, proportionality, non-arbitrariness—whose meanings remain ambiguous and inconsistently applied. Two solutions are proposed: (1) clarifying treaty provisions with detailed criteria to guide states and tribunals; (2) allowing state counterclaims against investors to offset compensation and balance obligations. Clearer rules and counterclaims could reconcile regulatory autonomy with investment protection and reduce geopolitical risks.

Keywords International investment arbitration · Environmental protection · Exception clause · Indirect expropriation · Proportionality · Counterclaim

11.1 Recent Trends in International Investment Arbitration

The regulatory measures taken by a state to protect the environment may be challenged in international investment arbitration as violations of international investment protection agreements. This study analyzes these cases.

The first step in this inquiry was to examine the trends in investment arbitration cases that have emerged in recent years.

The following examples illustrate instances in which state environmental protection regulations were alleged to violate investment agreements, resulting in the issuance of investment arbitration awards after 2010 (it should be noted that this list

S. Shintani (✉)
University of Tokyo, Tokyo, Japan
e-mail: sshintani@g.ecc.u-tokyo.ac.jp

J. Nakagawa et al. (eds.), *Geopolitical Risks and Geoeconomics in International Economic Law*, Economics, Law, and Institutions in Asia Pacific,
https://doi.org/10.1007/978-981-95-6996-0_11

does not include cases involving changes in national policies related to renewable energy).

- Occidental Petroleum v. Ecuador[1]
- Clayton v. Canada[2]
- Al Tamimi v. Oman[3]
- Copper Mesa Mining v. Ecuador[4]
- Aven v. Costa Rica[5]
- Eco Oro v. Colombia[6]
- AsiaPhos v. China[7]
- Rockhopper Exploration v. Italy[8]
- Lee-Chin v. Dominican Republic[9]
- Red Eagle Exploration v. Colombia[10]
- Gabriel Resources v. Romania[11]
- Montauk Metals v. Colombia[12]

Notably, these cases were not extracted artificially. They demonstrate that a significant proportion of petitions pertain to the mineral mining sector in relation to the states' environmental protection regulations. This phenomenon is probably attributable to the high level of national interest in the pivotal industry of mineral resource development, as well as pervasive vigilance toward foreign companies. This provides a substantial incentive for some form of interference through regulations.

A review by United Nations Conference on Trade and Development (hereinafter UNCTAD) revealed that at least 175 Investor-State Dispute Settlement (hereinafter ISDS) were brought against state measures that are related to environmental protection, amounting to about 15% of all 1190 known ISDS cases based on International Investment Agreements (hereinafter IIAs) from 1987 to 2021.[13]

[1] Occidental Petroleum Corporation and Occidental Exploration and Production Company v. The Republic of Ecuador, ICSID Case No. ARB/06/11.

[2] William Richard Clayton, Douglas Clayton, Daniel Clayton, and Bilcon of Delaware, Inc. v. Government of Canada, PCA Case No. 2009–04.

[3] Adel A Hamadi Al Tamimi v. Sultanate of Oman, ICSID Case No. ARB/11/33.

[4] Copper Mesa Mining Corporation v. Republic of Ecuador, PCA No. 2012–2.

[5] David R. Aven and Others v. Republic of Costa Rica, ICSID Case No. UNCT/15/3.

[6] Eco Oro Minerals Corp. v. Republic of Colombia, ICSID Case No. ARB/16/41.

[7] AsiaPhos Limited and Norwest Chemicals Pte Ltd v. People's Republic of China, ICSID Case No. ADM/21/1.

[8] Rockhopper Italia S.p.A., Rockhopper Mediterranean Ltd, and Rockhopper Exploration Plc v. Italian Republic, ICSID Case No. ARB/17/14.

[9] Michael Anthony Lee-Chin v. Dominican Republic, ICSID Case No. UNCT/18/3.

[10] Red Eagle Exploration Limited v. Republic of Colombia, ICSID Case No. ARB/18/12.

[11] Gabriel Resources Ltd. and Gabriel Resources (Jersey) v. Romania (I), ICSID Case No. ARB/15/31.

[12] Montauk Metals Inc. (formerly known as Galway Gold Inc.) v. Republic of Colombia, ICSID Case No. ARB/18/13.

[13] UNCTAD (2022, p. 2).

According to this UNCTAD report, environmental ISDS cases have been more often brought against developed regions (67%) as opposed to the general trend whereby developing countries are the most frequent respondents in ISDS overall.[14] This phenomenon can be attributed to the numerous ISDS cases that have been initiated in response to legislative changes concerning renewable energy in developed countries such as Spain.

Excluding cases related to renewable energy policy, developing countries remain the most frequent respondents in the ISDS environmental cases. Upon examining the Annex in the UNCTAD report,[15] I identified a discernible trend. Latin American countries are more frequently surveyed than other regions. Specifically, the number of environmental cases brought against Latin American countries totaled 43, constituting 24.6% of all environmental cases. Within Latin America, Mexico emerged as the most frequent respondent with 8 cases, followed by Peru, Costa Rica, and Ecuador, each with 5 cases. Given that Brazil, the largest nation in Latin America, has only 3 bilateral investment treaties currently in effect, and considering that Bolivia, Ecuador, and Venezuela withdrew from the International Centre for Settlement of Investment Disputes (hereinafter ICSID) in 2007, 2009, and 2012, respectively (Ecuador reentered it in 2021), the incidence of international investment arbitrations involving these countries is relatively limited. However, the potential for international investment disputes may be significantly higher.

Latin America is recognized as a region with abundant natural resources. However, when considering other resource-rich regions such as Africa and ASEAN countries, the trends observed in Latin America are not similar. According to the same Annex, these regions do not exhibit comparable patterns. In African nations, a single ISDS environmental case had been initiated against each of the following countries: Tanzania, Lesotho, Mauritius, South Africa, and Senegal. Similarly, within the ASEAN region, one case each was filed against Thailand, Indonesia, Vietnam, and Sri Lanka.

It is widely acknowledged that Latin American countries encounter significant challenges related to environmental pollution. Given the critical importance of the Amazon forests, these nations are expected to implement effective environmental protection regulations worldwide. A plausible explanation for the high incidence of investment arbitration claims against these nations is their proactive stance toward addressing environmental issues. Conversely, resource-owning governments may employ environmental regulations to exert their influence, thereby manifesting resource nationalism through environmental policy measures.[16]

In either case, a high number of international investment arbitrations are closely linked to geopolitical risks in this area. Political instability has contributed to the rapid changes in policies and regulations.

Environmental degradation represents a significant challenge in both Africa and the ASEAN region. However, geopolitical risks do not manifest in the same manner

---

[14] *Ibid.*, p. 3.

[15] *Ibid.*, Annex 1, pp. 8–13.

[16] Michot Foss et al. (2024, p. 6).

in environmental ISDS cases as in Latin American countries. This discrepancy may be attributed to the relatively lower global environmental interest in these regions compared to Latin America, and resource nationalism is often exercised through alternative forms of state power such as direct expropriations.

Anyway, environmental ISDS cases have led to new geopolitical risks. If environmental protection regulations by the state make mineral mining impossible after the project has started, the result will be soaring mineral prices and supply instability. Although reducing state interference could minimize geopolitical risks and stabilize mineral prices and distribution, the state has the power to enforce such regulations. State interference is used to protect critical industries and their environments. The challenge is striking a balance between state regulatory power and investment protection. In recent years, environmental regulations have increased because of growing environmental concerns and interest in this area. This study addresses this issue.

11.2 Nature of the Conflict

Before examining this issue, I first identify the conflicts between environmental and investment protection.

The conceptualization of "conflict" varies among commentators. For instance, Pauwelyn argued that "two norms are ... in a relationship of conflict if one constitutes, has led to, or may lead to, a breach of the other.[17]" According to this definition, normative conflict exists when there is simultaneously a norm that obligates one to take a particular action and a norm that prohibits taking said action.

Notably, a significant number of environmental treaties do not impose specific obligations on the parties involved. Instead, these treaties establish objectives aimed at environmental preservation. The determination of the measures to be adopted for the implementation of the treaty is entrusted to state parties. For instance, Article 3.1 of the Stockholm Convention on Persistent Organic Pollutants (POPs) stipulates:

1. Each Party shall:
    a. Prohibit and/or take the legal and administrative measures necessary to eliminate:
        i. Its production and use of the chemicals listed in Annex A subject to the provisions of that Annex; and
        ii. Its import and export of the chemicals listed in Annex A in accordance with the provisions of paragraph 2; (...)

Consequently, the measures to be implemented are delegated at the discretion of each party, and there is no obligation to adopt measures that contravene investment protection agreements to implement environmental treaties. Furthermore, States may implement environmental treaties by adopting measures that do not violate IIAs.

[17] Pauwelyn (2003, pp. 175–176).

Environmental treaties and investment protection agreements are not inherently in conflict with each other. In this context, there is no direct contradiction between legal norms, meaning that normative conflicts do not exist.

It is worth noting that this is an erroneous assumption that conflicts are non-existent. In international investment arbitrations, when compensation is ordered against a state, the amount is often extremely high. Even if a state implements a measure as an environmental protection regulation, if investment arbitration finds a violation of an investment protection agreement, the state will have to pay a large amount of compensation. Developing countries that cannot afford such compensation may be reluctant to implement environmental protection measures for fear of being subjected to arbitration. This would have the consequence that the implementation of investment agreements would impede the implementation of environmental treaties. Therefore, even if no normative conflicts have arisen, *de facto* conflicts still exist.

To address these *de facto* conflicts, it is necessary to clarify the actions of a state that are determined to be violations of investment agreements in investment arbitration. It is imperative to guarantee that states implement suitable regulatory measures by elucidating the scope of measures that do not constitute violations of investment agreements; that is, those that can be executed without payment of compensation.

11.3 Approaches Adopted by the International Investment Arbitration Tribunals in Addressing the Problem

Recent investment protection agreements include provisions that define the relationship between investments and environmental protection. For instance, although somewhat dated, Article 1114 of NAFTA stipulates the following.

Article 1114: Environmental Measures

1. Nothing in this Chapter shall be construed to prevent a Party from adopting, maintaining or enforcing any measure otherwise consistent with this Chapter that it considers appropriate to ensure that investment activity in its territory is undertaken in a manner sensitive to environmental concerns.
2. The Parties recognize that it is inappropriate to encourage investment by relaxing domestic health, safety or environmental measures. Accordingly, a Party should not waive or otherwise derogate from, or offer to waive or otherwise derogate from, such measures as an encouragement for the establishment, acquisition, expansion or retention in its territory of an investment of an investor. If a Party considers that another Party has offered such an encouragement, it may request consultations with the other Party and the two Parties shall consult with a view to avoiding any such encouragement.

These exception clauses are intended to ensure that environmental regulatory measures by the state are not considered violations of the agreement by prioritizing environmental protection over investment. Therefore, the question arises as to whether incorporating such exceptions into investment protection agreements effectively resolves *de facto* conflict. To elucidate this, it is necessary to examine the positions adopted by investment arbitration tribunals.

In the case of Aven v. Costa Rica, the issue was whether the suspension of the development of a resort area due to environmental regulations adopted by the state violated the DR-CAFTA. The applicable law, DR-CAFTA, contains a provision similar to that of NAFTA Article 1114. In this case, the Arbitral Tribunal holds[18];

412. Although the express terms of Article 10.11 essentially subordinate the rights to investors under Chapter Ten to the right of Costa Rica to ensure that the investments are carried out "in a matter sensitive to environmental concerns," this subordination is not absolute in the view of the Tribunal. It requires that the actions to be taken by the States Parties to DR-CAFTA act in line with principles of international law, which require acting in good faith. It is not a question of "not-applying" those provisions under Chapter Ten, but rather giving preference to the standards of environmental protection that were stated to be of interest to the Treaty Parties at the time it was signed.

413. Although Respondent argues that when Article 17.2(1)(b) establishes discretionary powers to the Treaty member Party with respect to investigatory, prosecutorial, regulatory, and compliance for enforcement of environmental matters, this implies a manner of ensuring that a Party can, as it sees fit, implement its own environmental laws without fear of violating DR-CAFTA, the Tribunal believes that this is not an absolute right either that may be exercised in any manner Respondent desires. By signing the Treaty, Respondent has agreed that there are limits to the manner in which a Party may implement and enforce its own environmental laws. It must do so in a fair, non-discriminatory fashion, applying said laws to protect the environment, following principles of due process, not only for its adoption but also for its enforcement.

The arbitral tribunal in question, while evidently favoring environmental protection, signaled that it did not possess the authority to grant the state the unmitigated freedom to formulate environmental protection regulations. The arbitral tribunal's decision indicates that the signing of the treaty by the respondent signifies their consent to the constraints imposed on the manner in which a party may implement and enforce its environmental laws. In this sense, the concept of a "preference to the standards of environmental protection" remains ambiguous, suggesting that the adoption of environmental protection regulations by parties is not as autonomous as previously assumed.

In Eco Oro v. Colombia, the central issue was whether the prohibition of the development of a gold and silver mine for environmental protection after the issuance of a permit to develop the mine violated the Free Trade Agreement (hereinafter FTA).

---

[18] David R. Aven and Others v. Republic of Costa Rica, ICSID Case No. UNCT/15/3, Award of the Tribunal, 18 September 2018, paras. 412–413 (footnote omitted).

The applicable law, the Canada-Colombia FTA, contains the following exception clause[19];

> "(3) For the purposes of Chapter Eight (Investment), subject to the requirement that such measures are not applied in a manner that constitute arbitrary or unjustifiable discrimination between investment or between investors, or a disguised restriction on international trade or investment, nothing in this Agreement shall be construed to prevent a Party from adopting or enforcing measures necessary:
>
> (a) To protect human, animal or plant life or health, which the Parties understand to include environmental measures necessary to protect human, animal or plant life and health;
>
> (b) To ensure compliance with laws and regulations that are not inconsistent with this Agreement; or
>
> (c) For the conservation of living or non-living exhaustible natural resources."

The Arbitral Tribunal determined that Colombia's environmental regulatory measures constituted a legitimate exercise of police power and did not amount to indirect expropriation. However, the Tribunal concluded that Article 805, which stipulates a minimum standard treatment obligation, had been violated.[20] Having determined this, the Arbitral Tribunal construed Article 2201(3) (the environmental protection exception clause) as being permissive, ensuring that a Party is not prohibited from adopting or enforcing a measure to protect human, animal or plant life and health, provided that such measures are not arbitrary or unjustifiably discriminatory between investments or between investors or a disguised restriction on international trade or investment.[21] The Arbitral Tribunal acknowledges the rights of states to adopt or enforce the measures in question. Concurrently, the Tribunal recognizes the right of investors to seek restitution. Specifically, the Tribunal interprets Article 2201(3) to mean that while a State may implement or enforce a measure in accordance with the objectives outlined in Article 2201(3) without violating the FTA, this does not preclude an investor from asserting a claim under Chapter Eight that such a measure warrants compensation.[22]

Therefore, States must provide compensation for implementing legitimate regulatory measures. At this juncture, the award was subjected to significant criticism.[23] Nevertheless, interpreting this award in such a manner appears contradictory to its determination of damages, which states the following[24];

829 In ascertaining the quantum of loss suffered by Eco Oro, it is unarguable that inherent in the reparation standard is the principle that a claimant can only recover for losses which it has established to have been caused by an internationally wrongful

[19] Article 2201(3) of Free Trade Agreement between Canada and the Republic of Colombia (signed on 21 November 2008 and entered into force on 15 August 2011).

[20] Eco Oro Minerals Corp. v. Republic of Colombia, ICSID Case No. ARB/16/41, Decision on Jurisdiction, Liability and Directions on Quantum, 9 September 2021, paras. 384–821.

[21] *Ibid*., para. 829.

[22] *Ibid*., para. 830.

[23] For example, Heath (2021).

[24] Eco Oro Minerals Corp. v. Republic of Colombia, ICSID Case No. ARB/16/41, Award on Damages, 15 July 2024, para. 299.

act. A loss caused by other factors, including any act which has been found to be lawful, is not recoverable. To this end, in identifying the losses which are caused by the acts found by the majority of the Tribunal to amount to a breach of Article 805, it is necessary to exclude those losses which would have been suffered in any event as a result of measures found by the majority of the Tribunal to be lawful. This requires the Tribunal to distinguish between the measures that have been found to be a breach of Article 805, on the one hand, and the loss that has been suffered by Eco Oro as a result of such measures, on the other. The question for the Tribunal is therefore: what losses were caused as a result of the breach of Article 805?

This paragraph rejects the notion that states must compensate for legitimate regulatory measures. Specifically, the Arbitral Tribunal did not calculate compensation for such measures when they were determined to not constitute indirect expropriation. These two decisions appear to contradict each other. However, it is uncommon for an arbitral tribunal comprising the same individual to issue contradictory awards, which suggests that an alternative interpretation may be reasonable. If this is the case, the award on merits should be considered to convey the same conclusion as the arbitral award in the case of Aven v. Costa Rica. While exception clauses acknowledge the authority of states to implement regulatory measures, they do not guarantee that such measures, when enacted as state regulations, will consistently comply with the Agreement.

It is evident from these arbitral awards that such exceptions do not diminish the likelihood of state regulatory measures being exempted from the obligation to provide compensation. While the exception grants the state the authority to implement regulatory measures and stipulates that *bona fide* regulatory measures are not subject to compensation obligations, it does not confer upon the state discretion to determine the *bona fides* of the regulation or the propriety of its implementation. Although states may have included such exceptions to completely exempt themselves from the obligation to compensate for regulatory measures, investment arbitration awards do not express this understanding.

As Garden asserted, the intentional inclusion of explicit treaty language by treaty drafters aimed at balancing states' environmental obligations with foreign investors' rights does not seem to have achieved anticipated clarity or outcomes.[25] These exception clauses do not mitigate the inherent *de facto* conflict between environmental and investment protection; rather, they exacerbate it.

Therefore, it is imperative to explore alternative solutions to this issue.

11.4 Suggestions for Problem Solving

Two approaches are proposed to address this issue.

[25] Garden (2022, pp. 17–24).

11.4.1 Clarification of the Content of Each Provision

The first approach involves clarifying the content of each provision and determining the state measures that violate it. This can be achieved by detailing the articles during the treaty-making process. An example can be observed in the expropriation provisions (Article 6 (2)(c)) within the Bilateral Investment Treaty (hereinafter BIT) between Hungary and Turkmenistan, which prescribes:

(c) non-discriminatory measures that the Contracting Parties take for legitimate reason of public purpose including for reasons of public health, safety, and environmental protection, which are taken in good faith, which are not arbitrary, and which are proportionate and reasonably connected to the stated purpose, shall not constitute indirect expropriation.

This Article asserts that non-discriminatory measures implemented by Contracting Parties for legitimate public purposes, including public health, safety, and environmental protection, do not constitute indirect expropriation. Furthermore, the Article delineates additional criteria for a regulation to be classified as one that does not amount to indirect expropriation. These criteria include actions taken in good faith, actions that are not arbitrary, and actions that are proportional to and reasonably related to the stated purpose. According to this Article, regulatory measures are not exempt from the obligation to provide compensation merely because they are enacted on a non-discriminatory, public-purpose basis, and additional criteria must also be satisfied.

Similarly, Annex 15.11(e) of the Costa Rica-Ecuador Trade Association Agreement stipulates (original text in Spanish only)[26];

(e) salvo en circunstancias excepcionales, como cuando una medida o serie de medidas son desproporcionadas a la luz de su objetivo de forma tal que no pueda considerarse de manera razonable que fueron adoptadas y aplicadas de buena fe, las acciones regulatorias no discriminatorias de una Parte que son diseñadas y aplicadas para proteger los objetivos legítimos de bienestar público, tales como salud pública, seguridad y medio ambiente, no constituyen una expropiación indirecta.

Currently, an increasing number of agreements incorporate provisions asserting that non-discriminatory regulatory actions undertaken by a party aimed at safeguarding legitimate public welfare objectives, such as public health, safety, and environmental protection, do not constitute indirect expropriation. Some agreements further stipulate this with the caveat "except in rare circumstances." However, broadly defined exception clauses fail to address this underlying issue. As evidenced by the previously discussed arbitral awards, a regulatory measure adopted indiscriminately by a state does not absolve its obligation to provide compensation. Therefore, a

[26] Translation:

Except in exceptional circumstances, such as when a measure or series of measures are disproportionate in light of their objective in such a way that they cannot be reasonably be considered to have been adopted and applied in good faith, non-discriminatory regulatory actions of a Party that are designed and applied to protect the legitimate public welfare objectives, such as public health, safety and the environment, do not constitute an indirect expropriation.

broadly defined exception is meaningless. Consequently, it is more efficacious to specify additional requirements, such as proportionality, at the treaty's inception. By delineating these requirements at the conclusion of the treaty, states are better informed of the regulatory measures they should consider to avoid contravening the agreement and arbitral tribunals are provided with guidance in their decision-making processes during investment arbitration. In this context, articulating detailed requirements for regulations that can be implemented without compensation is a potentially effective approach to resolve this issue.

Certain article categories aim to elucidate domestic legal standards by integrating them into the conventions. For instance, Article 10.13, which pertains to the expropriation provision of the Regional Comprehensive Economic Partnership Agreement (hereinafter, the RCEP Agreement), is supplemented by Annex 10B. Paragraph 3 of Annex 10B stipulates the following.

3. The determination of whether an action or series of related actions by a Party, in a specific fact situation, constitutes an expropriation of the type referred to in subparagraph 2(b) requires a case-by-case, fact-based inquiry that considers, among other factors:

(a) the economic impact of the government action, although the fact that an action or a series of related actions by a Party has an adverse effect on the economic value of an investment, standing alone, does not establish that such an expropriation has occurred;
(b) whether the government action breaches the government's prior binding written commitment to the investor, whether by contract, licence, or other legal document; and
(c) the character of the government action, including its objective and context.[2]

[2]For Korea, a relevant consideration could include whether the investor bears a disproportionate burden, such as a special sacrifice that exceeds what the investor or investment should be expected to endure for the public interest. This footnote does not prejudice the determination of the character of the government action of any other Party.

The Republic of Korea maintains that compensation for the infringement of property rights, necessitated by public necessity, requires the loss incurred to constitute a "special sacrifice." This provision of the RCEP Agreement is currently applicable only to South Korea. However, it offers the advantage of allowing parties to anticipate, to some degree, the nature of the compensation required for various state measures by referencing their own domestic systems.

It is important to acknowledge that the inclusion of such detailed provisions does not resolve all issues. While these clauses may enhance the predictability of the parties involved, they do not guarantee that the outcomes align precisely with their expectations. For instance, regarding the concepts of "proportionality" and "arbitrariness" as stipulated in these provisions, it is challenging to predefine in detail within the Convention the state measures that will be deemed "proportional" or "arbitrary." Consequently, the determination is left to the arbitral tribunals' discretion.

Historically, arbitral tribunals have not consistently adjudicated on matters such as "proportionality." For example, in Tecmed v. Mexico, proportionality was employed to assess the applicability of indirect expropriation in this case.[27] Conversely, in Eco Oro v., Colombia, the Arbitral Tribunal, after recognizing the state measure as a legitimate regulatory action, applied the proportionality test to ascertain whether the measure fell within the category of "except in rare circumstances."[28]

An in-depth examination reveals that the application of the proportionality test to investment arbitration has been inconsistent with varying interpretations of its purpose. However, this issue has not been addressed yet. In the case of Casinos Austria v. Argentina, the Arbitral Tribunal stated that proportionality is laid down as a principle of (public) law in the domestic laws of a large number of countries, and in the practice of their domestic courts, and is used and applied as a principle of international law in the practice of numerous other international courts and tribunals, both within the investment treaty context and beyond, thus confirming that proportionality qualifies as a general principle of law in Article 38(1)(c) of the ICJ Statute whose purpose it is to reconcile competing interests, such as investment protection as well as environmental protection, labor standards, human rights, or any other public interest, including the prevention of money laundering.[29] It is indisputable that the principle of proportionality is embedded in the public law frameworks of numerous countries and is reflected in the practices of their domestic courts. In this context, proportionality can be regarded as an established general principle of law. Nevertheless, as noted previously, the specific content of the proportionality test remains inconsistent, particularly in the context of investment arbitration. Even if proportionality could be acknowledged as a general principle of law, there is no consensus regarding its precise application. However, this has not yet been fully acknowledged.

Disparities in the interpretation of proportionality are evident not only among arbitrators but also more broadly. Bücheler, for instance, associates proportionality with the necessity of "assessing the relationship between means and ends and choosing the means that cause the least infringement," thereby framing it as strict proportionality.[30] He argues that proportionality is widely applied across various domains, including human rights, the use of force, and international investment law, and contends that it has been recognized as an independent rule of customary international law. Conversely, Henckels perceives proportionality analysis in investment arbitration as a mechanism for balancing the state's regulatory autonomy.[31] She proposes that proportionality analysis should be restructured as an "institutionally sensitive"

---

[27] Técnicas Medioambientales Tecmed S.A. v. The United Mexican States, ICSID Case No. ARB(AF)/00/2, Award, 29 May 2003, paras. 95–151.

[28] Eco Oro Minerals Corp. v. Republic of Colombia, *supra* note 20, paras. 623–699.

[29] Casinos Austria International GmbH and Casinos Austria Aktiengesellschaft v. Argentine Republic, ICSID Case No. ARB/14/32, Award of the Tribunal, 5 November 2021, para. 351.

[30] Bücheler (2015).

[31] Henckels (2015).

approach, highlighting the following three (+1) stages: legitimate objective, suitability, necessity, and proportionality stricto sensu. Henckels emphasizes that arbitral decisions should demonstrate deference—respect for the state—to avoid unduly infringing on the state's discretion. Additionally, Vadi examines proportionality in close connection with reasonableness and the standard of review.[32] Her approach integrates comparative constitutional law and legal theory, underscoring the risks and limitations associated with the "legal transplantation" of proportionality from domestic law to international investment law. She notes that special care is required when transplanting constitutional concepts and that understanding the normative context is crucial when applying proportionality. She also observes that proportionality "reflects the human desire for aesthetic balance," underscoring its relationship with value systems.

Even among a mere trio of scholars, there exist significant divergences in the comprehension of proportionality. Consequently, it is unsurprising that investors, host countries, and arbitrators each possess distinct interpretations of proportionality as well. From the negotiation of IIAs to the issuance of arbitral decisions, a diverse array of stakeholders is involved. During the treaty negotiation process, representatives from both nations participate in the negotiations. Upon reaching a consensus on a treaty draft, it is typically submitted to the national legislature of each country for approval before being enacted, although this procedure is not universally applicable to all treaties. In the event of investment arbitration, the host state, the investor, their respective legal counsel, and the arbitrators are all engaged in the proceedings. Each stakeholder has distinct interests encapsulated in the term "proportionality." It is unsurprising that these stakeholders may interpret "proportionality" differently. In this context, even if both the investor and the host country concur on the application of proportionality, the arbitrators' interpretation and application may diverge significantly from the expectations of either party.

Similar considerations apply to other criteria, such as arbitrariness. Therefore, it is imperative to accurately identify this issue and determine the appropriate criteria. This task should be undertaken by investment arbitration in the future and is also a crucial endeavor for researchers.

Consequently, the initial approach to resolving the conflict between environmental and investment protection encompasses two dimensions: one to be addressed by the state, and the other by the arbitral tribunal and researchers.

11.4.2 Permitting State Counterclaims Against Investors

An alternative approach for reconciling the conflict between environmental and investment protection is to implement a framework that permits states to file counterclaims against investors. The existing ISDS system is predominantly structured to

---

[32] Vadi (2018).

favor investors and is often perceived as one-sided because of the unilateral imposition of obligations solely on the state.[33] Within the current ISDS framework, the sole avenue for addressing investor violations of environmental and human rights laws is through procedures that align with the domestic laws of the host country. However, adopting such procedures may lead to arbitration allegations that the act in question constitutes a breach of IIA. Nevertheless, investment arbitration lacks a mechanism for adjudicating violations committed by investors.

Scholars have discussed counterclaims to address existing inequality between disputing parties in investment arbitration. A counterclaim is an autonomous claim by which the host state seeks a remedy on grounds that are separate from, but closely related to, those for principal claims, and, in this sense, is distinguished from pleadings to set-off.[34]

Counterclaims offer numerous advantages. Notably, enforcement under international investment arbitration is facilitated by the ICSID Convention and the New York Convention, making it more straightforward than the enforcement of domestic court judgments.[35] Furthermore, counterclaims can integrate external norms into IIAs, such as environmental and human rights obligations, into the dispute resolution process. Additionally, the acceptance of counterclaims may deter frivolous claims by claimant investors and frivolous objections by defendant states.[36]

If an investor declares bankruptcy, even a favorable ruling for the Host State in a domestic court may not result in compensation. However, if a state's counterclaim is upheld in investment arbitration, it may be possible to offset damages despite the absence of direct compensation. In instances in which an investor's property rights are adversely affected by a state's environmental regulatory measures, the state may be more inclined to implement such measures if they can mitigate the compensation owed to the investor through counterclaims. Counterclaims serve as a direct mechanism for addressing the conflict between environmental and investment protection.

To date, there have been few instances in which the jurisdiction and admissibility of counterclaims by states against investors in investment arbitration have been admitted, and it is improbable that such admissions will occur under the current ISDS regime.[37] The UNCITRAL Working Group III is currently deliberating on reform proposals for the existing ISDS system, with a particular focus on enabling states to file counterclaims against investors. For instance, WP.219 was discussed during the 45th session in September 2022, which included a draft article on counterclaims identified as Proposal D. Paragraph 1 of this proposal affirms that a respondent state may raise a counterclaim and outlines the potential conditions or grounds for doing so.[38]

---

[33] Ishikawa (2022, p. 8).

[34] *Ibid.*, p. 58.

[35] *Ibid.*, pp. 63–64.

[36] *Ibid.*, pp. 64–65.

[37] *Ibid.*, p. 117.

[38] UNCITRAL Working Group III (2022).

If counterclaims are accepted in the future, the inherent *de facto* conflict between environmental and investment protection may progress toward resolution.

11.5 Conclusion

This study demonstrates the inherent *de facto* conflict between environmental and investment protection. This study suggests that this conflict can be resolved by clarifying the content of each provision and permitting the state to counterclaim the investors. Two potential resolutions to this conflict involve implementing measures that ensure a balance between the state's right to regulate and investment protection. Achieving an appropriate balance between these two elements could mitigate the impact of the geopolitical risks identified in Section I of this study.

※This work was supported by JSPS KAKENHI (Grant Number JP24K16252).

References

Article by DOI

Garden, R (2022) Eco Oro v Colombia:1 The Brave New World of Environmental Exceptions. ICSID Review - Foreign Investment Law Journal 38(1): 17–24. https://doi.org/10.1093/icsidreview/siac020.

Book

Bücheler, Gebhard (2015) Proportionality in Investor-State Arbitration. Oxford University Press, Oxford, UK.

Henckels, Caroline (2015) Proportionality and Deference in Investor-State Arbitration: Balancing Investment Protection and Regulatory Autonomy. Cambridge University Press, Cambridge, UK.

Ishikawa, Tomoko (2022) Corporate Environmental Responsibility in Investor-State Dispute Settlement: The Unexhausted Potential of Current Mechanisms. Cambridge University Press, Cambridge, UK.

Pauwelyn, J (2003) Conflict of Norms in Public International Law: How WTO Law Relates to other Rules of International Law. Cambridge University Press, Cambridge, UK; New York, USA.

Vadi, Valentina (2018) Proportionality, Reasonableness and Standards of Review in International Investment Law and Arbitration. Edward Elgar Publishing, Cheltenham, UK; Northampton.

The Text of the Proposal D. paragraph 1 is as follows;

1. The respondent may make a counterclaim:

a) arising directly out of the subject matter of the dispute;

b) in connection with the factual and legal basis of the claim; or

c) that the claimant has breached its obligations under [this or any other applicable treaty, international law, domestic laws or investment contracts].

Online document

Heath, J. Benton (2021) Eco Oro and the Twilight of Policy Exceptionalism. Investment Treaty News. https://www.iisd.org/itn/2021/12/20/eco-oro-and-the-twilight-of-policy-exceptionalism/. Accessed on 29 October 2025.

Michot Foss, Michelle, et al. (2024) Political Risk and Resource Nationalism in Latin American Mining and Minerals. Rice University's Baker Institute for Public Policy. https://www.bakerinstitute.org/research/political-risk-and-resource-nationalism-latin-american-mining-and-minerals. Accessed on 29 October 2025.

UNCTAD, Treaty-based investor–State dispute settlement cases and climate action. IIA Issues Note, No. 4, September 2022, https://investmentpolicy.unctad.org/publications/1270/treaty-based-investor-state-dispute-settlement-cases-and-climate-action. Accessed 29 October 2025.

UNCITRAL Working Group III (2022) (Investor-State Dispute Settlement Reform), Possible reform of investor-State dispute settlement (ISDS) Draft provisions on procedural reform Note by the Secretariat (A/CN.9/WG.III/WP.219), http://undocs.org/en/A/CN.9/WG.III/WP.219. Accessed 29 October 2025.

Part III
Data Governance, Digital Sovereignty, and Regional Norm-Building in Asia

Chapter 12
Digital Silk Road or Cyber Silk Curtain? Geo-Economics and Legal Dynamics of China's Belt and Road Initiative Within ASEAN Under the RCEP Framework

Intan Innayatun Soeparna and Sheva Atha Nugroho

Abstract China's expanding Digital Silk Road (DSR) poses a significant challenge to ASEAN's digital sovereignty, exploiting gaps in the Regional Comprehensive Economic Partnership (RCEP), particularly in data governance and cybersecurity. This influence is magnified by fragmented regulations and varied infrastructure levels across ASEAN Member States, creating geopolitical and economic imbalances. To counter these challenges and internal divisions, ASEAN is developing the Digital Economy Framework Agreement (DEFA). This pivotal initiative aims to establish a legally binding framework for a unified regional digital economy. DEFA is explicitly designed to surpass RCEP by fostering deeper integration, harmonization, and interoperability among members. It addresses areas where RCEP was ambiguous, signaling a move toward more robust, binding rules. By creating a cohesive and progressive digital ecosystem, DEFA is anticipated to provide ASEAN nations with a strategic pathway to manage external influences like the DSR. Ultimately, this agreement seeks to strengthen ASEAN's relevance and centrality, allowing the bloc to navigate the complexities of the global digital landscape more effectively and secure its own digital future.

Keywords ASEAN · China · RCEP · Digital trade · Legal dynamic · Geo-economics

---

I. I. Soeparna (✉) · S. A. Nugroho
Faculty of Law, Universitas Airlangga, Surabaya, Indonesia
e-mail: intan@fh.unair.ac.id

J. Nakagawa et al. (eds.), *Geopolitical Risks and Geoeconomics in International Economic Law*, Economics, Law, and Institutions in Asia Pacific,
https://doi.org/10.1007/978-981-95-6996-0_12

12.1 Introduction

China's 2013 Belt and Road Initiative (BRI) expanded into the digital sphere in 2015 with the Digital Silk Road (DSR).[1] The DSR aims not only to strengthen China as a tech superpower but also to transform global digital governance by exporting its digital standards, infrastructure, and regulatory models, covering everything from 5G and cloud computing to AI.[2] ASEAN is a key region for the DSR, with heavy Chinese investment from tech giants like Huawei and Alibaba rapidly reshaping its digital landscape.[3] While these projects offer significant economic advantages, such as enhanced connectivity and e-commerce, they also introduce profound geopolitical and security challenges.[4] The growing dependence on Chinese technology raises acute apprehensions about digital sovereignty. ASEAN nations are now forced to navigate the complex challenges of data localization, cybersecurity vulnerabilities, and regulatory interoperability with China's distinct legal and political ecosystem.[5]

Compounding these concerns is the Regional Comprehensive Economic Partnership (RCEP). Signed on November 15, 2020, by the ten ASEAN countries and partners (Australia, China, Japan, Korea, and New Zealand), RCEP is a landmark achievement in global economic cooperation, creating the world's largest free trade zone.[6] However, while RCEP is vast, its digital trade provisions (primarily in Chapter 12) have been widely criticized as weak.[7] The agreement lacks robust, binding regulations on critical issues like cross-border data flows, data localization, and cybersecurity interoperability.[8] Many of its digital provisions are "best-endeavor" clauses, lacking the stringent commitments or dispute-settlement mechanisms needed to create a truly harmonized digital market. This regulatory vacuum is significant, as it inadvertently allows China to leverage RCEP's gaps to solidify its influence, pushing its own DSR-aligned standards into an otherwise undefined space.

This confluence of dominant DSR infrastructure and a permissive RCEP framework has engendered mounting apprehensions of a "Cyber Silk Curtain". This term describes a potential reality where ASEAN finds itself digitally siloed under China's sphere of influence, constraining its capacity to engage openly with the global digital marketplace.[9] Such isolation could hinder ASEAN nations from participating in equitable and transparent digital trade with economies beyond China's influence, thereby limiting technological collaborations and opportunities for economic diversification. Furthermore, the potential for economic and digital fragmentation within ASEAN

[1] Zeng (2019, pp. 207–216). See also Shen and Bingqin (2019, pp. 23–4 5).

[2] Insikt Group (2021, p. 4).

[3] Mochinaga (2021, p. 4). See also Su and Flew (2021, pp. 67–86).

[4] Khor et al. (2021, pp. 21–58).

[5] Mochinaga, (2021, p. 5).

[6] Regional Comprehensive Economic Partnership Agreement (RCEP), (November 15, 2020). See also Khan et al. (2022, pp. 175–189).

[7] Rimmer (2021, p. 6).

[8] Liu (2023, pp. 153–164).

[9] Jasuma and Paksi (2021, pp. 35–6 0).

itself is heightened, as certain member states, particularly those heavily reliant on DSR investments, may gravitate more fully toward China's digital framework, while others resist.[10]

To address digital challenges, ASEAN initiated the Digital Economy Framework Agreement (DEFA). It aims to enhance regional sovereignty by creating unified rules for cybersecurity, e-commerce, and data flows.[11] DEFA seeks a balanced, independent digital economy, reducing reliance on single powers like China and strengthening global integration. However, significant challenges remain as China continues to expand its economic ties.

This paper analyzes the rapid expansion of China's DSR within ASEAN, highlighting the challenge this poses to the digital sovereignty that ASEAN is striving to establish. A key focus is an examination of gaps in RCEP's digital trade provisions, especially those related to data governance and cybersecurity, and their potential to allow Chinese influence over ASEAN's data governance, cybersecurity policies, and digital trade regulations. The analysis assesses regional regulatory vulnerabilities that foster imbalanced legal dynamics and impact ASEAN's geopolitical and economic landscape. Finally, addressing these concerns, the paper explores whether ASEAN can mitigate such risks through alternative legal frameworks like the DEFA.

12.2 The Penetration of DSR China in ASEAN

China's DSR has rapidly penetrated the digital infrastructure and ecosystems of ASEAN member states, positioning China as a dominant external actor in the region's digital transformation. One of the clearest indicators of DSR penetration is the widespread deployment of Chinese telecommunications infrastructure. Companies such as Huawei and ZTE have built or co-developed 5G networks and broadband systems in nearly all ASEAN countries. Huawei is now the largest 5G provider in Southeast Asia, with operations in Thailand, Malaysia, Indonesia, and the Philippines.[12] These network deployments are often bundled with generous financing from Chinese policy banks, allowing ASEAN governments to expand digital infrastructure rapidly. However, these arrangements have also sparked concerns over technological dependence and potential cybersecurity vulnerabilities.

In addition to telecommunications, Chinese tech firms have deeply embedded themselves into ASEAN's cloud computing and e-commerce ecosystems. Alibaba Cloud, for instance, has established data centers in Indonesia and Malaysia, while Tencent and JD.com have invested heavily in Southeast Asian startups and digital payment platforms.[13] Through these platforms, Chinese firms are able to collect vast

[10] Mochinaga (2021, p. 10).

[11] ASEAN (2023c) Leaders' Statement on the Development of the ASEAN Digital Economy Framework Agreement (DEFA), p. 5.

[12] Mochinaga (2021, p. 5).

[13] Ji et al. (2023, p. 16).

amounts of consumer and transaction data, often stored on servers managed under Chinese-led systems, which raises concerns over data sovereignty and regulatory oversight.[14]

12.3 Challenges to ASEAN's Digital Sovereignty

The discussion on digital sovereignty within the ASEAN region takes on specific nuances shaped by the unique region's characteristics and priorities. While drawing on global definitions, ASEAN interpretations frequently emphasize ensuring that citizens' data is stored domestically and managed under national regulatory standards. Safeguarding critical national infrastructure against foreign interference and cyber threats is paramount, alongside efforts to reduce reliance on foreign technological capabilities. National security consistently emerges as a primary justification cited by ASEAN member states pursuing policies aimed at increasing digital sovereignty.

However, ASEAN's approach is also conditioned by its institutional culture, often referred to as the "ASEAN Way", which prioritizes consensus, non-interference in internal affairs,[15] and the principle of ASEAN centrality.[16] This manifests in regional governance efforts that often rely on confidence-building measures, capacity-building programs, and non-binding frameworks rather than supranational enforcement. While preserving unity among diverse member states, this approach can limit the effectiveness of achieving the deep regulatory harmonization that is often required for robust digital sovereignty or seamless regional integration. This becomes a challenge over ASEAN digital sovereignty as a regional association.

Meanwhile, China embraces the concept of digital or cyber sovereignty, asserting that a state has sovereign rights in internet governance. This concept is founded on three core principles. First, the government possesses exclusive control over online activities within the borders, superseding claims of universal rights. Second, the government holds ultimate authority over all non-state actors, whether domestic or foreign, thus rejecting a multi-stakeholder governance model. Third, all states are considered equal in internet governance, opposing any single nation's hegemonic power, a position particularly aimed at the United States. These principles are operationalized through three converging strategies: territoriality, which extends national control over the internet within a state's jurisdiction by regulating data and infrastructure; indigenization, which promotes domestic technology and standards to foster a self-reliant internet ecosystem; and investment, which dedicates significant resources to building the capabilities required for territoriality and indigenization. Collectively, these strategies aim to establish a nationally controlled and largely independent cyberspace for China.[17]

[14] Su and Flew (2021, p. 67).

[15] Soeparna (2019, p. 292).

[16] Mueller (2019, pp. 177–198).

[17] Creemers (2020, pp.107–142).

China and ASEAN have different approaches on digital sovereignty. It lies in the degree of centralization and underlying philosophy. China's model is highly centralized, state-centric, and prioritizing national security and control over information flows, rejecting multi-stakeholders and emphasizing indigenization.[18] In contrast, ASEAN's approach is more decentralized, balancing national interests with regional cooperation, economic growth, and a degree of openness to multi-stakeholder participation and international trade, although this varies among member states.[19] Stemming from two distinct concepts of digital sovereignty, China's cyber sovereignty poses a challenge to ASEAN's digital sovereignty due to the inherent power imbalance and China's growing influence in the region.

12.4 Digital Trade Under the RCEP Framework

Although China and ASEAN maintain distinct understandings of digital sovereignty, this difference has not hindered their ability to establish a digital trade relationship under the RCEP. The results of the digital trade negotiations within RCEP highlight a notable compromise achieved by powerful actors with differing approaches to the digital economy, data management, and regulation.[20] Beyond its sheer size, the RCEP also distinguishes itself as the most comprehensive and high-level multilateral framework for digital trade in the Asia Pacific Region. This is evident in its forward-looking provisions, which addresses a wide range of digital commerce aspects, including e-commerce facilitation, cross-border data flows, online consumer protection, and the promotion of paperless trading.

The digital trade rules embedded within RCEP place a significant emphasis on the importance of information disclosure as a cornerstone of transparency. This commitment to transparency is crucial for protecting the rights of governments in maintaining regulatory oversight, for businesses in ensuring fair market access and predictable operating environments, and for other stakeholders, such as consumers, in fostering trust and security within the digital marketplace. Furthermore, the focus on information disclosure is instrumental in upholding a fair competition framework within the digital market by reducing information asymmetry and promoting accountability among digital service providers. Ultimately, this commitment to information disclosure is a key mechanism for maintaining a fair competition framework within the rapidly evolving digital market, preventing anti-competitive practices and promoting a more equitable online environment.[21]

[18] Chen and Yang (2022, pp. 48–65).

[19] ASEAN Secretariat (2021, p. 5), ASEAN Telecommunications and IT Ministers Meeting (2018, p. 4).

[20] Kelsey (2022, pp. 119–144).

[21] Rui (2024, pp. 196–205).

Recognizing the burgeoning digital trade landscape between China and ASEAN, RCEP effectively addresses the critical need for harmonized governance and cooperation standards in this evolving domain, particularly within their unique economic and regulatory context. This is achieved through a comprehensive set of provisions designed to streamline processes, foster investment, and build mutual recognition in the digital sphere. For instance, Article 12 Section B, focusing on trade facilitation measures for certified operators, establishes a framework for trusted traders to benefit from expedited customs procedures, thereby fostering smoother cross-border digital transactions. Similarly, Article 10.17 on investment facilitation aims to create a more predictable and attractive environment for digital economy investments across the region. The promotion of paperless trade, as outlined in Article 12.5, directly reduces bureaucratic hurdles and costs associated with traditional trade documentation, paving the way for more efficient digital exchanges. Furthermore, the establishment of a framework for domestic electronic transactions (RCEP Article 12.10) lays the groundwork for greater interoperability and trust in online transactions within each member state, which is crucial for seamless regional digital trade. Finally, the regulations on electronic authentication and signatures (Article 12.6) provide a legal basis for secure and recognized digital transactions across borders, building confidence and facilitating the growth of digital commerce between China and ASEAN.[22]

12.4.1 Data Governance Issues

Despite the RCEP presenting itself as having comprehensive rules on digital trade, a closer examination reveals that several weaknesses exist within this framework, potentially limiting its effectiveness in truly fostering a seamless digital economy across the region.[23] Notably, RCEP lacks a specific definition for "e-commerce" and "digital product". While its provisions clearly encompass traditional trade facilitated by digital technologies, the absence of a precise definition can lead to ambiguity in interpreting the scope and application of the rules, particularly as digital business models evolve. It might also foster the incorrect assumption that every economic activity performed electronically falls under the agreement's coverage. The resulting potential assumption that all electronic activity is covered complicates implementation, particularly for developing and least-developed countries.[24]

In terms of data protection and localization, RCEP extends significantly beyond narrow cross-border online commercial transactions. They delve into broader governance issues like personal data protection (Article 12.8). In this concern, ASEAN countries implement a diverse range of data protection regulations. These frameworks are often analyzed by categorizing them into rules for domestic versus cross-border

[22] RCEP [Art. 12].

[23] Kelsey (2022, p. 120).

[24] Mitchell and Gyanchandani (2023, pp. 98–150).

data flows, frequently covering both personal and non-personal data protection.[25] Central to these regulations are the distinct concepts of "data processing" (any operation on personal data) and "data protection" (the measures safeguarding such data). Fundamentally, data protection seeks to ensure that personal data processing is fair, lawful, transparent, and conducted according to established principles.[26]

Processing personal data within ASEAN countries requires a valid legal justification. While consent is a common basis, the specific requirements, such as whether consent must be explicit or can be deemed (implied), differ from country to country. Beyond consent, other legal justifications can be used, like needing the data to fulfill a contract or pursuing legitimate interests. However, whether these alternatives are accepted and the specific rules governing them vary significantly across the region.[27] For example, the "legitimate interests" justification, which requires carefully balancing different factors, is recognized in countries like Singapore, Indonesia, the Philippines, and Thailand, but its application differs. This regulatory diversity means that organizations operating across ASEAN must understand the specific data protection laws of each individual country. This is particularly critical when handling sensitive personal data (like health or race information), as stricter rules almost always apply, typically demanding explicit consent from the individual.[28]

On the surface, RCEP appears progressive by including provisions intended to ensure data can move freely across borders for business purposes (Article 12.14) and generally prohibiting member countries from requiring businesses to use or locate computing facilities (like servers) within their territory as a condition of doing business (Article 12.15). However, these potentially impactful rules against data localization are substantially undermined by broad and flexible exceptions.[29] Member countries retain the right to restrict data flows or impose localization requirements if they deem such measures necessary to achieve a "legitimate public policy objective" or to protect "essential security interests" (Article 12.14(3) & 12.15(3)). Crucially, the interpretation of these exceptions emphasizes self-judgment, which allows more protective measures for individual, public, and national interests. However, the unclear scope and criteria for these exceptions remain a key issue, leaving application largely to the discretion of each individual member state.[30] While these articles include an exception to accommodate countries with diverse digital regulation policies, exemplified by China's consistently stringent cyber-sovereignty approach, this provision generates considerable uncertainty for digital businesses that routinely conduct cross-border electronic transactions within the RCEP region. Furthermore, the data localization policies in various member countries remain unchallenged under

[25] Watanabe et al. (2025).

[26] Bentotahewa et al. (2022, p. 183).

[27] Khumon (2018, pp. 1–24).

[28] Liu et al. (2024, pp. 129–158).

[29] Zhai (2024, pp. 24–45).

[30] Zhang (2023, pp. 36-45).

the RCEP agreement. The RCEP excludes dispute resolution processes over the interpretation of the exemption clause, leaving it to the parties to determine the limits themselves.[31]

12.4.2 Cybersecurity Concerns

The weakness also includes cybersecurity provision while cybersecurity serves as a fundamental pillar for the growth and sustainability of digital trade. Nevertheless, there is growing concern that disparate legislative and policy approaches ostensibly aimed at cybersecurity, and frequently framed within a national security context, have effectively created new barriers to trade in recent years.[32] A review of cybersecurity laws across six ASEAN nations shows that while most have legislation covering platform liability, cybercrime, and data protection, the development and content of these laws vary significantly. Key differences include copyright enforcement methods (Notice and Takedown in Singapore and Malaysia vs. judicial action elsewhere like Indonesia, Philippines, Thailand, Vietnam), the nature of cybercrime legislation (with Indonesia lacking a specific cybersecurity law), and the scope of data protection (Thailand and Indonesia drafting unified laws, Malaysia excluding government data, and Vietnam having a single comprehensive data security law).[33]

Acknowledging the diverse cybersecurity policies among its parties, including the ASEAN members, the cybersecurity provision under RCEP is framed as a "soft commitment". Given the complex nature of cybersecurity and the capacity gaps among economies, such clauses typically take the form of non-binding, unenforceable "soft law" rather than "hard law".[34] Unlike stricter trade disciplines, these commitments prioritize encouraging cooperation, sharing best practices, and building national capabilities for computer security incident response. They aim to foster a more uniform and integrated approach to cybersecurity among the parties, rather than imposing legally binding obligations and measures or establishing formal dispute-settlement mechanisms.[35]

However, like most Free Trade Agreements (FTAs), RCEP is silent on cybersecurity measures such as common standards or rules to ensure such measures are binding and represent the least trade-restrictive alternatives. This gap is significant, as the expanding scope of cybersecurity measures and the increasing economic importance of the digital economy necessitate a greater articulation of cybersecurity-specific trade rules.[36] Therefore, the divergence in cybersecurity standards can collectively weaken cybersecurity and become barriers to domestic companies especially Small

[31] Mishra et al. (2023, pp. 489–513).

[32] Lennon et al. (2023, pp. 184–204).

[33] Sunkpho et al. (2018).

[34] Lennon et al. (2023, p. 186).

[35] Mitchell and Mishra (2023, pp. 1–30).

[36] Meltzer (2020, p. 15).

Medium Enterprise (SMEs). For instance, differing standards between manufacturers lead to interoperability issues, demanding costly extra gateways for devices to communicate. This environment, lacking effective and common standards, impedes market entry for SMEs.[37] In addition, different laws and policies introduced in the name of cybersecurity, combined with broad interpretations of the RCEP exemption clause (which are sometimes framed as national security issues), can raise trade barriers among the parties. In essence, while RCEP acknowledges the importance of cybersecurity for digital trade, its provisions prioritize flexibility and cooperation over strict, enforceable rules. This approach, while facilitating agreement among diverse economies, can lead to significant variations in cybersecurity standards, data protection laws, and incident response capabilities across the RCEP region. This inconsistency creates potential weak points exploitable by cyber threats and adds complexity for businesses operating across multiple jurisdictions.

12.5 Digital Silk Road Within the RCEP

12.5.1 The Legal Dynamics

The landscape of digital trade rules under RCEP is likely to remain highly dynamic since it involves navigating the complexities of the digital economy while respecting national regulatory autonomy.[38] While RCEP includes provisions on electronic commerce, including a ban on localization measures and commitments to free cross-border data flows, it generally prioritizes a flexible, cooperative approach rather than strong enforceable legal obligations. This is reflected in the broad exemptions for "legitimate public policy" and "essential security interests", and exclusion of the e-commerce chapter from dispute settlement in RCEP. If disagreements arise regarding the interpretation of Chapter 12 of Electronic Commerce, the parties will resolve it through consultation only. This is a critical aspect of the legal dynamic of digital trade rules in RCEP.

China and ASEAN see RCEP as the right mechanism to cooperate in strengthening the regional economy. The RCEP outcome reflects a compromise between powerful states that have divergent positions on the digital economy, data, and regulation. However, the RCEP also reflects the pursuit of China to its commercial and nationalist aims, which are central to its DSR strategy, emphasizing the development of digital infrastructure and a comprehensive digital ecosystem.[39] This is consistent with China's "dual circulation" strategy that aims to boost economic growth by focusing

[37] Peng (2018, pp. 445–469).

[38] Mirra (2025, pp. 146–167).

[39] Bora L.Y (2020, pp. 1–19).

on its internal market potential and advancing domestic technology.[40] While prioritizing internal strengths, this approach also seeks to strongly link domestic demand with international markets. To support this, the government encourages participation in global e-commerce and digital trade, helping Chinese companies become more competitive internationally.[41]

The RCEP agreement also appears to have shortcomings in data governance, largely due to its extensive exemption clause. Speculation exists that China, driven by its recent laws aimed at data sovereignty, may have required this undisputed exemption clause as a non-negotiable term for joining the pact.[42] The extensive data regulation enacted by China, established through core laws like the Cybersecurity Law, Data Security Law, and Personal Information Protection Law, as well as specific sectoral rules (e.g., for mapping, credit, automotive data, overseas listings), could potentially exceed the scope of exceptions permitted under RCEP for "legitimate public policy" or "essential security".[43] These comprehensive Chinese regulations create a complex, tiered system mandating data localization and security assessments for critical operators and large data handlers, while imposing varying conditions like assessments, certifications, standard contracts, and mandatory individual consent for other cross-border transfers of personal and important data, potentially challenging RCEP's intended balance on data flows.[44]

Furthermore, the lack of harmonized digital standards and cybersecurity regulations across RCEP member countries can create barriers to digital trade, potentially enabling China to promote its own established standards and infrastructure within the region. For example China's past imposition of its unique WAPI (Wireless LAN Authentication and Privacy Infrastructure) Wi-Fi security standard, which differed from the international IEEE/ISO standard and effectively acted as a trade barrier by requiring vendors to adopt the China-specific protocol.[45] This practice of creating national ICT standards that diverge from international norms has raised substantial concerns, prompting industry calls for China to harmonize with globally recognized, market-driven standards instead.[46]

The legal dynamic within the digital trade rules under RCEP reflects the way participating countries frame their laws around technology. This dynamic is also a reflection of their broader economic, political, and strategic directions. These legal frameworks within RCEP are more than just tools for governance; they also function as significant expressions of national social and political identity, directed both inward and outward. Whether these legal expressions aim for aspirational goals or merely practical outcomes, the resulting rules inevitably reveal aspects of each member state's political character and its relationship, actual or intended, with global

[40] Yunling (2022).

[41] Zhang (2024, pp. 1–27).

[42] Wang and Sharma (2021, pp. 40–62).

[43] Deane et al. (2024, pp. 154–179).

[44] Zhang (2023, pp. 36–45).

[45] Cromer (2005, pp. 1–13).

[46] Peng (2018, pp. 445-469).

issues and influential powers.[47] Thus, despite the digital trade provision in RCEP aiming to establish common ground in a rapidly evolving area, their legal dynamics may exacerbate economic and geopolitical disparities between the highly developed digital economy of China and the diverse digital landscape across ASEAN member states.

12.5.2 Geo-Politic and Economic Landscape

RCEP was strategically created by ASEAN with the goals of strengthening regional trade liberalization and boosting Asia's economic growth prospects worldwide. When it was finalized, it was distinct as the only ongoing, credible multilateral effort globally that could provide a strong counterforce to the worldwide shift away from globalization toward protectionism.[48] It is also driven by the notion of ASEAN centrality, aims to bolster cooperation with regional partners, including those seeking to operate with a degree of independence from China and the US (or the Quad). However, RCEP is unlikely to reinforce ASEAN's central role. Instead, the RCEP agreement reflects a changing reality in East Asian trade, where power is more distributed and ASEAN's traditional role as the central pivot and standard-bearer is reduced. Additionally, ASEAN is struggling to take a leading role in newer vital policy areas for regional integration, such as the development of infrastructure, often referred to as connectivity.[49] In this domain, other actors, particularly major economies with significant financial and technological resources, have taken a more prominent and proactive role. China's BRI, for example, has gained considerable momentum, often operating outside of ASEAN-led frameworks. This is challenging for ASEAN to assert itself as the central coordinator or norm-setter in the crucial area of regional connectivity, further impacting its ability to maintain overall centrality in the evolving regional landscape.

The legal dynamic of digital trade rules under RCEP foster legal fragmentation and undermine cohesiveness, particularly within ASEAN. This trend erodes ASEAN's "substantial centrality" which refers to its capacity to effectively lead regional agenda-setting and rule-making.[50] Such internal disunity, in turn, creates opportunities for external powers to exert greater influence within the geo-political landscape. Therefore, although ASEAN's geography provides a foundation for integration, the ultimate success and direction of regional cooperation depend critically on managing the interplay between the bloc's internal unity and the pressures of external influence.[51]

---

[47] Dahdal and Ghafar (2025, pp. 1–26).

[48] Armstrong and Drysdale (2022).

[49] Mueller (2019)

[50] Wu (2020, pp. 97–117).

[51] Fadzili et al. (2024, pp. 1–22).

The DSR deeply integrated with China's digital economy policy, yields significant geopolitical and economic consequences. RCEP, despite being economic cooperation, can be dominated by political rather than purely economic objectives. While many ASEAN members joined for trade advantages, major powers like China often use such agreements for agenda-setting and rule-making.[52] Under RCEP, China aims to expand its influence through setting standards and promoting digital economic policies, thus boosting its competitive edge in technology and innovation.[53] Therefore, RCEP offers more than economic gains; it has major geo-political implications, enabling China to reinforce its regional economic leadership, enhance relations with neighbors, and consolidate its political and geopolitical power.[54] China's DSR gives considerable influence in shaping regional digital norms and standards, potentially aligning ASEAN more closely with China interests or approaches such as data governance and cybersecurity. China's strategy regarding digital trade rules and its engagement within the regional system is defined by three main characteristics. First, its position on governing digital trade has typically been cautious, though recent shifts toward more openness are noticeable. Second, China actively influences digital trade governance by promoting specific digital standards. Third, security issues are given considerable weight in China's digital trade approach.[55]

12.6 ASEAN Framework of Digital Economy

Issues concerning digital trade under RCEP, primarily related to data governance and cybersecurity, facilitate the penetration of China's DSR into the ASEAN digital landscape. This is largely due to the fragmented regulations and varying levels of infrastructure development across ASEAN Member States.[56] These inconsistencies create significant impediments to seamless digital economic integration, posing tangible barriers to cross-border e-commerce, the free flow of data, and the expansion of digital trade.[57] Recognizing these challenges, ASEAN needs a strategy to overcome internal fragmentation and deepen digital integration.

Currently, ASEAN is negotiating the Digital Economy Framework Agreement (DEFA), a landmark initiative focused specifically on deepening digital integration within the ASEAN bloc. DEFA represents a strategic response to the perceived fragmentation of the existing digital landscape across Southeast Asia, characterized by disparate national regulations and varying levels of digital readiness among member states.[58] Its formal introduction and the subsequent launch of negotiations mark a

---

[52] Chong (2021).

[53] Wei (2024, pp. 145–155).

[54] Tan and Soong (2021, pp. 1–14).

[55] Gao and Chen (2024, pp. 1–20).

[56] Chong et al. (2023, pp. 139–149).

[57] Lee et al. (2025, pp. 81–96).

[58] ASEAN (2023a, b, c).

significant milestone in ASEAN's journey toward a more cohesive and digitally empowered future. DEFA is unlikely to be an isolated event but rather the culmination of a long-term regional commitment to economic cooperation. For over 25 years, ASEAN has been dedicated to digital transformation. This long-term commitment, guided by roadmaps and master plans like the 2021 ASEAN Digital Masterplan 2025 (ADM2025), aims to build a leading digital community.[59]

The DEFA represents a strategic shift. Unlike past agreements, DEFA is designed to prevent implementation gaps. Its core difference is flexibility, featuring a "two-tiered" system that allows nations to adopt commitments at varying speeds based on their digital readiness. Furthermore, DEFA makes proactive capacity building a central pillar, actively helping less-developed members comply. This pragmatic, private-sector-driven design aims for effective and inclusive regional integration.

12.6.1 The Objective and Core of DEFA Negotiation

The DEFA has ambitious objectives focused on creating a cohesive digital ecosystem. Its key aims are to accelerate digital trade growth, improve interoperability between national systems, ensure online security, and, importantly, boost the participation of SMEs so they gain greater benefits from the regional digital economy. The DEFA strives to align policies across member economies to maximize these benefits, which involves harmonizing rules and standards for artificial intelligence, data regulations, and open government data.[60]

The core negotiations of DEFA aim to establish a thriving digital economy[61] by focusing on foundational elements such as Digital Trade, which seeks to create a conducive environment with paperless processes and harmonized rules, and Cross-border E-Commerce, designed to build a seamless ecosystem for online transactions.[62] These efforts include harmonizing Digital Payments and E-Invoicing to improve efficiency, recognizing that the promotion of e-payments in ASEAN Countries is crucial for advancing the region's digital economy.[63] Moreover, the development of Digital ID and Authentication systems to ensure trusted online interactions for individuals and businesses to secure cross-border online transactions.[64] Collectively, these pillars aim to streamline and secure the fundamental aspects of digital economic activity across the region.

Complementing these foundational elements, the negotiations address critical enablers and governance. Cybersecurity is paramount, with a focus on regional

59 Isono and Prilliadi (2023, p. 1 8).

60 Cheung and Taojun (2023, p. 52).

61 ASEAN (September 2023).

62 Lee et al. (2025, p. 87).

63 Mizan et al. (2019, pp. 113–119).

64 Chen (2007, pp. 176–183).

cooperation, common standards, and joint responses to cyber threats.[65] A particularly vital and complex area is Cross-border Data Flows and Data Protection, which strives to balance the essential free flow of data with robust privacy and security, a linchpin for the agreement's overall success.[66] Looking forward, the framework includes Emerging Topics like AI to foster innovation responsibly, Talent Mobility and Cooperation to develop and share skilled digital human capital, and Competition Policy to ensure a fair and innovative digital marketplace.[67]

Compliance monitoring for the ASEAN DEFA is expected to align with the established ASEAN Economic Community (AEC) framework. A multi-tiered system will likely be used. The ASEAN Coordinating Committee on Electronic Commerce and Digital Economy (ACCED) is anticipated to handle day-to-day monitoring. Ultimate oversight will fall to the ASEAN Economic Community Council (AECC), supported by the ASEAN Secretariat's monitoring directorate (AIMD) for technical analysis and reporting. This approach integrates DEFA into the existing AEC structure, ensuring a systematic and coordinated implementation of this pivotal digital trade agreement.

12.6.2 Redress Challenge on Data Governance and Cyber Security Under RCEP

The comprehensive nature of DEFA's negotiation objectives signals an understanding that a thriving digital economy requires more thorough and potentially binding rules for digital trade. The DEFA negotiations are centered on provisions deemed critical for achieving meaningful regional digital integration. Among the most prominent discussion points are mechanisms for cross-border data flow, which remains a particularly contentious area as negotiators strive to balance the economic imperatives of data movement with legitimate national privacy and security concerns.[68] This is particularly noteworthy because RCEP, for example, lacks strong disciplines that prevent barriers to cross-border data flows or prohibit data localization mandates,[69] underscoring the need for DEFA's more robust approach. DEFA explicitly includes a pillar aimed at facilitating cross-border data flows while establishing data protection frameworks. While the RCEP requires its Parties to adopt what it terms "appropriate and necessary" measures to safeguard personal information, a directive that explicitly acknowledges and accommodates the diverse national data protection systems already in place, this approach inherently allows for considerable variation in regulatory stringency and enforcement across member countries. This flexibility, while respecting national sovereignty and existing legal frameworks, can

65 Estiyovionita and Sitamala, (2022, pp. 79–86).
66 Lee et al. (2025, p. 90).
67 ASEAN (September 2023).
68 Watanabe et al. (2025).
69 Reinsch et al. (2019).

also present complexities for businesses attempting to navigate multiple compliance regimes and may not always ensure a uniformly high level of data protection for individuals throughout the expansive RCEP region.[70]

In what appears to be a more focused effort toward harmonization, the DEFA aims to establish more clearly defined and potentially robust data protection frameworks.[71] This initiative is significantly shaped and propelled by stakeholders, including businesses and digital rights advocates, who are strongly pushing for the development and adoption of common data protection standards across participating nations. Their advocacy extends to fostering greater interoperability between different national data systems, which is crucial for facilitating smoother, more secure, and more efficient cross-border data flows essential for a vibrant digital economy. Furthermore, there is a significant emphasis on creating and implementing mutual recognition mechanisms, such as regionally recognized trust marks or data privacy certification schemes, which would serve as verifiable indicators of compliance with agreed-upon high standards, thereby simplifying cross-border operations for businesses and building greater consumer trust in the digital ecosystem.

In terms of cyber security, while RCEP is framed as a "soft commitment",[72] DEFA includes Online Safety and Cybersecurity as a core pillar, aiming for improved cooperation and a secure online environment. This includes establishing common security standards, strengthening national and regional Computer Emergency Response Teams (CERTs), and collaboratively addressing cross-border cyber threats such as online scams and disinformation campaigns. ASEAN recognizes the importance of cybersecurity and has taken steps to establish a regional CERT to enhance cybersecurity cooperation and information sharing among AMS. Ensuring the accuracy and reliability of information circulating on digital platforms is also considered vital, as misinformation can have serious negative consequences for businesses, governments, and individuals. Ultimately, building and maintaining trust in digital systems is paramount for the sustained growth and adoption of digital services. Cybersecurity, therefore, is not merely a technical issue but a foundational challenge that DEFA must address comprehensively to foster a safe and reliable digital environment.[73]

12.6.3 Building ASEAN Centrality

Beyond its internal impact, the ASEAN DEFA possesses the potential to significantly influence the broader landscape of digital trade governance. If successfully concluded as a high-quality agreement, DEFA could establish a new de facto baseline for digital trade rules in the Indo-Pacific, positioning ASEAN as a potential rule-shaper, not

[70] Khumon (2018, pp. 1–24).

[71] ASEAN Framework on Personal Data Protection (2012).

[72] Lennon et al. (2023).

[73] Kasih (2023).

just a rule-taker.[74] This could establish an "ASEAN model" as a "third way" for digital governance, distinct from state-centric Chinese models. By prioritizing inclusive development and balanced data governance, this approach could be particularly appealing to other developing nations.

However, realizing this ambition faces a critical internal challenge: the deep strategic divergence among members regarding China. Countries like Cambodia and Laos, heavily integrated with China's Digital Silk Road, are wary of high standards that could jeopardize Chinese investment. To navigate this and prevent a regional fracture, DEFA employs strategic flexibility. A proposed "two-tiered" implementation allows these nations to adopt foundational rules first, delaying commitment to sensitive areas like cross-border data flows.

This pragmatism reflects a broader reframing of DEFA's purpose from geopolitics to geo-economics. Recognizing that ASEAN's political unity is weak, the goal is not to counter China but to ensure ASEAN's collective economic survival by creating a competitive, unified digital market. This is an attempt to reclaim "digital centrality" in an era where the region risks fragmentation between US and Chinese spheres of influence. Consequently, DEFA is not expected to be a "toothy" agreement with strong enforcement against external powers. Instead, it aims to be pragmatically influential. Its success hinges on the long-term bet that the economic benefits of a cohesive ASEAN digital market will be so compelling that all members eventually find it in their interest to align with its standards, reaffirming ASEAN's centrality and securing the region's position as a global growth epicenter.

ASEAN's pursuit of digital sovereignty through the DEFA is fundamentally challenged by the reality of infrastructure control. Rule-making alone cannot guarantee sovereignty when servers and networks are predominantly controlled by a single external power, such as China. The effectiveness of DEFA's legal framework is constrained by this physical control, especially given foreign laws like China's 2017 National Intelligence Law. This law can compel Chinese companies to cooperate with state intelligence, creating a direct conflict with data privacy rules. A legal right to privacy in Jakarta is challenged if the data, flowing through Chinese-built networks, can be accessed under Beijing's jurisdiction.

DEFA pushes back by first establishing a unified legal basis to regulate all digital service providers operating within ASEAN, subjecting them to local laws and audits regardless of their origin. Second, it can mandate high technical standards for cybersecurity and data handling as a condition of market access, focusing on operational compliance. Third, by creating a large, integrated market, DEFA aims to counterbalance dependence by attracting a diverse range of global tech providers from the US, Europe, and beyond. This market-driven diversification is the most practical long-term strategy to enhance sovereignty. Finally, DEFA provides a collective bargaining position, preventing a "divide and conquer" scenario and allowing ASEAN to negotiate digital standards from a position of strength.

---

[74] Honey (2025).

12.7 Conclusion

By pioneering the comprehensive DEFA, ASEAN is undertaking a landmark initiative with dual objectives. Internally, it aims to craft a sophisticated framework tailored to the unique economic and developmental diversity of its ten member states. Externally, this ambitious project is positioned to become an influential template for other developing nations navigating digital transformation.

The DEFA is explicitly designed to transcend the foundational, flexible digital trade principles established in RCEP. Where RCEP offers general guidelines, DEFA seeks deeper, binding commitments. Its focus on harmonizing rules for cross-border data flows, establishing interoperable digital identity systems, standardizing e-invoicing, and securing a moratorium on customs duties for electronic transmissions represents a significant leap toward a seamless regional digital market. This elevates the status of DEFA to that of an intended "RCEP-plus" agreement, specifically tailored for ASEAN's aspirations.

This interplay introduces a clear legal hierarchy. For digital trade occurring exclusively between ASEAN members, DEFA's more detailed provisions will take precedence, ensuring deep integration goals are not diluted. Conversely, for transactions between an ASEAN member and a non-ASEAN RCEP signatory (like China or Japan), RCEP's Chapter 12 rules will govern.

Ultimately, DEFA is a strategic maneuver by ASEAN to fortify its internal cohesion. By establishing a unified rulebook, ASEAN proactively mitigates the risk of fragmentation that could arise if members adopted disparate standards from external partners. This integration is crucial for strengthening the bloc's collective economic power.

If successful, DEFA could set a new global benchmark for developing economies. A unified ASEAN, speaking with one voice, could establish itself as a significant third pole in international rule-making, offering a distinct model that balances economic openness with regulatory sovereignty. This enhances the bloc's strategic agency in the contested Indo-Pacific, providing a strategic pathway to manage external influences like China's DSR.

Bibliography

Armstrong S, Drysdale P (2022) The Implications of the Regional Comprehensive Economic Partnership (RCEP) for Asian Regional Architecture, ERIA Discussion Paper Series No. 454.

ASEAN (2012) ASEAN Framework on Personal Data Protection.

ASEAN (2023a) ASEAN launches world's first region wide Digital Economy Framework Agreement.

ASEAN (2023b) Framework for Negotiating ASEAN Digital Economy Framework Agreement.

ASEAN (2023c) Leaders' Statement on the Development of the ASEAN Digital Economy Framework Agreement (DEFA), p. 2.

ASEAN Secretariat (2021) ASEAN Digital Masterplan 2025, p. 5

ASEAN Telecommunications and IT Ministers Meeting (2018) Joint Statement on Multi stakeholder Cooperation in Cybersecurity, p. 4

Bentotahewa V, Hewage C, Williams J (2022) the Normative Power of the GDPR: A Case Study of Data Protection Laws of South Asian Countries, SN Comput. Sci. 3: 183. https://doi.org/10.1007/s42979-022-01079-z

Bora L Y (2020) Challenge and Perspective for Digital Silk Road, 7 Cogent Business & Management 1: 1 -19. https://doi.org/10.1080/23311975.2020.1804180

Chen X, Yang Y (2022) Different Shades of Norms: Comparing the Approaches of the EU and ASEAN to Cyber Governance, 57 the International Spectator 3: 48–65. https://doi.org/10.1080/03932729.2022.2066841

Chen Z (2007) A Scenario for Identity Management in Daidalos, Fifth Annual Conference on Communication Networks and Services Research (CNSR '07), Fredericton, NB, Canada. Pp. 176–183. https://doi.org/10.1109/CNSR.2007.6.

Cheung P, Taojun X (Eds.) (2023) the ASEAN Digital Economy: Towards an Integrated Regional Framework (1st ed.), Routledge. Pp. 52. https://doi.org/10.4324/9781003308751

Chong M T, Puah C H, Mansor S A, The C S (2023) Digital Connectivity Bridging Digital ASEAN, 17 International Journal of Economics and Management 1: 139–149. https://doi.org/10.47836/ijeam.17.1.10

Chong W Y (2021) Regional Comprehensive Economic Partnership (RCEP) – The Geopolitical and Economic Implications on Malaysia, International Conference on Economics, Business, Social, and Humanities (ICEBSH). https://doi.org/10.2991/assehr.k.210805.068.

Creemers R (2020) China's Conception of Cyber Sovereignty: Rhetoric and Realization, In Broeders D. & Berg B. Van Den (Eds.), Governing Cyberspace: Behavior, Power, And Diplomacy, Digital Technologies and Global Politics. Lanham: Rowman & Littlefield, pp.107 – 142.

Cromer Z K (2005) China's WAPI Policy: Security Measure Or Trade Protectionism?, 4 Duke Law & Technology Review 1: 1–13. https://scholarship.law.duke.edu/dltr/vol4/iss1/17

Dahdal A M, Ghafar A A (2025) The Digital Silk Road: 'Tech-Diplomacy' as a Paradigm for Understanding Technological Adoption and Emerging Digital Regulations in MENA, Asian Journal of Law and Society: 1–26. https://doi.org/10.1017/als.2024.30

Deane F, Woolmer E, Cao S, Tranter K (2024) Trade in the Digital Age: Agreements to Mitigate Fragmentation, 14 Asian Journal of International Law 1: 154–179. https://doi.org/10.1017/S204425132300036X.

Economic Partnership on E-Commerce, in Dynamism of East Asia and RCEP: The Framework for Regional Integration, Kimura, F., S. Urata, S. Thangavelu, & D. Narjoko (eds.): 119–144, Jakarta, ERIA

Fadzili M A F B M, Norependi H H B, Azman A Y B,Yuki W, Hassan M S, Ali F A R (2024) Regional Comprehensive Economic Partnership (RCEP) as Geopolitical Strategy, 20 Geopolitics Quarterly (Special Issue): 1–22. https://doi.org/10.22034/igq.2024.476068.1946

Gao X, Chen X (2024) The regime complex for digital trade in Asia and China's engagement. 23 Asia. Eur. J 393–413 https://doi.org/10.1007/s10308-024-00705-0

Honey S (2025) Navigating digital trade fragmentation in the age of geoeconomics. https://www.hinrichfoundation.com/research/article/digital/navigating-digital-trade-fragmentation-in-the-age-of-geoeconomics/

Insikt Group (2021) China's Digital Colonialism: Espionage and Repression Along the Digital Silk Road, Recorded Future, p. 4. https://www.recordedfuture.com/research/china-digital-colonialism-espionage-silk-road

Isono I, Prilliadi H (2023) ASEAN's Digital Integration: Evolution of Framework Documents, Economic Research Institute for ASEAN and East Asia (ERIA).

Jasuma N B, Paksi A K (2021) China's Digital Silk Road: The Loss for Indonesia, 4 Nation State: J. Int'l Stud. 1: 35–60. https://doi.org/10.24076/nsjis.v4i1.513.

Ji M, Gao X, Liang Y (2023) Opportunities and Challenges of Cross-Border E-Commerce Development Cooperation between China and Southeast Asian Countries—Based on the Perspective of

the Entry into Force of RCEP, 5 Acad. J. Bus. & Mgmt 13: 133–139. https://doi.org/10.25236/AJBM.2023.051319.
Kasih M C (2023) Fostering ASEAN's Digital Future through Cybersecurity Policies and Human Empowerment, ERIA Policy Brief No. 2023–02.
Kelsey J (2022) Opportunities and Challenges for ASEAN And East Asia from The Regional Comprehensive Estiyovionita K, Sitamala A (2022) ASEAN's Role In Cybersecurity Maintenance And Security Strategy Through An International Security Approach, 4 Lampung. J. Int. Law. 2: 79–86. https://doi.org/10.25041/lajil.v4i2.2556
Khan H U, Ali S, Shah S S A (2022) The Regional Comprehensive Economic Partnership (RCEP): An Analysis of Its Potential Benefits for China, 6 Liberal Arts and Social Sciences International Journal (LASSIJ) 2: 175–189. https://doi.org/10.47264/idea.lassij/6.2.10
Khor H E, Poonpatpibul C, Foo S Y (2021) Belt and Road Initiative: A Framework to Address Challenges and Unlock Potential for High-Quality and Inclusive Growth, 66 the Singapore Economic Review (SER) 1: 21–58. https://doi.org/10.1142/S0217590819410029
Khumon P (2018) Regulation for Cross-Border Privacy in Southeast Asia: An Institutional Perspective, 29th European Regional Conference of the International Telecommunications Society (ITS): "Towards a Digital Future: Turning Technology into Markets?", Trento, Italy, 1st–4th August 2018, International Telecommunications Society (ITS), Calgary
Lee B T F, Đinh L d, Sims J P, Ali S (2025) ASEAN Digital Economy Framework Agreement (DEFA): Implications for Digital Trade and Regional Economic Integration, 8 Journal of Strategic and Global Studies 1: 81–96. https://doi.org/10.7454/jsgs.v8i1.1166
Liu J, Sengstschmid U, Yixuan G (2024) Facilitating Data Flows across ASEAN: Challenges and Policy Directions, In Data Governance and the Digital Economy in Asia, Routledge, pp.129–158
Liu W (2023), Comparative Analysis of Digital Trade Terms Under RCEP and CPTPP Agreements, Highlights in Business, Economics and Management 17: 153–164. https://doi.org/10.54097/hbem.v17i.11080
Meltzer J P (2020) Cybersecurity, digital trade, and data flows: Re-thinking a role for international trade rules, ERIA Global Economy & Development Working Paper No. 132.
Mirra B (2025) Digital Trade: New Design Elements In Preferential Trade Agreements, in Claussen K, Elsig M, Polanco R, (eds.), the Concept Design of a Twenty-First Century Preferential Trade Agreement: Trends and Future Innovations, Cambridge University Press, pp. 146-167.
Mishra N, Valencia A M P (2023) Digital services and digital trade in the Asia Pacific: An alternative model for digital integration? 31 Asia. Pac. Law. Rev. 2: 489–513. https://doi.org/10.1080/10192557.2023.2216058
Mitchell A D, Gyanchandani V (2023) Convergence & Divergence in Digital Trade Regulation: A Comparative Analysis Of CP-TPP, RCEP, And EJSI, 19 South Carolina Journal of International Law and Business 2, Article 6: 98–150. https://scholarcommons.sc.edu/scjilb/vol19/iss2/6
Mitchell A D, Mishra N (2023) A New Digital Economy Collaboration in the Indo-Pacific: Negotiating Digital Trade in the Australia-India CECA, 57 Journal of World Trade 1: 1–30 https://doi.org/10.54648/trad2023001.
Mizan N S M, Ma'arif M Y, Satar N S M, Shahar S M (2019) CNDS-Cybersecurity: Issues and Challenges in ASEAN Countries, 8 International Journal of Advanced Trends in Computer Science and Engineering 1.4: 113–119. https://doi.org/10.30534/ijatcse/2019/1781.42019
Mochinaga D (2021) The Digital Silk Road and China's Technology Influence in Southeast Asia, Keio Research Institute at SFC: 4 https://www.cfr.org/blog/digital-silk-road-and-chinas-technology-influence-southeast-asia
Mueller L M (2019) ASEAN centrality under threat – the cases of RCEP and Connectivity, 8 Journal of Contemporary East Asia Studies 2: 177–198. https://doi.org/10.1080/24761028.2019.1691703
Peng S Y (2018) "Private" Cybersecurity Standards? Cyberspace Governance, Multistakeholderism, and the (Ir)relevance of the TBT Regime, 51 Cornell International Law Journal 2, Article 4: 445–469. https://scholarship.law.cornell.edu/cilj/vol51/iss2/4
Regional Comprehensive Economic Partnership Agreement (RCEP), (November 15, 2020).

Reinsch W A, Lydia Murray L,Caporal J (2019) At Last, An RCEP Deal. https://www.csis.org/analysis/last-rcep-deal

Rimmer M (2021) A Submission to the Joint Standing Committee on Treaties on the Regional Comprehensive Economic Partnership (RCEP), pp 1–80. https://doi.org/10.31219/osf.io/3mvd9

Rui Z (2024) China-ASEAN Bilateral Digital Trade under the RCEP Digital Trade Framework: Current situations, Challenges, and Responses, 14 Frontiers in Business, Economics and Management 2: 196–205. https://doi.org/10.54097/kckpj871

Shen G, Bingqin L (2019) The Digital Silk Road and the Sustainable Development Goals, 50 IDS Bull. 4: 23–45. doi.org/https://doi.org/10.19088/1968-2019.137

Soeparna I (2019) ASEAN Investment Dispute Settlement: A Challenge to the ASEAB Enhanced Dispute Settlement Mechanism, in Ma Y J (ed.), Chinese (Taiwan) Yearbook of International Law and Affairs 37, Brill Nijhoff, Leiden/Boston, pp. 289–307 https://doi.org/10.1163/9789004443297_013

Su C, Flew T (2021) The Rise of Baidu, Alibaba and Tencent (BAT) and Their Role in China's Belt and Road Initiative (BRI), 17 Global Media and Communication 1: 67–86. doi.org/https://doi.org/10.1177/1742766520982324

Sunkpho J, Ramjan S, Ottamakorn C (2018) Cybersecurity Policy in ASEAN Countries, 17th Annual Security Conference - Securing the interconnected world, Las Vegas, USA

Tan W, Soong J J (2021) The Political Economy of China's Rising Role in the Regional Comprehensive Economic Partnership (RCEP): Strategies and Instruments of Chinese Way, 55 The Chinese Economy: 1–14. https://doi.og/https://doi.org/10.1080/10971475.2021.1972547.

Wang C, Sharma V (2021) India's RCEP dilemma with China: Beyond the legal texts, 36 Pacific Focus 1: 40–62 https://doi.org/10.1111/pafo.12180

Watanabe S, Ogura E, & Keita Oikawa K (2025) Current Status of ASEAN Data Governance and Its Implications for the Digital Economy Framework Agreement. ERIA Discussion Paper Series 2024–32, No 539.

Wei K (2024) the Impact of RCEP Tariff Concessions on Intra-Regional Trade: An Analysis of Trade Creation and Diversion, 31 Highlights in Business, Economics and Management: 145–155. https://doi.org/10.54097/9fpgy060

Wu C H (2020) ASEAN at the Crossroads: Trap and Track between CPTPP and RCEP, 23 Journal of International Economic Law: 97-117. https://doi.org/10.1093/jiel/jgz032.

Yunling Z (2022) China and the Regional Comprehensive Economic Partnership: An Economic and Political Perspective, ERIA Discussion Paper Series No. 434.

Zeng J (2019) Narrating China's Belt and Road Initiative, 10 Global Policy 2: 207–216. doi.org/https://doi.org/10.1111/1758-5899.12662

Zhai D (2024) RCEP Rules on Cross-Border Data Flows: Asian Characteristics and Implications for Developing Countries, 33 Asia Pacific Law Review 1: 24–45. https://doi.org/10.1080/10192557.2024.2417949.

Zhang C (2023) RCEP Basic Security Exceptions for Cross-Border Data Flows and China's Response, 14 Journal of Education, Humanities and Social Sciences: 36–45. https://doi.org/10.54097/ehss.v14i.8793

Zhang D (2024) Understanding the evolution of China's approach to digital trade: interests, ideas, and institutions, 3 ARPE 7: 1–27. https://doi.org/10.1007/s44216-024-00026-4

Chapter 13
Bamboo in the Storm: A Vietnamese Perspective on Data Sovereignty and Trust in the Digital Economy

Hien Xuan My Nguyen and Vy Thao Nguyen Ngo

Abstract Developing legal systems are strengthening regulations on digitalization and cross-border data flows, yet transitional countries still face significant legal and institutional challenges in meeting the stringent commitments of modern Free Trade Agreements (FTAs). For example, the EU's FTAs with Singapore and Vietnam, and ongoing negotiations with other ASEAN countries, reflect its motivation for a region-to-region framework tied to global data-governance standards, centered on the GDPR's Article 45(3) adequacy requirement. While normatively influential, the GDPR's strict requirements and severe penalties pose considerable compliance burdens for developing economies. For ASEAN countries such as Vietnam, legal transplantation from the EU may also risk "legal imperialism" if external models are adopted without regard to local institutional capacities and infrastructural constraints. Vietnam's legal framework, currently grounded in cybersecurity and state control, provides solid roots for data governance. Yet to thrive in the evolving digital ecosystem, these roots must be complemented by new branches of trust, transparency, and interoperability that extend beyond national borders. This article analyzes Vietnam's legislative progress on cross-border data flows, identifies practical implementation challenges, and considers implications for future digital trade agreements. Drawing on Japan's trust-based approach, the article proposes a balanced, model-rooted, resilient yet adaptable roadmap for Vietnam to build trust for cross-border data flows in line with domestic capacity and regional cooperation.

Keywords Data Free Flow with Trust · Data sovereignty · Japan · Vietnam · Cross-border data flows · Digital trade agreement

H. X. M. Nguyen (✉)
International Law Faculty, Ho Chi Minh City University of Law, Ho Chi Minh City, Vietnam
e-mail: nxmhien@hcmulaw.edu.vn

V. T. N. Ngo
Vietnamese Journal of Legal Sciences, Ho Chi Minh City University of Law, Ho Chi Minh City, Vietnam
e-mail: nntvy@hcmulaw.edu.vn

J. Nakagawa et al. (eds.), *Geopolitical Risks and Geoeconomics in International Economic Law*, Economics, Law, and Institutions in Asia Pacific,
https://doi.org/10.1007/978-981-95-6996-0_13

13.1 Introduction

In recent years, many developing legal systems have made significant progress in addressing the complexities of economic and digital activities. Countries are adopting varied approaches to manage cross-border data flows and safeguard personal data while integrating into international markets. These advancements not only reflect efforts to integrate into the global framework but also demonstrate a commitment to meeting international standards.

However, countries in transition often face a "storm" of legal and practical challenges, driven by the pressures of international commitments. By 2023, the European Union (EU) secured Free Trade Agreements (FTAs) with Singapore and Vietnam while pursuing negotiations with other ASEAN nations, reflecting its strategic ambition to establish a region-to-region FTA, a move that underscores the growing interplay between trade agreements and evolving global standards, including those for data governance and digital trade. To maximize the benefits of trade agreements like the EU FTA framework, these nations must improve their legal frameworks to align with stringent requirements such as the European Union's General Data Protection Regulation (GDPR). The GDPR poses one of the most significant challenges with Article 45(3), which mandates "adequacy status" for non-EU countries to enable the seamless transfer of personal data across borders. This adequacy requirement underscores the EU's normative authority in global data governance while avoiding reciprocity obligations. To date, only 15 third countries and territories have achieved this status. While the GDPR aims to protect personal data, its severe penalties under Article 83 present significant compliance challenges for businesses worldwide.

However, transplanting advanced legal models from developed countries does not always bring optimal efficiency. Vietnam, along with other ASEAN countries influenced by Asian collective identity and communitarian values, may face the risk of "legal imperialism" from the EU, where external legal models, particularly in personal data protection, are imposed without adequately considering their unique cultural and societal contexts. In addition, limitations in digital infrastructure and a lack of uniformity in law enforcement continue to be major barriers to the effective implementation of new regulations.

This article examines the legislative progress on cross-border data flows in Vietnam, evaluates practical challenges, and explores implications for advancing digital trade agreements. In this process, referring to Japan's "*trust-based*" model is a potential recommendation that emphasizes the role of trust, transparency, and commitment of stakeholders in drafting digital trade agreements. Based on these analyses, inspired by the symbol of bamboo—"*strong roots, stout trunk, flexible branches*", the article emphasizes the balance between transplanting legal frameworks from international experience, adapting to the global context, and protecting intrinsic legal values.

13.2 Struggling to Harmonize Cross-Border Data Flow Amid Fragmentation: Vietnam's Effort to Walk a Fragile Tightrope

In the digital economy, data has emerged as the foremost commodity, underpinning various sectors and driving innovation. Since the Internet was established, it has allowed data to be transferred from a user's device to other devices, creating complex data flows that have crossed international borders, connecting countries and regions around the world.[1] Therefore, the concept of free data flow is consistent with the vision of a globally interconnected society and is associated with promoting trade liberalization. Nevertheless, states also express concerns about data privacy, national security, and digital sovereignty associated with cross-border data flows. In this context, several data flow restrictions have been imposed to require companies to store data within the country or impose additional requirements for transferring data abroad. These restrictions vary significantly in design and implementation depending on the country or region, reflecting a wide range of economic, social, political, institutional, and cultural perspectives and values. One of the most salient discrepancies pertains to the divergent approaches to cyber sovereignty adopted by China (Security, Personal Data Protection, and Free Flow Balance Model) and the Russian Federation, in marked contrast to the United States' advocacy for the free flow of data (US—Trade-First Free Flow Model). Notably, the EU maintains a distinctive rights-based digital sovereignty model, recognizing and protecting privacy as a fundamental right (EU Human Rights and Digital Trade Balance Model).[2] This discrepancy has given rise to concerns regarding the potential for fragmentation of the Internet and the data-driven digital economy.

Although there has been an effort to harmonize the cross-border data flow management model at the multilateral level, WTO members have negotiated a "*stable text*" of the Electronic Commerce Agreement within the WTO.[3] Notably, the agreement does not contain provisions on cross-border data or localization requirements. Furthermore, the agreement contains a self-judging exception in its Article 25, which allows WTO members to restrict data transfers on subjective grounds.[4] As a result, efforts at multilateral harmonization have paradoxically increased the fragmentation of national policies related to data governance and privacy protection.

The fragmentation of the digital economy poses significant risks for developing countries, mainly when they are influenced by and dependent on individual national data management models, reinforced by FTAs. As FTAs between major global

[1] National Agency for Science and Technology Information (2023, p. 3), Dat, H.L.N.T. & An, C.T.T. (2024).

[2] Nabiebu et al. (2025, p. 175).

[3] However, the United States, Brazil, Colombia, El Salvador, Guatemala, Indonesia, Paraguay, Taiwan, and Türkiye have not signed this version. Patrick Leblond, *Is the WTO's New E-commerce Agreement Really a Game Changer?*, 2024, https://www.cigionline.org/articles/is-the-wtos-new-e-commerce-agreement-really-a-game-changer/.

[4] Global Data Alliance (2024), para. 62.

powers, including the EU, the US, and China, provide a range of data governance frameworks, they exert a spillover effect that pushes developing countries to adopt or conform to these models. In the context of developing countries, the lack of bargaining power often forces these countries to choose a model that suits their main trade relationships.[5] The current situation may therefore create a dependence on regulations issued by major powers, thereby complicating the protection of their regulatory autonomy in data management.

To illustrate, Vietnam signed an FTA with the EU to have opportunities to access the EU market. However, to fully leverage the benefits of trade agreements such as the EU FTA framework, Vietnam must undertake essential reform to its legal frameworks to comply with stringent requirements such as the EU's GDPR. One of the most significant challenges of the GDPR is Article 45(3), which requires "*adequacy*" for non-EU countries to allow seamless cross-border transfers of personal data. It can be observed that the model bypasses reciprocal obligations, as the EU demands compliance while refraining from engaging with non-European countries on equal terms.

Since 2019, Vietnam has embarked on a comprehensive reform of its data and cybersecurity legal framework, beginning with the implementation of the 2018 Cybersecurity Law and its guiding Decree No. 53/2022/ND-CP, which imposed obligations on data localization, cross-border data transfers, and critical information infrastructure. The adoption of Decree No. 13/2023/ND-CP on Personal Data Protection marked a significant step toward GDPR-style regulation by codifying lawful processing bases, data subject rights, and restrictions on overseas transfers.[6] Building on these foundations, recently, Vietnam has passed the standalone 2024 Data Law, 2025 Personal Data Protection Law, and complementary instruments, including the 2025 Law on Digital Technology Industry, to align more closely with EU standards and support future adequacy recognition. However, the direct transplantation of advanced legal models from developed countries may not yield the most effective results in the Vietnamese context. Vietnam's unique characteristics as a developing country and its relatively limited technological advancement compared to more developed countries require a tailored approach to data governance. At the same time, Vietnam's considerations go beyond compliance with EU standards; significant national security and sovereignty concerns also need to be addressed in the framework design process.

This article, firstly, focuses explicitly on the Regional Comprehensive Economic Partnership (RCEP) and the Comprehensive and Progressive Trans-Pacific Partnership (CPTPP) to assess the prevailing regulatory trends concerning this issue. In this vein, a particular focus is placed on Vietnam's legislative advancements, showcasing efforts to align its regulatory framework with GDPR while safeguarding national security and digital sovereignty. Lastly, the authors identify potential challenges facing Vietnam in regulating cross-border data transfers and propose adopting Japan's

---

[5] Drahos (2003, p. 79), Azmeh (2024, pp. 375–397), and Musoni et al. (2023).

[6] Hang NHB (2024, p. 18).

"*trust-based*" model, which prioritizes trust, transparency, and commitment from stakeholders in developing legal frameworks and digital trade agreements.

13.3 A Comparative Analysis of Cross-Border Data Flow Regulations in the Comprehensive and Progressive Trans-Pacific Partnership and the Regional Comprehensive Economic Partnership

13.3.1 The Comprehensive and Progressive Trans-Pacific Partnership

The CPTPP was adopted in 2017 among 11 countries in the Asia–Pacific region and entered into force on December 30, 2018. Although the US withdrew from the agreement at the beginning of the Trump administration, the CPTPP's e-commerce chapter reflects US efforts to secure digital trade obligations. It is an exact reiteration of the e-commerce chapter in the earlier Trans-Pacific Partnership (TPP).[7]

According to Article 14.11, the provision on "*cross-border transfers of information by electronic means*" acknowledges the fundamental principle that "*each Party shall permit the cross-border transfer of information by electronic means, including personal information*". It reflects the principle of trade liberalization in international trade, which has been established in the provisions of the WTO and other international trade agreements. The provision also stipulates that "*each Party may have own regulatory requirements concerning the transfer of information by electronic means*", provided that such measures are for a legitimate public policy objective, provided that such measures: "*(i) are not applied in a manner that would constitute a means of arbitrary or unjustifiable discrimination or a disguised restriction on trade; and (ii) do not impose greater restrictions on the transfer of information greater than required to achieve the objective*". While this article urges for transparent domestic regulations that explicitly govern conditions of cross-border data flow, vagueness in terms such as *"arbitrary"*, *"reasonable"*, *"disguised restriction"* may frustrate the provision's intention. Such ambiguity risks inconsistent interpretation and application across jurisdictions, potentially leading to disputes among member states.

Furthermore, Article 14.13 mandates that "no party *shall require a covered person to use or locate facilities in that Party's territory as a condition for conducting business in that territory*". Nevertheless, akin to the restrictions stated in Article 14.11, a party may not comply with the above provision if it meets the requirements in Article 14.13.3 CPTPP. In effect, this clause strives to balance between the principles of market openness and regulatory sovereignty, granting states limited flexibility

---

[7] MOFCOM (2021), http://www.mofcom.gov.cn/article/zwgk/bnjg/202101/20210103030014.shtml.

to impose localization requirements when justified by public interests such as data security, privacy protection, or law enforcement needs. Thus, while the CPTPP seeks to prevent protectionist data policies, it recognizes each member's right to regulate for legitimate policy objectives at the same time, thereby reflecting the ongoing tension between economic integration with digital sovereignty. Upon this, Article 14.8 of the CPTPP guides ongoing negotiation and future establishment of the common personal data protection standards, by requiring each Party to adopt or maintain a legal framework for personal data protection that takes into account principles and guidelines from relevant international bodies. It can be inferred that Article 14.8 of the CPTPP integrates privacy protection into the architecture of digital trade, advancing a model of "data flow with trust" before that term gained traction in global discussions. By emphasizing the purpose of "enhancing consumer confidence in electronic commerce" in its first paragraph, the CPTPP positions data protection not as a trade barrier but as a trade-enabling trust mechanism. At the same time, the article's use of soft language such as "shall endeavour" and "should encourage" reveals its non-binding, flexible character, reflecting the reality that CPTPP members possess uneven regulatory capacities. For developing members like Vietnam, this provision allows gradual institutional development toward internationally compatible data protection standards while preserving policy space.

13.3.2 The Regional Comprehensive Economic Partnership

RCEP was signed on 15 November 2020 by 15 countries, including China, Japan, South Korea, Australia, New Zealand, and ASEAN (ten countries). On 1 January 2022, RCEP officially came into effect. Chapter 12 of the agreement in question pertains to electronic commerce. The chapter is composed of 17 articles, the majority of which bear a resemblance to previous FTAs. In Section IV, RCEP explicitly addresses the contentious subjects of cross-border data flows under two articles: 12.14 and 12.15.

The primary purpose of Article 12.14 is to facilitate cross-border data flows and avoid creating barriers to international digital trade by requiring data localization or local infrastructure. Article 12.14, titled "*Location of Computing Facilities*", employs a language similar to that of the CPTPP, stipulating that RCEP contracting parties must permit the free flow of data across borders, including personal data. Moreover, Article 12.15, which addresses the "*cross-border transfer of information by electronic means*", stipulates that such information must be capable of being transferred without restrictions across borders. However, these provisions are accompanied by Article 12.14.3 and 12.15.3, which allow Parties to interpret their public policies and apply restrictions on the location of computer infrastructure, as well as cross-border transfer of information by electronic means for "*public policy objective*". Notably, footnotes 12 and 14 also emphasize that: "*The Parties affirm that the necessity behind the implementation of such legitimate public policy shall be decided by the implementing Party*". It can be seen that the RCEP seeks to balance the promotion of digital trade with the sovereignty of individual countries to protect their national interests, particularly regarding security and public policy. The explanation in footnotes appears to be in line with the WTO's practice in its General Agreement on Tariffs and Trade (GATT) Article XX and General Agreement on Trade in Services (GATS) Article XIV, where "necessity" is subject to the responding Member's burden of proof by making a *prima facie* case that its measure is "necessary",[8] and as long as it does not constitute arbitrary discrimination or a restriction on trade.[9] However, this does not fundamentally prevent fragmentation in cross-border data management policy because the RCEP's dispute settlement mechanism does not apply to Chapter 12 on electronic commerce, according to its Article 12.17.3.[10] Thus, it is unclear whether the principles and interpretation within the WTO framework have a binding effect when applying and interpreting the RCEP clauses. Only if, after a future review under Article 20.8, the RCEP parties mutually agree to extend dispute-settlement coverage to Chapter 12, will those rules become enforceable between consenting members. In this circumstance, the RCEP's Article 19.4 (2) explicitly regulates that: "*With respect to any provision of the WTO Agreement that has been incorporated into this Agreement, the panel shall also consider relevant interpretations in reports of WTO panels and the WTO Appellate Body, adopted by the WTO Dispute Settlement Body*". Yet, it only imposes the obligation on the RCEP dispute settlement panel to refer to the WTO reports with the aim of ensuring predictability and consistency in the international trade framework, but does not prevent such a panel from adopting different interpretations, especially in newly emerging topics such as e-commerce and data-engaged services. Consequently, in any situation, the RCEP still enables these parties to apply data localization requirements with restrictions to a certain extent.

13.4 Comparative Analysis of Digital Trade Provisions Under the RCEP and CPTPP

From the above analysis, there are several key differences between RCEP and CPTPP, particularly regarding provisions related to the location of computing facilities, cross-border electronic information transfer, source code, and dispute settlement. In these areas, RCEP's Chapter 12 is notably more political than CPTPP's Chapter 14 due to its non-justiciable character and skepticism in cross-border data governance policy, rendering its provisions less effective in liberalizing cross-border digital trade and data flows. Noteworthily, Vietnam's position under both the CPTPP and the RCEP reflects the country's transitional approach to balancing digital trade liberalization with regulatory sovereignty. At the time CPTPP and RCEP entered into force, respectively in 2019 and 2022, Vietnam's privacy-related provisions were scattered across multiple instruments, including the 2015 Law on Cyberinformation Security and

[8] *Appellate Body Report, US—Gambling, paras 291, 309–311.* See more at: Du (2016, pp. 846–847).

[9] Huang and Li (2023, p. 27).

[10] Leblond (2020).

the 2018 Cybersecurity Law, which were not fully aligned with global privacy norms. Both agreements acknowledge Vietnam's developing institutional capacity in personal data protection and cross-border data governance, and accordingly provide it with special and differential treatment to allow gradual compliance with international commitments. To be more specific, footnote 5 of the CPTPP's Article 14.8 stipulates that Vietnam and Brunei Darussalam were granted a transitional exemption, meaning they are not required to apply Article 14.8 until they have implemented their own domestic legal frameworks for personal data protection. This clause acknowledges Vietnam's previous absence of a comprehensive and standalone privacy law before 2023, when Decree No. 13/2023 on Personal Data Protection was officially enacted, and the need for regulatory and technical capacity building before assuming binding commitments. Similarly, while RCEP's Article 12.15(3) addresses the free flow of cross-border data for business purposes, its footnote 13 explicitly exempts Cambodia, Lao PDR, Myanmar, and Vietnam from applying this rule for a five-year transitional period, with an optional three-year extension for the least-developed members. For Vietnam, this provision delays the obligation to liberalize cross-border data flows, allowing it to retain certain localization or approval requirements during the transitional phase. Unlike CPTPP's "*until implementation*" exemption, RCEP's flexibility is time-bound, and once the period expires, compliance becomes mandatory regardless of domestic readiness.

Taken together, these differentiated treatments illustrate how Vietnam occupies a transitional role in the digital economy, navigating between commitments to global trade liberalization and the protection of national regulatory space. Accession to such regional trade agreements requires a strategic balancing act in Vietnam's legal modernization—seeking to enhance digital competitiveness while preserving sovereignty over data governance and privacy regulation. It is akin to planting a bamboo, which is rooted in clear legal philosophies and governance principles to seize international trade opportunities, while firmly preserving regulatory autonomy amid any uncertain situation.

13.5 Vietnam's Legislative Progress on Cross-Border Data Flows

With its active integration into international trade agreements as a member country of both CPTPP and RCEP, Vietnam recognizes the important role of data management in digital commerce. With its strategic geographical position and dynamic economic policies, the country has the potential to emerge as a significant hub for data centers in Asia.[11] Although Vietnam has not yet received adequacy status from the EU, it has recently undertaken efforts to supplement and revise its data protection laws.

Before the 2024 Data Law, Vietnam had applied several measures affecting cross-border data transfers, including data storage requirements under Article 26 of Decree

[11] Thanh Niên (2024).

No. 53/2022/ND-CP, personal data transfer requirements under Article 25 of Decree No. 13/2023/ND-CP, and technical infrastructure requirements under Decree No. 147/2024/ND-CP. However, the regulations were often sectoral, focusing on specific areas such as cybersecurity and online content management.

To be more specific, Article 26.1 of Decree No. 53/2022/ND-CP stipulates that covered enterprises must store certain types of data[12] in Vietnam for a minimum period of 24 months at the request of the Minister of Public Security. Although Decree 53/2022/ND-CP focuses primarily on the requirement to store data domestically, implementing this requirement means restricting the ability to freely transfer such data abroad. According to these laws and regulations, foreign companies operating in specific sectors, such as telecommunications, data storage and sharing, e-commerce, and online payment, are mandated to establish a representative office or branch in Vietnam and store localized data within the country for a minimum of 24 months.

Decree No. 13/2023/ND-CP, issued on April 17, 2023 and effective from July 01, 2023, establishes a comprehensive legal framework on personal data protection. This decree applies to Vietnamese agencies, organizations, individuals, foreign organizations, and individuals involved in personal data processing activities in Vietnam. The scope of regulation of Decree 13/2023/ND-CP is broader than Decree 53/2022/ND-CP, focusing on protecting individuals' privacy in the digital environment. Regarding the conditions for transferring personal data abroad, Article 25 of the Decree stipulates that the transfer of personal data must comply with strict conditions. The prerequisite is the consent of the data subject. In addition, organizations or individuals transferring data must conduct a personal data transfer impact assessment (TIA) and provide this assessment record to the Ministry of Public Security. The Decree also clearly stipulates cases where data transfer may be restricted or suspended, such as when the data is used for activities that are harmful to national interests, when TIA requirements are not complied with, or when personal data of Vietnamese citizens is leaked. Specifically, data localization requirements for foreign data service providers may arise when their services involve cybersecurity violations, as announced by the Department of Cyber Security and High-Tech Crime Prevention.

In addition, Vietnam also provides for a temporary ban on cross-border data transfers under Article 25.8 of Decree No. 13/2023 and business-to-government (B2G) data sharing under Article 20 of Decree No. 53/2022, prioritizing public interest and "national security concerns". Notably, Decree No. 13/2023 is a significant step forward in Vietnam's efforts to strengthen cybersecurity, closely aligning with the provisions set out in the 2018 Law on Cybersecurity, which emphasizes the need to protect personal data as an essential component of the national cybersecurity strategy. Articles 3(1) and 4(1) of the 2018 law highlight the important role of cybersecurity in

[12] (i) data relating to personal information of service users in Vietnam which is defined to mean information in form of signs, characters, numbers, pictures, voice or similar information used to identify an individual; (ii) data generated by service users in Vietnam which includes account name of service users, time of using service, information of credit card, email address, IP address of most recent login/log out, the registered telephone number associated with the account or data; and (iii) data on the relationship of service users in Vietnam which includes friends and groups with whom users connect or interact.

a variety of areas, including national defense, security, socio-economic development, science and technology, and foreign affairs.[13]

The implementation of Decree No. 147/2024/ND-CP, effective from December 25, 2024, marks a significant regulatory framework governing the management, provision, and utilization of Internet services and online information in Vietnam. This Decree is pertinent to both domestic and international entities engaged in activities related to the Internet within the Vietnamese context. The primary focus of Decree 147 is regulating the online environment, emphasizing the importance of information security and maintaining social order in cyberspace. Particularly noteworthy are the technical infrastructure requirements outlined in Articles 34, 35, 54, and 74, which mandate that domestic enterprises offering information content services via mobile telecommunications networks, online gaming platforms, and local social networks must possess a minimum of one or two server systems located within Vietnam.[14]

In this context, the Data Law, enacted in late November 2024 and set to take effect on July 1, 2025, marks an important step toward a more comprehensive legal framework that covers all types of digital data and establishes common data governance principles. The 2024 Data Law aims to establish a national consolidated database and data center for state management. Thus, it expands the scope of control over cross-border data transfers, not only limited to personal data as in Decree 13/2023/ND-CP but also including non-personal data of national importance. This trend reflects a shift in Vietnam's approach from imposing *ad hoc* local storage requirements to building a strategic data management system based on the importance and risk of the data.

Notably, the 2024 Data Law sets out important conceptual frameworks in relation to data classification, notably the distinction between "*important data*" and "*core data*". "*Important data*" is described as information that is likely to impact important aspects of the national interest, including defense, security, foreign relations, macroeconomic stability, social cohesion, public health, and safety (Article 3.6). In contrast, "*core data*" includes a subset of critical data, namely data that has a direct and significant impact on these important areas (Article 3.7).

Unlike the previous approach, Article 23 of the 2024 Data Law establishes that, in principle, agencies, organizations, and individuals are free to transfer data from abroad to Vietnam and process international data in Vietnam. However, for core or important data, the transfer abroad must comply with regulations to ensure security, protect public interests, and the rights of data subjects. The 2024 Data Law stipulates three forms of transferring important and core data abroad, including transferring data from domestic systems abroad (clause a), transferring data of Vietnamese organizations/individuals to foreign parties (clause b), and using international platforms to process data (clause c). Currently, the government is drafting three detailed guiding decrees: the Draft Decree on Data Products & Services, the Draft Decree on Core Data & Important Data, and the Draft Framework Decree. Those by-law instruments are anticipated to include detailed provisions regarding these data transfer processes,

[13] Ngo and Nguyen (2025, pp. 317–341).

[14] DLA Piper (2025, pp. 16–18).

which may involve the relocation of data from domestic storage systems to international servers or the use of global cloud platforms. While specific regulations have yet to be released, stricter requirements are expected for transferring such data. These may involve conducting risk assessments, reporting on impact evaluations, and potentially obtaining approval from relevant authorities.[15]

In addition, Vietnam has also enacted the Law on Personal Data Protection in 2025, which is expected to take effect from January 1, 2026. The law not only focuses on protecting the personal data of Vietnamese citizens, but also expands the scope of application to the collection and processing of personal data of foreigners in Vietnam. Article 20 of the law stipulates cases of transferring personal data abroad. Specifically, data transfer includes: (i) transferring personal data stored in Vietnam to a data storage system located outside of Vietnam; (ii) Vietnamese agencies, organizations and individuals transferring personal data to foreign organizations and individuals; and (iii) Vietnamese agencies, organizations and individuals using platforms located outside of Vietnam to process personal data. The law also requires that the TIA of personal data transfer abroad must be carried out only once during the entire operation period and updated as prescribed in Article 21. The data transferor is responsible for preparing the TIA File and must be ready to provide this file to the personal data protection authority upon request, and send an original copy to this authority within 60 days from the commencement of processing of personal data. In addition, the personal data transferor is also responsible for notifying the personal data protection authority of the details related to the data transfer and the contact information of the responsible organization or individual after the data transfer is completed.

The government authority has the right to assess and request the personal data controller or processor to complete the TIA file if the file is incomplete or does not comply with the regulations. The parties involved must also update and supplement the TIA dossier when there is any change in the submitted content. After that, the personal data protection authority has the right to conduct periodic (once a year) or *ad hoc* inspections of the transfer of data abroad if it detects violations of the law on personal data protection or incidents of disclosure or loss of personal data of Vietnamese citizens. In particular, this authority has the right to request the suspension of data transfer abroad if it detects that the data is used for activities that violate Vietnam's national interests and national security. Hence, akin to Decree 13, the Law on Personal Data Protection does not mandate prior approval from the relevant authority prior to the transfer of data. Instead, it establishes that the Ministry of Public Security can request to suspend transferring data if the enterprise fails to amend its records in response to official notifications. Thus, the law applies an *ex-post* model, which indicates that the enterprise retains the autonomy to decide on the international transfer of data, while the competent authority subsequently undertakes an examination of the records post-transfer. Enterprises bear responsibility for any inaccuracies found in their records. It should be noted that the following cases are exempted from the obligations to conduct a personal data cross-border transfer impact assessment: (i) transfers carried out by competent state agencies, (ii)

[15] Trần and Nguyễn (2025).

storage of employees' personal data by agencies or organizations on cloud computing services, and (iii) self-initiated cross-border transfer of their own personal data by data subjects; (iv) in other cases as stipulated by the government. On one hand, this clause recognizes the global nature of digital infrastructure (cloud or individual use). On the other hand, it reinforces state control in defining when data flows are regulated or exempted. This open-ended provision offers regulatory flexibility, but such an approach may compromise legal certainty and predictability, particularly if future exemptions are issued through administrative instruments without clear legislative safeguards or public consultation.

In short, the enactment of the 2024 Data Law, along with the 2025 Law on Personal Data Protection represents a significant advancement in the legal framework governing data management in Vietnam, transitioning from fragmented sectoral regulations, which primarily emphasized local data storage, to a more comprehensive data governance system. This approach is particularly relevant for data deemed to have national importance, thereby illustrating Vietnam's commitment to safeguarding core national interests in the context of a rapidly evolving global digital economy. The 2024 Data Law and the 2025 Law on Personal Data Protection also align well with the mentioned provisions outlined in the RCEP, CPTPP, and the WTO e-commerce Agreement. From this, it can be inferred that Vietnam uses trade-agreement commitments as an external catalyst for reform, but retains extensive regulatory autonomy (especially on data flows) for sovereignty, security, and public interest reasons.

13.6 Strengthening the Bamboo in Storm: Challenges for Vietnam

Despite the perspective of certain enterprises that new regulations may present significant opportunities for enhancing management capabilities, boosting competitiveness, and fostering trust among stakeholders, many businesses in Vietnam are confronted with an array of challenges. Specifically, two controversial legal issues are related to cross-border data transfers: (i) the ambiguous definition of core data and important data and (ii) the definition of cross-border data transfers.

Data classification is important in establishing a solid legal framework and facilitating systematic data management and monitoring by government agencies. This classification benefits businesses because it allows for the development of effective internal data governance strategies, thereby minimizing legal risks and enhancing information security. However, the current definitions of "*important data*" and "*core data*" are often too broad and vague, leading to significant challenges without clear guidance. The possibility of many types of information being unnecessarily classified as "*important*" or "*core*" can lead to undue restrictions on data use. Furthermore, the lack of clarity on data classification criteria and specific processes for determining the rights and obligations of relevant parties raises concerns about "*inadvertent violations*". As a result, businesses may face uncertainty in regulatory compliance, which may reduce their competitiveness in a globalized market.

Second, the scope of cross-border data transfers is broadly defined, covering most global digital transactions. For example, if a multinational company in Vietnam stores employee data on international cloud platforms such as Amazon Cloud or Mediafire, with servers located abroad, this would be considered a cross-border data transfer. Similarly, if a parent company abroad accesses data from servers in Vietnam, this activity could also be subject to the provisions of the 2024 Data Law. This provision places significant pressure on businesses that are making an effort to optimize their data management processes using cloud technology.[16]

Thus, although the measures in the 2024 Data Law are designed to walk on the tightrope of complying with the commitments in the FTA and invoking the security exception in necessary situations, their implementation remains controversial. It is particularly evident when analyzed together with the Cyber Security Law 2018, especially Article 26.3, which applies to domestic and foreign enterprises providing telecommunications networks, Internet services, and value-added services in cyberspace in Vietnam that collect, exploit, analyze, or process personal data, user relationship data, or data generated by users in Vietnam, storing such data in Vietnam for a period prescribed by the government and further requiring foreign enterprises to establish branches or representative offices in Vietnam. Moreover, Articles 17.đ and 19.1 of the 2025 Law on Personal Data Protection grant state authorities broad powers to require access for security purposes. In parallel, Decree No. 13/2023/ND-CP on Personal Data Protection and the 2025 Law on Personal Data Protection establish GDPR-inspired obligations, such as Article 11 (lawful bases for processing), Articles 9–10 (data subject rights, including access, correction, and erasure), and Article 21 (conditions for cross-border data transfers). It creates significant disadvantages for businesses, especially when the actual effectiveness of these measures is still unclear. Uncertainties in the implementation process can increase costs and legal risks for businesses while weakening competitiveness in the global environment.

While Vietnam strongly emphasizes national security and seeks to preserve broad regulatory autonomy in its domestic legal framework, which is an approach well aligned with the exceptions permitted under the CPTPP and RCEP, such reliance on these exceptions is not desirable as a long-term strategy. Invoking a public objective exception may undermine investor confidence and the predictability of cross-border data governance, especially when the criteria for arbitrary, unjustifiably discriminatory, or disguised restrictions on trade are not clearly established in the context of cross-border data flow. When invoked, these exceptions risk being perceived as policy shields rather than proportionate safeguards, thereby weakening Vietnam's commitment to the principles of free cross-border data flows and creating a chilling effect on foreign investment and digital innovation. Thus, Vietnam, as well as other developing countries with concerns alike, is in need of a common framework that can balance

[16] Ibid.

sovereignty concerns with its treaty obligations and enhance trust among its regional and global digital partners.

13.7 From Sovereignty to Trust: Can Japan's DFFT Framework Be a Feasible Pathway for Digital Governance

With the trend of expanding policy space on cross-border data transfer through exceptions and carve-outs in FTAs, along with GDPR adequacy requirements that restrict and condition data transfers, developing countries may face significant compliance and harmonization challenges, thus expressing apprehension regarding the potential erosion of their "information sovereignty" or "data sovereignty".[17] Notably, while conditions of genuine public interests and necessity of the invoked cross-border data flow restriction measures embedded in GATS and FTAs remain vague and varied,[18] the unilateral adequacy decision can be withdrawn anytime by the CJEU at the EU level, as shown by the *Schrems I* and *Schrems II* decisions.[19] In this context, power asymmetries in international negotiations may marginalize developing countries, causing a sense of exclusion that contributes to widespread distrust and resistance.

In this context, the concept of Data Free Flow with Trust (DFFT) was proposed by former Japanese Prime Minister Shinzo Abe as a means to balance data privacy and security with the promotion of cross-border data flows.[20] First introduced at the 2019 G20 Osaka Summit, the DFFT model aims to promote cross-border data flows by creating trust among nations and businesses, which is built on mutual recognition of established data-protection regimes such as Asia–Pacific Cross-Border Privacy Rules (APCR) and the GDPR, thereby promoting international cooperation and economic development.[21] This is an innovative and distinctive approach to the GDPR's central purpose, which is to safeguard personal data and ensure accountability in how organizations process it, grounded in the fundamental-rights- and privacy-based protection. With different legal philosophy and serving purpose, the DFFT's focus is on enabling data mobility as a non-binding law and policy-driven framework,[22] thus encouraging cooperation, communication, and interoperability among countries' data regimes to build mutual recognition of standards and creating international "data bridges" through voluntary agreements and multi-stakeholder dialog, often coordinated by the G7, OECD, and DEPA (Digital Economy Partnership Agreement).[23] It, therefore, offsets some of the limitations of GDPR's adequacy model as a unilateral decision,

[17] Guo and Li (2025, p. 1).

[18] Ngo and Nguyen (2025, pp. 325–326).

[19] Christakis (2024).

[20] Arasasingham and Goodman (2023), Takemasa (2023).

[21] Du (2024).

[22] Ministry of Foreign Affairs of Japan (2019).

[23] Ibid.

which is often reached after long negotiations.[24] Therefore, the DFFT model not only reduces fragmentation in national data policies by bridging the gap between open data economies and privacy-centric regimes like the EU's, but also lays the foundation for a highly interoperable global data governance system.[25] Consequently, this approach enhances the protection of personal data and fosters economic and digital cooperation among nations, thereby contributing to the future global data governance frameworks that balance sovereignty, human rights, and technological advance.

While the DFFT model offers a promising framework for balancing data freedom with necessary safeguards for privacy, national security, and intellectual property, there remain noteworthy challenges. The core component of DFFT is "*trust*", but this concept is often vaguely defined. This vagueness can lead to countries having different interpretations of what constitutes trustworthy data handling practices, causing inconsistencies and conflicts during implementation.[26] Although the goal of DFFT is to create a highly interoperable global data governance system, achieving regulatory harmony among different legal systems remains a significant challenge, especially in jurisdictions with varying levels of regulatory capacity and resources.[27] Without effective negotiations and communications in establishing common applicable standards, provisions in digital trade agreements may place unfair demands on developing countries, forcing them to comply with standards and regulations that do not consider differences in economic, political, and cultural conditions. It thereby increases the fragmentation of international data governance and could also create an environment where privacy and personal freedoms are threatened under the guise of data protection commitments.[28] Consequently, transplanting the DFFT concept from a principle to actionable and enforceable regulations requires significant effort.

It should be further noted that at the time of the model's proposal, Japan distinguished itself through its established technological infrastructure and its capability to adhere to the two preeminent data protection frameworks currently in existence: the Asia–Pacific Cross-Border Privacy Rules (APCR) and the GDPR. This recognition by the international community highlights Japan's effectiveness in implementing robust data protection measures. When transplanting the DFFT model to the Vietnamese context, major challenges may arise. With the priority in promulgating cybersecurity and cyberinformation security laws years before passing the personal data protection regulations, this clearly reflects that Vietnam's governance structure emphasizes state control over data as a strategic resource, aligning with a model closer to "data sovereignty" than "data free flow". From this, the government views data as an integral part of public order and national interests. Legal instruments are primarily designed to assert state authority and preserve regulatory autonomy, rather than to foster cross-border interoperability or mutual recognition of data protection

[24] Christakis (2024).

[25] Lippoldt (2023, pp. 7–9).

[26] Arasasingham and Goodman (2023).

[27] Du (2024).

[28] Dale and Aizawa (2024, p. 9).

standards, thus placing less emphasis on "trust". From this, the government has legitimate concerns that, when "trust" lacks a clear operational definition, it can easily be exploited as a means for technologically advanced countries to set the rules of the game according to their interests. Additionally, the so-called "harmonization" in the DFFT is not always a neutral mutual adjustment but operates under pressure in an asymmetric negotiation context. When incorporated into digital trade agreements, the DFFT-inspired provisions risked imposing undue compliance costs on developing countries, bypassing infrastructure and legal constraints. Thus, while the current approach of Vietnam enhances domestic oversight, it may hinder participation in trust-based mechanisms that require mutual recognition and reciprocal openness to facilitate cross-border data-engaged trade.

Nonetheless, the strong point of the DFFT is that this is not solely a "club" reserved for countries that already have trust in each other. Its value also lies in transforming trust from a political label into verifiable and gradually implemented principles, such as the OECD principle on the right to assess data by state agencies, the global CBPR/PRP certification scheme, and the ASEAN contractual regulatory frameworks.[29] Vietnam's membership in the CPTPP and the RCEP, in which Japan is also a member state, offers pathways toward gradual convergence with DFFT principles. Under Article 14.8 of the CPTPP and a five-year grace period provided by the RCEP, Vietnam is required to develop a comprehensive framework for personal data protection consistent with international standards, and, in fact, it has recently done so. Throughout the years since the accession to these agreements, Vietnam has progressively operated three pillars: (i) legal regulations; (ii) international cooperation within multilateral frameworks; and (iii) self-regulation within the industry.[30] Regarding legal regulations, until October 2025, Vietnam has enacted all significant regulatory frameworks on cyberinformation, cybersecurity, data governance and personal data protection, with the Law on Artificial Intelligence, the revised Law on Cyber Security, and other detailed guiding by-laws are to be discussed by the National Assembly in 2026. Thus, in its present stage, Vietnam is partially prepared to implement the DFFT. It can contribute to the trust dimension through stronger privacy safeguards, cybersecurity measures, and consumer protection, although it is still facing challenges in realizing the free flow aspect. The key barriers include mandatory data localization, the lack of an independent enforcement body, and the absence of mechanisms such as participation in the APEC Cross-Border Privacy Rules (CBPR) system.

Beyond legal instruments, the absence of robust cross-border cooperation mechanisms with unprepared industry-led compliance practices indicates that the latter two pillars have yet to be effectively implemented. Overcoming these limitations would require institutional reforms that promote transparency, inter-agency coordination, and cooperation with international privacy frameworks. To be more specific, in the short term, at least until 2027 and no later than 2030, when the grace period of RCEP runs out, to promote self-regulation within the industry, Vietnam should encourage the creation of sector-specific codes of conduct, certification schemes,

[29] OECD (2023, p. 29–30).

[30] IPS (2024).

and privacy compliance programs led by professional associations or chambers of commerce. In the long term, which is the next 5–10 years, international cooperation in privacy and data protection regulation will create a harmonized global regulatory landscape, helping to maintain high data protection standards and develop a sustainable digital economy.[31] Engaging with established international organizations, such as the OECD, Global Privacy Assembly, and ISO, as well as in exploratory dialogs on DFFT, would help promote interoperability between Vietnam's domestic data protection regime and international standards. This also allows Vietnam to adopt best practices in data protection from more developed economies. In that sense, DFFT is not only a framework for countries that already have trust but also a foundation for Vietnam to build trust in a roadmap in line with domestic capacity and regional cooperation. Hence, the DFFT model presents a valuable framework for enhancing Vietnam's digital trade agreements and domestic data law.

13.8 Concluding Remarks

In the context of increasing global uncertainty and fragmentation of cross-border data flow regulations, Vietnam's continued enactment of cybersecurity and personal data protection laws since 2015 can be regarded as a significant milestone in establishing a robust framework for national data governance. This policy promotes trade liberalization within the digital economy while ensuring national security and upholding citizens' rights. However, it is easier said than done. While direct commitment to the DFFT model may not be immediately feasible, it is essential that the Vietnamese legal framework gradually aligns with its standards while maintaining a firm stance on national security and digital sovereignty. In other words, the country's legal framework, currently grounded in cybersecurity and state control, provides the solid roots of this bamboo grove. Yet to thrive in the evolving digital ecosystem, these roots must be complemented by new branches of trust, transparency, and interoperability that extend beyond national borders. This approach will allow Vietnam not only to protect its national interests but also to rise with a trusted and sustainable data governance.

References

Arasasingham A, Goodman MP (2023) Operationalizing Data Free Flow with Trust (DFFT). CSIS. https://www.csis.org/analysis/operationalizing-data-free-flow-trust-dfft. Accessed 30 Sept 2025

Azmeh S (2024) Developing Countries and Joint Statement Initiatives at the WTO: Damned if You Join, Damned if You Don't? *Development and Change* 55: 375–397. https://doi.org/10.1111/dech.12836

[31] OECD (2023, p. 30).

Christakis T (2024) Data free flow with trust: current landscape, challenges and opportunities. *Journal of Cyber Policy*, *9*(1): 95–120. https://doi.org/10.1080/23738871.2024.2421838

Dale JG, Aizawa N (2024) Data Free Flow with Trust: Japan's Struggle to Integrate Democracy and Human Rights into Digital Trade Policy. *Frontiers in Sociology*, 25 Sept 2024: 1–12. https://doi.org/10.3389/fsoc.2024.1397528

Dat HLNT & An CTT (2024) The Regulation of Data Transmission in the Digital Era: From the European Union's Perspective and Implications for Vietnam. *Vietnamese Journal of Legal Sciences* 11(2): 1–13. https://doi.org/10.2478/vjls-2024-0007

DLA Piper (2025) *Data Protection Laws of the World Handbook: Vietnam*. DLA Piper, London

Drahos P (2003) When the Weak Bargain with the Strong: Negotiations in the World Trade Organization. *International Negotiation* 8: 79–109. https://doi.org/10.2139/ssrn.418480

Du M (2016) The Necessity Test in World Trade Law: What Now? *Chinese Journal of International Law* 15(4): 817–847, https://doi.org/10.1093/chinesejil/jmw036

Du R (2024) Multilateral and Regional Cooperation in Digital Trade Rules with a Focus on Agreements in the Asia-Pacific Region. *Online Research Conference Inclusive and Sustainable Development through Digital Trade and E-commerce*, 1–20

Global Data Alliance (2024) World Trade Organization publishes agreement on electronic commerce. https://globaldataalliance.org/news/world-trade-organization-publishes-agreement-on-electronic-commerce. Accessed 30 Sept 2025

Guo S, Li X (2025) Cross-border Data Flow in China: Shifting from Restriction to Relaxation? *Computer Law & Security Review* 56: 106079. https://doi.org/10.1016/j.clsr.2024.106079

Hang NHB (2024) Addressing Fragmentation in Vietnam's Data Protection Laws: Recommendations for a Unified Legal Framework. *Vietnamese Journal of Legal Sciences* 11(2): 14–26. https://doi.org/10.2478/vjls-2024-0008

Huang X, Li J (2023) An Analysis of China's Rules for Cross-border Data Flows under RCEP Framework. *IOSR Journal of Business and Management* 25(4, Ser. V): 24–28

Institute for Policy Studies and Media Development (IPS) (2024, October 28) Cross-border personal data governance: Promoting accountability and advancing multilateral cooperation. https://www.ips.org.vn/en/news/cross-border-personal-data-governance-promoting-accountability-and-advancing-multilateral-cooperation-ct401.html Accessed 30 Oct 2025

Leblond P (2020) Digital Trade: Is RCEP the WTO's Future? CIGI, 23 Nov 2020. https://www.cigionline.org/articles/digital-trade-rcep-wtos-future/. Accessed 30 Sept 2025

Leblond P (2024) Is the WTO's New E-commerce Agreement Really a Game Changer? CIGI. https://www.cigionline.org/articles/is-the-wtos-new-e-commerce-agreement-really-a-game-changer/. Accessed 30 Sept 2025

Lippoldt D (2023) Mitigating Global Fragmentation in Digital Trade Governance: A Case Study. *CIGI Papers* No. 270, Jan 2023, pp. 7–20

Ministry of Foreign Affairs of Japan (2019) G20 Osaka Leaders' Declaration. https://www.mofa.go.jp/policy/economy/g20_summit/osaka19/en/documents/final_g20_osaka_leaders_declaration.html. Accessed 30 Oct 2025

Musoni M, Karkare P, Teevan C, Domingo E (2023) *Global Approaches to Digital Sovereignty: Competing Definitions and Contrasting Policy*. ECDPM Discussion Paper No. 344, May 2023. https://ecdpm.org/application/files/7816/8485/0476/Global-approaches-digital-sovereignty-competing-definitions-contrasting-policy-ECDPM-Discussion-Paper-344-2023.pdf. Accessed 30 Sept 2025

Nabiebu M, Ijiomah A, Ekpo ME, Agube N (2025) Harmonization vs. Fragmentation: The Struggle to Govern Cross-Border Data in Trade Agreements. *Advances in Law, Pedagogy, and Multidisciplinary Humanities (ALPAMET)* 3(1): 175–196

NASATI (2023) *Triển vọng phát triển kinh tế số dựa trên dữ liệu*. National Agency for Science and Technology Information, No. 21, Vietnam, pp. 1–30

Ngo NTV, Nguyen XMH (2025) The Quest of Balancing Data Regulatory Autonomy with International Trade Commitments: Assessing the GATS and the EVFTA. In: *European Yearbook of International Economic Law*. Springer, Cham, pp. 317–341. https://doi.org/10.1007/8165_2024_135

OECD (2023) *Moving Forward on Data Free Flow with Trust: New Evidence and Analysis of Business Experiences*. OECD Digital Economy Papers No. 353, Apr 2023, pp. 1–50

Takemasa S. (2023) 'Legal Framework for Data Free Flow with Trust (DFFT): Trade Agreements as Incubators to Enhance Trust of Data Transaction' in Yokomizo, D., Tojo, Y. and Naiki, Y. (eds.) *Changing Orders in International Economic Law Volume 2: A Japanese Perspective*. Abingdon: Routledge, pp. 201–220

Thanh Nien (2024) Việt Nam – miền đất hứa cho các trung tâm dữ liệu. https://thanhnien.vn/viet-nam-mien-dat-hua-cho-cac-trung-tam-du-lieu-185240518174952332.htm. Accessed 30 Sept 2025

Trần QT, Nguyễn TKT (2025) Chuyển dữ liệu xuyên biên giới trong Luật Dữ liệu 2024. *Saigon Times*. https://thesaigontimes.vn/chuyen-du-lieu-xuyen-bien-gioi-trong-luat-du-lieu-2024/. Accessed 30 Sept 2025

Chapter 14
"Soft" Law on Cybersecurity and Data Governance: Strengthening Asia's Digital Economy

Trang Anh Mac

Abstract The Asia Pacific region has been targeted by cybercriminals for the reasons of digitalisation of its economy, a young society, the Internet-connected working environment and the evolution of online platforms and hardware manufacturing (Gullapalli, Why is the Asia Pacific region a target for cybercrime - and what can be done about it? 2023). It is one of the significant geopolitical threats to countries' digital sovereignty, causing economic and security concerns. While the European Union is worried about the dependence on semiconductor manufacturing mainly in Asia and lays down technical requirements and legislative initiatives to protect its regional common market (Farrand et al., International Affairs:2379–2397, 2024), Asian countries, especially in South-East Asia, experience serious cyberattacks, data breaches and a lack of security infrastructure. This paper aims to analyse the gaps amongst different parts of Asia regarding policy, legislation and infrastructure: the dominance of China in technology, technical infrastructure and serious cybercrimes in South-East Asia (Segal et al., Asia Policy:57–115, 2020). Amongst the proposed solutions, such as establishing multilateral collaboration across the region and building capacity to fight against cybercriminals, etc. (Socquet-Clerc et al., Cybersecurity Governance in Southeast Asia. Thematic SSG Brief. Geneva: DCAF - Geneva Centre for Security Sector Governance, 2023), the growth of "soft" law and its elasticity have been demonstrated as a potential solution in addition to the reinforcement of technical obligations imposed on the online-service providers, such as social and e-commerce platforms, banking services, etc. and infrastructure readiness.

Keywords Soft law · Digital economy · Asia Pacific · Cybersecurity · Data governance · Information and Communication Technology (ICT)

T. A. Mac (✉)
Ho Chi Minh City University of Law, Ho Chi Minh City, Vietnam
e-mail: mtanh@hcmulaw.edu.vn

J. Nakagawa et al. (eds.), *Geopolitical Risks and Geoeconomics in International Economic Law*, Economics, Law, and Institutions in Asia Pacific,
https://doi.org/10.1007/978-981-95-6996-0_14

Abbreviations

BC	Budapest Convention
CIRTs	National Computer Incident Response Teams
ENISA	European Union Agency for Network and Information Security
GGE	Group of Governmental Experts
ICT	Information and Communication Technology
ITU	International Telecommunication Union
UN	United Nations
UN ESCAP	United Nations Economic and Social Commission for Asia and the Pacific
UNCC	UN Convention against Cybercrime
UNCTAD	United Nations Trade and Development
WCI	World Cybercrime Index

Recent thought-provoking research has addressed the cybercrime around the globe, categorised by the types of cyberattacks and geopolitical region. Unsurprisingly, many countries in the Asia–Pacific region are listed in the top results, such as Russia (1st), China (3rd), North Korea (7th), India (10th), Iran (11th), etc. based on the survey on 5 categories of most critical cybercrime menaces—technical product/service, attacks/ extortion, data/ identity theft, scams and money laundering.[1] Furthermore, the gaps of legal instruments, technical capacities, organisation manners, capacity growth and collaboration[2] are significant amongst the countries across Asia–Pacific region. Russia, China and North Korea with different pursuits remain the most significant menaces leading to cyberwar across the region and global.[3] This article addresses the intertwining relation between the notions of cybersecurity and data governance, the actual policies, legislations of 58 countries across the region in addition to their cybercrime and security diverse nature. Finally, it analyses the development and position of the "soft" law[4] in the context of cybersecurity and data governance in Asia.

[1] Bruce M et al. (2024, p. 7–23).

[2] The International Telecommunication Union (2024).

[3] Segal A et al. (2020, p. 57–114).

[4] The concept of "soft" law is varied and controversial; therefore, within this research, its regulatory approaches, referred to as "soft" ones, should comprise (i) "regulatory guidance" (including informal guidance on case-by-case basis, e.g. preliminary warnings, informal station, initial guidance to new regulations and regime clarifying broader application of existing legal frameworks), (ii) "self-regulation" (developed voluntarily by private actors to observe, ensure its compliance and enforcement, e.g. codes of conducts, ethical codes, industry protocols), (iii) "co-regulation" (collaboratively established by public-private actors, e.g. harmonised European standards and certification regimes under the EU Regulation 1025/2012 on European Standardisation (European Parliament and the Council, 2012b), which were introduced in the EU's "Better Regulation" Agenda, known as "meta-regulation". See COM (2007), Brooks E (2025), OECD/KDI (2021), and ENISA (2015).

14.1 Cybersecurity, Data Governance and Inextricable Intertwinement Between Them

The conceptual foundation of computer security was first laid down around 1960s-1970s, through the works of Donald Davies—Packet switching, the U.S. Department of Defense—ARPANET, the Internet’s ancestor, followed by their technical report “Security Controls for Computer Systems”, commonly known as the “Ware Report”. The first “non-self-replicating benign” virus program called the Creeper was written in 1971. The first antivirus program example, called the Reaper, created by Ray Tomlinson in 1973 chased and deleted the Creeper, marked a milestone in the emergence and evolution of cybersecurity.[5] In our modern days, “cybersecurity” refers to technologies, practices and policies deployed by organisations, individuals to protect networks, devices and data from unauthorised access or criminal use, to reduce the risks of cyberattacks.[6]

Meanwhile, the concept of data emerged and evolved in research fields since the establishment of scientific journals in the seventeenth century, for instance the journal Philosophical Transactions of the Royal Society.[7] As the subset of “data management”, “data governance” refers to data management discipline ensuring data is secure, private, accurate, available and usable. It sets out internal policies, standards, procedures for gathering, storing, processing, using and disposing of data.[8] In the late twentieth century, the recognition of data’s value by the organisation resulted in the emergence of “data governance” notion.

With time, these two concepts have developed an interrelationship where the significant position of data governance in the strategy performance of the organisation’s security, including that of cybersecurity, is established. As the complexity of new information technologies, such as cloud computing, big data and artificial intelligence, the cybersecurity and data governance become essential for security of data assets and maintenance of the society’s trust.[9] The good understanding of sensitivity, value, location of and access to the data set may allow the organisations to well control and protect the information security from any attack, damage and unauthorised access or cyber risks.[10]

The complexity of cybersecurity is composed of many factors, including the unsettled conditions caused by the geopolitical strains. The cyber menaces, including the business disturbance, internet-spying and exposure of sensitive or intellectual property information, financial and reputation damages, loss of customer trust, costs of

[5] MaryVille University (2024), Shahid Alam (2022)

[6] National Cyber Security Centre, America’s Cyber Defense Agency (2021), and Lindemulder G et al. (2024).

[7] Leonelli S (2019, p. 3).

[8] Google Cloud (2025); Holdsworth J et al. (2025)

[9] Thomson Reuters (2023).

[10] Queenan M (2021).

preventive measures, responses to incidents, misinformation, etc. impact the security strategies of 60% of organisations,[11] and states. Politics and crimes can drive the motivation of cyberattacks. For example, the Indonesian flag printed upside down in the Southeast Asian Games guidebook initiated the cyberwar between Malaysian and Indonesian hackers attacking Malaysian websites.[12]

14.2 Asia–Pacific Countries' Policy, Legislation and Infrastructure

The paper has surveyed 58 countries in the Asia–Pacific region, there are 44 countries (76%) having the cybercrime/cybersecurity legal framework. There are only 4 countries (7%) which are in the stage of drafting and 10 countries (17%) where there is a limit of information about the cybercrime legislation. Most of these 14 countries are also found in the Tier 5—Building of the Cybersecurity Index and even not in the list of this Index. In general, the cybersecurity policy approaches are much similar across the Asia–Pacific countries (cf. Table 14.1). The main approaches focus on the establishment of both legal binding and non-binding (standards, norms, guidelines, codes of conduct) instruments, public awareness and trust, expert training and public–private relationship. They have demonstrated the progressive adoption of "soft" law in most of the countries in the region under the major forms of standards and guidance.

The "soft" regulatory approaches have been adopted by countries categorised in different Tiers of Cybersecurity Index, from top to bottom. This reality has demonstrated a great potential and adaptability of "soft" law which have been seen and exploited by various mature, developing and less developed jurisdictions. It can be metaphorically defined, in the application of specific regulations, the GDPR for instance, as an intermediate floor, bridging the roof which is sovereign rules and legally binding laws and the base which is technology development standardised specifications (*lex informatica*).[13] However, it also leaves an uncertainty whether this "intermediate floor" can hold the whole "house" lacking both the foundation and rooftop, such as the countries at the bottom of Cybersecurity Index.

It is noteworthy that the strong economies also nurture the ambition to gain regional and global influence in the cybersecurity policy and legislation, for example, China and India. Indeed, the approaches of some countries are allegedly inspired by Chinese cyberspace sovereignty policy, such as Vietnam. In the case of the Russian Federation, the digital sovereignty principles applied to both information and internet infrastructure. 17/58 countries surveyed are listed in the top 50 countries having the highest cybercrime score in the world. Many of them are present in the top tiers of the cybersecurity index. China and Russia are ranked as the first and third highest

---

[11] Moschetta G et al. (2025).

[12] BCC (2017)

[13] Porcedda M G (2026), Reidenberg J R (1997).

Table 14.1 Legislation, policy of cybercrime/cybersecurity and data governance in the Asia–Pacific countries[14]

Countries	Cybercrime/ cybersecurity,[15] data governance[16] legislation	International Cooperation/ Commitments	Policy of cybercrime/cybersecurity and data governance	Cybersecurity index[17] (Tier)
China (#3 in WCI)[18]	Cybersecurity Law (2017), Data Security Law (2021), Personal Information Protection Law (2021)	UN GGE (2019/2021), CERT member UNCC	Cybersecurity Law protects Chinese cyber sovereignty, critical information infrastructure, personal data and privacy, requiring personal (crucial) data collected/generated in China to be domestically stored.[19] The data localisation obligations cover a wide range of data affecting economics, national security, public, corporate and individual interests.[20] The related laws provide extensive security measures of monitoring resident censors, removing harmful content, etc. Its Personal Information Security Specification (GB/T 35273-2017) interpreting personal data policies was characterised as "soft" law.[21] Its cybersecurity rules concentrate on people-centric development, internet improvement, innovation and law-based management, openness, international collaboration, digital transformation and sharing of cyber governance experiences and knowledge[22]	T2

(continued)

14 UN Economic and Social Commission for Asia and the Pacific (2025).

15 UNCTAD (2025a).

16 UNCTAD (2025b), Foreign Policy Analytics (2021).

17 The International Telecommunication Union (2024). Tier (T1: Role-Modelling, T2: Advancing, T3: Establishing, T4: Evolving, T5: Building).

18 Bruce M et al. (2024).

19 KPMG China (2017).

20 Belli L (2021).

21 Jiang M (2020, pp.195–197).

22 The State Council Information Office of the People's Republic of China (2023)

Table 14.1 (continued)

Countries	Cybercrime/ cybersecurity, data governance legislation	International Cooperation/ Commitments	Policy of cybercrime/cybersecurity and data governance	Cybersecurity index (Tier)
	Cybersecurity Law (2017), Measures for the Administration of Scientific Data (2018), E-Commerce Law (2019), Cryptography Law (2019), Opinions of State Council on Strictly Crackdown on Securities Illegal Activities in accordance with the Law (2021), Several Provisions on Car Data Security Management (Trial) (2021), Data Security Law (2021), Personal Information Protection Law (2021), Cybersecurity Review Measures (2022), Internet Information Service Algorithmic Recommendation Management Provisions (2022), Security Assessment Measures on the Cross- Border Transfer of Data (2022)		Beijing's State-centric data governance policy prioritises "digital economy", "cyber sovereignty", referring to cyberspace, data and networks as "sovereign territory subject". More restrictive personal data protection, especially cross-border data transfer is imposed. The Chinese Communist Party's goals include the impact on worldwide data governance rules and standards[23]	
North Korea (#7)[24]		UNCC		T5

(continued)

[23] U.S.-China Economic and Security Review Commission (2022, p. 1).

[24] North Korea has been better known for their alleged cyberattacks rather than its cybersecurity policy for good. Hwang J et al. (2021, pp. 4–24).

Table 14.1 (continued)

Countries	Cybercrime/ cybersecurity data governance legislation	International Cooperation/ Commitments	Policy of cybercrime/cybersecurity and data governance	Cybersecurity index (Tier)
Hong Kong	Protection of Critical Infrastructures (Computer Systems) Ordinance (2025)		The approaches distinguish the public and private sectors, including practical guides for the government's activities, regarding security, risk assessment, audit, incident handling[25] and efforts to raise awareness on information security in the community.[26] The bill empowers regulating authorities to issue respective code of practices providing recommended standard framework[27]	
	The Personal Data (Privacy) Ordinance (Cap. 486) (1996/2012)		The principles of open data, data sharing, foster the data quality, reliability, data flow and data protection, promotes data-driven, people-centric, outcome-based digital public service and companies' data ownership are adopted. The government supports the deployment of data for innovation and digitalisation, facilitates open data and cross-border data flow from Mainland to Hong Kong[28]	

(continued)

[25] Digital Policy Office (2025a).

[26] Digital Policy Office (2025b).

[27] Liu T et al. (2025).

[28] Digital Policy Office (2024, pp. 1–3).

Table 14.1 (continued)

Countries	Cybercrime/ cybersecurity, data governance legislation	International Cooperation/ Commitments	Policy of cybercrime/cybersecurity and data governance	Cybersecurity index (Tier)
Japan	Act on prohibition of unauthorized computer access	BC (2012), UN GGE member CIRT	5 main principles are committed: "cybersecurity for all", simultaneous advancement of digitalisation and cybersecurity, "enhancing initiatives from the perspective of national security", guarantee of global safety, security of cyberspace, guarantee of the "free, fair and secure cyberspace".[29] Its Hiroshima Process International Code of Conduct for Organizations Developing Advanced AI Systems (HCOC) promoted international technical standards[30]	T1
	Act on the Protection of Personal Information (Act No. 57 (2003/2017)		National policies and rules are used to foster data use and generation of value from data, provide essential regulations governing cross-border data flow, "data security", "data maturity", mitigating risks of utilisation of AI and other advanced technologies[31]	
Macao	Cybersecurity Law No. 13/2019		Guidelines on cyber risks, resilience in several sectors, such as finance,[32] insurance[33] are provided	
	Personal Data Protection Law No. 8/2005 (2005)		As part of the governance of data flow across Mainland, Guangdong, Hong Kong and Macao, Macao's policies concentrate on the security of cross-border data transfer and data security[34]	

(continued)

29 National Centre of Incident Readiness and Strategy for Cybersecurity (2021).

30 Habuka H et al. (2024, pp. 11, 24).

31 Digital Agency (2025).

32 Circular No. 017/B/2023-DSB/AMCM Guideline on Technology and Cyber Risk Management.

33 Circular No. 015/B/2019-DSG/AMCM Guideline on Cyber Resilience for Insurance Sector.

34 The Government of the Hong Kong Special Administrative Region (2023).

Table 14.1 (continued)

Countries	Cybercrime/ cybersecurity, data governance legislation	International Cooperation/ Commitments	Policy of cybercrime/cybersecurity and data governance	Cybersecurity index (Tier)
Mongolia	Criminal Code, Law on Cyber Security (2021)	CIRT	Law on Cybersecurity considers information security as part of national security, provides instruments to address, reduce risks of cybercrime, unauthorised data breaches and other cybersecurity menaces[35]	T3
	Law on Personal Data Protection		National politics are changing from socialist system to democracy, facing governmental and social challenges, requiring the creation of a "resilient digital economy". Due to the importance of data, the National Data Governance Roadmap focuses on the data governance structure, data integration, risk mitigation and standards of quality and privacy[36]	
South Korea (#36)	Criminal Act	Observer to the BC, CIRT	The national plan envisages a free, safe cyberspace supporting national security, economy's prosperity, emphasising rule of law, human rights balance and establishing collaboration in cybersecurity.[37] The country demonstrated its support for "soft" law approaches as the sensitivity of security issues[38]	T1
	Personal Information Protection Act (2020)		The policy promotes individualised integrated public services, AI and data-driven administration, a "data economy ecosystem", secure data use and sharing[39]	

(continued)

35 Cyber Security Council of Mongolia (2024, pp. 6–7).

36 UN Department of Economic and Social Affairs (2024a, pp. 16–18).

37 National Security Office (2019, p. 12).

38 Ebert H et al. (2020, pp. 23, 28).

39 UN ESCAP (2024a).

Table 14.1 (continued)

Countries	Cybercrime/ cybersecurity, data governance legislation	International Cooperation/ Commitments	Policy of cybercrime/cybersecurity and data governance	Cybersecurity index (Tier)
Armenia	Criminal Code (2021), Draft Law on Cybersecurity	BC (2007), CIRT	*Ad-hoc* cybersecurity measures regime requires development of security systems, infrastructure, promotion of inter-institutional collaboration and clarified mandates.[40] Draft cybersecurity law consists of standards for service providers[41]	T4
	Law on the Protection of Personal Data		Digitalisation Strategy promotes, advances data-sharing mechanism, data-driven innovation with "only once" principle requiring information to be submitted solely once to the administrative bodies.[42] The Data Protection Authority issued over 10 "soft" law guides, one published with UNICEF's support within a program aimed at ending violence against children[43]	
Azerbaijan	Criminal Code	BC (2010) member CIRT UNCC (with reservation)	Special bodies are formed to respond to information security incidents, coordinate information infrastructure activities to provide information and assistance and collaborate with local/international governments[44]	T2
	Law on Personal Data (2010) Law "On Official Statistics" (amendment proposal)		Data registers are used across public sectors by many administrative bodies for the purposes of enhancing evidence-based policymaking processes.[45] The amendment draft of law "On Official Statistics" has considered "soft" law as its appropriate approach[46]	

(continued)

[40] World Bank (2021a, pp. 14–15).
[41] Badasyan et al. (2025).
[42] World Bank (2021a) note 46, p. 13.
[43] Armenia (2021, p. 190).
[44] World Bank (2021b, p. 12).
[45] World Bank (2021b) note 48, p.12.
[46] Aliyeva I (2024).

Table 14.1 (continued)

Countries	Cybercrime/ cybersecurity, data governance legislation	International Cooperation/ Commitments	Policy of cybercrime/cybersecurity and data governance	Cybersecurity index (Tier)
Georgia	Bill—SB 315—Computer crime, Information Security Act	BC (2012) member CIRT EU-Georgia Association Agreement (2017–2020)	Cybersecurity is strengthened by enhancing defence capacities, effective cybercrime neutralisation, creating cyber-culture to support resilience to cyber threats, incidents, sustainability of a cybersecurity governance system, public–private cooperation, growing a strong cyber workforce and promoting the country's position as a net contributor to international cybersecurity at an international scale[47]	T2
	Law on Personal Data Protection		Georgia establishes multilateral approaches to data governance, enhancing data sharing, implementing international standards of data management and use, supporting data quality, reliability (ethical, equitable, safe, secure, accurate data)[48]	
Kazakhstan (#21)	Criminal Code (Chapter 7)	UN GGE member CIRT UNCC	To reduce the country's vulnerability to cyber threats, Cybersecurity Concept develops a trusted solution register, international collaboration, legal framework, digital culture and specialist training. Cybershield 2.0 program integrates private sector, law enforcement, security and defence[49]	T2
	Law No. 94-V ZRK on Protection of Personal Data (2013)		As part of PforR program, its Digital Era Lifestyle program lays out data-driven public sector strategy, facilitates the generation of user-centric framework of delivering digital public services[50]	
Kyrgyzstan	Chapter 40 "Cyber security crimes" Criminal Code (2021)	Member-state of the Shanghai Cooperation Organisation, CIRT	The approaches include strategies, security principles, guarantees, risks management, insurance, training, practices and technologies to ensure infrastructure integrity, availability and confidentiality[51]	T3
	Law on Personal Data No.58 (2008)		The law was adopted based on international principles, norms to ensure the protection of human, civil rights, freedoms related to personal data collecting, processing and use[52]	

(continued)

47 Spînu N (2020, pp. 7–9).
48 UN ESCAP (2022).
49 OECD (2023, pp. 51–52).
50 World Bank (2021c, p. 12).
51 Maralbaeva A (2024, pp. 138–147).
52 Maralbaeva A (2024, p. 142).

Table 14.1 (continued)

Countries	Cybercrime/ cybersecurity, data governance legislation	International Cooperation/ Commitments	Policy of cybercrime/cybersecurity and data governance	Cybersecurity index (Tier)
Russia Federation (#1)	Criminal Code (amendments in 2021), Chapter 28. Crimes in the Sphere of Computer Information	UN GGE member CIRT UNCC	Digital sovereignty (*tsifrovoi suverenitet*), as one of Russian information space's principles, includes *electronic sovereignty* encompassing Internet infrastructure protected from cyber threats, and *information sovereignty*, a self-sufficient control of information and resistance to information attacks. Russian Internet (RuNet) is a Russian language-based, relatively closed segment of the Internet consisting of popular research engines, social media sites (Yandex, Vkontakte and Odnoklassniki)[53]	T2
	Federal law No. 149-fz on information, informational technologies and the protection of information (2006), Data Protection Law No. 152 (2006) (amended in 2014, 2022, 2023)		Russia's enforcement action is focused on its data localisation obligation (local storage and processing). Data operators must store, process Russians' personal data in Russia and provide Roskomnadzor (the Federal Service for Supervision of Communications, Information Technology and Mass Media) with documentation. Roskomnadzor oversees cross-border data transfer through notification and seeking-approval regimes[54]	

(continued)

[53] NATO Strategic Communications Centre of Excellence (2021, p. 12).

[54] Giardini T et al. (2023).

Table 14.1 (continued)

Countries	Cybercrime/ cybersecurity, data governance legislation	International Cooperation/ Commitments	Policy of cybercrime/cybersecurity and data governance	Cybersecurity index (Tier)
Tajikistan[55]	Criminal Code (section xii. crimes against information security, chapter 28), Code on Administrative Offences No. 455 (2008)			T4
	Law No. 1537 on Personal Data Protection (2018)		The country's policy is to use statistics to provide "evidence-based policy" and govern the policy conduct[56]	
Turkmenistan[57]	Criminal Code No. 222-1 (1997) (amended in 2019)		The U.S. allegedly reported that the country's cybersecurity policy is influenced by Russia's and China's ones, including monitoring Internet activities[58]	T4
	Law on Information on Private Life and its Protection No. 519-V			
Uzbekistan	Law "on Cybersecurity" No. ЗРУ-764 (2022)	CIRT UNCC	The law defines authority of the State Security Service, its sector-specific regulations, focusing on protection of computers, networks, programs and data from unauthorised/unintended access, duty of subjects to report cybersecurity incidents, cybercrimes and enforce preventive measures[59]	T2
	Law No. ZRU-547, On Personal Data, (2019)		Data governance mechanisms have not been formed[60]	
American Samoa				

(continued)

55 The country faces and experiences cybersecurity challenges, incidents, lacks technical expertise, resources and an inadequate legal framework. Its cyberspace is vulnerable to cyber-attacks and disruptions in the telecommunications sector. Kedia S (2023, p. 441).

56 UN ESCAP (2024b).

57 The country's risk of cyberattack is low (2%–0%). Orumbayeva M et al. (2022), Santisteban A S et al. (2020, p. 776).

58 IREX (2024).

59 Abdullaeva D K et al. (2023, pp. 1–2).

60 Ministry of Digital Technologies of the Republic of Uzbekistan (2024, p. 13).

Table 14.1 (continued)

Countries	Cybercrime/ cybersecurity, data governance legislation	International Cooperation/ Commitments	Policy of cybercrime/cybersecurity and data governance	Cybersecurity index (Tier)
Australia (#34)	Criminal Code Act No. 12 (1995) (amended in 2024)	BC (2013), UN GGE member CIRT UNCC	Australian Action Plan supports small businesses and individuals to strengthen their cybersecurity, defend against cyber threats, provides guidance, ensures technological safety, protects valuable data assets, shares information, blocks the global threats, protects critical infrastructure, enhances sovereign capabilities, maintains a resilient region and global leadership[61]	T1
	Privacy Act (1988), Information Privacy Act (2009)		The Public Data Policy Statement formalised the government's commitment to open data, data-driven innovation, mandated it to optimise the use and reuse of public data and to make non-sensitive data publicly accessible. Its vision puts forward delivery of simple, secure and connected public services for all through the best data and digital capabilities[62]	
Cook Islands			The Action Plan forecasts to enhance the country's capacity, measures to assess, mitigate cyber risks, establish administrative bodies, develop legislation (by passing Cybersecurity Bill[63]), strategy and participate in international conventions on cybersecurity[64]	
			During the establishment of a data governance framework, the all-of-Government approach will be carried out and maintained[65]	

(continued)

[61] Australian Government (2023, pp. 4–22).

[62] UN ESCAP (2024c).

[63] Cook Islands (2024, p. 33).

[64] Cook Islands (2023, pp. 48–49).

[65] Government of the Cook Islands (2023, p. 61).

Table 14.1 (continued)

Countries	Cybercrime/ cybersecurity, data governance legislation	International Cooperation/ Commitments	Policy of cybercrime/cybersecurity and data governance	Cybersecurity index (Tier)
Fiji	Cybercrime Act (2021), s.340–s.346 Crimes Decree (2009)	BC member (2024)	National legislation does not adequately govern the complexity and diversity of cyber offences[66]	T4
			Fiji's plan aims to enhance public records management, data dissemination, data collection capacity, expand subject-specific databases, improve data security and reduce vulnerability to cyber threats[67]	
French Polynesia				
Guam				
Kiribati	Cybercrime Act (2021)	BC (2024) member CIRT	National legislation combats criminal abuse of information, communication technology, cybercrime, develops technical minimum standards of cybersecurity, aims to establish a secure environment protecting fundamental rights, balance approaches in line with international and regional best practices[68]	T3
			Policy and legal instruments are needed to support electronic transactions, regulate privacy, data protection, cybersecurity and keep users, especially vulnerable groups (women, children), safe online[69]	
Marshall Islands	National Security Act (2024), Cybersecurity Act (2025), Digital Transformation and Identity Verification Act (2025)			T5
Micronesia				T5

(continued)

66 Tamanikaiwaimaro S (2021, pp. 14–20).

67 UN ESCAP (2024).

68 Minister of Information, Communication, Transport and Tourism Development (2020, pp. 3–4).

69 World Bank (2021d, p. 9)

Table 14.1 (continued)

Countries	Cybercrime/ cybersecurity, data governance legislation	International Cooperation/ Commitments	Policy of cybercrime/cybersecurity and data governance	Cybersecurity index (Tier)
Nauru	Cybercrime Act (2015)	UNCC	A national cybersecurity framework is being developed, establishing cybersecurity policies, regulations, technologies and infrastructure, providing cybersecurity training and awareness programs across all sectors[70]	T4
New Caledonia				
New Zealand	Crimes Act (1961)	CIRT	National strategy supports increase of engagement, involvement of society in cybersecurity issues, tackles information gaps to provide evidence-based policy, modernises, enhances operational structures, information flows amongst the agencies. It initiates the representation, promotion of the country's interest globally, assists other Pacific partners fostering their capacities[71]	T3
	Privacy Act (1993/2020)		The country's lead agency of government-held data (Stats NZ) expectedly provide quality, trustworthy data, statistics for the purposes of evidence-based decisions. The government maintains data governance policy, transparency, trust, integrity on the base of data and decentralisation of government. Its model grants agencies autonomy separate from the Executive Branch[72]	
Niue				
Northern Mariana Islands				

(continued)

70 Nauru Government (2025, pp. 16–24).

71 New Zealand Government (2023, p. 4).

72 UN ESCAP (2024d).

Table 14.1 (continued)

Countries	Cybercrime/ cybersecurity, data governance legislation	International Cooperation/ Commitments	Policy of cybercrime/cybersecurity and data governance	Cybersecurity index (Tier)
Palau	Title 17 PNC Chapter 31	UNCC	Palau's strategy focuses on cybersecurity, digital residency, extending global collaboration, strong "cyberspace borders", protection of citizens, society, public officials, diplomates and investment from cyber threats[73]	
Papua New Guinea	Cybercrime Code Act (2016)	CIRT UNCC	Legal instruments enable crime investigating, prosecution, sanctions for non-compliance, breach of law, protect security, citizens' rights against abuses by others, misuse of the latest technologies and provide minimum standards of behaviours, establish cybersecurity capacities[74]	T3
Samoa	Crime Act (2013)	CIRT	Samoa is developing "incident-response capability" with the national cybersecurity strategy related to national risk priorities, business development, which are still vague on risks, priorities and objectives[75]	T4
			Samoa lacks a governance framework[76]	
Solomon Islands	Penal Code (Cap. 26), Par. 17 of the Telecommunications Act (Cap. 115)		The nation's strategy aims to protect critical infrastructure, create a robust legal framework, enhance national capacity to manage incidents, foster collaborative, multi-stakeholder approaches involving Government, the private sector and international partnerships to address cyber threats[77]	T5

(continued)

73 Republic of Palau (2022, pp. 11–15).

74 The Independent State of Papua New Guinea (2024, pp. 23–25).

75 Nagyfejeo E et al. (2018, p. 7).

76 UN Department of Economic and Social Affairs (2024b, pp. 1–2).

77 UN (2025a, p. 70).

Table 14.1 (continued)

Countries	Cybercrime/ cybersecurity, data governance legislation	International Cooperation/ Commitments	Policy of cybercrime/cybersecurity and data governance	Cybersecurity index (Tier)
Tonga	Computer Crimes Act (2019)	BC (2017), CIRT	Its plan provided basic principles protecting confidentiality, integrity, availability of governmental e-services and IT systems, including their security, connectivity, interoperability, portability, innovation, accessibility, customer focus, standardisation, redundancy and whole-of-government approach[78]	T4
Tuvalu	Cybercrime draft law		The Government designs to advance laws to regional, international standards, emphasise cultural values, develop defensive, offensive cyber-capabilities through legislation on cybersecurity, data protection, privacy and related areas[79]	T4
Vanuatu	Cybercrime Act No. 22 (2021)	CIRT	The goal includes regional collaboration, determination of security standards for critical infrastructure, establishment of reliable legal framework, demonstrating domestic characteristics and international practices for an open, safe environment, delivery of training and support of international organisations[80]	T3
Brunei	Computer Misuse Act, Revised (2007)	CIRT UNCC	The Act protects the integrity, security of computer systems and data, criminalises offences including unauthorised access, modification, use/ interception, obstruction, disclosure of computer, its materials, codes, etc[81]	T3

(continued)

[78] Tonga (2022, p. 7).

[79] Ministry of Justice (2021, pp. 27–32).

[80] Republic of Vanuatu (2013, pp. 7–11).

[81] Computer Emergency Response Team (2023, p. 9).

Table 14.1 (continued)

Countries	Cybercrime/ cybersecurity, data governance legislation	International Cooperation/ Commitments	Policy of cybercrime/cybersecurity and data governance	Cybersecurity index (Tier)
Cambodia	Draft Cybercrime law (2014/ 2023)	CIRT UNCC	The draft tackles standard cybercrimes (illegal access, data espionage and intellectual property theft), punishments and was criticised for free speech restriction[82]	T4
	Article 32 Law on Electronic Commerce (2019)		In the absence of a data legal framework, several related laws, policies have been planned, drafted. Their officials' mindset has shifted from "default model" with the government's conservative "data concealment" culture, lack of will to use, share data, towards the recognition of data as an "added value"[83]	
Indonesia (#29)	Law No.19/2016 (Electronic Information and Transactions Law)	UN GGE member CIRT	In the absence of specific adequate legislation tackling computer misuse, its policy and strategy need to be improved, to protect its critical information infrastructure and digital assets[84]	T1
	Law No. 27 (2022) on Personal Data Protection, Law No. 11 (2008) regarding Electronic Information and Transactions (EIT Law), Law No. 19 (2016) regarding the Amendment of EIT Law, Government Regulation No. 71 (2019) Regarding Provisions of Electronic Systems and Transactions[85]		The policy seeks to improve the framework governing data accuracy, access, accountability, accessibility, improving data use in policymaking based on data standards, metadata standards, inter-operationality and reference code[86]	

(continued)

[82] Cambodia Development Resource Institute (2020, pp. 7–9).
[83] UN Department of Economic and Social Affairs (2024c, pp. 35–36).
[84] Computer Emergency Response Team (2023, pp. 15–16).
[85] Foreign Policy Analytics (2021).
[86] UN ESCAP (2024e).

Table 14.1 (continued)

Countries	Cybercrime/ cybersecurity, data governance legislation	International Cooperation/ Commitments	Policy of cybercrime/cybersecurity and data governance	Cybersecurity index (Tier)
Lao (#46)	Law No. 61/NA on Prevention and Combating Cybercrime	CIRT UNCC	The law provides principles, legal instruments to prevent, combat, eliminate cybercrime, to protect data, critical infrastructure, information and communication systems[87]	T4
	Law on Electronic Data Protection, Law on Electronic Transactions (2012), Law on Cyber Crime (2015), Penal Code (2017)		Despite plans, regional/ global collaborations, the country lacks methods, interoperability, exchange, coordination, standards, legislation, technology, infrastructure and experts[88]	
Malaysia (#26)	Computer Crimes Act (1997), other acts	CIRT UNCC	4 pillars govern cybersecurity including more effective governance, better legislation and enforcement, more competitive technology, advanced cybersecurity capacity, awareness and global collaborations[89]	T1
	Personal Data Protection Act (2010)/Law No. 2014-038 relating to protection of personal data (2015)		Digital Economy Blueprint provides principles of inclusivity, ethics and trust, promotes data sharing for data-driven policymaking to boost transparency, citizen-centric service delivery and digital economy growth[90]	
Myanmar (#43)	Cyber Security Law (Draft)	CIRT	Myanmar's cybersecurity legislative draft proposal is reportedly inspired by the Chinese policy[91]	T3
			Comprehensive data governance with quality standards, access protocols, security systems is needed to ensure information security and privacy[92]	

(continued)

[87] World Bank (2022, p. 5).

[88] UN DESA (2023).

[89] Malaysia (2020, pp. 28–81).

[90] UN ESCAP (2024f).

[91] U.S.-China Economic and Security Review Commission (2022).

[92] The Asia Foundation (2020, pp. 9–22).

Table 14.1 (continued)

Countries	Cybercrime/ cybersecurity, data governance legislation	International Cooperation/ Commitments	Policy of cybercrime/cybersecurity and data governance	Cybersecurity index (Tier)
Philippines (#27)	Cybercrime Prevention Act (2012)	BC (2018) member CIRT UNCC	National cyberspace security is based on trust, security of assets and reliability of Information and Communications Technology products[93]	T2
	Republic act 10173 data privacy act (2012), The Philippine Statistical Act (2013)		They focus on digitalisation, technology deployment in public services, "streamline governance" and support for competitive economic growth[94]	
Singapore	Cybersecurity Act No.9/2018	UN GGE member CIRT	National goals are strengthening security, digital infrastructure, open, secure, stable, accessible, peaceful and interoperable cyberspace,[95] international coordination and collaboration[96]	T1
	Personal Data Protection (Amendment) Act (2020), Statistics Act (1973) (revised, amended 2020–2021), The Official Secrets Act (1935)		Singapore's Secure, Smart Nation strategy takes the "whole-of-nation approach", taking data and digitalisation, deploying digital technologies for modernisation of government operation, using AI, data as a strategic asset, enriching its value, improving digital infrastructure and services[97]	

(continued)

93 Department of Information and Communications Technology (2024, pp. 5–6).

94 UN ESCAP (2024g).

95 Cyber Security Agency of Singapore (2021, p. 2).

96 Cyber Security Agency of Singapore (2016, pp. 4–5).

97 UN ESCAP (2024h).

Table 14.1 (continued)

Countries	Cybercrime/ cybersecurity, data governance legislation	International Cooperation/ Commitments	Policy of cybercrime/cybersecurity and data governance	Cybersecurity index (Tier)
Thailand (#32)	Computer Crimes Act (No. 2) B.E. 2560 (amended in 2017), Cyber Security Act (2019)	CIRT UNCC	Thailand prioritises stronger cyber resilience, higher security standards, mitigation of cyber threats and protection of critical information infrastructure[98]	T1
	Personal Data Protection Act, B. E. 2562 (2019), Digitalization of Public Administration & Services Delivery Act (2019), Statistics Act (2007)		The objectives are to modernise, optimise public services by digitising data, integrating agency data exchange, providing guidelines, standards of data governance and open access data[99]	
Timor-Leste				T5
Vietnam (#22)	Cyber Information Security (2015), Cybersecurity Law (2018), Cybersecurity, Decree No. 53/2022/ND-CP (2022)	CIRT UNCC	The strategy strengthens the Communist Party's leadership, State's management, legal framework, cyberspace sovereignty, critical information infrastructure, information systems, trust, technology self-reliance, expert training, public awareness, international collaboration and investment resources[100]	T1
	Personal Data Protection Law, Decree No. 13/2023/ND-CP on protection of personal data (2023)		Vietnam's legislation reportedly reflects a considerable influence from China's data governance policy,[101] concentrating on e-government development through adequate public services, wide-ranging public engagement, enhanced government activities, economic growth, position of e-government, digital government and open data[102]	

(continued)

98 Directorate of Security Policy and Plan, Office of the National Security Council (2022).

99 UN ESCAP (2024i).

100 Decision No. 964/QD-TTg of the Prime Minister: Approving the National Cyber Security Strategy, proactively responding to challenges from cyberspace to 2025, vision 2030, dated August 10, 2022. Ministry of Science and Technology (2022).

101 U.S.-China Economic and Security Review Commission (2022, p. 1).

102 UN ESCAP (2024j).

Table 14.1 (continued)

Countries	Cybercrime/ cybersecurity, data governance legislation	International Cooperation/ Commitments	Policy of cybercrime/cybersecurity and data governance	Cybersecurity index (Tier)
Afghanistan	Cyber Crime Code—Section 12	CIRT	The strategy builds a resilient cyber ecosystem, legal framework, including standards, practices, certificate and testing body, secure e-government, expert training and safeguard of data privacy[103]	T5
Bangladesh	National Digital Security Act No.46/2018	CIRT	11 actions are identified, public awareness, cybercrime mitigation, incident response capacity, critical infrastructure protection, cybersecurity framework, skills development, experts training and public–private partnership[104]	T1
	Data Protection Act (Draft) (2023)			
Bhutan	Penal Code under Chapter 31 (Computer Offences), Chapter 17, 20, 21—Information Communication and Media Act of Bhutan (2018)	CIRT	The draft strategy addresses cybersecurity challenges (low public awareness, lack of experts, stakeholders' support, funding).[105] 7 goals cover national cybersecurity governance, coordination, legal framework harmonised with economic roadmap and other legislation, protection of critical information infrastructure, enhancement of public awareness, incident-response and child online safety[106]	T3
	Bhutan Information, Communications and Media Act 2018, E-Governance Policy (2019), National Digital Identity Act (2023)		A robust legal, policy framework underpins data management across public and private sectors. The inconsistent law, policy and the legal instruments' coordination challenges hinder full transparency and accessibility of data which is promoted by the Interactive Data Portal[107]	

(continued)

[103] Ministry of Communications and IT (2014).

[104] Agrafiotis I et al. (2018, p. 23).

[105] Royal Audit Authority, Bhutan Integrity House (2023, p. 10).

[106] Bhutan Infocomm and Media Authority, Royal Government of Bhutan (2020).

[107] UN DESA, Government Technology (GovTech) Agency, Royal Government of Bhutan (2024).

Table 14.1 (continued)

Countries	Cybercrime/ cybersecurity, data governance legislation	International Cooperation/ Commitments	Policy of cybercrime/cybersecurity and data governance	Cybersecurity index (Tier)
India (#10)	The Information Technology Act (2000) (amended in 2008—ITA)	UN GGE member CIRT	India's comprehensive strategy addresses securing a large-scale digitisation of many aspects of public and private sectors, strengthening structure, institutions, governance, technology development, incident and crisis management, data security and governance, synergising internet infrastructure, standards development, cyber insurance, position and brand of India at both domestic and global platforms, cyber diplomacy and cybercrime investigation[108]	T1
	Digital Personal Data Protection (DPDP) Bill (2023), Information Technology Act (2000), Collection of Statistics Act (2008)		The practice of "*data-led governance and policymaking*" for the purposes of policy interventions, evidence-based decision and real-time data requires to collect data for new measurable parameters, improve efficiencies in data-collecting processes, expand data centres, make data available for the public, integrate data analysis and interactive data visualisation in the policymaking process[109]	
Iran (#11)	Law No. 71063 on Computer Crimes	CIRT UNCC	Iran's approach demonstrates the complex dynamics of its national security intersection, domestic control and resource limitations. It is alleged that Tehran prioritises robust offensive cyber capabilities, uses cyber tools as cost-effective and discrete measures to control the society[110]	T3
	Bill—Protection of Data and Privacy in the CyberSpace (2018), Law on Publication and Access to Data (2009), Electronic Commerce Law (2004), Cybercrime Law (2009)			

(continued)

[108] Data Security Council of India (2020)

[109] UN ESCAP (2024k).

[110] Gerami N (2024).

Table 14.1 (continued)

Countries	Cybercrime/ cybersecurity, data governance legislation	International Cooperation/ Commitments	Policy of cybercrime/cybersecurity and data governance	Cybersecurity index (Tier)
Maldives[111]	Maldives Penal Code (2023 amendment)	UNCC		T5
	Privacy and Personal Data Protection Bill (Draft)			
Nepal	Draft of Information Technology and Cyber Security Bill 2080 (2024)	CIRT		T3
	Article 28 of the Constitution of Nepal, 2072 BS, Individual Privacy Act, 2018 (2075), Statistics Act, 2079 (2022)		The 15th Plan's targets are to enhance data management mechanisms, credibility, accessibility of data, its employment in policy-producing, decision-making processes, and development of inter-agency, inter-government statistics[112]	
Pakistan (#44)	Prevention of Electronic Crimes Act (2016)	CIRT		T1
	Personal Data Protection Bill (2021), Prevention of Electronic Crimes Act (2016)		"One Nation One Vision" administrative reforms (2024) promote data collection, access, sharing and cybersecurity. "Digital Pakistan" enhances access, connectivity, digital infrastructure, government digital services, innovation and entrepreneurship[113]	

(continued)

[111] Policy, strategy or legal framework for cybersecurity has not been produced. World Bank Group (2024, p. 32).

[112] UN ESCAP (2024l).

[113] UN ESCAP (2024m).

Table 14.1 (continued)

Countries	Cybercrime/ cybersecurity, data governance legislation	International Cooperation/ Commitments	Policy of cybercrime/cybersecurity and data governance	Cybersecurity index (Tier)
Sri Lanka	Computer Crime Act No. 24 (2007)	BC (2015) member CIRT UNCC	The strategy aims to build a resilient, trusted cybersecurity ecosystem through governance, legal instruments, policies, standards, workforce training, resilient digital government, infrastructure, public awareness and public–private partnership[114]	T2
	Personal Data Act No. 9 (2022)—Draft		A framework sets policies for data sharing, classification, management, quality, privacy, security, supporting decision-making, trust and misuse prevention[115]	
Türkiye (#28)	Penal Code (Articles 243, 244, 245)	BC (2015) member CIRT UNCC	Requirements include protecting critical information infrastructure, integrating cybersecurity across service, production, supply, adhering to "confidentiality-integrity-availability" balance and "need-to-know" basis principles, establishing legal framework and fostering research & development[116]	T1
	Law on the Protection of Personal Data No. 6698 (2016)		A data-driven government structure, user-oriented public services are envisaged to remove hindrance of data sharing inter-institutions, provide high quality, value-added integrated services[117]	

114 Sri Lanka Computer Emergency Readiness Team (2018, pp. 5–19).

115 Ministry of Technology, pp. 8–9.

116 Ministry of Transport and Infrastructure (2020, pp. 18–19).

117 UN ESCAP (2024n).

cybercrime scores. It is likely that the more cyber threats the countries have to face, the more security measures they develop. The influence of leading countries targets on the standards, as part of "soft" regulatory approaches at all levels, from global, regional to national ones. It is expected to observe more serious efforts of these big countries to exert effects on other jurisdictions, maintain their leading positions in technical advancement in cyberspace, regulatory development and reinforce their geopolitical advantages. For developing and least developed countries, the harmonisation of standards in cyberspace and cross-border data governance may allow them to quickly follow and adapt to the security and data management requirements of their trading or political partners. Nevertheless, it contributes to the complexity of geopolitical competition, cyber sovereignty within the region.

A similar survey on data governance policy and legislation in these countries has been conducted. In 24/58 (41%) countries, the information of the data protection and privacy legislation is limited. In comparison with the legislation on cybersecurity, Asian countries are likely to focus less on data governance. Accordingly, only 04/58 (07%) countries are in the stage of drafting the law and 30/58 (52%) countries have the data protection and privacy legislation. While Japan seems to cover most of the private, industrial sectors, most of the countries deploy data governance as the evidence base for decision-making processes in the public sectors, focusing on the public and government interests. The role of data governance in the cybersecurity guarantee is significant. However, the inadequacy and imbalance between the cybersecurity and data governance regulations and policies exist across the Asia–Pacific region. Amongst the leading countries, there exists a fragmentation of data governance frameworks, for example Schrems II saga.[118] However, in the case of the Asia–Pacific region, there are a few countries building cross-border data governance mechanisms and the geopolitical influence race then takes place amongst major trading partners, particularly China, the U.S. and the EU. In the context of transnational data flows, "soft" law has been proposed as a solution to support the domestic traditional regulatory frameworks, harmonising the data governance rules amongst the countries. G20 initiated the soft law Digital Stability Board mandated the right to agree standards, coordinating the development of data governance policies, principles and norms.[119] "Soft" law instruments were proposed to balance out digital sovereignty and international collaboration.[120]

[118] C-311/18—Facebook Ireland and Schrems.

[119] Arner D W et al. (2021, pp. 10–11).

[120] Balarabe K (2024, p. 11).

14.3 Position of "Soft" Law in the International and Regional Context

Only 11 countries in the survey are members of the Budapest Convention, one is the Convention's observer; and 8 countries are members of the UN Group of Governmental Experts 2019/2021 (cf. Table 14.1). In addition, the network of the National CIRTs (known as Computer Emergency Response Teams (CERTs)) covers 36/58 Asia–Pacific countries.[121] The "Cooperation Measures" scores of most Asian countries in 2024 are majorly corresponding to their international collaboration through international cybersecurity conventions and CIRT network. Most recently, on 25 Oct 2025, 21/58 countries surveyed with other 44 signatories, signed the UNCC in Hanoi, Vietnam.[122] This shows a global engagement to the fight against cybercrime. However, to a certain extent, these international and regional cooperation efforts have not successfully yet proved its efficiency and capabilities to resolve the cybersecurity concerns of the Asia–Pacific countries. In addition to international conventions, the measure of international, regional and national standards, norms and guidelines has been endorsed by many Asian countries' governments (cf. Table 14.1). It supports the viewpoint that the "soft" law may promote international cooperation, experience and knowledge sharing across countries with different ICT infrastructures and bridge the gaps of maturity, legislation and policy amongst the countries.[123] The "soft" law's non-binding nature expectedly facilitates international, regional agreement-reaching progress. The UNCC also emphasises its support for harmonising, exchanging skills, expertise, capacity and technical capability information to build common standards.[124]

As ICT subsectors, cybersecurity and data governance face the same regulatory challenges as the technology in general does. The circumstance of transnational operations of tech companies and other actors, particularly cross-border data transfer and cybersecurity, the phenomena of shopping for applicable law and forum are unavoidable. In addition to the technology acceleration, the fragmentation of governing frameworks and the transnational characteristic of ICT activities have created a need (a) to find a balance point of (i) protection of fundamental rights, (ii) rules of law, (iii) sovereignty, other backbone principles of each legal systems and maintenance of technological neutrality, development; and, (b) to initiate an international regulatory collaboration.[125] Further, the survey also showed an absence of private actors' involvement and consideration of their interests in some countries despite the fact that they can contribute to identifying and investigating cyber threats, developing technologies and technical standards against cybercrimes (*lex informatica*)

[121] ITU.

[122] UN (2025b).

[123] Fu S et al. (2023).

[124] UNCC.

[125] OECD/KDI (2021, p. 19).

and self-regulations controlling cyber risks.[126] The development of "soft" regulatory approaches, especially co- and self- regulations with the involvement of private actors and the use of their technical/financial resources in the design, enforcement phases may resolve the challenges more rapidly.

Despite being a flexible instrument, "soft" law is difficult to determine with a sole definition. Historically, it can be found as "*normative provisions contained in non-binding texts*".[127] The notion of "soft" law is controversial with multiple propositions in the context of international law. As earlier defined, this notion in this research is already broad and mixed with varied regulatory approaches. The co-regulation concept, as a "soft" law, set a first foundational element of its enforceability in the security and data governance operations in cyberspace. For example, the European Commission issued the best practices for business-to-business, business-to-government data sharing based on the contractual relations.[128] Or, in the form of self-regulation,[129] the "soft" law becomes more effective not only amongst private actors, but also their relations with third parties. It is undeniable that the debate surrounding "soft" law, its applicability, implementation and effectiveness will not end soon. However, the adoption of "soft" law should be taken with reservations, the EU scholars and practitioners have witnessed the gaps amongst interpretation and application of the binding provisions of the AI Act (as the rooftop), the "soft" regulatory approaches (as the middle floor) and technology development (as the ground).[130]

The surveys maintain some biases and lack of adequate information due to the limited access to documents in the local languages other than English. The outline of connections and patterns of cybersecurity and data governance policies, legislative approaches amongst the Asia–Pacific countries is complicated under the impacts of extraneous, intravenous factors, e.g. from geopolitical threats, competitions to ICT infrastructure, including legal framework and technology advancement. However, they arouse the hope and expectation for the advancement of legislation in these areas in near future. They also show the requirement of quick adaptation to the changes in technology and the rising cybercrime wave related to the ICT activities for the legislators. For now, the involvement of "soft" law helps harmonise the domestic legal instruments of cybersecurity, data governance, quickly resolves technological challenges in cyberspace and allows the governments to balance their strategies and sovereign priorities.

---

126 Keck M (2022).

127 Shelton D et al. (2000), Fajardo T (2014).

128 European Commission (2018), Policy Department for Citizens' Rights and Constitutional Affairs, Directorate-General for Internal Policies (2022, p. 44).

129 Carletti C (2021, pp. 125–150).

130 Lewis D et al. (2025).

References

Book

Porcedda M G (2026) The GDPR as Mid-Atlantic Regulation [in] Part III. European Privacy and Digital Law: The Role of Trust and of the Transatlantic Digital Economy [in] Orrù E et al. (2026) Conceptions of Data Protection and Privacy, Hart Studies in Information Law and Regulation ISBN: 9781509983728 pp. 167–189

Journal Article

Abdullaeva D K et al (2023) Cybersecurity Issues in Uzbekistan, International Journal of Business Diplomacy and Economy ISSN: 2833–7468 2(7):1–2

Kedia S (2023) Cyber Security in Global World: A Comparative Analysis. IJSDR 8 2 ISSN: 2455–2631:441

Reidenberg J R (1997) Lex Informatica: The Formulation of Information Policy Rules through Technology 76 Tex. L. Rev. 553 (1997–1998) pp. 553–593

Santisteban A S et al (2020) Analysis of National Cybersecurity Strategies IJACSA 11(12):771–779

Segal A et al. (2020) Roundtable - The Future of Cybersecurity across the Asia-Pacific. Asia Policy 15 2:57–115

Shelton D et al (2000) Commitment and Compliance: The Role of Non-Binding Norms in the International Legal System (Introduction) GWU Legal Studies Research Paper No. 2013–50

Article by DOI

Arner D W et al (2021) The Transnational Data Governance Problem. Berkeley Technology Law Journal (forthcoming) University of Hong Kong Faculty of Law Research Paper 2021/039:10–11 https://doi.org/10.2139/ssrn.3912487

Balarabe K (2024) Digital Borders and Beyond: Establishing Normative Grounds for Cybersecurity and Sovereignty in International Law 11 https://doi.org/10.2139/ssrn.4876617

Belli L (2021) Cybersecurity policymaking in the BRICS countries: From addressing national priorities to seeking international cooperation. The African Journal of Information and Communication (AJIC) 28:8–9 https://doi.org/10.23962/10539/32208

Brooks E (2025) Unpacking the ideas that shape the health policy process: A genealogy of the EU's Better Regulation agenda Journal of Critical Public Health, Online First https://doi.org/10.55016/ojs/jcph.vi.79497

Bruce M et al (2024) Mapping the global geography of cybercrime with the World Cybercrime Index. PLoS ONE 19(4):7–23 https://doi.org/10.1371/journal.pone.0297312

Fajardo T (2014) Soft Law https://doi.org/10.1093/OBO/9780199796953-0040

Farrand B et al (2024) The new geopolitics of EU cybersecurity: security, economy and sovereignty. International Affairs 100 6:2379–2397. https://doi.org/10.1093/ia/iiae231

Fu S et al (2023) International Soft Law Governance of Artificial Intelligence: Advantages, Approaches, and Credibility Journal of Business Theory and Practice 11(3) https://doi.org/10.22158/jbtp.v11n3p35

Habuka H et al (2024) Enhancements and next steps for the G7 Hiroshima AI Process: Toward a common framework to advance human rights, democracy and rule of law. Cambridge Forum on AI: Law and Governance (2025) 1 e15 1–26 https://doi.org/10.1017/cfl.2024.5

Hwang J et al (2021) North Korean cyber-attacks and policy responses: An interdisciplinary theoretical framework. International Journal of Cybersecurity Intelligence and Cybercrime 4(2):4–24 https://doi.org/10.52306/04020221NHPZ9033
Leonelli S (2019) Data Governance is Key to Interpretation: Reconceptualizing Data in Data Science. Harvard Data Science Review 3 https://doi.org/10.1162/99608f92.17405bb6
Maralbaeva A (2024) E-justice and Cyber Security: Balancing between Openness of the Courts and Data Protection in Kyrgyzstan 138–147 https://doi.org/10.5771/9783748918271-123
Nagyfejeo E et al (2018) Cybersecurity Capacity Review - Independent State of Samoa. 7 https://doi.org/10.2139/ssrn.3658469
OECD (2023) Improving Framework Conditions for the Digital Transformation of Businesses in Kazakhstan. OECD Publishing. 51–52 https://doi.org/10.1787/368d4d01-en
OECD/KDI (2021)Case Studies on the Regulatory Challenges Raised by Innovation and the Regulatory Responses OECD Publishing 19–23 https://doi.org/10.1787/8fa190b5-en
Orumbayeva M et al. (2022) Cybersecurity and Current Global Threats in Central Asia Мемлекеттік Басқару Және Мемлекеттік Қызмет, халықаралық ғылыми-талдау журналы 2 (81) https://doi.org/10.52123/1994-2370-2022-657

Online Documents

Agrafiotis I et al (2018) Cybersecurity Capacity Review Bangladesh 2018 bcc.portal.gov.bd/sites/default/files/files/bcc.portal.gov.bd/publications/733ea39f_8a40_4e85_8b9e_58500ee89f79/2020-10-20-00-13-3a751045bb7027fc505e59dfda762514.pdf Accessed 15 May 2025
Aliyeva I (2024) Emerging Legal Issues Around AI, Synthetic Data, Machine Learning UNECE/EFTA Workshop on Modernizing Statistical Legislation Working paper no. 3 unece.org/sites/default/files/2024-05/2024_Legislation_WP3_Azerbaijan_IAliyeva.pdf Accessed 30 Oct 2025
America’s Cyber Defense Agency (2021) What is Cybersecurity? cisa.gov/news-events/news/what-cybersecurity Accessed 3 May 2025
Armenia (2021) Rationale for Actions Ensuring Implementation of the 2021–2026 Action Plan of the Government of the Republic of Armenia https://www.gov.am/files/docs/4901.pdf Accessed 30 Oct 2025
Australian Government (2023) 2023–2030 Australian Cyber Security Strategy—Action Plan 4–22 homeaffairs.gov.au/cyber-security-subsite/files/2023-cyber-security-strategy-action-plan.pdf Accessed 11 May 2025
Badasyan et al (2025) Data Protection & Privacy 2025: Armenia, Trends and Developments practiceguides.chambers.com/practice-guides/data-protection-privacy-2025/armenia/trends-and-developments Accessed 30 Oct 2025
BCC (2017) Malaysia sites hacked after blunder over Indonesian flag bbc.com/news/world-asia-40996126 Accessed 15 May 2025
Bhutan Infocomm and Media Authority, Royal Government of Bhutan (2020) Study report on Cybersecurity bicma.gov.bt/data/reports/other-reports/Study_Report_on_Cybersecurity_2020.pdf Accessed 15 May 2025
Cambodia Development Resource Institute (2020) Cyber Governance in Cambodia: A Risk-Based Approach to Cybersecurity. CDRI Special Report No. 18. 7–9 cdri.org.kh/storage/pdf/SP18_cybersecurity_1620204216.pdf Accessed 13 May 2025
Carletti C (2021) Digital Technology: Protection and/or Economic Value for Personal Data Knowledge and Management and Conformity to Soft Law Norms. Peace Human Rights Governance 5(1) phrg.padovauniversitypress.it/system/files/papers/PHRG%E22021%E21%E205.pdf Accessed 15 May 2025
COM (Commission of the European Communities (2007) Report from the Commission “Better Lawmaking 2006” pursuant to Article 9 of the Protocol on the application of the principles of

subsidiarity and proportionality 14th report eur-lex.europa.eu/LexUriServ/LexUriServ.do?uri=COM:2007:0286:FIN:EN:PDF
Computer Emergency Response Team (2023) Cyber Security Laws for OIC Members. 9, 15–16 oic-cert.org/en/download/OIC-CERT%20Member%20Cybersecurity%20Order%20v4.pdf Accessed 13 May 2025
Cook Islands (2023) Cook Islands National Security Policy 2023–2026 pacificsecurity.net/wp-content/uploads/2023/09/APSC-Cook-Islands-National-Security-Policy-2023-2026-1.pdf Accessed 11 May 2025
Cook Islands (2024) National Digital Strategy 2024 - 2030 pmoffice.gov.ck/wp-content/uploads/2024/02/CI-National-Digital-Strategy-v10.pdf Accessed 11 May 2025
Cyber Security Agency of Singapore (2016) Singapore's Cybersecurity Strategy isomer-user-content.by.gov.sg/36/5d93ef97-4e61-4a73-8c04-e42b743b275e/SingaporeCybersecurityStrategy.pdf Accessed 14 May 2025
Cyber Security Agency of Singapore (2021) The Singapore Cybersecurity Strategy 2021 ccdcoe.org/uploads/2018/10/Singapore_Cybersecurity_Strategy_2021.pdf Accessed 14 May 2025
Cyber Security Council of Mongolia (2024) The Organisation's Introduction Handbook pubcert.mn/sites/default/files/2024-04/Cyber%20book.pdf Accessed 14 May 2025
Data Security Council of India (2020) National Cyber Security Strategy 2020 dsci.in/files/content/knowledge-centre/2023/National-Cyber-Security-Strategy-2020-DSCI-submission.pdf Accessed 15 May 2025
Department of Information and Communications Technology (2024) National Cybersecurity Plan 2023–2028 cms-cdn.e.gov.ph/DICT/pdf/NCSP-2023-2028-FINAL-DICT.pdf Accessed 14 May 2025
Digital Agency (2025) International Data Governance Study Group (the fifth) digital.go.jp/en/councils/global-data-governance/d7dea47d-32f6-44d1-aff6-95f4e3c664da Accessed 8 May 2025
Digital Policy Office (2024) Principles of Data Governance digitalpolicy.gov.hk/en/our_work/data_governance/policies_standards/policy/doc/principles_of_data_governance_en.pdf Accessed 8 May 2025
Digital Policy Office (2025a) Digital Infrastructure, Information and Cyber Security Within the Government. digitalpolicy.gov.hk/en/our_work/digital_infrastructure/information_cyber_security/government/ Accessed 14 May 2025
Digital Policy Office (2025b) Digital Infrastructure. digitalpolicy.gov.hk/en/our_work/digital_infrastructure/information_cyber_security/community/ Accessed 14 May 2025
Directorate of Security Policy and Plan, Office of the National Security Council (2022) Executive Summary National Security Policy and Plan B.E. 2566–2570 (2023–2027) nsc.go.th/wp-content/uploads/2023/09/ExecutiveSummaryEN.pdf Accessed 15 May 2025
Ebert H et al (2020) Cyber Resilience and Diplomacy in the Republic of Korea: Prospects for EU Cooperation https://eucd.s3.eu-central-1.amazonaws.com/eucd/assets/iXvfE20z/digital-dialogue-rok.pdf Accessed 30 Oct 2025
ENISA (2015) Cyber Security Information Sharing: An Overview of Regulatory and Non-regulatory Approaches enisa.europa.eu/sites/default/files/publications/Regulatory%20and%20Non-regulatory%20Approaches%20to%20Information%20Sharing.pdf Accessed 31 Oct 2025
European Commission (2018) Guidance on sharing private sector data in the European data economy SWD/2018/125 final eur-lex.europa.eu/legal-content/EN/TXT/?uri=celex:52018SC0125 Accessed 15 May 2025
Foreign Policy Analytics (2021) Global Data Governance Power Map foreignpolicy.com/2020/10/06/global-data-privacy-collection-laws-database-surveillance-cybersecurity-governance/ Accessed 8 May 2025
Gerami N (2024) Navigating Cybersecurity and Surveillance: Iran's Dual Strategy for National Security docs.publicnow.com/viewDoc?filename=129076%5CEXT%5C0E61CCF9F8E4D7400B0078FB503DA73ED29106E2_E54003DDAC47543C6A12ADEAD72FF6EBC7DB58C0.PDF Accessed 15 May 2025

Giardini T et al (2023) DPA Digital Digest: Russia. Digital Policy Alert digitalpolicyalert.org/digest/dpa-digital-digest-russia Accessed 10 May 2025
Google Cloud (2025) What is data governance? cloud.google.com/learn/what-is-data-governance?hl=en Accessed 5 May 2025
Government of the Cook Islands (2023) National ICT Policy 2023–27 pmoffice.gov.ck/wp-content/uploads/2023/08/National-ICT-Policy-2023.pdf Accessed 11 May 2025
Gullapalli V (2023) Why is the Asia Pacific region a target for cybercrime - and what can be done about it? weforum.org/stories/2023/06/asia-pacific-region-the-new-ground-zero-cybercrime/ Accessed 24 Dec 2024
Holdsworth J et al. (2025) What is data governance? ibm.com/think/topics/data-governance Accessed 5 May 2025
IREX (2024) Vibrant Information Barometer 2024 - Turkmenistan. A study funded by USAID irex.org/sites/default/files/VIBE_2024_Turkmenistan.pdf Accessed 11 May 2025
ITU National CIRTs worldwide : 139/195 itu.int/en/ITU-D/Cybersecurity/Pages/CIRTs/List-of-National-CIRTs.aspx
Jiang M (2020) Cybersecurity Policies in China cyberbrics.info/wp-content/uploads/2020/11/CyberBRICS-Book-FINAL-author-version-1.pdf Accessed 14 May 2025
Keck M (2022) UNCDF The role of cybersecurity and data security in the digital economy policy accelerator.uncdf.org/all/brief-cybersecurity-digital-economy Accessed 31 Oct 2025
KPMG China (2017) Overview of China’s Cybersecurity Law assets.kpmg.com/content/dam/kpmg/cn/pdf/en/2017/02/overview-of-cybersecurity-law.pdf Accessed 14 May 2025
Lewis D et al (2025) Mapping the Regulatory Learning Space for the EU AI Act arXiv:2503.05787v2 [cs.CY]
Lindemulder G et al (2024) What is cybersecurity? ibm.com/think/topics/cybersecurity Accessed 3 May 2025
Liu T et al. (2025) Fortifying the Future: Hong Kong’s new cybersecurity laws to protect critical infrastructure lexology.com/library/detail.aspx?g=743c63e6-555a-44d1-b947-67722aef092f Accessed 30 Oct 2025
Malaysia (2020) Malaysia Cyber Security Strategy 2020–2024 Introduction asset.mkn.gov.my/wp-content/uploads/2020/10/MalaysiaCyberSecurityStrategy2020-2024.pdf Accessed 14 May 2025
MaryVille University (2024) The History of Cybersecurity online.maryville.edu/blog/history-of-cybersecurity/ Accessed 5 May 2025
Minister of Information, Communication, Transport and Tourism Development (2020) Kiribati National Cybersecurity Strategy mict.gov.ki/download/file/fid/300 Accessed 11 May 2025
Ministry of Communications and IT (2014) National Cyber Security Strategy of Afghanistan itu.int/en/ITU-D/Cybersecurity/Documents/National_Strategies_Repository/Afghanistan_2014_National%20Cybersecurity%20Strategy%20of%20Afghanistan%20%28November2014%29.pdf Accessed 15 May 2025
Ministry of Digital Technologies of the Republic of Uzbekistan (2024) Uzbekistan Digital Economy Overview and Vision 2030 aict.uz/caict_uzbekistan_digital_economy_overview_vision_2030.pdf Accessed 11 May 2025
Ministry of Justice (2021) Communication and Foreign Affairs, Draft of National ICT Policy pp. 27–32 finance.gov.tv/wp-content/uploads/2022/08/National-ICT-Policy-2021.pdf Accessed 13 May 2025
Ministry of Science and Technology (2022) Approval for Strategy of National Security and Cybersecurity mst.gov.vn/phe-duyet-chien-luoc-an-toan-an-ninh-mang-quoc-gia-197154876.htm Accessed 15 May 2025
Ministry of Technology. Digital Sri Lanka 2030 - A National Digital Strategy for Sri Lanka mot.gov.lk/assets/files/National%20Digital%20Economy%20Strategy%202030%20Sri%20Lanka-bc77184e0b6035d235cd0bb1ebf75707.pdf Accessed 14 May 2025

Ministry of Transport and Infrastructure (2020) National Cyber Security Strategy 2020–2023 hgm.uab.gov.tr/uploads/pages/siber-guvenlik/national-cyber-security-strategy-2020-2023.pdf Accessed 15 May 2025

Moschetta G et al (2025) Geopolitical tensions, AI and more are complicating the cyberspace. Here's what to know. World Economic Forum weforum.org/stories/2025/01/global-cybersecurity-outlook-complex-cyberspace-2025/ Accessed 15 May 2025

National Centre of Incident Readiness and Strategy for Cybersecurity (2021) Japan's Cybersecurity Strategy 2021 (Overview) nisc.go.jp/pdf/policy/kihon-s/cs-senryaku2021-gaiyou-en.pdf Accessed 14 May 2025

National Cyber Security Centre. What is cyber security? ncsc.gov.uk/section/about-ncsc/what-is-cyber-security Accessed 3 May 2025

National Security Office (2019) National Cybersecurity Strategy itu.int/en/ITU-D/Cybersecurity/Documents/National_Strategies_Repository/National%20Cybersecurity%20Strategy_South%20Korea.pdf Accessed 14 May 2025

NATO Strategic Communications Centre of Excellence (2021) Russia's strategy in cyberspace. 978-9934-564-90-1 vaemergency.gov/aem/blue-book/reading-corner/nato-cyber-report-11-06-2021.pdf Accessed 10 May 2025

Nauru Government (2025) Nauru National Digital Transformation Strategy 2025–2030 nauru.gov.nr/media/204028/nndts_final_version_2025.pdf Accessed 11 May 2025

New Zealand Government (2023) Department of the Prime Minister and Cabinet. Cyber Security Strategy Annual Report 2022/2023. 4 dpmc.govt.nz/sites/default/files/2023-09/cyber-security-strategy-annual-report-2022-23.pdf Accessed 13 May 2025

Policy Department for Citizens' Rights and Constitutional Affairs, Directorate-General for Internal Policies (2022) IPR and the use of open data and data sharing initiatives by public and private actors europarl.europa.eu/RegData/etudes/STUD/2022/732266/IPOL_STU(2022)732266_EN.pdf Accessed 15 May 2025

Queenan M (2021) The Role of Data Governance in Cybersecurity. Cybersecurity Magazine cdn.naspo.org/Cybersecurity%20Page/The%20Role%20of%20Data%20Governance%20in%20Cybersecurity.pdf Accessed 6 May 2025

Republic of Palau (2022) National Security Strategy of the Republic of Palau pitiviti.org/storage/dm/2022/08/rop-2022-national-security-strategy-20220813191012624.pdf Accessed 13 May 2025

Republic of Vanuatu (2013) National Cyber. 7–11 digital.gov.vu/images/policies/Cybersecurity-Policy-EN-FR-BI.pdf Accessed 13 May 2025

Royal Audit Authority, Bhutan Integrity House (2023) Performance Audit Report on Preparedness for Cybersecurity bhutanaudit.gov.bt//wp-content/uploads/2023/07/Final-PA-Report-on-Cybersecurity-9.5.23.pdf Accessed 15 May 2025

Shahid Alam (2022) Cybersecurity: Past, Present and Future arxiv.org/pdf/2207.01227 Accessed 5 May 2025

Socquet-Clerc K et al (2023) Cybersecurity Governance in Southeast Asia. Thematic SSG Brief. Geneva: DCAF—Geneva Centre for Security Sector Governance dcaf.ch/sites/default/files/publications/documents/Cybersecurity_Governance_in_Southeast_Asia_Thematic_Brief.pdf Accessed 24 Dec 2024

Spînu N (2020) Georgia Cybersecurity Governance Assessment dcaf.ch/sites/default/files/publications/documents/GeorgiaCybersecurityGovernanceAssessment.pdf Accessed 14 May 2025

Sri Lanka Computer Emergency Readiness Team (2018) Coordination Centre (CERT CC), Draft version 7 of Information and Cyber Security Strategy of Sri Lanka 2018–2023 sherloc.unodc.org/cld/uploads/res//treaties/strategies/sri_lanka/lka0001s_html/Information_and_Cyber_Security_Strategy_of_Sri_Lanka_20182023.pdf Accessed 15 May 2025

Tamanikaiwaimaro S (2021) Cybersecurity in the Republic of Fiji diplomacy.edu/wp-content/uploads/2021/06/IGCBP2010_2011_Tamanikalwalmaro.pdf Accessed 11 May 2025

The Asia Foundation (2020) Developing Myanmar's Local Data Ecosystem themimu.info/sites/themimu.info/files/documents/Report_Developing_Myanmars_Local_Data_Ecosystem_Mar2020.pdf Accessed 14 May 2025

The Government of the Hong Kong Special Administrative Region (2023) LCQ9: Data governance system info.gov.hk/gia/general/202311/15/P2023111500270.htm Accessed 9 May 2025

The Independent State of Papua New Guinea (2024) National Cyber Security Strategy 2024–2030. 23–25 ict.gov.pg/wp-content/uploads/2024/policies/Final%20PNG%20NCSS-%20rev%2004-04-24.pdf Accessed 13 May 2025

The International Telecommunication Union (ITU) (2024) Global Cybersecurity Index 2024 5th Ed. itu.int/en/ITU-D/Cybersecurity/Documents/GCIv5/2401416_1b_Global-Cybersecurity-Index-E.pdf Accessed 4 May 2025

The State Council Information Office of the People's Republic of China (2023) China's Law-Based Cyberspace Governance in the New Era http://scio.gov.cn/zfbps/zfbps_2279/202303/t20230320_709283.html Accessed 15 May 2025

Thomson Reuters (2023) Understanding Data Governance and Cyber Security insight.thomsonreuters.com.au/legal/posts/understanding-data-governance-and-cyber-security Accessed 6 May 2025

Tonga (2022) Tonga National Cybersecurity Framework. Cyber Security Consultancy Services for Developing and Supporting Information Systems. 7 digitaltransformation.gov.to/wp-content/uploads/2022/08/Tonga_National_Cybersecurity_Framework_final.pdf Accessed 13 May 2025

U.S.-China Economic and Security Review Commission (2022) China's Evolving Data Governance Regime. uscc.gov/sites/default/files/2022-07/Chinas_Evolving_Data_Governance_Regime.pdf Accessed 8 May 2025

UN (2025a) Technical and statistical report Gap Analysis of Cyberlaws in Pacific Small Island Developing States. 70 unctad.org/system/files/official-document/dtlecde2024d6_en.pdf Accessed 15 May 2025

UN (2025b) Status of Treaties. UN Convention against Cybercrime treaties.un.org/pages/ViewDetails.aspx?src=TREATY&mtdsg_no=XVIII-16&chapter=18&clang=_en Accessed 31 Oct 2025

UN Department of Economic and Social Affairs (2024a) Ministry of Digital Development Innovation and Communications (2024) Draft Outcome Report - Capacity Development Workshop on National Data Governance Framework and Digital Government in Mongolia pp.16–18

UN Department of Economic and Social Affairs (2024b) Capacity Development and Consultation Workshop on Samoa National Data Governance Framework. Concept Note publicadministration.desa.un.org/events/capacity-development-and-consultation-workshop-samoa-national-data-governance-framework-0?page=2 Accessed 13 May 2025

UN Department of Economic and Social Affairs (2024c) Compendium of Baseline Studies on the National Data Governance Frameworks. Draft Working. UN Peace and Development Fund Project on Digital Data Management and Data Governance. pp 35–36 publicadministration.desa.un.org/sites/default/files/list-of-files/2024/Compendium%20of%20Baseline%20Studies%20of%20National%20Data%20Governance%20Frameworks_CLEAN_21April2024.pdf Accessed 12 May 2025

UN DESA, Government Technology (GovTech) Agency, Royal Government of Bhutan (2024) Bhutan National Data Governance Baseline Report tech.gov.bt/wp-content/uploads/2025/03/Bhutan-National-Data-Governance-Baseline-Report-2024-FINAL.pdf Accessed 14 May 2025

UN DESA. Ministry of Technology and Communications (2023) Initial Findings of a baseline study of Lao PDR National Data Governance. Capacity Development and Consultation Workshop on Lao PDR - National Data Governance Framework publicadministration.desa.un.org/sites/default/files/list-of-files/2025/1.2.2%29%20Piya%20-%20UN%20DESA%20Lao%20PDR%20Baseline%20Survey.pdf Accessed 4 May 2025

UN Economic and Social Commission for Asia and the Pacific (2025) Asia and the Pacific SDG Progress Report un-ilibrary.org/content/books/9789211071559c010 Accessed 3 May 2025

UN ESCAP (2022) Country Statement - Georgia unescap.org/sites/default/d8files/event-documents/5b_Georgia_CST8.2022.pdf Accessed 9 May 2025

UN ESCAP (2024a) Republic of Korea: Data governance profile unece.org/sites/default/files/2024-05/S3_7_ESCAP_RMunkHansen.pdf Accessed 10 May 2025

UN ESCAP (2024b) Tajikistan: Data governance profile unescap.org/sites/default/d8files/event-documents/Tajikistan-datagovernance-profile.pdf Accessed 10 May 2025
UN ESCAP (2024c) Australia: Data governance profile unescap.org/sites/default/d8files/event-documents/Australia-datagovernance-profile.pdf Accessed 10 May 2025
UN ESCAP (2024d) New Zealand: Data governance profile unescap.org/sites/default/d8files/eventdocuments/New_Zealand-data-governance-profile.pdf Accessed 10 May 2025
UN ESCAP (2024e) Indonesia: Data governance profile unescap.org/sites/default/d8files/event-documents/Indonesia-datagovernance-profile.pdf Accessed 10 May 2025
UN ESCAP (2024f) Malaysia: Data governance profile gdhelppage.gdcatalog.go.th/data/0_01/files/Malaysia-data-governance-profile.pdf Accessed 14 May 2025
UN ESCAP (2024g) Philippines: Data governance profile gdhelppage.gdcatalog.go.th/data/0_01/files/Philippines-data-governance-profile.pdf Accessed 14 May 2025
UN ESCAP (2024h) Singapore: Data governance profile gdhelppage.gdcatalog.go.th/data/0_01/files/Singapore-data-governance-profile.pdf Accessed 14 May 2025
UN ESCAP (2024i) Thailand: Data governance profile gdhelppage.gdcatalog.go.th/data/0_01/files/Thailand-data-governance-profile.pdf Accessed 14 May 2025
UN ESCAP (2024j) Vietnam: Data governance profile unescap.org/sites/default/d8files/event-documents/Viet_Nam-data-governance-profile.pdf Accessed 14 May 2025
UN ESCAP (2024k) India: Data governance profile unescap.org/sites/default/d8files/event-documents/India-data-governance-profile.pdf Accessed 14 May 2025
UN ESCAP (2024l) Nepal: Data governance profile unescap.org/sites/default/d8files/event-documents/Nepal-data-governance-profile.pdf Accessed 14 May 2025
UN ESCAP (2024m) Pakistan: Data governance profile unescap.org/sites/default/d8files/event-documents/Pakistan-data-governance-profile.pdf Accessed 14 May 2025
UN ESCAP (2024n) Türkiye: Data governance profile gdhelppage.gdcatalog.go.th/data/0_01/files/Türkiye-data-governance-profile.pdf Accessed 14 May 2025
UNCTAD (2025a) Cybercrime Legislation Worldwide unctad.org/page/cybercrime-legislation-worldwide Accessed 3 May 2025
UNCTAD (2025b) Data Protection and Privacy Legislation Worldwide unctad.org/page/data-protection-and-privacy-legislation-worldwide Accessed 8 May 2025
World Bank (2021a) South Caucasus GovTech for Armenia: A Whole of Government Approach as a Key Foundation for the Digital Economy in Armenia 14–15 openknowledge.worldbank.org/server/api/core/bitstreams/adf64e95-24ce-58b1-a9a0-2177c625efd8/content Accessed 9 May 2025
World Bank (2021b) South Caucasus GovTech for Azerbaijan: A Whole of Government Approach as a Key Foundation for the Digital Economy in Azerbaijan 12 documents1.worldbank.org/curated/en/454321623769098198/txt/South-Caucasus-GovTech-for-Azerbaijan-A-Whole-of-Government-Approach-as-a-Key-Foundation-for-the-Digital-Economy-in-Azerbaijan.txt Accessed 9 May 2025
World Bank (2021c) Resilient Digital Kazakhstan Program (P176295) documents1.worldbank.org/curated/en/400941617469177523/pdf/Concept-Stage-Program-Information-Document-PID-Resilient-Digital-Kazakhstan-Program-P176295.pdf Accessed 9 May 2025
World Bank (2021d) Kiribati Digital Government Project (P176108) documents1.worldbank.org/curated/en/164781631299073813/pdf/Concept-Project-Information-Document-PID-Kiribati-Digital-Government-Project-P176108.pdf Accessed 11 May 2025
World Bank (2022) Positioning the Lao PDR for a Digital Future Priority Measures to Accelerate Digital Economy Development thedocs.worldbank.org/en/doc/c01714a0bc2ca257bdfe8f3f75a64adc-0070062022/original/Positioning-The-Lao-PDR-for-a-Digital-Future-11-10-22.pdf Accessed 13 May 2025
World Bank Group (2024) Technical Note, Digital Financial Inclusion and Financial Consumer Protection, Maldives Financial Sector Assessment Program documents1.worldbank.org/curated/en/099060624144515101/pdf/P18010018ba7020fc1bd1b12ee8ea7e80dc.pdf Accessed 15 May 2025

Chapter 15
Normative Reconstruction of Data Governance in Asia Amid Geopolitical Shifts

Hiroshi Kataoka

Abstract Cross-border data flows are essential for economic growth and innovation, particularly in Asia's rapidly developing digital economies in which digital trade drives regional integration. However, varying national priorities—such as digital sovereignty, privacy protection, economic competitiveness, and national security—have led to significant regulatory fragmentation across Asia. This regulatory diversity, combined with complex geopolitical dynamics, including China's growing influence and the relative decline of U.S. leadership, has created barriers to seamless data exchange. In this shifting landscape, the rise of digital protectionism in Asia is increasingly undermining the role of the "Free Flow of Data" as a principle of international cooperation. Diverging approaches among regional powers and unilateral regulatory strategies by major powers are deepening asymmetries in global and regional data governance. Without coordinated frameworks, excessive fragmentation risks slowing economic growth, constraining innovation, and reducing opportunities for cross-border collaboration. To address these challenges, middle and emerging powers should form plurilateral partnerships to reconstruct data governance norms. By adopting a risk-based approach under Data Free Flow with Trust (DFFT), they can balance sovereignty with interoperability. Japan can lead this process through the "Tokyo Effect," whereby shared principles among such partnerships draw major powers into an inclusive global framework.

Keywords Cross-border data governance · Digital protectionism · Data Free Flow with Trust (DFFT) · Plurilateral partnerships · Contextual Risk-Based Minimization Model (CRM Model) · Tokyo effect

---

H. Kataoka (✉)
Azabudai Kataoka Legal and Economic Affairs Office, Tokyo, Japan
e-mail: gaku@azabudai.net

J. Nakagawa et al. (eds.), *Geopolitical Risks and Geoeconomics in International Economic Law*, Economics, Law, and Institutions in Asia Pacific,
https://doi.org/10.1007/978-981-95-6996-0_15

15.1 Introduction

A shift in the United States (U.S.) trade leadership has become increasingly evident. Its unilateral approach to trade—marked by higher tariffs and withdrawal from multilateral agreements—has fueled the perception that it is retreating from its traditional role as a global champion of free trade.

In recent years, the influence of the U.S. over negotiations on electronic commerce (e-commerce) in Asia has declined, particularly following its withdrawal from TPP.[1] In the aftermath, the remaining members proceeded to establish CPTPP[2] without U.S. participation, while RCEP[3] emerged with more flexible provisions on data transfers and localization, reflecting the preferences of countries such as China.

Amid these developments, the geopolitical landscape of digital trade in Asia has grown more complex, shaped by strategic rivalry among major powers. As a result, the region is witnessing a proliferation of regulatory models, reflecting divergent approaches among CPTPP, RCEP and other trade agreements, rather than convergence toward a unified framework.[4] Countries like Japan and Singapore have taken a more prominent role in shaping regional norms, notably serving as co-convenors of the Joint Statement Initiative (JSI) on e-commerce within the World Trade Organization (WTO).[5]

As digital economies expand, cross-border data governance has emerged as an increasingly critical and complex policy challenge. While governments seek to safeguard privacy, ensure national security, and preserve sovereign authority over critical data, these objectives have, in some jurisdictions, evolved into explicit forms of digital protectionism, understood here as state-imposed measures restricting cross-border data flows to assert sovereign control.[6] States are adopting increasingly stringent rules on cross-border data transfers, thereby fragmenting digital markets, undermining interoperability, and eroding mutual trust.

Yet, not all restrictions on data transfers are inherently protectionist. In certain circumstances, narrowly defined data localization measures may still be warranted—for example, to safeguard critical infrastructure or to ensure the availability of health-related data for public health protection. Consequently, the principle of the "Free Flow of Data," once regarded as a foundational norm of the global digital economy, is losing coherence.[7] Diverging national policies and the growing prevalence of unilateral restrictions have progressively eroded its status as a universal standard.

---

[1] Trans-Pacific Partnership Agreement (2016), signed 4 February 2016.

[2] Comprehensive and Progressive Agreement for Trans-Pacific Partnership (2018), signed 8 March 2018.

[3] Regional Comprehensive Economic Partnership Agreement (2020), signed 15 November 2020.

[4] APEC Policy Support Unit (2025, pp. 38–39).

[5] WTO (n.d., p. 2).

[6] Aaronson (2019, pp. 545–550), Yakovleva (2024, pp. 142–149).

[7] Cory and Dascoli (2021, p. 2).

To address these challenges, cross-border transfer norms should be reconstructed under the guiding principle of Data Free Flow with Trust (DFFT).[8] This approach both respects diverse legal frameworks through which sovereign authority is exercised and enables secure, rules-based, trust-oriented cross-border collaboration.[9]

15.2 Digital Protectionism in Asia

Geopolitical shifts across Asia have fundamentally reshaped national approaches to data governance. Intensifying concerns over digital sovereignty, strategic autonomy, and national security have prompted Asian governments to reconceptualize data not merely as an economic resource but as a strategic asset central to both security and competitiveness.[10] Once viewed as inherently non-territorial and globally mobile, data is now increasingly subjected to territorial control, with governments asserting regulatory authority over data generated within their jurisdictions.[11] This transformation signals a broader regional shift toward digital protectionism, marked by stricter controls on outbound data flows and heightened domestic oversight of digital infrastructure and critical systems.[12] Such frameworks are increasingly criticized for erecting structural barriers to the free flow of data, undermining interoperability across jurisdictions, and exacerbating regulatory fragmentation.[13]

15.2.1 Adverse Effects of Digital Protectionism

While state-led data regulation is gaining recognition internationally, regulatory discretion over cross-border data flows must be exercised with caution. When such measures become excessively restrictive—regardless of whether they are justified on grounds of personal data protection or national security—they can generate significant economic, societal, institutional, political, and geopolitical harms, which are especially pronounced in Asia.

1. **Economic Impacts** Stringent data localization mandates and outbound transfer restrictions can prevent both foreign and domestic firms from leveraging offshore cloud services, forcing redundant infrastructure investments and inflating operational costs. This not only stifles innovation and undermines competitiveness

[8] Digital Agency, Government of Japan, Data Free Flow with Trust (DFFT). https://www.digital.go.jp/en/policies/dfft/ (accessed 8 October 2025).

[9] Organisation for Economic Co-operation and Development (OECD) (2019, pp. 17–19).

[10] Center for Strategic & International Studies (2021, pp. 1–2).

[11] OECD (2019, pp. 88–90).

[12] Center for Strategic & International Studies (2021, pp. 3–5).

[13] Burri (2023, pp. 88–90).

but also creates de facto barriers to market entry, disproportionately harming emerging Asian digital economies.[14]

2. **Societal Consequences**. Restrictive cross-border data frameworks impede transnational collaboration in critical sectors such as research, healthcare, and finance, thereby reducing the shared benefits of digital interconnectivity.[15]
3. **Institutional Fragmentation**. Uncoordinated or unilateral rules contribute to regulatory fragmentation, generate legal uncertainty, and discourage long-term digital investment—effects that are particularly pronounced within Asia's diverse regulatory landscape.[16]
4. **Political Tensions**. Opaque or arbitrary enforcement of data restrictions can weaken democratic norms, undermine public trust, and exacerbate regional diplomatic frictions, especially in states with fragile rule-of-law systems.[17] Such practices not only risk enabling domestic repression but also complicate cross-border relations.
5. **Geopolitical Asymmetries**. Asymmetric data practices—where some countries restrict outbound transfers while freely collecting and exploiting foreign data—further exacerbate global digital power imbalances. China's regulatory model, which restricts outbound transfers on national security grounds while enabling relatively expansive inbound flows, is often cited as a paradigmatic example. This asymmetry enhances its AI development capacity and contributes to heightened geopolitical tensions.[18]

In sum, digital protectionism creates systemic risks that extend beyond individual economies. In Asia, continuing regulatory fragmentation erodes trust, limits market integration, and obstructs the formation of coherent governance.[19] Addressing these problems calls for regional frameworks that are both balanced and interoperable, together with effective mechanisms for policy harmonization and mutual recognition.

15.2.2 Legitimate Data Protection and Digital Protectionism

The rise of digital protectionism is particularly evident in Asia, where competing priorities of economic openness, regulatory autonomy, and sovereign control over data have resulted in diverse and sometimes conflicting approaches to cross-border data governance.[20] While the legitimate protection of personal information, national security, and public interests remains a core responsibility of the modern state, it

[14] Cory (2017, pp. 4–5).
[15] OECD (2019, pp. 60–71).
[16] Deane et al. (2024, pp. 165–168).
[17] Freedom House (2025).
[18] Zhang (2024, pp. 7–10).
[19] Cory and Dascoli (2021, pp. 1–4).
[20] United Nations Development Programme (2021, pp. 12–19).

is crucial to distinguish such genuine objectives from protectionist measures that unduly restrict data flows for economic or political leverage.[21]

Despite official commitments to digital trade liberalization, several governments in the region have adopted stringent data localization mandates and outbound transfer restrictions. Although these measures are frequently justified on the grounds of privacy or security, when applied excessively or disproportionately they shift from legitimate data protection to digital protectionism.

Against the backdrop of rapidly intensifying geopolitical transformations, the institutional fragmentation of data governance frameworks has become a critical concern in Asia. Where regulatory fragmentation stems primarily from protectionist objectives rather than genuine risk mitigation, such fragmentation undermines interoperability, hinders digital cooperation, and constrains the growth of regional digital economies.[22]

Therefore, a clear distinction between legitimate data protection and digital protectionism is indispensable for building balanced and interoperable governance frameworks.[23] Such clarity enables policymakers to design proportionate and transparent measures that protect fundamental rights while preserving cross-border data flows. Without it, regulatory overreach risks deepening institutional fragmentation, widening disparities in access to global digital opportunities, and undermining efforts to establish internationally consistent data governance regimes.

15.3 International Negotiations on Cross-Border Data Transfer Rules

The formulation of international rules on cross-border data transfers has long been debated within the context of negotiations on e-commerce under the WTO and various regional trade agreements.[24] Among the key provisions considered essential for ensuring the free flow of data are: (i) provisions prohibiting members from imposing restrictions on cross-border data transfers for business purposes (hereinafter Data Transfer Clause); and (ii) provisions prohibiting requirements to locate computing facilities within a Party's territory (hereinafter Localization Prohibition Clause).

The Data Transfer Clause establishes a foundational rule aimed at preventing states from banning or limiting cross-border data transfers for business purposes, thereby discouraging data protectionist measures. Similarly, the Localization Prohibition Clause seeks to prevent states from mandating the establishment or use of domestic computing infrastructure as a prerequisite for business operations, thereby effectively prohibiting data localization measures.[25]

[21] Naef (2023, pp. 423–427).

[22] Arner et al. (2022, pp. 643–645).

[23] Burri (2023, pp. 94–96).

[24] Mishra (2024, pp. 184–214).

[25] López et al. (2022, p. 12).

While such provisions have been incorporated into various international agreements, their effectiveness in curbing digital protectionism has remained limited, owing to the broad scope of exceptions and the inherently subjective nature of their interpretation. At present, negotiations within the WTO have reached an impasse, and even under regional trade agreements, assertive unilateral positions taken by major powers are increasingly shaping institutional frameworks.

15.3.1 WTO Negotiations on Cross-Border Data Transfer

With the global expansion of e-commerce, the regulation of cross-border data transfers has emerged as a critical issue within the WTO framework. The initial step can be traced back to the adoption of the Work Programme on Electronic Commerce in 1998,[26] and a turning point came in 2017 at the Eleventh WTO Ministerial Conference, where a group of member states launched the JSI.[27] This initiative marked the beginning of a concerted effort to develop comprehensive international trade rules governing e-commerce, including those related to cross-border data transfers.

As of July 2024, the JSI includes 91 participating countries and regions, with Japan serving as a co-convenor alongside Australia and Singapore.[28] In the same month, the JSI released a stabilized text consisting of 38 provisions, reflecting progress in areas such as electronic payment facilitation as well as the continuation of the moratorium on customs duties on electronic transmissions.[29]

Nonetheless, the stabilized text omitted the Data Transfer Clause and the Localization Prohibition Clause (hereinafter collectively referred to as the "Two Fundamental Clauses")—both of which are widely regarded as essential to ensuring the free flow of data. These omissions resulted from persistent divisions among key participants, particularly the U.S., which declined to endorse the text owing to the lack of language addressing its national security concerns.[30]

Consequently, efforts to establish international rules regarding cross-border data transfers have stalled at the WTO level. In practice, regional trade agreements—both bilateral and plurilateral—now serve as the primary venues where more concrete rule-making takes place.

---

[26] WTO (1998).

[27] WTO (2017).

[28] WTO (n.d., pp. 5–6).

[29] Ministry of Economy, Trade and Industry, Japan, Stabilised text achieved in WTO Joint Statement Initiative on electronic commerce (26 July 2024). https://www.meti.go.jp/english/press/2024/0726_001.html.

[30] U.S. Mission to the International Organizations in Geneva, Statement by Ambassador María L. Pagán on the WTO e-commerce Joint Statement Initiative (26 July 2024), para 4. https://geneva.usmission.gov/2024/07/26/statement-by-ambassador-maria-l-pagan-on-the-wto-e-commerce-joint-statement-initiative/.

15.3.2 Contentious Issues in Regional Trade Agreements

Following the U.S. withdrawal from TPP in 2017 under the Trump administration,[31] Japan assumed a leading role in concluding CPTPP. Subsequently, it concluded several key agreements, including JEEPA,[32] USJDTA,[33] and RCEP. All of these agreements incorporate the Two Fundamental Clauses.[34] On their face, these texts suggest that the European Union (EU), the U.S., and China all oppose restrictions on cross-border data transfers and mandatory data localization requirements.

However, each of these major powers has embedded exception clauses or carve-outs that reflect their respective domestic regulatory priorities, thereby allowing unilateral regulatory assertions to be accommodated within the framework of these agreements.

15.3.2.1 Cross-Border Transfer of Personal Data

A significant point of contention in international negotiations over the Data Transfer Clause concerns whether the free flow of personal data should be protected under such provisions. The U.S. and the EU have adopted sharply divergent positions on this issue. In U.S.-concluded regional trade agreements, including USMCA[35] and USJDTA, the term "information," as used in prohibitions of cross-border data transfer restrictions, is explicitly defined as "information, including personal information" thereby confirming that personal data falls within the category of information whose free flow must be guaranteed.[36]

In contrast, the EU takes the position that the transfer of personal data should be regulated under a distinct legal framework, separate from transfers conducted for commercial purposes. This approach is exemplified in JEEPA Art. 8.81(4), which expressly preserves the right of each Party to impose transfer restrictions on the grounds of personal data protection. The EU's stance reflects the framework under the General Data Protection Regulation (GDPR),[37] which subjects cross-border transfers

[31] Office of the U.S. Trade Representative, The United States officially withdraws from the Trans-Pacific Partnership (23 January 2017). https://ustr.gov/about-us/policy-offices/press office/press-releases/2017/january/US-Withdraws-From-TPP.

[32] Agreement Between the European Union and Japan for an Economic Partnership (JEEPA), signed 17 July 2018.

[33] Agreement Between the United States of America and Japan Concerning Digital Trade (USJDTA), signed 7 October 2019.

[34] CPTPP Arts. 14.11(2), 14.13(2); USJDTA Arts. 11(1), 12(1); RCEP Arts. 12.14(2), 12.15(1); JEEPA Art. 8.81(1), (2).

[35] United States-Mexico-Canada Agreement (USMCA), signed 30 November 2018.

[36] USMCA Art. 19.11; USJDTA Art. 11(1).

[37] Regulation (EU) 2016/679 of the European Parliament and of the Council of 27 April 2016 on the protection of natural persons with regard to the processing of personal data and on the free movement of such data, and repealing Directive 95/46/EC, O.J. L 119, 4.5.2016, p. 1 (General Data Protection Regulation, GDPR). https://eur-lex.europa.eu/eli/reg/2016/679/oj.

of personal data to specific safeguards, including adequacy decisions and appropriate contractual clauses.[38]

Furthermore, USJDTA Art. 15(4) addresses concerns over excessive regulation of personal data transfers by explicitly adopting a risk-based approach (providing that any restrictions on personal data transfers must be "proportionate to the risks presented"). This approach stands in marked contrast to post-Schrems II[39] practices by certain EU Member State data protection authorities (DPAs), which have rejected risk-based assessments under the GDPR's rules on international data transfers. Instead, they have effectively adopted a so-called "zero-risk standard," under which even hypothetical risks—regardless of their actual or contextual likelihood—are deemed sufficient to prohibit a data transfer.[40]

15.3.2.2 Exception Clauses and Dispute Settlement Frameworks

Two of the most consequential exception clauses affecting cross-border data transfers are: (i) those invoked to pursue "legitimate public policy objectives" (hereinafter Public Policy Exception), and (ii) those designed to safeguard "essential security interests" (hereinafter National Security Exception). While the conditions and scope of these exceptions vary across agreements, their broad application seriously risks undermining the normative force of the Two Fundamental Clauses, effectively enabling or legitimizing data protectionist practices.

With respect to the Public Policy Exception, the term "legitimate public policy objectives" remains undefined in the texts of the agreements, providing neither substantive criteria nor procedural safeguards.[41] This ambiguity creates a significant risk that states may invoke the exception in an arbitrary or expansive manner, thereby weakening the effectiveness of the agreements.

In the context of the National Security Exception, notably under RCEP—whose provisions have been widely characterized as reflecting a regulatory approach consistent with China's digital governance model[42]—the Electronic Commerce Chapter grants each Party broad discretion to determine the necessity of national security measures, while expressly excluding such determinations from dispute settlement procedures.[43] Similarly, the U.S. has adopted a comparable interpretative position

---

[38] GDPR, Arts. 44, 46.

[39] Court of Justice of the European Union (CJEU), Case C-311/18, Data Protection Commissioner v. Facebook Ireland and Maximillian Schrems, Judgment of 16 July 2020, ECLI:EU:C:2020:559, paras. 93–95.

[40] Christakis (2024, pp. 18–23).

[41] CPTPP Art. 14.11(3); USMCA Art. 19.11(2); USJDTA Art. 11(2); JEEPA Art. 8.81(3); RCEP Arts. 12.14(3)(a), 12.15(3)(a).

[42] Yakovleva (2024, pp. 23, 194).

[43] RCEP Arts. 12.14(3)(b), 12.15(3)(b), 12.17(3).

with respect to Art. XXI of the GATT and Art. XIV bis of the GATS,[44] interpreting it as conferring sole authority on the invoking Member to determine the necessity of national security measures.[45]

Such growing reliance on the National Security Exception enables major powers to undertake unilateral measures insulated from external challenge, thereby undermining the predictability and stability of the international legal order.[46] To mitigate this risk, it is essential to define the institutional scope and limits of such exceptions and to ensure their disciplined and transparent application. In practice, however, major powers—by leveraging their military or economic influence—can readily assert the legitimacy of these unilateral measures, thereby rendering existing international frameworks increasingly ineffective in constraining such unilateral measures.[47]

15.4 Normative Reconstruction of Cross-Border Data Governance

The principle of the "Free Flow of Data" has long served as a foundational norm underpinning the global digital economy, discouraging unjustified restrictions on cross-border data transfers while fostering innovation and economic growth.

In recent years, however, this foundational norm has come under growing strain. Geopolitical tensions, the assertion of digital sovereignty, and increasing regulatory divergence have collectively undermined its normative and institutional coherence, deepening the fragmentation of the global governance landscape. Consequently, the rise of digital protectionism is accelerating, forcing policymakers to confront the structural limitations and inconsistencies embedded within existing legal and institutional frameworks for global data governance.

Given the substantial divergences in governance structures, regulatory philosophies, and institutional designs across jurisdictions, establishing a framework for cross-border data transfers that both respects national sovereignty and ensures international interoperability requires a neutral and objective approach, insulated from political or subjective value judgments.[48] From this perspective, DFFT can serve

[44] WTO, General Agreement on Tariffs and Trade 1994, Art. XXI, Apr. 15, 1994, Marrakesh Agreement Establishing the World Trade Organization, Annex 1A, 1867 U.N.T.S. 187. https://www.wto.org/english/docs_e/legal_e/06-gatt_e.htm; WTO, General Agreement on Trade in Services, Art. XIV bis, Apr. 15, 1994, Marrakesh Agreement Establishing the World Trade Organization, Annex 1B, 1869 U.N.T.S. 183. https://www.wto.org/english/docs_e/legal_e/26-gats_01_e.htm; Hrynkiv and Delimatsis (2020, pp. 8–10).

[45] United States–Certain Measures on Steel and Aluminum Products, First Written Submission of the United States, paras 1–2, WT/DS544 (June 12, 2019). https://ustr.gov/sites/default/files/enforcement/DS/US.Sub1.%28DS544%29.fin.%28public%29.pdf.

[46] Dimitropoulos et al. (2025, pp. 22–27).

[47] Alford (2011, pp. 726–729).

[48] Kuzio J et al. (2022, Sect. 1 and Sect. 4).

as a guiding principle, providing a normative foundation rooted in interoperability and mutual trust while accommodating states' sovereign control over data. To reconstruct a shared normative foundation for data flows under DFFT, adopting a risk-based approach is essential to ensuring effective implementation.

15.4.1 Erosion of the Principle of the "Free Flow of Data"

Originally rooted in the U.S. vision of an open internet economy in the 1990s, the principle of the "Free Flow of Data" embodied the belief that unrestricted cross-border data transfers would drive innovation and trade.[49] Supported by its burgeoning tech sector, the U.S. placed this principle at the core of its trade policy.[50]

However, its status as a shared global norm has gradually eroded, as shown by the following developments:

First, escalating U.S.–China tensions over economic and technological dominance have prompted a strategic recalibration by both countries. In response to national security concerns, the U.S. has restricted Chinese telecommunications equipment, tightened controls on foreign cloud services, and imposed targeted sanctions,[51] marking a clear shift from its earlier liberal stance. Conversely, China has strengthened its data localization regime under the banner of "cyber sovereignty," reinforcing state control over data.[52]

Second, the EU's stringent data-protection framework challenges the principle of the "Free Flow of Data." The GDPR adopts a default prohibition on international transfers of personal data, allowing them only under narrowly defined conditions—such as adequacy decisions or appropriate safeguards—making free flow the exception rather than the rule.[53]

Third, rapid advances in artificial intelligence and growing state efforts to access private-sector data have amplified both economic and rights-based concerns over cross-border data transfers. These trends heighten security and human rights risks, fueling calls for digital sovereignty and stronger privacy protections, and prompting a reassessment of the normative foundations of unrestricted data flows.[54]

Fourth, the U.S. has increasingly distanced itself from the WTO framework it once championed, undermining the coherence of global trade rules. The return of the Trump administration in 2025 revived tariffs as a strategic tool, eroding the

---

[49] Meltzer (2015, pp. 90–91).

[50] Burri (2017, pp. 87–93).

[51] Congressional Research Service (2022), U.S. restrictions on Huawei Technologies: National security and foreign policy considerations, R47012, 5 January 2022, p. 12. https://www.congress.gov/crs-product/R47012.

[52] Hung (2025, pp. 22–25).

[53] Voss (2020, pp. 506–509).

[54] UNESCO, Recommendation on the Ethics of Artificial Intelligence (2021), Arts. 7, 28–30. https://unesdoc.unesco.org/ark:/48223/pf0000380455.

predictability underpinning free trade and the digital economy.[55] By effectively disabling the WTO dispute settlement system, the U.S. also weakened the institutional foundation for shaping multilateral rules, particularly in the digital economy.[56] This shift is widely regarded as a deliberate retreat from the normative basis of the multilateral trade regime once advanced by the U.S.[57]

Taken together, these developments raise serious concerns about the legitimacy of U.S. participation in shaping rules on digital trade and cross-border data transfers, as well as the growing risk of regulatory backlash. States now regulate cross-border data flows according to their own priorities and frameworks, with many tightening domestic regimes and expanding notions of digital sovereignty. Consequently, the U.S. stance is increasingly viewed as undermining efforts to build a coherent and equitable framework for international data governance.[58]

15.4.2 DFFT as a Guiding Principle

In today's multipolar environment, the principle of the "Free Flow of Data" no longer serves as a universally accepted premise for international negotiations.[59] Rebuilding a common foundation for cross-border data transfers requires more than simply reaffirming the normative value of free flow; it demands the design of innovative institutional frameworks grounded in regulatory interoperability, mutual accountability, and trust.

DFFT has gained traction in international fora such as the G7 and OECD,[60] reflecting an emerging consensus on the need to reconcile the promotion of cross-border data flows with robust, trust-based regulatory frameworks. However, DFFT remains inherently polysemous, encapsulating an internal tension between its two elements— "data free flow" and "with trust." Measures restricting data transfers on grounds such as national security may conform to the trust component while simultaneously undermining the principle of free flow. As a result, the implementation of DFFT is necessarily shaped by each jurisdiction's institutional context and

---

[55] Executive Order No. 14257, Regulating Imports with a Reciprocal Tariff to Rectify Trade Practices that Contribute to Large and Persistent Annual United States Goods Trade Deficits, 90 FR 15041 (7 April 2025). https://www.federalregister.gov/documents/2025/04/07/2025-06063/regulating-imports-with-a-reciprocal-tariff-to-rectify-trade-practices-that-contribute-to-large-and.

[56] Carneiro de Castro (2024, pp. 1–3).

[57] Bacchus (2020, pp. 9–12).

[58] Burri et al. (2024, pp. 192–194, 198–199).

[59] OECD (2023, pp. 11–15), Dimitropoulos et al. (2025, pp. 17–24).

[60] G7 Digital Ministers, G7 Vision for Operationalizing Data Free Flow with Trust (2023 Vision Annex endorsed at the Hiroshima Summit). https://www.soumu.go.jp/main_content/000879099.pdf; OECD, 2024 Ministerial Council Statement (May 3, 2024), pp. 1–2. https://www.oecd.org/content/dam/oecd/en/events/2024/5/oecd-ministerial-council-meeting-2024/2024-Ministerial-Council-Statement.pdf; OECD (2023, p. 3).

regulatory posture, and its effective operationalization depends on deliberate and well-calibrated institutional design.[61]

To embed DFFT within institutional frameworks, it is essential to reconstruct the operational rules and mechanisms through which shared baseline principles—such as purpose limitation, necessity, proportionality, data minimization, transparency, and accountability—are translated into practice, thereby ensuring their consistent application across diverse legal systems. Many of these principles are already partially codified in existing domestic and international frameworks.[62] Within the EU, for example, several are embedded in the Charter of Fundamental Rights[63] and the GDPR; however, the extraterritorial application of these norms often introduces regulatory rigidity and imposes disproportionate burdens on jurisdictions with fewer resources or differing institutional structures.[64]

Accordingly, the challenge lies in recalibrating these operational mechanisms so as to respect institutional diversity while enhancing international interoperability. This effort must avoid the unilateral transplantation of the EU model and instead reposition the underlying principles as shared international norms capable of broader acceptance. Such recalibration is essential for the institutional realization of DFFT through fostering trust-based, interoperable and cooperative frameworks for cross-border data governance.[65]

Realizing this vision ultimately requires the development of risk-based, context-sensitive mechanisms that translate shared principles into concrete norms and institutional structures. These mechanisms should serve as the foundation of a coherent and trusted architecture for cross-border data governance under DFFT.

15.4.3 A Risk-Based Approach as an Operational Framework

A risk-based approach provides a framework for assessing the nature, severity, and likelihood of risks while evaluating the proportionality of regulatory measures adopted in response.[66] By doing so, it offers a common basis for decision-making that can be applied across jurisdictions, irrespective of differing legal traditions or policy objectives. This enables states to maintain sovereign control over data while achieving international coherence and fostering mutual trust in cross-border data governance.

---

[61] OECD (2023, pp. 15–17), Dale and Aizawa (2024, pp. 3–5).

[62] GDPR Art. 5(1)(a)–(f); OECD (2013), Organization of American States, Updated Principles on Privacy and the Protection of Personal Data (2021). https://www.oas.org/en/sla/iajc/docs/Publication_Updated_Principles_on_Privacy_and_Protection_of_Personal_Data_2021.pdf.

[63] Charter of Fundamental Rights of the European Union, 2012 O.J. (C 326) 391.

[64] Kuner (2017, pp. 892–895).

[65] OECD (2023, pp. 15–18), Aaronson (2023, pp. 102–105).

[66] Breitbarth (2021, pp. 542–545).

Recent international discourse increasingly recognizes the importance of risk-based methodologies in shaping cross-border data governance. Paragraph 18 of the 2013 Revised OECD Privacy Guidelines reflects this trend by requiring that any restrictions on cross-border data transfers be proportionate to both the level and the likelihood of risks involved.[67] USJDTA Art. 15(4) also incorporates a provision aligned with a risk-based approach.[68]

Academic scholarship similarly supports adopting a risk-based framework. Breitbarth emphasizes the need to construct a flexible regulatory architecture that considers both the likelihood of risks and the effectiveness of safeguards, and to apply restrictions on data transfers accordingly.[69] Christakis argues that the GDPR should be interpreted as endorsing a risk-based approach, applying this both to international data transfers and to the assessment of government access risks regarding data stored in Europe, an interpretation that he links to the EU principle of proportionality.[70] According to this perspective, supplementary measures should be guided by context-sensitive risk assessments rather than rigid technical standards. Collectively, these arguments directly challenge the emphasis of the European Data Protection Board (EDPB) on uniform compliance obligations—such as mandatory encryption or standardized contractual clauses—while neglecting contextual risk factors.[71]

These international and academic trends were further underscored by a July 2024 decision of the Traunstein Regional Court in Germany. The court rejected the EU authorities' position that personal data collected by a global social networking provider could not be transferred to the U.S. and must instead be stored within the EU. It held that such transfers were lawful if they complied with Art. 6(1)(b) of the GDPR (contract performance) and met its Chapter V requirements.[72] The ruling has been widely interpreted as adopting a risk-based approach under the GDPR, marking a potential institutional shift within EU jurisprudence.[73]

Taken together, these developments signal a significant shift toward embedding risk-based approaches within both international and domestic frameworks[74]—underscoring the urgent need for robust and interoperable architectures capable of balancing sovereignty, innovation, and trust.

---

[67] OECD (2013), para 18.

[68] USJDTA Art. 15(4) (stipulated as "proportionate to the risks presented").

[69] Breitbarth (2021, pp. 542–545).

[70] Christakis (2024, pp. 58–62).

[71] European Data Protection Board (EDPB) (2021), Recommendations 01/2020 on Measures That Supplement Transfer Tools to Ensure Compliance with the EU Level of Protection of Personal Data (Final Version), paras 42–47 (June 2021). https://edpb.europa.eu/system/files/2021-06/edpb_recommendations_202001vo.2.0_supplementarymeasurestransferstools_en.pdf (hereinafter EDPB Recommendations 2021) .

[72] LG Traunstein, Judgment of 8 July 2024, 9 O 173/24. https://gdprhub.eu/index.php?title=LG_Traunstein_-_9_O_173/24.

[73] Christakis et al. (2024), German court decision signals move towards risk-based approach to data transfers. Cross-Border Data Forum, 16 Oct 2024. https://www.crossborderdataforum.org/german-court-decision-signals-move-towards-risk-based-approach-to-data-transfers/.

[74] Christakis (2024, pp. 2–7, 15–20).

However, institutional models such as the APEC Cross-Border Privacy Rules (CBPR) system[75] highlight the limitations of current practice. Although CBPR pioneered the operationalization of risk-based governance, its lack of binding legal force, limited interoperability, and vulnerability to geopolitical asymmetries undermine its broader legitimacy.[76]

To embed risk-based approaches effectively in future cross-border data governance, it is essential to establish binding and interoperable frameworks that replace voluntary schemes with enforceable obligations and enable mutual recognition across jurisdictions.

15.5 Implementation of Reconstructed Normative Frameworks

In reconstructing normative frameworks for cross-border data transfer, effective implementation is pivotal, particularly within Asia's diverse regulatory landscape.

15.5.1 Operationalizing Contextual Risk Assessment

The EU's Artificial Intelligence Act (AI Act)[77] provides an illustrative precedent for codifying a risk-based regulatory framework. It establishes a tiered structure of AI systems ranging from unacceptable risk to minimal risk. Within this framework, high-risk AI systems are defined in Art. 6(2) and Annex III across sectors such as education, employment, and law enforcement. Obligations for AI systems—set out in Title III of the Act—vary according to their potential impacts on fundamental rights, imposing graduated requirements concerning safety, transparency, and accountability.[78] While Annex III presumes certain systems to be high-risk, Art. 6(3) allows exceptions where no significant risk is demonstrated, underscoring the context-sensitive design of the Act.

This model offers valuable insights for cross-border data governance. Embedding contextual risk assessment within a holistic risk-based governance framework provides a more neutral and geopolitically resilient alternative to adequacy-based

---

[75] Asia-Pacific Economic Cooperation (2017), APEC Cross-Border Privacy Rules (CBPR) System: Policies, Rules and Guidelines. APEC Secretariat, Singapore. https://www.apec.org/docs/default-source/Groups/ECSG/CBPR/CBPR-PoliciesRulesGuidelines.pdf.

[76] Greenleaf (2009, pp. 33–36).

[77] Regulation (EU) 2024/1689 of the European Parliament and of the Council of 13 June 2024 laying down harmonized rules on Artificial Intelligence (Artificial Intelligence Act), Official Journal of the European Union, L 168, p. 1. https://eur-lex.europa.eu/legal-content/EN/TXT/?uri=CELEX:32024R1689.

[78] Artificial Intelligence Act, Art. 6(2), Annex III, and Arts. 8–29, 51–54.

approaches that focus solely on the destination country's legal system. By evaluating both risk attributes (e.g., sensitivity, identifiability, criticality) and use contexts (e.g., law enforcement, medical research, statistical analysis), regulatory frameworks can operationalize the principle of proportionality. This principle—comprising suitability, necessity, and balancing (*proportionality stricto sensu*)[79]—ensures that restrictions are neither overbroad nor underinclusive. Such an approach enables regulators to impose graduated conditions, ranging from unconditional transfer to absolute prohibition, with intermediate options such as minimum safeguards, standard safeguards (contractual or technical), and strict regulatory preconditions.[80]

Reconstructing operational norms in this manner moves beyond uniform adequacy standards while balancing sovereignty with interoperability. By grounding transfer conditions in contextual risk assessments, regulators can build an adaptive regulatory architecture that more closely aligns with the vision of DFFT[81] and, in the Asian context, fosters interoperability across diverse legal and institutional settings. Moreover, this framework operationalizes core principles such as purpose limitation, necessity, proportionality, and data minimization. It also promotes transparency and accountability through mechanisms such as mutual recognition systems and mandatory disclosure regimes.

15.5.2 Contextual Risk-Based Minimization Model (CRM Model)

Building on the preceding analysis, this paper proposes the Contextual Risk-Based Minimization Model (CRM Model) as a framework for reconstructing cross-border data governance through the operationalization of a risk-based approach. The CRM Model integrates contextual risk assessment with the principle of data minimization,[82] ensuring that both data collection and regulatory requirements remain confined to what is strictly necessary, thereby preventing overly broad or formalistic restrictions. It evaluates risk based on the nature of the data and the context of its use, limiting collection to the minimum necessary and calibrating restrictions on cross-border transfers in line with contextual risk and safeguards.

Unlike the general proportionality principle, the CRM Model prioritizes identifying less restrictive alternatives; where such alternatives exist, proposed restrictions cannot be regarded as genuinely "minimal" and thus become impermissible. Transfers of high-risk data may be permitted when rendered irreversibly anonymized

---

[79] Gerards (2013, pp. 467–470).

[80] European Risk Forum (2020, pp. 3–4).

[81] OECD (2019, pp. 15–18).

[82] GDPR Art. 5(1)(c) (data minimization principle); European Data Protection Board (EDPB) (2020), Guidelines 4/2019 on Article 25 Data Protection by Design and by Default, paras. 29–34 (Version 2.0, Oct. 20, 2020). https://www.edpb.europa.eu/our-work-tools/our-documents/guidelines/guidelines-42019-article-25-data-protection-design-and_en.

and accompanied by robust safeguards, while even low-risk data transfers can be restricted where concerns over irreversible harm cannot be ruled out.

Existing Transfer Impact Assessments (TIAs) under the GDPR offer only partial precedents and remain structurally limited, focusing mainly on recipient-country frameworks while neglecting data characteristics and contextual use.[83] In contrast, the CRM Model evaluates dimensions such as risk attributes, purpose of use, and protective measures, enabling more context-sensitive, balanced decisions. By rejecting formalistic prohibitions and combining risk-based assessment with data minimization, the CRM Model creates a flexible but principled institutional framework that ensures the coherent governance of both personal and non-personal data.

Effective implementation requires a shared risk classification system and clear correspondence between categories and safeguards. Defining high-, limited-, and minimal-risk data based on attributes such as identifiability and sensitivity ensures predictability, consistency, and transparency. Codifying these correspondences in statutes or supervisory guidelines enables interoperability while respecting regulatory diversity.[84] A shared taxonomy of risks and safeguards mitigates operational misunderstandings and supports a coherent evaluative framework. Institutionalizing these principles through regulatory cooperation frameworks or international agreements is therefore essential.

The CRM Model further adopts a modular architecture, establishing mandatory core modules for general principles and dispute resolution procedures, while sector-specific modules (e.g., law enforcement, medical research, finance) apply differentiated regulatory measures based on contextual risk assessments. To balance flexibility with administrative feasibility, the number of modules should remain limited, with only core principles codified in the main modules and technical requirements set out separately in implementation guidelines. This two-tiered governance ensures transparency, adaptability, and interoperability, enabling jurisdictions to operationalize the CRM Model within their own legal and technical infrastructures.

By fostering a shared evaluative architecture and a flexible modular structure, the CRM Model reduces reliance on static adequacy assessments and establishes a dynamic, interoperable, and trust-based framework for cross-border data governance, while ensuring regulatory measures remain proportionate and firmly grounded in contextual risk assessments.

15.5.3 Federated Data Governance

Federated data governance is a distributed model in which entities retain control over their datasets while enabling collaborative analysis or model training through

---

[83] EDPB Recommendations 2021, paras 42–45.

[84] OECD (2019, pp. 23–27).

secure coordination.[85] Rather than aggregating information centrally, each participant processes data locally and shares only model parameters or encrypted outputs. This model complements the CRM Model by supporting cross-border collaborative computation through technologies such as federated learning[86] and secure multiparty computation,[87] without transferring raw data. It preserves institutional autonomy, reinforces data minimization, and promotes interoperability across regulatory systems. Initiatives such as GA4GH[88] and GAIA-X[89] underscore their growing relevance in sensitive sectors such as health and finance.

Nonetheless, significant technical challenges persist, including computational efficiency, standardization, and security resilience. Even under current frameworks such as the GDPR, pseudonymized or aggregated data in federated settings may still constitute a "cross-border transfer," thereby triggering compliance obligations.[90] The CRM Model addresses this by replacing formalistic transfer notions with contextual assessments based on risk and safeguards, permitting only minimal and necessary data movement under robust protections. Embedding such risk-based, context-sensitive criteria into legal frameworks is essential to enable large-scale deployment of federated models without imposing disproportionate regulatory burdens.

15.5.4 Plurilateral Partnerships and the "Tokyo Effect"

The growing complexity of cross-border data governance—driven by tensions among privacy, human rights, national security, digital sovereignty, and regional cooperation—has exceeded the institutional capacity of traditional economic and trade fora, including the WTO and regional trade agreements.[91] Recent initiatives—such as

85 Wider et al. (2024, pp. 10–11).

86 McMahan et al. (2017, pp. 1273–1274).

87 Lindell (2021, pp. 86–88).

88 Global Alliance for Genomics and Health (GA4GH). https://www.ga4gh.org (accessed 8 October 2025).

89 GAIA-X European Association for Data and Cloud AISBL (2022), Gaia-X Architecture Document—22.10 Release, sec. 2.1. https://docs.gaia-x.eu/technical-committee/architecture-document/22.10/overview.

90 EDPB (2025), Guidelines 01/2025 on Pseudonymisation, paras. 22, 45–50, 63–67 (16 Jan. 2025). https://edpb.europa.eu/system/files/2025-01/edpb_guidelines_202501_pseudonymisation_en.pdf; EDPB (2023), Guidelines 05/2021 on the interplay between the application of Article 3 and the provisions on international transfers as per Chapter V of the GDPR, Example 12 (adopted 18 November 2021, last revised 14 February 2023). https://edpb.europa.eu/system/files/2023-02/edpb_guidelines_05-2021_interplay_between_the_application_of_art3-chapter_v_of_the_gdpr_v2_en_0.pdf.

91 Irion et al. (2020), sec. II.

the G7's DFFT framework[92] and the Global CBPR Forum[93]—reflect attempts to explore alternative pathways through plurilateral cooperation. However, these efforts remain fragmented, often shaped by the unilateral preferences of major powers, underscoring the need for a neutral, inclusive forum to address multidimensional challenges beyond trade. Such a framework should foster normative development across divergent models and recognize data not only as an economic asset but also as a digital public good, anchored in proportionality, transparency, accountability, and contextual risk assessment at its core.[94]

To be effective, this forum must incorporate a robust dispute settlement mechanism capable of delivering neutral and predictable decisions on transfer restrictions and exceptions.[95] Objective assessments grounded in shared risk classifications and contextual safeguards would constrain unilateral interpretations, curb regulatory dominance by major powers, and strengthen the rule of law in global data governance.[96]

Within this structure, plurilateral partnerships among middle powers and emerging economies are pivotal.[97] While bottom-up norm-building may face coordination difficulties, geopolitical fragmentation, and disparities in legal infrastructure, these challenges can be mitigated through modular agreements, shared standards, and regulatory capacity-building. Historical precedents such as the EEZ regime under UNCLOS,[98] the CBDR principle in climate governance,[99] and the SDGs[100] illustrate how sustained coalitions and shared problem awareness can gradually overcome asymmetries and institutionalize norms from the bottom up. These examples reinforce the feasibility of norm diffusion driven by smaller coalitions when backed by pragmatic design and mutual trust.

Japan, leveraging its leadership in DFFT, is well-positioned to guide this process by hosting mechanisms such as a secretariat and dispute resolution body. This paper conceptualizes the bottom-up institutionalization of interoperable frameworks in cross-border data governance as the "Tokyo Effect," led by plurilateral partnerships among middle and emerging powers. In contrast to the "Brussels Effect,"[101] where norms are exported unilaterally through regulatory dominance, the Tokyo Effect

---

[92] Ministerial Declaration: The G7 Digital and Tech Ministers' Meeting, Takasaki, Gunma, 30 April 2023, para. 6. https://g7g20-documents.org/database/document/2023-g7-japan-ministerial-meetings-ict-ministers-ministers-language-ministerial-declaration-the-g7-digital-and-tech-ministers-meeting.

[93] Global Cross-Border Privacy Rules Forum (2022), Global CBPR Declaration, 21 April 2022. https://www.globalcbpr.org/wp-content/uploads/Global-CBPR-Declaration-2022.pdf.

[94] UNCTAD (2021, pp. 7–10).

[95] Burri (2017, pp. 130–133).

[96] Viljoen (2021, pp. 637–645).

[97] Dimitropoulos et al. (2025, pp. 6–13).

[98] Beckman and Davenport (2012, pp. 3–5).

[99] Harris (1999, pp. 27–28).

[100] United Nations General Assembly (2015), Transforming our world: the 2030 agenda for sustainable development. G.A. Res. 70/1, 25 September 2015. https://docs.un.org/en/A/RES/70/1.

[101] Bradford (2020, pp. 1–4).

describes bottom-up diffusion of interoperable norms developed through such coalitions. By advancing inclusive normative development, this framework combines legitimacy, enforceability, and interoperability, thereby incentivizing acceptance—even among major powers—and fostering a more coherent, credible, and balanced system of global data governance.

15.6 Conclusion

This paper examined how recent geopolitical transformations have fueled the rise of digital protectionism and exacerbated governance asymmetries, particularly in Asia where competing regulatory frameworks shape cross-border data governance. To address these challenges, it proposes reconstructing operational norms by adopting a risk-based approach as a neutral and interoperable evaluative framework under the guiding principles of DFFT. As a concrete implementation pathway, it introduces the CRM Model, based on contextual risk assessment and the principle of data minimization, and operationalized through modular frameworks, federated data governance architectures, and a dispute settlement mechanism to ensure predictability and accountability. These elements enable tailored rules across sectors, decentralized yet trusted governance, and enforceable remedies for data-related disputes. This structure allows regulatory responses to be calibrated to the nature of data and its use context, avoiding one-size-fits-all obligations. It also enhances interoperability by aligning safeguards with actual risks, facilitating legitimate cross-border data flows without undermining sovereignty or privacy.

Against the backdrop of intensifying competition over data as a strategic resource, unilateral regimes designed by major powers risk deepening global fragmentation. In this context, establishing a new international forum holds strategic value. By emphasizing fairness, transparency, and enforceability, such a framework would institutionalize mechanisms to reconcile the tension between state sovereignty and global interoperability.

Plurilateral, bottom-up normative development offers an effective and neutral pathway toward inclusive, sustainable institutional design. Challenges—coordination burdens, legal diversity, capacity gaps—can be addressed through modular rulemaking, shared standards, and enforceable procedures. Sustained cooperation among smaller coalitions, as with UNCLOS, CBDR, and SDGs, can yield widely accepted norms.

The "Tokyo Effect" describes the diffusion of interoperable norms forged through plurilateral partnerships. Japan, uniquely positioned through its DFFT leadership, is well placed to advance such cooperation. These principles, developed in trusted coalitions, can gain legitimacy and form the foundation of a coherent, inclusive global regime for cross-border data governance.

References

Aaronson SA (2019) What are we talking about when we talk about digital protectionism? World Trade Review, 18(4):541–577. https://doi.org/10.1017/S1474745618000198

Aaronson SA (2023) Building trust in digital trade will require a rethink of trade policy-making. Oxford Review of Economic Policy 39(1):98–109. https://doi.org/10.1093/oxrep/grac046

Alford RP (2011) The self-judging WTO security exception. Utah Law Review 2011(3):697–759. https://scholarship.law.nd.edu/law_faculty_scholarship/330

APEC Policy Support Unit (2025) Study on convergences and divergences of free trade agreements in the APEC region. APEC Secretariat, Singapore. https://www.apec.org/docs/default-source/publications/2025/1/225_psu_study-on-convergences-and-divergences-of-ftas-in-the-apec-region.pdf

Arner DW, Castellano G, Selga ĒK (2022) The transnational data governance problem. Berkeley Technology Law Journal 37(2): 621–700. https://doi.org/10.15779/Z38GF0MX5G

Bacchus J (2020) Might Unmakes Right: The American assault on the rule of law in world trade. CIGI Papers No. 229, Centre for International Governance Innovation. https://www.cigionline.org/publications/might-unmakes-right-american-assault-rule-law-world-trade/

Beckman R, Davenport T (2012) The EEZ regime: Reflections after 30 years. In: Scheiber HN, Kwon MS (eds) Securing the ocean for the next generation: Papers from the Law of the Sea Institute, UC Berkeley–KIOST conference, Seoul, May 2012. Law of the Sea Institute, University of California, Berkeley, 1–36. https://www.law.berkeley.edu/files/Beckman-Davenport-final.pdf

Bradford A (2020) The Brussels Effect: How the European Union Rules the World. Oxford University Press, Oxford. https://doi.org/10.1093/oso/9780190088583.001.0001

Breitbarth P (2021) A risk-based approach to international data transfers. European Data Protection Law Review 7(4):539–549. https://doi.org/10.21552/edpl/2021/4/9

Burri M (2017) The governance of data and data flows in trade agreements. UC Davis Law Rev 51:65–133. https://lawreview.law.ucdavis.edu/archives/51/1/governance-data-and-data-flows-trade-agreements-pitfalls-legal-adaptation

Burri M (2023) Cross-border data flows and privacy in global trade law: Has trade trumped data protection? Oxford Review of Economic Policy 39(1):85–97. https://doi.org/10.1093/oxrep/grac042

Burri M, Vásquez Callo-Müller M, Kugler K (2024) The evolution of digital trade law: Insights from TAPED. World Trade Review 23(2): 190–207. https://doi.org/10.1017/S1474745623000472

Carneiro de Castro M (2024) Multilateralism's fragmentation: The United States' appeal into its own void. Yale Journal of International Affairs Online, April 2024. https://www.yalejournal.org/publications/multilateralisms-fragmentation

Center for Strategic & International Studies (2021) Governing data in the Asia-Pacific. https://www.csis.org/analysis/governing-data-asia-pacific

Christakis T (2024) The "zero risk" fallacy: International data transfers, foreign governments' access to data, and the need for a risk-based approach. Centre for Information Policy Leadership & Cross-Border Data Forum. https://www.informationpolicycentre.com/uploads/5/7/1/0/57104281/the_zero_risk_fallacy_-_t.christakis_feb24.pdf

Cory N (2017) Cross-border data flows: Where are the barriers, and what do they cost? Information Technology & Innovation Foundation, Washington, DC. https://itif.org/publications/2017/05/01/cross-border-data-flows-where-are-barriers-and-what-do-they-cost/

Cory N, Dascoli L (2021) How barriers to cross-border data flows are spreading globally, what they cost, and how to address them. Information Technology & Innovation Foundation (July 19, 2021). https://itif.org/publications/2021/07/19/how-barriers-cross-border-data-flows-are-spreading-globally-what-they-cost/

Dale JG, Aizawa N (2024) "Data Free Flow with Trust": Japan's struggle to integrate democracy and human rights into digital trade policy. Frontiers in Sociology, 9, 1397528. https://doi.org/10.3389/fsoc.2024.1397528

Deane F, Woolmer E, Cao S, Tranter K (2024) Trade in the digital age: Agreements to mitigate fragmentation. Asian Journal of International Law 14(1):154–179. https://doi.org/10.1017/S204425132300036X

Dimitropoulos G, Chen RC, Chaisse J (2025) Plurilateralism: A new form of international economic ordering? The Journal of World Investment & Trade 26(1–2):1–30. https://doi.org/10.1163/22119000-12340355

European Risk Forum (2020) Highlights note 12: Proportionality principle and the management of risk. Brussels: ERF. https://www.eriforum.eu/uploads/2/5/7/1/25710097/erif_highlights_12_-_proportionality_principle.pdf

Freedom House (2025) Data localization: A global threat to human rights online. Freedom House, 8 April 2025. https://freedomhouse.org/article/data-localization-global-threat-human-rights-online

Gerards J (2013) How to improve the necessity test of the European Court of Human Rights. International Journal of Constitutional Law 11(2):466–475. https://academic.oup.com/icon/article/11/2/466/698871

Greenleaf G (2009) Five years of the APEC privacy framework: Failure or promise? Computer Law & Security Review 25(1):28–43. https://doi.org/10.1016/j.clsr.2008.12.002

Harris PG (1999) Common but differentiated responsibility: The Kyoto Protocol and United States policy. NYU Environmental Law Journal 7:27–71. https://www.nyuelj.org/wp-content/uploads/2019/07/Harris_Common_But_DIfferentiated_Responsibility.pdf

Hrynkiv O, Delimatsis P (2020) Security exceptions under the GATS: A legal commentary on Article XIV bis GATS. TILEC Discussion Paper No. 2020–026, Tilburg University, 1–25. https://research.tilburguniversity.edu/en/publications/security-exceptions-under-the-gats-a-legal-commentary-on-article-

Hung HT (2025) Exploring China's cyber sovereignty concept and artificial intelligence governance model: a machine learning approach. Journal of Computational Social Science 8, Article 24, 1–31. https://doi.org/10.1007/s42001-024-00346-8

Irion K, Kaminski ME, Yakovleva S (2020) Privacy peg, trade hole: Why we (still) shouldn't put data privacy in trade law. University of Chicago Law Review Online,7 Oct 2020. https://lawreview.uchicago.edu/online-archive/privacy-peg-trade-hole-why-we-still-shouldnt-put-data-privacy-trade-law

Kuner C (2017) Reality and illusion in EU data transfer regulation post Schrems. German Law Journal 18:881–918. https://germanlawjournal.com/wp-content/uploads/04_Vol_18_No_04_Kuner.pdf

Kuzio J, Ahmadi M, Kim KC, Wang YF, Bullock J, Migaud MR (2022) Building better global data governance. Data & Policy 4: e25. https://doi.org/10.1017/dap.2022.17

Lindell Y (2021) Secure multiparty computation. Communications of the ACM 64(1):86–96. https://doi.org/10.1145/3387108

López González J, Casalini F, Porras J (2022) A preliminary mapping of data localisation measures. OECD Trade Policy Papers No. 262, OECD Publishing, Paris, 1–18. https://doi.org/10.1787/c5ca3fed-en

McMahan HB, Moore E, Ramage D, Hampson S, y Arcas BA (2017) Communication-efficient learning of deep networks from decentralized data. In: Proceedings of the 20th International Conference on Artificial Intelligence and Statistics (AISTATS 2017), JMLR: W&CP 54:1273–1282. https://proceedings.mlr.press/v54/mcmahan17a.html

Meltzer JP (2015) The Internet, cross-border data flows and international trade. Asia Pac Policy Stud 2(1):90–102. https://doi.org/10.1002/app5.60

Mishra N (2024) International Trade Law and Global Data Governance: Aligning Perspectives and Practices. Hart Publishing, Oxford

Naef T (2023) Data Protection without Digital Protectionism: The Right to Protection of Personal Data and Data Transfers in EU Law and International Trade Law. European Yearbook of International Economic Law Monographs. Springer, Cham. https://doi.org/10.1007/978-3-031-19893-9

OECD (2013), The OECD Privacy Guidelines: Revised 2013. OECD Publishing, Paris. https://www.oecd.org/sti/ieconomy/privacy.htm

OECD (2019) Enhancing access to and sharing of data: Reconciling risks and benefits for data re-use across societies. OECD Publishing, Paris. https://doi.org/10.1787/276aaca8-en

OECD (2023) Moving forward on Data Free Flow with Trust. OECD Publishing, Paris. https://doi.org/10.1787/1afab147-en

United Nations Conference on Trade and Development (UNCTAD) (2021) Digital Economy Report 2021: Cross-border Data Flows and Development – For Whom the Data Flow. United Nations, Geneva. https://unctad.org/system/files/official-document/der2021_en.pdf

United Nations Development Programme (2021) Enabling cross-border data flow: ASEAN and beyond. United Nations Development Programme, Singapore. https://www.undp.org/sites/g/files/zskgke326/files/2021-10/enabling-cross-border-data-flow-asean-and-beyond-report.pdf

Viljoen S (2021) A Relational Theory of Data Governance. Yale Law Journal 131:573–654. https://www.yalelawjournal.org/feature/a-relational-theory-of-data-governance

Voss WG (2020) Cross-border data flows, the GDPR, and data governance. Washington International Law Journal 29:485–522. https://digitalcommons.law.uw.edu/wilj/vol29/iss3/7

Wider A, Jarmul K, Akhtar A (2024) Towards automating federated data governance. In: Proceedings of the 2024 IEEE International Conference on Web Services (ICWS), Shenzhen, 10–19. https://doi.org/10.1109/ICWS62655.2024.00019

WTO (1998) Work programme on electronic commerce (WT/L/274, 30 September 1998). Geneva: WTO. https://docs.wto.org/dol2fe/Pages/SS/directdoc.aspx?filename=q:/WT/L/274.pdf

WTO (2017) Joint statement on electronic commerce (WT/MIN(17)/60, 13 December 2017). Geneva: WTO. https://docs.wto.org/dol2fe/Pages/SS/directdoc.aspx?filename=q:/WT/MIN17/60.pdf

WTO (n.d.) Information on the agreement on e-commerce. Geneva: WTO. https://www.wto.org/english/tratop_e/ecom_e/information_on_agreement_ecom.pdf (accessed 8 October 2025)

Yakovleva S (2024) Governing Cross-Border Data Flows: Reconciling EU Data Protection and International Trade Law. Oxford University Press, Oxford

Zhang C (2024) China's privacy protection strategy and its geopolitical implications. Asian Review of Political Economy 3(1):1–17. https://doi.org/10.1007/s44216-024-00028-2

Part IV
Emerging Regulatory Challenges: AI, Health, and Finance

Chapter 16
The Case for the Development of an Asian Regional AI Framework—Expanding the Discussion on "Sovereign AI" to a Regional Level

Sungjin Kang

Abstract Since the introduction of generative AI, the debate for sovereign AI has been growing for the last decade. At the same time, there is a need for an Asian regional framework for artificial intelligence (AI) governance, reframing the conversation around "sovereign AI" to emphasize its importance in a broader, supranational context. There are many Digital Trade Agreements (DTAs) with provisions related to AI infrastructure. However, they are not sufficient to handle the complex regulatory issues that come with generative AI. As a result, there is a growing need for a comprehensive regional accord—one that would harmonize regulatory standards, support sustainable infrastructure development, and encourage shared investment in AI architecture, workforce training, and cybersecurity. In order to realize the regional AI framework, there need to be several provisions including establishing joint funding for local language data repositories, designing governance standards that reflect regional needs, and fostering AI ecosystems that are both competitive and culturally sensitive. Despite the significant challenges posed by Asia's varied technological capabilities and regulatory frameworks, strategic regional collaboration can make the most of the unique strengths each nation brings to the table. Ultimately, such a framework would not just further technological self-determination and balance national sovereignty with regional integration—it would also strengthen Asia's position as a global leader in ethical and responsible AI innovation.

Keywords Sovereign AI · AI tech stacks · Digital trade agreements (DTAs) · Regional framework · Cross-border data flows · Green AI

Foreign Legal Counsel, Kim & Chang; PhD, Korea University. The views and arguments expressed in this paper do not reflect Kim & Chang's official positions. All errors and mistakes are attributed to the author only. The author greatly appreciates the helpful comments and suggestions by Prof. Junji Nakagawa, Prof. Thibault Schrepel and Prof. Rodrigo Polanco.

S. Kang (✉)
Kim & Chang, Seoul, South Korea
e-mail: kangsj1977@gmail.com

J. Nakagawa et al. (eds.), *Geopolitical Risks and Geoeconomics in International Economic Law*, Economics, Law, and Institutions in Asia Pacific,
https://doi.org/10.1007/978-981-95-6996-0_16

16.1 Introduction

Since the release of ChatGPT in 2022, AI systems have become much closer to our daily lives. The AI-based translation systems are quickly replacing the need for human translators, and the spread of generative AI also benefits many industry sectors, including design, technical writing, business writing, etc.

At the same time, the emergence of commercial large language model (LLM) AI systems, such as ChatGPT, DeepSeek, and Google Gemini, makes governments concerned about cybersecurity, privacy, and cultural identity. In this regard, the term "Sovereign AI" refers to a nation's capabilities to produce artificial intelligence using its own infrastructure, data, workforce, and business networks, which is gaining increasing attention.[1] By developing a sovereign AI system, a country may gain a significant military advantage over its rivals. For example, it can be used to develop new technologies and products that could boost the economy. In addition, sovereign AI could be used to improve national security by, for example, detecting and preventing cyberattacks.

So far, the race for sovereign AI has been mostly based on the individual country level, with some initiatives that include cooperation in AI, including the EU-Japan Digital Partnership. However, there are few multilateral and regional frameworks for cooperation on AI development, still in a nascent stage with non-binding principles and guidelines.

This paper will discuss the need and feasibility of developing legal instruments for an Asian regional AI framework. The author will begin by surveying the ongoing discussion on sovereign AI, based on the classification of "AI tech stacks" consisting of 3 layers (AI model, AI infrastructure, and AI applications). (Part II) Then the author will review the existing digital trade agreements and limitations (Part III). The author will argue for the case for the development of a legal instrument on Asian regional AI development with a view to facilitating sovereign AI systems in Asia (Part IV). The author is of the view that the development of such regional agreements may be based on the existing digital trade agreements (DTAs), with additional provisions to address new situations resulting from the generative AI models. In this regard, the author is of the view that discussion for a regional AI framework will especially benefit Asian countries, by combining their strengths in different levels of AI tech stacks from hardware and software points of view.

[1] Kristian McCann, *What Is Sovereign AI and Why Is It Gaining Traction?* (AI Magazine, 27 October 2024), https://aimagazine.com/articles/what-is-sovereign-ai-and-why-is-it-gaining-traction (Accessed on 13 August 2025).

16.2 Discussions on Sovereign AI

16.2.1 Prologue—Why "Sovereign AI" Instead of "Independent AI"?

States use the term "sovereign AI" rather than "independent AI" when discussing the development of artificial intelligence at the state level because "sovereign" more accurately encapsulates the comprehensive control, authority, and strategic national interests they aim to assert over this transformative technology. "Sovereign AI" refers to a government's or organization's control over AI technologies and associated data. This often includes how the AI technologies are deployed and operated, including the hardware and software infrastructure used to build and operate the AI technologies, as well as the policies and personnel used to operate the AI technologies and protect the data.[2]

"Sovereign AI" emphasizes the development and use of AI in a way that reflects a nation's specific cultural context, languages, societal values, and national priorities.[3] This may include mitigating biases that might be present in commercial AI models trained on data from other regions and ensuring AI serves the public interest as defined by the nation.[4] This goes beyond mere technical independence to ensuring AI is a tool that reinforces national identity and strategic objectives.[5]

16.2.2 Beginning of the Discussion—"AI Tech Stacks"

Before discussing the sovereign AI, it is necessary to understand that there are some "tech stacks" or "layers" surrounding the AI systems. An AI stack is a collection of technologies, frameworks, and infrastructure components that facilitate using artificial intelligence (AI) systems.[6] The AI tech stack consists of interconnected layers that ensure system effectiveness and flexibility.[7]

---

[2] Alan Zeichick, *What Is Sovereign AI?* (Oracle Cloud, 14 April 2025), https://www.oracle.com/artificial-intelligence/sovereign-ai/ (Accessed on 1 June 2025).

[3] Johe Letzing, *What is "sovereign AI" and why is the concept so appealing (and fraught)?* (World Economic Forum, 13 November 2024), https://www.weforum.org/stories/2024/11/what-is-sovereign-ai-and-why-is-the-concept-so-appealing-and-fraught/#:~:text=An%20example%3A%20a%20place%20using, those%20values%20as%20a%20threat; (Accessed on 1 June 2025).

[4] *The Rise of Sovereign AI: National Strategies, Global Implications* (Alphanome AI, 27 April 2025), https://www.alphanome.ai/post/the-rise-of-sovereign-ai-national-strategies-global-implications (Accessed on 1 June 2025).

[5] See Footnote 1.

[6] Cole Stiker, *What is an AI stack?* (IBM), https://www.ibm.com/think/topics/ai-stack (Accessed on 1 June 2025).

[7] Lena Tyson, *Navigating the AI Tech Stack: An In-Depth Guide*, https://medium.com/@lenaztyson/navigating-the-ai-tech-stack-an-in-depth-guide-2f722ac88703 (Accessed on 1 June 2025).

In discussions on AI tech stacks, experts present that there are 3 interlinked layers: the application layer, the model layer, and the infrastructure layer. The application layer refers to the manifestation of user experience, encapsulating elements from web applications to REST APIs that manage data flow between client-side and server-side environments. The model layer refers to language models and other machine learning tools, which constitute the "engine room" for decision-making and data processing. Lastly, the infrastructure layer refers to hardware and software components used for machine training and inference.[8]

The discussions on sovereign AI also use the 3-layer AI stack, as many governments publish their strategies to build their own sovereign AI models and sovereign AI infrastructure, using those 3-layer AI stacks.[9] In particular, the governments may have the biggest influence by making a framework for AI infrastructure development, through strategic investment and industrial policy on AI.

16.2.3 How "Sovereign" an AI Should Be?

However, one must admit that achieving true sovereignty in AI remains almost impossible, because of the dependence of key AI technologies and advanced semiconductors on foreign countries, namely the United States, Taiwan, and/or South Korea. For example, the UAE's Falcon model was trained on Amazon Web Services (US) infrastructure.[10] In addition, the most important AI hardware, advanced AI chips, are designed by Nvidia (US), and manufactured by TSMC (Taiwan), using High Bandwidth Memory (HBM) chips manufactured by SK Hynix (South Korea) and Micron (US).

Nevertheless, governments pursuing sovereign AI can influence longer-term outcomes in positive and negative ways. For example, sovereign AI could establish countries as attractive hubs for AI-focused capital and talent that can help them compete in the global AI arena. In addition, sovereign AI models could serve as high-profile examples of how to develop an LLM ethically, and sovereign AI infrastructure might support greater and more equitable resource access to AI. Furthermore, the emphasis on open-source development could promote more accessibility and innovation in AI technologies.[11] However, the pursuit of sovereign AI may result in a form of technological fragmentation that hinders international collaboration and exacerbates

---

[8] Rajeev Sharma, *AI Tech Stack: A Complete Guide*, (Markovate, 25 March 2025), https://markovate.com/blog/ai-tech-stack/ (Accessed on 1 June 2025).

[9] Pablo Chavez, *Sovereign AI in a Hybrid World: National Strategies and Policy Responses* (Lawfare Media, 7 November 2024), https://www.lawfaremedia.org/article/sovereign-ai-in-a-hybrid-world--national-strategies-and-policy-responses (Accessed on 1 June 2025).

[10] See Chavez (2024).

[11] See Chavez (2024).

geopolitical tensions, promotes censorship and propaganda, and threatens human rights, including privacy and freedom of expression.[12]

In any case, it is important to admit that 100% sovereign AI is impossible without foreign components and technologies. Instead, the pursuit of sovereign AI should not leave such foreign companies out of the sovereign AI strategy, and accept them as crucial partners, while avoiding over-reliance on 1 or 2 private sector partners.

In this regard, it may be more reasonable to argue that efforts to build AI models and AI infrastructures on the individual government level, private sector level, and the regional/multilateral level must go hand in hand, and policymakers must understand that such efforts should be viewed as "complementary" rather than "competing." Moreover, governments and international organizations must also coordinate their efforts and rules for AI regulation. In this regard, the author considers that it is useful and important to consider the existing digital trade agreements (DTAs) and discuss the room for further developments at the Asian regional level in the next parts.

16.3 The Existing Digital Trade Agreements and Their Limitations in Development

16.3.1 DTAs with Explicit Reference to AI[13]

One may consider whether the existing digital trade agreements (DTAs) can catch up with the rapid development of AI technologies. The existing DTAs have been working to address the issues that arise from the rise of data-driven digital trade. However, the author considers that it is time to consider a new version of DTA with the development of "regional" sovereign AI tech stacks in mind. The regional sovereign AI may require provisions related to the joint development of the three tech stacks.

The Digital Economy Partnership Agreement (DEPA),[14] as well as the Australia-Singapore Digital Economy Agreement (ASDEA),[15] were two of the first agreements with specific provisions on AI governance. First, Module 8 of the DEPA includes provisions on "emerging trends and technologies," which comprise artificial intelligence (AI) governance. In these agreements, the parties recognized the importance of AI in the digital economy, and the development of an "ethical and governance framework for the trusted, safe and responsible use of AI technologies."[16] In particular, the parties agreed to promote "the adoption of ethical and governance frameworks

[12] See Chavez (2024).

[13] Among the various agreements with explicit reference to AI, the author chose a few agreements as examples.

[14] Digital Economy Partnership Agreement (DEPA), signed on June 12, 2020.

[15] Australia-Singapore Digital Economy Agreement (ASDEA), signed on Aug. 6, 2020.

[16] See Article 8.2(1) and (2) DEPA; Annex A, art 31(1) and (2) ASDEA.

that support the trusted, safe and responsible use of AI technologies (AI Governance Frameworks),"[17,18] considering internationally recognized principles or guidelines, including explainability, fairness, and human-centered values.[19] However, the DEPA provides no further details on AI governance and therefore, DEPA members introduced their own AI governance models and AI bills. Chile has introduced an AI bill in 2024, pending approval by the Chilean parliament,[20] while Singapore also introduced a model AI governance framework for generative AI.[21] In addition, New Zealand also introduced AI framework for use by public service.[22]

In the case of the ASDEA, Australia adopted an AI Ethics Framework,[23] but it did not adopt a comprehensive AI governance framework like Singapore.[24] However, the governments of Australia and Singapore signed an MOU on cooperation on AI to implement the principles under the ASDEA.[25] The governments identified AI development and deployment, sharing workforce and talent, ethics, and governance as priority areas for collaboration.[26] Then the two governments also agreed to hold joint strategic dialogues to identify collaborative opportunities in AI technology, exchange information about best practices, and catalyze investment and trade opportunities in AI technologies.[27] Based on the ASDEA and the MOU on AI, the author anticipates that the DEPA parties will also sign a similar MOU to provide the framework for collaboration among the current and future parties.

Similarly, the Korea-Singapore Digital Partnership Agreement (KSDPA)[28] has provisions explicitly related to AI similar to the DEPA and ASDEA. Annex A, Article 14.28(1) of the KSDPA provides that the governments of South Korea and Singapore recognize that "the use and adoption of Artificial Intelligence ("AI") technologies are

[17] See Article 8.2(3) DEPA.

[18] See Annex A, Article 31.1 ASDEA.

[19] See Article 8.4 DEPA.

[20] Proyecto de Ley que regula los sistemas de IA, https://www.minciencia.gob.cl/areas/inteligencia-artificial/Inteligencia-Artificial/Proyecto-Ley-regula-sistemas-IA/ Accessed on 13 August 2025.

[21] Singapore's Model AI Governance Framework for Generative AI (MGF-Gen AI). https://aiverifyfoundation.sg/wp-content/uploads/2024/05/Model-AI-Governance-Framework-for-Generative-AI-May-2024-1-1.pdf. Accessed 13 August 2025.

[22] New Zealand government releases AI framework for use by public service (IAEAI News). https://iaeai.org/tpost/vgu1nvluh1-new-zealand-government-releases-ai-frame. Accessed 13 August 2025.

[23] Australia's Artificial Intelligence Ethics Framework < https://www.industry.gov.au/data-and-publications/australias-artificial-intelligence-ethics-framework/australias-ai-ethics-principles > Accessed on 11 July 2022.

[24] Gilbert & Tobin (2022) AI Governance within Your Organization. https://www.gtlaw.com.au/insights/heres-great-toolkit-artificial-intelligence-ai-governance-within-your-organisation, Accessed on 11 July 2022.

[25] Memorandum of Understanding Between the Government of Australia and the Government of the Republic of Singapore on Cooperation on Artificial Intelligence (AUS MOU on AI), signed on 23 March 2020.

[26] See paragraph VI AUS MOU on AI.

[27] See paragraph V AUS MOU on AI.

[28] Korea-Singapore Digital Partnership Agreement (KSDPA), entered into force on 13 January 2023.

becoming increasingly important within a digital economy offering significant social and economic benefits to natural persons and enterprises." The parties also recognized the importance of "developing ethical governance frameworks for the trusted, safe and responsible use of AI technologies that will help realize the benefits of AI," and the importance of aligning with international standards.[29] In order to achieve such benefits, the parties agreed (1) to collaborate on and promote the development and adoption of frameworks that support the trusted, safe, and responsible use of AI technologies ("AI Governance Frameworks"); (2) considering internationally recognized principles or guidelines in developing AI Governance Frameworks; and (3) cooperation through dialogues and sharing each party's experience on regulation, policies and initiatives related to the use and adoption of AI technologies.[30]

In addition, the Korean Ministry of Science and ICT signed an MOU with Singapore's Ministry of Communication and Information to promote practical collaboration and the development of reasonable use of AI across the government.[31] The purpose of the MOU is to "1) Encourage the sharing of best practices among the AI ecosystem at the government, institutional, academic, and industry levels of the participants; 2) Facilitate increased access to AI technology, talent, and markets; 3) Build linkages between research and industry activities to support the commercialization of AI applications; and 4) Foster a human-centered approach to AI, including by developing and adopting governance and regulatory frameworks for the development and use of safe, trustworthy, and responsible AI technologies."[32] The MOU provides that the forms of cooperation include facilitation of information and best practice exchange, development of R&D collaboration, cooperation in international fora on AI, etc.[33] Then, the MOU provides that the areas of cooperation include AI ethics and governance, AI startups, AI talent development and attraction, establishment of multi-site test-beds for new innovations, joint projects for sectoral research in AI and data, etc.[34]

In addition, Article 12.24 of Australia—United Arab Emirates Comprehensive Economic Partnership Agreement (Australia—UAE CEPA)[35] provides for similar rules as the agreements described above. The parties agreed to cooperate with their respective relevant policies, through 1) sharing research and industry practices related to AI technologies and their applications and governance; 2) promoting and

---

[29] See Annex A, Article 14.28(2) KSDPA.

[30] See Annex A, Article 14.28(3) KSDPA.

[31] Memorandum of Understanding Between the Ministry of Science and ICT of the Republic of Korea and Ministry of Communications and Information of the Government of Singapore on Cooperation on Artificial Intelligence (KS MOU on AI), signed on 6 December 2022.

[32] See Article 2 KS MOU on AI.

[33] See Article 3(1) KS MOU on AI.

[34] See Article 3(2) KS MOU on AI.

[35] Australia-UAE Comprehensive Economic Partnership Agreement (AUCEPA), entered into force on 1 October 2025.

sustaining the safe and responsible development, deployment and use of AI technologies by businesses and across the community; and 3) encouraging commercialization opportunities and collaboration between researchers, academics and industry.[36]

The Parties also recognized the importance of developing governance and regulatory frameworks for the trusted, safe, and responsible use of AI technologies to realize the benefits of AI and mitigate risks. In view of the cross-border nature of the digital economy, the Parties further acknowledge the benefits of ensuring that such frameworks are internationally aligned as far as possible.[37] The Parties then agreed to 1) collaborate on and promote the development and adoption of frameworks that support the trusted, safe, and responsible use of AI technologies ("AI Governance Frameworks"), through relevant regional and international fora; and 2) take into consideration internationally recognized standards, principles, or guidelines when developing such AI Governance Frameworks.

16.3.2 DTA Provisions Related to AI Infrastructure

Based on the previously discussed 3-layer AI tech stack, the author will discuss the provisions under the existing DTAs related to the AI infrastructures, including cross-border transfer and data localization. The existing DTAs provide mostly for rules governing software and data transfer, enabling the AI systems, while they do not often provide for rules governing hardware infrastructures.

16.3.2.1 Cross-Border Transfer of Information by Electronic Means

The DEPA, the ASDEA, and several other regional digital trade agreements recognize that "each Party may have its own regulatory requirements concerning the transfer of information by electronic means."[38] On the other hand, the parties may take measures inconsistent with the preceding paragraph, if it is "necessary to achieve a legitimate public policy objective."[39] However, even in such cases, the parties should not apply the measures in a manner constituting a means of arbitrary or unjustifiable discrimination or a disguised restriction on trade; and they should not impose restrictions on cross-border transfers of information "greater than are necessary to achieve the

[36] See Article 12.24(1) AUCEPA.

[37] See Article 12.24(2) AUCEPA.

[38] Comprehensive and Progressive Agreement for Trans-Pacific Partnership (CPTPP), entered into force on December 30, 2018, Article 14.11(1); Regional Comprehensive Economic Partnership, entered into force on 1 January 2022. Article 12.15(1); Annex A, Article 23(1) ASDEA; Article 14.10(1) AUKFTA.

[39] Agreement between the United States of America, the United Mexican States, and Canada (USMCA), signed on Dec.10, 2019, Article 19.11(2); Article 14.11(3) CPTPP; See Article 12.15(3)(a) RCEP; Agreement Between the United States of America and Japan Concerning Digital Trade (USJDTA), entered into force on 1 January 2020, Article 11.2; Article 14.10(3) AUKFTA.

objective."[40] The drafting of this provision is similar to Article XX of the GATT, allowing a two-tier analysis.

On the other hand, Korea-EU Digital Trade Agreement[41] provides, "The Parties are committed to ensuring cross-border transfer of data to facilitate digital trade, while recognizing that each Party may have its own regulatory requirements in that regard,"[42] by prohibiting measures including data localization, except for measures to achieve legitimate public policy objectives.[43]

16.3.2.2 Personal Information Protection

The DEPA defines "personal information" as "information, including data, about an identified or identifiable natural person."[44] In most RTAs, the parties are required to adopt or maintain a legal framework to ensure the protection of personal information.[45] They also recognize that the parties may take different legal approaches in their domestic laws on personal information. Therefore, the parties are required to take into account "international standards, principles, guidelines and criteria of relevant international organizations or bodies."[46] In addition, the DEPA parties must take into account key principles to follow, including "limitation on collection; choice; data quality; purpose specification; use limitation; security safeguards; transparency; individual participation; and accountability"[47] to develop a legal framework for personal information protection. In addition, the DEPA and ASDEA provide for non-discriminatory practices to protect users from violations occurring in their jurisdictions.[48]

The DEPA also has provisions on "data protection trust marks." First, the DEPA parties are to encourage the adoption of data protection trust marks by businesses to

---

[40] See Article 19.11(2)(a) and (b) USMCA; Article 14.11(3) (a) and (b) CPTPP; Article 12.15(3)(a) RCEP; Article 11.2(a) and (b) USJDPA; Annex A, Article 23(3) ASDEA; Article 14.10(3)(a) and (b) AUKFTA.

[41] Agreement on Digital Trade between the European Union and the Republic of Korea (K-EU DTA), agreed in principle in March 2025.

[42] See Article 5(1) K-EU DTA.

[43] See Article 5(2) and 5(3) K-EU DTA.

[44] See Article 1.3 DEPA; Article 14.1 CPTPP; Article 19.1 USMCA; Article 1(dd) USJDPA; Article 14.1 AUKFTA. On the other hand, Article 4(q) of K-EU DTA defines "personal data" as "any information relating to an identified or identifiable natural person, including personal credit data."

[45] See Article 4.2(2) DEPA; Korea-Vietnam Free Trade Agreement (VKFTA), entered into force on 1 December 2015, Article 10.6(1), first sentence; Article 14.8(1) CPTPP; Article 19.8(1) USMCA; Article 15(1) USJDPA; Article 12.8(1) RCEP; Article 6.2 K-EU DTA.

[46] See Article 4.2(2), second sentence DEPA; Article 10.6(1), second sentence KVFTA; Article 19.8(2) USMCA; Article 12.8(2) RCEP; Article 14.12(2) AUKFTA.

[47] See Article 4.2(3) DEPA; Article 19.8(3), first sentence USMCA; Annex A, Article 17(3) ASDEA; Article 14.12(2) AUKFTA.

[48] See Article 4.2(4) DEPA; Article 19.8(4) USMCA; Annex A, Article 17(4) ASDEA; Article 14.12(3) AUKFTA.

help verify conformance to personal data protection standards and best practices.[49] The DEPA parties agreed to exchange information on and share experiences on the use of such data protection trust marks, and they endeavor to mutually recognize the other Parties' data protection trust marks as a valid mechanism to facilitate cross-border information transfers.[50] This is a unique provision under the DEPA.

The DEPA and the ASDEA provide for encouraging the development of interoperability/compatibility mechanisms.[51] At the same time, the parties are required to publish information on the personal information protection for users of electronic commerce, including the ways for individuals to pursue remedies and for businesses to comply with legal requirements.[52] Juridical persons/enterprises are also "encouraged" to publish their privacy policies.[53] In addition, as cross-border data flow becomes an important issue, some RTAs also recognize the necessity to take adequate level of safeguards for cross-border data transfers.[54] In addition, the ASDEA recognizes that the APEC Cross-Border Privacy Rules ("CBPR") are a valid mechanism to facilitate cross-border information transfers,[55] and they agreed to endeavor to jointly promote the CBPR system.[56] Further, the Office of the Australian Information Commissioner and the Personal Data Protection Commission of the Republic of Singapore signed an MOU on personal data protection cooperation.[57] The MOU provides for the parties' intention to cooperate through sharing experience, expertise, intelligence, and information on best practice in relation to the protection of personal information.[58] However, the MOU does not provide for the exchange of personal information within its scope of collaboration.[59]

16.3.2.3 Data Localization

The CPTPP, the DEPA, the ASDEA, and the RCEP provide that "each Party may have its own [measures/regulatory requirements] regarding the use of computing facilities, including requirements that seek to ensure the security and confidentiality

---

[49] See Article 4.2(8) DEPA.

[50] See Article 4.2(9) and (10) DEPA.

[51] See Article 4.2(6) DEPA; Article 19.8(6) USMCA; Article 15(3) USJDPA; Annex A, Article 17(7) ASDEA; Article 14.12(6) AUKFTA.

[52] See Article 14.8(4) CPTPP; Article 19.8(5) USMCA; Article 15(2) USJDPA; Article 14.12(4) AUKFTA.

[53] See Article 12.8(4) RCEP; Annex A, Article 17(6) ASDEA; Article 14.12(5) AUKFTA.

[54] See Article 10.6(2) KVFTA.

[55] See Annex A, Article 17(8) ASDEA.

[56] See Annex A, Article 17(9) ASDEA.

[57] Memorandum of Understanding between the Office of the Australian Information Commissioner and the Personal Data Protection Commission of Singapore on Cooperation in Personal Data Protection (AUS MOU on Personal Data Protection), signed on 20 March 2020.

[58] See paragraph 2, AUS MOU on Personal Data Protection.

[59] See paragraph 2, AUS MOU on Personal Data Protection.

of communications."[60] They further provide that neither party requires a person from the other party "to use or locate computing facilities in that Party's territory as a condition for conducting business in that territory."[61] Then, they provide for an exception for legitimate public policy, while they should not apply the measures in a manner constituting a means of arbitrary or unjustifiable discrimination or a disguised restriction on trade[62]; and they should not impose restrictions on cross-border transfers of information "greater than are necessary to achieve the objective."[63]

In addition, the RCEP also recognizes essential security exceptions on data localization.[64] Such exceptions in the CPTPP, the DEPA, the ASDEA, and the RCEP may stem from objections raised by some countries that have domestic laws prohibiting the transfer of geographic information or other sensitive information from their territory.[65]

In contrast, most of the US-led RTAs required the parties not to adopt data localization measures,[66] while the USJDPA provided for exceptions in financial service suppliers.[67] However, the U.S. withdrew proposals made in 2019 by the Trump administration insisting that WTO e-commerce rules allow free cross-border data flows and prohibit national requirements for data localization and reviews of software source code.[68] As a result, the US also backed off from digital trade discussions under the Indo-Pacific Economic Framework (IPEF).[69] On the other hand, K-EU DTA explicitly prohibits data localization and other regulatory requirements to require local data processing,[70] except for the measures to achieve legitimate public policy objectives.[71]

---

[60] See Article 14.13(1) CPTPP; Article 12.14(1) RCEP; Annex A, Article 24(1) ASDEA; Article 14.11(1) AUKFTA.

[61] See Article 14.13(2) CPTPP; Article 4.4(2) DEPA; Annex A, Article 24(2) ASDEA; Article 14.11(2) AUKFTA.

[62] See Article 14.13(3) CPTPP; Article 12.14(3)(a) RCEP; Annex A, Article 24(3) ASDEA; Article 14.11(3) AUKFTA.

[63] See Article 14.13(3) CPTPP; Article 14.11(3) AUKFTA.

[64] See Article 12.14(3)(b) RCEP.

[65] For example, Korean law still prohibits cross-border transfer of digital geographical information to servers located abroad, which is still subject to US criticism in annual National Trade Estimate reports by the USTR. USTR, 2024 National Trade Estimate Report on Foreign Trade Barriers (April 2025), p. 253.

[66] See Article 19.12 USMCA; Article 14.13(2) CPTPP; Article 12.1 USJDPA; Article 12.14(2) RCEP.

[67] See Articles 12.2 and 13 USJDPA.

[68] US drops digital trade demands at WTO to allow room for stronger tech regulation (Reuters, 26 October 2023).

[69] U.S. suspends Indo-Pacific talks on key aspects of digital trade -lawmakers (Reuters, 3 November 2023).

[70] See Article 5(2)(b), (c), (d) K-EU DTA.

[71] See Article 5(3) K-EU DTA.

16.3.2.4 The Limits of Existing DTAs

The author is of the view that existing Digital Trade Agreements (DTAs) offer a framework covering only basic principles for cooperation in artificial intelligence (AI) and related domains. While these agreements touch upon crucial areas such as data transfer, the protection of personal data, and data localization, their scope remains largely introductory. They provide foundational principles and guidelines. However, in their current form, they lack the comprehensive detail and specificity required to effectively govern international collaboration and address the complex challenges and nuances presented by the rapidly evolving AI landscape.

Crucially, the author emphasizes that DTAs should reflect the accelerating pace of AI technological advancement. This unprecedented speed of development outstrips the capacity of the current, basic DTA provisions to effectively guide and support international cooperation in this dynamic field. Consequently, there is an urgent call to consider and implement more "advanced" and "specific" legal and cooperative provisions. The timing is critical; now is deemed the opportune moment to establish these detailed guidelines specifically designed to facilitate and harmonize the collective effort among Asian countries toward developing their respective sovereign AI capabilities in a coordinated manner.

16.4 Proposal for Asian Regional AI Agreement

16.4.1 Current Status of Sovereign AI Development in Asia

Asia has become the world's leading region for digital connectivity based on Internet and smartphone user numbers. This digital foundation potentially enables the development of "sovereign AI" in Asia with key elements including: (1) advanced digital infrastructure with data centers, high-speed networks, and cloud platforms; (2) significant investment in AI development, as seen with Deepseek (China) and Clova X (Korea); (3) government policies and legal frameworks, including Singapore's National AI Strategy and Korea's "Framework Act on the Development of Artificial Intelligence and the Establishment of Foundation for Reliability" (referred to as the "AI Basic Act")[72]; and (4) diverse industrial capabilities from basic IT manufacturing to advanced semiconductor production and specialized technical expertise.[73]

These developments highlight the need for a coordinated framework for regional cooperation in AI research, development, and deployment across Asia. The increasing number of Digital Trade Agreements (DTAs) and Memoranda

---

[72] Basic Act for Development of Artificial Intelligence and Building Trust, etc., Act No. 20676, adopted on 21 January 21, expected to enter into force on 22 January 2026.

[73] OECD, National AI policies & strategies, https://oecd.ai/en/dashboards/overview (Accessed on 10 July 2025).

of Understanding (MOUs) between Asian countries creates a need for consistent rules governing AI. While existing regional agreements like the Comprehensive and Progressive Agreement for Trans-Pacific Partnership (CPTPP) and the Digital Economy Partnership Agreement (DEPA) address AI governance, cross-border data transfer, data protection, and data localization, these provisions are not comprehensive enough.

In this regard, the author proposes some provisions that may be useful to be included in the future regional agreements governing regional cooperation and joint development of "Asian regional AI systems" in the future. The author is of the view that additional regulatory elements should be included in any regional AI agreement in Asia, though the exact content of these elements requires further examination, keeping abreast with the technological and regulatory developments.

16.4.2 Proposal for Asian Regional AI Framework

16.4.2.1 Purpose and Objectives

The objective of the regional-level artificial intelligence (AI) agreement is not to replace existing or prospective domestic legislation, nor to override current international agreements. Rather, this regional framework is intended to complement individual nations' efforts to develop sovereign AI capabilities by establishing harmonized rules and principles that facilitate such endeavors.

Furthermore, the Asian regional AI framework agreement should promote collaboration with these foreign entities, recognizing them as essential partners in the AI ecosystem. The agreement should also aim to enhance the attractiveness of participating countries as investment destinations for large technology firms by fostering greater transparency and predictability within regulatory environments. To this end, the proposed agreement must incorporate provisions that ensure cooperation among parties in promoting transparency, good governance, and multi-level stakeholder engagement.

Moreover, as evidenced by legislation such as the European Union's AI Act and the Republic of Korea's AI Basic Act, an increasing number of domestic laws assert extraterritorial jurisdiction over AI operators located beyond national borders. This trend raises the potential for jurisdictional conflicts in enforcement.[74] Consequently, it may be necessary for the regional agreement to include mechanisms designed to mitigate such conflicts and promote legal coherence across jurisdictions.

---

[74] For example, Article 4 Korean AI Basic Act: This Act shall apply to acts committed outside the country if they affect the domestic market or users.

16.4.2.2 Provisions Related to Asian Regional AI Infrastructure Development

Among the 3 layers of AI tech stacks, governments may have the biggest influence in the construction of AI infrastructure. In addition, this may be an area where the Asian countries may provide for principles, including climate change and sustainability. Asian countries appear positioned to establish fundamental principles prioritizing climate change mitigation, sustainability, and regional cooperation in AI development.

Foundational Principles for Asian AI Infrastructure: Sustainability and Good Faith Cooperation

The establishment of a resilient and globally competitive AI ecosystem in Asia necessitates the foundational embedding of core principles, primarily the proactive consideration of climate change and sustainability, alongside a steadfast commitment to good faith cooperation among nations. The substantial environmental footprint of AI technologies, particularly the vast energy and water consumption of data centers, mandates an urgent and collective pivot toward "Green AI." Modern AI systems, with their intensive computational demands, contribute significantly to carbon emissions, a concern amplified in Asian regions where electricity grids may still heavily rely on fossil fuels. In response, several Asian governments and technology firms are already giving force to green AI practices, including the development of energy-efficient data centers, the increased utilization of renewable energy sources, and the formulation of national strategic plans like Singapore's Green Plan 2030.[75]

The Association of Southeast Asian Nations (ASEAN) Guide on AI Governance and Ethics serves as a salient example, promoting alignment and interoperability of AI regulatory frameworks across diverse jurisdictions.[76] The proposal for an "AI third way," envisioning multilateral cooperation among Asian middle powers to develop common AI infrastructure and products, is fundamentally predicated on this principle of good faith, aiming to reduce dependency on dominant global AI influences.[77] Integrating sustainability is not merely an ethical consideration but a long-term economic and strategic advantage; regions heavily reliant on fossil fuels face heightened carbon intensity and potential regulatory burdens, while proactive investment in green data centers and renewable energy can reduce operational expenditures, mitigate resource scarcity risks, and attract environmentally conscious global investment. Similarly, good faith cooperation is the primary mechanism for Asian nations to overcome

[75] Government of Singapore, Singapore Green Plan, https://www.greenplan.gov.sg/ (Accessed on 15 May 2025).

[76] ASEAN Secretariat, ASEAN Guide on AI Governance and Ethics, https://asean.org/book/asean-guide-on-ai-governance-and-ethics/ (Accessed on 27 May 2025).

[77] J Taylor and J Tan, Asia needs an AI third way (East Asia Forum, 13 April 2025), https://eastasiaforum.org/2025/04/13/asia-needs-an-ai-third-way/ (Accessed on 27 May 2025).

individual limitations in resources and market scale, enabling them to compete globally and ensure AI development aligns with shared regional values, thereby fostering a stable and predictable AI landscape conducive to long-term investment.

Strategic Regional Investment in Core AI Architecture: Funding, Datacenters, and Chips

To translate these principles into tangible advancements, strategic regional investments in the core physical and digital architecture of AI are imperative. This involves a multi-pronged approach focusing on the establishment of a regional AI infrastructure fund, collaborative ventures in the development and utilization of hyperscale datacenters, and cooperative strategies for AI chip procurement and research. A regional AI infrastructure fund, potentially modeled on consortia of national laboratories or public–private partnerships, can serve as a vital mechanism to pool financial resources, distribute risks, and channel investments toward common objectives. The involvement of Multilateral Development Banks (MDBs) like the Asian Infrastructure Investment Bank (AIIB), which has already demonstrated interest in funding digital and sustainable infrastructure projects in Asia, could provide structural support and financial leverage to such a fund. Financing for these large-scale endeavors can be drawn from diverse sources, including public–private partnerships (PPPs), innovative land value capture schemes, capital recycling, and credit enhancement tools designed to attract private sector capital, with blended and concessional finance being particularly crucial for pioneering green data centers. Joint investment in and collaborative use of hyperscale datacenters are critical, given the booming demand in Asia to support cloud computing and AI workloads, which necessitate investments exceeding US$100 billion for the currently planned APAC data center pipeline.[78]

Furthermore, joint procurement of AI chips—the essential computational hardware for AI systems—can enhance negotiating power and ensure supply stability, a crucial consideration amidst global supply chain vulnerabilities and export control regimes. Beyond procurement, regional collaboration in AI chip research and development, potentially expanding on the principles of specialization and ecosystem enablement demonstrated by Taiwan's semiconductor industry, is vital for fostering indigenous innovation and reducing reliance on external suppliers. This could involve leveraging the distinct semiconductor strategies and R&D strengths of nations like South Korea, Japan, and India to create a distributed network of excellence. An "expanded Taiwan model" for AI chip R&D, therefore, signifies more than manufacturing diversification; it implies the cultivation of a comprehensive regional high-tech

[78] Cushman & Wakefield, Asia Pacific Data Centre Investment Landscape, https://cushwake.cld.bz/investmentlandscape-06-2025-apac-regional-en-content-datacentres#:~:text=21%25%20Share,46%2C759 (Accessed on 10 July 2025).

ecosystem encompassing collaborative design, advanced research, talent development, and specialized manufacturing capabilities, thereby uplifting the technological capacity of the entire region.

Bolstering Enabling Ecosystems for AI Development: Cybersecurity, Human Resources, and Export Controls

The successful development and operation of regional AI infrastructure depend critically on bolstering ancillary capabilities, notably through joint investments in cybersecurity, strategic human resource development, including enhanced talent mobility, and the establishment of coordinated export control mechanisms. As AI systems become increasingly integrated into critical national and regional infrastructure, their security against sophisticated cyber threats is paramount. The Asia–Pacific region, like other parts of the world, faces specific AI-enabled cyber risks, including the empowerment of malicious actors, heightened threats to critical infrastructure, and increased espionage activities. In this regard, joint regional investment is essential to fund shared cybersecurity operational centers, establish robust threat intelligence sharing platforms, and collaboratively develop AI-powered defensive tools that are localized to address regional languages and specific threat vectors.

Concurrently, a highly skilled workforce is indispensable for the design, development, deployment, and ethical oversight of AI systems, yet a significant AI talent gap persists across Asia. National AI strategies across the continent uniformly emphasize the critical need for AI talent development and the attraction of global experts. Measures to facilitate the mobility of AI engineers, such as harmonized visa and residency permit processes—exemplified by Singapore's Tech.Pass[79] and ONE Pass[80] initiatives—are crucial for addressing immediate skill shortages. ASEAN's Responsible AI Roadmap[81] further underscores this by prioritizing the advancement of AI skills across the regional workforce. However, such mobility must be balanced with strategic efforts to build and retain talent within the region, preventing a "brain drain" and ensuring that mobile talent contributes to indigenous capability building.

Cybersecurity in this interconnected AI ecosystem is a shared responsibility; joint investments and intelligence sharing build collective resilience and the trust necessary for deeper collaborations in data sharing and R&D. Similarly, cooperation on export controls serves as a geopolitical navigation tool, allowing Asian nations to align with

---

[79] Tech.Pass is a visa that allows established global tech talent, including entrepreneurs, leaders or technical experts, to take on multiple economic activities and plug into Singapore's tech ecosystem. Singapore Economic Development Board, Tech Pass, https://www.edb.gov.sg/en/incentives-and-programmes/incentives-and-facilitation-programmes/tech-pass.html (Accessed on 1 September 2025).

[80] Singapore Ministry of Manpower, Overseas Networks & Expertise Pass (ONE Pass), https://www.mom.gov.sg/passes-and-permits/overseas-networks-expertise-pass (Accessed on 1 September 2025).

[81] ASEAN Responsible AI Roadmap (2025–2030), https://asean.org/book/asean-responsible-ai-roadmap-2025-2030/ (Accessed on 1 September 2025).

international norms, manage relations with major tech powers, and safeguard access to critical technologies while protecting their own innovations.

16.4.2.3 Provisions Related to AI Models

Development of regional sovereign AI models requires freer cross-border data flows and open local language archives. In addition, the risk-based approaches explored by the EU AI Act and Korean AI Basic Act may be a useful tool to balance between different areas of application, different levels of cybersecurity, and different needs of stakeholders.

Regional Frameworks Governing Cross-Border Data Flows

The proliferation of artificial intelligence technologies has created unprecedented challenges for traditional territory-based legal systems, particularly regarding data governance across national boundaries. While dominant AI regulatory frameworks from North America and Europe often emphasize individual privacy rights and corporate compliance, they inadequately address the unique concerns of regions with diverse linguistic, cultural, and religious contexts. As a result, there is a need for regional cooperation frameworks that establish "freedom of movement of data" principles while respecting legitimate public policy objectives (LPPO),[82] including national security, sovereignty concerns, and cultural diversity. The author is of the view that regionally negotiated data flow agreements can establish reciprocity mechanisms, shared security protocols, and mutual recognition systems that enable beneficial AI development while maintaining appropriate jurisdictional oversight. These frameworks must balance competing interests: facilitating the free flow of non-sensitive data necessary for AI advancement while establishing a clear delineation of sensitive data categories that warrant heightened protection.

Joint Fund for Local Language Archives

The linguistic homogenization observed in current AI systems threatens significant cultural and epistemological loss, as underrepresented languages receive insufficient attention in model development. The author proposes the establishment of joint regional funds specifically dedicated to digitizing local libraries, archives, and oral traditions to ensure linguistic and cultural diversity are preserved and represented within AI systems. There are already some projects including the Endangered

---

[82] Mirra Burri and Kholofelo Kugler, *Regulatory Autonomy in Digital Trade Agreements*, Journal of International Economic Law (Vol. 27, 2024), pp. 417–419.

Languages Archive to serve as a digital repository for preserving multimedia collections of endangered languages.[83] However, the author proposes that the proposed agreement must include joint funds to make digital repositories for non-endangered languages with a smaller volume of historic archives like Thai, Bahasa, and Tagalog. Such initiatives serve multiple complementary purposes: preserving endangered linguistic and cultural knowledge, creating valuable training resources for language-specific AI development, and reducing the inherent biases that emerge when systems are trained predominantly on resources from dominant languages.

Therefore, the proposed regional AI agreement should outline potential funding structures that combine governmental contributions with academic partnerships and private sector participation through mandatory contribution requirements or tax incentive programs. The proposed funding mechanism would prioritize standardized digitization protocols, ensuring interoperability across repositories while maintaining appropriate intellectual property protections for culturally sensitive materials. By creating accessible, high-quality datasets in diverse languages, such initiatives address fundamental inequities in current AI development trajectories while simultaneously preserving invaluable cultural heritage that might otherwise face digital extinction. Regional cooperation in this domain presents opportunities for cost-sharing that make comprehensive digitization economically viable, where individual national efforts might prove prohibitively expensive.

Joint Development of AI Governance Standards as Trust-Building Mechanisms

The swift expansion of generative AI in Asia demands regulatory frameworks that balance innovation and safety. Adopting a risk-based approach—like those in the EU AI Act[84] and South Korea's AI Basic Act[85]—allows for tiered regulations, with stricter oversight for systems posing higher risks to critical infrastructure, public health, or democratic processes. This strategy enables emerging economies and smaller developers to join the AI ecosystem without overwhelming compliance burdens, while ensuring robust protections where essential. Coordinated, region-wide risk frameworks also offer regulatory consistency for cross-border development, while honoring each nation's sovereign right to set acceptable risk thresholds.

Equally important is the collaborative creation of AI governance standards, which can serve as trust-building measures in a region marked by diverse histories and power balances. A multi-stakeholder approach—engaging governments, academia, civil

[83] The Endangered Languages Archive, https://www.elararchive.org/ Accessed on 23 August 2023.

[84] REGULATION (EU) 2024/1689 OF THE EUROPEAN PARLIAMENT AND OF THE COUNCIL of 13 June 2024 laying down harmonized rules on artificial intelligence and amending Regulations (EC) No 300/2008, (EU) No 167/2013, (EU) No 168/2013, (EU) 2018/858, (EU) 2018/1139 and (EU) 2019/2144 and Directives 2014/90/EU, (EU) 2016/797 and (EU). 2020/1828 (Artificial Intelligence Act, EU AI Act) (OJ L 2024/1689, 12.7.2024).

[85] See Basic Act for Development of Artificial Intelligence and Building Trust, etc.

society, and private sector actors from multiple jurisdictions—is crucial for developing standards that reflect regional realities and diverse perspectives. This participatory process helps surface region-specific challenges, legitimizes the resulting policies, and ensures that marginalized voices are heard.

Regional standards could address contentious issues such as autonomous weapons, facial recognition, predictive policing, and social credit systems, all of which raise significant ethical dilemmas shaped by cultural and political values. Effective governance would require established mechanisms for dispute resolution, independent assessments, and phased enforcement. To ensure the success of these standards, capacity-building efforts must accompany implementation, providing all jurisdictions with the technical expertise and institutional resources needed for effective oversight.

In summary, a risk-based, collaborative approach to AI governance—combining regulatory nuance with inclusive standard-setting—can foster innovation, reinforce trust, and ensure responsible AI development adapted to the complexities of Asia's diverse technological landscape.

16.4.2.4 Provisions Related to AI Applications

Building a Pro-Competitive AI Software Ecosystem

The development of pro-competitive AI software ecosystems requires legal frameworks that simultaneously stimulate innovation while preventing excessive market concentration—a particularly challenging balance given the network effects and economies of scale inherent to AI systems. Traditional competition law frameworks, designed primarily for industrial and early digital markets, prove increasingly inadequate for addressing the unique characteristics of AI markets, including data network effects, intellectual property concentrations, and algorithmic competition dynamics. We propose that effective pro-competitive frameworks must operate across multiple regulatory domains: intellectual property regimes must evolve to balance proprietary protection with necessary knowledge sharing; competition authorities require enhanced technical capabilities and new analytical frameworks for evaluating market power in AI contexts; and interoperability requirements may need codification through technical standards and mandated interfaces. The concept of the "essential facilities" doctrine merits reconsideration for core AI infrastructure components where market dominance creates substantial barriers to competition. Furthermore, open source AI development presents a potentially powerful pro-competitive force, though one that simultaneously raises complex questions regarding responsible deployment and safety governance. Regulatory approaches that incorporate graduated oversight—with heightened scrutiny for dominant market participants and streamlined compliance pathways for new entrants—offer promising directions for promoting competitive ecosystems without stifling early-stage innovation. Emerging regulatory experiments, including the European Union's Digital Markets Act and various national AI regulatory frameworks, provide preliminary insights into effective governance approaches, though their long-term impacts on competitive market structures remain uncertain. Without proactive governance frameworks specifically addressing AI market dynamics, existing market concentration trends may accelerate, potentially leading to innovation bottlenecks and raising significant democratic concerns regarding concentrated control over increasingly consequential technologies.

Cultural Sensitivity in AI Application Development

Cultural sensitivity in AI application development has primarily been framed as an ethical consideration rather than a legal requirement—a distinction that has limited its practical implementation amid competitive pressures and technical complexity. This regulatory gap appears increasingly untenable as AI applications mediate increasingly significant aspects of social, economic, and political life across diverse cultural contexts. The author proposes that cultural sensitivity obligations must transition from voluntary ethical frameworks to enforceable legal requirements with appropriate compliance mechanisms.

Such frameworks would establish mandatory cultural impact assessments for AI applications deployed across diverse cultural contexts, focusing particularly on systems making consequential decisions affecting individual rights and opportunities. Legal frameworks should differentiate between inadvertent cultural insensitivity arising from training data limitations and more problematic systematic biases in algorithmic design or implementation that consistently disadvantage specific cultural groups.

However, implementation challenges are substantial: defining actionable cultural sensitivity metrics remains methodologically complex; balancing universally applicable standards with culturally-specific expectations creates inherent tensions; and enforcement across jurisdictional boundaries presents significant coordination challenges. Nonetheless, the development of culturally sensitive AI applications not only serves ethical imperatives regarding equal treatment and dignity, but also enhances product effectiveness across diverse markets and reduces legal liability under existing non-discrimination frameworks—creating alignment between ethical practices and market incentives when properly structured.

16.5 Conclusion

Building a sovereign AI system has emerged as a critical imperative for nations seeking to address multifaceted security challenges in the digital age. National sovereignty in artificial intelligence encompasses not merely technological self-sufficiency but the capacity to safeguard against increasingly sophisticated cybersecurity threats, economic vulnerabilities, and informational manipulation. The contemporary security landscape demands that nations maintain significant control over critical AI infrastructure, applications, and data governance frameworks.

This recognition has driven an acceleration of bilateral Digital Trade Agreements (DTAs) and the implementation of domestic legislation with deliberate extraterritorial application, as nations attempt to secure advantageous positions across one or more layers of sovereign AI systems. These legal frameworks frequently address cross-border data flows, intellectual property protections for AI innovations, and conditional market access provisions. However, the inherent limitations of bilateral and unilateral approaches are becoming increasingly apparent as AI systems grow more complex and resource-intensive, suggesting the necessity for more comprehensive regional cooperation frameworks, particularly among Asian nations with complementary technological capabilities and shared regional concerns.

The time has arrived for Asian countries to contemplate a more sophisticated and comprehensive regional AI agreement that transcends the limitations of existing bilateral arrangements. While acknowledging the substantial obstacles to such cooperation—including significant disparities in technological development, divergent regulatory philosophies, and complex geopolitical alignments—a regional framework remains both necessary and achievable through graduated implementation approaches. The initial phases might emphasize non-binding cooperative mechanisms focusing on less contentious domains such as research collaboration, talent development, and technical standardization, gradually evolving toward more formalized arrangements as trust and integration deepen.

Rather than pursuing the technically and economically unfeasible goal of complete AI sovereignty (a "100% sovereign AI"), Asian nations would benefit from strategic regional cooperation that preserves essential sovereign controls while enabling resource pooling in areas requiring substantial scale. This balanced approach recognizes that meaningful AI sovereignty in the contemporary context requires strategic alliances rather than technological isolation, with carefully delineated sharing arrangements that protect core national interests while enabling essential collaboration.

Such proposed regional frameworks need not emerge ex nihilo but can be constructed upon the foundation of existing Digital Trade Agreements, expanding and adapting their provisions to address novel challenges presented by generative AI technologies. Current DTAs typically establish baseline provisions regarding data localization, intellectual property protection, and algorithmic transparency that can serve as building blocks for more comprehensive governance frameworks. However, generative AI introduces distinct regulatory challenges—including ownership questions regarding AI-generated content, liability frameworks for hallucinations or harmful outputs, and appropriate guardrail mechanisms for increasingly autonomous systems—that require innovative legal approaches. Regional frameworks could address these emerging issues while harmonizing divergent national approaches to reduce compliance complexity for developers and deployers. Additionally, sector-specific provisions might be developed for particularly sensitive domains such as healthcare, finance, and critical infrastructure, where generative AI applications pose unique risks and opportunities. The evolutionary development of such frameworks, building upon existing legal instruments while incorporating novel provisions specifically addressing generative AI capabilities, represents a pragmatic pathway toward meaningful regional cooperation.

Regional sovereign AI frameworks would particularly benefit Asian nations by creating synergistic relationships that leverage complementary strengths across different layers of the AI technology stack. East Asian economies with advanced semiconductor capabilities, Southeast Asian nations with substantial data processing infrastructure and linguistic diversity, and South Asian countries with significant software development expertise could create integrated ecosystems that compete effectively with other global AI powers.

At the same time, the complementary strengths described above may simultaneously present major impediments, hindering the realization of such a regional AI framework in Asia. As explained above, there is the vast diversity in digital readiness, economic development, and regulatory landscapes among Asian nations. This disparity creates a fragmented approach to AI governance, which raises concerns over privacy, ethical risks, and the potential exploitation of AI technologies for strategic advantage by dominant players. Hence, while regional AI cooperation in Asia is ideologically supported, achieving harmonized, enforceable frameworks remains hindered by socioeconomic, political, and infrastructural disparities.[86]

Despite such impediments and challenges, the author is of the view that Asian countries can still jointly establish mechanisms for joint research initiatives, shared AI infrastructure investments, coordinated regulatory approaches, and specialized talent development programs tailored to regional priorities. This approach acknowledges the reality that different Asian nations possess distinctive advantages at various levels of the AI stack—from hardware manufacturing to algorithm development to application deployment—creating natural opportunities for mutually beneficial specialization. Furthermore, regional cooperation could establish distinctively Asian approaches to AI ethics and governance that better reflect shared cultural values and social priorities compared to frameworks developed primarily in Western contexts. By developing coordinated sovereign AI strategies that combine individual national strengths while respecting legitimate sovereignty concerns, Asian nations could establish technological self-determination in a domain increasingly central to economic prosperity, national security, and cultural identity.

References

ASEAN Secretariat (2025) ASEAN Responsible AI Roadmap. https://asean.org/book/asean-responsible-ai-roadmap-2025-2030/ (Accessed on 1 September 2025)

[86] Hpone Thit Htoo, Beyond the Matrix: AI Governance Gaps in Southeast Asia (CSIS, 26 August 2025), https://www.csis.org/blogs/new-perspectives-asia/beyond-matrix-ai-governance-gaps-southeast-asia (Accessed on 7 October 2025).

Australia's Artificial Intelligence Ethics Framework (2022) https://www.industry.gov.au/data-and-publications/australias-artificial-intelligence-ethics-framework/australias-ai-ethics-principles (Accessed on 11 July 2022)

Burri M and Kugler K (2024) Regulatory Autonomy in Digital Trade Agreements, Journal of International Economic Law 397–423. https://doi.org/10.1093/jiel/jgae025

Chavez P (2024) Sovereign AI in a Hybrid World: National Strategies and Policy Responses (Lawfare Media). https://www.lawfaremedia.org/article/sovereign-ai-in-a-hybrid-world--national-strategies-and-policy-responses (Accessed on 1 June 2025)

Cushman & Wakefield (2025) Asia Pacific Data Centre Investment Landscape. https://cushwake.cld.bz/investmentlandscape-06-2025-apac-regional-en-content-datacentres#:~:text=21%25%20Share,46%2C759 (Accessed on 10 July 2025)

Gilbert & Tobin (2022) Here's Great Toolkit: AI Governance in Your Organization, https://www.gtlaw.com.au/insights/heres-great-toolkit-artificial-intelligence-ai-governance-within-your-organisation (Accessed on 11 July 2022)

Hpone T H (2025) Beyond the Matrix: AI Governance Gaps in Southeast Asia. https://www.csis.org/blogs/new-perspectives-asia/beyond-matrix-ai-governance-gaps-southeast-asia (Accessed on 7 October 2025)

Letzing J (2024) What is 'sovereign AI' and why is the concept so appealing (and fraught)? (World Economic Forum). https://www.weforum.org/stories/2024/11/what-is-sovereign-ai-and-why-is-the-concept-so-appealing-and-fraught/#:~:text=An%20example%3A%20a%20place%20using,those%20values%20as%20a%20threat (Accessed on 1 June 2025)

McCann K (2024) What Is Sovereign AI and Why Is It Gaining Traction? (AI Magazine). https://aimagazine.com/articles/what-is-sovereign-ai-and-why-is-it-gaining-traction (Accessed on 13 August 2025)

New Zealand government releases AI framework for use by public service (2025) https://iaeai.org/tpost/vgu1nvluh1-new-zealand-government-releases-ai-frame (Accessed 13 August 2025)

Proyecto de Ley que regula los sistemas de IA, https://www.minciencia.gob.cl/areas/inteligencia-artificial/Inteligencia-Artificial/Proyecto-Ley-regula-sistemas-IA/ (Accessed on 13 August 2025)

Sharma R (2025) AI Tech Stack: A Complete Guide. https://markovate.com/blog/ai-tech-stack/ (Accessed on 1 June 2025)

Singapore Economic Development Board (2025) Tech Pass. https://www.edb.gov.sg/en/incentives-and-programmes/incentives-and-facilitation-programmes/tech-pass.html (Accessed on 1 September 2025)

Singapore Ministry of Manpower (2025) Overseas Networks & Expertise Pass. https://www.mom.gov.sg/passes-and-permits/overseas-networks-expertise-pass (Accessed on 1 September 2025)

Singapore's Model AI Governance Framework for Generative AI (2024) https://aiverifyfoundation.sg/wp-content/uploads/2024/05/Model-AI-Governance-Framework-for-Generative-AI-May-2024-1-1.pdf (Accessed 13 August 2025)

Stiker C, What is an AI stack? (2025) https://www.ibm.com/think/topics/ai-stack (Accessed on 1 June 2025)

The Endangered Languages Archive (2023) https://www.elararchive.org/ (Accessed on 23 August 2023)

The Rise of Sovereign AI: National Strategies, Global Implications (Alphanome AI, 27 April 2025). https://www.alphanome.ai/post/the-rise-of-sovereign-ai-national-strategies-global-implications (Accessed on 1 June 2025)

Tyson L (2025) Navigating the AI Tech Stack: An In-Depth Guide. https://medium.com/@lenaztyson/navigating-the-ai-tech-stack-an-in-depth-guide-2f722ac88703 (Accessed on 1 June 2025)

Zeichick A (2025) What Is Sovereign AI? (Oracle Cloud). https://www.oracle.com/artificial-intelligence/sovereign-ai/ (Accessed on 1 June 2025)

Chapter 17
Technology Transfer in the Health Sector: Between Voluntary Licenses and Competition

Francisco Hernández Fernández

Abstract Article 7 of the Agreement on Trade-Related Aspects of Intellectual Property Rights (TRIPS) links the protection and enforcement of intellectual property rights (IPRs) to the transfer and dissemination of technology. Yet, the concept of "technology transfer" remains undefined in international law, becoming an all-purpose term often invoked without precision. In the health sector, the urgency of effective technology transfer has intensified, particularly after the COVID-19 pandemic underscored the need to diversify supply chains and promote local manufacturing. The WTO Ministerial Declaration on the Response to the COVID-19 Pandemic reaffirmed the role of the multilateral trading system in expanding and diversifying the production of essential goods. Achieving this objective is impossible without technology transfer. Voluntary licenses, agreements allowing patent holders to authorise others to use, produce, or market patented medicines, remain the most common mechanism. Initiatives such as the Medicines Patent Pool (MPP), the mRNA Technology Transfer Programme, and the Drugs for Neglected Diseases Initiative (DNDi) exemplify efforts to enhance manufacturing capacity and access in developing countries. However, competition policy also matters. Article 40 of TRIPS recognises that licensing practices may impede the dissemination of technology. This chapter examines major health-sector initiatives and explores national measures in Asia to ensure that licensing practices support, rather than hinder, both competition and technology transfer.

The author previously served as a Legal Affairs Officer in the Intellectual Property, Government Procurement and Competition Division of the World Trade Organization Secretariat. This paper reflects the author's own views and does not represent the position or opinion of the WTO Secretariat, nor does it prejudice the rights or obligations of WTO Members under the WTO agreements. Any errors are the author's sole responsibility. The analysis contained in this chapter discusses policy debates purely from an academic perspective. It does not advocate or recommend any course of action by WTO Members or by the WTO as an institution.

F. Hernández Fernández (✉)
Unified Patent Court, Luxembourg City, Luxembourg
e-mail: fhfozz@gmail.com

J. Nakagawa et al. (eds.), *Geopolitical Risks and Geoeconomics in International Economic Law*, Economics, Law, and Institutions in Asia Pacific,
https://doi.org/10.1007/978-981-95-6996-0_17

Keywords Technology transfer · Voluntary licensing · Intellectual property rights (IPRs) · TRIPS Agreement · Competition law · Health sector

17.1 Introduction

The concept of "technology transfer" in the health sector has long been acclaimed as a panacea for improving access to medicines, yet it remains an elusive and vague concept. The Agreement on Trade-Related Aspects of Intellectual Property Rights (the TRIPS Agreement) proclaims in Article 7 that protection and enforcement of intellectual property (IP) should contribute to the transfer and dissemination of technology. In addition, Article 66. 2 of the TRIPS Agreement indicates that "developed country Members shall provide incentives to enterprises and institutions in their territories for the purpose of promoting and encouraging technology transfer to least-developed country Members in order to enable them to create a sound and viable technological base".

Despite its importance, no universally accepted legal definition of "technology transfer" exists. In practice, the term is invoked broadly, sometimes idealistically, as a catch-all solution for various development challenges, without a clear consensus on its scope or meaning. In principle, international technology transfer should be understood in terms of technical knowledge acquired from foreign sources through commercial relationships,[1] often through licensing of intellectual property rights (IPRs). Still, the lack of a clear definition has tangible consequences: it creates uncertainty about what obligations (if any) States or companies have to share technology, and it impedes the development of concrete legal tools to facilitate the transfer of know-how and manufacturing capabilities.

This ambiguity became more than a theoretical problem during the COVID-19 pandemic. The crisis starkly exposed the unequal access to vaccines and other medical technologies that can occur when manufacturing know-how is concentrated in only a few countries. This leads to a situation described by some commentators as "vaccine nationalism",[2] under which some developed countries and some manufacturing companies control the production of vaccines. In 2022, World Trade Organization (WTO) Members acknowledged these shortcomings. A WTO Ministerial Declaration on the COVID-19 Pandemic[3] noted the importance of expanding and diversifying the production of essential health goods as part of pandemic preparedness. In a similar vein, the World Health Assembly of the World Health Organization (WHO) called, in its COVID-19 response declaration, for scaling-up production "of safe, effective, quality, affordable diagnostics, therapeutics, medicines and vaccines for

---

[1] Tang (2009, p. 3 1).

[2] Chimpango (2021, p. 16 7).

[3] *Ministerial Declaration on the WTO Response to the COVID-19 Pandemic and Preparedness for Future Pandemics. Adopted on 17 June 2022. WT/MIN(22) /31 WT/L/1142*, (2022).

the COVID-19 response, including, existing mechanisms for voluntary pooling and licensing of patents to facilitate timely, equitable and affordable access to them".[4]

In a similar vein, in a recent report of the Office of the United Nations High Commissioner for Human Rights on key challenges in ensuring access to medicines, vaccines and other health products in the context,[5] among the conclusions and recommendation was "to take measures to encourage the mutual learning and the transfer of technology to ensure the widest possible access to medicines, vaccines and other health products". Efforts to scale up global production capacity during emergencies may risk falling short without a meaningful technology transfer mechanism.[6] At the same time, technology transfer has been an important factor in making production feasible and competitive in some developing and least developed countries.[7] COVID-19 served as a catalyst, reigniting debate over how to ensure equitable access to medicines and raising fundamental questions about the interplay among IP rights, voluntary cooperation, and competition law in enabling access.

At the same time, it is now widely recognised that technological differences across countries are a significant determinant of income levels. The comparative advantage that underpins the need for countries to trade is slowly being replaced by a "competitive advantage".[8] Recent studies carried out by the World Intellectual Property Organization (WIPO) have concluded[9] that innovation remains highly concentrated in either high-income countries (such as the United States, France, Germany, Japan, and the Republic of Korea) or large economies (such as China and India). These countries account for 50 per cent of exports, 60 per cent of scientific publications, and 80 per cent of international patenting. In other words, only a small number of countries are responsible for most of the world's technologies. As a result, for countries lacking innovation capacity, which includes the vast majority, technological progress can only be achieved and measured in terms of technological absorption and adaptation. Therefore, some authors argue that policy in these countries may usefully focus on encouraging technology transfer from foreign firms.[10] In this sense, trade is also essential since it leads to international technology diffusion, part of the overall technology transfer, because (a) it makes available for production technologically advanced intermediate goods, (b) it makes intermediate and final goods available for

[4] COVID-19 Response. Seventy-Third World Health Assembly. WHA73.1. (2020), para 8.

[5] Analytical study on key challenges in ensuring access to medicines, vaccines and other health products in the context of the right of everyone to the enjoyment of the highest attainable standard of physical and mental health Report of the Office of the United Nations High Commissioner for Human Rights. A/HRC/56/28 (2024), p. 16.

[6] Technological Needs for Pharmaceutical and Vaccine Production in Low-And Middle-Income Countries. An African Perspective., p. viii.

[7] Local Production of Pharmaceuticals and Related Technology Transfer in Developing Countries: A Series of Case Studies by the UNCTAD Secretariat. (2011), p. 12.

[8] Porter (1990).

[9] World Intellectual Property Report 2024: Making Innovation Work for Development, p. 12.

[10] Cheng (2021, p. 5 6).

the study of their technological specifications, and (c) it favours person-to-person communication.[11]

Against this backdrop, this article examines the relationship between two key mechanisms for facilitating technology transfer in the pharmaceutical field: voluntary licensing of IP rights and the enforcement of competition law. Voluntary licenses, agreements in which patent holders allow others to produce or use their innovations, have become the dominant vehicle for industry-led sharing of medical technology. Yet voluntary licensing, while essential, may not fully ensure equitable technology dissemination. Competition law, on the other hand, provides governments with a tool to address IP abuses that hinder technology transfer, as explicitly recognised in Article 40 of the TRIPS Agreement. This duality raises important policy questions: Are these frameworks complementary or in tension with each other? Can reliance on goodwill through voluntary licenses be balanced with regulatory oversight to prevent anti-competitive constraints on the diffusion of technology?

Scholarly literature[12] has emphasised that initiatives on technology transfer operate within broader structural asymmetries between developed and developing countries, particularly regarding innovation capacities. This chapter does not attempt to provide a comprehensive account of these asymmetries. Still, it acknowledges them as part of the global background against which the Asian experiences examined here take place. The objective of this paper is to explore how voluntary licensing and competition law interact in practice and to assess the "policy space" that states, particularly in Asia and other developing regions, have to ensure that technology transfer actually occurs effectively. Part II begins by analysing voluntary licenses as a prevalent mechanism for technology transfer in health, highlighting both their achievements and structural limitations. Part III then examines the role of competition law in policing licensing practices that impede the dissemination of technology, including an analysis of TRIPS Article 40 and examples of national approaches (focusing on Asian jurisdictions) to curbing anti-competitive licensing. Part IV offers policy reflections for WTO members on leveraging both approaches, suggesting how multilateral and national initiatives can be rethought to promote genuine technology transfer. The conclusion synthesises the findings, emphasising that a more coherent legal strategy is needed to link IP, competition, and public health, thereby fulfilling the long-standing promise of technology transfer in the health sector.

17.2 Voluntary Licensing: A Necessary but Incomplete Tool

Voluntary licensing is the primary mechanism by which pharmaceutical patent-holders share technology on their own terms. In legal terms, a voluntary license is a private contract in which an IP owner (the licensor) authorises a third party (the

[11] Trade and Transfer of Technology. Background Note by the Secretariat. Working Group on Trade and Transfer of Technology. WT/WGTTT/W/1. (2002), para 24.

[12] Nguyen (2010, p. 161).

licensee) to use, manufacture, or sell an IP right, typically subject to defined conditions. Voluntary licenses can enable the production of cheaper generic versions of medicines before patent expiry, thereby expanding supply and access. They are often presented as a win–win: the licensee gains knowledge and market opportunities, the licensor earns royalties or other benefits, and patients in low-income markets receive the products they need. The appeal of this approach lies in its flexibility; parties can tailor the terms to their specific needs. In recent years, several high-profile initiatives have harnessed voluntary licenses to broaden access to medicines in developing countries. In particular, as has been argued,[13] one key outcome of the pandemic response has been the establishment of many new voluntary licensing and/or technology-transfer partnerships between pharmaceutical companies and generic manufacturers for COVID-19 health products and technologies.

One leading example is the Medicines Patent Pool (MPP), an organisation established in 2010 with UN backing to negotiate public-health-driven licenses for critical medicines. MPP has struck 22 voluntary licensing agreements with major pharmaceutical companies for HIV/AIDS treatments, hepatitis C, tuberculosis, and, more recently, COVID-19 treatments. These licenses have enabled 56 generic manufacturers in countries such as India, Pakistan, and South Africa to produce affordable versions of patented drugs for distribution in dozens of low- and middle-income countries. Between January 2012 and December 2023, MPP's license portfolio facilitated the supply of 43.56 billion doses of treatments benefiting 148 countries, while also yielding royalties to the originator companies, evidence that voluntary licensing can advance global health imperatives without undermining industry incentives. A joint study by the World Intellectual Property Organization (WIPO) and MPP found that[14] "if done in the right conditions, use of voluntary licensing for medicines and vaccines could increase patient reach for biopharmaceutical companies and could contribute to reducing global health inequalities, while being economically viable".

One ongoing initiative is the mRNA Technology Transfer Programme (or "mRNA hub") established by the World Health Organization (WHO) and partners in 2021. This programme was created in response to the COVID-19 pandemic. Based in South Africa, the mRNA hub seeks to develop and transfer mRNA vaccine manufacturing know-how to multiple recipient countries. By mid-2022, the hub had begun training scientists and sharing technology with production "spokes" in various low- and middle-income countries, including India, Pakistan, Vietnam, Indonesia, and Bangladesh. The goal is to establish sustainable regional manufacturing by enabling these countries to independently produce mRNA vaccines (for COVID-19 and other diseases). Notably, this transfer programme operates through negotiated agreements and partnerships, essentially involving a voluntary sharing of technical knowledge. It represents a groundbreaking multilateral technology transfer model that diverges

[13] Intellectual Property, Voluntary Licensing and Technology Transfer. Communication from the United Kingdom. Council for Trade-Related Aspects of Intellectual Property Rights. IP/C/W/704/Rev.1 (2023), para 4.

[14] Medicines Patent Pool (2024), Voluntary Licensing. Right for Health. Smart for Business. How voluntary licensing advances global health while being economically viable for biopharmaceutical companies, p. 8.

from the traditional bilateral licensing approach. This model is not without some IP challenges,[15] partly because of the landscape of mRNA patents.[16]

Voluntary licensing has also been part of product development partnerships for neglected diseases. For instance, the Drugs for Neglected Diseases initiative (DNDi) is a non-profit R&D organisation that explicitly structures collaboration agreements to ensure that resultant technologies are widely accessible. DNDi operates via a "virtual" model,[17] it does not own manufacturing facilities but partners with public and private entities to develop drugs through product development partnerships (also known as PDPs). It secures licensing terms that guarantee affordability and access. In practice, DNDi's agreements with pharmaceutical collaborators include provisions granting DNDi non-exclusive, royalty-free, and irrevocable rights to co-developed products, allowing it to subsequently license production to generic manufacturers for all endemic countries in need. This model enabled DNDi to help develop and disseminate new treatments for diseases such as leishmaniasis and Chagas disease, for which commercial actors would otherwise have little incentive to invest. It demonstrates how voluntary licenses can be designed to align explicitly with public health objectives. Indeed, DNDi has published its model licensing clauses to illustrate how access-friendly terms (such as requirements to share research data, commitments to affordability, and non-exclusive rights for follow-on manufacturing) can be embedded in technology transfer agreements.

However, there are many other initiatives at the international level that promote public–private partnerships and encourage technology transfer, such as the African Pharmaceutical Technology Foundation established by the African Development Bank in 2023, the International Vaccine Institute, and the Global Health Innovative Technology Fund. In addition, the WHO Health Technology Access Programme (HTAP)-formerly known as the COVID-19 Technology Access (C-TAP) who recently[18] helped to reach a deal to develop a new generation of diagnostic test from a South Korean firm (SD BioSensor) to a Nigerian health tech firm (Codix Bio) are examples of efforts to ensure geographically diversified and sustainable access to health products.

Despite these successes, voluntary licensing remains a useful yet incomplete approach for achieving equitable technology transfer. Structural limitations inherent in the voluntary nature of these agreements often restrict their impact:

- *Patent-holder discretion*: The decision whether to offer a license, to whom, and on what terms lies almost entirely with the patent owner. A company may simply refuse to license a critical health technology or delay negotiations if it perceives that exclusivity is more profitable.

[15] Adekola and Mercurio (2025, p. 6–8).

[16] Adekola (2023, p. 87 3).

[17] Junod Moser et al. (2023, p. 32 3).

[18] *WHO and Medicines Patent Pool Announce Sublicensing Agreement for Rapid Diagnostic Test Technology*, https://www.who.int/news/item/09-05-2025-who-and-medicines-patent-pool-announce-sublicensing-agreement-for-rapid-diagnostic-test-technology (last visited Jun. 1, 2025).

- *Restrictive clauses in license agreements*: When licenses are granted, they sometimes contain conditions that limit their effectiveness in achieving broad transfer. Common restrictive provisions include territorial restrictions (the license may allow production for certain countries but exclude others, often middle-income markets where needs are also significant), quantity caps or export restrictions, and field-of-use limitations (the technology can only be used for specific diseases or indications).
- *Lack of transparency*: Many voluntary license deals remain confidential. Aside from initiatives like MPP (which publishes its licenses on the website), the details of private licenses are often not publicly disclosed. The notable exceptions in Asia are China and Thailand,[19] where patent licensors/licensees are required to register/record their licensing agreements, and not only to enforce them against their parties, as is usually the case. Another rare industry exception is Gilead, which provides access to its voluntary licensing agreements on its website.[20] This opacity makes it difficult for governments and global health actors to determine who has the right to produce what and under what conditions. Non-transparency also obscures potentially anti-competitive arrangements.
- *Power asymmetries*: Voluntary license negotiations may be influenced by the parties' differing bargaining positions. Manufacturers or public health agencies typically have limited bargaining power against a multinational patent holder, unless they face external pressure. They may simply agree to terms that may not fully meet their local production and access needs, such as high royalties or restrictions mentioned above, to gain access to the technology. This asymmetry can result in situations where the license permits supply to the poorest countries but excludes many emerging economies, reinforcing inequitable access patterns. In some cases, a license might allow the use of the patent but does not include the transfer of the associated trade secrets or clinical data needed to manufacture the product effectively. Thus, the license on paper might not translate to a full technology package in practice. Furthermore, the licensing arrangement may create a dependency on the licensor depending on the licensee's expertise, experience, and infrastructure. During the license term, the licensor may have no incentive or may be prohibited (by the terms of the agreement) from developing a market share within the allocated territory or territories. In addition, the licensor may become reliant on the revenue stream generated by the licensee.[21]
- *Lack of an enabling environment*. An enterprise that wishes to acquire technology will be more reluctant to enter into a commitment to pay royalties for its use in an environment where the legal regime does not provide guarantees against local competitors gaining access to the same technology at no cost. Thus, in the absence of IP protection, the enterprise that possesses the technology and the enterprise

---

[19] WIPO Survey on the Antitrust Dimension of Intellectual Property Licensing Agreements in Support of Technology Transfer (2015).

[20] Gilead Sciences Global Access Partnerships, https://www.gilead.com/responsibility/global-health-and-access/access-in-low--and-middle-income-countries/access-partnerships

[21] Meiselles and Wharton (2018, p. 37 6).

that seeks it may be more reluctant to enter into a contract for its transfer.[22] An effective IP regime creates a psychological sense of security, a sort of safety net for those transferring technologies; in its absence, voluntary licensing may be disincentivised or less likely to occur.

- *Lack of specific regulation.* In many jurisdictions, the contractual freedom framework offers flexibility but may pose challenges in addressing specific access concerns. It is often overlooked that there is no uniform law governing IP licensing transactions in many jurisdictions, such as in the European Union, despite complex intellectual property licensing issues having been litigated.[23] The existing legislation in place remains minimal. Only the Commission Regulation (EC) No 316/2014 on the application of Article 101(3) of the Treaty to technology transfer agreements ("TTBER"), which will expire on 30 April 2026, and the Guidelines on the application of Article 101 of the Treaty to technology transfer agreements ("Technology Transfer Guidelines") provide some guidance. Similar regimes exist in other Asian jurisdictions. For example, Chinese Taipei's Fair Trade Commission has promulgated the Guidelines on Technology Licensing Arrangements, setting forth codes of conduct for entities in the technology industry seeking to license their technologies to others. The reason is that most jurisdictions have opted to grant the parties the freedom to contract, leaving them to agree on any terms in the agreement, provided there is no unfair competition or violation of public policy.

In summary, voluntary licenses have become a dominant tool for facilitating technology transfer in the health sector, exemplified by initiatives such as MPP, the WHO mRNA hub, and DNDi's partnerships. They have demonstrated potential to expand drug production in lower-income settings and have provided important learning-by-doing opportunities for manufacturers in those regions. However, their voluntary and contractual nature means they ultimately depend on the goodwill and strategic calculations of patent holders. Where that goodwill is absent or insufficient, voluntary licensing alone cannot guarantee equitable outcomes. As the next part discusses, competition law and related government interventions are crucial for addressing situations in which reliance on voluntary measures fails to deliver the necessary access to technology, or, worse, when licensing practices become obstacles to competition and hinder further technology dissemination.

---

[22] Factors Affecting Transfer of Environmentally-Sound Technology. Note by the Secretariat. Committee on Trade and Environment. WT/CTE/W/22. (1996), p. 5–6.

[23] de Werra (2012, p. 91).

17.3 The Role of Competition Law in Enabling Technology Transfer

Competition law, or antitrust or antimonopoly law in the USA,[24] can serve as a corrective mechanism when IP rights are exploited to hinder technology transfer and access.

Under the current WTO framework, there is no dedicated competition agreement. Instead, several provisions scattered throughout various WTO agreements contain some principles or references to competition. For this reason, at the 1996 Singapore Ministerial Conference, a decision was made to establish a working group on trade and competition. From 1997 to 2004, a Working Group on Trade and Competition Policy was established to develop a competition framework within the WTO. Still, negotiations collapsed at the Fifth Ministerial Conference at Cancun in 2003. Although the reasons are complex and multiple, at that time, some delegations believed that trade liberalisation could serve as a substitute for competition policy.[25] Furthermore, while trade policy was traditionally focused on measures at the border, competition policy regulated competitive conditions and the behaviour of enterprises within the country.[26] Hence, WTO Members were not able to bridge this conceptual difference. Nevertheless, at some point, WTO Members will have to address the issue of competition, as competition restraints may inevitably operate as a countermeasure to the trade liberalisation achieved through the WTO's trade negotiations.[27]

Despite this, during negotiations on the Uruguay Round leading to the establishment of the WTO in 1995, negotiators were aware of and discussed in great detail governmental restrictions on the terms of licensing agreements. Technology is disseminated in various ways. Besides foreign direct investment, technology can spread to new users through joint ventures, licensing agreements, and international trade. It is an open question which of these other transfer modes is the most important, because comparing the technological content of the different transactions[28] is difficult. However, from the IP perspective, licensing is the main channel. However, it is essential to recognise that technology licensing is not necessarily equivalent to technology transfer. The fact that two parties reach a licensing agreement does not mean that the subject matter of the agreement is actually transferred. It becomes an actual transfer when the licensor delivers the technology and knowledge to the

---

[24] Herdegen (2024, p. 41 3).

[25] Synthesis Paper on the Relationship of Trade and Competition Policy to Development and Economic Growth. Note by the Secretariat. Working Group on the Interaction between Trade and Competition Policy. WT/WGTCP/W/80. (1998), p. 20.

[26] Report (1998) of the Working Group on the Interaction Between Trade and Competition Policy to the General Council. WT/WGTCP/2. (1998), para 23.

[27] Matsushita (2002, p. 30 7).

[28] The Effects of Foreign Direct Investment on Development: Technology and Other Know-How Transfers and Spillovers. Note by the Secretariat. Working Group on the Relationship between Trade and Investment. WT/WGTI/W/65 (1998), para 7.

licensee, and the licensee learns how to effectively use, adapt, and, where possible, improve the technology and knowledge.[29]

In 1987,[30] negotiators of what would become the TRIPS Agreement discussed a system under which licensing agreements are subject to government authorisation and are approved only if their terms conform to certain conditions. These concerns included: restrictions on the royalty rates payable; conditionality of trademark licensing on the transfer of technology; non-approval of the licensing of foreign trademarks in joint ventures with foreign companies; obligations on the licenser to bear the responsibility if the technology in question infringes patents of a third party; restrictions on the duration of licenses for know-how; conditionality of the renewal of contracts on the offer of improved technologies; obligation to grant patents to the licensee without compensation after the termination of the licensing agreements, even before the expiration of the terms of the patents. Furthermore, negotiators identified specific practices in licensing agreements that were considered abusive or anti-competitive, such as those covering countries for which patents have not been granted; incorporating tie-in commitments on non-patented articles; incorporating restrictions on the export of the goods in question; and incorporating commitments on the importation of inputs for the manufacture of the goods in question.

The debate continued in 1990, when Members analysed national legislation and practices deemed restrictive concerning IP rights.[31] Negotiators seemed to have reached an understanding that the mere existence of conditions on the use, licensing, or assignment of IP rights is not necessarily deemed to be restrictive; generally, such conditions have to go "beyond" what is considered to be the scope of the intellectual property right in question or be the "unreasonable" exercise. Licensing, therefore, is generally regarded as pro-competitive as it multiplies the number of users of the IPR or technology. In other words, it is not the existence of IPR rights that constitutes a problem, but rather the exercise of those rights on a case-by-case basis (called the rule of reason in the US legal framework). Even though some Members supported[32] the idea that licensing, for example, proprietary information, in other words, confidential information, shall not be discouraged or impeded, voluntary licensing of proprietary information by imposing excessive or discriminatory conditions on such licenses or conditions that dilute the value of such proprietary information. In other words, parties should not take measures to discourage the licensing of IP rights, even those that ought to remain a secret by definition.

---

[29] World Intellectual Property Organization, Successful Technology Licensing 6–7 (2015).

[30] Compilation of Written Submissions and Oral Statements. Prepared by the Secretariat. Negotiating Group on Trade-Related Aspects of Intellectual Property Right, including Trade in Counterfeit Goods. MTN.GNG/NG11/W/12 (1987), p. 22–23.

[31] National Legislation and Practices Deemed Restrictive in Connection with Intellectual Property Rights. Note by the Secretariat. Negotiating Group on Trade-Related Aspects of Intellectual Property Rights, including Trade in Counterfeit Goods. MTN.GNG/NGH/W/64 (1990).

[32] Draft Amendment to the General Agreement on Tariffs and Trade on the Protection of Trade-Related Intellectual Property Rights. Communication from Switzerland. Negotiating Group on Trade-Related Aspects of Intellectual Property Rights, including Trade in Counterfeit Goods. MTN.GNG/NG11/W/73 (1990), p. 17.

As a result of those negotiations, Article 40 was incorporated into the TRIPS Agreement and explicitly recognises that certain conditions in IP licenses "*may have adverse effects on trade and may impede the transfer and dissemination of technology*". The inclusion of this article was an explicit acknowledgement by WTO members that licensing practices might be used anti-competitively, thus warranting scrutiny. While this provision of the TRIPS Agreement highlights that the primary rationale of the WTO rulebook is to be an enabler, fostering a level playing field across the membership by establishing the same regulatory burdens or evenly distributing this burden among actors and the supply chain across different jurisdictions.[33] It also proves that the TRIPS Agreement was not only concerned about establishing minimum standards of IP protection and enforcement, but the TRIPS Agreement also sought to strike a balance that could accommodate broader policy considerations such as competition, which plays a fundamental role to the point that some WTO Members have argued that promoting fair competition is a key aspect of their culture and value system, part of their public morals.[34] So, then what kinds of licensing practices restrain competition and impede tech transfer?

Article 40(2) of TRIPS provides illustrative examples: exclusive grant-back conditions, conditions preventing challenges to patent validity, and coercive package licensing could each be problematic. An exclusive grant-back is a type of license that requires the licensee to grant the licensor exclusive rights to any improvements or new inventions developed using the licensed technology. This practice can stifle follow-on innovation by others and prevent improvements from falling into competitors' hands. No-challenge clauses bar the licensee from contesting the validity of the IP, potentially perpetuating a weak or illegitimate patent and deterring its removal, thus locking up technology unnecessarily. Coercive package licensing refers to tying arrangements in which a licensor requires the licensee to license a bundle of patents or technologies, even if the licensee wants only one; this can block competitors in a specific technology market who might otherwise have developed alternatives. These examples, referenced in TRIPS, are not exhaustive but do indicate a range of abuses where a patent holder's superior bargaining position imposes terms that suppress competition and limit the diffusion of technology.

In the pharmaceutical sector, licensing agreements are generally perceived as pro-competitive.[35] Still, competition authorities and courts around the world have identified several broad categories of anti-competitive licensing behaviour relevant to the pharmaceutical sector:

- *Refusals to license essential technology*: In some situations, a single company's control of a technology is so critical that a refusal to license it can eliminate competition. In the pharmaceutical industry, a refusal to license a patented drug manufacturing process or a key research tool could, in theory, prompt antitrust intervention if the technology is indispensable for producing any competing product and

[33] Tokas (2024, p. 5).

[34] United States-Certain Tax Credits Under the Inflation Reduction Act (DS623). First Written Submission of the United States of America. (2025), para 64–68.

[35] Moullet (2019, p. 17 7).

there is no legitimate justification for exclusivity. However, competition law has traditionally been cautious in this area, often viewing outright refusals as within a patent holder's rights, except in exceptional circumstances. Nevertheless, in some jurisdictions, such as Article 145 c) of the Law on Intellectual Property of Vietnam, of 2005, the refusal to license IPRs without any qualification ultimately amounts to issuing a compulsory license.[36]
- *Excessive or exploitative pricing*: While high drug prices alone are not typically considered an antitrust violation in many jurisdictions, especially the US, which generally does not regulate excessive pricing under antitrust law, some competition regimes do treat the excessive pricing of a patented medicine as a possible abuse of dominance. The theory is that when a company holds a patent, prices can be a vital medicine at levels far above reasonable benchmarks, such as production cost plus a reasonable margin, which may constitute an abuse of its dominance, particularly if patients or healthcare systems have no alternative.
- *Conditional licensing and restrictive covenants*: Aside from the TRIPS-listed examples, a prevalent practice is territorial market division (e.g., a licensor permitting a generic producer to supply drug X only in Africa but not in Asia, while another licensee is restricted to Asia, and so on). If done among competitors, this could be seen as market allocation. Even though patents are territorial, when a company with a patent in multiple jurisdictions divides markets among licensees, competition concerns may arise if the arrangement primarily prevents parallel competition. Similarly, exclusive licensing agreements, where only one licensee is granted rights for a large region or globally, might draw scrutiny if they foreclose other potential entrants and are not justified by pro-competitive efficiencies. Patent pooling or cross-licensing agreements among multiple firms can also trigger antitrust analysis if the pooling is done to shut out rivals or fix prices. However, patent pools can be pro-competitive when they integrate complementary technologies (which is more relevant for platforms such as vaccines or diagnostics). Competition authorities will typically evaluate these conditions under a rule-of-reason approach, weighing potential justifications such as efficiency gains or the need to recoup research and development costs against the anti-competitive harm.

The legal frameworks in many countries empower competition agencies to act against such practices. Because our focus is especially on Asia, it is instructive to look at how certain Asian jurisdictions have incorporated competition-law tools to promote technology transfer and access to medicines:

- **Japan**: Japanese law does not have a statute explicitly enumerating forbidden licensing clauses; however, the Japan Fair Trade Commission (JFTC) has issued

[36] Refusal to License IP Rights—A Comparative Note on Possible Approaches. Prepared by the Secretariat. World Intellectual Property Organization (WIPO) (2013), p. 7.

Guidelines on Patent and Know-how Licensing Agreements under the Antimonopoly Act. These guidelines (first issued in 1999[37] and subsequently updated) detail which licensing practices may violate Japan's Antimonopoly Act. For example, the guidelines consider practices such as territorial restrictions or field-of-use limitations to be potentially problematic if they substantially restrain competition in a market. Japan has used the general competition law framework to evaluate IP licensing, often under the rubric of unfair trade practices. Japanese authorities have more frequently dealt with patent-related competition issues in the context of drug cartels or bid-rigging, rather than through compulsory licenses; however, the legal tools exist should an IP license be used to block generic competition contrary to the public interest.

- **South Korea**: Korea's Monopoly Regulation and Fair-Trade Act, enforced by the Korea Fair Trade Commission (KFTC), explicitly covers abuse of intellectual property rights such as: restrictions on prices of contracted products; on suppliers of raw materials; on purchasers of contracted products; trade in competing goods or technology; tie-in sales; imposition of no-challenge obligation; improving technology and research activities; on use after expiration of patent rights; and on termination of contract or disputes.[38] Korea has pursued cases in which pharma companies were found to be blocking generic entry through abusive litigation or improper Orange Book listings (e.g., the GlaxoSmithKline Korea case concerning the abuse of the patent system to delay generics). While those are not licensing practices per se, the KFTC also published guidelines on the Review of Unfair Exercise of Intellectual Property Rights, which mirror concerns similar to those in TRIPS Art 40. For instance, the KFTC has indicated that it would consider a patent pool or cross-licensing among major manufacturers to be illegal if it involves price-fixing or market division. In one notable Korean case, the KFTC in 2011 ordered several drug companies to cease certain patent settlement agreements that paid generics to delay entry (a so-called "pay-for-delay" situation regarded as anti-competitive in many jurisdictions, including under US and EU law). Although pay-for-delay is primarily about settlement, rather than licensing, it illustrates how competition law intervenes when patent exclusivity is leveraged to restrain competition beyond the patent's legitimate scope.

An alternative outcome of the Uruguay Round could have been a proposal submitted by the Republic of Korea[39] in 1991, which called for establishing a dispute-prevention system concerning the transfer of technologies. Under the Korean proposal, private undertakings of different Members engaged in the negotiation of a voluntary licence agreement involving patent and/or know-how may, through their

---

[37] Roger D Blair and D Daniel Sokol (eds), 'Intellectual Property and Antitrust in Japan' in Masako Wakui, The Cambridge Handbook of Antitrust, Intellectual Property, and High Tech (1st edn, Cambridge University Press, 2017) 143.

[38] Lee (2017, p. 16 6).

[39] Proposal for the Establishment of Dispute Prevention System in Respect of Transfer of Technologies. Communication from the Republic of Korea.Negotiating Group on Trade-Related Aspects of Intellectual Property Rights, including Trade in Counterfeit Goods. MTN.GNG/TRIPS/W/1 (1991).

respective government, may have requested the Committee on Trade-Related Aspects of Intellectual Property Rights (which ended up being named as TRIPS Council) for an advisory opinion with regard to whether such licence agreement, either in part or as a whole, constitutes an abuse of the patents and/or know-how or has an adverse effect on competition in international trade. The advisory opinion would have been issued by a Licence Review Board established under the aegis of the TRIPS Committee. Furthermore, the proposal proposed a guideline for preventing abusive practices in patent and/or know-how license agreements, to be promulgated two years after its first meeting. Unfortunately, the proposal did not gain much traction during the negotiations, with the notable exception of Colombia,[40] which expressed its support for the proposal as an "adequate mechanism".

In subsequent meetings, the representative of the Republic of Korea said[41] that the successful conclusion and implementation of an agreement on TRIPS would be dependent, among other things, on whether such an agreement, if adopted, would help facilitate the international transfer of technology; and whether it would provide rules by which the game of international transfer of technology was to be played. In that respect, it would be an omission if it did not commit all parties to jointly formulate and establish a supra-national norm and system capable of regulating or discouraging anti-competitive practices which might occur in connection with the international transfer of technology. However, other negotiating Members did not share Korea's approach at the time. In this sense, several months before, several of them[42] indicated that this should remain at the national level. Giving each Party the freedom to take the measures it deems appropriate to prevent the abuse of intellectual property rights or resort to practices which unreasonably restrain trade or adversely affect the international transfer of technology. For some authors,[43] the rules on competition policy embedded in the TRIPS Agreement merely constituted a "concession" to Members, recognising their residual sovereignty regarding this public policy area. As such, these rules could not be transformed into affirmative obligations.

Nevertheless, there was an understanding that there was a need to enter into consultation with other Party to discuss practices which restrain competition limit access to the technology or markets or foster monopolistic control, and which are engaged in by licensors, may have harmful effects on trade and transfer of technology among their countries to ensure that IPR owners, who are nationals or domiciliary of its country, comply with the obligations prescribed in this respect by the national legislation of the Party granting them such rights. For this reason, article 40. 3 of the TRIPS

---

[40] Communication from Colombia. Negotiating Group on Trade-Related Aspects of Intellectual Property Rights, including Trade in Counterfeit Goods. MTN.GNG/TRIPS/W/2. (1991), p. 6.

[41] Meeting of Negotiating Group of 16 and 20 September 1991. Chairman: Ambassador Lars E. R. Anell (Sweden). Note by the Secretariat. Negotiating Group on Trade-Related Aspects of Intellectual Property Rights including Trade in Counterfeit Goods. MTN.GNG/TRIPS/2. (1991), p. 1.

[42] Communication from Argentina, Brazil, Chile, China, Colombia, Cuba, Egypt, India, Nigeria, Peru, Tanzania and Uruguay. Negotiating Group on Trade-Related Aspects of Intellectual Property Rights, including Trade in Counterfeit Goods. MTN.GNG/NG11/W/71 (1990), p. 8.

[43] Ullrich (2005, p. 733–734).

Agreement indicates that WTO Members shall enter consultations with other WTO Members that have cause to believe that an IP right owner, national or domiciliary of the Member for which consultation has been addressed, is undertaking practices violating the requesting Member's laws and regulations. In this event, consultation shall be carried out by supplying publicly available, non-confidential information, subject to applicable domestic law, and upon the conclusion of an agreement safeguarding its confidentiality. Empowering WTO members to adopt laws to prevent or control anti-competitive licensing practices, Article 40 of the TRIPS Agreement permits countries to cooperate to address such practices.

17.4 Rethinking Policy Approaches: Way Forward

The following considerations synthesise options discussed in academic and policy literature and do not amount to proposals for institutional reform or negotiated outcomes.

The interplay between voluntary licensing and competition law in the context of health technology is a complex issue. When these frameworks operate in harmony, competition law pressures can lead to more voluntary licenses, and well-structured voluntary licenses can alleviate competition concerns. In other instances, they may collide with voluntary agreements used tactically to pre-empt regulatory action, or with antitrust enforcement stepping in to override inadequate private arrangements. This section explores tensions and complementarities, illustrating that an optimal approach will combine elements of both.

It is no secret that a complex relationship exists between IP and antitrust law, often described as a conflict of laws. The reason for such a characterisation is easy to see. Antitrust law, simply put, aims to protect consumers from the harms of monopolisation. Intellectual property law, in contrast, seeks to enhance incentives to innovate by granting time-bound proprietary rights over inventions or expressions of ideas. However, as pointed out by some authors,[44] this is an overly simplistic description, although some have argued that antitrust and IP law are in conflict in the short run but not in the long run, since in the long run, both areas of the law attempt to maximise the set of choices available to consumers. As it has been characterised[45] back to the negotiations of the TRIPS Agreement, IP rights promote innovation and intellectual creativity, and strong protection improves and expands the industrial base. Unlike what has been preconised by global health actors like UNITAID, IP is not a barrier to access to medicines and diagnostics.[46] In sum, contemporary policy thinking tends

[44] Hylton (2017, p. 8 1).

[45] Suggestion by the United States for Achieving the Negotiating Objective. Negotiating Group on Trade-Related Aspects of Intellectual Property Rights, including Trade in Counterfeit Goods. MTN.GNG/NG11/W/14 (1987).

[46] Unitaid (2016), p. 4. Unitaid's Approach to Intellectual Property, available at: https://unitaid.org/uploads/Unitaids-approach-to-intellectual-property.pdf.

towards a more coherent and integrated approach to the relationship between IP and competition policy.[47] In this sense, as it has been argued[48], developing states were prepared to agree to standards of IP rights protection being prescribed, provided this was counterbalanced by a commitment from developed states to ensure that IP rights protection would lead to a transfer and dissemination of technology benefiting developing states. Competition law was intended to serve as a potential instrument to ensure the implementation of the commitment.

Although for some WTO Members,[49] competition law is one of the least-discussed flexibilities within the WTO's TRIPS Agreement, it should be perceived as an integrated strategy to achieve technology transfer and access. Voluntary licenses bring speed, flexibility, and cooperation; competition law brings equity, oversight, and the power to break impasses. When leveraged together, they can drive a more effective transfer of health technologies: encouraging originator companies to share innovations broadly (under threat of legal action if they do not), and ensuring that when technologies are shared, they truly take root in a competitive environment rather than creating new monopolies under different guises.

Despite these tensions, there are clear synergies that can be harnessed. Voluntary licenses can be structured to address competition concerns, effectively designing pro-competitive licenses proactively. For instance, licensors can offer non-exclusive licenses to multiple independent manufacturers, thereby fostering competition among them to supply various markets (as opposed to a single exclusive licensee). They can refrain from imposing resale restrictions, allowing licensees to export to other markets where there is no patent or where the patent holder isn't serving demand, thereby preventing artificial segmentation. Licensors can also include clauses permitting the license to expand (to additional licensees or a broader geography) if certain supply benchmarks are not met, introducing a competitive check on the initial licensee's performance. All of these features have been present in some MPP licenses. By design, MPP licenses are non-exclusive and permit combinations with other licenses, aiming to stimulate a competitive generic market. The need for antitrust intervention diminishes when licenses are designed to be competition friendly. Indeed, a public-health-minded licensor has nothing to fear from competition law—the law is triggered only by practices that unduly restrain competition.

The role of states in aligning voluntary licensing with competition policy is crucial. Governments (especially when funding research or negotiating purchase agreements) can insist that any resulting licensing arrangements include conditions to facilitate technology transfer and competition. For example, when a state contributes public funding to vaccine development, it can require the developer to commit to licensing the vaccine to multiple producers and to share knowledge, effectively incorporating

[47] Taubman (2021, p. 16 7).

[48] Beiter (2023, p. 74 8).

[49] Intellectual Property and the Public Interest: Promoting Public Health Through Competition Law and Policy. Communication from China and South Africa. Council for Trade-Related Aspects of Intellectual Property Rights. IP/C/W/643. (2018), para 7.

pro-competitive and pro-transfer terms into the deal. This was debated during the pandemic for state-funded innovations. Some high-income countries did not impose such conditions on vaccine makers, leading to calls later for open technology sharing. In the future, states could implement what some analysts refer to as "public interest licensing": making public R&D grants conditional on non-exclusive licensing and access provisions. On the procurement side, governments (or international agencies like GAVI) buying medicines could negotiate with suppliers to grant licenses to other manufacturers to secure secondary supply sources, using their buyer power to induce voluntary tech transfer and ensure competition, so the government is not solely dependent on one supplier.

A dual approach, incentivising voluntary technology transfer while retaining robust oversight through competition law, is necessary to fulfil the promise of technology transfer in health. Multilateral and national policy measures can be rethought to better link IP, competition, and public health objectives. The following considerations are relevant to WTO members in general, with a particular focus on Asian countries seeking to expand local pharmaceutical production or enhance the multilateral framework.

a. **Strengthen multilateral frameworks for competition oversight of licensing**

   Article 40 of the TRIPS Agreement could offer opportunities to address competition concerns in licensing practices. While the extent of its use varies across jurisdictions, the provision remains a flexible tool whose scope continues to be discussed in WTO fora.[50] While Article 40 recognises the problem, it leaves implementation entirely to domestic law. In practice, many developing countries have limited experience or capacity in applying competition law to IP. A possible initiative, perhaps via the TRIPS Council or the Working Group on Trade and Transfer of Technology, is to develop guidelines or best practices on anti-competitive licensing. These could serve as a reference for national authorities to identify problematic clauses and determine appropriate remedies. Such guidelines might, for example, state that exclusive grant-backs and no-challenge clauses are generally suspect in health-related licenses and should be avoided or narrowly tailored. They could also encourage information sharing among competition authorities regarding pharmaceutical licensing cases. While competition law cooperation exists through forums like the International Competition Network (ICN), a WTO-backed effort focused on the impact of trade and tech transfer could elevate the issue's importance. A stronger international understanding would ultimately empower more countries to confidently use competition law when needed to enforce technology transfer commitments.

b. **Increase transparency of licensing deals affecting global health**

   As noted, one challenge is the secrecy surrounding many voluntary licenses. Improving transparency around pharmaceutical licensing practices has been discussed in various international forums, including the WHO's Global Strategy and Plan of Action on Public Health, Innovation, and Intellectual Property, as well

[50] World Trade Organization, Intellectual Property and the Public Interest: Communication from China and South Africa (IP/C/W/643, 11 June 2010).

as its 2024–2026 Implementation Plan. One proposal that has emerged in this broader policy context involves the voluntary development of a global database, possibly managed by a neutral body such as WHO, WIPO, or in collaboration with the WTO, where key licensing terms relevant to access to essential medicines could be disclosed. The feasibility and scope of such an initiative remain under discussion.[51] Egypt has suggested this idea on behalf of the African Group in a recent meeting of the WTO Working Group on Technology Transfer.[52] The proposal is to establish a dedicated WTO technology transfer platform that would serve as a central, transparent space where technologies are listed by sector, along with relevant details on patent holders, licensing terms, associated fees, and incentives offered by home countries to license patents to developing countries. This platform, if created, could aim to streamline and simplify the technology transfer process, ensuring that it occurs on mutually agreed terms and fosters equitable access to innovation across developing countries.

Already, the MPP publishes its agreements; expanding this norm to bilateral licenses (perhaps those stemming from public funding or the settlement of patent disputes) would shed light on restrictions that might merit regulatory attention. In this broader debate, WTO Members might, for example, explore whether a ministerial declaration or General Council decision could invite industry to voluntarily report such licenses, tying it to corporate social responsibility during pandemics. Transparency of information would aid competition authorities and public health agencies in identifying when a license leaves significant populations uncovered or competition suppressed, enabling timely action. Other, more ambitious ideas include linking reporting to certain trade-related incentives or procurement eligibility, although these proposals remain controversial and would ultimately depend on Members' views.

c. **Model contractual clauses and legal provisions for pro-competitive licensing**

One option often mentioned in policy discussions is that States might, where appropriate, propose that international organisations support the development of voluntary model clauses to encourage licensing terms that promote competition and access in the context of technology transfer. Such illustrative provisions might address, for example, non-exclusivity, equitable access to improvements, or pricing mechanisms designed to ensure affordability and accessibility. Naturally, these ideas would be subject to the differing interpretations and views among the States themselves regarding how best to operationalise such approaches.

d. **Leverage public funding to mandate technology transfer conditions**

The WHO Pandemic Agreement includes provisions that encourage Parties to incorporate access-oriented licensing terms into publicly funded research and

---

[51] World Health Assembly, Global Strategy and Plan of Action on Public Health, Innovation and Intellectual Property (WHA Res 61.21, 24 May 2008); World Health Organization, GSPA-PHI Implementation Plan 2024–2026 (WHO 2024) https://iris.who.int/handle/10665/375187 accessed 12 May 2025.

[52] Note on the Meeting of 12 November 2024. Chairperson: H.E. Raimondas Ališauskas (Lithuania). Working Group on Trade and Transfer of Technology Seventy-fourth Session. WT/WGTTT/M/74. (2024), para 5.11.

development arrangements. In line with this, States may choose to adopt national or regional policies that include, for example, affordable pricing mechanisms, non-exclusive licensing, or technology transfer conditions to facilitate equitable access to pandemic-related health products. While approaches may differ, the inclusion of such provisions reflects a growing recognition of the public-interest dimension in publicly funded biomedical innovation.[53] The Philippine Technology Transfer Act of 2009 foresees this. This could mean requiring that any vaccine or drug developed with substantial public funding be licensed non-exclusively to manufacturers in developing regions. Countries like the United States have debated using "march-in" rights under the Bayh-Dole Act (a form of compulsory license for federally funded inventions) to ensure access, but have hesitated to use them. A more proactive stance would avoid the need to march in later: bake the requirement in from the start. For Asian countries building domestic pharma innovation capacity, this approach is vital—it ensures that partnerships with foreign firms or local private developers yield public health returns. At the WTO, members could share experiences on this front, perhaps in the context of the WTO's pandemic response work or the upcoming discussions on a Pandemic Treaty at the WHO. The key is creating a norm that public investment equals public access, operationalised through licensing requirements that allow multiple producers and knowledge sharing.

e. **Empower and resource national competition authorities**

Many developing countries have competition laws on paper that could address IP abuses, but enforcement is often weak due to resource constraints or political pressure. It is particularly important for Asian countries to strengthen the expertise of their competition agencies in IP-intensive sectors. This may involve training staff in pharmaceutical market analysis, hiring or consulting with patent experts, and establishing dedicated units to investigate the pharmaceutical and technology sectors. International donors and technical assistance providers (such as the OECD, UNCTAD, or bilateral aid agencies) can support these efforts. Additionally, competition agencies should forge cooperative relationships with domestic health regulators and IP offices. For example, suppose a health ministry becomes aware of a restrictive vaccine supply contract. In that case, it should be able to refer it to the Competition Commission for evaluation of potential anti-competitive effects. Some jurisdictions have established public-interest review mechanisms that enable third parties (e.g., consumer groups, health NGOs) to initiate reviews of licensing practices. Such participatory provisions could be adopted to ensure that concerns are addressed. An active and capable competition authority serves as a credible deterrent to companies that impose licensing restrictions that hinder the diffusion of technology.

[53] World Health Organization, Proposal for the WHO Pandemic Agreement: Onscreen Text Reflecting Progress up to 16 April 2025 (WHO, 16 April 2025) https://www.keionline.org/40717 accessed 12 May 2025.

17.5 Conclusion

Technology transfer in the health sector has been much invoked and promised. The COVID-19 pandemic highlighted the crucial importance of decentralised manufacturing capacity for medical products and the limitations of existing mechanisms in achieving it. This article has examined how two seemingly distinct legal approaches, voluntary IP licensing and competition (antitrust) law, can be more effectively harnessed in concert to achieve the goal of effective technology transfer.

Several key findings emerge. First, voluntary licensing, while indispensable, has clear limits. It operates at the discretion of patent holders and is often circumscribed by restrictive terms, leaving many countries without access to crucial technology. The lack of a binding definition or obligation for technology transfer in international law leaves voluntary initiatives to fill the void. Second, competition law provides a necessary counterweight, a means for the public's interest in dissemination to override private interests in exclusivity when the latter are abused. Article 40 of TRIPS and national laws based on it acknowledge that in some instances, licensing practices that are not adequately scrutinised may unintentionally limit innovation and market access, thereby directly impeding technology transfer. Enforcement of competition law in such cases is not a deviation from the IP system, but a part of its design to balance incentives with access.

The interplay between these tools can produce better outcomes than either alone. Voluntary licenses induced or broadened under the pressure of competition oversight tend to be more impactful and fairer. Likewise, competition law interventions that result in the issuance of new licenses or the entry of generics can achieve what voluntary measures have failed to do. However, the article also cautions that poorly coordinated use of these tools can undermine effectiveness. Suppose authorities are too lenient, hoping that the industry will self-regulate through voluntary licenses. In that case, they may permit arrangements that do not fully facilitate the dissemination of broad-based technology. Conversely, overly stringent or inconsistent enforcement might deter companies from engaging voluntarily. Thus, a nuanced approach is needed.

For policymakers, various actors, including the European Parliament[54] and parts of the pharmaceutical industry,[55] have called for the establishment of a new WTO Committee on Trade and Health. Whether such an initiative will materialise remains an open question for Members. In these debates, some have suggested that an overarching WTO trade and health initiative could play a determining role in preparing guidelines on how governments can implement existing exceptions and flexibilities in international trade law to increase public health security, and what mechanisms must be put in place to improve the global response to health emergencies and to

---

[54] European Parliament resolution of 7 July 2021 on the trade-related aspects and implications of COVID-19 (2020/2117(INI)) (2021), para 22.

[55] Trade and Health Agenda: A Meaningful World Trade Organization Roadmap to Strengthen Global Health. (2025), https://www.ifpma.org/publications/trade-and-health-agenda-a-meaningful-world-trade-organization-roadmap-to-strengthen-global-health/.

lay the groundwork for a trade pillar for the negotiations on a future international treaty on the pandemic response remains a possibility. The negotiating history of the TRIPS Agreement also reveals an interest and the need by some WTO Members to further collaborate in determining good licensing practices. An overarching WTO trade and health initiative could play a determining role. In the meantime, the discussions among WTO Members will continue at the TRIPS Council following a recent communication[56] that aims to explore the relationship between IP, innovation, and technology transfer.

While this chapter has focused on policy-oriented proposals, it should be recognised that their implementation would occur within a complex environment in which soft-law instruments, market incentives, and political economy factors shape the effectiveness of voluntary licensing and competition law. Ultimately, ensuring effective technology transfer is about designing a more coherent legal and policy ecosystem that links IP rights with the conditions and expectations for sharing, and aligns competition law with public health imperatives. This coherence has been lacking; IP, competition, and health have sometimes evolved in parallel without full integration. A change is underway, prompted by global health crises and the recognition of inequities, towards breaking down these silos. The considerations discussed in this article, from greater transparency and model licensing terms to stronger competition enforcement, are presented as possible avenues explored in academic and policy debates to move towards such coherence.

In conclusion, technology transfer can move beyond aspirational rhetoric and be operationalised through the effective use of legal tools. It can be realised through deliberate legal design and enforcement that marries the strengths of voluntary initiatives with the safeguards of competition law. For WTO members, particularly in the developing world, leveraging this dual approach will be crucial in building local capacity for health innovation and production. The stakes could not be higher: at issue is the ability of all countries to access life-saving innovations and to collaborate on an equal footing to address health challenges. By combining incentives for voluntary cooperation with vigilant oversight against anti-competitive hindrances, states can move closer to a world in which critical health technologies flow more freely across borders, advancing the objectives underlying international commitments on technology transfer.

References

Adekola, T.A. 2023. When mRNA technology meets patent law: innovation, barriers and public health. *Journal Of Intellectual Property Law and Practice* 18, 867–877

[56] Intellectual Property and Innovation: Technology Transfer Case Studies. Communication from Australia; Canada; the European Union; Israel; Japan; Korea, Republic of; New Zealand; Singapore; Switzerland; the Separate Customs Territory of Taiwan, Penghu, Kinmen and Matsu; the United Kingdom and the United States of America. Council for Trade-Related Aspects of Intellectual Property Rights. IP/C/W/717 (2025).

Adekola, T.A. and Mercurio, B. 2025. mRNA Technology Transfer Hub and Intellectual Property: Towards a More Equitable and Sustainable Model. *World Trade Review*, 1–19, https://doi.org/10.1017/S147474562400020X

Beiter, K.D. 2023. Reductionist Intellectual Property Protection and Expansionist (and 'Prodevelopment') Competition Rules as a Human Rights Imperative? Enhancing Technology Transfer to the Global South. In C. Godt and M. Lamping (eds.), *A Critical Mind. Hanns Ullrich's Footprint in Internal Market Law, Antitrust and Intellectual Property.* Springer, 733–783

Blair, R.D and Sokol, D.D. 2017. Intellectual Property and Antitrust in Japan. In M. Wakui (ed.), *The Cambridge Handbook of Antitrust, Intellectual Property, and High Tech* (1st edn). Cambridge University Press. 143

Cheng, T.K. 2021. *The Patent-Competition Interface in Developing Countries.* Oxford University Press

Chimpango, B. 2021. Vaccine nationalism and equitable access to COVID-19 pharmaceuticals: TRIPS Agreement under trial (again). *Journal of International Trade Law and Policy* 20, 166–183, https://doi.org/10.1108/JITLP-03-2021-0012

Herdegen, M. 2024. *Principles of International Economic Law.* Oxford University Press

Hylton, K.N. 2017. Antitrust and Intellectual Property: A Brief Introduction. In R.D. Blair and D.D. Sokol (eds.), *The Cambridge Handbook of Antitrust, Intellectual Property, and High Tech,* Cambridge University Press, 81–91

Junod Moser, D., Boulet, P., Childs, M., Shieh, M., and Pécoul, B. 2023. Striking fair deals for equitable access to medicines. *Journal of Intellectual Property Law and Practice* 18, 323–335, https://doi.org/10.1093/jiplp/jpad025

Lee, H. 2017. Competition Law and Intellectual Property in Korea. In R.D. Blair and D.D. Sokol (eds.), *The Cambridge Handbook of Antitrust, Intellectual Property, and High Tech,* Cambridge University Press, 158–180

Matsushita, M. 2002. Competition Policy in the Framework of WTO. In P.C. Mavroidis, A. von Bogdandy, and Y. Mény (eds.), *European Integration and International Co-ordination: Studies in Transnational Economic Law in Honour of Claus Dieter Ehlermann.* Kluwer Law International

Meiselles, M. and Wharton, H. 2018. *International Licensing Agreements: IP, Technology Transfer and Competition Law.* Wolters Kluwer

Moullet, P. 2019. The Competitive Assessment of IP Licensing Agreements in the Pharmaceutical Sector. In P. Figueroa and A. Guerrero (eds.), *EU Law of Competition and Trade in the Pharmaceutical Sector*, Edward Elgar Publishing, 175–218

Nguyen, Tu Thanh. 2010. *Competition Law, Technology Transfer and the TRIPS Agreement: Implications for Developing Countries.* Edward Elgar Publishing.

Porter, M. 1990. *The Competitive Advantage of Nations.* Free Press

Tang, Y.S. 2009. *International Trade Policy for Technology Transfers: Legal and Economic Dilemmas on Multilateralism versus Bilateralism.* Wolters Kluwer

Taubman, A.S. 2021. The Competition Policy Roots of Intellectual Property Law: A Reflection. In R.D. Anderson, N. Pires de Carvalho, and A. Taubman (eds.), *Competition Policy and Intellectual Property in Today's Global Economy*, Cambridge University Press, 162–198

Tokas, M. 2024. The concept of the level playing field in International Economic Law. *Journal of International Economic Law* 27, 1–19, https://doi.org/10.1093/jiel/jgae026

Ullrich, H. 2005. Expansionist intellectual property protection and reductionist competition rules: A TRIPS perspective. In K.E. Maskus and J.H. Reichman (eds.), *International Public Goods and Transfer of Technology Under a Globalised Intellectual Property Regime,* Cambridge University Press

Chapter 18
Principles of Sustainable Finance Regulation and Their International Investment Law Implications: The Case of Hong Kong and Its Taxonomy for Sustainable Finance

Lee Soo-Hyun

Abstract This paper examines how Hong Kong's Taxonomy for Sustainable Finance (HKT) interacts with its international investment law (IIL) regime, focusing on the regulatory principle of Do No Significant Harm (DNSH). While the HKT recognizes DNSH as a core principle, it prioritizes market usability over rigorous integration, emphasizing only "Foundations of DNSH" without interpretive guidance. This subdued approach reflects alignment with the Common Ground Taxonomy (which excluded DNSH) and prioritizes green finance market development. Hong Kong's IIL regime—comprising 23 BITs and 10 treaties with investment provisions—lacks definitional clarity on sustainability, risking incomplete assessments by arbitral tribunals in disputes involving public interest measures. The paper argues this gap constrains Hong Kong's right to regulate. By expanding the HKT's remit to substantively integrate DNSH, Hong Kong can fill the lacuna between IIL and sustainable development, providing a basis to interpret and enforce investment law-sustainability interactions while strengthening its position as a global sustainable finance hub.

Keywords Do no significant harm (DNSH) · Sustainable finance taxonomy (HKT) · Right to regulate · Policy incoherence · Subdued approach · Interoperability

---

S.-H. Lee (✉)
College of Management Engineering, University of Suwon, Hwaseong-Si, South Korea
e-mail: shigotoba@protonmail.com

Asia Centre, Future Earth Programme, Seoul National University, Seoul, South Korea

J. Nakagawa et al. (eds.), *Geopolitical Risks and Geoeconomics in International Economic Law*, Economics, Law, and Institutions in Asia Pacific,
https://doi.org/10.1007/978-981-95-6996-0_18

18.1 Introduction

The Hong Kong Taxonomy for Sustainable Finance (HKT) released in May 2024 is a notable feature of the sustainable finance regulatory ecosystem of Hong Kong. While still in its draft phase, with its Phase 2A revealed in September 2025, the HKT is distinct in that rather than primarily serving the function to further align Hong Kong's regulatory and policy ecosystem in the direction of capital flows, it instead identifies the public policy priorities of Hong Kong and how they correspond with taxonomic definitions of sustainable finance offered. In this regard, the HKT poses a persistent legal doctrinal question: what applications can the HKT have in the international investment law regime of Hong Kong?

This chapter is part of a series of research[1] that examines how de facto principles of sustainable finance influence, and are influenced by, instruments of international economic law. These "de facto principles of sustainable finance" through their regulatory diffusion have adopted soft law characteristics, travelling across global value chains to come into effect even where there is no formal legislative process to serve as the legal foundation for such application. The close integration of national champions into global value chains also means that even without de jure application, major private sector economic entities through voluntary adherence results in national and transnational compliance.

Based on this approach, this paper examines the interaction between the sustainable finance and international investment regulatory ecosystems of Hong Kong to understand how the diffusion of sustainable finance principles encounters those systems. From this analysis, the paper concludes that policy incoherence between Hong Kong's sustainable finance regulatory ecosystem and that of its foreign direct investment regime can constrain the right to regulate for the public interest of Hong Kong. This occurs as overlapping regimes, namely that of domestic sustainable finance regulation and Hong Kong's foreign direct investment-related obligations are used to define the objective and purpose of investment alongside the rights and protections of both the investor and the host state.

This is especially troublesome in regulatory spaces where sustainable investment, or more broadly, the role of investment in sustainable development, are not clearly defined. This is the case for Hong Kong's international investment law regime, which instead of comprehensive national legislation relies on international investment agreements to carve out spaces for the interaction between international investment and sustainability. However, the interpretation and implementation of sustainability in international investment law, as an interstitial principle of the international public interest,[2] such as through investment treaty arbitration, remain ad hoc and oftentimes render incomplete assessments. It is within this context that regulatory principles of sustainable finance can provide the substantive basis to interpret, implement, and enforce constructive interactions between investment law and sustainability in working towards advancing sustainable development with real-world impact.

---

[1] See, for instance, Lee (2022).

[2] Lowe (1999, p. 21).

18.2 Methodological Framework

The research that fits under this series deconstructs the encompassing theme of sustainable finance[3] into individual governance concepts to identify and examine recurrence across diverse jurisdictions. These are referred to as "regulatory principles," recognizing that while they do not embody instruments of international law, they share legislative, substantive, and procedural aspects across different jurisdictions. The proliferation of these concepts and the similarities in their implementation are indicative of substantive regulatory principles that are becoming transnationally apparent in the legislation, implementation, and enforcement stages.

Identifying such regulatory principles requires an observation of regulatory diffusion and the prominence of diffused concepts in sustainable finance governance systems, examining for instance, the extent to which they are substantively overlapping. In doing so, this project seeks to understand the interaction between sustainable finance regulatory principles and international investment law regimes, such as the de jure or de facto application or implementation of such regulatory principles in international investment law instruments. This crossover between sustainable finance, which remains largely in the realm of private sector finance and portfolio investment, and international investment law, which deals with foreign direct investment, share a commonality that serves as the logical basis of this work: the ad hoc nature of sustainability and sustainable development.

Regulatory or policy diffusion involves the laws and/or policies in one jurisdiction influencing laws and/or policies in another jurisdiction or across multiple jurisdictions.[4] Alternatively, for agencies or entities in the private sector, regulatory diffusion would involve adopting a similar corporate policy or strategy in an effort to emulate certain results or processes.[5] Bringing these together, we have a third type of regulatory diffusion, which takes place between originating actors and private sector actors. In the literature, a few common characteristics of regulatory diffusion are identified. For instance, diffused regulation tends to demonstrate upward stickiness. Once the originating state regulation is diffused to the state or non-state actor, returning to more lenient regulation is difficult if the motivations for regulatory diffusion continue to exist.[6]

The diffused regulatory principle examined in this paper is do no significant harm (DNSH) in application to the HKT. The operative substance of DNSH is briefly explored in the next section.

---

[3] While a full scoping is not featured, the evolution of "sustainable finance" can be traced from its earliest derivations found in fiduciary duty, shareholderism, and the social responsibility of the business, moving then into stakeholderism and the universal owner. See Markowitz (1959), Friedman M (1970) The Social Responsibility of Business is to Increase its Profits. The New York Times Magazine, Jensen and Meckling (1976), Hansmann and Kraakman (2000), Hawley and Williams (2002); Stout (2012), and Hart and Zingales (2017).

[4] Vogel (1997).

[5] Simmons et al. (2007).

[6] Vogel (1997).

18.3 Understanding the Do no Significant Harm as a Regulatory Principle

Do No Significant Harm (DNSH) is one of the most ubiquitous principles in sustainable finance taxonomies, though perhaps its most robust application is found in the EU. DNSH is defined in Article 3b of the EU Taxonomy Regulation,[7] which states the following:

> For the purposes of establishing the degree to which an investment is environmentally sustainable, an economic activity shall qualify as environmentally sustainable where that economic activity […] does not significantly harm any of the environmental objectives [...]

This definition of DNSH is premised on objectives that are elsewhere established in the taxonomical instrument. In the case of the EU, DNSH is in application to the six environmental objectives of the EU Taxonomy Regulation. DNSH applies to an economic activity, such as investment, which would contravene the principle if it is demonstrated to have caused significant harm of the six objectives. They are reproduced as such[8]:

1. Climate change mitigation, such as by resulting in an increase in the amount of covered emissions;
2. Climate change adaptation, such as by resulting in reduced adaptive capacities of societies and ecosystems and exacerbating the adverse impacts of climate change;
3. Sustainable use and protection of water and marine resources, such as by resulting in the detriment of the status and/or potential of bodies of water;
4. Circular economy, such as by resulting in reduced circularity over the lifecycle of the good(s) and/or service(s) involved;
5. Pollution prevention and control, such as by resulting in increased pollution of air, water, or land; and
6. Protection and restoration of biodiversity and ecosystems, such as by resulting in detrimental effects to the condition, resilience, and/or conservation of habitats and ecosystems.

The European Commission observed that while an individual investment might partially contribute to one of the environmental objectives, it could also negatively impact another objective. To assist in evaluating each measure for adherence to the

---

[7] EU taxonomy for sustainable activities. In: European Commission—European Commission. https://ec.europa.eu/info/business-economy-euro/banking-and-finance/sustainable-finance/eu-taxonomy-sustainable-activities_en. Accessed 21 November 2020.

[8] Adapted from European Commission, *Technical guidance on the application of "do no significant harm" under the Recovery and Resilience Facility Regulation*, C(2021) 1054 final, 2 December 2021a, p. 2.

DNSH principle, the European Commission provided general interpretative guidance. According to this guidance, a measure that meets any of the specified conditions is likely considered compliant.[9]

1. The measure by design presents clear benefits to one of the environmental objectives while presenting "no or an insignificant foreseeable" negative impact on any of the other environmental objectives.
2. The measure is tracked with a "100% coefficient" as supporting either a climate change or environmental objective.
3. The measure "contributes substantially" to an environmental objective as defined in the Taxonomy Regulation.

"Substantial contribution" in connection to an economic activity finds broad definition in Articles 10 to 16 of the Taxonomy Regulation. Article 13(k) states that an economic activity may contribute "substantially to the transition to a circular economy, including waste prevention, re-use and recycling, where that activity [...] avoids and reduces litter." Both EU Member States and private sector organizations have consistently highlighted concerns regarding the insufficiently detailed criteria established by the Taxonomy Regulation, especially due to the potential risk of widespread greenwashing. For instance, the European Supervisory Authorities (ESAs) requested clear guidelines on promoting environmental and social characteristics and whether funds need a threshold of sustainable investments to comply with the Taxonomy Regulation.[10]

Where the above three conditions are not applicable, adherence to DNSH mandates that the economic activity incorporates specific guiding principles from the outset. Compliance with DNSH should be clearly established prior to the implementation of the economic activity, such as the admission of an investment, during the promissory or negotiation stage. These guiding principles can be summarized as follows:

1. Does the measure have direct environmental impact resulting from the economic activity itself? Or does it have "primary indirect" impacts, such as increased future emissions resulting from the use of the economic activity once it is complete?
2. Does the measure take into consideration the whole lifecycle of the good or service?
3. Does the measure promote greater climate-neutral energy infrastructure through electrification as a means of climate change mitigation?
4. Does the measure have a technologically and economically feasible alternative that is closer in its environmental impact to taking no measure at all? If not, does the measure follow the "best available environmental performance" in its sector?

---

[9] European Commission, *Technical guidance on the application of "do no significant harm" under the Recovery and Resilience Facility Regulation*, C(2021) 1054 final, 2 December 2021b, pp. 3–4.

[10] Pell EH (2022) European Commission moves ahead with plans to classify gas and nuclear as sustainable in EU Taxonomy. In: Responsible Investor.

The adherence to these guidance principles is assessed based on technical criteria established by other EU regulations.[11] For example, identifying the direct or primary indirect impacts of a measure related to the use and protection of water and marine resources aligns with Directive 2000/60/EC (October 23, 2000), which establishes a framework for action in the field of water policy for the European Community.[12]

In instances where specific EU criteria are absent or insufficient for guiding the application of the DNSH principle, the Taxonomy Regulation adopts a science-based methodology. This approach is frequently utilized in science-based targets by private sector entities aiming to address their environmental impact.[13] This is demonstrated in the general criteria for DNSH in relation to climate change adaptation, which guides the assessment of climate change adaptation against the threshold of the "state-of-the-art science for vulnerability and risk analysis and related methodologies in line with the most recent Intergovernmental Panel on Climate Change reports [and] scientific peer-reviewed publications."[14]

The DNSH principle supports affirmative compliance in substantial contributions while also serving as a safeguard measure that can be applied retrospectively to determine compliance post fact, as well as proactively to deny an economic measure for plausible concern of future non-compliance with the Taxonomy Regulation. However, the question of how the DNSH principle retains interoperability outside of the EU's regulatory milieu remains a difficult one. EU-wide directives, regulations, and harmonized standards incubate an ecosystem that is conducive to the level of integration required to enforce a DNSH.

The Korean Green Taxonomy, for instance, integrates DNSH against six environmental objectives, in this case referencing the EU Taxonomy Law directly.[15] This emphasis on interoperability is important to economic interests of Korea because the EU is Korea's third largest export destination market and EU entities leading foreign direct investment into the economy.[16] A modified diffusion of DNSH can be found in the ASEAN Taxonomy for Sustainable Finance, which includes DNSH as the first Essential Criterion benchmarking the EU Taxonomy Regulation, but working off four

[11] European Commission, *Technical guidance on the application of "do no significant harm" under the Recovery and Resilience Facility Regulation*, C(2021) 1054 final, 2 December 2021b.

[12] See Appendix B ("Generic criteria for DNSH to sustainable use and protection of water and marine resources"). Further examples include Appendix C ("Generic criteria for DNSH to pollution prevention and control regarding use and presence of chemicals") and Appendix D ("Generic criteria for DNSH to protection and restoration of biodiversity and ecosystems").

[13] See, for instance, the Science-based Targets initiative (SBTi), a self-regulating initiative led by the private sector and broadly supported by the United Nations seeking to orient their corporate sustainability objectives on decarbonization pathways defined in the Paris Agreement and defined against a threshold of the most recent scientific research.

[14] Appendix A ("Generic criteria for DNSH to climate change adaptation").

[15] Ministry of Environment, Republic of Korea (2021) Korea Taxonomy Guideline, p. 11.

[16] Delegation of the European Union to the Republic of Korea, *2025 EU-ROK Trade and Investment Relations*, 21 April 2025.

environmental objectives that are more aligned with the Southeast Asian context.[17] DNSH diffusion is also seen in the South African Green Finance Taxonomy with the exception that DNSH criteria are applied within each objective in what is identified as the Do Not Significant Harm Criteria.[18]

The next necessary component for this analysis is to examine the HKT, particularly as it relates to DNSH and its diffusion.

18.4 Hong Kong Taxonomy for Sustainable Finance

The Hong Kong Taxonomy for Sustainable Finance is a green classification framework established by the Hong Kong Monetary Authority (HKMA) with the support of the Climate Bonds Initiative (CBI) for implementation within the local market. Initially released as a prototype in May 2023, the taxonomy was refined based on feedback from market consultations and subsequently published as the official Hong Kong Taxonomy for Sustainable Finance. The Taxonomy aims to standardize the classification of financial products and investments based on their environmental sustainability. It helps investors identify activities with positive environmental impacts and avoid those with negative effects.

Continuing from the methodological approach and scope defined above, this section has the task of investigating the manner in which DNSH has been integrated into the sustainable finance and sustainability performance regulations of Hong Kong. There are three distinctive characteristics of DNSH and its integration into the HKT, which when ratified will be a foundation to its sustainable investment regulatory system.

First, the HKT identifies DNSH as one of its five core principles, but rather than establishing DNSH as a standalone principle, the HKT instead emphasizes the "Foundations of the DNSH" without offering further interpretive guidance:

> (5) Foundations of Do No Significant Harm and Minimum Social Safeguards (MSS). While the Hong Kong Taxonomy primarily focuses on climate change mitigation, it acknowledges the interconnectedness of sustainability issues. The importance of DNSH and MSS is recognized and will be explored in future development.

In the discussion paper published a year before the release of the HKT, the EU Taxonomy regulation is recognized as a benchmark for the construction of national taxonomical systems and that the DNSH was a "well-developed" criterion.[19] To that

---

[17] ASEAN Taxonomy Board, *ASEAN Taxonomy for Sustainable Finance Version 2*, 9 June 2023, p. 169; ASEAN Taxonomy Board, *ASEAN Taxonomy for Sustainable Finance Version 3*, 20 December 2024, p. 33.

[18] National Treasury, Republic of South Africa., *South African Green Finance Taxonomy*, March 2022.

[19] Hong Kong Monetary Authority (HKMA), Climate Bonds Initiative (CBI), *Prototype of a Green Classification Framework for Hong Kong*, 30 May 2023, p. 7.

regard, the HKT was meant to "outline the foundations for DNSH and MSS"[20] while also adding, "experience shows that if not properly operationalised, DNSH and MSS can become a burden and hinder the development of the green finance market. A careful balance of stringency between these requirements and the usability of the taxonomy as a whole should be achieved."[21]

Should the discussion paper and consultations serve as travaux préparatoires in the legal interpretation of DNSH within the HKT, then a clear interpretive hierarchy is drawn out, placing the development of the green finance market as a priority over ensuring that fundamental regulatory principles such as DNSH are properly installed. The ramifications of such are explored in the discussion section of this paper.

The second characteristic of DNSH integration is that the HKT identifies compliant economic activities categorized under public policy interests of Hong Kong, such as power generation, transportation, construction, and water and waste management. While the rigour of how DNSH is applied to economic activities that are categorized under such public policy interest areas is unclear, particularly in contrast to the extent to which investments may advance the public policy interests, investments under the economic activities are confronted by fewer requirements, such as an indirect environmental impact or lifecycle assessment. This poses potential conflicts with DNSH as a regulatory principle because economic activities within these designated economic activities may, in future renditions of the HKT, undergo limited DNSH review. Without the substantiation of DNSH at the inception of the HKT, questions of co-benefit generation and interaction between policy priority areas will remain key factors affecting the stable and predictable application of HKT—an important issue in application to other areas of regulation such as international investment law.

Lastly, a third characteristic of the HKT is that its technical criteria are closely aligned with the Common Ground Taxonomy (CGT), which was an effort by the European Union and China to enhance interoperability of their respective sustainable finance regulation.

The CGT made clear that there were key differences between the taxonomical approach to defining environmentally sustainable investments that could not—or did not—translate. Most notably, the exclusion of DNSH and Minimum Social Safeguards.[22] To that end, CGT was criticized for the absence of DNSH alongside other key principles in sustainable finance, such as a best available science.[23] The extent to which the CGT could be operationalized was also questioned due to data limitations needed to calculate certain key performance indicators that were covered in

---

[20] Ibid., p. 8.

[21] Ibid., p. 17.

[22] Hong Kong Green Finance Association et al., *Understanding Use Cases of the Common Ground Taxonomy*, 22 September 2022, p. 9.

[23] Principles for Responsible Investment (PRI), *PRI Consultation Response: Common Ground Taxonomy*, 14 January 2022.

the review.[24] At the same time, despite its name, the CGT is not a taxonomy that is legally binding, rather a comparison between the green taxonomy regulations of the EU and China as an exercise to identify differences in views towards environmentally sustainable investments.[25]

While the CGT may not have been designed to be legally binding or serve as a functional taxonomy, there was subsequent regulatory diffusion, such as to the HKT. Indeed, the supplemental guideline to the HKT describes it as having been "developed with the aim of operationalising the CGT."[26] Furthermore, the CGT was identified as the "major taxonomy referenced" as the starting point of interoperability.[27] In effect, irrespective of the legal basis of CGT, it has nevertheless experienced transmission through regulatory diffusion.

The divergence between the EU and Chinese taxonomies on DNSH were such that they were not included into the CGT exercises, raising questions of whether this decision to exclude DNSH was made largely on methodological or technical grounds, such as matters of political economy. Yet it is important here to note that the Chinese green taxonomy is more stringent in some areas than the EU and vice versa. In this manner, it is "descriptively inaccurate to claim that one taxonomy is generally more stringent than another in absolute terms."[28]

Nevertheless, if Hong Kong bases the interpretation of DNSH on the CGT, then the fate of DNSH may largely rest on the evolutionary direction of the HKT: closer adherence with the European Union standard of DNSH or alternatively to maintain closer interoperability with China and the interpretation of such regulatory principles therein.

In its initial form, however, the HKT features a subdued role for DNSH and based on existing information, the future of DNSH in the HKT remains unclear. When the Hong Kong Monetary Authority released the HKT in May 2025, it also released a record of consultations that it undertook with stakeholders. These comments outlined "next steps" for the HKT, of which item (vii) identified that "some respondent expressed the need to include DNSH elements and suggested that the Taxonomy incorporate the EU Taxonomy criteria for DNSH."[29] The response provided by HKMA to these concerns is telling. In point 3.1.4 under Sect. 18.3 ("Way Forward"), the HKMA offers the following response:

> On the one hand, the incorporation of DNSH and [minimum social safeguards] requirements could help sustainable finance initiatives align with holistic environmental and social

---

[24] Hong Kong Green Finance Association et al., *Understanding Use Cases of the Common Ground Taxonomy*, 22 September 2022, p. 28.

[25] International Platform on Sustainable Finance Taxonomy Working Group, *Common Ground Taxonomy—Climate Change Mitigation: Instruction Report*, 2022, p. 6.

[26] Hong Kong Monetary Authority (HKMA), Climate Bonds Initiative (CBI), *Hong Kong Taxonomy for Sustainable Finance: Supplemental Guidance*, May 2024, p. 12.

[27] Hong Kong Monetary Authority (HKMA), Climate Bonds Initiative (CBI), *Prototype of a Green Classification Framework for Hong Kong*, 30 May 2023, p. 7.

[28] Chan et al. (2025, p. 8).

[29] Hong Kong Monetary Authority (HKMA), Climate Bonds Initiative (CBI), *Consultation Report: Prototype for a Green Classification Framework for Hong Kong*, May 2024, p. 11.

considerations. On the other hand, there are concerns that their inclusion might be complex in practice for investors and financial institutions. We would explore the incorporation of both components in the future development of the Taxonomy, bearing in mind the principles of interoperability and usability.[30]

From these supplementary and preparatory works, it is clear that the HKMA could not easily reconcile the high bar set by the DNSH as diffused from the EU Taxonomy Regulation with the public policy interests identified in the HKT, as well as the broader national strategic interest of ensuring a stable and predictable regulatory ecosystem conducive to foreign investment.

As to the future of the HKT, its current interoperability-centred trajectory would most likely place it in a middle area between two influential sustainable finance regulatory regimes, namely the EU and Mainland China. This middle ground has been shown to result in capital leakages in areas where those different taxonomies apply.[31] This would also mean that taking any substantive position on DNSH would not be feasible in the short- to intermediate-term without the HKT reconciling the fact that it had not included DNSH, a fundamental regulatory principle in sustainable finance regulation. One such position would maintain Hong Kong's position as a global financial centre while also by inference meaning that potentially large volumes of investment that would have otherwise needed to have observed DNSH at an EU threshold could be HKT-compliant while paying minimal or no consideration to DNSH.

The discussion and final section of this analysis addresses how the international investment law regime of Hong Kong, e.g. its international investment agreements, engagement with investment treaty arbitration, and domestic laws related to the treatment of foreign direct investment, confronts questions of sustainability. Building from this foundation, this paper provides an analysis of sustainability as a concept across two regulatory regimes (sustainable finance and international investment law) in helping to determine whether they are coherent. As issues of sustainability saturate the world of not only foreign portfolio but also direct investment, confronting questions of policy coherence between international and sustainable investment becomes inevitable. This paper examines the approach of Hong Kong to this balancing act in an effort to understand how one of the world's primary financial hubs will plan its future.

18.5 Discussion

The extent to which regulatory principles like DNSH can be diffused into the international investment law regime of Hong Kong is the final theoretical question of this paper, applying the above methodology in this context. To this end, this section examines the extent to which DNSH and sustainability performance as defined and

30 Ibid., p. 15.

31 Chan et al. (2025, pp. 16–18).

interpreted in those regulations are coherent with matters of sustainability more broadly in the international investment law regime of Hong Kong. In doing so, this section offers an assessment of the level of law and policy coherence between Hong Kong's approach to international investment and sustainable investment.

18.5.1 Placing DNSH in Hong Kong's International Investment Law Regime

As explored in the previous section, the question of DNSH diffusion is an interesting one for Hong Kong. The HKT can potentially become the first regulatory system in connection to investment to apply the principle within the public interests of the national context. In respect to international investment law, relevant national legislation is limited to the Basic Law, which serves primarily to lay out a broad legal foundation for Hong Kong to set out its own economic law and policymaking towards maintaining a liberal investment regime.[32] As a result, Hong Kong remains one of the most liberal trade and investment legal regimes in the world. This regime is comprised of a nexus of international investment agreements; ratification of key multilateral conventions including the World Trade Organization system and the International Centre for Settlement of Investment Disputes (ICSID) Convention; harmonized monitoring, reporting, and verification standards; and a national legal system under Chapter V of the Basic Law[33] that guarantees legitimate expectations of minimum standards of treatment for investors.

In terms of treaties, Hong Kong's international investment law regime is constituted of 23 bilateral investment treaties and its 10 treaties with investment provisions. A conventional definition of an IIL regime would typically include national laws on foreign direct investment as well as interpretation that arise from investment treaty arbitration awards. However, in the case of Hong Kong, the lack of a specific legislation on foreign direct investment[34] as well as unclear application of mainland China IIAs in connection to Hong Kong entities in investment treaty arbitration[35] render the inclusion of these elements a more complicated exercise. Regarding the latter, investment treaty arbitration involving a Macanese entity under the China-Laos BIT resulted in an unclear determination as to whether BITs involving China can apply to Macao and Hong Kong. Without explicit inclusion of Macao and Hong Kong into the jurisdiction of Chinese BITs, it has generally been seen that applying those BITs to Macao and China would be inconsistent under an interpretation offered by the Vienna Convention on the Law of Treaties, Article 29 (the "moving treaty frontier" doctrine).

---

[32] Chaisse (2024, p. 37).

[33] (1997) The Basic Law of the Hong Kong Special Administrative Region of the People's Republic of China.

[34] Chaisse (2024, p. 17).

[35] In specific reference to the Sanum Investments cases.

DNSH would become relevant in assessing the consistency of a government measure affecting the foreign direct investment with the prevailing treaty instrument should the measure seek to address.

Within the scope of Hong Kong's international investment law regime defined, issues of sustainability or sustainable development are included in several instruments, either at the preambular and/or the operative text:

1. Hong Kong—New Zealand CEPA (2010),
2. EFTA—Hong Kong FTA (2011),
3. Chile—Hong Kong FTA (2012),
4. Canada—Hong Kong, China SAR BIT (2016),
5. Georgia—Hong Kong, China SAR FTA (2018),
6. Australia—Hong Kong Investment Agreement (2019),
7. Hong Kong, China SAR—Mexico BIT (2020)
8. Hong Kong, China SAR—Türkiye BIT (2023)
9. Bahrain—Hong Kong, China SAR BIT (2024).

Notable amongst these is the inclusion of "recognizing the need to promote investments based on the principles of sustainable development" in both the Canada-Hong Kong (2016) and Chile-Hong Kong (2016) BITs, an affirmation of commitment to sustainable development treaties in Article 8.1 of the EFTA-Hong Kong FTA (2011). Hong Kong's other IIAs also refer to sustainable development and widely reflect Draft Provision 12 of UNCITRAL Working Group III.[36] For instance, Articles 15 and 16 of the Australia-Hong Kong Investment Agreement (2019) and Articles 12.1 and 13 of the Hong Kong – Mexico BIT (2020) contain clauses that safeguard parties' right to regulate for environmental, health or other regulatory objectives. The Chile (2012), Mexico, and Australia IIAs also encourage enterprises to voluntarily incorporate international standards and guidelines of corporate social responsibility. Overall, an overview of Hong Kong's IIAs that mention issues relevant to sustainable development has included new generation features, though this is not particularly indicative since recent IIAs, such as that with the United Arab Emirates (2019), which remains a largely conventional IIA as it relates to the right to regulate.

Additionally, IIAs that Hong Kong remains signatory to also contain GATT Article XX (General Exception) safeguards in Article 18 of the China—Hong Kong CEPA Investment Agreement, Chapter 19 of the Hong Kong—New Zealand CEPA, and Article 5 of the Hong Kong, China SAR—Türkiye BIT. The significant contribution criterion is present in an even wider gamut of the IIAs including those with Georgia, France, Macao, and Mexico.

While altogether one in every 2.5 of Hong Kong's IIAs can be associated to the sustainability performance and impact of foreign direct investment, the manner in which sustainability (or sustainable development) can be defined within the international investment law space represents a much-contested frontier in the subject.

---

[36] United Nations Commission on International Trade Law (UNCITRAL), *Possible reform of investor-State dispute settlement (ISDS): Draft provisions on procedural and cross-cutting issues*, A/CN.9/WG.III/WP.231, 26 July 2023.

While this paper does not delve further into the subject, firmly held convictions on the limitations of international investment law, especially in the format of investment treaty arbitration, when considering matters that may be interpreted as extra-legal, such as those of the public interest, have led many to view that international investment law, if unable to adapt to present realities such as anthropogenic climate change, will result in its irrelevance.[37]

While regulatory principles in sustainable finance are introduced through diffusion into the Hong Kong sustainable finance regulatory ecosystem, their application do not carry over mutatis mutandis into its international investment law regime. This research argues that this poses both risk and opportunity.

Within this landscape, sustainable finance regulatory principles like DNSH, which, as examined in Section Four, serve as a prerequisite in evaluating the sustainability contribution of an investment, would best fit in general exceptions related to sustainable development or more broadly the public interest.

Another potential setting for DNSH may be under corporate social responsibility provisions where they exist, given the shared provenance of DNSH and the governance of the conduct of private sector entities. However, given that the practice of integrating corporate social responsibility into international investment agreements has hitherto largely been a means for self-regulation, stronger language would be needed to ensure first-order optimality.[38] Two variations of this clause broadly refer to voluntary corporate social responsibility standards and a second with stronger language but indirect reference to corporate social responsibility, emphasizing instead fiduciary duty and integrity.

The first type has been a common trend in the recent practice of international investment agreements,[39] which is the inclusion of self-governance standards. Article 13 (Corporate Social Responsibility) of the Hong Kong, China SAR—Mexico BIT (2020), for instance, includes such language:

> Each Contracting Party may encourage enterprises operating within its area or subject to its jurisdiction to voluntarily incorporate into their internal policies internationally recognised standards, guidelines and principles of corporate social responsibility that are supported by that Contracting Party.

There are two important observations that are pertinent here. The first is that the Hong Kong, China SAR—Mexico BIT (2020) does not offer investment treaty arbitration as a means of dispute settlement for both general exception (Article 12) and corporate social responsibility (Article 13), leaving national courts as the means to settle such claims. The second is that Article 13 itself, while emphasizing the voluntary nature of observing any such provisions related to corporate social responsibility, also makes it quite simple (normatively) for the insertion of sustainable finance principles such as DNSH. This would include, for instance, following "international recognized standards," adding therein DNSH as a definitive example.

[37] See, for instance, Burgstaller (2021), Beverelli et al. (2020), Aust (2016), Brauch et al. (2019), Gehring and Segger (2015), and Sornarajah (2015).

[38] See, for instance, Dubin L (2018) Corporate Social Responsibility Clauses in Investment Treaties.

[39] See, for instance, Levashova (2018).

However, in cases where Contracting Parties have diverging sustainable finance regulation or taxonomies to scaffold Article 13, it would seem that the obligation to observe DNSH where it is not explicitly defined or required would make its application to such investments procedurally challenging. In the case of the HKT, unless the transnational corporate entity has mandatory DNSH requirements through home country standards, such as through the EU Taxonomy Regulation, it would remain unclear where and to what extent DNSH would apply to the contracting parties.

As per the second type, one may see this language in the Bahrain—Hong Kong, China SAR BIT (2024),[40] Article 8(3) takes positive list approach to general exceptions as seen in the GATT and Article 8(4) adds a more comprehensive corporate social responsibility component. Article 8(4) safeguards the right to regulate for "prudential reasons," which includes fiduciary duties owed by financial institutions; the safety, soundness, integrity or financial responsibility of financial institutions; and the integrity and stability of financial systems. The wording in Article 8(4) is constructed in a manner that host and home country standards of fiduciary duty would apply, meaning that in the context of Hong Kong and HKT, an obligation to observe DNSH would not necessarily exist. Integrating DNSH in Article 8(4), might include adding two new subclauses, perhaps after the current Article 8(4)(b), as:

Article 8(4)(c): "the observation of financial regulation, such as taxonomies, in governing the economic activities of financial institutions and their extra-financial effects, namely those affecting the public policy considerations of the Contracting Parties as identified in Article 8(3)".

Article 8(4)(d): "the observation of widely held standards in sustainable finance regulation, such as do no significant harm, where applicable national financial regulation does not exist in whole or in part".

In Chile—Hong Kong, China SAR BIT (2016) and Canada—Hong Kong, China SAR BIT (2016), for instance, both types are included. While Article 16 of the Chile—Hong Kong BIT and Article 17 of the Canada—Hong Kong BIT provide for similar substance as Article 13 of the Hong Kong—Mexico BIT, they provide more comprehensive language that is more conducive to including sustainable finance regulatory principles like DNSH.

Article 18(2)(a), the Chile—Hong Kong BIT, for instance, includes a wider range of stakeholders, including "financial market participants, policy-holders, policy-claimants, or persons to whom a fiduciary duty is owed by a financial institution," which makes the question whether the national financial regulatory context provides for a modern fiduciary duty that extends to questions of double materiality that include both financial and sustainability concerns. Poignantly, Article 18(3) carves out further right to regulate flexibilities for Contracting Parties:

> Notwithstanding Article 11.1 and 11.2 (Transfers), a Party may prevent or limit transfers by a financial institution to, or for the benefit of, an affiliate of or a person related to that institution, through the equitable, non-discriminatory and good faith application of a measure relating

[40] The same observations apply to Hong Kong, China SAR—Türkiye BIT (2023).

to maintenance of the safety, soundness, integrity or financial responsibility of financial institutions.

A normative reading of this provision would indicate that economic activities of financial institutions may face restrictions imposed by the host state in situations related to the maintenance of the integrity of financial institutions. If read in combination with Article 18(2), further enhanced by a DNSH requirement, this dimension of the Chile—Hong Kong FTA would provide for a robust platform for the integration of best-in-class sustainable finance regulatory principles.

One albeit limited alternative is exceptions that defer substantive obligations to those of regional economic integration. In Finland—Hong Kong, China SAR BIT (2009) and Hong Kong, China SAR—Thailand BIT (2005), for instance, articles on exception (in both cases Article 7), there is deferment to regional trade agreements. In such cases, applicable standards of sustainable finance may refer then to applicable regional regulation or taxonomies, such as the EU Taxonomy Regulation or the ASEAN Taxonomy Board's ASEAN Taxonomy for Sustainable Finance (Draft 3). Both documents have clearly established governance architecture that recognizes DNSH. As examined earlier, the EU Taxonomy Regulation includes DNSH as a minimum safeguard required for all undertakings (Article 18). In the ASEAN Taxonomy, DNSH is included as an essential criterion (Article 3.2).

In such cases, it would seem that DNSH would apply via these applicable instruments and as a result would raise uncertainties concerning how the HKT, wherein DNSH lacks a clear legal ambit, would interact with EU or in the future ASEAN-based investors.

18.5.2 Challenges and Looking Ahead

The opportunity is that substantive and operative components of sustainability, whether in the context of a treaty interpretation or the settlement of a dispute, can refer to sustainable finance regulatory principles to ensure that interpretation is aligned with the public interest objectives, such as those defined in the HKT. Carving out clear legal application and interpretation of regulatory principles can help to Hong Kong not only align with the quickly evolving and (less quickly) harmonizing standards of understanding that correlation but also take the prerogative in shaping its own public policy flexibilities when it comes to sustainable development-related policies.

The alternative is to allow the international investment law-sustainable development nexus remain undefined, which is consistent with Hong Kong's regulatory trajectory to date. This permits parties, or in the case of a dispute arbitral tribunals, considerable discretion in defining sustainability where it is otherwise left undefined in the prevailing international investment law instrument. The risk therein is the extent to which parties or tribunals are willing and able to interpret sustainability in connection with national public policy priorities. For instance, in many cases, investment treaty arbitration tribunals have in many cases resorted to incomplete assessments of sustainability.

An incomplete assessment occurs when a strictly legal interpretation of sustainability as it is operationalized in an international investment law instrument confronts limitations arising from uncertain norms to the level of indeterminacy. These instances are most commonly found in application to measures related to the public interest, such as sustainability. In such circumstances, assessments must extend beyond the traditional ambit of legal interpretation in substantiating those norms. This view is not uncommon in the literature.[41]

One such a view necessarily calls for international investment law as a legal science to expand beyond its conventional boundaries, integrating interdisciplinarity methods as an exercise of cross-fertilization across different social, natural, and engineering sciences.[42]

Hong Kong's current approach permits individual international investment agreements following this business-as-usual approach to defining the substantive rights and obligations between itself as the host state and putative covered investments. It is herein that the HKT, should it significantly expand its remit to key sustainable finance regulatory principles like DNSH, can encapsulate an important function in filling the substantive lacuna that exists between international investment law and sustainability development. In doing so, Hong Kong may retain crucial policy flexibilities as it continues to position itself as a popular destination for international investment, of which an increasing proportion will be based on double rather than single materiality.

Carving out such definitions can create obstacles to investment as spacious right to regulate determinations can result in unpredictable variables, resulting in investors avoiding sectors where those variables hold the most weight. This is particularly relevant considering the lack of differentiation between foreign and domestic investors within the Basic Law. While this serves to strengthen investor confidence under Hong Kong's WTO obligations, the difference lies in the fact that foreign investors have a separate forum to contest government measures implemented in the public interest, investment treaty arbitration, which is subject to such incomplete assessment risk.

The HKT will invariably become more refined in the future and in and of itself embodies an accomplishment in tightening the correlational nexus between international investment and sustainable development. This is purely in the fact that the release of the HKT has begun this discussion in Hong Kong. Future editions of the HKT will face scrutiny and criticism, but these are necessary steps as Hong Kong expands its role from a global financial hub to a global hub of sustainable finance. The Administration already has this goal in its horizon. For example, in October 2024, the HKMA released its Sustainable Finance Agenda, which outlines eight goals to support banks to increase their engagement in sustainable finance.[43] While

[41] See, for instance, Cordonier Segger (2021), Marcoux (2020), Gaukrodger D, *Business Responsibilities and Investment Treaties*, 15 January 2020, and Krajewski (2020).

[42] Sands (1998).

[43] Hong Kong Monetary Authority (HKMA) (2024) Sustainable Finance Action Agenda.

this takes a largely capacity-based approach, if Hong Kong implements incentivization or investment promotion schemes to attract sustainable investment or investment in sustainability-related activities—as per the purpose of the HKT—then it will become crucial to establish a stable and predictable regulatory ecosystem to continue to attract investors to Hong Kong while ensuring that inbound and outbound sustainable investment is high-quality with real-world impact.

References

Aust HP (2016) Investment Protection and Sustainable Development What Role for the Law of State Responsibility? In: Hindelang S, Krajewski M (eds) Shifting Paradigms in International Investment Law: More Balanced, Less Isolated, Increasingly Diversified, 1st edn. OUP, pp 204–226

Beverelli C, Kurtz J, Raess D (eds) (2020) International Trade, Investment, and the Sustainable Development Goals: World Trade Forum. CUP

Brauch MD, Touchette Y, Cosbey A, et al. (2019) Treaty on Sustainable Investment for Climate Change Mitigation and Adaptation: Aligning International Investment Law with the Urgent Need for Climate Change Action. Journal of International Arbitration 36:7–35

Burgstaller M (2021) Investment Protection and Sustainable Energy Projects in the Age of Climate Change. In: Hobe S, Scheu J, Boknik B, Nikolov P (eds) Evolution, Evaluation and Future Developments in International Investment Law: Proceedings of the 10 Year Anniversary Conference of the International Investment Law Centre Cologne. Bloomsbury, pp 107–119

Chaisse J (2024) Hong Kong as an Actor in International Economic Law: Multilateralism, Bilateralism and Unilateralism, 1st edn. Hart Publishing

Chan KJD, Mok LW, Lau PCC (2025) Leakage in the common ground: how misalignment in sustainable finance taxonomies impacts cross-border capital flows. Journal of Sustainable Finance & Investment 1–26. https://doi.org/10.1080/20430795.2025.2481954

Cordonier Segger M-C (2021) Crafting Trade and Investment Accords for Sustainable Development: Athena's Treaties, First edition. OUP, Oxford

Dubin L (2018) Corporate Social Responsibility Clauses in Investment Treaties. https://www.iisd.org/itn/2018/12/21/corporate-social-responsibility-clauses-in-investment-treaties-laurence-dubin/

Gehring MW, Segger M-CC (2015) Overcoming obstacles with opportunities: Trade and investment agreements for sustainable development. International Investment Law and Development: Bridging the Gap 93–124

Hansmann H, Kraakman R (2000) The End of History for Corporate Law Essay. Geo LJ 89:439–468

Hart O, Zingales L (2017) Companies Should Maximize Shareholder Welfare Not Market Value. Journal of Law, Finance, and Accounting 2:247–274

Hawley JP, Williams AT (2002) The Universal Owner's Role in Sustainable Economic Development. Corporate Environmental Strategy 9:284–291. https://doi.org/10.1016/S1066-7938(02)00056-8

Jensen MC, Meckling WH (1976) Theory of the Firm: Managerial Behavior, Agency Costs and Ownership Structure. Journal of Financial Economics 3:305–360

Krajewski M (2020) Framing the broader context of business and human rights: the impact of trade agreements on human rights. In: Deva S, Birchall D (eds) Research Handbook on Human Rights and Business. Edward Elgar Publishing Limited, UK, pp 269–289

Lee S (2022) "Do No Significant Harm" as a Core Principle in Sustainable Finance Regulation in the ASEAN Draft and Singapore Taxonomies. Journal of International and Area Studies 29:21–38

Levashova Y (2018) The Accountability and Corporate Social Responsibility of Multinational Corporations for Transgressions in Host States through International Investment Law. ULR 14:40. https://doi.org/10.18352/ulr.441

Lowe V (1999) Sustainable Development and Unsustainable Arguments. In: Boyle A, Freestone D (eds) International Law and Sustainable Development: Past Achievements and Future Challenges. OUP, pp 19–38

Marcoux J-M (2020) Transnational Public Policy as a Vehicle to Impose Human Rights Obligations in International Investment Arbitration. The Journal of World Investment & Trade 21:809–846. https://doi.org/10.1163/22119000-12340188

Markowitz HM (1959) Portfolio Selection: Efficient Diversification of Investments. Yale University Press

Sands P (1998) Treaty, Custom and the Cross-fertilization of International Law. Yale Hum Rts & Dev LJ 1:85–106

Simmons BA, Dobbin F, Garrett G (2007) The Global Diffusion of Public Policies: Social Construction, Coercion, Competition or Learning? Annual Review of Sociology 33:449–472

Sornarajah M (2015) Resistance and Change in the International Law on Foreign Investment. CUP

Stout LA (2012) New Thinking on Shareholder Primacy. Accounting, Economics, and Law: A Convivium 2

Vogel D (1997) Trading up and governing across: transnational governance and environmental protection. Journal of European Public Policy 4:556–571. https://doi.org/10.1080/135017697344064

Chapter 19
Forging Trade Rules in the Age of AI: The Case for Special Labor Safeguards

Tsai-fang Chen

Abstract Artificial intelligence (AI) has the potential to reshape global labor markets, generating structural displacement across sectors through trade in AI-enabled goods and services. This chapter argues that the WTO's current safeguard regime is poorly equipped to address the distinctive character of AI-induced labor disruption. Rooted in a product-specific, sectoral logic, the Agreement on Safeguards fails to accommodate the cross-cutting, anticipatory nature of AI shocks, and excludes services altogether. To address this gap, the chapter proposes a new WTO instrument: a special safeguard mechanism specifically designed to enable members to respond to systemic employment dislocation linked to trade in AI-intensive products and services. It outlines the foundations for such a mechanism, proposes core design elements, and considers necessary guardrails to prevent protectionist misuse. Rather than eroding multilateralism, this approach seeks to preserve it: by equipping the WTO with tools that enable governments to manage labor transitions within a rules-based framework, this chapter aims to reaffirm the WTO's relevance in an era of general-purpose technological disruption.

Keywords Artificial intelligence · Job displacement · WTO · Trade and labor · Human-centered trade · Safeguards

Part of this research has been supported by a grant from National Science and Technology Council, Taiwan (NSTC 114-2410-H-A49-009-).

T. Chen (✉)
National Yang Ming Chiao Tung University, Hsinchu, Taiwan
e-mail: tfc@nycu.edu.tw

J. Nakagawa et al. (eds.), *Geopolitical Risks and Geoeconomics in International Economic Law*, Economics, Law, and Institutions in Asia Pacific,
https://doi.org/10.1007/978-981-95-6996-0_19

19.1 Introduction

Artificial intelligence (AI) has the potential to seriously displace workers, to threaten job security, and to reduce the demand for new hires, leading to higher unemployment rate and economic insecurity.[1] As firms adopt AI, labor markets are exposed to a new category of technology shock whose speed, scope, and cross-border transmission differ from earlier episodes of trade-induced adjustment. Confronting these pressures, governments may be forced to adopt trade measures affecting market access and competition conditions of imported AI products and services. The World Trade Organization (WTO) should better regulate the trade measures in response to these disruptions in line with the emerging principle of human-centered trade.[2]

In an earlier essay, I argued that existing WTO rules are structurally ill-equipped to manage AI-induced job displacement and advanced a broader "labor-sensitive AI trade framework" as a response.[3] That essay argues for policy space for members to adopt trade measures that protect workers from AI-driven dislocation.[4] It advanced

---

[1] MAURO CAZZANIGA ET AL., GEN-AI: ARTIFICIAL INTELLIGENCE AND THE FUTURE OF WORK 3, https://www.imf.org/en/Publications/Staff-Discussion-Notes/Issues/2024/01/14/Gen-AI-Artificial-Intelligence-and-the-Future-of-Work-542379 (arguing AI might pave way for large-scale job displacement); DANIEL SUSSKIND, A WORLD WITHOUT WORK: TECHNOLOGY, AUTOMATION AND HOW WE SHOULD RESPOND 3 (2020) (arguing that the threat of "technological unemployment" is now real); Anton Korinek & Donghyun Suh, *Scenarios for the Transition to AGI*, 37 (arguing that the effects of automation follow an inverse U-shape, first increasing wages by utilizing abundant capital but eventually decreasing wages due to labor displacement); Pawel Gmyrek, Janine Berg & David Bescond, *Generative AI and Jobs: A Global Analysis of Potential Effects on Job Quantity and Quality*; Lucian Cernat, *Trade, Jobs and Technological Change: What to Expect in the Next Five Years?*, https://ecipe.org/publications/trade-jobs-technological-change-next-five-years/ (Cernat notes that AI and robotics are reducing the number of jobs supported by exports—especially in countries reliant on trade for employment); Erik Brynjolfsson, Bharat Chandar & Ruyu Chen, *Canaries in the Coal Mine? Six Facts about the Recent Employment Effects of Artificial Intelligence*, 1 (2025) (finding that since the widespread adoption of generative AI, early-career workers in the most AI-exposed occupations have experienced a 13 percent relative decline in employment).

[2] Centenary Declaration for the Future of Work, Int'l Labour Conf., 108th Sess., I, §§ I(A)–(B), II(A)(i)–(iii) (June 26, 2019) (declaring that in further developing the ILO's human-centred approach to the future of work, "the ILO must direct its efforts to: (i) ensuring a just transition to a future of work that contributes to sustainable development in its economic, social and environmental dimensions; (ii) harnessing the fullest potential of technological progress and productivity growth, including through social dialogue, to achieve decent work and sustainable development, which ensure dignity, self-fulfilment and a just sharing of the benefits for all; (iii) promoting the acquisition of skills, competencies and qualifications for all workers throughout their working lives as a joint responsibility of governments and social partners ..."); WTO Director-General Ngozi Okonjo-Iweala described WTO as "a people-centered, rules-based organization delivering for working- and middle-class people everywhere ..." *Why the Developing World and All of Us Need Trade and the WTO* (2023), https://www.csis.org/analysis/why-developing-world-and-all-us-need-trade-and-wto.

[3] Tsai-Fang Chen, *AI, Job Displacement, and the WTO: Identifying Legal Gaps and Charting a Worker-Centered Path*, Feature Essay, YALE JOURNAL OF INTERNATIONAL LAW ONLINE (Nov. 10, 2025), https://yjil.yale.edu/posts/2025-11-10-ai-job-displacement-and-the-wto-identifying-legal-gaps-and-charting-a-worker.

[4] *Id.*

the idea of an "AI Shock" as a general-purpose technological disruption transmitted through trade, emphasized the inadequacy of the goods-services divide and technological neutrality in the GATS, and sketched a menu of reforms across rules on trade in goods, services, and contingency protection.[5]

This chapter takes up one part of that broader agenda and develops it in depth. It focuses on a special AI safeguard mechanism tailored to AI-induced labor displacement. Rather than revisiting the full range of reforms canvassed in the prior essay, this analysis here asks a more concrete institutional question: if WTO members were to design a dedicated safeguard to manage AI-linked employment shocks, what should that mechanism look like? The answer, I argue, requires a departure from the product-specific, industry-centered architecture of the existing Agreement on Safeguards in at least three aspects. First, any viable AI safeguard for labor displacement must reach goods, services, and good-service bundles, reflecting the ways in which AI is traded, i.e., physical products, cross-border digital services, or their bundles. Second, the injury standard must be explicitly keyed to serious labor displacement (or a threat thereof) in identified labor segments, rather than to the condition of a narrowly defined "domestic industry" producing a like or directly competitive product. Third, the mechanism should dispense with the "unforeseen developments" requirement and adjust the causation and compensation requirements to fit systemic, cross-sectoral shocks that are foreseeable in abstract but nonetheless destabilizing in practice.

A special labor safeguard mechanism is not a call for the WTO to manage the labor market. Instead, it is a proposal to preserve the credibility of the multilateral trading regime in the face of general-purpose technological change. Where the social and political costs of AI-induced dislocation are high, governments will act. The question is whether they will do so within a transparent, time-limited, and multilaterally supervised framework, or through arbitrary, *ad hoc* measures that erode trust in the system. A labor-sensitive safeguard, limited to AI-linked trade flows under stringent conditions, can function as a "release valve" that allows members to pace adjustment without abandoning the core commitment to trade liberalization. By recognizing job loss as an independent basis for "serious injury," and by tailoring causation to AI-embedded imports rather than to competition between like products, the proposed mechanism would focus the WTO contingency protection on the actual harm, i.e., labor displacement.

The structure of the argument is as follows. Part 2, drawing on and compressing the analytical foundations developed in the earlier essay of the author, sets out the channels through which AI generates cross-border employment shocks, explains why those shocks implicate WTO law, and identifies the main points of misfit in existing disciplines. Part 3 examines in greater detail the limitations of current WTO instruments. Part 4 advances the core proposal of the chapter: a special AI-labor safeguard mechanism. It explains the rationale and purpose of the instrument, defines its scope of application across goods, services, and bundles, specifies the triggering conditions (increased AI-linked imports, serious labor displacement, and causation),

[5] *Id.*

and outlines key design elements including temporal limits, cross-sectoral reach, and special and differential treatment. Part 5 concludes by reflecting on how a labor-sensitive safeguard mechanism can help the WTO navigate the AI shock while maintaining the legitimacy of multilateral trade governance in an era of general-purpose technological disruption.

19.2 AI's Impact on Job Displacement and the WTO

This section restates, in compressed form, the analytical premises that ground the special AI safeguards design later. It sets out how AI generates cross-border employment shocks and why those shocks implicate WTO law. I provided a fuller development of these premises in my earlier essay[6]; here they function as the factual and legal baseline for a safeguards-focused book chapter.

19.2.1 What AI Changes in Labor Markets

AI operates as a general-purpose technology. It reaches into higher-skilled, office-based work once thought resilient to automation[7] at a large scale.[8] Therefore, the impact of AI on jobs has become a serious policy concern. It usually is also a trade concern, as for many these are presented as an imported challenge: some workers may face threats of displacement or hiring freeze directly by AI imports; others face intensified competition as foreign producers deploy AI.[9]

AI-induced job displacement has gradually materialized, as demonstrated by the emerging corporate adoption of large-scale layoffs and hiring freezes under their

---

[6] *Id.*

[7] Cazzaniga et al., *supra* note 1 at 3; Janine Berg et al., Generative AI and Jobs: A Refined Global Index of Occupational Exposure 1 (2025), https://webapps.ilo.org/static/english/intserv/working-papers/wp140/index.html.

[8] Cazzaniga et al., *supra* note 1 at 7–8 (AI exposure affects nearly 40 percent of global employment, with advanced economies facing rates as high as 60 percent).

[9] Chen, *supra* note 3.

wider AI strategies. These include corporations such as Shopify,[10] IBM,[11] Salesforce,[12] Microsoft,[13] Accenture,[14] JP Morgan Chase,[15] and Amazon.[16] Though AI cannot yet fully replace human workers, corporate choices reveal a shift toward AI-driven efficiency, with early evidence of displacement in layoffs and hiring freezes tied to AI adoption.

19.2.2 Why This Becomes a WTO Problem

The WTO is not an international labor organization. It neither sets labor standards nor manages employment policy. Its mandate, however, covers the legality of members' measures affecting trade, including trade measures responding to economic shocks. The Marrakesh Agreement's preamble expressly refers to "raising standards of living

---

[10] *Shopify Says No New Hires Unless AI Can't Do the Job—WSJ*, https://www.wsj.com/tech/ai/shopify-says-no-new-hires-unless-ai-cant-do-the-job-81c34f1e (last visited June 2, 2025) (Shopify CEO Tobi Lütke stated that no new hires would be made unless it could be shown that AI could not do the job).

[11] Belle Lin, *IBM CEO Says AI Has Replaced Hundreds of Workers but Created New Programming, Sales Jobs*, WALL STREET JOURNAL, May 6, 2025, https://www.wsj.com/articles/ibm-ceo-says-ai-has-replaced-hundreds-of-workers-but-created-new-programming-sales-jobs-54ea6b58 (IBM has replaced hundreds of workers with AI and now reports that 94% of routine HR tasks are handled by AI).

[12] Brody Ford, *Salesforce Says AI Has Reduced Hiring of Engineers and Customer Service Workers*, BLOOMBERG.COM, May 28, 2025, https://www.bloomberg.com/news/articles/2025-05-28/salesforce-says-ai-has-reduced-hiring-of-engineers-and-customer-service-workers (Salesforce has reduced hiring for engineering and customer service roles due to productivity gains from AI, redeploying 500 service workers and increasing hiring in AI-focused sales positions).

[13] Brody Ford & Matt Day, *Microsoft Layoffs Hit Coders Hardest With AI Costs on the Rise*, BLOOMBERG.COM, May 14, 2025, https://www.bloomberg.com/news/articles/2025-05-14/microsoft-layoffs-hit-software-engineers-as-industry-touts-ai-savings (In early 2025, Microsoft announced major layoffs, with software engineers comprising over 40% of the approximately 2,000 positions cut. While not explicitly attributed to AI, the reductions coincided with growing reliance on AI tools—some projects now report up to 30% of code written by AI).

[14] *Accenture to 'Exit' Staff Who Cannot Be Retrained for Age of AI*, https://www.ft.com/content/a74f8564-ed5a-42e9-8fb3-d2bddb2b8675 (last visited Sept. 28, 2025).

[15] Chip Cutter and Haley Zimmerman, *CEOs Start Saying the Quiet Part Out Loud: AI Will Wipe Out Jobs*, THE WALL STREET JOURNAL (July 3, 2025), https://www.wsj.com/tech/ai/ai-white-collar-job-loss-b9856259 (JP Morgan Chase's CEO of consumer and community business, Marianne Lake told investors that she could see its operations head count falling by 10% in the coming years as the company uses new AI tools).

[16] *See, e.g., Amazon's Jassy Says AI Will Reduce Company's Corporate Workforce*, BLOOMBERG.COM, June 17, 2025, https://www.bloomberg.com/news/articles/2025-06-17/amazon-s-jassy-says-ai-will-reduce-company-s-corporate-workforce (Amazon CEO Andy Jassy has indicated that the company's workforce is expected to shrink over the next few years as AI takes on more tasks in retail and cloud operations).

and ensuring full employment,"[17] and the Agreement on Safeguards explicitly lists job loss as an element of "serious injury" justifying temporary protective measures.[18] Accordingly, employment and labor displacement fall within the WTO's competence whenever trade measures are used to manage pressures for adjustment.

WTO law already provides limited mechanisms to address risks to economic security arising from trade liberalization. Under the GATT, members may renegotiate tariffs[19] and invoke general[20] or security exceptions[21] to address broader threats to national economic stability. The Agreement on Safeguards permits temporary restrictions when a surge in imports threatens serious injury to a domestic industry. The GATS allows negotiated modification or withdrawal of market access commitments.[22] The GATS also contains various exceptions to provide policy spaces. These provisions show that structured flexibility is a core part of how the WTO reconciles openness with stability. Indeed, the existence of flexibility is critical in promoting commitments to liberalize trade. A calibrated framework for labor-related shocks would therefore develop, rather than depart from, the WTO's existing mandate.

Even if the long-term effect of AI on employment remains uncertain, periods of disruptive transition are unavoidable. Governments must navigate a dual challenge: to foster innovation while protecting workers from wage suppression and involuntary job loss. A purely passive approach of waiting risks social and political instability that can undermine commitment to trade itself. Yet unilateral reactions could be harmful, distorting markets and undermining the credibility of the multilateral trading system without solving the underlying problem. Members should acknowledge that trade-related labor measures are a legitimate object of WTO discipline and equip the system with orderly, transparent guardrails through which they can operate.

One might argue that domestic policy instruments, such as taxation of AI-related efficiency gains,[23] welfare and/or retraining schemes, are sufficient to address the labor displacement effects of AI, making trade reform unnecessary. Indeed, such national tools are indispensable for resilience and equity within economies. However, when displacement becomes systemic, cross-border, and asymmetric across countries, domestic measures alone cannot absorb the shock. Where job losses are transmitted through international trade in goods and services, the response necessarily implicates the WTO framework itself.

---

[17] Marrakesh Agreement Establishing the World Trade Organization, Preamble ("*Recognizing* that their relations in the field of trade and economic endeavour should be conducted with a view to raising standards of living, ensuring full employment....").

[18] Agreement on Safeguards, Art. 4.2(a).

[19] GATT Art. XXVIII:1.

[20] GATT Art. XX.

[21] GATT Art. XXI.

[22] GATS Art. XXI.

[23] *Navigating the Future of Work: A Case for a Robot Tax in the Age of AI*, BROOKINGS, https://www.brookings.edu/articles/navigating-the-future-of-work-a-case-for-a-robot-tax-in-the-age-of-ai/ (last visited Oct. 6, 2025).

19.3 What Is Missing Under Current WTO Rules

This section identifies the constraint that motivates a special AI safeguard. It proceeds in two steps: the services regime offers no temporary safety valve, and the safeguard available in the goods regime is architecturally mismatched to AI-linked labor shocks. There is no disciplined, time-limited instrument to manage trade-transmitted AI-induced employment shock across goods, services, and bundles.

19.3.1 The GATS

(a) Likeness and non-discrimination.

Two thresholds arise at the outset of any measure that differentiates among service types of suppliers: human-supplied vs AI-supplied services and automation-oriented vs complementary (augmenting) AI.[24] Any attempt to differentiate them will have to pass MFN (GATS Article II) (irrespective of specific commitments) and National Treatment (GATS Article XVII) (where a sector/mode is scheduled). Because likeness analysis in services turns chiefly on competitive substitutability,[25] AI-supplied and human-supplied services (e.g., translation, customer support, or back-office processing) will often be treated as "like," and the same may hold for automation vs complementary AI where outputs are substitutable. Non-discrimination rules may prevent governments from adopting measures to pace labor shocks.

(b) Technological neutrality and the reach of commitments

While MFN applies regardless of specific commitments, NT and Market Access under Art. XVI exposure turn on commitments. Under the prevailing view of technological neutrality, earlier made commitments extend to later-developed delivery methods, including Mode 1 AI supply, without explicit limitations.[26] Doctrine of technological neutrality thus expands coverage without supplying a relief mechanism, tightening constraints on potential human-first rules in committed sectors.

(c) The tariff instrument gap for digitally delivered AI services

---

[24] See Brynjolfsson, Chandar, and Chen, *supra* note 1 at 14 (finding that AI that automates and AI that augments have different effects on early-level employment).

[25] Appellate Body Report, Argentina—Measures Relating to Trade in Goods and Services (Financial Services) ¶ 6.25, WTO Doc WT/DS453/AB/R (adopted May 9, 2016).

[26] Panel Report, United States—Measures Affecting the Cross-Border Supply of Gambling and Betting Services, ¶ 6.285, WTO Doc WT/DS285/R (adopted Apr. 20, 2005) [*hereinafter* Panel Report, *US—Gambling*] (found that "a market access commitment for mode 1 implies the right for other Members' suppliers to supply a service through all means of delivery, whether by mail, telephone, Internet etc., unless otherwise specified in a Member's Schedule.")

For services, members have no tariff at their disposal, and the long-standing WTO moratorium on customs duties on electronic transmissions forecloses duties on cross-border digital delivery for now.[27] When AI services scale quickly across borders, governments cannot apply a rules-based price at the border. The adjustment burden shifts to non-tariff measures, such as licensing conditions, quantitative limits, human-in-the-loop mandates, or internal taxes, which sit squarely under MFN and, in committed sectors and modes, NT and potentially Market Access where they function as effective prohibitions or zero-quotas.

(d) No emergency safeguard in services

Unlike the GATT, the GATS contains no general emergency safeguard that would allow a member to temporarily suspend or roll back specific commitments in response to a surge of cross-border services that threatens serious injury.[28] Article X mandates negotiations on such a mechanism, but Members have never agreed on such rules. Therefore, the GATS does not provide the right to deploy time-limited and non-discriminatory restraints on service supply to pace adjustment. That inadequacy is acute in a rapid scale-up, Mode-1 delivered, cross-sector disruption of AI context. The alternatives[29] do not fix the problem: *ex ante* scheduling is irrelevant once commitments exist and neutrality reads AI delivery into them; modification or withdrawal of commitments is permanent, is sector specific and requires compensation; the necessity test and the chapeau make it difficult to invoke general exceptions under Article XIV; balance of payment safeguard under Article XII and the financial prudential carve-out targets financial stability only.

The GATS' combination of non-discrimination constraints, no tariff lever, stringent exception provisions, and no emergency safeguard leaves members with little space to phase AI-service shocks. This pushes them toward workarounds inconsistent with multilateral disciplines. In any event, this rigidity will prevent members from expanding their commitments in the area of service trade, even if for members whose current GATS commitments are limited.

---

[27] WTO, *Declaration on Global Electronic Commerce* (Second Ministerial Conference, Geneva, 20 May 1998) WT/MIN(98)/DEC/2.

[28] Mario Marconini, *Emergency Safeguard Measures in the GATS: Beyond Feasible and Desirable*, 8 (2005).

[29] Juan A. Marchetti & Petros C. Mavroidis, *What Are the Main Challenges for the GATS Framework? Don't Talk About Revolution*, 5 EUR BUS ORG LAW REV 511, 543–44 (2004), http://link.springer.com/10.1017/S1566752904005117.

19.3.2 The Agreement on Safeguards: Why the Existing Tool Cannot Carry AI Shocks

While the Agreement on Safeguards exists to afford members flexibility to deal with unexpected import surges, the Agreement is anchored in a particular physical product and a defined domestic industry producing a like or directly competitive product. The domestic industry that can be protected under the Agreement is limited to the producers of the specific physical product competing with the increased imports under Article 4.1(c) of the Agreement on Safeguards. The Agreement does not apply to services, the main import channel when it comes to AI. The Agreement on Safeguards, therefore, does not provide any space for responses against AI-induced job displacement through service import. But even when AI was imported through physical goods, the Agreement falls short due to the following reasons.

First, the product-specific nature of the Agreement on Safeguards does not solve issues caused by the general-purpose technology such as AI. AI's labor effects are horizontal, cutting across many goods, often via embedded functionality that does not present as an import surge under a discrete tariff-line. There is no safeguard keyed to a technology category, and fragmented relief across dozens of products is often impractical. The focus of the Agreement on competition between imported good and domestic like product also misses the point regarding concerns over AI-induced labor displacement, as the impacted labor are not necessarily employed by the domestic industry competing with the imported goods carrying AI functionality.

Second, the employment centered harm may not satisfy the domestic industry injury requirement. Safeguard measures can only be adopted based on a demonstration of serious injury to the domestic industry.[30] Serious injury is assessed on a composite of indicators, including "the rate and amount of the increase in imports of the product concerned in absolute and relative terms, the share of the domestic market taken by increased imports, changes in the level of sales, production, productivity, capacity utilization, profits and losses, and employment."[31] In AI settings, these indicators other than employment can remain stable or even rise while employment falls due to automation. Job loss alone may not satisfy the injury requirement, even where social harm is acute. The instrument can be blind to the very harm a labor-sensitive response must address.

Third, the unforeseen developments requirement is a hurdle for the effective utilization of the safeguard mechanism. The persistence of the "unforeseen developments" requirement[32] complicates action in an AI context where disruptions may be foreseeable.

Fourth, compensation burdens may be too costly for developing countries and least-developed countries. Safeguards must be applied on an MFN basis and trigger

---

[30] Agreement on Safeguards, Art. 4.

[31] Agreement on Safeguards, Article 4.2(a).

[32] GATT Article XIX:1(a).

compensation rights for affected Members.[33] Cross-sector, economy-wide labor shocks would entail broad measures with high compensation exposure, rendering the tool costly or even unusable, especially for less developed members.

Because the GATS offers no emergency safeguard and the Agreement on Safeguards is not sufficient for AI-induced labor displacement, the system lacks a coherent way to pace adjustment where AI is transmitted through trade. Members who could not tolerate labor shocks are forced to act outside the multilateral framework. This is the concern the special AI safeguard must be designed to fill.

19.4 A Case for Reform: A Special AI-Labor Safeguard Mechanism

As a general-purpose technology, AI carries wide-ranging implications for international trade. For the purpose of this chapter, it is useful to distinguish three channels through which AI can generate adjustment pressure through trade. First, domestic firms may adopt AI by importing it through, for example, cross-border AI-enabled services. In this "displaced by AI adoption" scenario, firms can substitute imported AI inputs for tasks previously performed by domestic workers, creating displacement pressures from imported AI.

Second, even where domestic firms do not adopt or integrate AI that causes labor displacement into their own operations, domestic firms and their workers may nonetheless face direct competition from foreign AI-service providers supplying the domestic market. Here, in this "displaced by AI competition" scenario, the competitive pressure operates through import competition in services: foreign AI-enabled services delivered cross-border increasingly perform functions that domestic suppliers and individual workers previously provided, displacing or undercutting them without any intervening decision by domestic firms to "use AI" as an input. These first two channels are those that the AI special safeguard proposal in this chapter is designed to address.

Third, domestic industries may face intensified competition because foreign competitors deploy AI to reduce costs, improve quality, or speed innovation, thereby expanding exports of downstream goods or services into the domestic market even if AI itself is not imported by the affected economy. In such cases ("displaced by indirect competition" scenario), the increased import competition occurred in the downstream product market, driven by foreign productivity gains. This third channel is outside the scope of the proposed AI special safeguard as framed in this chapter. Where the legal conditions are met, this type of competition is one that the traditional, sector specific safeguard architecture is designed to address.

---

[33] Agreement on Safeguards, Article 2.2; Article 8.

19.4.1 Why Special Safeguard Mechanism?

The gaps identified in the preceding section point to a broader problem that the WTO's existing rules are not calibrated for the AI-induced labor displacement. This section explains why, among the available reform options, a dedicated safeguard instrument is the most pressing. A threshold question is whether WTO rules could accommodate differential treatment of complementary AI that augments workers and automation-oriented AI that replaces them. As I have argued elsewhere, existing doctrinal tools offer some room for such distinction: likeness analysis, the chapeaux of general exceptions, and legitimate regulatory distinctions under Article 2.1 of the TBT Agreement do not foreclose the possibility for treating these categories differently. The practical difficulty, however, is that applying these provisions remains uncertain and fact-intensive. [34] Authoritative interpretations by WTO members confirming such distinctions would help, but securing consensus is likely to prove difficult.[35]

Nor would reforms to other pillars of WTO law, standing alone, fill the gap. On the services side, revising technological neutrality under the GATS could, in theory, create space for members to distinguish between human-delivered and AI-delivered services. Yet this chapter recognizes the substantial benefits of an innovation-friendly interpretive framework. Abandoning technological neutrality altogether would be an overly blunt and risky response, given the difficulty in obtaining concessions in today's negotiating climate. Drawing a principled line between human and AI services would also raise significant classification difficulties. As for the e-commerce moratorium, customs duties are not well suited as a tool for managing short-term technological disruption.

On the subsidy front, I have previously proposed a set of reforms to the SCM Agreement designed to address both sides of the AI challenge. That proposal called for expanded flexibility to shield subsidies aiming at retraining, upskilling, or incentivizing complementary AI technologies while at the same time tightening disciplines on subsidies whose principal effect is to accelerate automation-driven displacement.[36] These reforms remain important, but they do not, on their own, provide the kind of temporary, time-limited relief that governments need when confronted with sudden AI induced labor displacement.

What distinguishes a safeguard mechanism from each of these alternatives is its capacity to offer structured, time-bound breathing room. A special safeguard mechanism enables members to take temporary measures in response to labor harm, subject to multilateral conditions and oversight. Accordingly, whether or not the broader reforms are adopted, the case for a dedicated safeguard mechanism stands on its own, as none of the other reform options could provide this function. The Agreement on Safeguards, as demonstrated in the preceding section, is ill-suited

[34] Chen, *supra* note 3.

[35] Marrakesh Agreement Establishing the World Trade Organization, Art. IX:2.

[36] Chen, *supra* note 3.

to carry AI-induced labor shocks. The instrument proposed in the next section is designed to fill this gap.

19.4.2 Designing the Special AI-Labor Safeguard Mechanism

This chapter proposes a special safeguard mechanism that authorizes members to take temporary, targeted measures in response to AI-linked increases in imports that cause or threaten to cause serious labor displacement. The instrument applies to goods, services, and good/service bundles, dispenses with the "unforeseen developments" element in GATT Article XIX.1(a), and recognizes job loss and closely related labor-market harms as sufficient injury when causally linked to AI-related trade. Its function is to allow national determinations within multilaterally agreed guardrails, preserving the balance of rights and obligations while acknowledging the distinctive character of AI shocks.

Unlike the Agreement on Safeguards, the proposed special AI-labor safeguard mechanism is not applied against a like or directly competitive product for the protection of a domestic industry. It does not concern competition between an imported product and a domestic like product. Instead, it concerns labor displacement induced by imported AI product, services, or their bundles. In other words, the heart of the special mechanism is the competition between AI and human labor.

19.4.2.1 Rationale and Purpose

To address the limitations of the current safeguard regime, this chapter proposes a dedicated AI-labor safeguard mechanism narrowly tailored to the realities of AI-induced displacement. Unlike traditional safeguards, which are rooted in product-specific surges and narrow definitions of industry injury, a labor safeguard must be structurally and legally responsive to the unique attributes of AI-driven disruption. The mechanism should enable governments to act preemptively and proportionally in the face of labor shocks, while preserving the normative balance of rights and obligations within the WTO system.

The proposed special safeguard mechanism is not intended to manage competition between imported and domestic like products. Rather, it addresses a more fundamental tension: the competition between human labor and machine-based automation. The target of the special safeguard mechanism is not imported competing product, but the imported AI that threatens to cause large-scale labor displacement. While it is true that the WTO's mandate centers on market access rather than labor rights, the rationale underlying a labor-sensitive safeguard mechanism is not alien to the existing Agreement on Safeguards. Both aim to provide contingent protection in order to secure the market access commitments and the multilateral trading system.

At its core, the special safeguard mechanism offers a structured response to dislocation, enabling members to uphold their market access commitments while managing the social consequences of structural change. A labor-sensitive mechanism would preserve the core logic of WTO safeguards while adapting it to a new, cross-sectoral, and technologically driven form of threat against the will of members to further market liberalization.

When AI-induced labor displacement materializes, members could be forced to adopt measures with trade effects. The existence of the proposed special safeguard could function as a credible tool that prevents members from adopting unilateral and arbitrary trade measures that could lead to serious obstruction to international trade.

While the mechanism is intended to address only AI-induced labor displacement and takes the form of a single instrument, it can also be considered as part of the larger WTO reform relating to AI. While the chapter focuses on reform within the WTO, the proposed mechanism could also be adopted in regional trade agreements.

19.4.2.2 Scope of Application

The special safeguard mechanism must apply to trade in goods, services, and bundled forms of both. In addition to the form of standalone digital services, AI often enters the economy not as a standalone service or product, but as embedded functionality—within manufactured goods or hybrid service infrastructures. A safeguard mechanism limited to traditional goods classifications would fail to capture this layered reality. Accordingly, the new mechanism should adopt a technology-sensitive scope, enabling members to respond to job displacement regardless of the form of the underlying AI package. From this perspective, a safeguard mechanism under GATS alone is not sufficient.

The mechanism operates only where the measure would otherwise be inconsistent with the member's WTO obligations.[37] For measures on goods, it may include raising a tariff above a bound rate under GATT Article II or imposing a quantitative restriction under GATT Article XI. For measures on services, it may include introducing a numerical limitation or other GATS Article XVI:2 market access restriction in a scheduled sector/mode or according less favorable treatment to foreign services/suppliers contrary to Article XVII. The proposed mechanism does not authorize departures from MFN.

19.4.2.3 Conditions

Adopting the basic requirements of the Agreement on Safeguards, the special safeguard measures could be adopted when the following cumulative conditions are met: increased import, injury, and causation.

[37] GATT, art. XIX:1(a).

A member may act where (i) increased imports of AI-linked goods, services, or their bundles are shown in absolute or relative terms; (ii) a domestic competent authority determines serious labor displacement or threat thereof in identified labor segments; and (iii) the competent authority determines that the serious labor displacement or threat thereof is causally linked to the increased imports of AI and not primarily to other factors.

With regard to the element of increased import, the proposed special safeguard mechanism requires a showing of increased imports of AI-linked goods, services, or bundles in absolute or relative terms over a recent, representative period. This may include both "displaced by AI adoption" scenario as well as "displaced by AI competition" scenarios.

With regard to the element of serious labor displacement or threat thereof, this mirrors the structure of the Agreement on Safeguards while recognizing labor-market injury as the required harm. To be effective, the mechanism must recognize actual or potential job loss as a valid basis for action. Under the current WTO framework, serious injury is typically assessed through a composite of factors within a narrowly defined domestic industry such as declines in production, sales, profitability, and employment.[38] However, in the case of AI-induced displacement, labor loss may occur even when output remains stable or increases, due to productivity gains from automation. The proposed safeguard would treat job displacement itself as sufficient to satisfy the injury threshold, as long as it is clearly attributable to AI-linked import competition. Anticipatory use should also be permitted where governments demonstrate a credible threat of large-scale displacement. The causality requirement should be tailored to AI-embedded imports. The showing of the serious labor displacement could occur in identified labor segments, such as occupations or regions linked to imported AI functionality.

With regard to the element of causation, the rationale of Article 4.2(b) of the Agreement on Safeguards would be adopted. The adoption of the measure would require the establishment of a credible, evidence-based link between increased imports of AI technology, on the one hand, and serious labor displacement, on the other. Where several factors cause serious labor displacement at the same time, investigating authority of a WTO member should not infer the causal link between increased AI imports and serious labor displacement or threat thereof on the basis of the injurious effects caused by factors other than increased AI imports.[39]As the proposed special mechanism protects workers from AI-driven task substitution transmitted through trade instead of domestic product from imported like or directly competitive product, the proposed special safeguard mechanism does not involve a like or directly competitive product analysis. Instead, the causation requirement has to be satisfied based on the causal link between the imported AI and serious labor displacement or

---

[38] Agreement on Safeguards, art. 4.2.(a).

[39] *See* Appellate Body Report, United States—Definitive Safeguard Measures on Imports of Circular Welded Carbon Quality Line Pipe from Korea, ¶ 252, WTO Doc. WT/DS202/AB/R (Adopted Mar. 8, 2002) [*hereinafter* US—Line Pipe].

threat thereof. It is important to ensure that the special safeguard measure is indeed adopted to protect labor from AI.

The proposed special safeguard mechanism is not part of the existing Agreement on Safeguards and should dispense with the requirement of "unforeseen developments," which appears in GATT Article XIX.1(a), given that, in the context of AI, disruption may be foreseeable but still deeply destabilizing. In addition, for any further trade liberalization in the future, it would be difficult to argue that AI disruption is unforeseeable.

19.4.2.4 Requirements Regarding the Application of Special AI Safeguard Measures

The application of the special AI safeguard measure should follow those under Agreement on Safeguards. Measures authorized under the special AI-labor safeguard mechanism would be temporary and applied only to the extent necessary to remedy or prevent serious labor displacement and to facilitate adjustment. Its application would be non-discriminatory. Similarly, the types of measure permitted under the special safeguard mechanism should be flexible.

Different from those provided under the Agreement on Safeguards, the proposed special AI safeguard measure is not predicated on the competition between an imported product and a domestic industry producing like or directly competitive product and must permit cross-sectoral application. AI does not injure one industry alone—it reshapes workflows across multiple, often unrelated sectors. Restricting the safeguard to narrowly defined industries would render it ineffective against AI's systemic reach. A requirement that the special safeguard measure must be limited to the extent of necessity may be applied "only to the extent necessary to prevent or remedy serious injury and to facilitate adjustment."[40] The "serious injury" is those that have been determined to exist by competent authorities of a WTO member attributable to increased imports,[41] in this case, to increased AI imports that cause labor displacement or threat thereof. This requirement is critical to limit the abuse of the mechanism.

Given the asymmetries in fiscal capacity and technological preparedness among WTO members, the mechanism must include special and differential treatment for developing and least-developed countries. Most importantly, these members should be exempt from the compensation obligations typically triggered under Article 8 of the Safeguards Agreement. Without such a waiver, the mechanism would be legally available but politically and economically unusable.

---

[40] Agreement on Safeguards, Art. 5.1.

[41] *See* Appellate Body Report, US—Line Pipe (2002), ¶¶ 249, 260.

19.5 Conclusion

Artificial intelligence has brought about a global challenge, cutting across industries, transforming labor, and unsettling the assumptions that underpin global trade. The WTO must evolve to maintain its credibility and relevance. This chapter has argued for the establishment of a special AI-labor safeguard mechanism that offers a rules-based path toward adaptation through temporary, targeted, and principled measures. Equipping the multilateral trade regime with labor-sensitive instruments will be essential for preserving both market openness and legitimacy in the age of AI.

GPSR Compliance
The European Union's (EU) General Product Safety Regulation (GPSR) is a set of rules that requires consumer products to be safe and our obligations to ensure this.

If you have any concerns about our products, you can contact us on

ProductSafety@springernature.com

In case Publisher is established outside the EU, the EU authorized representative is:

Springer Nature Customer Service Center GmbH
Europaplatz 3
69115 Heidelberg, Germany

www.ingramcontent.com/pod-product-compliance
Ingram Content Group UK Ltd.
Pitfield, Milton Keynes, MK11 3LW, UK
UKHW020631260926
475829UK00003BA/19
9789819569953